About the Authors

Federico Mayor is the former director-general of UNESCO. He has served as Spain's minister of education and science, as president of the University of Granada and as a member of the European parliament.

Jérôme Bindé is director of UNESCO's Analysis and Forecasting Office. An alumnus of the Ecole Normale Supérieure in Paris, and member of the French University (*agrégé*), he was assistant professor at the Ecole Polytechnique.

This book is available in the following countries

Fiji: University Book Centre, University of South Pacific, Suva
tel: 679 313900, fax: 679 303265

Ghana: EPP Book Services, PO Box TF 490, Trade Fair, Accra
tel: 233 21 773087, fax: 233 21 779099

India: Segment Book Distributors, B-23/25 Kailash Colony,
New Delhi
tel: 91 11 644 3013, fax: 91 11 647 0472

Mozambique: Sul Sensacoes, PO Box 2242, Maputo
tel: 258 1 421974, fax: 258 1 423414

Nepal: Everest Media Services, GPO Box 5443, Dillibazar,
Putalisadak Chowk, Kathmandu, Nepal
tel: 977 1 416026, fax: 977 1 250176

Pakistan: Vanguard Books, 45 The Mall, Lahore
tel: 92 42 735 5079, fax: 92 42 735 5197

Papua New Guinea: Unisearch PNG Pty Ltd, Box 320, University,
National Capital District
tel: 675 326 0130, fax: 675 326 0127

Tanzania: TEMA Publishing Co Ltd, PO Box 63115, Dar Es Salaam
tel: 255 51 113608, fax: 255 51 110472

Uganda: Aristoc Booklex Ltd, Diamond Trust Building, Kampala Rd,
PO Box 5130, Kampala
tel: 256 41 344381, fax: 256 41 254867

Zambia: UNZA Press, University of Zambia, PO Box 32379, Lusaka,
Zambia
tel: 260 1 290409, fax: 260 1 253952

The World Ahead: Our Future in the Making

Federico Mayor in collaboration
with Jérôme Bindé

with the assistance of Jean-Yves Le Saux,
Ragnar Gudmundsson and the team of UNESCO's
Analysis and Forecasting Office

UPL
DHAKA

IPSR
SOUTH AFRICA

White Lotus
THAILAND

UNESCO Publishing
PARIS

Zed Books
LONDON • NEW YORK

The World Ahead: Our Future in the Making was first co-published by
Zed Books Ltd, 7 Cynthia Street, London N1 9JF, UK and Room 400,
175 Fifth Avenue, New York, NY 10010, USA and UNESCO Publishing,
7 Place de Fontenoy, 75352 Paris 07-SP, France in 2001.

Distributed in the USA exclusively by Palgrave, a division of St Martin's
Press, LLC, 175 Fifth Avenue, New York, NY 10010, USA.

Cover designed by Andrew Corbett
Set in Monotype Dante by Ewan Smith, London
Printed and bound in Malaysia

A catalogue record for this book is available from the British Library.

Library of Congress Cataloging-in-Publication Data
Mayor, Federico
    The world ahead: our future in the making / Federico Mayor in
  collaboration with Jérôme Bindé; with the assistance of Jean-Yves Le
  Saux ... [et al.].
        p. cm.
  Includes bibliographical references and index.
    ISBN 1-85649-874-3 (cased) – ISBN 1-85649-875-1 (limp)
    1. Social prediction. 2. Human ecology. 3. Sustainable development.
  I. Bindé, Jérôme. II. Title.
HM901.M39 2001
303.49'0905–dc21

                                  00-043901

ISBN 1 85649 874 3 cased
ISBN 1 85649 875 1 limp
UNESCO ISBN 92 3 103634 3 limp

Contents

Boxes

Team for the Preparation of the Book

§ THE report *The World Ahead: Our Future in the Making*, first published in French as *Un Monde nouveau*, UNESCO Publishing and Editions Odile Jacob, September 1999, was drawn up by Federico Mayor, director-general of UNESCO, in accordance with the programme and the budget of the organization for 1998–99. It was prepared in collaboration with Jérôme Bindé and with the assistance of the team of UNESCO's Analysis and Forecasting Office:

Director: Jérôme Bindé

Main collaborators: Jean-Yves Le Saux, Ragnar Gudmundsson

Research and editorial assistance: Philippe Ambrosi, Judit Carrera-Escudé, Dave Dewnarain, Julien Dubouloz, Hadewych Hazelzet, Marcel Kabanda, Angélique Khaled, Nadia Khouri-Dagher, Aurélien Kruse, Giuseppina Laezza, Alexandra Novosseloff, Rizwan Rahim, Lise Revol, Tracy Rotstein, Silvia Sala, Arianna Zorzato

Communication and media relations: Maud Glaizot, Anne-Marie Roth

Secretariat and administrative support: Anne Bonraisin, Anne-Marie Roth, Yannick Tschanz, Sabine Vayssières

Acknowledgements

§ THE preparation of this report would not have been possible without the support and valuable contributions of a large number of individuals and organizations. Many international organizations generously shared their experience, research and data: UNESCO and its specialized institutes, all agencies and programmes of the United Nations system, and the OECD.

The report benefited greatly from initial contributions by Michèle Aulagnon, Anne de Beer, Gérard Blanc, Néstor García Canclini, Daniel Cohen, Philippe Collomb, Emmanuel Decaux, Goéry Delacôte, Benjamin Dessus, Cyria Emelianoff, Christopher Flavin, Francis Godard, Guy Herzlich, Ethan B. Kapstein, Bo Kjellén, Pierre Laconte, Hervé Le Bras, Jean Le Dû, Gilbert D. Loescher, Jean Margat, Elikia M'Bokolo, Paul Metz, François Ost, Alain Pavé, Christian de Portzamparc, Philippe Quéau, Laurent Sagart, Saskia Sassen, Richard Sennett, Jean-François Soussana, Jacques Theys, Peter Weber, Ernst-Ulrich von Weizsäcker, Stephen A. Wurm.

The report also benefited greatly from discussions with and kind contributions from Michel Batisse, Boris Berkovski, José-Joaquin Brunner Ried, Teresa R. Caldeira, Stephen K. Chu, Edgar Da Silva, Jacques Delors, Leandro Despouy, Chedli Fezzani, Maryse Gaudier, Kenneth Gwilliam, Malcolm Hadley, Hugues de Jouvenel, Inge Kaul, Monique Mainguet, Malick M'Baye, Candido Mendes, Edgar Morin, Ernesto Ottone, Sue Parker, Eduardo Portella, Jonas Rabinovitch, Ándres Szöllösi-Nagy, Alphonse Tay, Wolfgang Vollmann.

The report benefited from presentations made during the 21st Century Dialogues organized by UNESCO's Analysis and Forecasting Office (16–19 September 1998). In this respect we would like to thank Arjun Appadurai, Miguel Azcueta Gorostiza, Jean Baudrillard, Hélé Béji, Claire Besset, Colin R. Blackman, Mohamed Larbi Bouguerra, Néstor García Canclini, Roger Cans, Roberto Carneiro, Philippe Collomb, Goéry Delacôte, Jean-Louis Deneubourg, Lord Desai, Souleymane Bachir Diagne, Cheik Modibo Diarra, Gloria Beatriz Durand Soria, Thierry Gaudin, Nilüfer Göle, Jean-Joseph Goux, Hisanori Isomura, Hugues de Jouvenel, Ethan B. Kapstein, Craig Kielburger, André Lebeau, Hervé Le Bras, Pentti Malaska, Jean Margat, Hans-Peter Martin, Eleonora Barbieri Masini, Peter H. Mettler, Jesús Moneo, Gertrude I. Mongella,

Nicole Morgan, Vitit Muntarbhorn, François Ost, Otto Piene, Eduardo Portella, Christian de Portzamparc, Ilya Prigogine, Amulya K. N. Reddy, Martine Rèmond-Gouilloud, Francisco Sagasti, Daniel Sala-Diakanda, Saskia Sassen, Richard Sennett, Igor A. Shiklomanov, Niels E. Skakkebaek, Stelarc, Tony Stevenson, Roger Sue, Amadou Toumani Touré, Kimon Valaskakis, Gianni Vattimo, Bill Viola, Stephen A. Wurm, Zeng Yi.

The report also drew on analyses presented during the series of 21st Century Talks organized at UNESCO headquarters since September 1997 by the Analysis and Forecasting Office. We would like to thank for their insights Jacques Attali, Boutros Boutros-Ghali, Manuel Castells, Mireille Delmas-Marty, Stephen Jay Gould, David L. Heyman, Axel Kahn, M. G. K. Menon, Luc Montagnier, Edgar Morin, Ramakanta Rath, Jeremy Rifkin, Mary Robinson, Joël de Rosnay, Pierre Sané, Philippe Sollers, Alain Touraine, Vassilis Vassilikos, Jean-Didier Vincent, Michael Walzer and Theodore Zeldin.

The team expresses sincere appreciation to UNESCO Publishing and the UNESCO Division of Statistics for their cooperation.

Abbreviations

ACDA	Arms Control and Disarmament Agency
AIDS	acquired immune deficiency syndrome
ASEAN	Association of South East Asian Nations
BICC	Bonn International Center for Conversion
CEDAW	Convention on the Elimination of All Forms of Discrimination Against Women
CFC	chlorofluorocarbon
DAW	Division for the Advancement of Women
ECOWAS	Economic Community of West African States
FAO	Food and Agriculture Organization (UN)
GDI	gender-related development index
GEF	Global Environment Facility
GMO	genetically modified organism
GOOS	Global Ocean Observing System
HDI	Human Development Index (of the UNDP)
HIPC	heavily indebted poor countries
HIV	human immunodeficiency virus
IEA	International Energy Agency
IFPRI	International Food Policy Research Institute
IGCP	International Geological Correlation Programme (UNESCO)
IHP	International Hydrological Programme (UNESCO)
ILO	International Labour Organization
IMF	International Monetary Fund
INCB	International Narcotics Control Board (UN)
INSTRAW	United Nations International Research and Training Institute for the Advancement of Women
IOC	Intergovernmental Oceanographic Commission (UNESCO)
IPCC	Intergovernmental Panel on Climate Change (UNESCO)
IPDC	International Programme for the Development of Communication (UNESCO)
IPPF	International Planned Parenthood Federation

IUCN	International Union for the Conservation of Nature and Natural Resources
LEISA	low external input sustainable agriculture
LPG	liquid petroleum gas
MAB	Man and the Biosphere programme (UNESCO)
Mercosur	Mercado Común del Sur (Common Market of the South)
MOST	Management of Social Transformation programme (UNESCO)
NGO	non-governmental organization
OECD	Organization for Economic Cooperation and Development
OSCE	Organization for Security and Cooperation in Europe
SADC	Southern African Development Community
SIPRI	Stockholm International Peace Research Institute
TOE	tons of oil equivalent
UNCED	United Nations Conference on Environment and Development
UNCTAD	United Nations Conference on Trade and Development
UNDCP	United Nations International Drug Control Programme
UNDP	United Nations Development Programme
UNEP	United Nations Environment Programme
UNESCO	United Nations Educational, Scientific and Cultural Organization
UNFPA	United Nations Population Fund (formerly United Nations Fund for Population Activities)
UNHCR	United Nations High Commissioner for Refugees
UNICEF	United Nations Children's Fund
UNIFEM	United Nations Development Fund for Women
UNPINC	United Nations Programme for International Narcotics Control
VNG	vehicle natural gas
WACLA	World Assembly of Cities and Local Authorities
WCCD	World Commission on Culture and Development
WEC	World Energy Council
WEU	Western European Union
WFMLA	World Federation of Modern Language Associations
WHO	World Health Organization
WMO	World Meteorological Organization
WTO	World Trade Organization
WWF	World Wide Fund for Nature

Let us expect nothing from the twenty-first century:
it is the twenty-first century which expects everything
from us.

Introduction

'We cannot predict the future, but we can prepare it,' observed Ilya Prigogine, Nobel prizewinner, physicist, chemist, philosopher and one of the great thinkers of our time. He added: 'As Paul Valéry has written, "the future is construction". Our human action depends on our memory of the past, our analysis of the present and our anticipation of the future.'[1]

§ WE cannot predict the future because the future will never be as before. We can prepare for it because, far from being inscribed in a book of destiny, the future is uncertainty, bifurcation, unpredictable creation. It is in our hands, because the future is freedom – for the most part, it will be exactly what we make of it. We can prepare for the future, but are we prepared for the twenty-first century?[2]

The specific aim of this work, which I have drawn up in collaboration with Jérôme Binde and with the assistance of Jean-Yves Le Saux, Ragnar Gudmundsson, and the team of UNESCO's Analysis and Forecasting Office, is to prepare us more thoroughly for the coming decades so that we may respond in good time to the challenges of the future. Tomorrow will always be too late.

The twenty-first century is in fact already upon us – and we are already a part of it, without realizing it. As one of the leading historians of our time, Eric Hobsbawm, notes, the twentieth century was a short century, which really began only in 1914 and ended some time around 1989.[3] It was an age of extremes, which began with the violence and fury of the First World War and broke up under the impact of pickaxe blows, which caused a wall to crumble. All the while, two major upheavals with long-term consequences were deeply changing our vision of the world and the very structure of our society.

The *scientific revolution* of our time has led us from an age of certainty and dogmatism into an ocean of uncertainties and doubts: in the relatively recent past we believed, with naive assurance, in the predictability of phenomena governed by the laws of a reliable and imperious science. Today, determinism is yielding to a concept of nature and history marked by randomness. For this reason, the twenty-first century could be less like a park designed in the French style and more like that 'garden of forking paths' beloved of Jorge

Luis Borges. But at the same time, as we face new paradigms of complexity, irreversibility, globalization and uncertainty, it is liberty and human creativity that come once again to the fore. In the words of Aminata Traoré, 'creativity is our hope – including, in the first instance, political creativity'.[4] Far from coming to an end, history continues, even if the script is no longer written in advance and the characters are in search of an author. A throw of the dice can never eliminate chance.

The *third industrial revolution* is radically transforming our societies.[5] This upheaval was all too hastily attributed to globalization, or rather to its most recent phase. Undoubtedly, that was mistaking cause for effect. In fact, it is the third industrial revolution, based on the information age and the rapid introduction of new technology into all facets of human life, that is changing the world. Built on the cyber revolution and on the order of codes – computer codes today, genetic codes tomorrow – the third industrial revolution is shaping the society of material production into a new, immaterial empire, into the world of signs of a 'programmed society'.[6] The advent of this society is being hastened by the rapid expansion of worldwide networks, private or public, which constitute the principal agents of globalization and accelerate its progress. If globalization today primarily concerns computers, telecommunications, financial markets, the media scene and networks, this is because globalization is first and foremost the outcome of the third industrial revolution. According to Daniel Cohen, two centuries after the first industrial revolution, that of the railways, and one century after the second industrial revolution, which was fuelled by the car, the aeroplane and electricity, the very fabric of society will from now on experience the consequences of the information revolution, which 'makes each one of us the motionless motor of an infinity of virtual shifts'.[7]

Each one of us? Well, not really. For the globalization that accompanies the third industrial revolution is in the process of splitting the world into two halves: at a time when the world of the 'globalizers' – that 'one-fifth' society that is itself under the hegemony of a self-confident 'hyperclass' – is savouring its triumph, are we going to forget the world of the 'globalized' – those four-fifths of humanity who are acted upon more than they are the actors in their destiny? But that is not all, as one of the co-authors of this work has noted elsewhere, how can we remain passive at the dawn of the twenty-first century in the face 'of the emergence of a paradoxical society, where social links will strangely depend on the severance of those same social links? *A spectre haunts the world: the dissociated society. A new age of segregation has begun to divide society, work, family, school and homeland.*'[8] Most analysts note this paradox without really explaining it: far from creating a homogeneous global society, whether desired or deplored, or bringing about the convergence of nations, the third industrial revolution and concomitant globalization subject societies to a logic of fracture. At work, they replace the Fordism of the second industrial revolution – a mechanism for integration that was at the origin of both the consumer society and the welfare state – with a flexible capitalism that ignores the work values of earlier times and in their place substitutes the double logic of precariousness and the very short term, and of 'assortative matching'.[9] This socially divisive logic widens the gap not only between qualified professionals and less qualified workers, but also between members of the same profession with practically the same qualifications. Values such as trust, loyalty and security of contract disappear, together with the temporal structure itself of human activity.[10] No longer does work represent salvation: not so long ago, it created social links; now it has become one of the most powerful factors in their disintegration, leaving a trail of exclusion, marginalization, flexibility and uncertainty.

This logic of assortative matching, of exclusive groupings, of separation, of disintegration and of disaffiliation – which means that in all spheres of activity the 'best' will only want to deal with the 'best', as was already the case in top-class competitive sport or in show-business – is affecting national identity, family structure and schooling. Institutions are breaking up and reconstituting themselves at an accelerating pace. Nations fall apart or undergo centrifugal movements that undo the existing combination of constituent ethnic groups. The rich no longer wish to support the poor. The world market slices up and splits national markets. Separatism is no longer penalized: instead, in many cases, the world market favours it. The new 'global cities' turn their backs on their national hinterland in order to play the game of competition or cooperation with other global cities. All too often, the family breaks up, under the same pressure of 'assortative matching'. Couples become the temporary mirrors of fragile socio-cultural and economic affiliations, marriages become unstable and single-parent families increase.

Even the school system is splitting up. Between 20% and 30% of students or more, depending on the individual society, remain trapped at the lowest levels of learning and hence are virtually excluded from this new society based on knowledge and education. Moreover, this rapidly expanding school and university apartheid now affects all socio-cultural categories. If adequate measures are not taken in time, this educational apartheid threatens to jeopardize the project of lifelong education for all, which lies at the very centre of UNESCO policy. Education was expected to make a decisive contribution to the redistribution of opportunities and qualifications, so as to promote the growth of societies based on the knowledge economy. It is education itself that has been forced off track by the reasoning that drives the privileged classes to isolate their children in 'good schools' and 'good secondary schools' and 'good universities' and to globalize their chances via the route of international schools and universities that bear the seal of educational elitism and consumerism. And this is occurring just at the time when managing exclusion and academic failure or presenting diplomas without value on the job market have become the unhappy tasks of national education systems. The third industrial revolution and its attendant globalization are the bearers of exclusion as certainly as storm-clouds are bearers of the storm. We allowed ourselves to be led by what we believed to be the self-regulating virtue of the 'market'. We were led astray. Without further delay, we must draw on human wisdom and experience. We will have to re-learn the art of piloting and of regulating societies, where we thought that *laisser-faire* policies alone would suffice.

At a time when most institutions are deeply shaken by the impetus of the third industrial revolution, an unprecedented wave of urbanization is disrupting the order of society, especially in the South which, in the span of one generation, has been invaded by the world of the mega-city.[11] The city itself is undergoing a remodelling process according to the logic of social and urban apartheid which, like other processes of assortative matching, begins the selection process by excluding. This self-generated apartheid – which in most regions of the world takes the form of new walled cities, with their ramparts and fortresses – calls into question the whole concept of public space, which is a component of democracy. It undermines the very foundations and promises of the social contract, as was highlighted in the 21st Century Dialogues organized by UNESCO's Analysis and Forecasting Office.[12]

Another threat hangs over democracy – the 'programmed society', as prophesied by the sociologist Alain Touraine nearly twenty years ago, now designs culture by industrial means, and has begun to manipulate the human being, 'with the risk of private appropriation of life and of human reproduction. The extraordinary growth, largely ensured by the private sector, in computer, cultural and biotechnological industries has already begun to replace classical methods of social control by new techniques in managing and governing human societies which threaten to elude governmental control and hence also to elude democracy.'[13] The social contract, already called into question by the logic of assortative matching, risks being broken a second time by a new model, which imposes private techno-structures on citizens, evading the control of elected representatives or of democratic sovereignty. Monolithic state structures are in the process of being replaced – through a game of liberalization, denationalization and concentration that produces mega-mergers – by huge, private, 'faceless' organizations, which are equally inaccessible.[14] A century and a half ago, Alexis de Tocqueville, one of the prophets of liberalism, worried about the emergence of a new industrial despotism[15] – will the twenty-first century witness the advent of a futurist version of this scenario?

Freud detected a 'discontent' in civilization. Is it possible to diagnose today, as some experts do, a 'discontent' in globalization? Some speak of a 'divorce between a sense of direction and power'. Others have referred to the loss of references, the erosion of principles, the vertigo they claimed would grip societies in transition around the third millennium. Should one prophesy a twilight of values? As Elias Canetti ironically surmised, has history, from a certain point, ceased to be real? Has the quarrel between the adherents of the 'end of history' viewpoint and advocates of 'the continuance of history' any greater purpose than a giant empty screen, crackling in front of drowsy television viewers? Has the endgame already taken place without our knowledge? Are we merely engaged in a parody of futile and vain 'extra time'? Is the whole of society given over to the cruel logic of make-believe? Has the empire of signs sucked the blood of the empire of reality and drained its life blood from the history of man?

We cannot fail to observe the increase in 'soul-sickness' at the very heart of the most prosperous societies and social categories which seem best protected from misfortune. The heart itself seems prey to a curious void, indifference and passivity grow, there is an ethical desert, passions and emotions are blunted, people's eyes are empty and solidarity evaporates. Grey areas expand, mafias work their way into the heart of states and of financial markets, and the law of the jungle prevails.[16] Amnesia wins out – the future seems unreadable. We witness the divorce between forecast and plan; long-term vision is discredited; obsession with the short-term, with precariousness, and with the tyranny of emergency situations has us in its grip and the twentieth century seems to be ending in a state of stress as we zap perpetually from one crisis to the next.

The governments of the wealthiest countries are almost exclusively preoccupied with economic affairs. They systematically reduce official development aid and their contributions to the United Nations organizations. Barring the odd exception, they are failing to honour their commitment to devote 0.7% of their GNP to public aid for development. We had the opportunity of building peace on the basis of greater sharing and of implementing international global cooperation programmes. This drive, which was undertaken within the framework of the major United Nations conferences that punctuated the last decade, is slowing down. The biggest powers call the tune. For all that, do we see world peace and order? The 1990s saw genocide recurring as though this century's end allowed horror to be rendered banal. Yet, in the age of globalization, such tragedies have taken on a new form. Societies that have lost their bearings seem to be searching for enemies, but the enemy is now diffuse and unattainable, ever-changing, everywhere and nowhere.

Now and then we become truly sick at heart. Will the twenty-first century be the century of artificial paradises, real hell and the overwhelming increase in depression hinted at by the present statistics? Will it be characterized by the massacres, anomie, violence, pandemics and the nightmarish universe predicted by Philip K. Dick in *Do Androids Dream of Electronic Sheep?*, later filmed as *Blade Runner*? Will childhood be exposed to the violence and cruelty of virtual perversions? Can we still avert the 'perfect crime' as evoked by Jean Baudrillard, where the real world is replaced by the world of simulacra, which he fears has already taken place?[17] Should we quickly relegate the twentieth century to the surplus store of history? Must we sell it off in the flea-market of oblivion?

However, hope springs eternal. If nothing else can guarantee a sense of history wagered on a radiant future, if the idea of secular salvation is no longer a winner, if, faced with the possibility of recession and regression, the very idea of progress seems to become blurred, that possibility of hope still remains. The new science of complexity, of which Ilya Prigogine was one of the inventors, and for which Edgar Morin established links with the social sciences, focuses on non-linear situations. While removing all credit from the idea that the future is given to us, the new science, with its notion of time pointer and the liberty it allows, repositions human creativity and imagination at the heart of history. Because choices and forking paths are available to us, because we can imagine history, the possibility of progress remains not as a certitude, but as a simple potentiality. The future, we used to say, is written nowhere. According to Prigogine, 'local fluctuations linked to instability can play a key role in the evolution of the system as a whole'. Perhaps we are not ready for the twenty-first century. But neither is the twenty-first century ready for us. It is neither ready to be taken on nor ready to be thought about. It remains to be imagined, sketched, moulded, dreamed, thought out and constructed, made, unmade and composed. The future is a multiplicity of trajectories and of plans. As Pier-Paolo Pasolini recalled in an epigraph to his film *A Thousand and One Nights*, the future resides not in a single dream, but in a multitude of dreams.

In the face of the strength of the powerful, only one power counts: that of the people. If we could restore their voice to millions and millions of silent people, if we could give them a real possibility of using their freedom of thought and of speech, if the voiceless people of today could get their voice back, then we would see a shift in decision-making. Then, those who are counted in or omitted from censuses, opinion polls or elections would really count when their future is being shaped. Our hope lies in the voice of the people, or democracy. Not democracy for a few, but democracy for all.

It must be acknowledged that, over the course of the past decades, humanity has advanced. Fifteen years ago, 70% of the planet lived under the cloak of oppression, of misery, deprived of their civil rights. Democracy has gained ground. The voice of the people may now be heard in places where, before, there was only silence. Peace, when it reigned, was that of safety. Today the safety of peace is beginning to prevail while the force of reason is getting the upper hand over the reason of force. Nevertheless, the reality underlying this growth in democracy deserves clear assessment, not the praises of globalization sung at conferences by the smiling storytellers of the end of history, whose edifying reports amount to a new version of children's tales. The fight against under-development has also made some progress, as shown in the annual *Human Development Reports*:

- In the course of the past 36 years, life expectancy at birth has increased by 16 years in developing countries, rising from 46 to 62 years.[18]
- The rate of infant mortality in developing countries has fallen by over 50% since 1960.[19]
- Between 1970 and 1995, the rate of literacy among adults in developing countries has increased by nearly a half, rising from 48% to 70%. Women's literacy has increased by over two-thirds in the past 20 years.[20]
- In the course of the past three decades, the number of individuals living in countries with a high rate of human development has gone from 429 million to 1.2 billion, and the number of those living in poorly developed countries has fallen from 1.9 to 1.7 billion.[21]

Invariably, however, it is the failures of the United Nations that are discussed. We forget to celebrate the successes achieved despite the regrettably frequent and widespread lack of political will. Yet should we not mention here the eradication of smallpox, or the elimination of polio, promised for the near future by the World Health Organization? Can we completely ignore the progress of vaccination or the rise in life expectancy, tragically under threat for several years now owing to AIDS in a number of African countries and owing to poverty or poor living conditions in a number of countries, such as the Russian Federation? Can we minimize the political successes represented by the end of institutional apartheid in South Africa or in Namibia? The end of war in Salvador, in Guatemala, in Mozambique or in Cambodia? Can we brush aside the hope which the confirmation of peace in Northern Ireland and the return of its fragile promise to the Near East could represent? Must we overlook, as if they were self-evident, the educational successes for which UNESCO has worked so hard, which have led to a tangible fall in the rate of illiteracy, achieved despite a considerable increase in actual population?[22] How can we disregard the progress in personal liberty, which has been most noteworthy in societies where the very notion of individual choice was practically inconceivable only four decades ago, and where the freedom of women, rapidly expanding today, was not so long ago regarded by realists merely as Utopian pipe-dreams?

It is well known that one talks only about generals who win or lose battles, never about those who manage to avoid them. Whatever we have been able to avoid and whatever never took place is invisible. Peace is invisible. We never see foresight, love or hope.[23] We do not see what we unwittingly escaped. Any forward-looking analysis must protect itself against the illusions of a media-dominated society. All too often, only the negative or the insignificant appear on television screens; in the foreground, we see exhausted refugees streaming by; a moment later, clowns, celebrations and contrived party joyfulness invade the screen. We see the violence that sells, and the myth of affordable happiness. This tale, to paraphrase Shakespeare, seems to be 'told by an idiot … signifying nothing'. Happiness, peace, health, knowledge and intelligence, real generosity and especially true love, whether secular, spiritual or sacred, have no image, as it were, on screen. They remain scarcely visible, only fleetingly glimpsed. They linger in the background, behind the set, or off the pitch, or they simply become image and fiction in the dream industry.

Likewise, globalization cannot be limited to computers, telecommunications, financial markets and organized crime, because it is not merely a question of globalization in 'real time', that is, in virtual time, but it also implies long-term globalization, and the perception of relationships within space and between individuals and nations.

Twenty-two centuries ago, the great historian of antiquity, Polybius, the first theorist of globalization, pointed out that, in the past, 'events which occurred in the world were not linked, now, they all form part of a single whole'. Globalization in the shape of world integration and the growth of interdependence breeds another form of globalization, which is the feeling of belonging to the world and of mutual interdependence. Interaction creates relations, even in a context where the relationship is an unequal one, as in any system dominated by a hegemony. In antiquity, at the heart of the Roman empire, the Stoic philosophers had thought out – centuries before Kant and with a keen sense of anticipation – the concept of cosmopolitanism, wherein can be found the ancestor of modern universalism. If globalization currently seems, at times, to call into question the classical form of universality, it also creates the globalization of self-awareness, which is today manifest in the numerous networks that exist to link the planet's citizens, regardless of political boundaries. The globalization of events creates the globalization of wills, demonstrated by the expansion of NGOs and international solidarity movements and, too, by the still rather fragile emergence of forms of world government – to which the United Nations summit bears testimony, as more and more often governments combine with key players in civil society, forecasting experts, the private sector and NGOs.

The growth of interdependence also gives rise to the globalization of society, marked by the still fragile construction of an international civil society and of international professional networks that evoke Arnold Toynbee's prophetic notion that culture encompasses three different circles: the universal, the national or local, and the transversal. In the face of the tragedies and scourges of the end of the twentieth century (inter-community massacres, rapid spread of organized crime, financial crises, growing poverty, inequality and exclusion), globalization gives rise moreover to the beginnings of a 'globalization of law and justice', first predicted by Mireille Delmas-Marty, among others.[24] The international agreement leading to an International Criminal Court is one of the first portents of this, should the states party to this agreement ratify it in coming months.

In short, globalization favours the growth of great ideas, until recently considered Utopian, but somehow compatible with certain states of citizenship, such as global citizenship, for which Edgar Morin brilliantly sketched the outline with his idea of 'earthling cosmopolitanism'.[25] Thus the ancient prophecy of the philosophers is fulfilled, according to which all men would share the same universal reasoning, necessitating a common destiny, common rights, but also common responsibilities. According to a maxim of ancient wisdom, 'Wherever he be in the world, noble man is in his homeland.'[26]

At the dawn of the twenty-first century, some attractive signs exist, uncertain and fragile, yet undeniable, allowing us to reject the hypothesis, already dismissed by Kant, according to which humanity is constantly evolving in the worst direction. To refute this thesis of 'moral terrorism', Kant furnished the following, indisputable case: he argued that, if humanity were constantly worsening, it would already have destroyed itself long ago.[27] The very possibility of a less gloomy future is essential, for what could we do, or know, or hope for, if humanity had no faith in humanity? We believe that the tenuous force of this hope is essential if we wish to tackle the four major challenges that lie at the very centre of this work's propositions, and which must be met in good time if humanity wishes to survive the coming century.[28]

The first of these challenges is peace, which constitutes the precondition for the achievement of all the other challenges, as Boutros Boutros-Ghali recalled in one of the 21st Century Talks we hold at UNESCO. The Cold War chapter has drawn to a close, but today we are experiencing – and this is a euphemism – 'hot peace'. Since the fall of the Berlin Wall, dozens of wars have continued to smoulder or have broken out and nearly thirty conflicts, of which the vast majority are taking place within states, have continued to devastate large parts of the world. The illusion that the end of the Cold War would immediately trigger a mechanism of perpetual peace and bring about the end of history, as well as an era of uninterrupted development guaranteed by the merits of *laisser-faire* politics, has well and truly evaporated. A fourth category of states has appeared on the international stage – in addition to the industrialized countries, the developing countries and countries in transition – namely, countries at war or emerging from conflict. A forgotten phenomenon has made its reappearance – the collapse and violent dissolution of a certain number of states, who founder in genocide, inter-community massacres or in wars that are so far from civil as to merit the term uncivil war.

Second challenge: will the coming century witness the rise of a new kind of poverty, the victims of which, like ghostly nocturnal shapes, will stare through the windows of social and urban apartheid, at an unprecedented wealth, enclosed behind the high walls of paradises sold by mail order? Will the twenty-first century be synonymous with growing and vertiginous in-equalities? Will the proliferation of exclusions destroy the very notion of public space, by sapping the very foundations of democracy, both within nations as well as on an international scale? Let us take a straight look at the facts:

- Between 1980 and the crisis of 1997–98, about fifteen countries enjoyed strong economic growth, which brought about an average but very un-equally distributed rise in income for the large part of the billion and a half inhabitants who live there, i.e. around one-quarter of humanity.
- During the same period, one hundred countries suffered either economic decline or stagnation, which brought about a fall in average income for one billion six hundred million people, i.e. more than one-quarter of the world's population.
- In Asia, and also in Russia, in Latin America and in a number of the world's countries, a series of financial crises triggered recession that had dramatic consequences for the populations of countries, many of which had been cited as success stories up until then.
- At the dawn of the twenty-first century, more than one billion three hundred million individuals live in absolute poverty (less than $1 per day), and their number continues to increase;[29] some reputed experts even estim-ate this figure at two billion. More than three billion people, in other words, more than half of humanity, live in poverty, with less than $2 per day.
- According to the United Nations Development Programme (UNDP), 'The poorest 20% of world citizens share the miserable fraction of 1.1% of world revenue, as opposed to 1.4% in 1991 and 2.3% in 1960, while the richest 20% shared 70% of world revenue in 1960 and 85% in 1991. Today, the net worth of the ten greatest fortunes is US$133 billion, which is more than one and a half times the total national revenue of the total number of least developed countries.' The ratio of the share of revenue held by the richest 20% compared to the poorest 20% has grown from 30:1 in 1960 to 61:1 in 1991 and to 82:1 in 1995[30] – thus we see the consolidation of the 'one-fifth' society described by Hans-Peter Martin in The Global Trap.[31]
- Over eight hundred million people are either starving or under-nourished, while two billion people suffer from nutritional deficiencies.

- Over one billion have no access to health care.
- Eight hundred and eighty million people in the world are illiterate, 866 million of these being from developing countries.
- Over one billion four hundred million have no direct access to drinking water.
- Two billion are not linked to an electricity network.
- Some 80% of the planet's population – i.e. over four and a half billion individuals – have no access to basic forms of telecommunications, that is, to the means that open the door to new technology, which holds the key to distance learning and to the new virtual economy.
- Two-thirds of the world population of those in absolute poverty are under 15 years old and 70% are women and girls.
- As one of the co-authors of this report underlines, 'today we boast of the success of the Internet, but we will still live for a long time to come in a world of *information highways* and *information subways*, of *electronic highways* and blocked *subways*. And it is the future itself which appears compromised. A future which is absent, receding and unreadable in the North, where most of the rich countries scarcely produce children any more. A future which is spoiled or already mortgaged in the South, because it is the children who, together with women, live in dire poverty.'[32]

According to a study by the United Nations Conference on Trade and Development (UNCTAD), in view of the UN anticipated growth in world population, world GDP would have to quintuple in 50 years for per capita revenue to increase by 3% per annum in developing countries, an increase that would demand considerable and sustained growth over a half-century.[33] This growth would have to be particularly strong in those places where poverty is currently worst, which may seem a fragile hypothesis in many world regions, particularly in sub-Saharan Africa. From these forecasts it is clear that *laisser-faire* policies alone will not overcome misery and poverty. Human development strategies, which give priority to education and to primary health care, are all the more crucial, even in the context of weak economic development, as they bring about a considerable improvement in the quality of life of the population.[34]

Third challenge: sustainable development and the wise management of the global environment. According to a Canadian study, it would require three Earths for the entire world to attain the degree of development and the current consumer lifestyle of North America. Our development models, based on extravagant, unlimited use of non-renewable resources, compromise in advance, perhaps irreparably, the development of future generations to whom, through selfishness and temporal short-sightedness, we deny their rights, whereas ancient Rome was capable of recognizing the rights of children not yet born in its inheritance legislation. The question is loud and clear: how much will suffice to satisfy us?[35] Everywhere, humanity is draining today the resources that would have fed the generation of tomorrow. Because it has the technical capacity to commit collective suicide, humanity now realizes that it is mortal. Who will stop this spiral? Who can teach us ecological wisdom? Who can show us the way towards another type of development, one that is more economic, more intelligent, more caring? Who can teach us, in the words of the French philosopher Michel Serres, to assume the 'mastery of mastery'? Which democratic force can halt the hand of the sorcerer's apprentice?

Fourth challenge: the 'drunken boat syndrome'.[36] As Seneca wrote, and as wise sailors say, 'There is never a favourable wind for the one who doesn't know where he is heading.' Nor is there a favourable wind for the captain who is unable to read charts or for the helmsman who has broken his rudder. Are we setting our course for the future? Do we have a direction and a long-term plan? Do we still have the tiller and the navigation equipment to remain on course? We may well ask. As a result of globalization, many states appear to have mislaid their maps, compass, piloting equipment, even the will to aim for a horizon. If they are still afloat and not already sinking, they are tossed about by the waves, as though history had fallen into the hands of 'anonymous masters',[37] the abstractions that no one can control any longer, such as financial markets, exchange rates, interest rates, mineral or agricultural markets in raw materials, indices or statistical artefacts of every kind.

At a time when the power of states often seems to have been eroded, while it may be the very nature of their function that is being transformed, what can we observe? Most problems know no borders and become international issues. It is impossible today to solve the problems of water, energy, global climate change, pollution in all its forms, food security, or development itself solely at national level. Financial transactions, the laundering of dirty money, organized crime, drug smuggling, epidemics or factors that degrade the global environment do not come to a halt at Customs or border posts. Nor do radioactive clouds. The problems of the end of the twenty-first century, which, if they are not treated in time, will become open wounds, are nomadic, stateless and without passports. They are already global problems, or will soon become such, as demonstrated by the rapid expansion of the AIDS pandemic or the contagion of the 1997–98 financial crises.

Jean Baudrillard has said that the twenty-first century will be viral. If that is true, forward thinking should focus on prevention and the invention of 'political vaccines' on the only scale on which the illness can be checked, the global scale. Which worldwide policies should we now put in place so as to render effective the cooperative initiatives that have been launched at an international level? The major conferences that were organized by the United Nations during the 1990s, such as the summits at Rio, Vienna, Cairo, Copenhagen, Beijing or Istanbul and the Kyoto Summit on the Reduction of Greenhouse-effect Gas Emissions, represent the first steps forward. General de Gaulle said, 'The Supply Corps will follow.' Alas, it did not. The follow-up did not follow through.

It is for the planet's citizens to demand this follow-up from their governments, while being aware that it will not be enough. Because it is not only action that is lacking, but vision and political courage: we refuse to acknowledge the full magnitude of problems. In the future, should nations call former leaders to account for decisions they made or adopted too late, just as today, citizens in the USA are claiming compensation from the tobacco industry for the damages caused to their health? Would it not be wise to implement as of now the decisions taken at global level? In ten years' time, in twenty years' time at the very most, won't we have to go a great deal further, much further than at Rio or Kyoto, Vienna, Cairo, Istanbul or Beijing? If states had already honoured the commitments to eradicate poverty made at Copenhagen, then we could say that we have really begun to prepare for the twenty-first century.

Here and there, a few embarrassed apologies are tendered: sorry, the poorest say, we can't afford to act. So, they turn to those richer than themselves, who echo: sorry, we don't have the means to act, we can't allow ourselves the luxury of action. So, too many governments choose to do nothing. But that was not the only option available to them. A great number of countries have begun to make education a priority and to free funds from their national budgets to finance it. Some states, such as India, have committed themselves to raising their investment in education to 6% of GDP. Overcoming inertia will be one of the main issues at stake in the run-up to 2020.

The means do exist. While public aid for development has steadily dwindled – to the point of falling in the OECD countries, to an average figure of 0.22% of GDP,[38] although the industrialized countries solemnly undertook at several United Nations conferences to raise this to 0.7% – we continue to invest in anti-development. While the Cold War ended nearly ten years ago, we continue to invest in insecurity on a grand scale, instead of funding, as a matter of priority and a preventive measure, the construction of peace. On a global scale, despite an uneven decline over the course of the 1990s, military expenditure still accounts for US$700 to US$800 billion per year, and the military budgets of some major powers are again beginning to increase. It is not possible to pay the price of war and the price of peace simultaneously. As Wally N'Dow, secretary-general of the Istanbul Summit on the City, has stressed, there are resources to give everyone 'a roof, clean water, and basic sanitary facilities at a cost of less than one hundred dollars per person'. For the 1.3 billion individuals living in a state of absolute poverty, this effort would represent US$130 billion. On the one hand, US$130 billion have been held back, while on the other hand, US$700 to US$800 billion have been spent. Are there then two sets of rules? But let us say clearly that this question does not only concern the industrialized countries. It also concerns a great number of developing countries, including some of the least developed countries, whose leaders spend a considerable part of the national budget on military expenditure, to the detriment of education and human development.[39]

Taking up the four challenges we have set out here will be the major task of the first half of the twenty-first century, and particularly for the first 20 years. The moment of truth has arrived – in one or two decades, the fate of the human race itself may be at stake, so weighty will be the combination of dangers jeopardizing the future. The issue at stake is indeed clear. Professor Ethan Kapstein, member of the Council on Foreign Relations in New York, formulated it in these terms: 'The world is heading inexorably towards one of those tragic moments about which historians of later periods ask themselves why nothing was done in time. Have the elite economists not figured out towards which abyss economic and technical change is heading? And what has prevented them from taking the necessary steps in order to avoid a world social crisis?'[40]

As Albert Einstein said, 'in moments of crisis, only imagination is more valuable than knowledge'. Before this eminent scientist, whose discoveries illustrate the spirit of the twentieth century, other prophets and poets had expressed similar intuition. 'Where danger lurks, salvation also lies,' wrote Friedrich Hölderlin. The first condition of such a rescue by imagination is anticipation, foresight and long-term vision, which should translate into forward planning and preventive action.

There are those who will say: 'The future is too complex and uncertain, let's concentrate on the present. There's no point in anticipating. We'll go wherever the wind or the current carries us.' To these people, we reply that it is too easy to shut our eyes, or to wait until difficulties arise before attempting to provide responses that would be nothing more than stop-gaps, or to act only in hasty and improvised reaction. This short-term logic, this tyranny of emergency and this shrinking of time where the present cancels out the past and remains blind to the future, all these have had disastrous effects today, reminiscent in some ways of how our predecessors reacted in the 1930s in the face of mounting danger. The dictatorship of 'real time' and the short-term view, and the absence, unique in history, of thought and of vision, condemn us to chronic lack of preparation, futile frenzy, the impossibility of transmission to future generations and tragic surprises. The hegemony based on short-term gain and temporal short-sightedness offers individuals no other choice but to yield to the iron whims of the despot of the day, or forever to adapt to events when it is already too late.

To avoid being at the mercy of circumstances in a complex and uncertain future, to be master of one's fate once more, to escape routine and obsolescence, or the intoxication of uncontrollable technology that leaves us at the mercy of cruel destiny, we must reinstate the long-term approach. We must set our sights as far ahead as possible. We must anticipate trends, detect here and now the snags looming in the future, and change in order to accommodate or reorient them. How could we ever face our children's reproaches that we were such poor captains who, instead of rising to the challenge of our times, steered the ship of humanity straight onto well-charted rocks?

Thucydides said: 'A political leader must have more than clean hands, he must have clear vision.' We must follow the example of Native Americans by placing our ear to the ground to hear from afar the approaching earthquake, or to listen for the light step of the traveller, maybe the bearer of news. Governments, international institutions, research institutes and universities should, if they have not already done so, greatly strengthen their facilities for looking ahead in the next few years, as should local and regional community organizations, key institutions of civil society and, of course, the private sector which, in the large multinational corporations, is perhaps in the forefront in this area. For its part, UNESCO has been working on this reform since 1994, through the complete renewal of its entire forecasting programme, the setting up of an Analysis and Forecasting Office, the strengthening of monitoring functions and the scientific and intellectual debates on the future within its own programme, notably through the organization of the 21st Century Talks and the 21st Century Dialogues.

Good anticipation allows for early identification of challenges, risks, promising trends, parameters and key variables and, depending on the changes predicted or the scenarios sketched, makes it possible to determine which solutions should be implemented if we wish to come closer, through a series of projects and activities, to a future that is perceived as desirable rather than unavoidable. The words of Hölderlin, cited above, take on their full meaning: when faced with rising danger and the multiplication of risks, our ability to forecast and to avert danger increases. In the last few years, forecasting capabilities have greatly increased within the scientific community – we need only think of the forecasting of world climate change, energy or water supply. Capabilities within ministerial departments as well as those of key social actors have also increased. From now on, we know that solutions exist and that awareness of problems is heightened. Only political will is really lacking, as it remains prisoner of very short-term considerations, of the fear of losing the next election and of the working of pressure groups who bring all their weight to bear, usually behind the scenes, to the detriment of public good and general welfare. As we have emphasized, globalization will never remain confined only to the networks, telecommunications, computers, the media world or markets. It will have to be based on the consolidation of a public democratic space worldwide, and on its permanent monitoring at national level. It will have to rest on an anticipatory concept of democracy that combines the synchronic demands of the social contract with the diachronic demands of responsibility towards future generations and transmission. If it can incorporate all these elements, globalization could lead to a larger, international democracy, where freedom and equality, those rival siblings, will be reconciled – to use Bergson's term – through fraternity, in other words, through sharing.

What are the cornerstones of this new order in the twenty-first century? What are its starting premisses? We are convinced that globalization cannot be reconciled with universal considerations (which it currently tends to replace) if we fail to strengthen, as was the case in 1945 when the United Nations was founded, the link between people and countries in order to avert violence and war. 'We, the people of the United Nations, resolved to preserve future generations from the scourge of war.' Thus begins the UN charter. That was in 1945 in San Francisco. With horror still present in their eyes, the peoples of the world thought of their children and their descendants and decided to spare them the heartbreaks that they had experienced.

Was it merely coincidence that 1945 also saw the growth of a strong movement towards globalization (termed 'internationalization' at that time)? As Ethan Kapstein has shown, this wave of post-war globalization included new risks and challenges for workers in many countries.[41] Governments of the time, under pressure from public opinion but also with great vision, invented the welfare state, which, in supplementing the salary benefits linked to Fordism, or mass production, would give rise to a new social contract based on negotiation, on social insurance and security and on the new caring society of the welfare state. To a great extent, this social contract corresponded to de Tocqueville's inspired forward thinking when, a century earlier, he had anticipated the triumph of the welfare state. In *On Democracy in America*, he had prophesied the growth of the social democratic state, in which, as a convinced liberal, he saw the ghost of a benevolent despotism that, if carried to extremes, could spare us 'the trouble of thinking and the worry of living'.[42]

As we are all too aware, the social contract of 1945 has not aged well. Its costs have risen significantly, its efficiency is questioned, its principles have been constantly and unremittingly attacked by the supporters of *laisser-faire* policies. The apostles of globalization and of 'the end of history' based their hopes on the prospect that the dynamics of the market economy would be strengthened by new technologies. They also wagered that a new Utopia would emerge, or rather, that on an old illusion from the eighteenth and nineteenth centuries – the market society updated by the new Dr Panglosses of blind optimism – would become reality. This Utopia was based on the idea that society would ultimately be self-regulating, with the market economy somehow pervading the social sphere, and through an active policy of dissolution, reduction or dismantling of all mediation, whether political, social and cultural or associated with the inconvenient heritage of history (social, national or religious conflicts, cultures and traditions, etc.). Basically, this was the peaceful and hyper-liberal version of the old Marxist political Utopia – the withering away of the state. The market society's Utopia saw only advantages in the reversal of the state's position and in the erosion of democratic sovereignty – in particular, it counted on the victory of market liquidity and of a democracy of customers based on direct transactions over the spectres of populism. While retaining its dogmatic prestige within the economics departments of a fair number of universities, this Utopia has today reached its limits, and seems to have been relegated increasingly to the dusty museum of ideologies, even by those economists who continue to espouse *laisser-faire* and extreme free-market policies. This is because the crisis of 1997–98 has again made obvious the necessity for regulation. When put to the test by world financial crises and relapses, the euphoric belief in the principles that challenged the 1945 social contract did not hold water. As for the idea that the new, reputedly unsinkable programmed societies could, when fully privatized and with all public services (education, health, etc.) dismantled, manage without the social contract and any form of regulation – this has already foundered on the reef of history.[43]

For all that, we do not believe – for economic as well as cultural and social reasons, which stem from the great transformation of society in the course of the last few decades – that we can restore the old 1945 contract to its original state. Over and above the economic and political obstacles, there would be the human obstacle: it would be impossible not to see that the emergence of individualism and the demand for autonomy and liberty, which are linked to the emergence of the network society and the third industrial revolution, would be violently opposed to the restoration of such a contract. The globalized world is also the individualized world where the subject, to use Alain Touraine's term, reverts to a multitude of personal trajectories, plans and intivdual itineraries, which combine memory, reason and imagination, the retrospective and the prospective.

However, the idea is beginning to emerge – this was also one of the main themes of the 21st Century Dialogues organized at UNESCO in September 1998 – that 'the third industrial revolution and the globalization that accompanies it have not yet found the new social contract that they require'. The societies of the twenty-first century will have to invent it rapidly, because the contract of the second industrial revolution and of 1945 – Fordism, or mass production, in the economic sphere and the welfare state in the social – continues to disintegrate before our very eyes.

In 1989 the fall of the Berlin Wall followed by the implosion of the Soviet system opened up numerous possibilities for change. The Iron Curtain had corroded – based on the idea of equality, it had left liberty to one side. We are today witnessing the economic success of a system based on the concept of liberty that has forgotten equality and solidarity alike. But this success in terms of book-keeping is virtually a political failure because it is coupled with an ethical vacuum and with an absolute lack of purpose. The power of globalization is meaningless. To render globalization humane, to make it into a truly universal promise and a plan, to give it meaning, this is the course we want to plot for the twenty-first century.

On the question of development, radical opposition is beginning to die out, as a growing number of experts note. Lines of convergence are being drawn. As observed by Amartya Sen, the idea is emerging that development in the twenty-first century is based on intelligence rather than on matter, and on education and knowledge rather than on 'blood, sweat and tears' and on the sacrifice of one or more generations.[44] Moreover, according to one economist:

> both the market and the State reach limits, so it is better to combine rather than to oppose their rationale. The State takes strategic decisions while the market may adopt the role of allocating goods on a day-to-day basis, which does not involve any social choices. Experience shows that 'State alone' leads to failure while 'market only' meets obvious limits in the field of work (unemployment and inequality), of finance (potentially destabilizing role of speculation) or of environment (necessity of collective norms). Micro-economic theories confirm the restrictive conditions in which a balanced market is the optimal situation. Analysis of endogenous technical progress re-confirms the importance of public intervention for development (education, innovation), while new political economics show that the State never plays the neutral role of a simple tool in development policies. Thus, the alternation of interventionist and liberal strategies is not unavoidable. The Asian countries' crisis begun in 1997 leaves us with hope for an original synthesis for the twenty-first century – the search for complementary relations between the State and the market, at the heart of institutional arrangements which are rich in other forms of coordination, as the basis for development.[45]

As Joseph Stiglitz, then first vice-president and chief economist at the World Bank, recognized:

> the crisis, in Asia and especially in Russia, revealed the importance for development of questions such as the financial institutions, corruption, and bankruptcy laws. The key to success, declared the 'Washington consensus' [the economists of the World Bank and of IMF], lay in large-scale equilibrium, in liberalization and in privatization. Countries have followed this programme but without any success. The Chinese decided that all of this was totally unnecessary. Instead

of privatizing, they concentrated on new enterprises, instead of freeing commerce, they concentrated on being competitive. And China now appears to be the country with the best economic balance! The rate of poverty has fallen from 66% to 22%! It is impossible to ignore this achievement. Privatization was, in theory, supposed to reduce corruption, but it was found that where there was no institutional framework, it tended instead to increase corruption. We have learned that to persist in transforming a country too quickly can destroy the social contract, undermine confidence, enrich the elite and impoverish the others. All of this causes damage which takes a long time to repair.[46]

Globalization must certainly be rendered humane. It must also be universal. The sceptics and the cynics will claim that this is merely a Utopian, pious hope. In fact, nothing can guarantee the advent of this order, except the desire, love, will and courage within each one of us: qualities that could restore meaning to the human experience if we only so decided. It is up to us alone to reject the bleak prophecies that predict voluntary slavery. It is up to us to build up a series of intermediate projects and activities, so as to bridge the arid gulf that separates realism from Utopia. For this, political responsibility is of paramount importance. At present, we all too often forget this. As Max Weber emphasized, it is the politician's task to structure time, to determine time-frames for action. It was Max Weber who wrote the inspirational phrase, 'the possible would never be achieved if, in the world, we did not constantly keep trying to achieve the impossible'.[47]

As futurists will have noticed, we have not formulated any scenarios in this Introduction, and very few will be put forward in the chapters of *The World Ahead*. Certainly, this work is not far removed from the future-oriented work carried out by the Analysis and Forecasting Office, which, within the framework of foresight exercises suggested by UNESCO's partners, was persuaded, with all usual precautions, to propose a number of scenarios. Nevertheless, we have chosen not to use this method in *The World Ahead*. Forecast models only too often display a propensity to lapse into futurology. It is a question of academic hypothesis, and historical reality has always consisted of a practical combination of scenarios, a 'cocktail' of versions of the future. On the other hand, we have sketched some images of possible futures and also of desirable futures. What matters is to anticipate, through our vision and action, the risks and chances in an uncertain world. It is a question of identifying the precise composition of the cocktail of trends that could develop their potential in the twenty-first century. What will be the hierarchy of principles in the future? Will cooperation be subordinated to competition, or, without totally abolishing it, can it become humane? Will organized crime networks take control of the engine-room, or will their influence be contained, and then gradually reduced or even eliminated without undermining democracy? Will chaos be limited to a minimum, or will it spread throughout the world? Will social and urban apartheid be contained and combated, or will it extend its logic of exclusion right through the social framework? Anticipation can, moreover, help us to clarify our policies regarding the steps which must be taken to favour the primacy of those trends, principles and values that seem likely to minimize risks and dangers and to achieve a future that is recognized as desirable.

It is at this point that we cannot avoid rethinking society, that the hypothesis of a new world contract arises, so as to humanize the third industrial revolution and its attendant globalization, because foresight cannot satisfy itself with the identification of certain trends, the formulation of certain hypotheses and certain scenarios, and the detection of certain future snags. Anticipation is the art of the desirable. It is also the art of converting the imagination into history, through the definition of a concrete scale of plans and action. In this way, it escapes the trap of Utopia and cynicism alike. Anticipation is the vision and the memory of the future.

Foresight is a duty, short-sightedness is a crime. For the time being, the globalization of computers, markets, telecommunications and viruses is a boat adrift. Even from a purely economic viewpoint, greater international democracy in tandem with the growth of a forward-looking concept of democracy will become imperative if we wish to avoid shipwreck, to rise to the four challenges we touched on, to chart a course for globalization, to restore a perspective to the plan and direction of the human experience, and to solve the concrete problems of humanity in time, rather than adopt a *laisser-faire* attitude and wait for crises to arise before attempting unsuccessfully to deal with them.

Four contracts should form the pillars of this new international democracy and *The World Ahead* proposes to explore some of its more concrete aspects, without aiming to be exhaustive. UNESCO, and others, will return to some of the major problems we have been unable to tackle or have merely touched on, such as the future of work from the viewpoint of the third industrial revolution, the future of the oceans, the multi-faceted threat of pollution, notably invisible and chemical pollution, the problems of bio-ethics in the face of breakthroughs in science and industry, or forward-looking approaches to development. All of these subjects are already, or will be, at the core of future deliberation by UNESCO. To paraphrase Shakespeare, there are more things in this world than *The World Ahead* can hold.

In our opinion, the twenty-first century, if it wishes to bring about a new alliance between nations, people and citizens in order to avert violence and war, must be based on four contracts – social, natural, cultural and ethical. According to the principle of the four contracts we propose for entry into the twenty-first century, we have tried to pave the way for a new social contract for the twenty-first century, not sliding backwards, but striding forward boldly with eyes wide open. Bearing in mind demographic forecasts and the constant growth of inequality, the first priority is to rebuild solidarity through the eradication of poverty and the reduction of the scandalous disparities that lead to despair and exclusion. What must the long-term policies be, the basis of which must be established without delay if we wish to eradicate poverty – in line with the commitment made at the Copenhagen Summit on social development? How can we fight against urban apartheid, how can we alter the city and thus change life? How can we turn to good account the third industrial revolution and humanize it before it is too late? How can we redistribute the dividends of globalization, in order to end the 'one-fifth' society that calls into question the very foundations of democracy? How can we fight against the anomie of drugs and organized crime that threaten humanity's future, since it is youth that pays the heaviest price for these scourges? How can we pave the way for a new social contract founded not on the exclusion of an increasingly large segment of humanity, but on greater respect for the dignity and legitimate aspirations of each individual? How can we give women their rightful place in society, and establish both equality and effective sharing in all spheres of human activity? In this regard, *The World Ahead* sketches out a number of recommendations for thought and action in order to translate the new social contract into effective commitments, going beyond national and international rhetoric and divergent viewpoints on politics or economics.

The second contract *The World Ahead* outlines is the natural contract, which must be founded on an alliance between science, development and environmental preservation.[48] How can we put into effect the commitments of the Rio Earth Summit or of the Kyoto Summit on the reduction of greenhouse-effect gas emissions? How can we reconcile the protection of the biosphere and the development of the sociosphere? How can we go beyond the social contract, negotiated among contemporaries, to conclude a natural contract for sustainable development and co-development with the Earth, based on the concept of an ethics of the future and the passing on of a heritage to the coming generations? How can we master mastery and free science from its Promethean complex of dominating nature? How can we mobilize the decision-makers and public opinion to resolve, through cooperation and negotiation, those problems that call for coordinated responses at both global and regional levels? How can we solve the problems of desertification and of land erosion? How can we prevent the twenty-first century from becoming the century of water wars, just as the twentieth century was too often that of oil wars? How can we guarantee that there will be food for everyone and that this food will be healthy and of good quality – how can we ensure food security from the point of view of both quantity and health? How can we control the revolution in agricultural biotechnology? How can we harness and diversify energy, while drawing ever closer to the idea of a revolution in ecological and developmental efficacy, theories developed by the Club of Rome in its report *Factor Four*? How can we place education and research at the service of sustainable development? Which infrastructures should we put in place so that cities are not only habitable and pleasant to live in, but may also last? How can we guarantee that Earth will once again be 'blue like an orange', in the prophetic words of the poet Paul Eluard? We have a home and a homeland in common – the planet. From now on, learning to preserve and respect it while managing its resources in a healthy and intelligent fashion is an absolute necessity. On that too, *The World Ahead* draws up a number of concrete pointers and recommendations so that the 'natural contract' may lead to real commitments to be negotiated, budgeted for and defined within a time-frame, beyond polemic and international disagreements on these issues.

The third contract is the cultural contract.[49] This contract is inextricably linked to the two previous contracts, and lifelong education for all will be one of its basic tenets. This is a vast endeavour that must be the great plan for the twenty-first century, and whose final target can only be realistically achieved towards 2100. This objective should be a top priority not only for governments but for society as a whole, for the private sector and for the players in the 'quaternary economy' currently in gestation, and for each citizen who, like Socrates, will never cease learning and learning to learn. But this horizon necessarily remains very far off, even if an early form of it already exists at the heart of industrial societies, and any attempt to universalize it will be riddled with obstacles and pitfalls. Moreover, it will not constitute a miracle solution in itself. To launch it, it will not be sufficient to free vital technical, human and financial resources. It will also be necessary to make lifelong education for all a basic facet of democracy and thus to do away with the burgeoning school and university apartheid and to rebuild education as a citizen's project for civil training and for the provision of equal opportunities for all. In the absence of any firm political will or of a genuine long-term plan for education, we could easily witness the division of lifelong education for all, according to a divisive logic in which a minority of 'chosen ones' would accede to the 'paradise of knowledge', while the 'damned', i.e. the victims of knowledge exclusion, would be doomed to stay in new educational ghettos and the intermediate masses to ineffective purgatories.

The revolution in new technology constitutes a fundamental challenge, but also a decisive tool at the heart of the cultural contract. How can we move from the information society to the knowledge society? How can we combat illiteracy? How can we provide quality secondary education universally, to benefit men and women on an equal basis? Faced with the rapid evolution of knowledge and of techniques, what will be the new methods of education that would favour an updating and a renewal of knowledge? What will the school of the future be like and what will be taught there in the twenty-first century? How can we reassert the value of technical and professional teaching? How can we completely redesign higher education, so that it will indeed be accessible to all on merit, and so that it may become a system of lifelong education for all?

How can we turn the promise of information highways and knowledge into reality for everybody? How can we promote the infrastructural development of a knowledge-based society in the South, in places where the telephone is still a luxury? How can we promote the growth of science and of technological applications in societies that are victims of the brain drain? What are the threats that new technology poses to the destiny of societies and of cultures? How can that same technology contribute to the strengthening of education, of scientific research, of the application of knowledge, of intercultural dialogue and of the free circulation of information and of knowledge? What does the future hold for books and reading? What is the future of linguistic diversity – the heritage stored within each individual? By 2020, will distance learning turn educational institutions into virtual worlds, or will it establish on-line education, which may include the excluded and reach the 'untouchables' of knowledge?

Will we be wise enough to draw up a cultural contract that will favour cultural plurality and comity rather than promoting cultural conformity? Are we heading for a clash of cultures or a process of cultural cross-fertilization? Will we be capable of bridging the cultural gap that, at the very heart of society, separates the privileged from the excluded, possibly by devising, as was recommended in an international report, a programme of action founded in particular on the extensive recourse to new technology and on the use of centres for communication and exchange, which should include schools, theatres, museums, cultural centres, citizens' networks and businesses?[50] Will we be capable of establishing, thanks to mass teacher exchanges negotiated at regional or international level, widespread trilingualism in primary education, at an age when it is so easy to learn the language and the culture of others? Will we also be able to introduce a cultural dimension into this development? Will we be able to promote cultural policies that will, by increasing the available cultural programmes, be able to create the demand for culture through education and through artistic and aesthetic training? Will we be better equipped to join up the three spheres of culture, the global, the national or local, and the transversal cultures that are rapidly growing in the age of networks? How can we reconcile creation, tradition and development? Will we be able to give development a soul and to place the human being, all too often nowadays a slave to it, once more at its heart?

The fourth contract is the ethical contract, which must reinvest the human experience with meaning and perspective. This contract should have three different aspects. In the first instance, how can we promote the growth of a culture of peace and of intelligent development, which, instead of keeping human beings down, would be synonymous with growth based on knowledge and on the networking of knowledge and of competency, which are, by definition, immaterial? How can we move from a logic of reconstruction, based on post-conflict surgery, to a logic of prevention, based on the antici-pation of conflicts and on the forecasting of crises? How can we encourage the emergence of a culture of peace, founded on the devaluing of violence, on the effective implementation of the full rights of man, on the active promotion of pluralism and of dialogue between all the components of society, and on ethical education towards peace, democracy and the respect of the other? How can we favour the progress of the application of human rights, beginning with the total abolition in all countries of the death penalty?

We must also give a firmer hold to democracy, by reintroducing the concept of the long term into development and the public space of the city. Democracy will, indeed, have to be anchored in the long term, by placing at the heart of institutions and of society this anticipatory and forward-looking concept of citizenship as a project, the necessity of which we have already underlined.[51]

This future-oriented democracy will have to reconcile the fundamentally contemporary nature of the contract with the necessity of long-term vision and responsibility for future generations. It will also have to extend democracy in space, through the introduction of appropriate forms of international democracy. As was stressed in the 21st Century Talks, the key questions of regulation and government will remain at the centre of world debate over the coming decades. Faced with the extent of the challenges already mentioned – and the reality of recent military intervention that was decided without the backing of the Security Council and outside the framework of the United Nations – can we put forward the hypothesis that we are advancing towards global democracy? Faced with the growth of a global market economy, will it be necessary to invent, one day, as one expert suggested, 'a democracy which, like the market, is not limited by territory, a democracy without borders in either space or time'?[52] Can we create modes of international integration equivalent to those of the European model, or is this pure illusion? From now on, faced with international problems such as people without state or passport, can we do without such a framework? We are convinced that, as has been the case in emerging nation-states, problems of government, of arbitration, of regulation and of fitness to decide the law at a global level will be central to our twenty-first-century agenda. These issues will attract the growing attention of states, but also of international civil society and of global citizen networks, which are already growing widely. They will render absolutely indispensable the reflection and actions of thoroughly transformed international institutions. For this reason, in The World Ahead, at the end of Chapter 18 we outline a few areas for reflection and action concerning the imperative reform of the United Nations.

The development of democracy on an international scale should also occur at the level of society through the dissemination of a new culture of democracy, which will settle conflicts by going beyond the aporia of assimilation and the fragmentation of identity, and through the spread of a new culture of association, which will allow us to go beyond the contradictions between state and market, through the rediscovery of the very basis of democracy – association, a founding concept for both Rousseau and de Tocqueville.[53]

But this new ethical contract may not be concluded without solidarity and sharing, therefore, without the redistribution of the benefits of globalization, which must benefit everyone and not just one-fifth of the population. Bringing the benefits of globalization to all was the objective which the G8 members set themselves at one of their recent summits.[54] This commitment must be accomplished within the reality of history. Redistribution

> should take place at the heart of every society, or of every group of societies, and at a global level – which presupposes, as Ethan Kapstein underlined in the *Twenty-first Century Dialogues*, a 'worldwide organization for taxation', without which any project of redistribution on a global scale would be swept away by market logic. Such an organization would at least include minimal thresholds for imposing taxation and short-term taxes on movements of capital, similar to those put in place by Chile. The cohesion of economic and social policies could be further aided by international organizations which were genuinely multilateral and adopted by all players.[55]

The redistribution of the benefits of globalization will also be indispensable if we wish to help Africa to make a new start – this is why we refer, in the fourth section of this work, to the crucial question for the coming decades: will the African miracle really take place? Democracy will not be strengthened in a lasting fashion unless, by restoring a sense of participation, we give back to citizens the taste for public affairs and the desire to exercise political rights. The 'cogito ergo sum' of the twenty-first-century citizen should become, 'I participate, therefore I am'.[56] If I fail to participate, I am counted in censuses and in polls, I am accounted for in election results, but do I really count? To exist in the twenty-first century will be to participate in it. Everyone must be aware of the enormous gulf that today separates democracies from this ideal, given the lack of interest or indifference that pervades many countries, and translates into abstention from voting and into a deficit of democratic activity within civil society and political movements. The choice must be made between citizen participation or the domination of professional democracy where decisions are moulded by pressure groups and taken by a select few.[57]

The third aspect of this new contract for peace and global government, which concludes *The World Ahead*, is directly linked to the preceding aspect. It is the vast area of ethics of the future, explored on the initiative of the International Council for Social Sciences and the Analysis and Forecasting Office. What political and ethical reference points will we need to establish in order to put an end to the tyranny of emergency, in the name of which we invest in enterprises doomed to failure, often with the best intentions in the world? How can we reinstate the long-term view and free ourselves from the hegemony of the short term? How, in this perspective, can we strengthen our ability to anticipate and foresee? Which policies should be adopted and applied so that evolving science is no longer divorced from conscience, which is also rapidly evolving? How can we ensure that in current political action, today's decisions cease to ignore all long-term vision in the name of blind pragmatism and of adjustment – raised to the status of dogma, in the name of decisions that nearly always favour the present and the powerful, in the name of a moral short-sightedness that tacitly assumes rights over future generations? How can we introduce into our children's education, from the beginning of the very next academic year, an ethics *of* the future which is not ethics *in* the future, indefinitely postponed, but rather an ethics of the present *for* the future? We have attempted to answer some of these questions in the conclusion.

At the dawn of the twenty-first century, we propose seven principles for the students of the future:

- *Trust the people*, unless you have proof that your confidence is misplaced – it is impossible to build a lasting future on mistrust.
- *Care for the planet*, not because it belongs to you, but because it has been given to you to hold in usufruct and you must pass it on to your children and to your children's children exactly as you found it.
- *Smart is beautiful*, because the future of the human race lies in the immaterial world of the spirit. The development of the twenty-first century will be founded on grey matter, on the growth of intelligence and on the blossoming of the soul and of wisdom.
- *Prepare for peace if you want peace*, because if you prepare for war, you will have war.
- *Give to others if you wish to receive*, because as the African proverb says, love is the only thing which grows when shared.
- *In a global world and market, we need a global democracy*: there will be no 'global village' while there is no citizenship of the nation Earth, mutually supportive and respectful of national citizenship and of local cultures.
- *Our future is not written in advance – it is in the hands of all of us.*

Some will ask whether have we quantified the contracts we propose for the twenty-first century. Throughout this work, we provide concrete indications for a certain number of priority measures. Will the cost be too high? Let us remember that global military expenditure represents more than US$700 billion per annum, and that we could make considerable savings by reducing this unproductive expenditure, by improving public service productivity, by streamlining administration, by abolishing a number of extravagant and ineffective subsidies and by fighting positively against corruption. Let us remember that the United Nations Development Programme (UNDP) estimates at only US$40 billion per annum the cost of achieving and maintaining universal access to basic education, to adequate nutrition, to drinking water and to elementary sanitary infrastructures, as well as to gynaecological and obstetric care. This sum represents less than 4% of the total wealth of the world's 225 largest fortunes. Is the price of peace and development too high? Is the price of democracy too high?

'Expect nothing from the twenty-first century,' said Gabriel Garcia Marquez. 'It is the twenty-first century that expects everything from you.'[58]

Notes

1. Ilya Prigogine 'Foreword' in F. Mayor, with the collaboration of T. Forstenzer, *The New Page*, Dartmouth Publishing/UNESCO, Paris, 1995.

2. Jérôme Bindé, 'Ready for the 21st century?', *Le Monde*, 29 July 1998, reproduced in over eighty newspapers and periodicals in different regions around the world.

3. Eric J. Hobsbawm, *Age of Extremes: The Short Twentieth Century 1914–1991*, Abacus, London, 1995.

4. Aminata Traoré, Minister for Culture in Mali, UNESCO, June 1999.

5. See Daniel Cohen, *The Wealth of the World and the Poverty of Nations*, trans. Jacqueline Lindenfeld, MIT Press, Cambridge, MA, 1998.

6. Alain Touraine, *Critique de la Modernité*, Fayard, Paris, 1992.

7. Cohen, *The Wealth of the World*.

8. Jérôme Bindé, 'Quelle société pour le XXe siècle?', Preface to the *Bilan du Monde*, 1999 edition, Le Monde, Paris, 1999.

9. 'Appariements sélectifs', in Cohen, *The Wealth of the World*, p. 63.

10. See particularly Richard Sennett and Roger Sue, communications to *21st Century Dialogues*, UNESCO, 16–19 September 1998, in Bindé (ed.), *Les Clés du XXIe siècle*, UNESCO Publishing/Éditions du Seuil, Paris, 2000.

11. See Chapter 3.

12. J. Bindé, 'Towards urban apartheid?', presentation to 21st Century Dialogues, September 1998, published in *Futuribles*, Paris, May 2000 and in Bindé (ed.), *Les Clés du XXIe siècle*.

13. Bindé, 'Quelle société pour le XXIe siècle?'.

14. Anaisabel Prera Flores, 'El poder sin rostro', UNESCO, May 1999.

15. Alexis de Tocqueville, *On Democracy in America*, Part 4, Chapter V, Paris, 1835–40.

16. *Business Week*, 'The Mob on Wall Street', 16 December 1996.

17. Jean Baudrillard, *Le Crime parfait*, Editions Galilée, Paris, 1995.

18. UNDP, *Human Development Report 1998*, Oxford University Press, New York, 1998.

19. Ibid.

20. Ibid.

21. UNDP, *Human Development Report 1996*, Oxford University Press, New York, 1996.

22. See Chapter 16.

23. Federico Mayor, 'The duty of remembrance (1945–1999)', *El País*, 22 April 1999, reproduced in many dozens of newspapers and periodicals in different regions worldwide.

24. Mireille Delmas-Marty, *Trois Défis pour un droit mondial*, Seuil, Paris, 1998; *Vers un Droit commun de l'humanité*, conversation with Philippe Petit, Textuel, Paris, 1996; *Pour un Droit commun*, Seuil, Paris, 1994.

25. E. Morin, 'Our common home', *UNESCO Courier*, November 1995.

26. This maxim of Stoic philosophy from antiquity, which is the forerunner of the idea of world citizenship and of cosmopolitanism, is quoted by Peter Coulmas, *Weltbürger: Geschichte einer Menschheitssehnsucht*, Rowolt Verlag, Hamburg, 1990.

27. Immanuel Kant, 'The Conflict of the Faculties (1798)', Paris, Vrin, 1998.

28. The argument that follows is inspired by analyses developed at the third session of *21st Century Talks*, by J. Bindé, synthesized in the article 'Ready for the 21st century?', and 'Quelle société pour le XXIe siècle?'. See also Bindé (ed.), *Les Clés du XXIe siècle*.

29. United Nations, Res. A/51/178.

30. UNDP, *Human Development Report*, Oxford University Press, New York, 1996, 1997, 1998.

31. H. P. Martin and H. Schumann, *The Global Trap: Globalization and the Assault on Prosperity and Democracy*, Zed Books, London, 1997.

32. Bindé, 'Ready for the 21st century?'.

33. UNCTAD, 1994, study quoted by Jacques Decornoy, 'Inquiétants nuages au-dessus de la FAO', *Le Monde diplomatique*, October 1995.

34. See Chapter 2.

35. Alan Durning, 'Asking how much is enough', *State of the World 1991*, Worldwatch Institute, Washington, DC, 1991.

36. Bindé, 'Ready for the 21st century?'.

37. Marc Ferro, 'Médias et intelligence du monde', *Le Monde diplomatique*, Paris, January 1993.

38. OECD, *Report of the Development Cooperation Development Assistance Committee 1998*, OECD, Paris, 1999.

39. See Chapter 18.

40. Quoted in Bindé, 'Ready for the 21st century?'.

41. E. Kapstein, Communication to 21st Century Dialogues, UNESCO, 16–19 September 1998, *Les Clés du XXIe siècle*.

42. De Tocqueville, *On Democracy in America*, Part 4, Chapter VI.

43. Anaisabel Prera Flores, 'Sociedad de mercado? No, gracias', *El País*, Madrid, August 1998.

44. Amartya Sen, 'Development thinking at the beginning of the twenty-first

century', in Louis Emmerij (ed.), *Economic and Social Development into the Twenty-first Century*, Interamerican Development Bank (IDB), Washington, DC, 1997.

45. Robert Boyer, 'Etat, marché, développement: une nouvelle synthèse pour le XXIᵉ siècle?', paper presented at conference 'Au-delà du Consensus de Washington', conference organized by the Ecole des hautes études en sciences sociales, in co-operation with UNESCO, UNESCO, Paris, 16–17 June 1999.

46. Joseph Stiglitz, 'Un hérétique à la Banque mondiale', *Libération*, Paris, 25 June 1999. See also J. Stiglitz, 'Towards a New Paradigm for Development: Strategies, Policies and Processes', Prebisch lecture at UNCTAD, 1998.

47. Max Weber, 'La Vocation du politique', in *Le Savant et le Politique*, Plon, Paris, 1959 (French translation of *Politik als Beruf*, 1919).

48. For the definition of this concept, see Michel Serres, *The Natural Contract*, University of Michigan Press, Ann Arbor, 1995.

49. See J. Pérez de Cuéllar, 'Le contrat', *Le Monde*, 12 December 1992; this article was also published in numerous leading newspapers in the different regions of the world. See also the Preliminary Outline of the *World Report on Culture and Development*, World Commission on Culture and Development, document CCD.III/94/Doc.2, UNESCO, February 1994.

50. Report of the Lisbon Group, *Limits to Competitivity*, Editions du Boréal, Canada, 1995.

51. This anticipatory conception of democracy has, in particular, been developed by Mihajlo Mesarovic, Meeting of Special Advisers, UNESCO, 11 March 1998.

52. J. Attali, Communication to the 21st Century Talks, 6 April 1998, quoted in *Le Monde*, 28 April 1998. See *Les Clés du XXIe siècle*.

53. Roger Sue, Communication to the 21st Century Dialogues, UNESCO, 16–19 September 1998, *Les Clés du XXIe siècle*.

54. G8, 'The Birmingham Summit', 15–17 May 1998.

55. Bindé, 'Quelle société pour le XXIe siècle?'

56. Federico Mayor, Opening Address of the 29th Session of the General Conference, UNESCO, 21 October 1997.

57. See Michael Walzer, 'What democracy for the future?', 21st Century Talks, UNESCO, 13 November 1997, see *Les Clés du XXIe siècle*.

58. Gabriel Garcia Marquez, speech to the forum 'Vision of the next generation: Latin America and the Carribean on the threshold of the new millennium', organized by UNESCO and the IDB, Paris, 8 March 1999.

. . . .

PART ONE

Towards a New Social Contract

. . . .

CHAPTER I

Population: Is a Time-bomb Ticking?[1]

§ FOR the ancient Chinese strategist Sun Tzu, war was 'the province of life and death, the road to survival or ruin'.[2] The same could be said for population. Are we then right to fear that a population time-bomb is putting the very survival of the human species and the biosphere at risk? The growth of the world population during the second half of the twentieth century has undoubtedly caused one of the biggest upheavals in human history. It took some 40,000 years since the time of Cro-Magnon man to reach the figure of 2.5 billion inhabitants in 1950, but a mere 37 years has been enough for that figure to double.[3] It has been estimated that the world's population reached 6 billion on 12 October 1999.[4] Numerous experts are afraid that this expansion, concentrated for the most part in the developing countries, and more particularly in the poorest among them, will provoke an 'explosion' of poverty and induce a rise in migrations, especially from the South to the North. Fortunately, the prospects have brightened a little, largely owing to progress in education over the last few years.

Time-bomb or Demographic Transition?

According to the United Nations Population Fund (UNFPA) the growth of the world's population 'has slowed down, is continuing to slow down and could continue to slow down even more in the coming decades'.[5] Currently the world population is increasing by about 80 million persons a year – the equivalent of almost one new Germany each year or a new South America every four years.[6] This figure is slightly less than the peak of 92 million reached in 1992. The decline in absolute terms is largely due to family planning and to the much higher proportion of girls attending schools, which rose from 59% to 76% between 1960 and 1995.

According to the 'median' projections of the United Nations, the world population is expected to reach 8 billion by 2025 and 9.4 billion by 2050, eventually stabilizing at slightly under 11 billion towards 2200.[7] These figures are based on a scenario in which fertility levels out at a reproduction rate of about two children per woman, as against the present rate of 2.96. Other projections arrive at 7.7 billion inhabitants (the 'low' variant) or 11.1 billion (the 'high' variant) by 2050, and forecast for 2150 a population of 3.6 billion ('low' variant) and 27 billion ('high' variant).[8] The big differences between the various projections are essentially due to different forecasts regarding the speed with which the fertility rate will decrease: if fertility remained at its present level, the human population would reach 14.9 billion by 2050 and 296 billion by 2150, an outcome that is obviously purely theoretical. The pace at which fertility declines is directly proportionate to education, level of training (especially for girls) and development. Indeed, the population growth of between 90 and 100 million persons a year, the figure in our minds at the World Conference on Education for All in Jomtien, Thailand in 1991, has not been reached: from this point of view, the present trends are the best news we have received as the twentieth century comes to an end.

Demographers have often been surprised by the actual turn of events in the last few decades, and some reputed specialists still regard the 'medium variant' of the United Nations as excessive and take the view that population growth will slow down sooner and more sharply. According to Hervé Le Bras, for example, we must prepare for 'a further radical change' to follow the one that has already taken place.[9] According to Jacques Vallin, 'it is not impossible that the low hypothesis will turn out to be the right one'.[10]

As the UNFPA stresses, world population growth reached a maximum (2%, and even 2.5% in less developed regions) in the years between 1965 and 1970 owing to the discrepancy between a still high birth rate (in some cases even higher as a result of the elimination of certain pathological causes of infertility) and a lower death rate as a result of technical advances in the fight against major endemic and infectious diseases and in environmental management.

Since the beginning of the 1990s, population growth for the planet as a whole has dropped to 1.48% per year (1990–95), the lowest rate recorded since the end of the Second World War.[11] For developing regions it is currently 1.77% and could well fall to 1.1% by 2020–25 and to 0.8% by 2040–50.[12] In Asia and Latin America, the annual growth in population is even beginning to decline in absolute figures. The majority of developing countries, however, will for a long time be faced with a rising population owing to the 'population explosion' of previous decades: of the 2.8 billion additional inhabitants for which the earth has had to make room between 1950 and 1990, 2.4 billion live in developing countries, where the age structures have been transformed. A 'giant wave' reached childbearing age in the 1980s. This effect of demographic inertia will clearly have a big impact, at least during the first few decades of the twenty-first century.

Depending on the country, life expectancy at birth has doubled or even tripled. In Sri Lanka, for example, the anti-malaria campaign achieved, in the space of two years (1946–48), a gain of twelve years in life expectancy. Since the 1950s there have been gains of 23 years in Asia, 20 in North Africa, 17 in Latin America and 15 in sub-Saharan Africa. In many countries one-third – or in the case of Africa one-half – of the population is now under 20 years of age. The younger generation has never been so numerous: 31.4% of the world's population is under 14 and 18% between 15 and 24.[13] The challenge is unprecedented. In the words of a demographer, 'for human beings, the twentieth century will have been that of their learning to gain control of their lives'. Having pushed back the moment of death, the task had become that of 'mastering life by choosing the number of children desired'.[14]

This downward trend in fertility has become virtually worldwide since the 1960s, due to the expansion of education and the fact that a growing number of countries throughout the world have introduced family planning policies. Their efforts have been sustained and guided by a vast network of financial and technical international assistance (1.3 billion dollars per year at the beginning of the 1990s) provided by United Nations agencies such as the UNFPA, UNICEF, the WHO or UNESCO and by the major NGOs. The countries untouched by the trend are now the exception: their populations represented only 8% of the world population in 1995 as against 71% in 1965. Between 1960 and 1990, the proportion of families in developing countries making use of contraception rose from 9% to 51%. The 'demographic transition' (the transition from high to low death rates and birth rates) is spreading. These factors, however, will have a different impact in different countries, even where the initial situations were comparable: world population trends might well, therefore, become increasingly diverse, and perhaps more fragmented and contrasting. As one demographer points out, 'there is no evidence that, at the continental or state level, inequality concerning death is regressing; nor is there any reason to believe that, once the decline in fertility has started, it can be halted at the level of replacement'. As a result, 'it is impossible to reason as if the trends observed at the end of this century will continue automatically, as if population changes would be unaffected by the human, cultural, social and economic environment foreshadowed on the eve of the third millennium'.[15]

In this case, we could in the very long term be confronted not with a worsening of the population explosion, long seen by numerous experts as the warning sign of an apocalypse, but with its opposite: within a few decades the world population might gradually 'implode', a development that is already beginning in certain countries where the population is declining.

Although the pace of growth has slowed down in many countries, it remains very high (2.9% per year on average) in Africa, where each woman bears an average of 5.7 children as against 3.3 for all developing regions taken together and 2.96 for the world as a whole.[16] By 2050, Africa might well be home to 22% of the world population, with nearly 2 billion persons; by 2025 it will contain 18% of all human beings (1.5 billion persons) unless the demographic projections are once again proved wrong – in other words, its population is expected to more than double in the space of 35 years.[17] In Africa, life expectancy at birth could rise to 71.9 years by 2050, a level still below that reached by the industrialized countries in 1995 (74.2 years).

The downward trend in fertility, however, which started from very high rates, appears to have commenced in a growing number of countries in sub-Saharan Africa: the latest findings of population and health surveys confirm a drop in fertility in Kenya, Botswana and Zimbabwe and also indicate a drop (of one to two children per woman in ten years) in Ghana, Guinea, Senegal, Côte d'Ivoire, the Central African Republic and Rwanda.[18] Are we moving towards the 'end of the African exception'?[19] If current trends are confirmed, scarcely any countries should still have a 'traditional' pattern of fertility by the first decades of the twenty-first century.

Although the terrible prospect of an uncontrollable population explosion appears to be fading, there is no cause for self-congratulation. Admittedly, the scenario according to which the world population will peak at around 8 billion inhabitants in about 2050 is not to be ruled out entirely. According to United Nations calculations, however, the international community will need to mobilize the sum of US$17 billion a year from 2000 if it is to prevent the world population from exceeding 7.8 billion inhabitants by the middle of the twenty-first century.

Above all, owing to 'demographic inertia' and the momentum of recent growth, which has produced more women of childbearing age, the world is about to experience a population increase in absolute terms beyond anything it has ever known before, in just one generation. Between now and 2015 the world population could increase by some 1.4 billion inhabitants, with most of this growth in developing countries. Moreover, the high proportion of very young people in most of the countries of the South – nearly 53.5% of the population in the least developed countries is under 25 years old[20] – will not only contribute to a very rapid increase in population but at the same time pose colossal challenges to development by amplifying needs in education, health, housing, employment and infrastructures and create unprecedented problems in regard to food supply and the management of natural resources. The 15–24 age-group, which today totals 1.05 billion persons, has never been so large.[21] Are we ready to devote the necessary resources to preparing their future, which is also our future? Probably never before in human history has the need to invest in the education of the young been so pressing, and never has the task been so overwhelming. The future of development and peace throughout the world will depend to a great extent on the determination of governments to meet this gigantic challenge.

Box 1.1 AIDS and the Future of the World Population: The Need for a Worldwide Response

The AIDS epidemic is much more serious than previously thought: as a November 1997 report by the Joint Programme on HIV/AIDS (UNAIDS) of the United Nations and the World Health Organization (WHO) has revealed, the new infections are twice as common and their victims 50% more numerous than previous estimates had suggested: 2.3 million persons die from AIDS each year and there are 16,000 new cases of contamination every day. In 1997, some 30 million persons were living with the virus – and there were 40 million in 2000; in some countries, more than a quarter of the adult population is infected. Some 1,600 children are infected each day and 350,000 died of the disease in 1996; around 1,200 are now dying of it every day. The repercussions of the AIDS epidemic will primarily affect developing countries, which now account for 90% of cases of HIV-positive individuals, mainly in sub-Saharan Africa and in South and South-East Asia. And yet 92% of the money being spent on the prevention and treatment of AIDS (over US$14 billion) is being spent in the industrialized countries.

According to the Population Division at the United Nations, the present high incidence of HIV in sub-Saharan Africa is already causing life expectancy at birth rates to stagnate and even to decrease in the most seriously affected countries. After Africa, home to 14 million HIV-positive men and women, Asia is the principal victim, with about half the total number of individuals currently infected by HIV. Quite apart from the immense human tragedy, the repercussions on development will be considerable: a UNDP study has recently estimated the cost of AIDS for the economies of Asia in the year 2000 at between US$38 and US$52 billion.

Since the AIDS pandemic is affecting the entire planet, the response to it must be on a world scale: a virus subject to rapid mutation and capable of developing resistance to new treatments cannot be tackled by each country independently. AIDS must be overcome in all countries or it will not be overcome at all. The fight will have to be conducted on four fronts:

1. *Information, education and prevention campaigns all over the world.* The often prohibitive cost of treating the disease highlights the absolute necessity of greater efforts in favour of education and information for the populations at risk, especially women. Unless their status is improved AIDS will not be defeated. Among those infected, only one person in ten is aware of the fact: we therefore need more campaigns of prevention and explanation concerning the disease and its modes of transmission and more research facilities in the developing countries through international

scientific cooperation. But victory over AIDS will be impossible without trans-sectoral policies that associate research, health policies, education and communication policies, social policies and cultural action.

2. *Access to treatment for everybody*. Unfortunately, tritherapies, which reduce the development of the disease a thousandfold, are very expensive (from US$5,000 to US$10,000 per year). Research is expected to come up with a less costly but just as effective treatment before long. Meanwhile, we must invest in the provision of universal access to treatment – for reasons of solidarity as well as for our collective security – and reject all forms of discrimination: all sick human beings are entitled to the same treatment. Otherwise, the Universal Declaration of Human Rights will remain no more than words on paper.

3. *Universal availability of preventive treatment*. Efforts must be focused on preventing mother-to-child transmission by anti-retroviruses such as AZT (US$1,500 for three months' treatment), on treating opportunistic diseases such as tuberculosis (US$15 per patient per year) and on carrying out the systematic screening of donated blood.

4. *The search for an effective vaccine*. As Luc Montagnier, co-discoverer of the AIDS virus, stressed in the 21st Century Talks, 'A vaccine is much less expensive than medication. The vaccine against poliomyelitis was distributed throughout the world thanks largely to international institutions … An anti-AIDS vaccine would therefore be used in every country. The problem is that it would be necessary to devote hundreds of millions of dollars to the research – and that is not yet happening.' At a time when the world is investing US$700 to US$800 billion in arms, a few thousandths of that sum devoted to the development of an anti-AIDS vaccine is not just a possibility but a moral duty.

Success on these four fronts will depend on our pursuing and stepping up the fight against AIDS at the international level, essentially through UNAIDS, the programme launched in January 1996 in partnership between the WHO, UNESCO, UNICEF, the UNDP, the World Bank and a number of NGOs and through UNESCO's World Foundation for AIDS Research and Prevention, which we established with Luc Montagnier in 1993.

The gravity and urgency of the AIDS epidemic in poor countries requires an unprecedented mobilization of international solidarity, which could take a lead from the proposal, made by France and supported by the G8 countries at their May 1998 summit in Birmingham, to set up an International Therapeutic Solidarity Fund with the purpose of making the new therapies available to developing countries and at the same time promoting training, public information and the search for an effective vaccine. This fund would be financed by voluntary contributions from states, major international funds, transnational pharmaceutical companies and private donations.

Sources: UNAIDS, November 1997; statements by Federico Mayor, Peter Piot and Luc Montagnier to the 154th session of UNESCO's Executive Board, 28 April 1998; Robert Pear, 'AIDS numbers make a giant leap', *International Herald Tribune*, 27 November 1997; Eric Ram, 'Children and the plague of AIDS', *International Herald Tribune*, 29–30 November 1997; *Afrique Médicine Santé*, May–June 1997, interview with Peter Piot; Patrick Festy and Eric Chevallier, *Futuribles*, No. 194, January 1995; IFRI, *Ramsès*, 1996; communiqué of the G8 Summit held in Birmingham, 17 May 1998; speeches by Mr Jacques Chirac, president of the French Republic and by Mr Bernard Kouchner, then French secretary of state for health to the tenth Conference on STD/AIDS in Africa (Abidjan, Côte d'Ivoire), 7–8 December 1997 and Declaration of Abidjan, 9 December 1997; Jean-Yves Nau, 'Sida: la France propose de créer un fonds international de solidarité thérapeutique', *Le Monde*, 9 December 1997; Laurent Aventin and Pierre Huard, 'VIH/SIDA et entreprise en Afrique', MOST document No. 19, UNESCO, 1998; Luc Montagnier, *Entretiens du XXIe siècle*, 'De quoi souffrirons-nous au XXIe siècle? La science face aux maladies émergentes et réémergentes', UNESCO, 16 December 1998. See Jérôme Bindé (ed.), *Les Clés du XXIe siècle*, Editions UNESCO/Seuil, Paris, 2000.

Population figures are not the only factor; also important is their distribution. The human population is very unevenly distributed, with over 60% of the world's inhabitants occupying 10% of its land. This unevenness is clearly revealed on the world population map recently prepared for UNESCO by the geographers Daniel Noin and Geneviève Decroix,[22] which shows that 'the world is no longer a mosaic of more or less favoured rural communities but principally a vast urban sprawl, hierarchically ranked and dominated by the major conurbations' whose growth 'is unrelated to the natural resources of their hinterland'.[23] Admittedly, the concept of density is of limited interest since 'high density does not in any way signify overpopulation'.[24] The differences in density, however, are striking. With 3.45 billion inhabitants, Asia alone contains 60% of the total population. Within each continent, some areas are unpopulated and others crowded. Four large centres of population contain the great majority of the world's population: East Asia, where one-quarter of the world population lives on less than 3% of its dry land; South

Asia, with one-fifth of the world's inhabitants on less than 2% of the land; Europe, with 12% on 4% of the land and North-East America, with 3.7% on 1.1% of the land.[25]

The distribution of the population, however, does not reflect the distribution of wealth. As Hervé Le Bras observes, 'there exist rich densely populated countries and poor sparsely populated ones and, conversely, rich but sparsely populated countries that contrast with poor densely populated ones – from Bangladesh to Rwanda and Burundi – which are household names'.[26] Wealth is very unevenly spread within most of the countries and even more so between quintiles of the population. These disparities are tending to get worse (see Chapter 2).

Finally, inequality has an influence on the future prospects of the population according to the level of development. Although, for life expectancy at birth, the gap between the countries of the North and South appears to be narrowing slightly, the figure for the richest countries is still almost double that recorded in some of the poorest, especially those in tropical Africa, where in one case at least – Sierra Leone – it does not exceed 40 years. Despite recent progress, human beings are still far from equal in this respect: life expectancy at birth ranges from 43 years in Afghanistan to nearly 80 years in Japan.[27] Even within a particular country the differences are considerable, both in the North and in the South: for blacks in the United States of America it is six years less than for whites.[28] But certain specialists, such as France Meslé and Jacques Vallin, are also troubled about a change in the general pattern of mortality and question the United Nations projections that forecast gains of twelve to fifteen years by 2025.[29] AIDS has added a new cause of death in developing countries. By 2005 it will have nearly doubled the death rate in Zimbabwe, increased it by nearly 50% in Burkina Faso, Côte d'Ivoire and Congo, and reduced the foreseeable population of Uganda and Zambia by some 6 to 7%. In the five most affected countries, life expectancy at birth fell by around 2000 to the level reached 30 years ago.[30]

As for the reduction of infant mortality, the progress achieved over the last 40 years has been considerable. However, the fall has been much slower in some Asian countries and especially in sub-Saharan Africa, where there are few countries with rates below 100 per 1,000 live births, i.e. ten times the rates for children born in North America or Europe.[31] In Africa and in certain countries of Asia, the fight against infectious diseases has not yet been won. The United Nations Conference on Population and Development, held in Cairo in 1994, invited all countries to reduce infant mortality by one-third and wherever possible to a rate below 50 per 1,000 (the rate in France in 1950) by the year 2000 and to 35 per 1,000 by 2015. This fight is essential not only for ethical reasons and for its positive impact on general well-being but also because of its repercussions on the birth rate: mothers are far more likely to have fewer children or to space out pregnancies when they realize that it is unnecessary to 'have ten children in order to keep five'. In any case, demographic inequality is simply the consequence of structural socio-economic inequality and inequality of opportunity for human development.

One last form of inequality will doubtless exert a profound influence on development and the future of the world population, and that is the ageing of the population – a trend that will not be confined to the North – and the drop in population in certain industrialized countries and several economies in transition. As a Canadian demographer remarks, the ageing process 'is an inevitable and general trend that will one day or another affect all societies'.[32] Between 1950 and 2025 the number of persons over 60 might well be multiplied by six and rise from 200 million to 1.2 billion. During the same period their proportion in the overall population will probably rise from 8% to 14%, and to 20% by 2050.[33] The growth and ageing of the population are in fact two aspects of the same phenomenon, operating at different points in time: as soon as the pace of growth slows down significantly the ageing process speeds up. This law is well illustrated by the case of China: the proportion of persons aged over 65 years, at present just below 10%, is expected to increase there to nearly 22% in 50 years' time, with the number of individuals leaping from 50 to 280 million between 1980 and 2050. For the world as a whole, the 1950 figure of 1.9 persons of working age for each dependant fell to 1.7 in 1965 and is not expected to return to 1.9 until 2010.[34]

However, the problems of ageing are quite different in the North and in the South. In the South, ageing poses problems concerning overall human development strategy and the pace of decrease in fertility and raises a crucial question: how is a country to respond to ageing in the absence of social protection systems founded on the welfare state, at a time when, as a result of urbanization and modernization, the ties of family solidarity are weakening? In the North, the ageing societies are haunted by the dread of depopulation which, in the absence of compensatory migration, could by 2025 seriously affect a good many countries, including Japan, Spain, Italy, Greece, Germany, Bulgaria, Hungary, Romania and Russia. In the long run, all developed, developing (e.g. Cuba) and 'emerging' countries where the average number of children per woman is under 2.1 will be affected, that is to say virtually the whole of Europe and a number of countries in Asia and North America. In the industrialized countries, ageing and the prospect of a decreasing population are already raising major problems: relations between the generations; financing of social security systems; potential decrease in overall dynamism, and critical social and ethical arbitration between the claims of different generations and between the quest for higher life expectancy and the possibilities of providing better care to an ageing population.

Ageing will affect the developing countries too, where it will be even more rapid than in Europe. Initially it will bring some relief – a smaller proportion of young people to provide with schooling and subsequent employment, a swelling of the population of working age. This situation has already been reached by countries that have introduced effective family planning policies.[35] For a good many experts, however, the major problem of the twenty-first century in the field of population will be not so much the excessive number of children as the huge number of old people as a result of progress in medicine, genetics and development in general. Hence the anxiety of certain specialists: 'Will we come to regulate death as we do birth?' one of them has even asked.[36] Will we end up with an apocalyptic situation in which our societies are tempted to encourage euthanasia rather than contraception?[37] Certain current indicators are ominous. At all events, not only must the rich countries now adjust to the ageing of their populations (lifelong training of workers, reorganization of careers, adaptation of public health and social security systems and policies), but the developing countries must also ready themselves to do the same and take advantage of 'the good years of declining fertility'.[38]

One factor may have a considerable impact on the situation: this is the question of international migration, which is very difficult to forecast, usually disregarded in world demographic projections and the subject of much questioning and debate among both experts and the general public. The total number of legal migrants is estimated at 100 million, to which must be added between 10 and 30 million illegal ones.[39] Although international migration has slowed down considerably in the last hundred years or so and the population policies of most countries in the North and South have tended in more recent times to reduce the flows by further concentrating them on specific labour needs and on the immigration of an increasingly skilled workforce, it cannot be assumed that this will remain the case in the face of a growing demographic imbalance by the next generation.

The second half of the twentieth century saw the end of the centuries-old movement that carried Europeans to other lands and the growth of South–North and South–South migration. All in all, more than two million persons – not counting illegal migrants – arrive each year in the countries of the North. In certain countries the number of the latter may be high: it has been estimated, for example, that as many illegal as authorized migrants enter the USA each year. But South–North migration makes us overlook the even greater currents between countries of the South: over the last 30 years some 35 million persons have moved from countries of the South to those of the North but, for the world as a whole, the International Labour Office estimates at 85 million, and the UNFPA at 100 million, the number of persons living in countries other than the ones in which they were born. These movements include in particular migration towards the Middle East and Gulf countries initiated by income from oil. The population of the United Arab Emirates includes 80% of migrant workers, that of Saudi Arabia 34%.[40] To this must be added more recent currents in Asia, where Thailand, the Philippines and Indonesia are supplying increasing contingents of workers not only to Australia and Japan but also to a good many other countries. For example, the number of foreign residents in Malaysia was estimated by the OECD – before the crisis of 1997–98 – at no less than one million, equivalent to one-eighth of the workforce, and at over two or three million by private organizations. The problems raised by the integration of foreigners are therefore not confined to the countries of the North.

The movements about which least is known are the ones that criss-cross Africa, owing to the absence of data for many countries and the imprecision of census returns. The figure of 35 million migrants advanced by an ILO study some ten years ago[41] is now regarded as plausible by World Bank experts.[42] It includes pilgrims, refugees and workers and their families. The proportion of foreigners varies from one country to another: in West Africa, foreigners make up 5% of the total population, a figure comparable to that found in France or Germany.[43]

All over the world, conflicts have displaced entire populations: more than 6 million Afghans – i.e. one-third of the population – fled abroad between 1979 and 1994;[44] more than a million Bosnians had been displaced within the Republic of Bosnia in December 1995;[45] in 1997, the United Nations High Commissioner for Refugees (UNHCR) registered 2.7 million Afghans[46] and 446,000 Somali refugees[47] living outside their respective countries. According to the UNHCR, one in 115 of the world's inhabitants has been forced to flee their home.[48]

How will migration develop in the years to come? The most widespread idea is that 'migration pressure' will build up in the countries of the North, particularly in Europe and the United States of America, because population growth is still strong in the South, especially in Africa and Central America, and inequalities between rich and poor countries are getting worse. As the industrialized countries are tending to close their frontiers because of un-employment and growing intolerance towards migrants, tensions are bound to heighten and illegal migration to rise.

This argument is rather too simplistic. In the first place, living standards and levels of development are tending to become more diverse in the South itself, thus creating new needs for labour; recent examples have been the case of Malaysia up until the crisis of 1997–98 and some earlier cases concerning countries in the Gulf and in Africa. The Democratic Republic of Congo and South Africa attracted numerous workers to their mining sectors, Gabon to its timber industry and Côte d'Ivoire to its cocoa and coffee sectors. Such migration flows were initially directed towards neighbouring countries or followed well-trodden routes that provided support networks. The Egyptians who had to leave Iraq in 1991 made not for Europe but for Libya, and it was also towards Libya more than towards Italy that Tunisian workers migrated in large numbers.

We can therefore expect increasingly diverse patterns of migration involving manual workers, technicians, engineers and teachers, as is already taking place in the Gulf, and an increase in South–South migration. In the OECD countries taken together migration is now tending to stabilize, and even to decrease.[49] This situation is of course due to the closing of frontiers and restrictions on the right of asylum but also to the hesitations of potential migrants faced with greater risks of insecurity and unemployment. One is struck, however, by the economic performance of countries – the USA is a case in point – with a strongly positive migration balance over the last few decades.[50] In the longer term, the slowing of population growth might have a similar impact: birth rates in the Maghreb, for example, are already falling and within a decade or so the number of persons entering the labour market will cease rising. Clearly, however, the further reduction of migration flows will depend primarily on improving the quality of life in the countries of origin: the host countries belonging to OECD could help matters by honouring their international commitments relating to public development aid.[51]

The Major Challenges

At the dawn of the twenty-first century, population experts and the international community regard three closely related problems as being of particular concern: the impact of population growth on food security; its impact on the environment and natural resources; and its impact on poverty and development in general.[52]

Food security How can we hope not only to put an end to malnutrition, which is today the lot of nearly 800 million persons, but also to feed the roughly 3.4 billion extra individuals that the United Nations foresees in the median variant of its projections? In other words, will there be enough to eat for everybody in a world in which the amount of arable land per person is shrinking? According to Paul Kennedy, it is expected to decrease from 2,800 m^2 at the beginning of the 1990s to 1,700 m^2 in 2025.[53] Will the population begin to exceed the earth's 'carrying capacity', defined by the Independent Commission on Population and Quality of Life as 'the maximal sustainable load that humankind can impose on the environment before it loses its capacity to support human activity'?[54]

Despite the fears of certain experts, such as Lester Brown and Paul Ehrlich, the evidence suggests that in this area there is no 'population bomb'.[55] The relation between needs and available supplies has, on the whole, improved since the 1960s.[56] As Nobel prizewinner Amartya Sen stresses, 'Not only in the two centuries since Malthus but also in the most recent decades, the growth of food production has constantly exceeded to a significant extent the expansion of the world's population.'[57] However, the 1998 UNDP *Human Development Report* emphasizes that the continuation of such efforts will depend on a further 'green revolution'[58] that introduces integrated rural development policies (agrarian reform, development of infrastructures, schooling), new methods of cultivation, the reform of agricultural pricing and marketing, and active measures to help peasant farmers.[59] But it will also depend on peace: food insecurity appears to be less related to population growth than to geographical, economic or political vicissitudes. Most of the African countries that have suffered from famine in the last 25 years have been riven by civil war or by serious political and social unrest.

Furthermore, if we exclude the case of Africa, the biggest increases in food production are being recorded in the South. A comparison of the three-year averages for 1979–81 and 1991–93 reveals that food production per inhabitant rose by 3% worldwide and by 2% in Europe but fell by 5% in North America. Per capita food production even increased by 22% in Asia (by 23% in India and by 39% in China). During the same period, on the other hand, it fell by 6% in Africa.[60] And between 1980 and 1990 food production per inhabitant fell in no less than 72 out of 113 developing countries while individual calorie intake declined in 37 of them.[61]

However, the key issue remains the distribution of available food resources. In certain regions of the world the increasing contrast between population growth and declining food production per inhabitant is posing the major problem of social access to food for populations whose poverty makes them unable to pay its price.[62]

The environment and natural resources[63] According to Amartya Sen, 'the effects of population growth on the environment could turn out to be much more serious than the problem of food, to which so much attention has been paid in writings inspired by Malthus'.[64] Here we need to distinguish between the short and the long term. In the short term, it is the North that is primarily responsible for environmental destruction: one-fifth of the world's population is consuming 58% of its energy and 65% of its electricity; petrol consumption averages 500 kg of oil equivalent per inhabitant per year in the industrialized countries, six times the average consumption per inhabitant (43 kg) in the developing countries; in 1994, commercial energy consumption per inhabitant in the industrialized world amounted to eight times that of developing countries (4,452 kg of oil equivalent as against 568 kg).[65]

In the long term, it is feared that the impact of population growth and of changing modes of production and consumption in the South will be particularly detrimental to the environment. As the emerging economies of the South develop, they will steadily increase their consumption: according to the UNDP, the developing countries will, within 15 years, be responsible for 60% of annual carbon dioxide emissions.[66] In the view of Amartya Sen, the developing countries will therefore, in the future, represent 'as great a threat to the enviroment as the present-day inhabitants of the rich countries'. In many regions of the world, especially in the arid zones, population growth has already had a serious impact on the natural environment as it often leads to the over-exploitation of natural resources, the degradation of soils, the pollution of water courses and desertification.

As early as 1795 the philosopher and economist Condorcet had the brilliant intuition that the danger of overpopulation, which might, he thought, result in a 'steady decrease in happiness', could be overcome by higher productivity, improved management and prevention of waste, and rapid progess in education, particularly for women. Discussing the threats of human settlement to the environment, he imagined solutions that are at the heart of the international debate today: 'the same product of industry', he wrote, 'will either require a lesser destruction of raw materials or be employed for a longer period'.[67]

It should be borne in mind that population density does not necessarily entail environmental destruction, which often arises from the modes of production and consumption. Small populations may be just as harmful. Generally speaking, itinerant cultivation or stockbreeding often turns out to be more harmful than farming on a fixed site. Similarly, the natural fauna and flora can adapt to dense concentrations of human beings subject to strict conditions of surveillance and control, as in national parks or biosphere reserves. Settlement along river banks, so long as it is properly regulated, may preserve aquatic life: salmon have returned to the Thames and the Rhine.

The responses to the environmental challenges posed by population growth must therefore be based on:

- an 'efficiency revolution' in the use of energy and natural resources (soils, water, oceans, etc.) founded on the principle of economy, recycling, waste disposal and the increasing use of renewable energies as a substitute for fossil fuels;
- the spread of food production methods more respectful of ecosystems;
- the sharing of knowledge, technology and know-how between North and South; and
- a change in lifestyles and in modes of production and consumption through education, the introduction of new patterns of development and the promotion of 'sustainable cropping'.

Urbanization[68] Another major trend will shape the future of human beings: the urbanization of the South. Shortly after the year 2000, the majority of the world's population will be living in cities,[69] thus ending the domination of an age-old pattern of existence. It is impossible to say exactly when this break with the past occurred: it happened a long time ago in Europe, the USA, Canada, Australia and New Zealand, and the turning point for Latin America came before 1970. Only Africa and Asia have yet to make the change, probably around 2020. The urbanization process will be mainly to the advantage of immense cities of over eight million inhabitants: there already exist 22 of them and the number could rise to 33 by 2015. Most of these megalopolises will be located in the South, first of all in Asia and later in Africa. And it is in the poorest countries that cities are expanding the fastest.

The shortage of resources and the speed of urban expansion, which leave scant leeway for planning, aggravate the problems of urbanization: not enough proper jobs, in contrast to the industrial and administrative development of former times; problems of drinking-water supply, of sanitation, of transport over steadily increasing distances; much greater pollution. Will the cities of the South be able to win the race between a growing population and construction of the necessary housing and facilities?

The situation, however, is not hopeless. The expansion of the megalopolises is already slowing down in many countries, such as India and Egypt, where the number of inhabitants is no longer rising except from 'natural growth'. Indeed, the population of Mexico City is decreasing.[70] Moreover, whereas it was estimated only twelve years ago that economies of scale linked to population density would cease to operate at a certain size (around 150,000 inhabitants), it is now thought that 'it is not the size of a city that counts but the way it is managed'.[71] To invent a balanced and decentralized system of management that encourages the participation of inhabitants in urban development and in the decisions that shape their immediate environment – that is the challenge of the next 20 years.

Development, employment and poverty In general, the relationship between economic wealth and population growth is tending to change: it was long held that the acquisition of wealth was not merely conducive to lower fertility (the cost of having a child being greater than its economic usefulness) but a prerequisite. Today the relationship is seen as being more complex: in the low-population oil-producing countries, the 'black gold' for a long time reduced the cost of raising children and contributed to continued high fertility. On the other hand, very poor territories – such as the state of Kerala in India – have succeeded in reducing fertility by pursuing appropriate human development policies centred on education, health and women.

In the next twenty-five years, however, countries of the South will have to find room on the labour market for at least one billion additional persons. Merely to absorb the new arrivals into the economy and simply maintain living standards at their present level, they will have to sustain an economic growth of 70%, or more than 2% a year.[72] A much higher rate would be needed to achieve a massive reduction in poverty, satisfy the immense needs of this extra population in terms of education, infrastructures, housing and health, and give each person significantly greater chances of self-fulfilment. It will therefore be necessary to change the scale and pace, but also the nature, of development, which should henceforth be centred on quality of life rather than on productivism and a blind and unsustainable hyper-consumption.

The challenge is made even more immense by the fact that, as the 1996 *Human Development Report* stresses, present-day economic growth is profoundly inegalitarian: the gap between rich and poor countries and even within nations is widening, and the phenomenon of 'jobless growth' is affecting industrialized and developing countries alike.[73] As the G7 summit in Lyons emphasized, we must now 'make a success of globalization for the benefit of all' and hence 'share the benefits of economic growth as broadly as possible'.

A Few Priorities for Action

Wealth creation is not essential for the reduction of fertility. Nor is a slower pace of population growth enough to secure a higher standard of living. The conjunction of these two trends is rather the outcome of an equitable growth giving precedence to providing universal access to education, health and opportunities for economic development.

Serious thought should be given to the example of several high-performance economies in East and South-East Asia (Republic of Korea, Taiwan, Hong Kong, Singapore, Indonesia, Malaysia) despite the serious crisis that has beset the region in 1997–98. These economies have experienced 30 years of economic growth of over 5.5% per year accompanied not only by a halving of the proportion of poor persons but also by a big drop in their number and, in most cases, by a noteworthy reduction in fertility. Their success is due mainly to their 'growth with equity' policy, which, for instance, increased spending on education, with resources allocated as a matter of priority to the provision of primary education for all and in particular to closing the gap between boys' and girls' access to education. As the 1998 UNFPA Report stresses, 'societies which invest in the fields of health, education and job creation find themselves better off economically, which will lead to a general improvement of the quality of life and lighten the burdensome obligation to support an elderly population'.[74] It has been shown in numerous countries, particularly in Asia, that efforts in education make it possible to slow down population growth while at the same time improving the standard and quality of individual lives. It is to be hoped that the economic problems encountered by numerous emerging countries will not weaken their commitment to human development: at a time of crisis, education remains the best investment for securing sustainable endogenous development.

To meet the challenges of population growth, policies at the beginning of the twenty-first century should therefore be guided by five priorities: education for women; empowerment of women; promotion of scientific and technical development; a change in lifestyles and new modes of production and consumption; and the promotion of growth with equity and of new partnerships for development.

Education for women If there is one fundamental means of achieving a reduction in fertility it is education, in particular for women. In many countries, the lengthening of schooling for girls is tending to raise the average age at marriage (now over 25 years in North Africa), to reduce sharply the number of early marriages (in Bangladesh, 48% of women are married by the age of 19 as against 89% 30 years ago) and, in consequence, to reduce 'automatically' the number of children. A longer period of schooling and delayed marriage are also tending, particularly in the Arab countries, to narrow the age difference in relation to the husband and to change relations within the couple. According to a study by the World Bank, women living in certain regions in which girls are excluded from secondary education have an average of seven children. Where the enrolment rate for girls exceeds 40%, that average drops to three children. The decline in fertility is slow when girls have access to primary education alone but gathers pace as they gain access to the further two levels of education.

It is clearly urgent to reach the women excluded from education – the approximately 29% of girls in the world who are not enrolled in primary schools, the 65% of the world's 880 million illiterates who are women. They will be reached by innovatory approaches that combine the universalization of primary education, effective compulsory schooling, distance education, interactive teaching methods and lifelong education for adults. At the same time, it is also necessary to provide secondary education for all, in particular for women, and to develop higher education.

UNESCO has made women one of its priority target groups for action. The 'Education for All' initiative launched by UNESCO at its Jomtien Conference in 1990, in partnership with the UNDP, UNICEF and the World Bank, lays emphasis on improved access to education and a higher quality of education for women. But we must go further: the nine most populous developing countries, meeting in New Delhi in 1993 at the initiative of UNESCO, adopted a plan for education specifically aimed at girls and women. India set the example by undertaking at that Conference to increase the proportion of its

GDP devoted to education, which was to rise from 3.4% to about 6% in 2025. We therefore propose that all countries that have not yet reached this target should set it for themselves without delay and urgently define how it is to be achieved – for instance, by reducing military and non-productive expenditure. Indeed, this was the course of action recommended by Michel Camdessus, director-general of the IMF, at the 1992 Earth Summit.

Empowering women As UNESCO stressed at the Cairo Conference, the slowing of population growth must not be based on coercion or orders from above. Nor should it involve the obligation to adopt foreign models or inter-ference along dogmatic lines. It can stem only from the informed choice of men and women in control of their lives and fully aware of their rights and dignity.

Besides the necessary expansion, at all levels of formal and out-of-school education, of programmes of instruction in population issues, specific action in favour of women is required. In this regard Nafis Sadik, executive director of the UNFPA, has identified three priorities:

- 'make available to women the information and services they need to bear and raise their children in good health and absolute security;
- support them in the choices they make concerning areas other than repro-duction, such as health and education for themselves and their children; and
- lastly, whatever choice they make, ensure that their interests, not as mothers or wives or as units of production or reproduction but as women, are given priority'.

Women must be given freedom and autonomy, which are essential not only to the slowing of population growth but also to the solving of problems related to the decline of fertility affecting the majority of industrialized countries. One of the few countries in the North that has displayed a marked increase – at least temporarily – in its fertility rates is Sweden, that is to say one of the countries that has gone furthest in the building of a welfare state and in the realization of effective sexual equality.

Promotion of scientific and technological development In view of the foresee-able population growth, we shall be unable to change the scale of development while at the same time achieving the objectives of sustainable development and food security for everyone without an unprecedented expansion of science and technology, which alone are capable of bringing about the necessary 'efficiency revolution' already referred to.[75] In this area, the countries of the South need to set themselves new priorities commensurate with the issues at stake and devote a much greater proportion of their GDP and national and local budgets to research, especially applied research. The dangers to the biosphere of population growth and industrial development need to be more closely monitored by the world scientific community. UNESCO is contributing to this work through several of its intergovernmental scientific programmes.[76]

A change in lifestyles and new modes of production and consumption It has become vital in this field to do better with less. Here the industrialized countries must set an example, since the endless expansion of non-sustainable patterns of consumption at present pursued by the North is rendered even more impossible to condone by the foreseeable increase in population. But the emerging economies also need to make an effort to avoid importing non-sustainable models of production and consumption *en bloc*.

Promotion of growth with equity and of new partnerships for development There can be no viable solution to the problems of population and development while economic growth continues to aggravate – as it is doing at present – the inequalities between and within nations. Such lop-sided growth is fraught with future conflict, boding violence as surely as storm-clouds bode a storm. We shall have to find new ways of sharing and a new form of development that combines growth, justice and equity. Today, solidarity must be the watchword not only geographically, between North and South and within each nation, but also in time, with regard to future generations: we do not have the right to squander their chances and their heritage.

At a time of declining public aid to development, which private investment, directed essentially towards approximately ten countries enjoying rapid economic development until the Asian crisis of 1997–98, will not be able to replace, we need to invent new partnerships for development, particularly for Africa and the least developed countries. This implies profound changes in the structure and forms of assistance by the rich countries, which must redirect their action towards the major priorities of human development. We were delighted to find these new partnerships for development placed at the heart of discussions at the 1995 Summit on Social Development in Copenhagen and the 1996 'Habitat II' Summit in Istanbul and to see them advocated by the G7.[77] But today, more than ever, words must become deeds and lead to positive action. Tomorrow, it will always be too late.

The challenge is twofold, with its quantitative and qualitative dimensions inextricably linked. It will be impossible for us to resolve the world population problem by approaching it solely in terms of births and deaths or of managing statistical flows and quantities of individuals, investments and resources. We shall resolve it only if we give precedence to quality over quantity, if we place the human being and an improved quality of life once again at the centre of development.[78] The 'caring capacity' is from this point of view more essential than the notion, itself highly controversial, of the earth's 'carrying capacity' or 'population limit'. As Shakespeare remarked, 'What is a city but its inhabitants?' What is the Earth if not first and foremost the life it sustains, that is to say the biosphere as a whole, over which the human species now weighs so heavily? Clearly, everything must be done to reduce the growth in population. But this demographic revolution must be founded on dignity, which is the most fundamental right of the human being. For it is indeed vital for us to be in a position to provide for all those who come to join us on this planet. We must be ready to offer them not only the quality of life they have a right to expect but also a friendly smile.

Pointers and Recommendations

- Educate girls and women and give them control over their lives (i) by providing universal and effective access to primary education and making secondary education generally available, especially to girls and (ii) by providing the information and facilities they need to bear and raise their children in good health and absolute security.
- Promote the scientific and technological development that are essential to a population growth respectful of the environment and to food security for all.
- Change lifestyles and patterns of consumption that are detrimental to sustainable development.
- Promote growth with equity and new partnerships for development.
- Promote new policies for the cities (see Chapter 3).
- Encourage the industrialized countries, especially the richest ones, to honour their commitments to contribute 0.7% of their GNP to public development aid and to favour the endogenous development of the least developed countries.

Notes

1. Further information on the prospects and issues connected with population changes is given in other chapters, particularly Chapters 2, 3, 5, 7, 8, 9, 10 and 11.

2. Sun Tzu, *The Art of War*, UNESCO collection of representative works, Oxford University Press, London, 1963.

3. Source: *The State of World Population 1997*, United Nations Population Fund (UNFPA), May 1997.

4. UNFPA website.

5. UNFPA, *The State of World Population 1998*.

6. Source: United Nations, 1998, op. cit. (figures for 1990–95) and UNFPA, *The State of World Population 1997* (the population of Germany was 82.2 million in 1997; that of South America as a whole 327.1 million).

7. This last figure is 0.7 billion lower than the previous estimate in 1992, mainly because of the unexpected rapidity of the decline in fertility in many countries. Source: United Nations, Department for Economic and Social Affairs, Population Division, *World Population Prospects: The 1996 Revision* (24 October 1996); *World Projections to 2150*, 1 February 1998. The 'median' version predicts a world population of 8 billion inhabitants in 2025, 10.4 billion in 2100 and 10.8 billion in 2150.

8. The 'high' and 'low' scenarios differ by only one child per couple (half a child above and half a child below the replacement rates).

9. Hervé Le Bras, *Les Limites de la planète*, Flammarion, Paris, 1994.

10. Jacques Vallin, *Dossiers du CEPED*, No. 26, Paris, 1994.

11. Figures for 1990–95. Source: United Nations, Population Division, 1996 estimates. Whereas growth exceeded 2% per year from 1965 to 1970, it was 1.72% per year between 1975 and 1990, before dropping to the current rate. The latter figure is lower than the 1994 forecast (1.57%). See Arkady Ostrovsky, 'Birthrate down, hardship up', *Financial Times*, 29 May 1997.

12. Developing regions, according to the classification of the United Nations Population Division, include Africa, Latin America and the Caribbean, Asia (excluding Japan), Melanesia, Micronesia and Polynesia.

13. Figures for 1996 (United Nations). This population is very differently distributed according to region: in the developed countries, children under 15 years make up 19.6% of the population, as against 43.9% in the least developed countries; in the developing countries, this age group is seven times more numerous than the over-65 age group (UNFPA 1998 and United Nations 1996).

14. Jean-Claude Chesnais, 'La transition démographique, trente ans de bouleversements (1965–1995)', CEPED, Paris, 1995 (*Les Dossiers du CEPED*, No. 34).

15. Jacques Dupâquier, *Le Monde*, 27 May 1999.

16. Jean-Claude Chasteland, *Le Monde*, 30 August 1994.

17. Medium projection of the United Nations.

18. *Chronique du CEPED*, July–September 1995 and *Le Monde*, 15 September 1995.

19. Thérèse Locoh, 'Familles africaines, population et qualité de vie', CEPED, Paris, March 1995 (*Les dossiers du CEPED*, No. 31).

20. Source: United Nations, Population Division, 1995 estimate for the less developed countries. The figure rises to 63.4% for the least developed countries.

21. 1998 UNFPA, *The State of World Population 1998*.

22. This world map appears in an appendix to the book by Daniel Noin, *L'Humanité sur la planète*, UNESCO, Paris, 1997.

23. Noin, *L'Humanité sur la planète*, p. 14.

24. Ibid., p. 20. See also Chapter 3.

25. D. Noin, *Géographie de la population*, Paris, 1995; cited in J. C. Grimal and G. Herzlich, *La Population du monde*, Le Monde and Marabout, Paris, 1995. D. Noin distinguishes 'three centres of dense population' in *L'Humanité sur la planète*: the Chinese area (1.2 billion inhabitants in 1990), the Indian sub-continent (1.1 billion around 1990) and Europe (around 650 million).

26. Le Bras, *Les Limites de la planète*.

27. There can be enormous differences between neighbouring countries: in South-East Asia there is a difference of almost twenty years between Cambodia or Laos and

Malaysia, in Africa ten years between Kenya and neighbouring Uganda. Conversely, life expectancy in Russia – particularly for men – is at roughly the same level as in some developing countries such as China.

28. Source: UNDP, *Human Development Report, 1994*, Chapter 5.

29. *Les Dossiers du CEPED*, No. 30, 15 February 1995. Hitherto the 'health transition' started slowly and then gathered speed once the often simple instruments for fighting infectious diseases or preventing epidemics had been set in place; it declined only when modern causes of death (from cancers to road accidents) had to be faced. France Meslé and Jacques Vallin observe a stagnation – even a regression – over the last few years in certain countries of tropical Africa (Zambia, Uganda) while others (Madagascar, Cameroon, Togo), which started from the same level, have gained ten years of life expectancy. At the same time, some developing countries already 'advanced' in the fight against death, such as Mexico, are finding it hard to bring about a fall in the death rate for adults. Parts of Eastern Europe, the countries of the former Soviet Union in particular, are in a comparable situation: their health systems have proved ill-suited to the fight against cardiovascular diseases and cancers and they are falling further behind the Western countries, which are gaining one year of life expectancy every five years.

30. These projections are themselves in dispute since there exist scarcely any reliable data on the extent of the epidemic or any reliable models of its propagation. 'AIDS is going to kill more people than died during the second world war,' states Malcolm Potts, a professor at the University of California, and Jacques Vallin calculates that 'in a country in which life expectancy has hitherto been rising at six months a year, a 1% prevalence would wipe out two years of progress, a 10% prevalence twenty years and a 15% one thirty years'. It will place a heavy burden on health systems that are already stretched.

31. *Populations: l'État de la démographie*, La Découverte, Paris, 1996.

32. Louise Lassonde, *Coping with Population Challenges*, Earthscan, London, 1997.

33. ICPQL, *Caring for the Future*, Report of the Independent Commission on Population and Quality of Life, Oxford University Press, Oxford/New York, 1996. At world level, the over-65s made up 1% of the population in 1900 and 6.2% in 1992; they are expected to make up 20% in 2050.

34. UNFPA, *World Population Report 1998*.

35. In Tunisia, for example, the under-fifteens now make up only 36% of the population as against 42% two decades earlier. In China, the fall is spectacular: between 1975 and 1990, the proportion dropped from 40% to 26% and is expected to decrease further to 12% in 2020. At that time it will average 25% in South-East Asia and Latin America.

36. William McGurn, *Far Eastern Economic Review*, Hong Kong, cited in Louise Lassonde, *Coping with Population Challenges*.

37. Norman Macrae, 'Not too many babies, just too many oldies' in 'The World in 1995', a special issue of *The Economist*, London, 1994, pp. 137–8.

38. Jacques Vallin, *Dossiers du CEPED*, No. 26, 1994.

39. Michael Renner, 'Transforming security', *State of the World 1997*, Worldwatch Institute, W.W. Norton, London, 1997, pp. 124–5 (figures of the International Labour Organization).

40. Source: 'Conjuncture 97', cited in *Courrier International*, 4 December 1996.

41. Sergio Ricca, *International Migration in Africa*, International Labour Organization, Geneva, 1989.

42. Sharon Stanton Russell, Karen Jacobsen and William Dean Stanley, *International Migration and Development in SubSaharan Africa*, World Bank, Washington, 1990.

43. See *Le Monde*, 25 September 1996.

44. Source: UNHCR, May 1997.

45. Source: UNHCR, March 1997.

46. Source: UNHCR, May 1997.

47. Source: ibid.

48. 26 million exiles and 30 million persons displaced within their own countries (source: UNHCR, October 1998).

49. Source: OECD, *Trends in International Migration*, 1999.

50. 5.7 million in the 1980s, 3.3 million in the 1970s. Source: *1992 Statistical Yearbook of the INS*.

51. On this subject, see Chapter 2 and Part III, this volume.

52. As a separate chapter is devoted to each of these three subjects, they are here discussed succinctly.

53. Paul Kennedy, *Preparing for the 21st Century*, Oxford University Press, 1993.

54. ICPQL, *Caring for the Future*, Oxford University Press, 1996, Chapter 6, p. 97.

55. Amartya Sen, 'Il n'y a pas de bombe démographique', *Esprit*, No. 216, Paris, November 1995.

56. Philippe Collomb, 'L'alimentation de la population mondiale en 2050', *Populations et sociétés*, No. 312, April 1996, Paris, INED. The FAO is counting on a general increase in available food supplies per inhabitant by 2010: they would rise from 2,500 calories per day per person to over 2,700. The countries in the Near East, North Africa, East Asia and Latin America should reach or exceed 3,000 calories. Only sub-Saharan Africa would remain at very low levels (FAO, *World Dimension of Food, Agriculture and Food Security*). A study by the IFPRI arrives at comparable findings: supplies are expected to exceed 1970 and 1990 levels everywhere (*A 2020 Vision for Food, Agriculture and the Environment*, 1995).

57. Sen, 'Population: delusion and reality'. Agricultural techniques and developments of a commercial nature have made it possible to counter the obstacle of declining yields. During the last few decades, the introduction of high-performance agricultural techniques (irrigation permitting a second crop, more careful cultivation, use of high-yielding varieties) has enabled India and the island of Java to become self-sufficient despite an increasing population and a reduction in the size of holdings. The fall in the world production of cereals per inhabitant observed since 1984 is due less to technical progress running out of steam or soil fatigue than to technical adjustment measures such as the setting aside of land in a few large exporting countries (USA, Canada, European Union). At the local level, falls in production may indicate not the exhaustion of possibilities of cultivation but reconversion by farmers seeking profits, as in the case of a changeover from staple crop to cattle fodder in the Mexican state of Tabasco (Hervé Le Bras, *Les Limites de la planète*, 1994).

58. UNDP, *Human Development Report 1998*, pp. 10–11 and Chapter 4.

59. *Agricultures*, No. 4, July–August 1996: 'Sécurité alimentaire, enjeux et débats'.

60. Sen, 'Population: delusion and reality'.

61. FAO, *State of Food and Agriculture 1992*, Rome, 1992; cited in ICPQL, *Caring for the Future*, op. cit.

62. On this subject, see Chapter 10.

63. On this subject, see Chapter 7.

64. Sen, 'Population: delusion and reality'.

65. UNDP, *Human Development Report 1998*, Chapter 3 ('Consumption in a global village – inequalities and unbalances'), passim.

66. Ibid.

67. Condorcet, *Esquisse d'un Tableau historique des progrès de l'esprit humain* (1795), Vrin, Paris, 1970.

68. On this subject, see Chapter 3.

69. Source: United Nations Centre for Human Settlements (Habitat), *An Urbanizing World: Global Report on Human Settlements 1996*, Oxford University Press, Oxford/New York, 1996.

70. Source: ibid.

71. *Le Courrier du CNRS*, No. 82, June 1996.

72. See Hamish McRae, *The World in 2020*, HarperCollins, London, 1994.

73. UNDP, *Human Development Report 1996*, UNDP, New York, 1996.

74. UNFPA, *The State of World Population 1998*.

75. Ernst Ulrich von Weizsäcker, Amory B. Lovins and L. Hunter Lovins, *Factor Four: Doubling Wealth, Halving Resource Use*, Earthscan, London, 1997.

76. Man and the Biosphere Programme (MAB), Intergovernmental Oceanographic Commission (IOC), International Hydrological Programme (IHP) and the Management of Social Transformations (MOST).

77. 'Economic communiqué', G7, Lyons Summit (28 June 1996) (Section IV, pp. 9–12).

78. This is the message of the report *Caring for the Future*, prepared by the Independent Commission on Population and Quality of Life, chaired by Mrs Maria Lourdes Pintasilgo.

. . . .

CHAPTER 2

The Scandal of Poverty and Exclusion

§ THERE is no doubt that poverty has always existed and was once even considered inevitable. Today, it is nothing less than a scandal, in a world that produces more goods than are needed in order to feed all its inhabitants quite comfortably.[1] This is an assault on human dignity and a form of exclusion all the more serious since it results in wars, conflicts and violence.[2] No development strategy makes sense unless its primary aim is to eradicate poverty. The fight against this scourge demands that courageous political measures be taken without delay in three areas in particular: debt, often contracted as a result of imposed uniform development models; ownership and exploitation of natural resources; and the problem of disparities in land distribution, which results in the paradox of land without people and people without land. There should no longer be room for empty rhetoric devoid of concrete implications. Real change is now essential in the fight against poverty, a change without violence, a change that brings the full force of democracy to bear.

The last few decades have seen spectacular progress the world over. For example, the mortality rate in children under five years old has fallen, while the primary school enrolment rate and other social indicators have continued to progress in most countries. Since 1960, per capita income has been multiplied by 4.5 in eastern Asia, doubled in southern Asia and increased by 60% in Latin America.[3] In its 1997 *Human Development Report*, the UNDP pointed out that poverty had decreased more in the last 50 years than it had done during the previous five centuries.

However, the world has also seen the spectacular rise of poverty since the early 1980s. We are witnessing an exacerbation of worldwide inequalities, accompanied in most societies by an increase in the number of individuals living in absolute poverty. The regions most affected by poverty in the developing countries are Latin America and, more particularly, southern Asia and sub-Saharan Africa. The latter experienced a 21% cumulative reduction in per capita GNP between 1980 and 1989. Recent statistics for sub-Saharan Africa reveal that, out of a population of 590 million, 266 million now live below the poverty line.[4] According to the UNDP, nearly one-third of the inhabitants of the least developed countries – most of whom are to be found in sub-Saharan Africa – 'are statistically doomed to die by the age of 40'. The number of poor people increased from 14 million to 119 million in the countries of Eastern Europe and the Commonwealth of Independent States between 1988 and 1994.[5]

At the dawn of the twenty-first century, over 1.3 billion people live in absolute poverty (on less than $1 a day) across the globe, particularly in the developing countries, and their numbers continue to increase.[6] More than two out of three poor people are women. In a report on human rights and extreme poverty prepared for the United Nations Commissioner on Human Rights prior to the 1997–98 crisis, Leandro Despouy estimated that 1.5 billion people were desperately poor, with their numbers increasing by at least 25 million a year.[7] Over three billion people live in poverty on less than US$2 a day.[8] A further 1.5 billion lack access to drinking water, and more than two million receive no basic health care. The world financial crisis which broke out in Asia in 1997 is also plunging tens of millions of people into dire poverty, while the production of goods and services continues to increase worldwide.[9]

A real chasm has opened up between rich and poor. According to the UNDP, the poorest 20% of the world's population must today share a derisory 1.1% of global revenue, as against 1.4% in 1991 and 2.3% in 1960.[10] The ratio of the income of the richest 20% to that of the poorest 20% rose from 30:1 in 1960 to 61:1 in 1991, reaching a dizzying 82:1 in 1995. The number of the world's billionaires in US dollars increased from 157 to 447 between 1989 and 1996. Today the net worth of the ten largest fortunes is US$133 billion, or more than one and a half times the total national income of all the least developed countries.[11] The world's three richest people possess a fortune larger than the total GDP of the 48 poorest countries, and the property of the 84 richest is greater than the GDP of China (1.2 billion inhabitants).[12] The distribution of wealth is globally more inegalitarian than it is within any single country.[13]

Numerically speaking, the hardest-hit groups are women and children. Poverty, food deficiencies and unsafe water are responsible for the deaths of millions of children every year.[14] Resources diminish as family size increases; this means that two-thirds of the world's population living in absolute poverty are probably under 15 years of age. These young people's future prospects are even bleaker than those of their parents.[15] What is more, in most cases it is poverty that induces parents to send their children out to work, often in intolerable conditions, which means that they do not attend school, even in the most favourable scenario, in which basic education for all is provided free of charge. UNESCO estimates that 130 million children throughout the world are still not enrolled in schools, and the ILO estimates show that today there are 250 million working children between the ages of 5 and 14, half of them in full-time employment. Is not acceptance of child labour in the name of so-called economic imperatives – the very ones invoked to justify it in the industrialized countries in the nineteenth century – a renunciation of the objective of basic education for all and lifelong education? Is it not acceptance of the replication of poverty from one generation to another?

In fact, poverty is often handed down: it becomes the fruit of a family's past or of large-scale structural inequalities. But it is also the result of a new dynamic of growing inequalities. We are witnessing the emergence of unheard-of forms of poverty in the industrialized and developing countries alike. In March 1998, the ILO estimated that the Asian crisis had resulted in the loss of 24 million jobs in eastern Asia, and that between 1996 and 1998 unemployment had probably doubled in Hong Kong, China and the Philippines, and tripled in Indonesia, North Korea and Malaysia.[16] Other experts, including Sidney Jones of Human Rights Watch, are concerned about the consequences of the crisis for millions of Asians working outside their countries of origin, and the risk that the deterioration in living conditions of the most underprivileged could translate into an increase in prostitution.[17] Half the population of Indonesia and the Philippines already live on about $2 a day. The World Bank has looked at the way in which income reduction affects poverty and growth in four countries: Indonesia, the Philippines, Thailand and Malaysia. It studied the impact of a 10% reduction in income between 1997 and 2000, establishing the poverty threshold at $1 per capita per day for Indonesia and the Philippines and at $2 per capita per day for Thailand and Malaysia. World Bank simulations have shown that, should income distribution remain unchanged, poverty would double in Indonesia and increase by 35% to 50% in the Philippines, Thailand and Malaysia. With an increase in inequality equivalent to a 10% reduction of the Gini coefficient (an indicator measuring the level of inequality in income distribution), the incidence of poverty would triple in Indonesia and double in Thailand. Conversely, with a more egalitarian income distribution, in the form of a 10% increase in the Gini coefficient, the incidence of poverty would remain virtually unchanged in Indonesia, the Philippines and Malaysia, and be reduced in Thailand.[18]

The vast social gap no longer divides just North and South, but exists within each country, since much of the South can now be found within the North, and a great deal of the North is to be found within the South. Developing countries show signs of an emergent middle class that has reaped the fruits of development even as the situation of the poorest has worsened. Official figures mask enormous inequalities in income. According to Alan B. Durning of the Worldwatch Institute, 60% to 70% of most countries' inhabitants earn less than the national average. In the vast majority, the poorest 20% of homes do not even receive 10% of the national income, while the richest 20% normally earn half. Since 1950 the gap between rich and poor nations has widened, mainly because the rich are becoming richer. But since 1980, in many developing countries, the poor have also begun to get poorer.[19]

In the industrialized nations over 100 million people live in financial poverty in the OECD member countries alone, which also have 37 million unemployed and over 100 million homeless, a scandalously high figure for rich countries.[20] According to the UNDP, approximately 400,000 people in London are homeless.[21] For 20 years 'the number of jobs in industrial countries has increased at only half the rate of GDP growth and failed to keep pace with the growth in the labour force' making for the exclusion of young people and women in particular.[22] However, the extent of human poverty in the industrialized countries bears no automatic relation to income and employment levels. As it is, the USA, where the population has the highest per capita income in terms of purchasing power parity of the 17 industrialized countries studied by the UNDP, and where, according to official statistics, unemployment affects only some 5% of the active population, is also the country where human poverty is the most widespread, accounting for 16.5% of the population. The Netherlands and the United Kingdom, with almost identical per capita incomes, display very different poverty levels of 8.2% and 15% respectively. Of the 17 industrialized countries, it is in Sweden that human poverty is least widespread, with 6.8%.[23] It is quite obvious that in the industrialized countries the poverty level depends on the level of state intervention, redistribution policies, and the nature and effectiveness of measures adopted. The survival of fledgling democracies also depends on their economic skills, but more particularly on their political aptitude to respond to the challenge of ever-increasing poverty.

Poverty also has an impact on environment-friendliness. According to the UNDP, 'About three-quarters of the world's poorest people live in rural areas, dependent on agricultural activities for their livelihoods.'[24] More than 500 million poor people live in ecologically fragile zones. This situation is likely to worsen as demographic growth encourages more intensive cultivation of the land, which often leads to reduced yield. Chances of sustainable development recede as deprived populations are forced to struggle for survival, while vast tracts of land are given over to unbridled industrial activity that does not benefit the local populations themselves. As Alan Durning points out, 'economic degradation and ecological degradation combine to form a maelstrom, a downward spiral that threatens to engulf more and more victims for ever'.[25]

The reasons for this new explosion of poverty are, first and foremost, economic: increased foreign debt; inappropriate structural adjustment programmes; economic transitions carried out inconsiderately and based on erroneous assumptions; unequal distribution of wealth between town and country; inability to establish fair systems of taxation; lack of monitoring of capital flow at international level, etc. These changes are often exacerbated by

Box 2.1 Street Children

In the little world in which children have their existence, there is nothing so finely perceived and so finely felt, as injustice. (Charles Dickens, *Great Expectations*, 1861)

As long ago as 1986, UNICEF estimated that over 30 million children lived on the streets. Their numbers are increasing daily owing to the flight from the countryside, unplanned urban growth, the disruption of traditional family structures and the expansion of absolute forms of poverty. UNICEF's latest estimates, also presented by the WHO, indicate the existence of 100 million street children, of whom 40 million live in Latin America, 25 to 30 million live in Asia and 10 million live in Africa. Contrary to a common assumption, street children are not necessarily orphans or runaways. Some have parents and a home, but migrant families are often obliged to live in shanty towns in extremely cramped conditions. Children either seek refuge on the streets, forced there by poverty, ill-treatment and sexual abuse, or are placed on the pavements by parents to beg.

The plight of street children is one of the most horrible manifestations of the injustice of poverty and exclusion. Street children are the anonymous victims of widespread indifference and are forced to live without any kind of security, often in utter destitution and with no access to schooling or work. Very often, they turn to drugs and especially to inhaling solvents such as glue, which can have extremely serious pathological effects on brain functions. Drug addiction marginalizes them still further and con-stitutes a danger to their health that is all the greater as they have practically no access to any health services. They face major risks: they are the choice targets, or the tools, of the prostitution market, drug gangs and criminal organizations. They may even be liable to execution by contract killers or 'death squads', usually financed by informal associations of merchants or entrepreneurs bent on 'social' cleansing of city centres and business or shopping districts. Urgent measures are needed to solve the problem of street children, otherwise, as Susanna Agnelli emphasizes in the Report to the Independent Commission on Humanitarian Questions, 'their numbers will increase in proportion to the growth of large towns. Their frustration and the violence it entails will increase in proportion to their destitution.'

Governments, in an effort to maximize the scope of their actions, should specifically endeavour to enforce the provisions of the Convention on the Rights of the Child, signed in November 1989 and ratified in September 1990, and to that end establish more constructive relations with the private sector and the non-profit associations, including NGOs. Primary schools should be more effectively integrated into the community and greater contact between parents and teachers encouraged so as better to perceive their role in child development and stimulate parental control. What is called for is not charity or dependence on humanitarian aid – both of which can only be temporary measures – but political decisions and specific budgetary measures (such as earmarking 0.05% of the GDP for a six-year period) with the support of parliament, trades unions and associations. If we are to overcome this collective shame to society, we must all work together.

Professional training for all persons – social workers, doctors, nurses, public officials, the police, etc. – likely to come into contact with street children must include familiarization with the problem. Street children must be taken charge of by district associations, NGOs and appropriate institutions, with financial support from governments and international donors. There must be more structures, intelligently conceived, to enable those children to escape from their wretched condition, avoiding as far as possible structures that involve shutting them up in boarding schools or 'correction centres', which, by turning street children into outcasts, hinder their reintegration as adults. As Franklin Roosevelt said in his Philadelphia address on 20 November 1940, 'We cannot always prepare our children's future, but we can always prepare our children for the future.'

Sources: Working with Street Children: Selected Case-studies from Africa, Asia and Latin America, UNESCO/ICCB, 1995. A One-way Street? Report on Phase 1 of the Street Children Project, Programme on Substance Abuse, WHO, 1993. UNICEF, Convention on the Rights of the Child, 1989, in Street Children: A Growing Urban Tragedy, Report for the Independent Commission on International Humanitarian Issues, 1986. International Herald Tribune, 23 May 1995. Human Development Report, UNDP, 1993.

rapid population growth. Globalization, which, as Jean-Paul Fitoussi notes, stems from a political choice, 'just as refusal to organize it is a political choice', is implicated in the growth of poverty and inequality. Financial globalization increases structural inequalities because it brings with it a new division between profits and wages to the detriment of the latter, at least in industrialized countries. At the same time, market globalization increases the dynamic inequalities of wages and employment, widening the gap between skilled and unskilled workers.[26] According to Daniel Cohen, the inequality explosion is also explained by the effects of the third industrial revolution, which is linked to the upsurge of computer science and the new production technologies. This leads to the expansion of the logic of 'assortative matching', that is, to an explosion of inequalities within each age group and each socio-professional category. Hence, in the world of work, small differences in qualifications between two workers signify immense differences in wages and output. The outcome is that workers are grouped according to the level of their skills, with a gap between the elite and other wage-earners. These wage and productivity disparities may also be observed among countries with different levels of qualification.[27]

According to Philippe Engelhard, these factors all make for an 'increasingly glaring disparity between growth and improved collective welfare'. But, as the same expert asks, 'What point is there in growth that does not help the majority of the population?'[28] What is more, the idea that growth is necessarily unequal is erroneous: in the Republic of Korea, for instance, growth is relatively egalitarian, and Malaysia has made considerable progress in this area: in 1993 only 14% of its population were poor, as opposed to 60% in 1970.[29] In China, the poverty rate has gone down from 66% to 22%.[30] As Philippe Engelhard notes, the question is, in fact, 'less whether growth is unequal than whether it enables the poorest strata to improve their situation'.

Improving the Measurement of Poverty

According to the Indian economist Amartya Sen, winner of the 1998 Nobel Prize for economics, a distinction must be drawn between absolute poverty – the level below which an individual cannot provide for his or her basic needs – and relative poverty, defined by social inequality and the sense of having fewer material resources than others. As countries become richer, they have a different perception of the acceptable minimum level of consumption, by which the poverty threshold is determined. Amartya Sen also thinks that a person's vulnerability must be taken into account: poverty is linked to the degree of moral suffering it entails.[31] Hence any measurement of inequality and poverty depends on a choice of extremely diverse and sometimes highly subjective variables, whether in terms of income, wealth or even happiness. Where poverty is concerned, the real challenge is to increase people's choices and hence their freedom.[32]

Amartya Sen's analysis shows that it is extremely difficult to arrive at a reliable estimate of poverty. Three main criteria are currently applied: the incidence of poverty, which assesses the ratio of poor households or individuals to the total number of households or individuals; the degree of poverty, which measures the average income disparity per poor inhabitant as compared to the poverty threshold; and unequal poverty, which distinguishes different degrees of poverty and proposes a sort of poverty scale.[33]

However, the problem of accurate measurement and whether it is even possible to make pertinent comparisons on an international scale remains intact. For example, Pierre Salama and Jacques Vallier indicate that income statistics do not take sufficient account of 'auto-consumption' and ethnic solidarity, which are especially important in the least developed countries. The use of highly relevant data is therefore essential for discerning and grasping the new realities of poverty. The United Nations is aware of this problem: Commitment 2 of the Copenhagen Summit for Social Development, which deals with the eradication of poverty, stresses the need for each country not only to prepare national methods and indicators for measuring all forms of poverty (especially absolute poverty), but also to evaluate and monitor the situation of people with precarious livelihoods.[34]

However, Morgenstern quite rightly points out that the degree of precision of certain indicators was quite often disproportionate to the information we really need for forecasting and acting.[35] More important than measuring poverty is measuring the capacity to counter poverty. As Philippe Engelhard inquires, would a quantitative measurement of the capacity to reintegrate marginalized or excluded population groups not be a genuine criterion of performance?[36] What does it actually matter whether GNP grows by 2%, 3% or 5% if that growth benefits only a tiny minority of the population, as it does in many countries today?

Anti-poverty Initiatives

The fact that poverty is hard to measure should not defer immediate implementation of strategies designed to eradicate it and to reduce the suffering of the marginalized. According to the World Bank, the transfer of resources needed to eliminate poverty in the world was only 3% of the developing countries' total consumption in 1985, while 1% would have sufficed to eliminate extreme poverty.[37] More recently, the UNDP estimated that a $40 billion annual investment between 1995 and 2005, i.e. less than 0.2% of world revenue, would be sufficient to give all the inhabitants in the developing countries access to basic social services – health, water and primary education.[38] Is that investment beyond us, when we know that cigarette consumption in Europe alone absorbs $50 billion every year,[39] and that every year Americans spend $5 billion on dietary products to cut down their calorie intake, while '400 million human beings suffer so seriously from under-nourishment that both body and mind are impaired'?[40] As Wally N'Dow, secretary-general of the City Summit, points out, 'the resources exist for providing a roof, clean water, basic sanitary facilities, at a cost of under $100 per person, for every man, woman and child on this planet'. For the poor inventoried in national statistics alone, this effort would represent $130 to $150 billion. By way of comparison, it is worth recalling that military spending worldwide is estimated at $690 billion to $800 billion per year. The Cold War is over and yet we continue to invest massively in arms instead of making preventive investments in peace-building.

Poverty eradication has been on the agenda for over 150 years! Must we wait another century and a half before it is attained? Solutions do exist and specific initiatives indicate the course to be followed. Maryse Gaudier of the ILO reports that:

> Several countries, with the help of the big international financial institutions, drew up compensatory programmes designed to assist the poor and protect vulnerable groups ... in some developing countries, especially in Latin America, measures were initiated with a view to adapting institutional social security to population groups hardest hit by the effects of the economic crisis and structural adjustment ... Various countries like Bangladesh, Lesotho and Chile launched emergency employment programmes, with a view to ensuring the transfer of income to families in a situation of absolute poverty.

In the industrialized countries, anti-poverty measures have basically taken the form of special programmes to guarantee resources and vocational and social integration projects. Given the inadequacy of these policies, there has also been an increase in private action with voluntary-association systems, as in the developing countries.[41]

Access to credit likewise plays a fundamental role in integrating into economic life those who are excluded from conventional financing systems and enabling them to play an active role in the implementation of development policies. The Executive Board of UNESCO has stressed the need to put in place institutions that would give the world's poorest inhabitants access to credit, paying special attention to the needs of women and deprived groups. The best-known example of such an institution is the Grameen Bank in Bangladesh, established by Mohammed Yunus in 1983. Specializing in microcredit, this bank today lends to more than two million rural inhabitants, 94% of them women, with a loan reimbursement rate of over 98%.[42] Mohammed Yunus underlines that the Grameen Bank has received no international aid in the last three years, that it covers all operating costs on its own and that it employs 13,000 people. In 1995, at the Beijing Summit, UNESCO and the Grameen Bank signed a memorandum of understanding calling on UNESCO to provide for this bank's clients a lifelong education programme focusing on day-to-day activities, literacy and health. Another interesting initiative was taken by the Société d'investissement et de développement international (SIDI) in France. Also established in 1983, SIDI is run as a joint investment fund in which investors relinquish any profit over the inflation rate, the surplus being reinvested to help create businesses in poor countries.[43]

Education is a cornerstone of any long-term anti-poverty strategy. The overwhelming majority of the poor are deprived of access to information and knowledge that could help them emerge from their wretched condition. To combat poverty is to offer individuals choices; it is to give each citizen a chance to determine his or her own destiny; it is to give every man and woman the possibility of playing an active part in local and national public life. From that perspective, enhancing human resources and adapting education and training systems are priorities for any anti-poverty scheme.[44] This requires a new approach to adult education, one that takes into account the new employment prospects in such varied fields as environmental protection, development of renewable energies, water and natural resource management, cultural and natural eco-tourism, not forgetting public relations, and radio and television, with their increasing number of programmes in local languages. As emphasized in the British government's recent report on poverty eradication, the poor have assets, whether their skills, their social institutions, their culture or their knowledge of their environment.[45] It is vital to ensure that these assets are recognized and made use of.

States must, in the first instance, rely on their own assets. With that in view, it is essential that the countries themselves alter their priorities. They have everything to gain from financing education themselves whenever they are able to do so, rather than resorting to loans that cost them a great deal in the long run. India, with more than one-third of the world's illiterates, undertook in 1993 to increase the share of its GDP devoted to education to 6% by 2000–05 and has already achieved excellent results: from roughly 1.9%, the figure has gone up to 3.5%. Furthermore, India taught 64 million adults to read and write between 1989 and 1997. In Bangladesh, the primary school enrolment rate rose from 60% to 78% between 1990 and 1996, while the school drop-out rate fell from 60% in 1990 to 37% in 1996. Secondary education must influence another factor closely linked to poverty: population growth. According to the World Bank, Brazilian mothers who never attended school have an average of 6.5 children, as opposed to 2.5 among those who attended secondary school.[46] Education is the best means of controlling births and spacing pregnancies. In order to control demographic growth, it is necessary to open schools, colleges and universities: those are by far the most effective 'contraceptives'.

In the fight against poverty, it is therefore necessary to extend the range of choices rather than imposing constraints. The real challenge is to train the poor without steering them towards either low-status jobs or jobs likely to become obsolete. This calls for genuine reform of education centred on quality and efficiency: the schools of the future must teach how to learn and how to participate. To move on to the society of knowledge and of knowledge for all, the most deprived population groups must be assured of the opportunity – based on merit – to receive higher education, as stipulated in Article 26 of the Universal Declaration of Human Rights. Jacques Delors emphasized this point when he said: 'A society incapable of guaranteeing equal access for all to its essential functions, especially employment or activity, is a society that is losing its coherence.'[47]

UNESCO, through its action in the field of education, therefore plays an undeniable role in the fight against poverty. It addresses the problem on two fronts: that of basic education, essential if every individual is to be integrated into, and advance in, society, and that of lifelong education for all, the purpose of which is not only to prepare individuals for new economic developments, but above all to enable everyone to acquire the qualifications needed to find a niche in society. Through education, UNESCO also aims at helping each individual to realize his or her own capacities, for without self-respect and respect for others, nothing can be achieved. We can learn to live together only if we understand that we are all equal, united by certain universal values, yet at the same time all different. In this context, UNESCO supports the integration of cultural minorities, often the prime victims of poverty.

In a word, the problem today is not to alleviate poverty engendered by a dynamic of unequal growth through ineffective emergency or assistance measures, but rather 'to make the war on poverty a force for growth, wagering on long-term action'.[48] Unfortunately, it must be admitted that society suffers from apathy regarding the future and moral shortsightedness – both dangerous conditions. We continue to invest immoderately in arms, experiments in space and unnecessary material goods, whereas we should be investing in research into vaccines to treat sicknesses, in the fight against AIDS and prions, in programmes for street children, and in protecting the environment. We bear a terrible weight of responsibility. If we remain passive in the face of poverty, our children and grandchildren will reproach us for having failed to take the necessary steps in time.

We must therefore act without delay by taking brave political decisions. This means strengthening confidence instead of destroying it: there will be no sustainable development without confidence, and thus without a degree of social cohesion, which makes 'sense' by allowing us to situate ourselves *vis-à-vis* others and the world.

We must be fully aware that poverty, violence and instability are mutually reinforcing processes; eradicating poverty thus constitutes a major challenge for the future of democracy and one to which every citizen, without exception, must respond.

The Role of the International Community

Assistance from the rich countries must go in the first place to projects prepared by the beneficiary countries themselves. The international community must show its solidarity, particularly by reviewing the problem of the poorest countries' debt repayment. A study carried out by the International Monetary Fund and the World Bank shows that if nothing is done the multilateral debt service alone will account for 10% of the exports of 23 poor countries between 2005 and 2014; for seven other poor countries, the rate will be over 20%.[49] A minimalist vision of international cooperation is no longer acceptable. Let us have the courage to reduce the burden of both bilateral and multilateral debt radically and immediately, particularly in the least developed countries and in Africa.

In this respect, the efforts already made in the context of the initiative HIPC (heavily indebted poor countries) are particularly welcome: this initiative, which aims at wiping out up to 80% of the public debt of 41 of those countries, had by April 1999 already benefited seven countries (Bolivia, Burkina Faso, Côte d'Ivoire, Guyana, Mali, Mozambique and Uganda). More recently, in June 1999, the G7 countries decided to cancel the public debt of the poorest countries by some further US$70 billion, in the framework of the Cologne initiative. The latter aims in particular at increasing the number of countries eligible for reduction of their debt from the current figure of 29 to 36, and to reduce from six to three the number of years during which those countries must follow economic adjustment policies. Furthermore, any financial benefit from reduction of their debt must serve to fund education and health services. All in all, these measures to lighten the burden of debt should make it possible to reduce the nominal value of the poorest countries' debt, which currently stands at US$230 billion, by US$139 billion.[50] However, it is essential to go further than this, and faster; otherwise, there is a risk that the world's poor – who are not interested in the minute details or the logic of international finance or structural adjustment plans, and who were not invited to the meetings and ceremonies held recently for the purpose of proffering explanations and regrets on the subject – will lose their patience. Even with a change of political will and vision concerning action at international level, it too often happens that the procedures chosen are suited neither to people's way of life, particularly that of people living in extreme poverty, nor to considerations of an ethical nature.

As Pope John Paul II stressed in his message on the occasion of the World Day of Peace, 1 January 1999, 'an immediate and vigorous effort is needed, as we look to the year 2000, to ensure that the greatest possible number of nations will be able to extricate themselves from a now intolerable situation'.

The burden of debt is a major obstacle to any effort to eliminate poverty, all the more so since the interest rates paid on their loans by the poorer, more fragile and less solvent countries are manifestly higher than those paid by the industrialized countries.[51] In 1992, the developing countries paid their creditors more than two and a half times the amount they received in official development assistance. Today, official development assistance from the OECD member countries is at its lowest in a quarter of a century: 0.22 % of GNP,[52] while the minimum objective repeatedly agreed on by states the world over in the framework of the United Nations is 0.7%. There is something shocking about the fact that, between August 1997 and December 1998, the international financial community was capable of raising US$190 billion and of paying out US$63 billion for a rescue operation to safeguard the interests of creditors in Brazil, Indonesia, the Republic of Korea and Thailand, while the total sum of governmental aid at world level amounted in 1998 to US$32.7 billion.[53] Furthermore, such aid often returns to the donor countries, since they are the ones who supply the equipment and infrastructure for development projects. Is it poverty's role to finance wealth?

Inclusion of social clauses and anti-poverty measures in structural adjustment programmes must be ensured. Such measures not only serve as safety mechanisms in times of crisis, but are investments in the future.[54] We must repeat that the persistence of poverty and inequalities curbs development. It is to be hoped that as poor populations gain access to education and health services and are able to improve their skills, growth will be here to stay.[55] In this respect, it is noteworthy that the human and social dimensions of development are now taken into account by the World Bank. The president of the World Bank, James Wolfensohn, recently declared: 'There can be no adequate development without social progress.'[56] Reacting to the financial crisis besetting Asia – due to a large extent to a system that can be summed up as 'I lend, I supply, I implement; you get in debt', without any real improvement in micro-economic conditions – James Wolfensohn stressed the importance for the countries concerned to improve the workings of their institutions (both governmental and private), to establish social welfare systems for those living in poverty and to maintain the financing of basic education and social sectors in national budgets that risk being downsized.[57] That is something that UNESCO has always recommended, and it was reiterated at the 1993 session of its General Conference. Furthermore, serious thought must be given to the adoption of measures that would allow the indebted countries to replace part of their public debt repayment with investments of equivalent value in basic education ('debt–education swaps').

At the World Summit for Social Development (Copenhagen, 1995), the governments of the world undertook not only to reduce poverty, but to eradicate it. It is worth reminding ourselves of the terms of that solemn promise: 'We commit ourselves to the goal of eradicating poverty in the world, through decisive national actions and international co-operation as an ethical, social, political and economic imperative of humankind.' We must respect this commitment and fulfil it through measures based on a long-term vision and long-term objectives. Though often necessary, the emergency measures adopted have only a limited impact on poverty, and sometimes increase it in the medium or long term. While humanitarian or charitable treatments temporarily assuage suffering, only development based on solidarity will put an end to poverty once and for all: the shared prosperity of human-kind relies on justice.

What do we really want to pass on to our children: chronic poverty or the hope of a better future? The abject poverty of shantytowns, the scandal of street children and man's inhumanity to man are our collective responsibility which must be acknowledged by the affluent, victims of a mental blind spot that has accustomed them to tolerate the intolerable and see poverty as an irremediable phenomenon. Development will be sustainable only if it is shared.

Pointers and Recommendations

- Improve and complete the political, legislative and administrative measures to combat poverty at the national, regional and international levels.
- Protect the most vulnerable strata of the population by increasing the share of national budgets devoted to education and other social investments.
- Provide young people and the unemployed with training in keeping with the needs of society.
- Involve the beneficiaries directly in any anti-poverty strategy.
- Encourage and increase initiatives aiming at abolishing the public debt of the poorest and most deeply indebted countries, and promote 'debt-swap' arrangements that favour human development.
- Promote access to micro-credit for population groups who may not have access to other forms of borrowing.
- Encourage a radical change in the official development assistance policy of industrialized countries, reversing the tendency to reduce it, and aim once more at the minimum target of 0.7% agreed upon in the framework of the United Nations system, and devote most of that assistance to human development (education, health and basic social services).
- Mobilize $40 billion per year for ten years, in accordance with the UNDP recommendations, for providing universal access to basic services – health, water and primary education – following redefinition of the countries' domestic priorities and an increase in official development assistance directly allocated to human development.

Notes

1. See Kimon Valaskakis, 'Mondialisation et gouvernance', *Futuribles*, No. 230, Paris, April 1998. As the author points out, an overabundant economy of 'buffets' today coexists with its antithesis, the economy of the 'soup-kitchen'.

2. A recent study by the World Institute for Development Economics Research that studied 124 developing countries shows that a doubling of income would translate into a 13% reduction of the risks of humanitarian crisis, and that more than half of the countries that suffered such crises during the 1990s had experienced a drop in average income during the 1980s; *Financial Times*, 21 January 1998.

3. *Le Monde*, 7 March 1995.

4. UNDP, *Human Development Report*, Oxford University Press, New York, 1997.

5. Ibid. In this case, however, the data for the period prior to the fall of the Berlin Wall may not be entirely reliable.

6. United Nations, Res. A/51/178.

7. Leandro Despouy, *Enjoyment of Economic, Social and Cultural Rights, Final Report on Human Rights and Extreme Poverty*, Commission on Human Rights, Sub-Commission against Discrimination and for the Protection of Minorities, E/CN.4/Sub.2/1996, 13 June 1996.

8. Masood Ahmed, Michael Walton, I. Subbarao and Parita Suebsaeng, *Poverty Reduction and the World Bank, Progress in Fiscal 1996 and 1997*, World Bank, Washington, DC, 1997.

9. *Le Monde*, 18–19 October 1998.

10. UNDP, *Human Development Report 1997*, Oxford University Press, New York.

11. Ibid.

12. UNDP, *Human Development Report 1998*, New York, Oxford University Press.

13. Hamid Tabatabai, 'Poverty and inequality in developing countries: a review of the evidence', in Garry Rodgers and Ralph van der Hoeven (eds), *The Poverty Agenda: Trends and Policy Options, New Approaches to Poverty Analysis and Policy*, International Institute for Labour Studies, Geneva, 1995.

14. Jean-Pierre Langellier, 'L'immense planète des délaissés', *Le Monde, Bilan du monde*, 1998 issue.

15. Alan B. Durning, 'Halt to poverty', *State of the World 1990*, Worldwatch Institute, Washington, DC.

16. *Le Monde*, 18 March 1998.

17. *Financial Times*, 26 January 1998.

18. Tamar Manuelyan Atinç, Michael Walton and Stephen Commins, *Social Consequences of the East Asian Financial Crisis*, World Bank, Washington, DC, September 1998.

19. Durning, 'Halt to poverty'.

20. UNDP, *Human Development Report 1998*.

21. UNDP, *Human Development Report 1994*, New York, Oxford University Press.

22. Ibid.

23. UNDP, *Human Development Report 1998*.

24. UNDP, *Human Development Report 1997*.

25. Durning, 'Halt to poverty'.

26. Jean-Paul Fitoussi, 'Mondialisation et inégalités', *Futuribles*, No. 224, October 1997.

27. Daniel Cohen, *The Wealth of the World and the Poverty of Nations*, trans. Jacqueline Lindenfeld, MIT Press, Cambridge, MA, 1998; Michael Kremer, 'The O-Ring Theory

of Economic Development', *Quarterly Journal of Economics*, Vol. 58, No. 3, August 1993.

28. 'Face à la croissance de la pauvreté', interview with Philippe Engelhard, *Esprit*, May 1997.

29. UNDP, *Human Development Report 1997*.

30. *Libération*, 'Un hérétique à la Banque mondiale', 25 June 1999. Stiglitz notes that 'the Chinese have refused to deregulate and to privatize – and their balance sheet is healthier'.

31. Amartya Sen, *Levels of Poverty: Policy and Change*, World Bank, Washington, DC, 1980.

32. Amartya Sen, *Inequality Re-examined*, Russell Sage Foundation, New York and Clarendon Press, Oxford, 1992.

33. Maryse Gaudier, *Poverty, Inequality, Exclusion: New Approaches to Theory and Practice*, International Institute for Labour Studies, Geneva, 1993.

34. United Nations, *World Summit for Social Development, Programme of Action*, Chapter II: Eradication of poverty, 1995.

35. Morgenstern, *Précision et Incertitudes des données économiques*, quoted by Philippe Engelhard, 'Face à la croissance de la pauvreté'.

36. Engelhard, 'Face à la croissance de la pauvreté'.

37. *World Development Report*, World Bank, Washington, DC, 1990.

38. UNDP, *Human Development Report 1997*.

39. Sylvie Brunel, 'L'enfer des inégalités', *Le Monde*, 18–19 October 1998.

40. Durning, 'Halt to poverty'.

41. Gaudier, *Poverty, Inequality, Exclusion*.

42. *International Herald Tribune*, 28 February–1 March 1998.

43. *Le Monde*, 25 April 1995.

44. Gaudier, *Poverty, Inequality, Exclusion*.

45. *Eliminating World Poverty: A Challenge for the 21st Century*, White Paper on International Development, Secretary of State for International Development, November 1997.

46. *Le Monde*, 22 December 1993.

47. Jacques Delors, 'Giving a new dimension to the fight against exclusion', final address to the Copenhagen Seminar, Commission of the European Communities, 1993.

48. Engelhard, 'Face à la croissance de la pauvreté'.

49. *Le Monde*, 15 September 1995.

50. The present value of the poorest countries' public debt is estimated at US$127 billion. Following the Cologne initiative, the set of measures to lighten the debt should make it possible to reduce it by US$71 billion.

51. In its *Human Development Report* for 1997, the UNDP reports that during the 1980s, 'the poorer countries paid interest rates four times as high as those charged rich countries'.

52. *Le Monde*, 18–19 October 1998.

53. World Bank, *Global Development Finance 1999*, World Bank, Washington, DC, 1999.

54. Garry Rodgers and Ralph van der Hoeven (eds), *The Poverty Agenda: Trends and Policy Options, New Approaches to Poverty Analysis and Policy*, International Institute for Labour Studies, Geneva, 1995.

55. Michael Lipton, 'Poverty – are there holes in the consensus?', *World Development*, Vol. 25, No. 7, 1997.

56. *Le Monde*, 16 February 1996.

57. *Financial Times*, 29 January 1998.

CHAPTER 3

. . . .

Humanizing the City

§ SOME figures speak for themselves. It is estimated that in 2000, 75% of the population of the industrialized countries, representing 0.9 billion people, lived in cities, against 73% in 1990. The urban population in the developing countries increased from 37% to 45% over the same period, representing 2.3 billion people. By 2025, if current trends do not change, the proportions should amount in the North to 84% (1 billion inhabitants) and in the South to 57% (4 billion inhabitants).[1] The urban population worldwide is now growing two to three times more quickly than the rural population.

We are all aware of the gigantic scale of the urban revolution under way. In the space of 40 years, we shall have to build the equivalent of a thousand cities of three million inhabitants, approximately as many cities as there are today! This urban revolution, first and foremost demographic in nature, will mostly affect the developing countries.[2] In 2025, the rate of urbanization could be as much as 85% in Latin America, 54% in Africa and 55% in Asia. According to the World Bank, the cities of the developing countries alone are thought to be growing at a pace of 65 million inhabitants per year – which amounts to adding to the planet a city the size of Turkey every year.[3] It is probable that by 2025, 80% of the urbanized population will be living in developing countries. Furthermore, this urban gigantism is moving south, as two-thirds of the world population in mega-cities will be concentrated in the least developed regions: in the year 2000, six of the ten largest cities in the world were in Asia, two in North America and two in Latin America. By 2015, only one of the ten most populated cities in the world will be in the North (Tokyo) and none in the West. Urban problems will therefore have to be solved in a context very different from the past and, at the same time, very differentiated. Urban growth is now highest in the poorest regions – in which case it is unrelated to effective development – but also in those areas that are experiencing the most rapid economic development: in this case, the urban 'boom' often seems synonymous with uncontrollable chaos. It would therefore seem evident that if current trends continue, they will bring considerable pressure to bear on natural resources – particularly water and energy. They will also seriously threaten the organization and management of social structures. Therefore we must all aim, through a major alliance, to ensure that demographic forecasts do not come true. They are not inevitable but, if they are to be proved wrong, then educational infrastructure must be set up more quickly and the quality of life in urban and rural environments improved.

A New Approach to the City: A New Challenge for Development

In the coming decades, the city will present one of the major challenges of development, which will be increasingly urban. The fact is that urban infrastructure does not match the needs of populations, particularly as far as water, energy and transport are concerned, especially in the South, where most urban growth is concentrated. Furthermore, according to United Nations estimates, more than 600 million city-dwellers in the world are homeless or live in unhealthy conditions; 600 million people also have to put up with similarly precarious circumstances in the countryside and their drift towards the cities often merely converts rural poverty into urban poverty.[4] According to World Bank statistics, at least one inhabitant in every four in the cities of the South was living in poverty in 1996; in 2000, this proportion doubled;[5] in some regions such as Latin America, the number of poor in urban areas exceeds that of the poor in rural areas.[6] It is no accident that one of the last United Nations conferences in the twentieth century, which was held in Istanbul in June 1996, was entitled the City Summit (Habitat II).

The Istanbul Conference made it quite plain that urban patterns of consumption were unsuitable as they cause unprecedented damage to the urban environment and, more broadly, to the ecosystems on which those cities depend. All the indicators – energy consumption, production of greenhouse gases, mileage of roads built or used, numbers of cars, volume of domestic waste, atmospheric, chemical and radioactive pollution and pollution of water and the soil – show that, particularly in the industrialized countries, the idea of sustainable development has not yet reached the urban culture. An American citizen makes more demands on the natural environment than 20 inhabitants of Bangladesh. From an ecological standpoint, many countries of the North are distinctly more overpopulated than India or China.[7] The 'ecological mark' that rich countries leave on the earth is in no way proportional to their population size: three planets of the size of the Earth would be necessary to provide for six billion Canadians.[8]

The Istanbul Conference brought together two contrasting visions, that of the Habitat I Conference in Vancouver (1976), which saw habitat first and foremost as a 'human settlement' and that of the Earth Summit in Rio in 1992, which gave pride of place in habitat to the ecosystem.[9] This synthesis did, however, leave some ambiguity: in the twenty-first century, would cities be built that would be no more than merely inhabitable? Or would cities be somewhere where all would enjoy living?[10] As pointed out by Candido Mendes, '"human habitat" is political as its intrinsic biodiversity is related to human values and lifestyles'. This means that strategies have to be adopted that take the defense of cultural pluralism, the relationship between preservation and development, and the relationship between ecology and democracy into account.[11]

Above and beyond the definition of terms, what is at stake is a new concept of development that combines the various approaches that have been explored during the past decade: 'sustainable development';[12] 'human development';[13] and 'social development', which is the extension of the collective dimension of human development.[14] If urban problems are to be dealt with in all their complexity, we must attempt to invent a form of development that encompasses all specific forms of development as defined by the international community and goes beyond them. Incorporating the city in 'sustainable development' means seeing it as a major trend, requiring long-term prospective policies and a strong sense of solidarity between generations; but it also means recognizing the fact that the city has become a living environment interacting with the natural environment. Promoting 'human development' in the city also involves bearing in mind that for many underprivileged populations, the drift from the countryside to the city represented a quest for dignity that should not remain a mere mirage. Finally, making of the city a framework for 'social development' can remind us of how Aristotle referred to man as a 'political animal', that is to say an inhabitant of the *polis* or City, in other words, an 'urban being'. Is not the city 'natural' to humans insofar as humans are social beings? Adopting a new approach to the city would also mean making it or refashioning it as a framework for the construction of citizenship, society and civility.

The Istanbul Conference confirmed the need for convergence between these various approaches to development by considering that cities should become both 'inhabitable', which requires respect for the ecosystems on which the city depends, and 'liveable', which presupposes a culture of citizenship in the city, based on solidarity and participation and due respect for the dignity of those who live there. As emphasized by Henry Cisneros, who then was minister of housing and urban development in the United States administration, 'environmental problems have clearly become of critical importance for the future of our communities. Today, in the United States as in other countries, many people like ourselves are trying to set up the concept of "sustainable communities" by attempting to incorporate environmental problems in problems of social and economic justice'.[15]

Let us go even further: the distinction between the various problems of development has become largely artificial; we cannot solve some of them without solving the others. In urban terms, sustainable development, human development and social development are not only complementary but inseparable. The urban challenge of the twenty-first century requires us to adopt a new vision. What lies at stake in this synthesis is the future, which can no longer be examined separately from urban societies and the biosphere.

The growing complexity of the urban phenomenon requires the immediate implementation of global, innovative, interdisciplinary and integrated policies and, above all, a change in the scale of the development strategies of the actors involved, both public and private.[16] The city is more than a set of buildings, it is a way of life. It has even become a living environment, one that humans have built, and has become 'second nature' and even, all too often, the antithesis of nature. It is because the complexity of the urban phenomenon has too often been denied that so many cities have now become inhospitable. Interpenetration between the city and the ecosystem that supports it – particularly at a time when the globalization of trade and population movements has considerably increased the scale of that ecosystem – has become such that the city is now a melting-pot into which all the contradictions of our societies flow and out of which must emerge a new concept of development.

In the future, development aid should take account of the urban factor when establishing links between all the partners and all levels of development. The World Bank has already undertaken investing US\$15 billion over five years in urban policies and strengthening the links between the various actors in the city. One of the lessons of the Istanbul Summit is that the mayors of major conurbations will in the future exert greater influence in the economic, social and political life of countries. It is worth noting in this regard that the World Assembly of Cities and Local Authorities (WACLA) has decided to set up a permanent coordination body at international level. It is to be hoped that such cooperation will give rise to common initiatives, and more particularly to a common vision, and will nurture real solidarity between cities, perhaps through the development of economic and cultural twinning.

A global urban policy requires, first and foremost, that every inhabitant should have a roof over his or her head. However, a city must also offer lifelong opportunities and regain its civic purpose. Seeking the opinion of every citizen, enabling the variety of opinions in any city to be expressed in the public arena of urban democracy, implementing in the city the full range of human rights recognized in the Universal Declaration of Human Rights and the two international pacts relating to human rights, and translating into reality the decisions taken at the Istanbul Summit and other conferences organized by the United Nations during the past decade: these are the inescapable bases of a new urban contract that must be concluded immediately if the challenges of the future are to be met.

What City for the Twenty-first Century?

If all people are to have a roof over their head, it will be necessary, as we pointed out, to build over 40 years the equivalent of a thousand cities of three million inhabitants or rebuild many existing cities. The Istanbul Conference took a decisive step forward by unanimously proclaiming the right to a dwelling, henceforth included among human rights of a universal nature. The Final Declaration adopted at the City Summit stipulated in this regard:

> We reaffirm our commitment to the full and progressive realization of the right to adequate housing as provided for in international instruments. To that end, we shall seek the active participation of our public, private and non-governmental partners at all levels to ensure legal security of tenure, protection from discrimination and equal access to affordable, adequate housing for all persons and their families. We shall work to expand the supply of affordable housing by enabling markets to perform efficiently and in a socially and environmentally responsible manner, enhancing access to land and credit and assisting those who are unable to participate in housing markets.

A dwelling is now recognized as a human right. Furthermore, the definition of a home that underlies the Istanbul Declaration goes well beyond the idea of a roof over one's head. Housing policy should now include an ethics of housing. A human dwelling has nothing to do with a mere shelter. Finding somewhere to live is far more than just a need. A roof over one's head, a home of one's own, play a vital symbolic and practical role in the development of every human being: they are necessary to help him or her establish their identity as an individual in relation to others and to society.

A dwelling is the space where every individual's identity is fashioned, and therefore the feeling of human dignity that underlies any personal development and all social development. It must therefore offer minimum conditions of hygiene, material and human security and privacy which go hand in hand with the concept of dignity. It is an economic as much as an ethical imperative: a residential district is not viable without infrastructure, particularly supplies of drinking water, a sewerage system, the removal of urban waste, communications and transport, which link it to the way a city operates as a whole.

It is not enough, however, to reaffirm this right. If it is to be applied, we must build the cities of tomorrow and determine in what sort of city we wish to live with our children. Unfortunately, cities are often built without city-dwellers, if not actually to their detriment. For individuals, the city is not and should be not a destiny but a choice. The city is often perceived as a cruel, destructive chaos or as the modern version of hell. A more pragmatic and determined stance should be adopted and the city should be seen as a form of development and a history that are for us to invent and write together.

In the opinion of experts, urban growth is focusing at the beginning of the twenty-first century on mega-cities and conurbations with over one million inhabitants, particularly if that figure includes the population of peripheral areas.[17] According to United Nations estimates, 13 cities exceeded 10 million inhabitants in 1992. Their gigantic scale, due to natural urban growth and the drift from the countryside, is a supplementary obstacle to the adoption of sustainable patterns of development and consumption, while making urban planning and management extremely difficult. This phenomenon is not specific to the industrialized countries – quite the contrary. Over 20 years, between 1970 and 1990, the list of the 10 largest cities has varied considerably, as London, Paris and Beijing were replaced by Bombay, Calcutta and Seoul. As already mentioned, 18 of the 25 largest cities in the world will be in the South in 2025.[18] The 'model' of the polycentric city, very extensive and expanding constantly, is tending to become more frequent outside the USA and could become the predominant model on a world scale, even in regions where economic development is inadequate to support the development of urbanization. For 2015, the following ranking has been forecast: Tokyo (28.7 million), Bombay (27.4 million), Lagos (24.4 million), Shanghai (23.4 million), Djakarta (21.2 million), São Paulo (20.8 million), Karachi (20.6 million), Beijing (19.4 million), Dhaka (19 million) and Mexico City (18.8 million).

As the scale of cities changes, so does their appearance. Contrary to the hopes entertained by certain experts, the development of new means of communication and information does not seem likely to reduce the flow of urban movements in the short term or to slow down the process of urban concentration. Instead, it is causing a concentration of sophisticated economic activities – as was the case during previous technical revolutions since industrialization – and therefore a flow of people and wealth around the connections between the transport and communication networks.

By virtue of this, cities are tending to become independent, not only of their hinterland but also of the nation to which they belong. As shown by Saskia Sassen in what is already a classic work, metropolises such as New York, London and Tokyo have become 'global cities', in other words, connection points for worldwide networks.[19] 'The global city', according to Manuel Castells, the sociologist and town planner, 'is not a place but a process to which the advanced centres of production and consumption of services, together with local societies which are dependent on them, are linked through a global network'. The new form of urbanization tends to create a 'flow area' that has a distinct rank within the global network of regional interactions and interdependence.[20] What is more, the geography of global cities and their networks makes no distinction between industrialized and developing countries. São Paulo and Mexico City, for example, have now become major economic centres that have established close links with North America and the world's financial centres.

This new urban geopolitics or rather 'metapolitics', which links many cities 'belonging' to different regions and countries or rather belonging to them less and less, cannot be perfectly incorporated in the economy of the city and in the daily needs of its residents. The new urban boom frequently handicaps medium-sized centres that have not been able to become part of the networks or even the peripheral areas around major cities. As pointed out by Castells,

> the territories surrounding these hubs play an increasingly subordinate, in-adequate role, to the point at times of dysfunctioning: for example, the *colonias populares* (the shantytowns where newcomers initially settled) account for ap-proximately two-thirds of the population of the Mexican capital but no longer play any particular role in the international business centre which Mexico City has become. *Being globally connected and locally disconnected, physically and socially, such is the feature which distinguishes mega-cities, the new urban form* [emphasis added].[21]

To meet the urban challenge, we need from now on, according to Néstor García Canclini, 'to revive the public space' and to recover 'the overall meaning of urban social life': otherwise, 'we are faced with the risk of ungovernability: the explosive potential of destructuring and destructive trends could lead to greater authoritarianism and repression'.[22]

Are we to conclude that 'megapolization' is an irreversible phenomenon? Will the secession announced by Robert Reich between the symbolic analysts in global cities and the other social classes relegated to their periphery or imprisoned in their ghettos also be unavoidable?[23] On the contrary, it would seem possible, provided we wanted it, to control urban development and to halt the disintegration of cities. As more than half of the increase in the urban population is the result of natural demographic growth, we surely cannot rely solely on policies for combating the population drift from the countryside which, in point of fact, would have little chance of succeeding unless radical agrarian reform and large-scale rural development policies were implemented. After all, in spite of the loss of traditional solidarities, the city often represents an opportunity for an individual to escape harsh living con-ditions in the rural environment and the loss of land or of other means for surviving there with dignity. Urban development can also be regarded to some extent as the result of economic and social development as the drift from the countryside is largely the result of the rise in agricultural productivity.

We are convinced that the solutions to urban problems must start with the humanization of the cities themselves, which should become, as pointed out by Jorge Wilheim, deputy secretary-general of the Habitat II Conference, 'centres of peace, freedom, justice, creativity and solidarity'.[24] 'Changing the city' does not mean merely changing the 'style' of life, it implies a particular view of the world as ultimately reflected in our daily behaviour. From that viewpoint, the brutality of urban life in many parts of the world should not conceal the existence of certain exemplary initiatives, unfortunately still too infrequent, based on original solutions in the fields of urban transportation and access to water, the recycling of waste, housing, education, participatory development and town planning. In Latin America, reference can be made to Villa El Salvador in Peru and to Curitiba in Brazil (see Box 4.1) for transport and to Porto Alegre for the introduction of a participatory municipal budget drawn up with the cooperation of ordinary citizens. It is to be hoped that urban partnerships on a world scale will facilitate the rapid transposition of these examples of urban innovation and participatory development.

It would also seem salutary to propose other methods of development and town planning than those that often lead to an inhuman urban explosion. Rural development and the medium-sized city can offer two alternatives to the mega-city that would preserve our chances of keeping urbanization on a human scale.

Improving the quality of life in the countryside could prevent rural populations from migrating first to the outer suburbs of major cities and then abroad. In spite of the industrialization of agriculture, many societies are and will continue in the foreseeable future to be largely agricultural: this is particularly true of Africa, India and China, where 70% of the population still live in the countryside. Housing policy is not necessarily urban. The first priority for controlling urban growth is the improvement of living conditions, formal and informal education and employment in rural areas. On the African continent, where urbanization affects only 30% of the population, villages still constitute the core of social organization and their productivity could be doubled by applying more modern economic methods.[25] Regenerating African agriculture would also require national policies and economic initiatives more favourable to the rural populations.[26] In some regions, particularly in a number of Latin American countries, a policy of vast agrarian reforms is required that would enable peasant farmers to acquire ownership of their holdings.[27]

Solving the age-old problem of the drift from the countryside calls for lucidity and the courage to tackle the fundamental issue of human beings without land and land without human beings. Many present-day conflicts are rooted in the existence of paramilitary forces in charge of 'guarding the land' which, little by little, become an uncontrolled army, and commit acts of violence and terrorism. In 1998, Pope John Paul II rightly pointed out that 'more frequently, it is poverty and the lack of prospects for development which spur individuals and families to go into exile'.[28]

In the developing countries, cheaper services and more reliable food supplies, hygiene and security are enough to create a vision of the city as a place of salvation and abundance, at the price of a hazardous gamble: the city does not necessarily provide the right jobs, nor does it necessarily enable new city-dwellers to provide for their subsistence and that of their families. It would be fairer to offer those families, without forcing them in any way, more equitable opportunities of development in the rural areas. It should be borne in mind that in a number of countries, relative poverty in a rural environment, on condition that it is not below a particular level of dignity, may be preferable to the dire poverty and insecurity of urban ghettos.

A new approach to the city also means a new approach to the countryside. This involves reconsidering the mutual links between the urban and rural worlds, bringing these two environments within the same compass and re-defining their relationships. In the industrialized countries, it is important to integrate the rural areas into the national economy while preserving the complementarity and specificity of the rural environment in relation to the urban one, through carefully targeted regional production and the development of the heritage, ecology and culture of the countryside. In the developing countries as well as in the industrialized ones, new vocations have to be found for agricultural land. The development of biotechnologies and the exploitation of biomass and of solar or wind energy could offer the rural world a new opportunity for both economic growth and sustainable development. Tourism can also be exploited as a source of profit, provided there is adequate respect for the ecosystems.

On the other hand, medium-sized cities, such as those in Northern Europe, can offer the image of a city on a human scale thanks to more limited geographic expansion and urban development that is mindful of the natural environment. Nevertheless, it is far from certain that the policy of a con-centrated city can be easily applied to other regions of the world or that this 'agora-city', to be found in Europe in competition with the American-style city whose residential districts extend around its outskirts, constitutes the only model of sustainable development. High-density urbanization requires specific conditions for controlling the property market and political willpower, together with the effective coordination of all the actors involved. Furthermore, urban concentration, while it has the advantage of reducing traffic density, creates a gap between the city and nature that may have a negative influence on the quality of life. In the view of some experts, the 'enhancing of the heritage' of small and medium-sized cities and the creation of artificial economic centres are false solutions.[29] While some companies can be encouraged to locate in small cities, multinational corporations and strategic company centres cannot stray too far away from the decision-making centres and communication hubs. Saskia Sassen has underlined the recent trend among major transnational companies, at a time when they are apparently decentralizing and becoming world enterprises, to relocate their head offices or at least their key departments (finance, marketing, advertising and communication, strategic planning and foresight) preferably to global cities.

As regards medium-sized cities, it is probable in the longer term that only small towns that have succeeded in finding a role to play in the way a conurbation functions by becoming secondary residential or employment areas will actually succeed in finding their niche in the economy of the future. It would then seem that the dissemination of means of communication and trade is one of the fundamental factors underlying urban development as it encourages development around major conurbations of dense networks of smaller towns that often prove to be more dynamic than the metropolis itself.[30]

The City, a Living Environment

The revolution in the information and communication technologies has subjected the city to tension between the areas of rapid exchange and the areas that are enclaved or neglected in physical as well as symbolic terms. Opening up the city to its peripheral areas would seem to be a priority for development. But the need to strengthen means of communication within the city and between it and its hinterland seems to enter into contradiction with the ecological preservation of the urban environment.

New metropolises make up a new landscape with an alternance of central and peripheral areas. They often exceed the framework of a single city and bring together several centres linked to each other via high-speed communication systems. The traditional contrast between town and country, although it has not disappeared, has become overshadowed by the contrast between neighbourhoods or, on a larger scale, between core and satellite urban centres.

Restructuring a city in a loosely woven urban fabric requires a policy that seeks to reconcile development and the environment. It is a matter of re-defining the solidarities in which the city should find its place. Solidarity with future generations requires urbanization that takes heed of the needs of ecological development based on the notion of forward-looking democracy. In that field, where much damage has already been done, a resolutely forward-looking approach is required. The global vision of the city should lead to an overall plan of action, inspired by a spirit of foresight. It is a matter of defining a plan for sustainable development that takes account of interactions between citizenship, the economy, the level of resources and the global environment. A number of pilot experiments and successful urban ventures, such as that of Curitiba, could serve as guiding examples. New concepts, namely those of 'sustainable cities' and 'efficient cities' could provide inspiration for new urban policies.[31]

Provision should also be made at every level of urban planning for the prevention of natural or man-made disasters, in order to reduce their consequences, particularly through a better distribution of fire-fighting and earthquake mitigation infrastructures and hospital facilities. A new approach to urban security is required that could be supported by the security forces, one of whose tasks is precisely to help to provide vital communication and transport services in the event of an emergency and to bring immediate assistance to populations in the event of disasters.

The city should also prepare itself for the efficiency revolution. Consumption patterns related to the affluent society of the industrialized countries are neither sustainable nor indefinitely extendable in a context of ever faster urbanization. According to the Worldwatch Institute, 'today's cities are no longer in harmony with nature and can no longer provide their residents with stability. In the industrialized countries and the Third World alike, urban growth, both chaotic and uncontrolled, is gobbling up more and more land, water and energy drawn from neighbouring areas.'[32, 33]

Let there be no mistake in this regard. Principle VIII of the Rio Conference stipulates that 'to achieve sustainable development and a better quality of life for all, States must reduce and eliminate unsustainable methods of production and consumption'. The Istanbul Declaration reaffirmed that priority. It called upon signatory states to tackle 'unsustainable methods of consumption and production, particularly in the industrialized countries'. It could not be made more clear.[34] That is where the vital role of education makes itself felt, particularly education related to the urban environment and sustainable development, which can bridge the gap between human development and sustainable development.

The metropolis, with its high population density, should be able to provide efficient management of natural resources, but it has become, at the dawn of the twenty-first century, a place of wastage, particularly of water and energy. The opportunities that mega-cities seem to offer their populations are costly in environmental and health terms – all the more costly where urbanization was not prepared but rather improvised. While that cost is clearly visible not only in the cities (poor housing, massive air and water pollution, a proliferation of domestic waste, noise and nuisance, the chaos of urban transport), but also outside the cities, no account of it is taken in economic statistics. Furthermore, the city is very demanding in terms of space. In Cairo, for example, the city absorbs over 600 hectares of agricultural land each year while the arable surface area of Egypt accounts for less than 5% of national territory.[35] Over the last 25 years, Dakar has expanded by 20 kilometres and Kinshasa by 40 kilometres. The consequences of the drift from the countryside on the human and natural environment are catastrophic. In addition to its demographic desertification, the hinterland has also undergone cultural desertification with the loss of family solidarities, the decline of traditional languages and the disappearance of the skills, species and cultural patterns linked to traditional ecosystems.

Sustainable Energy for the Cities of the Twenty-first Century[36]

Supplying energy to conurbations requires the mobilization of very varied forms of energy, which are currently transported over vast distances across the entire world. Cities are very demanding in energy. While it is difficult to generalize, large or medium-sized cities, which are more compact, have slightly higher energy efficiency than smaller cities. Nevertheless, the energy 'bill' is globally high. In the OECD countries, for example, cities use 60% to 80% of the national energy budget. This proportion is slightly lower in the developing countries but is rising gradually in line with rapid urban growth in those countries.[37] One of the most visible signs of urbanization at the beginning of the twenty-first century is the creation of micro-climates around major conurbations.

The efficiency revolution in energy advocated by two reports to the Club of Rome, *Taking Nature into Account*[38] and *Factor Four*,[39] focuses primarily on the urban environment. In this instance, the development of revolutionary techniques, such as the introduction of energy-saving double-glazing and a new generation of refrigerators and motors, needs to be encouraged. Measures could be taken to encourage the recycling of the biomass and methane from urban waste in order to replace fossil fuels.

Energy efficiency has now become a key to sustainable development and respect for the environment. Most cities have become heat-generating plants, where vegetation has been replaced by dark roofs and tarred streets. A study carried out in Los Angeles has shown that the use of white roofs and coloured concrete surfaces and the planting of 10 million trees could lower the temperature of the city by 3°C (at 3 p.m.) and reduce the smog due to ozone by 12%, thereby resulting in considerable energy savings (by making air-conditioning less necessary) and a reduction in costs attributable to the ozone layer. The creation of parks is therefore a human, ecological and economic necessity. The development of 'smart architecture', more in tune with the climate, could also enable energy to be used more efficiently (photovoltaic tiles and walls, better thermal insulation, etc.). A commitment to reducing greenhouse gas emissions, with clearly defined objectives and deadlines, is also indispensable in urban areas. The Toronto City Council is now committed to lowering carbon dioxide emissions by 20% by 2005 in relation to their 1988 level.

The Istanbul Declaration reaffirmed the priority of sustainable development. Applying this principle to a policy for the right to housing requires reducing the consumption of the building industry itself. One of the 'hidden costs' of urban growth stems from the enormous consumption of natural resources linked to the construction and running of buildings and the demands they make on the environment's 'natural capital'. According to Nicholas Lenssen and David Malin Roodman, experts at the Worldwatch Institute, the building industry produces or 'consumes' approximately 40% of the materials used in the world economy each year and is thought to be largely responsible for the destruction of forests and rivers, water and air pollution and climate change.[40] In 1992, buildings accounted for one-third of energy consumption worldwide, without taking account of what is required for the production and transport of building materials.

As regards urban construction, we shall have to learn to find inspiration in local building traditions and to use vernacular housing that is less costly in resources and better adapted to local natural environments. We should now work on new forms of architecture that combine traditional structures and the most advanced technologies to erect buildings that are less costly, more efficient, safer, more 'sustainable' and more pleasant to live in without depriving ourselves of modern conveniences. Advocated several decades ago by a visionary precursor, the Egyptian Hassan Fathy,[41] the revival of earth architecture, in many countries where it is the traditional habitat, would provide a dwelling adapted to climatic conditions, at a very reasonable cost, and would be particularly suitable for social programmes for the homeless, who could acquire the expertise for building them themselves.[42]

For Reduced Urban Water Consumption[43]

As pointed out by Professor Obasi, secretary-general of the World Meteorological Organization (WMO), at the Habitat II Conference, 'water is indisputably the vital element for the survival of cities'. In worldwide terms, at least 170 million city-dwellers do not yet have access to drinking water near their dwelling and only 25% have access to water in their home or in the courtyard of their buildings.[44] Industrial, agricultural and human waste are the cause of the pollution of many springs and of ground water. This is a public health issue.[45] It is also a geopolitical issue, probably one of the major international issues of the twenty-first century. As pointed out by Wally N'Dow, secretary-general of Habitat II, water is 'one of the most determining factors' in conflicts. An urban policy for water should be conducted in order to prevent wastage due particularly to defective mains systems and illegal parallel networks, which makes water more expensive for the poorest section of the population (see Chapter 9). The installation of modern collection and distribution infrastructure is one of the key elements of any sound urban management.

More economical use of water is therefore necessary. In addition to the various possibilities outlined in Chapter 9, water should be systematically included in urban planning. According to Obasi, 'town-planners often forget that it is necessary to install efficient systems for collecting and treating hydrological resources and providing services for monitoring flooding and drainage'; in terms of standards, the Beijing Declaration of March 1996, drafted at the end of the International Conference on the Management of Water Resources in the Urban Environment, sets out the main principles to which the Istanbul Summit gave its approval.

Urban Transport: Efficiency and Cost Integration

The energy issue is closely linked to that of transport. In mega-cities, internal traffic poses a crucial problem. The great conurbations of North America and Europe have to contend with intense internal commuter traffic owing to the distances between job locations and residential areas. In the longer term, economic activity centring upon new technologies could lead to less traffic congestion in city centres through greater flexibility in working schedules. Nevertheless, the growing speed of commuters' transport in the current phase of urban development has had the paradoxical consequence of lengthening commuting distances and therefore their duration.

This trend raises the problems of managing means of communication and transport, which are dealt with in detail below.[46] Several solutions, which are by no means incompatible, could help to solve the serious difficulties caused by congestion and pollution in cities. One would consist in imposing tariffs and levying taxes on transport that reflect their real cost in terms of accidents, noise, atmospheric pollution and climatic upheavals as well as in terms of public health. The environmental costs have been estimated by the OECD to be 70% on average of total costs related to transport in 31 European countries. This also includes the costs of congestion, estimated at 7% of the total, costs that are not covered by the infrastructure and operating of public transport, estimated at 23% of the total.[47] Another solution consists in giving priority to public transport. In optimal utilization conditions, in the space of one hour, an underground railway can carry 70,000 people at a given point, a fast light railway 50,000, trams and buses 30,000 while the private car can carry only 8,000, and that with four passengers in each vehicle. Public transport therefore does have considerable potential.[48] As we have suggested elsewhere,[49] the physical congestion and, more particularly, the enormous pollution caused by urban transport call for new measures: minimal occupation of urban space by private cars; the use of electric or hybrid (electricity/petrol-powered) cars; the introduction of new types of fuel such as hydrogen; and the creation of monorail systems, which are fast, can provide a 'web-like' network, do not pollute and are less costly than an underground railway.

This raises the longer-term issue of town planning. Sprawling urbanization seems to be the underlying principle behind the development of rapidly industrialized cities such as Seoul and Buenos Aires and conurbations with steady demographic growth such as Bombay. The compact city, where jobs, services and homes are near to each other and can be serviced by public transport, offers an alternative to the 'car is king' approach. It is the more compact cities that are best able to offer alternatives to the private car.[50] It should also be said that compact cities are also more conducive to sociability and usually offer a better framework for fighting against exclusion. However, as we have already said, only proactive and concerted policies, and not the current *laisser-faire* approach, could spread the pattern of high-density cities outside specific regions (Europe) or locations (Singapore and Hong Kong) where it prevails.

The Rise of 'Urban Apartheid'

The compact city can also provide an opportunity for fighting against social disparities. Indeed, the movement of traffic is more than a material problem. The over-extension of urban territory generates new social structures. A feature of the mega-cities is the growing individualization of urban life. The city is at the same time a place where individuals can express their freedom and personal initiative, and a place where relationships are anonymous, a climate of general indifference prevails and there is a loss of traditional, particularly family-based, solidarities. In the industrialized countries, the reign of the individual has led to a breakdown in neighbourly relationships related to work and housing. Shaped by 'zoning' policies and by the market, the choice of where to live is now based on practical reasons, income or the sense of belonging to a particular class as revealed by the address.

All too often, diversity translates into social, economic, ethnic and cultural barriers and in the growth of ghettos in the South as well as in the North. Consequently, privileged neighbourhoods have appeared that are more and more insulated from the outside, whether in historic centres, as in many European cities, or in suburban areas, as in North America. A privileged group of citizens, those to whom Robert Reich refers as the 'symbols analysts', has access to most of the services provided by the city, whether they be housing, consumption or employment, and bases its solidarity not only on physical proximity but on the sharing of privileged social and cultural space, while claiming to belong to a cosmopolitan culture and an international lifestyle. Another group finds itself completely excluded from the flows of movement and condemned to confinement. This dualism and urban segregation lead to the formation of small isolated communities, which often find themselves at odds with the codes, rules and even laws of the dominant society. Between these two groups is a median category, which attempts to become integrated but is constantly threatened with 'social disqualification'.

Attracted by 'city lights', millions of people leave the poverty of rural life in order to live in the wretched 'mass solitude' of major conurbations where they often find themselves deprived of the most basic services in a situation of distress and exclusion, which is often a seedbed for violence and extremism. In the face of this tragedy, it should be recalled that practices as fundamental in the history of humanity as 'civic spirit', 'urbanity', 'civilization' and 'politics' came into being in the urban environment, a fact reflected in their etymology. Our task must be to recover that humanizing vocation of the city by seeking to reinforce the three interactive poles that are peace, democracy and development.[51] If the phenomenon of segregation into districts is to be avoided, the notion of urban citizenship must be developed, which means that a policy of inclusion must be undertaken in such a way as to integrate the excluded.

Do we need to be reminded of the role which lifelong education for all could play in encouraging the effective exercise of citizenship? Along with the NGOs, such as the International Movement ATD Fourth World, which do splendid work in integrating the excluded, we should say to all those who feel rejected: 'Take heart. Education is a lifelong business. You haven't missed education once and for all, you are not excluded forever. You have other opportunities to gain access to education and training.'

The disintegration of social fabric has diminished the notion of collective interest and has increased sectional interests based on a particular class, cultural group or religion or a carefully delineated local community. This leads to mutual indifference as expressed in the 'nimby' (not in my backyard) syndrome whereby those in the most privileged areas deny the less privileged access to community facilities and infrastructure.

Nevertheless, urban segregation today tends to go far beyond that which most societies and historical periods have experienced to varying degrees. A new spectre is now haunting the cities of the South as it has already haunted many of those in industrialized countries, particularly North America: urban apartheid. There is a risk that the city of the future might become the city of all divisions, whether they be social, economic, cultural or political. As is pointed out by Teresa Caldeira, who has made a special study of the case of São Paulo, spatial and social segregation in contemporary cities has given rise to a new phenomenon: that of 'fortified enclaves', guarded by private militia, or 'private towns', which are culturally and socially homogeneous, and whose multiplication is contributing to marginalizing and gradually eradicating the idea of public space on which the very notion of citizenship is founded.[52]

In many countries, 'closed communities' living in walled cities are spreading. In the USA, between four and eight million people, according to some estimates, are thought to live in ultra-protected residential areas. However, according to an OECD report published in 1996, there are 35 million Americans living in 150,000 communities managed by private associations.[53] Mike Davis has described the conditions of social violence which prevail in Los Angeles. In that city, as elsewhere, there are more and more 'gated cities', neighbourhoods that are closed to the public and protected by heavily armed private police forces, working with the police departments, while all those excluded from prosperity are pushed out to the periphery.[54] In these enclaves, protected by strict internal regulations and by electronic surveillance, the streets are private, the schools are private and the sewers and community facilities are private. Some communities have completely seceded and have proclaimed themselves independent *vis-à-vis* the local communities.[55] These neighbourhoods operate like microcosms of a city, offering a limited population all the advantages of urban life. There is evidence to suggest that in some cities there is an extremely worrying trend towards privatization of public areas. Pedestrian walkways and squares are included in the confines of shopping malls accessible only to a privileged section of the population, and the streets are laid out like corridors linking different centres and reserved for automobiles.

Such forms of urban apartheid are by no means a privilege of North America or Latin America. They are also prospering in Africa, as in the case of Lagos and Durban, and in Asia, where authentically private cities are being built in some countries.[56]

This eliminates any sense of freedom of movement and enjoyment of public spaces, regarded normally as a place for exchange and social mixing, the lifeblood of city life. Can there be a 'social contract' whether there is no 'social contact'?[57] The obsession with security and law and order then becomes the cause of real social violence. Urban apartheid forces us to 'imagine a world where we can be born, be educated, live, work, get married, have children, retire from active life and die in a closed world, "behind glass", without almost ever bumping into a poor person who is not an employee of the service industries'.[58]

In this extreme form of segregation, separation is displayed as a sign of wealth and social status, which is vaunted, sometimes on ecological grounds, by the developers of private cities. As observed by Thérèse Spector, public territory is then 'gradually left to those who have no chance of living, working and shopping in the new private enclaves. Day by day, it is left increasingly to the homeless and the street urchins. Contrary to its initial vocation, it is structured according to principles of separation and the highlighting of irreconcilable differences. Private territory on the one side, public territory increasingly restricted and reserved for the poor on the other, and more and more crime.'[59]

The development of urban apartheid has undoubtedly encouraged the spread of inequality that has gone hand in hand with the third industrial revolution and the increased insecurity that is the result of a growing social rift and the boom in drug trafficking and organized crime. To what type of political and social organization does the anti-model of urban apartheid correspond? To that of democracy? It seems unlikely.

The disquieting emergence of this phenomenon calls for fundamental responses that go well beyond urban policies: legislative measures regarding public areas; policies for social justice and the redistribution of the dividends of the third industrial revolution; adequate prevention policies for fighting against urban insecurity, drug trafficking and organized crime. This problem should not conceal the broader issue of relations between centre and periphery. The compact city in the European style should not be an isolated one, a haven protected at the heart of an urban area – the extensive city in the American style is all too often no more than a series of ghettos isolated from each other and separated by invisible frontiers. Town planning policies should therefore be aimed at tearing down the walls of isolation, silence and misunderstanding, by giving priority to relations between different neighbourhoods, between people and different professions, by encouraging the enhancement and creation of public areas, supported by an urban transport and communication policy. Urban development must clearly strike a balance between diversity and unity. To do that, the city should produce a social bond but with due consideration for the autonomy and expression of every individual.

Governance means inclusion: it means making sure that citizens 'matter'. 'Learning to live together' – as recommended by the Delors Commission on Education in the Twenty-First Century – is *the* major challenge. Diversity is our great asset, just as unity is our strength. The 'hybrid', pluri-cultural, pluri-religious and pluri-ethnic city is our future and our hope. But citizens must be free and delinquents securely behind bars. The opposite is all too often the rule today and citizens, having become their own prisoners, are forced to shut themselves up under the protection of alarm systems, codes and barbed wire, on account of the deficiency of the judicial and security systems. Freedom is total, and security nil. In that regard, ensuring the safety of city-dwellers is fundamental. All too often, it is only the frontiers that are guarded. Out of inertia, we invest billions to arm ourselves against a potential 'enemy', often fanciful or purely historical. But the investment that could ensure the security of citizens and establish a rapid and effective judicial framework – at least in the case of flagrant or repeated crime – is reduced to a mere pittance.

Building a Civic City for the Twenty-first Century

According to *laisser-faire* theorists, urban chaos, the unbridled growth of cities and deficient urban planning are the inevitable prices we have to pay for adapting to a change in production patterns, to rural exodus, to industrialization, to new methods of communication and to the changes in social mores. We must reject this vision of the unplanned 'natural city'.

Building the civic city of the twenty-first century means attempting today to strike a balance between diversity and unity. This balance we believe rests upon citizenship, upon the participation of every citizen in the building, management and governance of the city. It is because too many city-dwellers are no longer citizens or are not yet so that the city is in a state of crisis today.

Respect for diversity is primarily a challenge for urban planning. The city should now be seen as a living heritage favourable to the growth of a common purpose, a feeling of solidarity between citizens. It is therefore necessary to give the city a new face that reconciles technical progress and humanity and shows respect for its origins and culture, without being stifled by our desire to preserve existing buildings.

The architect Christian de Portzamparc has heralded the beginning of a third age for the city.[60] The first age was that of the compact historic city, with a tightly woven fabric based on alternate volumes and on monumentality, civility and urbaneness. The second age, that of Le Corbusier's modernism, is the age of urban Utopias and the car, which separates architecture and town planning and makes buildings independent, solitary objects, detached from their environment. It is the age of standardization, functionalism and an international style which, in spite of a degree of success, has led to the fragmentation of urban forms and solidarities. Christian de Portzamparc believes that the third age of the city must be that of 'urban tailoring', which would re-create urbanity without ideal models. It is a question of reconstituting a fragmented urban landscape, virtually in tatters, according to an approach that does not deny the past but is more synthetic and recreational, inspired by an unrestricted conception of a continuously evolving urban heritage. In a similar vein, Cyria Emelianoff refers to urban development that would be of a topological nature, that would put down the roots of solidarities in the neighbourhood or proximity and give pride of place to all forms of urban continuity whereby a building would be adapted to a street, a street to a neighbourhood, neighbourhoods to each other and the city itself to its surrounding region.[61]

Furthermore, while seeking to preserve existing buildings, it is necessary to make the city a living, continuously evolving heritage, by encouraging the functional and social diversity of the neighbourhoods. Giving the city back to its inhabitants, encouraging all forms of appropriation of the urban landscape by the citizen, such should be the new course for urban policies on the threshold of the twenty-first century. Citizens' involvement in the city is conditioned by a feeling of belonging to the place and of pride in its urban heritage. It should also be expressed through a new form of local democracy, therefore through effective participation in the governance of the city. One of the most promising innovations to emerge at the Istanbul conference, making it undoubtedly the first summit of the twenty-first century rather than the last of the twentieth century, is the emergence of civil society as a player in the city. Civil society was able to make its voice heard at the consultative forums (NGOs, forecasting experts, private enterprise, young people and women, etc.) that, for the first time, were an integral part of a United Nations conference and reported to the governments at the plenary session. The mayors and representatives of local authorities also played a major role in the conference and attention was drawn to their central position in managing sustainable and harmonious development. A number of courageous proposals were put forward at the conference by representatives of civil society and local authorities, reflecting their desire to contribute actively to the destiny of the city, an area in which some states had failed or given up.

That its citizens should play a decisive part in this is by no means a new idea. As pointed out by Jorge Wilheim, deputy secretary-general of the Istanbul conference: 'In the past, governments were expected to solve all problems. Today, people are tired of that attitude and many are coming together to rebuild a neighbourhood themselves. This auto-organization can be observed in many countries in Latin America, Africa and Asia. On a more complex level, cooperation between city councils, residents' associations, NGOs and universities can improve life in the shantytowns.'

In fact, the informal building sector accounts for 80% of building in the developing countries. This informal or people-based economy is one of the most dynamic sectors in the countries of the South and is the sign that inhabitants are ready to take charge of their city. Nevertheless, this approach reflects an uncontrolled and often dual process of urbanization, opposing the 'legal city' and the 'illegal city', either the shanty town without facilities or town centres well provided for. In countries where the provision of public services is inadequate or where the population is too poor for chargeable public services to be created, the population has sometimes undertaken to provide a number of emergency services itself. These practices can lead to a democratic partnership that inspires optimism between the authorities and local government, provided that the local initiative is the subject of institutional and financial support on the part of the political authorities.

At the urban level, the development of urban 'governance' cannot serve as an attractive façade for *laisser-faire* policies. It requires that a clear definition be given to the respective fields of competence of the public authorities, at national and local level, the local communities and other players in society – NGOs and associations, private enterprise and professional bodies. Careful thought needs to be given in particular to ways of ensuring greater decentralization of the main civic responsibilities – education, health and justice, etc. – towards local authorities. For it is first and foremost in the framework of the city that citizens can participate, play a full part in democratic life, exercise their rights and fulfil their obligations. Rather than through one-sided policies imposed from above, it is by carrying out 'strategic town-planning' schemes that a sense of belonging to the city can be created. 'Strategic town planning' proposes decision-making based on the practice of consensus, on the active participation of citizens and all partners concerned and on flexible processes of negotiation between public and private actors. With this in mind, the role of mayors would include managerial duties, arbitration between the economic and social actors and guaranteeing the collective interest.

Attention must also be drawn to the responsibility of the public authorities, particularly governments, when it is a question of taking decisions which will have an effect on several generations. 'The state continues to represent politically the democratic will of the community and a striving for equality. We do not seek to diminish the role of the state but rather to modify it. It must adapt to a new phase of worldwide development.'[62] If partnerships with local authorities, NGOs and various international bodies and the private sector have emerged as a balanced and democratic method of city management, the political authorities cannot wash their hands of their strategic role on the market, particularly in the field of infrastructure such as roads, water supplies and drainage and subsidized housing. A new conception of the state is emerging, that of the state as a strategist, which coordinates the desires of various partners in the name of solidarity between citizens, between territories and between generations.

Rapid urbanization does have an advantage: it facilitates access to goods and services (particularly in the field of health and education), thereby creating new development opportunities. These possibilities remain no more than a mirage, however, if those who could benefit from them are prevented from doing so by poverty, 'urban apartheid', new forms of delinquency and corruption, overpopulation, pollution and the inertia or ineffectiveness of public administrations.

Our task is to reinvent a city culture that is the product neither of international stereotypes nor of antagonisms and ghettoization. Educating people in city life should therefore be encouraged both in formal education, where more time could be allocated to it in school and university curricula, and in informal education. Today, the city is all too frequently a sort of 'non-place'. Whereas immigrants used to keep up their cultural customs for a long time and maintain strong links with their region or village of origin, the phenomenon of 'colonization' of the city, while it may still exist, scarcely lasts longer than a single generation today. Once the link with the group of origin or its representatives in the city has been severed, the solidarities that brought together individuals in an ethnic, local or religious group disappear. Furthermore, solidarities with the extended family gradually break up in an increasingly extensive urban fabric.

The city must be in a position to offer a culture that makes up for these lost solidarities. It must provide public and collective space to which an individual can feel physically and symbolically attached, without losing his or her bearings in a city split up into small communities that at best ignore each other and at worst hate each other. It should be built as a living heritage, tracing a link between past and future. The city must offer a collective framework for the exercise of individual freedom and should enable every individual to participate as he or she pleases, without exclusion or isolation.

A new urban culture could come into being in the twenty-first century. It is a question of political willpower rather than a technical issue. The message that UNESCO brought to Istanbul could be expressed in three words, which served as a motto to the document submitted to the Summit: *humanizing the city.* 'There are two things that we forget only when we die', we are reminded by the Turkish poet Nazim Hikmet, 'our mother's face and the face of our city.' Everyone in Istanbul hoped that it would be a human face. The city is not a mere amalgam of techniques, buildings, producers and consumers and excluded people. In the words of Christian de Portzamparc, the city 'contains time': the past and the future, our ancestors and our children. Living in a city should mean living in a particular place and saying 'this is my life, here is where my children are or where they will be born'.[63] In his poem 'Buenos Aires', Jorge Luis Borges wrote 'this city, which I thought was my past, has become my future'. There are too many uninhabitable cities today where dignity has been lost, where we can no longer meet others. Giving back the city what it rightfully deserves, making of it a place of civility for the future, will be one of the challenges for the city in the twenty-first century. As a place where citizenship emerged, the city should be repossessed by democracy. Otherwise, the right to a dwelling, among other examples, will remain a dead letter and cities will continue to surround themselves with new walls: those of urban apartheid. Changing the city means changing life.

Pointers and Recommendations

- Give new impetus to urban forecasting and the strategic planning of the city and urban fabric.
- Give priority to implementation of the right to a dwelling for all and to a housing policy that is not an abdication on the part of local and national authorities in the face of the informal economy and *laisser-faire*. Housing policy must be combined with a policy for infrastructure in communication, transport, the supply and drainage of water, education and health.
- Promote the city as a living environment, that is to say, formulate the principles and policies for urban ecology that promote the development of 'sustainable' practices but also integrate the city in its natural environment in order to create symbiosis between neighbouring cities and greater harmony between town and country.
- Promote a comprehensive policy relating to public and collective space. This means encouraging all forms of appropriation by citizens of urban

territory in order to put a stop to trends towards fragmentation, ghettos and urban apartheid. An efficient democratic public transport and communication policy should be devised with due respect for ecological factors.

- Create a living urban heritage focused on transmission to future generations. The city should be seen as a framework for and a driving force behind solidarities between social groups and generations. Love of the city as a source of cohesion and creativity should be founded on town planning and architecture. The policies of the city should, to that aim, reconcile town planning and architecture, which have too often been kept separate during the second half of the twentieth century.
- Encourage all forms of participation and collaboration on the part of civil society, local authorities, associations and national and international bodies so that the city might not simply be experienced as a fact of life, but claimed as a common project founded on the notions of urban citizenship and civility. Ensure better security for the inhabitants in the face of delinquency and organized crime.
- Promote lifelong education for all and particularly education focused on the city: teach ecological methods for preserving the city as a habitat, teach practices based on dialogue and civic participation to make of the city a place of citizenship, teach the history of the city and respect for its heritage, train town planners in order to nurture pride in the city so as to ensure that the city can offer each of its inhabitants opportunities for personal fulfilment.
- Conceive the city as a foundation stone for building a culture of peace in the twenty-first century, particularly through conviviality, solidarity and sharing, but also through a democratic dialogue and the exercise of citizenship by all.

Notes

1. Source: United Nations Centre for Human Settlements (Habitat), *An Urbanizing World: Global Report on Human Settlements 1996*, forward-looking summary report prepared by the Analysis and Forecasting Office of UNESCO, for a position paper presented by the director-general of UNESCO at the United Nations Conference on Human Settlements (Habitat II), 1996.

2. Federico Mayor, 'Gouvernabilité démocratique et développement urbain', *Dialogo*, UNESCO, July 1998. Jérôme Bindé, 'Sommet de la ville: les leçons d'Istanbul', *Futuribles*, No. 211, July–August 1996, Paris. Published as 'The city summit' in *Futures*, Vol. 29, No. 3, pp. 213–27, 1997.

3. Source: *United Nations, World Urbanization Prospects: The 1994 Revision*, United Nations, New York, 1995.

4. United Nations Centre for Human Settlements (Habitat), *An Urbanizing World*, introduction. The homeless living in the streets, public places and shelters are thought

to number 100 million worldwide. The number of homeless throughout the world could be as much as 1 billion if account is taken of all instances of precarious housing (squatters, inhabitants of refugee camps and temporary shelters, etc.); see pp. 229 ff.

5. World Bank, *Livable Cities for the 21st Century*, World Bank, Washington, DC, 1996.

6. *World Resources, A Guide to the Global Environment: The Urban Environment, 1996–1997*, official publication of Habitat II, Oxford University Press, 1996, p. 12.

7. E. U. von Weizsäcker and A. B. Lovins, L. Hunter Lovins, *Faktor Vier*, Report to the Club of Rome, Droemer Knaur, Munich, 1995, p. 293. Eng. trans. *Factor Four: Doubling Wealth, Halving Resource Use: The New Report to the Club of Rome*, Earthscan, London, 1997.

8. Ibid., p. 244.

9. See Michael Cohen, 'Habitat II and the challenge of the urban environment: bringing together the two definitions of habitat', *International Social Science Journal*, March 1996, pp. 95–101. The work of the participants focused on two major lines of emphasis: 'adequate housing for all' and 'sustainable urban settlements in an urbanizing world'.

10. Bindé, 'Sommet de la ville'.

11. Candido Mendes, 'Conclusions', *Beyond ECO-92: Global Change, the Discourse, the Progression, the Awareness*, UNESCO, ISSC, Paris/Editora Universitária Candido Mendes, Rio de Janeiro, 1995, p. 226.

12. That is to say the capacity 'to meet the needs of the present without compromising the ability of future generations to meet their own needs' (according to the definition given by the Brundtland Commission; see report of the World Commission on the Environment and Development, *Our Common Future*, Oxford University Press, New York, 1987, p. 8).

13. That is to say, according to the UNDP definition, 'a process which leads to the broadening of the range of possibilities open to each person' (*World Report on Human Development, 1990*), by taking account not only of income but also of other factors that have major consequences for the quality of urban life: 'a suitable diet, access to drinking water, improved health care services, greater access for children to an education system of a higher standard, affordable public transport, the availability of suitable housing, a stable means of subsistence and access to productive and satisfying jobs' (*World Report on Human Development, 1996*, Economica, Paris, 1996, p. 5).

14. The 'Copenhagen Declaration', adopted by the World Summit for Social Development in 1995, had already begun a synthesis when it emphasized that economic development, social development and protection of the environment are interdependent components and are mutually strengthened by sustainable development. To borrow the terms of the Brundtland Commission in *Our Common Future*, 'a world in which poverty and inequity are endemic will always be prone to ecological and other crises'.

15. Henry Cisneros, 'Sharing responsibilities for inner-city problems', in *World Resources 1996–97 (the Urban Environment)*, a publication of the World Resources Institute, Washington, p. 13.

16. Bindé, 'Sommet de la ville'.

17. United Nations Centre for Human Settlements (Habitat), *An Urbanizing World*, pp. 17–21.

18. Source: *World Urbanization Prospects, 1990*, United Nations, New York, 1991.

19. Saskia Sassen, *The Global City: New York, London, Tokyo*, Princeton University Press, Princeton, NJ, 1991.

20. Manuel Castells, *La Société en réseaux*, Volume 1: *L'Ère de l'information*, Éditions Fayard, Paris, 1998, p. 435 (*The Rise of the Network City*, Blackwell, Oxford, 1996). See also Peter Hall, 'The global city', *International Social Science Journal*, March 1996, UNESCO/Blackwell, pp. 15–23.

21. Castells, *La Société en réseaux*.

22. Néstor García Canclini, 'Urban cultures at the end of the century: the anthropoligical perspective', *International Social Science Journal*, UNESCO/Blackwell, No. 153, September 1997, p. 345.

23. Robert B. Reich, *The Work of Nations: Preparing Ourselves for 21st Century Capitalism*, Vintage Books, New York, 1992. French trans. *L'Économie mondialisée*, Dunod, Paris, 1993.

24. Jorge Wilheim, 'Introduction: urban challenges of a transitional period', *International Social Science Journal*, UNESCO, Paris, March 1996, p. 14.

25. Interview given by James Wolfensohn, president of the World Bank in *Le Monde*, 16 February 1996.

26. Daniel Cohen, *The Wealth of the World and the Poverty of Nations*, trans. Jacqueline Lindenfeld, MIT Press, Cambridge, MA, 1998.

27. Pontifical Council for Justice and Peace, *Towards a Better Distribution of Land – The Challenge of Agrarian Reform*, Libreria Editrice Vaticana, Rome, 1997.

28. Message from the Pope on the occasion of World Migration Day, 1998.

29. See François Ascher, *Metapolis ou l'Avenir des villes*, Éditions Odile Jacob, Paris, 1995.

30. See United Nations Centre for Human Settlements (Habitat), *An Urbanizing World*, passim.

31. See Danielle Beauchemin and Yves Robertson, 'Des villes efficaces: un dossier prioritaire de la coopération France–Québec', *Liaison Énergie-francophonie*, No. 30, 1er trimestre 1996, pp. 6–10 (distributed at Habitat II).

32. Marcia Lowe, 'Shaping cities', in Lester R. Brown (ed.), *State of the Word*, Worldwatch Institute, Washington, 1992, p. 70.

33. In the words of Michel Serres, 'mega-cities have become physical variables; they neither think nor graze, they just weigh heavily on their environment'. Michel Serres, *The Natural Contract*, University of Michigan Press, Ann Arbor, 1995.

34. See also the report of the Independent Commission on Population and the Quality of Life (Pintasilgo Report, *Caring for the Future*, Oxford University Press, New York, 1996) which, in a similar spirit, advocates 'sustainable patterns of consumption'.

35. Source: Philippe Panerai, 'Demain la Terre', *Le Nouvel Observateur*, collection Dossiers, No. 11, Paris, 1992.

36. See also Chapter 12.

37. The ideas in this section are largely drawn from the Background Paper prepared for the Dialogue held at Habitat II on 'Sustainable energy in human settlements', 5 June 1996.

38. Wouter van Dieren, *Taking Nature into Account: Toward a Sustainable National Income*, Copernicus, New York, 1995.

39. E. U. von Weizsäcker, A. B. Lovins and L. Hunter Lovins, *Factor Four: Doubling*

Wealth, Halving Resource Use: The New Report to the Club of Rome, Earthscan, London, 1997.

40. Nicholas Lenssen and David Malin Roodman, 'Making better buildings', *State of the World 1995*, Worldwatch Institute, W.W. Norton, New York, 1997.

41. See in particular: Hassan Fathy, *Architecture for the Poor: An Experiment in Rural Egypt*, University of Chicago Press, Chicago, 1973; *Natural Energy and Vernacular Architecture: Principles and Examples with Reference to Hot and Arid Climates*, University of Chicago Press, Chicago, 1986.

42. Ibid.

43. This theme is dealt with in Chapter 9.

44. Martha Duenas-Loza, acting director, INSTRAW (United Nations International Research and Training Institute for the Advancement of Women), 'Overview of women's roles in water resources', document distributed at Habitat II, 14 June 1996.

45. According to INSTRAW, diseases transmitted by water are the most serious cause of infantile mortality: they are responsible for 1.5 billion cases of gastric disorders and 4 million deaths per year. Ibid., p. 11.

46. See Chapter 4.

47. Source: OECD, *Urban Transport and Sustainable Development*, OECD, Paris, 1995, p. 126.

48. Union Internationale des Transports Publics, *Des villes à vivre: le défi du transport public*, Pierre Laconte, editor-in-chief, UITP, Brussels, 1996, p. 12.

49. See Chapter 4.

50. Marcia Lowe, 'Shaping cities', in Lester R. Brown (ed.), *State of the World*, Worldwatch Institute, Washington, DC, 1993; see also, by the same author, 'Reinventing transport', *State of the World 1994*, Worldwatch Institute, W.W. Norton, New York, 1994.

51. Mayor, 'Gouvernabilité démocratique et développement urbain'.

52. Teresa P. R. Caldeira, 'Building up walls: the new pattern of spatial segregation in São Paulo', *International Social Science Journal*, March 1996, pp. 55–66. See also, by the same author: *City of Walls: Crime, Segregation, and Citizenship in São Paulo*, University of California Press, Berkeley, CA, 1995.

53. Edward J. Blakely and Mary Gail Snyder, 'Divided we fall: gated and walled communities in the United States', in Nan Ellin (ed.), *Architecture of Fear*, Princeton Architectural Press, New York, 1997, p. 85; Robert Lopez, 'Un nouvel apartheid social. Hautes murailles pour villes riches', *Le Monde diplomatique*, 1996. OECD, *Politiques Novatrices pour un développement urbain*, 1996, quoted by Francis Godard, 'Modes de vie urbains: Questions liminaires', in T. Spector and J. Theys (eds), *Villes du XXIe siècle*, Ministère de l'équipement, des transports et du logement, CERTU, Paris, 1999.

54. Mike Davis, *City of Quartz – Excavating the Future in Los Angeles*, Verso, London, 1990.

55. Lopez, 'Un nouvel apartheid social', summarized in T. Spector, 'La prospective urbaine. Un état des lieux', *Futuribles*, No. 229, March 1998.

56. See *International Social Science Journal*, March 1996, particularly the article by Michael Sutcliffe, 'La ville éclatée: Durban, South Africa', pp. 67–72.

57. Blakely and Snyder, 'Divided we fall', p. 86.

58. Jérôme Bindé, 'La croissance des villes au XXIe siècle au Sud', paper presented

at the seminar 'Viable Development' at the Ecole Normale Supérieure, Paris, 13 January 1997.

59. Spector and Theys, *Villes du XXIe siècle*.

60. Christian de Portzamparc, *La Ville Age III*, Conférences Paris d'Architectes, Éditions du Pavillon de l'Arsenal, Paris, 1993. See also Olivier Mongin, *Vers la troisième ville?*, Hachette, Paris, 1995, foreword by Christian de Portzamparc.

61. Source: Cyria Emelianoff, 'Trois scénarios de développement urbain', international symposium 'Quel environnement au XXIe siècle? Environnement, maîtrise du long terme et démocratie', 8–11 September 1996, Abbaye de Fontevraud, France.

62. Interview with Jorge Wilheim, *Le Monde*, 6 June 1996.

63. Christian de Portzamparc, communication to the 21st Century Dialogues, UNESCO, 16–18 September 1998, Jérôme Bindé (ed.), *Les Clés du XXIe siècle*, Editions UNESCO/Seuil, Paris, 2000.

CHAPTER 4

. . . .

The Future of Urban Transport: Safer, Cleaner, Closer

§ TRANSPORT is a major issue for the future: we are thinking first and foremost of surface transport and, more particularly, of urban transport. In this field, considerable progress can be made in terms of reducing emissions of greenhouse gas, whether such progress takes the form of research on new sources of energy or new and less polluting engines. In the case of air transport, it seems that little progress of note can be hoped for in the near future, since as yet no real alternative fuel to kerosene exists. For this reason, the main potential advances discussed here concern urban and surface transport.

Transport has long been approached in terms of mobility and its inexorable expansion: from this standpoint, transport infrastructure serves as a lever for the economy, stimulating demand through major construction projects and increasing the economic competitiveness that comes from better organization of flows of goods and people.[1] This approach is certainly important and has lost none of its relevance: better access to the destinations of their choice should, in principle, enhance people's well-being and the opportunities life offers them. Here, mobility equals freedom and is a key factor of development. However, the world has for decades been faced with the huge growth in urban transport, the adverse consequences of which have cast doubt on the traditional vision of progress via mobility. Whatever the size of towns, the total number of cars increases two or three times faster in urban areas than the rate of population growth, and automobile use grows even more rapidly in those areas. The problem is particularly alarming in the towns of developing countries, where rapid urbanization is still not accompanied by an expansion of the surface area devoted to roads. For instance, only 11% of Bangkok's urban space is given over to traffic, while the percentage for European towns is between 20% and 25%.[2] The trend towards individual journeys and the quest for more free time is therefore today confronted with two major obstacles: congestion and pollution.

The boom in car ownership favours growing distances between home, workplace, shopping centres and other focal points of urban living. This trend is exacerbated by the congestion of city centres and the creation of new infrastructure. These distances, in turn, create a network of dispersed journeys that 'conventional' public transport can cover only with great difficulty and enormous capital outlays. We have here a real vicious circle that leads to ever-increasing use of private cars. As long as traffic congestion, instead of limiting the use of private cars, leads to the construction of new infrastructures that encourage urban sprawl, this vicious circle can only result in our society's ever-growing dependence on automobiles.

The question many experts, including Marcia Lowe of the Worldwatch Institute, are asking is simple: do cars improve access to one's chosen destination? Or must people go ever further to reach markets, services, workplaces and other key sites of daily life?[3] Seen in this light, the expansion of motor transport involves considerable costs for society, such as atmospheric pollution, growing congestion, contribution to global warming, wasted travel time and disruption of the natural and living environment, which are increasingly resented by those living in the vicinity of the infrastructures.[4] Not to mention the high cost in terms of loss of life, permanent disabilities, and impairment of health: according to the World Bank, more than half a million people die every year in road accidents and even more are injured. Two-thirds of victims are pedestrians, of whom one-third are children. The numbers are even higher in the developing countries. In India, only 5% of victims of serious traffic accidents are motorists.[5]

Growing congestion means rush-hour traffic for 12 hours or more in Seoul and 14 in Rio de Janeiro.[6] In central Cairo noise is ten times higher than recommended health and safety norms, and in certain districts lead build-up in the atmosphere exceeds by five to six times the norms established by the World Health Organization.[7] Residents of the main urban areas in the USA lose between one and two billion hours per year in traffic jams, and the average speed in rush hours in Paris is less than 10 km/h.[8] According to a recent survey, the annual cost of congestion exceeds $16 billion in England.[9] Bangkok's metropolitan authorities estimate that traffic problems cause the city to lose 44 workdays on average per year.[10] According to the United Nations Environment Programme, pollution there accounts for $1 billion in medical expenses per year.[11] Worse still, this loss of time combined with medical expenditure, artificially, and obviously deceptively, swells the GDP of the countries concerned, highlighting the obsolescence of many economic indicators, which continue to record energy growth and the liabilities of development as assets.

According to a recent OECD report on urban transport, the economic, environmental and social costs of commuting may be currently estimated at approximately 5% of the GDP of the industrialized countries.[12] We should therefore do away with the simplistic notion that 'more cars' equals 'more economic growth'.

Automobiles are now the prime source of atmospheric pollution. They are largely responsible for the smog that covers most of the world's cities. This pollution can be fatal to infants, the elderly and asthmatics.[13] It is estimated in Mexico that the high levels of particles emitted by motor vehicles – particularly dangerous for the respiratory tract – are responsible for 12,500 deaths per year.[14] The French public health agency Société Française de Santé Publique estimates at over one thousand the number of deaths attributable to automobile pollution every year in France.[15] According to the World Bank, the annual cost of dust and lead pollution in Bangkok, Jakarta and Kuala Lumpur is $5 billion, i.e. 10% of those three cities' revenue; more serious still, 90% of children in major African towns and 29% of those in Mexico City are now said to be suffering from lead poisoning. In Bangkok, this scourge allegedly costs children four IQ points on average. Moreover, the World Bank assesses at 1.56 million deaths per year the cost to Asia of atmospheric pollution, an increasing share of which is caused by automobiles.

Car exhaust emissions account for one-half of urban pollution and over one-quarter of greenhouse effect emissions. They therefore constitute a major cause of the global warming diagnosed by most experts. Travel is the cause of nine-tenths of carbon monoxide emissions, three-quarters of nitrogen oxide emissions of known origin, and one-third of the particles emitted into the atmosphere.[16] The problem is all the more serious in the developing countries since fuel oils there are more polluting than in the industrialized countries. According to the World Bank, the lead content of the fuel oils used in the developing countries ranges from 0.8 to 1.1 g/l; in the industrialized countries, it is 0.15 g/l on average. The sulphur dioxide content of diesel oil is more than twice as high in the developing countries as it is in the industrialized countries.[17]

In the 1970s, there was one car to 18 of the world's inhabitants; today, there is one car for every 12. True, the growth rate of vehicles in circulation is lower than before 1970; all the same, every year 19 million cars are added to the world total. According to the OECD, the number of cars, which has already increased fourfold in the last 30 years (from 120 to 500 million), is likely to double to a billion by 2010. By way of illustration, it was estimated that in the former Soviet Union automobile production would quadruple between 1985 and 2010, increasing from 1.3 to five million cars per year.[18] In the Asia-Pacific region, the largest world producer with more than 15 million cars per year, recent investments to increase production capacities should, in principle, before the 1997–98 stock market crashes, have made it possible to produce six million additional cars per year. Competition is so keen that there are now fears of surplus production capacities on a world scale, reaching 22 million vehicles in 2000.[19] If it led to a significant drop in prices, it could bring about a substantial increase in automobile demand, infrastructure crowding and, consequently, worse urban congestion.

To the increasing number of cars must be added the increasing number of kilometres travelled. For instance, in 1990 Americans drove approximately 16% more kilometres to work than in 1969; 88% more for shopping and 137% more for their other personal needs. Conversely, journeys for entertainment and leisure fell by 1% in the USA. Under these circumstances, can we deduce that increased mobility has improved the quality of travel and access to chosen destinations?[20]

One German researcher at the Wuppertal Institute found that the priority assigned to mobility often entails truly absurd land use and organization of economic activity. Taking the example of strawberry yoghurt – extremely popular in Germany – which travels on average 3,500 kilometres across the country before it reaches the consumer, not counting the 4,500 kilometres of transport required for the distributors, this scientist advocates more localized production. This would be feasible if labour were cheaper and transport more expensive, thereby better reflecting their real costs from the point of view of the economy, sustainable development and quality of life.[21]

During the hours when people travel to and from work, there are on average only 1.3 passengers per car in urban areas throughout the world (1.1 in the United States). At a time when other sectors consuming large amounts of energy are increasingly resorting to less polluting alternatives, transport is consuming ever more petrol, in both absolute and relative terms. At the same time, if current trends persist, the number of kilometres travelled annually by all vehicles in the world could exceed the 1990 level by 66% in 2010, according to OECD.

Transport is a heavy-duty sector marked by technical inertia, 'in which decisions and implementation are long in coming and their consequences spaced out into the distant future, affecting areas that are sometimes very remote from the original area and the actors involved'.[22] A forward-looking approach is therefore called for, especially since any transport policy requires the installation of infrastructure that often has a lifetime of over 50 years. Pondering the impact of infrastructure choice on energy consumption, Benjamin Dessus stresses the importance of rail transport as one alternative. He points out that the energy consumed by a TGV (high-speed train) is 14 grams of oil equivalent per passenger-kilometre as against 36 grams for a car, and that 'all things being equal, during the 50 years in which the requisite infrastructure is used, the initial choice of rail produces, from the outset, a 60% energy saving over road transport'.[23]

New, responsible measures are needed: new partnerships involving the public sector, the private sector, scientists, experts and consumers should come up with solutions that partially replace cars and combat the scourges of urban congestion, energy wastage and ecological damage, all caused by the lack of long-term strategies. What options can we envisage?

More Efficient Cars?

Many experts are wagering on 'hyper-cars' – low-energy-consumption vehicles. Two advances would seem to bear them out. The first is the use of lighter, more aerodynamic and shock-resistant materials, making it possible to recover a fair portion of the 80% to 85% of energy consumed and totally wasted before reaching the wheels. The second innovation consists in introducing a hybrid electric and petrol-driven system, a process that would increase energy efficiency by 30% to 50%. In this way, the combination of two strategies favouring the hybrid and the ultra-light would be likely to increase a car's energy efficiency by five to 20 times its current level.[24] Research is now being directed towards fuel cells, which can produce electricity from hydrogen. These fuel cells would not only considerably reduce (and in the best-case scenario eliminate) pollution from engine emissions, but would also help solve one of the main problems of electric cars: the need to recharge their batteries frequently. The main difficulty is in storing the hydrogen, hence the idea of producing hydrogen inside the engine from fuels such as methane, natural gas or petrol.[25]

Another major step towards producing cars that would create less pollution would be the more widespread use of photovoltaic panels incorporated in the bodywork to recharge the batteries of electric cars.

Many experts are also displaying interest in the use of new fuels. One such is liquid petroleum gas (LPG), which does not emit particles (unlike diesel, which emits 0.05 grams per kilometre) and cuts carbon dioxide and carbon monoxide emissions by 13% and 50% respectively.[26] In the Netherlands, which has the highest number in Europe of service stations selling LPG, 8% of cars now use that fuel, a trend that public authorities should encourage by means of lower taxes than those levied on other fuels. Vehicle natural gas (VNG), also low-pollution, is another option, limited for the time being essentially to utilitarian and business vehicles because it requires a large tank to be installed on board.

There is no doubt that 'hyper-cars' and LPG- or VNG-fuelled cars would be an attractive anti-pollution tool. However, their success could be double-edged if it served to increase problems of urban congestion and very remote homes. Nor must one disregard the cost of these cars. A European Union survey shows that technologies currently exist to reduce the average consumption of petrol-run cars by 40%, but that the additional cost involved in producing them is about 940 to 2,270 euros.[27] Such a sizeable increase could, however, be sharply reduced once the new technologies are widely available on the market, with the initial support of the public authorities through subsidies and differentiated taxes.

In fact, as John Decicco and Marc Ross point out, one of the main obstacles to the adoption of technologies that would help cut energy consumption is precisely the scant interest hitherto displayed by the players in this market. According to these two experts, the market for the new vehicles has been stagnating for a dozen years, essentially because the price of fuels has remained low and manufacturers give priority to enhancing their cars' power and comfort rather than to increasing the autonomy of drivers. Hence the import- ance of incentive measures such as taxes on heavy-consumption vehicles.[28] There are, nevertheless, a few heartening signs. Many manufacturers – Toyota, General Motors, Volkswagen, Volvo, Renault, Peugeot-Citroën and Daimler- Chrysler – have recognized the importance of reducing their vehicles' polluting emissions and are now interested in producing hybrid or hydrogen-fuelled cars. All the same, as Daniel Sperling says, the amounts spent on perfecting these vehicles are still small, while the US automobile industry's annual advertising costs alone amount to around U\$3.3 billion.[29]

Although there are technological improvements, it must be borne in mind that we are witnessing both an increase in, and the ageing of, the total number of cars on the roads and that technological progress has a lower potential in towns in the USA and Japan, which have long been following policies aimed at reducing traffic pollution. An OECD study indicates that, in the USA, even if one million electric or hydrogen-powered cars were put on the road between now and 2010, the total reduction of carbon dioxide pollution would still be less than one per cent lower than the present rate.[30]

This is why progress with car energy efficiency, even if it is considerable, must be accompanied by other measures in the years to come.

Giving Priority to Public Transport

The priority solution for attenuating the problem of congestion is to strengthen the role of public transport in highly congested urban centres. When sufficient people use public transport it makes for more efficient use of space and energy, at a far lower cost than private cars, and considerably reduces pollution and greenhouse gas emissions. Public transport helps to ensure that the starting-point and destination of journeys are kept relatively central. It is therefore compatible with maintaining historical urban structures. It also helps to enhance the huge infrastructure and property investments made in city centres.

In the developing countries in particular, public transport systems often fail to meet potential demand. However, since 2000 the developing countries have contained 16 megalopolises with a population of over 12 million. It is therefore high time to make serious plans for improving existing systems or for putting them in place where they do not exist. As it is, the urban space used by pedestrians and public transport is almost one hundred times smaller than that used by a car and its parking place.[31] Public transport has been neglected in far too many towns and is now seen as a service for the poor who have no cars, which results in antiquated and inadequate facilities in bad repair.[32] That trend needs to be reversed.

Over the past 20 years, many very large towns in the developing countries, such as Mexico City, Shanghai and Cairo, have built subway systems, considerably easing city-centre traffic, which would otherwise be at saturation point. However, constructing a subway system is very expensive, and many developing countries consider that their resources would be inadequate for infrastructure on such a scale.

Public authorities are increasingly inclining towards construction or restoration of light tram-based networks. The construction of such networks is patently less expensive, as Marcia Lowe points out: it costs on average one-fifth the price of a railway system on the surface and one-tenth that of a subway system.[33] Unlike a railway, the lightweight network does not require construction of an exclusive track and can be incorporated into existing roads or streets. However, it is definitely wiser to envisage the use of a specific traffic lane in order to maximize the network's efficiency and encourage commuters to use it. In Manila, for instance, it takes passengers 15 minutes to travel 22 kilometres on the tramway, while the same journey takes up to two hours by motorway. The success of this line has also induced the government to plan the construction of three additional lines.

Another solution is to rehabilitate the rail networks by linking them to express bus lines. Dakar and Lagos have both re-established their suburban lines, using the existing tracks. In both cases the number of passengers has increased and the system makes a profit, which is rarely the case with public transport firms.[34] Hong Kong has modernized its suburban train system at a cost of $13.2 million per kilometre, or approximately 10% of the cost of its subway system. Likewise, Rio de Janeiro and São Paulo have renovated their suburban railway systems, which were quite extensive but in poor condition and are now able to transport over a million people per day in either city.

Intelligent transport development using telematic equipment can contribute to better regulation of transport flows; it also makes public transport more attractive. In the Netherlands, traffic lights are programmed in accordance with the number of cars on the road to give priority to buses: better performance by buses has increased their use and reduced operating costs. Telematics equipment can thus increase the capacity of existing road infrastructure by up to 10%, according to the experts,[35] but this would not suffice to solve the problem of urban congestion.

Box 4.1 Curitiba: A Low-cost 'Surface Subway'

Curitiba is the fastest-growing city in Brazil, with a population of 1.6 million inhabitants that has more than tripled in the past 25 years. It is nevertheless known for being one of the most livable cities in Brazil – a reputation it owes largely to an integrated transportation and land-use planning policy that structured the city along two axes, along which both commercial and residential infrastructure coexist. Each road is defined by three parallel parts: a central road for public transportation and two outer one-way roads for all other traffic. Before the original plan was approved in 1964, the city bought land along the roads in order to build low-income housing, ensuring access for everyone to the centre of the city. The city now has three more of such roads in addition to the original two.

One of the keys to Curitiba's successful development is its public transportation system, which is based on a network of buses using the central mass transit lanes and liberating the other lanes. The system has evolved to accommodate its increased use from 50,000 passengers per day in 1974 to over 800,000 passengers per day in 1994, and now handles more than four times the flow of conventional bus systems. The first fact that improved passenger flow was the use of exclusive lanes. The second was the introduction of articulated buses, increasing the passenger flow to two and a half times that supported by conventional bus systems. And the third was the invention of tube-shaped bus stations, closed at one end and with raised loading platforms, passengers paying as they enter the tube's open end. This speeds boarding and the bus needs no conductor. Tube-shaped stations improved flow of passengers to 3.2 times that of conventional bussing. The fourth factor was the introduction of a bi-articulated bus, resulting in a flow of passengers four times that of conventional bussing.

The public transport authorities adopted a flat 'social fare' valid for unlimited transfers, designed to avoid penalizing those living in the poorer outskirts of the city. In addition to this, garbage collected by the poorest can be exchanged for bus tickets, thus sparing them a heavy expense while reducing the municipal budget for garbage collection. Fares completely cover the costs of running the system, which is jointly run by private companies and the city. Bus companies are paid per mile of bus route covered, not per passenger, an incentive for covering the entire city area. The city builds and maintains the infrastructure but, remarkably, Curitiba's bus system itself is not subsidized. Nearly 70% of the population uses the bus system each day (28% of bus users used to travel in their cars). Benefits include a per capita gasoline consumption 30% lower than that of cities of comparable size in Brazil and the cleanest air of any Brazilian city.

Combined with other innovative educational initiatives (which use old buses as mobile classrooms) and trash collection, the city is demonstrating an ever-growing understanding of system-based problem-solving from which all other cities could learn.

Source: Jonas Rabinovich (Urban Development Unit, UNDP), 'Curitiba: towards sustainable urban development', *Environment and Urbanization*, Vol. 4, No. 2, October 1992; various papers presented in international meetings, 1992, 1994; preparatory studies of a draft report to the Club of Rome, *Factor Four*, 1995; Habitat II, *Information initiale sur les meilleures pratiques pour l'amélioration de l'environnement bâti*, United Nations, 1995.

François Ascher suggests another priority for public transport in the years to come: it will need to adapt to a changing society if it is to avoid a progressive and constant reduction in its use; it will need to be rethought or even reinvented. What we are observing is a greater spreading out of working hours, now much more diversified than they once were. Furthermore, more than one-half of all journeys nowadays are not work-related. Movements are spread out less uniformly and we have witnessed the extension of opening hours in towns.[36]

For Ascher, this is part of a general trend: the growing individualization of behaviour patterns and daily schedules. Thanks to the progress of technology, especially communication technology, time constraints can now be managed more efficiently; true, people do not move about in time, but they adapt it to their activities. If we do not want large towns to be given over entirely to one-person cars, a fresh look must be taken at public transport with a view to adapting it to weaker, but constant and more varied flows. This is perhaps one of the major challenges for the future and one that urban transport policy must address in the decades to come.

Encouraging Non-motor Transport

Another extremely simple way of avoiding the adverse consequences of congestion, pollution and energy wastage consists in facilitating, as a matter of priority, access by pedestrians and cyclists to public highways, making streets safer for bicycles and laying out cycle lane networks. This has already been done in certain towns, whose municipal authorities have decided either to deny cars access to town centres or drastically reduce such access.

In Copenhagen, for instance, parking is banned on streets in the centre and parking areas have been replaced with public squares laid out by landscape architects, while the number of bicycle parking places close to stations has been increased. In Harare, too, businesses in the town centre have asked the authorities to provide bicycle parking.[37] In France, more people are cycling in Strasbourg, with 15% of journeys as opposed to 3% for the rest of the country, because municipal policy stipulates that cars may not enter the city centre.

Nevertheless, a pro-bicycle attitude does not necessarily mean that cars are ostracized. For instance, the Worldwatch Institute cites the example of the Netherlands, which is not only the industrialized country where the authorities have adopted most pro-cyclist measures, with the highest cycle-lane density in the world, but also the country with the highest private car density, even though it has a very comprehensive public transport system.[38]

It is true that the image of cycling is still often linked in the public mind to a society that pre-dates affluence and prosperity. The use of bicycles must be transformed into a point of pride, with emphasis on its advantages as a silent, flexible, non-polluting means of transport, excellent for health and requiring little infrastructure. Bicycles are also often perceived as dangerous, although in France, for instance, this is not borne out by the statistics, as shown by the 1993 figures: two persons killed for every 100,000 bicycles, 24 in the case of private cars, 25 for mopeds and 86 for motorcycles. Information campaigns would therefore need to be launched to enhance the subjective perception of safety.

The OECD report *Urban Transport and Sustainable Development* states that unless specific incentive and management policies are elaborated, environment-friendly modes of travel such as walking and cycling will continue to lose ground.[39] This risk is even greater in Asia as the emerging economies attain the status of industrialized economies. As it is, an increase in available income is still most often manifested by the purchase of a car.

However, an inverse movement is already perceptible: as individuals and national and local communities – with towns in the lead – become aware of the drawbacks and dangers of dependence on the automobile – that strange form of 'automania' from which it is to be hoped that a higher level of education will progressively release us in the twenty-first century – we can expect the popularity of non-motorized transport to be revived.

Need one evoke the massive and traditional use of bicycles in China and other parts of Asia, which it is essential to encourage in the face of the temptation to ultra-motorization? Between 20% and 30% of urban commuting is done by bicycle in the Netherlands and Denmark. In the USA, the number of those regularly cycling to work has tripled in the last ten years and stands at three million today.[40] These are indeed heartening signs.

At the same time, the idea of urban planning that attaches greater importance to pedestrians and cyclists is all the more crucial since it would consolidate the war on poverty and exclusion: one household in four in the developing countries cannot afford to pay for public transport. This situation is the source of enormous inequalities of access to education, health, work, services and culture and of their transmission to succeeding generations. In Manila, for example, the poor must sacrifice as much as 14% of their income to get to work.[41] In that light, it is impossible to overstate the fact that urbanization policies founded on the extension of built-up zones over increasingly vast areas are most detrimental to the more vulnerable strata of the population, for it is they who most often live in districts furthest from the centre of economic activity. This problem underscores the importance of making special, subsidized transport tariffs available to the most disadvantaged parts of the population.

For Better Organization of Space

Transport and traffic policy is all too often dissociated from policy on the location of housing, jobs and equipment. Cities wear themselves out trying to adapt transport supply to demand, while they should also be working on demand by reducing commuting needs through better control of the locations of various urban functions. Individual mobility, a precious freedom, becomes an increasingly expensive economic, human and environmental constraint on individuals and communities alike. As Benjamin Dessus points out, town planning decisions directly influence energy consumption: the dispersal of housing entails greater costs. Hence, 'while an inhabitant of a very sparsely populated city like Phoenix, Arizona (ten inhabitants per hectare) consumes an average of 1.6 TOE (tons of oil equivalent) per year on commuting, an inhabitant of the Paris region (50 inhabitants per hectare) consumes 0.25 TOE per year and an inhabitant of Tokyo or Singapore (150 inhabitants per hectare) less than 0.15 TOE'.[42]

It is a matter of crucial importance to begin making projections for the future and to reinforce urban planning, not only with a view to improving transport systems but also because the health and quality of life of populations are at stake. Better anticipation of urban problems, combined with medium- and long-term strategic planning for their prevention, would make it possible, in particular, to cut down the number of traffic accidents and the diseases attributable to atmospheric pollution and, hence, to reduce infrastructure requirements in regard to hospitals, ambulance and fire services. Land-use management and urban design will therefore need to be reconsidered in the future. Current standards too frequently encourage longer routes and additional journeys in order to meet a specific need.[43] This dispersed urbanization, which goes hand in hand with excessive motoring, is expensive for the towns and for society as a whole. It pointlessly increases loss of land, impedes access to public services by expanding urban areas, and causes investment and tax revenue in the municipalities to fall as economic activities move closer to the periphery.

The second United Nations Conference on Human Settlements (Habitat II, Istanbul, June 1996) highlighted the need to bring urban transport under control by spreading mobility needs through better planning or remodelling of towns and cities (densification), improved and more appropriate transport systems, flexible working hours and 'telecommuting'. The World Bank has also stressed the importance of avoiding a land-use management policy founded on low settlement density, especially when the private cost of increased mobility is clearly lower than the social cost.[44]

Surveys in the major cities of Canada, the USA and the UK have shown that the doubling of population or settlement density translated into a 20% to 30% reduction in the annual number of kilometres travelled by car per person. And petrol consumption is inversely proportional to urban density.[45] Hence the importance attached to the densification of towns and the creation of efficient public transport networks and, as a consequence, to new interest in urban planning and better control of land and land-use management.

If there are no concerted policies by governments and municipalities, public and private decision-makers, experts and consumer associations, we shall see the multiplication on all continents of largely irreversible situations, as in Los Angeles, where urban development has favoured extreme dispersal and where two-thirds of urban space is now geared to automobile traffic, thereby reinforcing urban segregation. The idea is not to reject progress but, on the contrary, to use it sensibly in order to reduce 'car-mania' and make towns more urbane: more livable and more congenial, more town-like and therefore more civic.

Better Management of Transport's True Costs

In order to encourage the expansion of fast and efficient public transport, motorists must also be required to cover the actual cost to society of their increased mobility. What is needed, in fact, is to win acceptance for the idea that excessive car journeys are detrimental to the economy, the environment, the quality of life and, therefore, to development. This will be no easy task, so linked is the idea of development in twentieth-century imagery to that of the automobile and road infrastructure. Appropriate measures include increased petrol taxes, integrated parking fees and even a variable-rate tariff system. The revenue thus obtained could reasonably be used to improve public transport, car-pooling facilities, bicycle lanes and pedestrian precincts.

In Marcia Lowe's view, the ultimate aim of those measures would be to build 'a transport system in which the rule would be access, not excess'.[46] In the Philippines, high petrol and automobile taxes and improved public transport brought a 43% reduction in petrol consumption between 1976 and 1985, despite population growth and increased per capita income. Likewise, in areas served by public transport, time spent on the road has been cut by about one-third. Therefore even developing countries can combine energy control, a culture of sustainable development and improved transport and urban living.

Variable-rate tariff scales offer the advantage of charging cars higher rates during rush hours and in the more congested areas, thus reflecting each car's contribution to the congestion and penalizing traffic jams, which are a major source of pollution.[47] A survey conducted in San Francisco showed that a tariff system adjustable to congestion levels would increase the number of public-transport users by 10% to 20%. This system has been working in Singapore since 1975 and for the last five years in Norway; it is currently under study in a number of countries. In order to be accepted by motorists long accustomed to free road use, any measure that obliges them to pay for using their cars would need to be explained. Also, in order to avoid penalizing the less privileged inhabitants, it is important at the same time to improve the supply and operation of public transport.

Towards an Integrated Strategy for the Future

The idea that radical measures for reinventing transport policy and taking account of their impact on the environment are necessary and even urgent is gaining ground. For example, the report of the Royal Commission on Environmental Pollution in England recommended in 1994 a 9% annual increase in fuel taxes, a 50% reduction in motorway spending, a substantial increase in expenditures on public transport, and an end to the road-construction programme. In addition, according to a recent study by the British Road Federation, even if annual road investment were to increase by 50%, the congestion problem would nevertheless continue to grow worse.[48]

The OECD report *Urban Transport and Sustainable Development* stresses the importance of an integrated strategy that would combine better land-use management; improved traffic management that would encourage, *inter alia*, use of public transport; tolls along the more congested routes; and fuel taxes that would gradually increase each year 'in order to encourage the use of more economical vehicles, a reduction in the length and number of car journeys, fewer and shorter unaccompanied car journeys and greater use of environment-friendly modes of transport'.[49]

Better coordination and more dovetailing of the various modes of transport is absolutely essential for greater mobility and energy efficiency and for sustainable development. This is why comprehensive organization of journeys must include the installation of interface infrastructure that would allow the user to change transport modes with the least inconvenience and, therefore, always opt for the mode of transport that best caters to individual and community needs. Another enormous challenge for many developing countries is road maintenance. It is believed that for lack of adequate maintenance, these countries have lost the equivalent of $45 billion through deterioration of their infrastructure and equipment over the last 20 years.[50]

We are increasingly aware that the boom in mobility does not have only favourable repercussions on our societies and the environment. There too, we shall need to change our ideas about human beings and society. The challenge is enormous, so strongly have bigger incomes and improved living conditions been associated with increased mobility over the years. Andreas Schafer and David Victor stress the existence of a marked correlation between increased income and increased transport spending.[51] Education, the social and human sciences applied to urban policy, and communication and information are today called upon to play an essential role. But action must also include incentive policies that directly influence travel styles: the measures proposed here, far from delaying progress, would, on the contrary, use it to encourage energy control and make public transport systems more efficient. The objective of a modern transport policy must be to minimize damage to the environment, to guarantee individuals access to services and places and to help cities become a place of convivial interaction rather than a dispersed, polluted urban area that excludes the underprivileged. The technologies for attaining this objective do exist. But does the political will exist?

Pointers and Recommendations

* Encourage more forward-looking vision and better urban planning that takes account of demographic developments in order to avoid dispersed settlements that necessitate long journeys between home and work.
* Give priority to public transport and reconsider it in the light of social change.
* Use education, information and organization of safer traffic networks to enhance the role of non-motorized transport.
* Consolidate research for developing and marketing less polluting vehicles through incentive measures.
* Guarantee poor populations effective and very low-cost access to transport infrastructures.

Notes

1. Odile Heddebaut and Guy Joignaux, 'Le réseau européen de transports à l'horizon 2010. "Maillons manquants" et intégration territoriale', *Futuribles*, No. 195, February 1995.

2. Kenneth M. Gwilliam, *Transport in the City of Tomorrow: The Transport Dialogue at Habitat II*, TWU Papers, World Bank, Washington, DC, 1996.

3. Marcia Lowe, 'Reinventing transport', *State of the World 1994*, Worldwatch Institute, Washington, DC.

4. Emile Quinet, 'Vers une politique des transports', *Futuribles*, No. 195, February 1995.

5. World Bank, *Sustainable Transport: Priorities for Policy Reform*, Washington, DC, 1996.

6. Marcia Lowe, 'Rethinking urban transport', *State of the World 1991*, Worldwatch Institute, Washington, DC.

7. World Bank, *Sustainable Transport*.

8. Lowe, 'Reinventing transport'.

9. *The Economist*, 24 January 1998.

10. Lowe, 'Reinventing transport'.

11. *The Economist*, 18 June 1994.

12. OECD, *Urban Travel and Sustainable Development*, OECD, Paris, 1995.

13. Marcia Lowe, 'Rediscover rail', *State of the World 1993*, Worldwatch Institute, Washington, DC.

14. World Bank, *Sustainable Transport*.

15. *Le Monde*, 13 June 1996.

16. *Le Monde*, 19 July 1995.

17. World Bank, *Sustainable Transport*.

18. OECD, *L'Automobile à l'aube du 21ème siècle*, Paris, OECD, 1995.

19. *The Economist*, 'The coming car crash', 10 May 1997.

20. Lowe, 'Reinventing transport'.

21. E. von Weizsäcker, A. Lovins and L. Lovins, *Factor Four: Doubling Wealth, Halving Resource Use*, Earthscan, London, 1997.

22. Quinet, 'Vers une politique des transports'.

23. Benjamin Dessus, *Energie, un Défi planétaire*, Editions Belin, Paris, 1996.

24. Weizsäcker et al., *Factor Four*.

25. *Le Monde*, 'Comment réduire la pollution de l'air en ville', 15 November 1997; *The Economist*, 'At last, the fuel cell', 25 October 1997.

26. *Le Monde*, 17 April 1996.

27. Heddebaut and Joignaux, 'Le réseau européen'.

28. John Decicco and Marc Ross, 'La nouvelle génération d'automobiles', *Pour la Science, La science des transports*, special number, January 1998.

29. Daniel Sperling, 'Les véhicules électriques et hybrides', *Pour la Science, La science des transports*, special number, January 1998.

30. OECD, *Motor Vehicle Pollution: Reduction Strategies Beyond 2010*, OECD, Paris, 1995.

31. International Association of Public Transport, *Making Cities Liveable: The Public Transport Challenge*, ed. Pierre Laconte, IUPT, Brussels, 1996.

32. Brian Williams, *Transport in the City of Tomorrow*, Discussion Paper, Dialogue for the 21st Century, Habitat II, Second United Nations Conference on Human Settlements, Istanbul, June 1996.

33. Lowe, 1993, 'Rediscover Rail'.

34. Ibid.

35. *The Economist*, 'Living with the car', 6 December 1997.

36. François Ascher, 'La ville, l'individu et le temps concassé', *Libération*, 3 April 1996.

37. Lowe, 'Rethinking urban transport'.

38. Marcia Lowe, 'The bicycle: vehicle for a small planet', *State of the World 1990*, Worldwatch Institute, Washington, DC.

39. OECD, *Urban Travel and Sustainable Development*, OECD, Paris, 1995.

40. Lowe, 'Reinventing transport'.

41. World Bank, *Sustainable Transport*.

42. Dessus, *Energie, un Défi planétaire*.

43. Lowe, 1994, 'Reinventing transport'.

44. World Bank, *Sustainable Transport: Priorities for Policy Reform*, Washington, DC, 1996.

45. IUPT, *Making Cities Liveable*.

46. Lowe, 'Reinventing transport'.

47. The engine of a stationary car pollutes three times as much as that of a moving car, so that technical improvements that make cars 'cleaner' do not suffice to offset the increased pollution linked to increasing traffic jams. *The Economist*, 'Living with the car', 6 December 1997.

48. *The Economist*, 24 January 1998.

49. OECD, *Urban Travel and Sustainable Development*.

50. Kenneth M. Gwilliam, *Individual Sustainable Mobility – Priorities for Policy Reform and an Agenda for Action*, World Bank, Washington, DC, 1996.

51. Andreas Schafer and David Victor, 'L'évolution de la mobilité dans le monde', *Pour la Science, La science des transports,* special number, January 1998. These two experts also point out that regardless of economic, social and geographical conditions, time spent travelling has so far remained constant at an average of 1.1 hours per day. Accordingly, since 'people's mobility increases with income, they use faster means of transport; they then cover longer distances in the same time'.

CHAPTER 5

. . . .

Women Make the World Go Round

§ WHAT positive aspects of the twentieth century will we remember a century or two from now? Perhaps, as well as a few spectacular advances, the discreet beginnings of a great revolution: women's liberation.

In the beginning, this grassroots movement had virtually never been on the agenda of any party or institution. It gained momentum from history, from conflicts through the organized protest of women and from the evidence, abundant in times of war and national liberation struggles, that in the absence of men, women were more than capable of 'making things work'. Despite appearances, the change in the status of women has only very rarely been imposed by law: rather, it has imposed itself on laws. It is only fair to women to recognize the fact that their emancipation was, first and foremost, their own work, anonymous and silent, even though many enlightened men did make a decisive contribution to it.

This revolution, however, is far from over. For the most part, the voice of half the Earth is silenced.[1] Of course, here and there in some rich countries, in certain privileged metropolises, in some residential suburbs in the South, women have undoubtedly broken their chains. But even where society recognizes them as citizens, women are still mostly only 'emancipated'. The end of subservience has not yet, even in the most advanced countries, entailed full exercise of rights or real freedom and equality.

Elsewhere, liberation has barely begun. It begins with the rudiments of education, with the ABC of freedom written on a blackboard, in exercise books, on a school wall, with the gradual shedding of the veil of ignorance. But nothing is ever irreversibly acquired: even in industrialized countries, the temptation of a backlash has grown stronger in recent years. For the adversaries of sexual equality, feminists have 'gone too far'. Moreover, in some countries it is now on the road to school, on the path towards knowledge, that girls and young women are falling victim to blind fanaticism. The achievements, still fragile – such as schooling for girls or equal civic rights – may be jeopardized.

However, the undeniable improvement in the status of women over the last few decades still cannot conceal the flagrant disparities that persist today. As the UNDP points out, of all the inequalities of development, inequality between the sexes requires the most *specific* measurement and concerns *all countries*, even the most advanced and those most proud of their achievements in this field: in no nation, in no country do women really enjoy the same opportunities as men.[2] What is more, contrary to the generally accepted view, advances in sexual equality do not always depend on a country's affluence, or even – which is astonishing at first sight – on the level of what the UNDP refers to as 'human development'. Income is not the deciding factor here.

Observing the shortcomings of a concept of human development that does not clearly reflect the degree of sexual equality attained, the UNDP has refined its development index based essentially on three criteria (per capita income, standard of education and life expectancy) and has added a 'gender-related development index' (GDI), taking the differences between men and women in these areas into consideration. Since 1970, all countries have improved the status of women, but unequally, and without any automatic correlation with income. The 1998 ranking puts Canada and Norway ahead of the field, followed by Sweden and Iceland. However, 60 out of the 163 countries listed are ranked lower according to the GDI than they are according to the human development indicator, highlighting the disparities in the treatment of women. Even more interestingly, this ranking shows that many developing countries far surpass much richer countries. Thus, Barbados does better than Switzerland and Italy; China, with only half the per capita GDP, is ten places ahead of one rich oil-producing country; and Thailand comes just behind a member of the European Union which has a per capita income four times higher.[3] What is more, countries that have limited resources but display firm political commitment, such as China, Sri Lanka and Zimbabwe, have attained a high rate of literacy among adult women, while in the view of the UNDP 'many rich countries are lagging behind'.[4]

This means that the fight against sexual inequality cannot rely on the growth of national income alone. It is, first and foremost, a matter of vision and political will. And this effort is not necessarily very expensive. On the contrary, it can increase a nation's development opportunities. We must re-member that a society in which women are not placed on a footing of strict equality and parity with men, either *de jure* or *de facto,* is a diminished society performing below its real creative and productive potential, and does not address the challenges of the twenty-first century in optimum conditions.

Progress

Outstanding progress has admittedly been made worldwide in the past two decades, especially in UNESCO's fields of competence, the most noteworthy being in education: disparities between the sexes with regard to adult literacy and children's enrolment in schools were reduced by half between 1970 and 1990. The literacy rate among women, which was 54% that of men in 1970, rose to 74% in 1990. In primary education, 85 girls to every 100 boys currently attend school, as against 65% in 1960. Between 1970 and 1990, girls' enrolment in primary education increased by 1.7% per year in the developing countries and that of boys by only 1.2%. The enrolment rate for girls in primary and secondary education in the developing countries increased from 38% in 1970 to 68% in 1992. In higher education, the findings are equally impressive, where women's enrolment is now 70% that of men, whereas in 1970 it was only 50%.[5] There is a current consensus among the international community that education, especially women's education, is the best investment.[6]

Considerable progress has also been made in the field of health. Women's life expectancy has increased at a pace of more than 20% that of men in the last 20 years. The average fertility rate has dropped by one-third from 4.7 children per woman between 1970 and 1975 to three between 1990 and 1995, thus increasing women's freedom and choices while reducing their risk of death in childbirth or during pregnancy. In 20 years the mortality rate of women in childbirth has fallen by half. Over half of the women of child-bearing age have been using modern contraceptive methods since 1990, while in 1970 only one-quarter of them did so.[7]

On the subject of reproduction, the United Nations Conference on Population and Development (Cairo, 1994) and on Women (Beijing, 1995) promoted 'the recognition of the basic right of all couples and all individuals to decide freely and responsibly the number, spacing and timing of their children and to have the information and means to do so, and the right to attain the highest standard of sexual and reproductive health' (Beijing Platform of Action, paragraph 95). We consider such recognition to be paramount, for freedom and responsibility are inseparable in this area. Moreover, this responsibility is not only individual but collective, calling as it does for mobilization of resources for the promotion of women, children and families, especially in the fields of education, health and social services. The Universal Declaration of Human Rights rightly proclaims that 'motherhood and childhood are entitled to special care and assistance' (Article 25) and that 'the family ... is entitled to protection by society and the State' (Article 16).

At least in some developing countries the doors of political power are very slowly opening for women. In most regions of the world, it is becoming less rare for women to become members of government. The number of women ministers has doubled in the past ten years.[8] In Sweden, 40% of members of parliament are women, and there is almost the same figure in Norway.[9] In the USA, while a 1937 survey showed that 65% of voters polled were opposed to the idea of voting for a woman for president, however competent she might be, the figure had dropped to 12% in 1987. Such progress is even more noticeable in the South, despite some erroneous ideas on the matter: women are better represented on average in the parliaments of developing countries than in those of industrialized countries.[10]

In democracies, women are turning to new methods to make their voices heard. For example, if a women's association decides to announce in the press that, because of the violence in a particular television channel's programmes, its members are boycotting the products advertised on that channel, the latter may quite possibly decide to change its programmes from one day to the next.

Disappointments: Discrimination, Poverty and Violence

Despite these advances, we are still far from the effective equality to which women have rightly aspired for so long and which the United Nations recognizes as their right. Despite the tendency of some states to reject the notion of equality in favour of that of equity, it is worth recalling that *equal* enjoyment of human rights by women and men is a principle universally recognized by the UN Charter. That principle was reaffirmed by the Vienna Declaration adopted by 171 states at the 1993 United Nations Conference on Human Rights.

Disparities between men and women in education have admittedly been cut by half in the last 20 years, but can we afford to wait another 20 years for equal access to education to become an absolute reality? Intolerable inequalities persist. According to our statistics, nearly two-thirds of the 880 million or so illiterates in the world are women and one adult woman in three, most of whom live in rural areas, still cannot read and write.[11] Girls still account for 60% of the 130 million children lacking access to primary education. Furthermore, as the states participating in the Beijing summit observed, curricula and educational equipment are still 'largely tainted with sexist prejudice'. Not only do textbooks fail to deal with problems faced by women and girls on a daily basis, but worse, they are often silent on the subject of women's achievements.[12] In the USA, according to a study conducted by the American Association of University Women, boys are given preference in subjects such as mathematics, science and technology, while girls are dissuaded from taking up those subjects. This is the case in both industrialized and developing countries: women are under-represented in the scientific disciplines.[13] Moreover, greater participation of women in educational professions could promote enrolment of girls, since families in certain regions of the globe are somewhat reluctant to entrust their young girls to male teachers. Releasing children from non-educational tasks is as important as any school strategy.

At the advent of the twenty-first century, there is at least one piece of good news that can cheer us: there is an increasingly broad consensus within the international community, and not only in UNESCO, on the priority that should be assigned to women's education, including in budgetary terms. We now *know* – it is no longer a mere belief – that the upsurge of education for women makes a decisive contribution to development. The consequences can be directly perceived even in economic terms: according to several World Bank surveys in Kenya, if women's education were raised to the same level as that of men, food crop yields would increase by 9% to 22%, and by one-quarter if everyone were assured of primary education. Case studies on the impact of women's education on social development abound: in Brazil, mothers who had never been to school have an average of 6.5 children, as against 2.5 for those who received secondary education. In the Indian state of Kerala, which has all but totally eradicated illiteracy, the infant mortality rate is the lowest in the entire developing world, and the fertility rate is the lowest in India. Women in both South and North are therefore – as Edgar Morin so neatly described the Breton women of Plozévet 30 years ago – a 'secret agent of modernity'.

Despite their specific health and nutrition needs, women, especially Third World women, are still less well cared for than men.[14] According to the World Health Organization (WHO), nearly 600,000 women die every year from complications connected with pregnancy or delivery, 99% of them in the developing countries.[15] In addition, abortions performed in appalling sanitary conditions account for 100,000 deaths per year; the United Nations estimates that millions of women subsequently suffer permanent disabilities for that reason. Moreover, they are directly threatened by AIDS.[16] The number of women infected with the HIV virus is one and a half times greater than that of men. Women currently account for 40% of the new cases of this disease, as opposed to 10% ten years ago.[17]

The prime victims of poverty are women. More than two times out of three, poverty has the face of a woman – a silent, voiceless face, a face that one often does not even wish to look at, a face relegated to society's peripheral vision. Of the 1.3 billion people living in absolute poverty, 70% are women. Many experts consider that extreme poverty, often associated as it is with discrimination, causes the deaths of millions of women and girls every year, especially elderly women. As Michèle Aulagnon points out, 'the risk of being dragged into poverty is greater for a woman than a man, especially after a certain age, when social welfare systems are based on the principle of continuous paid employment'.[18]

The number of poverty-stricken women in rural areas has virtually doubled in 20 years to 564 million in 1988. Both urban and rural female poverty, like sexual inequality in general, have complex causes 'in which', as Guy Herzlich states, 'the public and private spheres, institutions and markets (the labour and marriage markets) permeate one another' – as corroborated by a recent World Bank report.[19] For example, women experience great difficulty in obtaining credit and purchasing goods, and they are often treated unfavourably in inheritance. In the South they occupy many jobs in the 'informal sector' and are therefore remunerated poorly, if at all, and given scant protection. For instance, in Peru in the 1980s four-fifths of women worked in that sector. In Africa, in particular, the crisis and the dearth of social and economic prospects have pushed women into the informal sector. According to UNICEF, nearly 60% of economically active women in sub-Saharan Africa work for themselves, the highest rate in the world. But for most of the time they are confined to small-scale, unprofitable activities. The Ivoirian economist Ginette Yoman estimates that in West Africa 30% of households are headed by a woman and that these are the poorest.[20]

The industrialized countries are not spared. While men and women have the same standard of education and training, women are much more threatened by poverty than men. Why is this? In the first place, because the burden of maintaining a family falls increasingly on them in an environment of social and financial hardship. More and more households are in fact headed by women without a partner: one in three, according to the United Nations, and the figure is even higher in the Caribbean and some African countries.[21] Furthermore, women continue to be the victims of discriminatory practices on the labour market.

On the work front, women's improved training has not yet resulted in higher income, effective equality of rights or social recognition. 'In all countries of the world, women continue to be paid less than men for the same work,' notes the International Labour Organization.[22] Available data indicate that the proportion of 'working' women has increased by less than four points in 20 years, moving from 36% in 1970 to 40% in 1990, and that their salaries on average are only three-quarters of those of men and account for 30% of overall salary income. Despite an educational standard comparable with that of men, especially in the industrialized countries, women are all too often still denied access to positions of responsibility, especially in the private sector. Directorships of firms and many senior posts in the civil service are often closed to them, although in Western countries more and more women are occupying positions quite close to the top. Their remuneration is far from comparable to that of men.[23] In short, the vast majority of women are confined to what some economists have dubbed the 'pink ghetto': services, subsistence agriculture and ill-paid office jobs.[24] At the same time, unemployment and under-employment affect women more than any other group in all regions of the world. According to the UNDP, 'for most women, access to an independent income is still a far-off goal'.

In the political arena, despite recent positive developments, it is still exceptional for a woman to accede to the highest office: since the Second World War, only 28 women have been elected head of state or government; in 1997, only two women headed a government and three others were heads of state.[25] On a world scale, women occupy only 11.8% of seats in parliament on average, and this proportion exceeds 30% in only four countries.[26] In 48 countries there is no woman minister; in 136 countries, there is no woman with a ministerial portfolio in the economics area and, worldwide, only 9.9 per cent of all junior ministerial posts are held by women.[27] Between 1975 and 1997, women's representation in the legislative organs therefore remained practically stable, since it was 12.5% 20 years ago. Moreover, worldwide, only 7% of ministerial posts are held by women (the average ranging from a mere 6% in the least developed countries to 13% in the industrialized countries). It is noteworthy that women's participation in the political and economic spheres is not necessarily linked to their country's level of development; in some developing countries, their rate of participation is higher than in certain industrialized countries. In this respect, Trinidad and Tobago are ahead of the United Kingdom and Ireland, Cuba and Costa Rica are ahead of France and Israel, while China and Mexico are doing better than Japan.[28]

Human rights should be interpreted as being the rights of the human being, of men and women, on the basis of strict parity. However, in many countries women still do not enjoy the same treatment as men when it comes to property rights, inheritance rights and rights connected with marriage and divorce. The Convention on the Elimination of All Forms of Discrimination Against Women (CEDAW), adopted by the United Nations in 1979, entered into force years ago to little avail; although it had been ratified by the end of 1998 by 161 states, many governments either failed to ratify it or expressed reservations regarding certain articles. In its 1995 report, the UNDP pointed out that 90 countries deemed themselves as yet unable to adopt all the provisions that make women and men equal before the law.

The shortcomings in women's rights are reflected in the moral and physical persecution and oppression to which they are subjected, in the unacceptable status all too often assigned them in society and in the juridical and practical acts of discrimination of which they are victims. Hence violence against women and rape as a weapon of war continue to be used to sow terror and intimidation during armed conflicts.[29] The process of down-grading, the UNDP points out, begins even before birth; it marks childhood, becomes a component of marriage, is often expressed through sexual abuse and can lead to murder and suicide. A more banal and everyday form of violence has been practised since the dawn of time within the home itself. According to studies conducted in Chile, Mexico, Papua New Guinea and the Republic of Korea, at least two-thirds of women have been subjected to some form of domestic violence in their lives. The UNDP estimates that in Germany, the phenomenon affects four million women every year; in France, two million women are reportedly beaten by their spouses; in the USA, the number is four million; in Canada, Japan and South Korea, 25% to 60% of women are reportedly abused by their partners.

According to available studies, such conjugal violence is the main cause of suicide among women. Other forms of violence exist: according to non-governmental sources, some 25,000 women in India are burned to death each year because of dowry disputes.[30] Other studies conducted in Canada, New Zealand, the United Kingdom and the USA estimate that one woman in six is raped during her life. According to United Nations estimates, one million children, mainly girls, are thrust each year into the hell of prostitution in Asia. Finally, according to the UNDP, 100 million girls suffer genital mutilation, of which two million girls are victims every year. In addition, of the 18 million refugees across the world, 80% are women. And what can one say about 'sexual tourism', the sexual exploitation of girls in early adolescence in the poorest countries? Of the scandal of organized networks of paedophiles? Of the degrading image of women on offer as 'slaves' in the classified ads of certain famous publications?

At the forefront of violence against women are selective abortion – which consists in eliminating female foetuses – and infanticide of little girls, practices particularly widespread in Asia.[31] Unfortunately, technological progress could worsen this situation if in our societies women continue to be portrayed as a source of problems rather than as an asset. On the basis of local surveys conducted in Asia, *The Economist* highlighted the major risks connected with abuse of ultrasound scanning for purposes of gender selection.[32] While in normal conditions 106 boys are born for every 100 girls, this is no longer the case in some Asian countries, where the sex ratio is normal for the first child but alters considerably with subsequent births. In China it is 120.9 boys to 100 girls for a second child and in the Republic of Korea 185 for a third child. Parents have the child's sex scanned and then decide whether they wish to abort or continue the pregnancy. The same problem occurs in India, where many parents fear being financially ruined by the dowry they must provide for their daughter's marriage. According to the *Journal of Family Welfare*, out of 8,000 abortions carried out in Bombay following ultrasound sex identification, only one foetus was male. China, India and South Korea have banned selective abortion, but the rules are difficult to enforce in everyday life: for the practitioner, a sign is often enough to reveal the sex of the foetus. All of this occurs in tacit complicity.

The results of these practices are, unfortunately, only too visible. In some regions of the world, men outnumber women by five to one. The economist Amartya Sen has tried to estimate the number of female foetuses aborted and that of female victims of infanticide. By his reckoning, these practices apparently account for the 'loss' of some 100 million women from the world's population. The male/female ratio in India has dropped since the early twentieth century, unlike the sex ratios observed in most countries. At the present time, there are only 929 women to 1,000 men as against 972 to 1,000 in 1901.[33] If this type of practice is to end, society must confer on women a genuine role and powers that finally allow them to be treated as men's equals.

The Beijing conference concluded that violence against women constitutes a violation of women's fundamental rights and freedoms and partially or entirely prevents them from exercising those rights and freedoms. It is clear that the mere amendment or stricter enforcement of the laws cannot suffice to improve such a bleak panorama. Only a necessarily slow but profound change in attitudes, only the instilling of a culture of peace in the minds of 'men', particularly through education, can make for mutual respect and a genuine dialogue between the sexes.

In this respect, it is important that society in the rich countries should be attentive to the experience of women who live in very different cultural and social contexts. It is equally important that women's contribution to our common heritage – whether literary, scientific, intellectual or artistic – should be clearly visible. In this field, the reviewing of school textbooks is a major priority and must be systematically undertaken in the next decade.

Women's Work

United Nations data show that in all countries of the world, except Australia, Canada and the USA, women work longer hours than men. The disparity in the number of hours worked is greatest in the poor countries. In the developing countries, women work an average of 12 to 18 hours per day on various paid or unpaid activities, as opposed to an average of eight to 12 hours for men.

According to the UNDP, two-thirds of the total time spent working by men in the industrialized countries is devoted to remunerated activities and the remaining one-third to unpaid activities. The reverse is true of women. In the developing countries men devote three-quarters of their working time to remunerated activity. They receive the bulk of income and enjoy social recognition for their contribution, while women's work is often underpaid, undervalued or ignored.[34] On the basis of complex calculations that take account of the value of women's unpaid work and the relatively underpaid work done by women on the labour market, the UNDP assesses at $11 trillion per year women's 'non-financial and invisible contribution', which is not reflected in economic accounting. That contribution is particularly substantial in the South. In a recent report, the World Bank estimates that 'in some countries unpaid work could represent one third of the gross domestic product'.[35] Even if the UNDP's figures were exaggerated, it would perhaps be wise for national statistics fully to reflect women's 'invisible' contribution: women would cease to be considered nonentities in economic statistics, and it would be more difficult for leaders to forget women when taking major decisions. The 'invisible nature' of women's contribution feeds society's perception of them as 'dependants' rather than producers.[36]

In many regions, women's work is essentially linked to the subsistence economy by which families are fed, but does not enter into the market framework. Consequently, such work is neither quantified nor expressed in monetary terms. Women are therefore often deprived of the status given by society to the producers of foodstuffs sold on the market and thus an essential contribution by women to the world's actual productivity goes unacknowledged. The cause, according to Jodi Jacobson, is sex discrimination.[37]

Moreover, women often do not possess land title or have only limited title, despite their crucial role in agriculture. They are impeded by inegalitarian laws in some cases and by excluding customs in others, sometimes even sexist agrarian reform laws.[38] This has important consequences, and not only in demographic terms. In fact, when women have little or no access to production resources and can neither plan nor control the family income, their social status and economic security depend on their children. The high rates of population growth that result from such precariousness 'feed a vicious circle of increased population, fewer resources and increased poverty'.[39]

Furthermore, in many developing countries, men's contribution to the family income has dropped because of factors such as increased male emigration to towns, low wage levels, divorce and desertion. Women are therefore increasingly pressured into subsidizing their family's needs, which can oblige them unknowingly to employ agricultural methods that are not ecologically viable in the long term, such as very short fallow periods. Because of scarcity, women now spend more time on tasks such as collecting fuel, fodder and water. A study conducted in strongly deforested regions in India has shown that women and their children spend an average of four to five hours a day collecting enough fuel to prepare the evening meal.

Women's rights must urgently be recognized and better integrated into society, so that their creative and productive potential can be more effectively and less precariously expressed. Women's exclusion from the cultivation of marketable crops and from technological progress, and the fact that their role is often limited to a subsistence economy, over which they have little or no control, underscore the many adverse effects that undervalued and underestimated work can have. Jodi Jacobson neatly sums up the problem:

> If in subsistence economies women are the main providers of foodstuffs, fuel and water for their families, and if at the same time their access to productive

resources diminishes, more people will be prey to hunger, malnutrition, disease and loss of productivity. If women have learnt ecologically viable agricultural techniques and acquired extensive knowledge on genetic diversity, as millions have done, and if at the same time they are denied any partnership in development, that wisdom will be lost.

The time has come to recognize women's rights of ownership and fully integrate them into the world of work, at a level of parity with men that would prevent the flagrant distortions that occur if their efforts are undervalued.

The imbalances that exist between men and women constitute one of the three major imbalances in the world (the other two being the imbalance of wealth, and the imbalance of scientific and technical knowledge and its transmission through education). As we have seen, their effects are often cumulative, since women usually suffer far more than men from poverty and lack of access to education, as well as, we might add, from wars and violence.

While the situation of women is unsatisfactory in general, it is particularly so wherever the unfair discrimination against them is institutionalized. Let there be no mistake about it, a regime that flouts women's most basic human rights to the point of denying girls the right to go to school should not be recognized by the international community. The institutionalization of discrimination against women must be severely condemned. Basic human rights are universal and 'Everyone is entitled to all the rights and freedoms set forth in' the Universal Declaration of Human Rights 'without distinction of any kind, such as race, colour, sex, language, religion, political or other opinion.'[40] The law cannot apply differently to two categories of citizens, depending on their sex. As stressed by Mary Robinson, United Nations High Commissioner for Human Rights, 'We must broaden the human rights language to incorporate the dimensions which have come to be recognised as indispensable: gender, sustainability, the environment, the rights of children, the obligations of big business.'[41]

From Exclusion to Integration: Women at the Centre of Development

Unfortunately, in many cultures, a family's resources are distributed in accordance with the family members' status rather than their needs, and men and boys are better treated than women and girls. In many countries, girls are less well educated than boys, who are given precedence. According to the World Bank, in 17 of the 29 countries for which recent statistics are available, the mortality rate among girls from one to four years of age is higher than that for boys in the same age group.[42] In many regions of India, as the economist Amartya Sen and many experts point out, boys are better fed and cared for than girls, preferential treatment that explains the excessive female mortality during the critical period from birth to five years of age. Indeed, with the exception of girls between 10 and 14, more Indian women than men die of preventable diseases up to the age of 35. This form of inequality in the allocation of family resources has also been observed in three other countries of Southern Asia, the Middle East and North Africa, and in some parts of sub-Saharan Africa.

Such discrimination against women is all the more distressing since it is they, for the most part, who change the world on a daily basis and are the key agents of true development. In fact, many studies show that more often than not they use the money they earn to cover their children's health and education costs or reinvest it in their professional activity, and that they keep less than men do for their personal use.[43] According to surveys conducted in all developing regions, it is the mother's income or food production rather than the father's, and the control she has over that income, that determine what her children eat. As James Gustave Speth, administrator of the UNDP, put it: 'From one end of the Third World to the other, in rural areas, it is on women that the local economy depends.'

In that connection, the innovative experience of financing for women's micro-enterprises by institutions such as the Grameen Bank, with two million clients, of whom 94% are women, leads to a clear conclusion: once women have access to micro-credit, they can play a much more active role than men in the fight against poverty. It has also been observed that women are better at repaying their debts and make better use of the funds they are loaned, doubtless owing to their lesser propensity to social pathologies and a better sense of management and economy acquired in the household. Women, perhaps because they are closer to their children, are better forward planners than men. Women's investments must therefore be considered one of the most promising agents of change for the future.[44] What is special about the Grameen Bank is that it lends only to the poor, mostly women. Today it employs 12,000 people. Known throughout the world, the Grameen Bank has been emulated in developing countries such as Malaysia, the Philippines and Burkina Faso.

Half of humankind's creative potential cannot be ignored. Women must be given the means not only for economic activity, but in all fields of intellectual and scientific life in which their talents and vision have been eclipsed for far too long and are still not recognized at their proper value. Since the creation of the Nobel Prize in 1901, only 28 women have been laureates, out of 634 personal awards. Who is Russia's twentieth-century poetic genius apart from Mayakovski? Very probably a woman: Marina Tsvetayeva. We have all heard of the former. But who, apart from poetry lovers and Russian-speakers, has heard of the latter? Nevertheless, the current popularity of Latin American women novelists such as Nelida Piñon and Laura Esquivel offers a fine example of women's potential contribution to our societies' cultural wealth and of their capacity to proffer different, original points of view and to display courage when men fail to do so. If we really wish to ensure the success of development strategies, we must first of all invest in women's education and health and make sure of their participation in society's economic, political, social and cultural arenas.

Woman is the Future of Mankind

Government and parliaments certainly have a fundamental role to play in promoting the status of women in society. This calls, first of all, for effective universalization of compulsory schooling for girls, real parity with boys in education, and guaranteed access of women to lifelong education which, in the most remote regions, can benefit from the advances of distance-education techniques, once the necessary investments in telecommunications infrastructure have been made. It is also vital to encourage equal access for men and women to all disciplines: there too, parity must be a fixed and quantifiable goal. Women are still under-represented in the field of 'hard' science, owing in part to an archaic perception of scientific culture, identified as a masculine stronghold. It is absolutely necessary to promote access of girls and women to scientific and technological education so that they may have their say in the debate on modernization. In that way, they will be able to participate actively in development, with their skills and responsibilities, on an equal footing with men.

Women's education must be lifelong education for all women. It is particularly important for the generations of women who have been excluded from the educational process to be able to benefit from education later on in their life. Women's education must benefit as a matter of priority from the latest developments in adult education. This approach, which UNESCO initiated several years ago, is the result of a long process, which led to the Jomtien Conference on Education for All (1990), the New Delhi initiative in favour of the nine high-population countries (1993), and to the International Conference on Adult Education, held in Hamburg (1997). Since then, this approach is acknowledged as having been a major turning-point in the field of education. It represents far more than an introduction to literacy: first, its aim is to improve adults' living conditions and quality of life through suitable teaching methods in the adults' own language. The advantages of this education are almost immediately tangible since, in the short term, it takes the form of activities that generate an income. In that way, it is not just one adult who benefits from it, but often a whole family or even an entire community:

through adult education, walls and wells are built in villages, sanitation is improved, daily life is made easier, and all children are able to attend school. In particular, because the results stem from action taken on their own initiative, it contributes to restoring their dignity to women.

Women must be assured of the same access as men to lifelong education. Adult education must not be the exclusive privilege of populations who for the most part go or have gone to school. Women and men of all countries can every day, if only for an hour, learn, retrain, progress and increase their technical and professional knowledge. In order to survive, to live better and to live better together, the men and women of the twenty-first century must be able to continue to learn throughout their lives.

In this field, the fact that certain member states have been successful through their own efforts probably constitutes UNESCO's own greatest success; they are the states who have understood the immense importance of redirecting their budgetary policies in favour of education and modified their national budgets in accordance with this new priority. India, Brazil, Bangladesh and several others have made significant commitments in this area. Just how effective this policy is can be seen clearly from the relationship between the increase of the share of GNP devoted to education and the decrease in population growth.

Women's contribution to the educational process and the handing down of values and principles cannot be overstated. As the prime educators, women must form an integral part of any overhaul of the education system that aims at mobilizing and enhancing a country's human resources with a view to the long term.

Where women's rights are concerned, the United Nations must continue to encourage initiatives aimed at the ratification and implementation of standard-setting instruments such as the 1979 Convention. The UN can also help women gain awareness of their real rights and the laws by which they are protected, by introducing 'juridical literacy' programmes at all stages of education.

In our view, women must be at the heart of the process designed to replace the culture of violence with a culture of peace. Rarely – though the case is not unknown in history – is it women who call for war or massacre: on the contrary, it is they who, as a general rule, attempt to preserve what remains of the social fabric and ensure the family's protection when men's murderous folly is unleashed. UNESCO, through its education programmes, seeks to strengthen the role of women in the transmission of positive cultural values that promote a spirit of tolerance.

Returning to an initiative taken in Beijing at the 1995 Summit Conference on Women, UNESCO has encouraged a number of prominent individuals to sign a declaration on women's contribution to a culture of peace in order to encourage, *inter alia*, the construction of a 'culture of peace, in private and public life, in the name of solidarity and compassion', attribution of more responsibilities to women and high-quality education on the rights of women and men. Over 1,000 leading figures, heads of state or government, Nobel Peace Prize laureates and heads of United Nations agencies have already signed this declaration. Improving the status of women is one of the top priorities of UNESCO's strategy.

It is not so much a matter of adopting a 'feminist' approach (i.e. women capable of doing things in a man's way) as a 'feminine' approach, which acknowledges both the equality of, and the differences between, the sexes, so that women may be fully autonomous in their actions, with their own way of looking at life and living it, without having to accept subservient status.

Admittedly, action in favour of the equality of women is still inadequate. However, the decisions of the Beijing summit provide us with a valuable overall framework for action – for the time has come to take action. Will we be able to identify the real priorities in this area? We are convinced that a forward-looking strategy in favour of women, centred on a few essential aspects, should be prepared and allocated adequate financing for its implementation over the next 20 years. For government intervention is necessary: given the interaction, often unfavourable to women, of market mechanisms, private pressures and public shortcomings, women will never break through the 'glass ceiling' that currently impedes their progress without structural reforms and informed measures that favour effective equality without falling into the intolerant excesses of 'political correctness' and 'anthropological correctness'.

Three institutions, it seems to us, are required to play an essential role in promoting women at national and international level, namely parliaments, the media and municipalities. Not only is it important for women to be represented in these sectors of public life, it is important for the future that these institutions address such questions as women's education, protection of their dignity, women's genuine participation in economic, social and cultural life, as well as improvement of their lot – which is often also the lot of their children.

In this context, the UNDP has put forward a programme that the international community would do well to implement without delay. In the first place, juridical equality should be achieved within the next ten years, with a precise timetable of action, culminating in the total ratification of the 1979 Convention. The use of violence against women as an instrument in a war should be acknowledged and punished as a war crime. Juridical literacy campaigns should be launched to make women aware of their rights. Country reports on the status of women and progress towards equality according to targets set by the international community and by governments could be prepared by the competent United Nations agencies.[45]

The capacity for choice and, hence, for freedom in their work should be promoted for women and men. For instance, men should be encouraged, through specific measures such as those applied in the Nordic countries, to participate in family care. It is also necessary to extend the notion of public service beyond education and health to day-care centres, school cafeterias and educational support (concerning school homework, etc.), as is already the case in a number of countries, if we do not wish education systems to impede the necessary promotion of women through work. Modification of tax brackets and social security regimes, in order to adjust to the evolution of women's role, is also important, as is the amendment of property, inheritance and divorce laws.

There will be no decisive change, however, so long as a critical threshold of at least 30% is not determined by each country as the minimum proportion of national policy-making posts that should be occupied by women. That target is not arbitrary, since it was recommended as long ago as 1990, following protracted deliberations, by the United Nations Commission on the Status of Women. In parliaments or governments, only the Seychelles, the Netherlands and four Nordic countries have exceeded that threshold. The most tangible progress with regard to posts of administrative responsibility and directorship is that 15 countries have already passed the 30% threshold. This minimum 30% target should be achieved in some key decision-making areas in every country, in accordance with a precise timetable.

Above all, priority programmes should be developed by each country to provide universal lifelong education for women, ensure better health for pregnant women and mothers and make credit more accessible to women. Those are perhaps the most decisive factors of a new deal. Naturally, experience has shown that these three areas require firm action and long-term policies so as gradually to abolish the barriers to equal opportunities for women and to development.

We have already mentioned the considerable benefits that the developing countries can expect from the education of women. The cost of such reforms is very small: it is derisory compared to the vast amount of unproductive spending the world over. For instance, according to United Nations estimates, an extra investment of $5 billion to $6 billion a year would suffice to provide universal schooling for girls in primary and secondary education for the next 15 years.[46]

Today, the international institutions, the development banks, the World Bank itself and, obviously, UNESCO, which has been the pioneer in this field, are putting their faith in women as the key to development. Women earn money and can be relied on to pay it back. More and more women are going into business; in the South, especially in the informal sector, micro-enterprises are increasingly in the hands of women.

If the twentieth century was the century of women's emancipation, the twenty-first century will be the century of their fulfilment. Meanwhile, however, women are living in a no-man's-land, in a period of transition in which all contrasts coexist, a time of stark *chiaroscuro*. It is hardly surprising, then, that at the turn of this century women so often cry out in pain and are so often given over to despair, unhappiness and revolt. Neither is it surprising that at the same time an exclamation of hope is heard when they occasionally succeed in enjoying a few rights or, even temporarily, in curbing their exploitation, oppression or exclusion by men.

However, like Claude Lévi-Strauss, the traveller with the detached look, who thought more than half a century ago that the tropics were sad, we are increasingly convinced that woman is the future of mankind.

It is quite obvious that, today, it is women who change the world. It is they who make the world go round. Women are not a problem but, above all, a solution and it is only together with women that a fairer, freer, more egalitarian world can be achieved, one in which there is greater solidarity. As pointed out by one of the advisers of the United Nations secretary-general for the preparation of the Beijing summit, Jack Lang, French minister of education, research and technology, 'it is time for all women on this planet to occupy their rightful place ... We must face up to facts: by liberating themselves women are called upon to liberate the world. Far from being a question, they will perhaps, first and foremost, be an answer. An answer to the problems of underdevelopment and population growth; an answer to the problems of peacekeeping; an answer to the problems of power and democracy.'[47]

Pointers and Recommendations

- Give priority to the education of women and girls in public investment and development aid in order to do away with the existing inequalities of access to all levels of education, to literacy, and to all disciplines without exception between women and men.
- Facilitate women's access to positions of political responsibility, supervision and guidance, particularly bearing in mind the target of at least 30% representation of women in parliaments, local and provincial community assemblies (town councils, local governments, etc.) and in public decision-making bodies.
- Review school curricula and textbooks to ensure adequate portrayal of the role of women, their achievements and their contributions; sensitize teachers and pupils to the problems of sex discrimination.
- Ensure equal access for women to credit and the processes of economic decision-making, and translate the principle of 'equal pay for equal work' into reality (Article 23, Universal Declaration of Human Rights).

- Resolutely combat violence against women, especially selective abortion, genital mutilation, domestic violence, economic and sexual exploitation or rape, particularly in times of war, and make provision for appeal to the competent national and international courts. Promote greater respect for women in the media, radio and television and on the Internet.
- Offer women equal access to health and nutrition; provide special aid and assistance for motherhood, as well as access to reproductive-health services; improve statistics on women's health; mobilize the resources needed by families for education, health and social services.
- Prepare country reports on the status of women and progress towards equality on the basis of the targets set by the international community and governments.
- Ensure the unconditional ratification, implementation and dissemination of the major international instruments on sexual equality, especially the 1979 Convention on the Elimination of All Forms of Discrimination against Women.
- Assure women of civic and civil equality, particularly with regard to poverty and inheritance law.

Notes

1. Source: Federico Mayor, 'Woman', poem composed on the occasion of the United Nations International Conference on Women (Beijing, 1995).

2. UNDP, *Human Development Report 1995*.

3. UNDP, *Human Development Report 1998*.

4. UNDP, *Human Development Report 1997*.

5. Certain advances make for great optimism throughout the world: in the Arab countries, between 1970 and 1990 the proportion of girls enrolled increased from 47 to 77 per 100 boys, and from 34 to 65 in higher education. Approximately 30% of female higher education students study the natural or applied sciences. In South-east Asia and the Pacific, the female higher education enrolment rate doubled between 1970 and 1990. In Southern Asia, the female illiteracy rate fell from 81% to 67% in two decades. In Latin America and the Caribbean, the number of girls enrolled in secondary education represent 97% of the number of boys, and as many women as men are engaged in higher education. In sub-Saharan Africa, the secondary school enrolment rate for girls quadrupled between 1960 and 1991 from 8% to 32% (UNDP, *Human Development Report 1996*).

6. 'Education: The best investment', joint declaration by Federico Mayor, James Wolfensohn, James G. Speth, Carol Bellamy and Nafis Sadik, *International Herald Tribune*, 11–12 May 1996.

7. UNDP, *Human Development Report 1995*.

8. From 3.4% in 1987 to 6.8% in 1996 (United Nations data, Division for the Advancement of Women, October 1997). See also *Courrier International*, special edition No. 10, October 1994.

9. 40.4% in Sweden, 36.4 in Norway (UNDP, *Human Development Report 1998*).

10. *Le Monde*, 31 August 1995.

11. In the developing countries, the proportion of illiterate women was 38.3% in 1995, while that of men was 21.1%. In the least developed countries, the proportions stood at 61.9% for women and 40.5% for men. In Niger and Yemen, the proportion of women who have not received education was 90%.

12. A 1997 French parliamentary report on the portrayal of men and women in text books concluded that 'unequal treatment of men and women still exists in school materials intended to transmit knowledge'. The authors recommend, *inter alia*, training students to be alert to sexism (Senate-National Assembly, report of Simone Rignault and Philippe Richert on the portrayal of men and women in school textbooks, March 1997).

13. Women are always under-represented in the 'hard' sciences. Women account for only 2% of higher-education physics students in Japan, 3% in Switzerland and Germany and 5% in the United States (UNESCO, *World Science Report 1996*). Only ten women have received the Nobel Prize for a scientific subject, as opposed to 300 men (*El País*, 18 March 1998).

14. World Health Organization (WHO), 1996 Report.

15. The executive director of UNICEF, Carol Bellamy, introducing the 1995 edition of the UNICEF Report, stressed that 'it is no overstatement to say that it is one of the most neglected tragedies of our times', since 1,600 women, including adolescents, die every day from pregnancy- or delivery-related ailments, leaving behind a million orphans per year 'with [an] extremely slim chance of survival'. She points out that 'for every women who succumbs, there are 30 more who sustain serious injuries', that is, over 15 million per year. According to the report, this objective is quite easy to attain since it is not very expensive. Even the poor countries can provide doctors, midwives and nurses basic training in providing such care (UNICEF, 1996 Report).

16. See Chapter 1.

17. UNICEF, 1996 Report. It is estimated that over 14 million women will be infected with the virus in the year 2000 and that four million of them will die from it.

18. *Le Monde*, 31 August 1995.

19. Ibid.

20. UNICEF Press Review, French Committee for UNICEF, 17 May 1995, 19 June 1995.

21. During the past decade, female unemployment has increased more rapidly than men's and women are more often constrained to accept unstable jobs. In France, nearly eight beneficiaries of the minimum integration income (RMI) out of ten are people living alone, most of them women. In the USA, nearly half of poor families who receive allowances are headed by women without a spouse or whose spouse is absent, and their income is on average 23% lower than the official poverty threshold.

22. International Labour Organization; see *Le Monde*, 26 August 1995.

23. An ILO study shows that in the past ten years, while women's salaries increased by 10% in the USA, they fell in relation to those of men in Germany, Denmark, Portugal, Japan and Turkey, and remained practically static in France, Belgium and the Netherlands. The same study estimates that in the industrialized countries 75% of women are employed in traditionally ill-paid jobs in the tertiary sector and that they are generally in the minority in high-level private-sector posts. See *Le Monde*, 26 August 1995.

24. *Le Monde*, 31 August 1995.

25. United Nations, Division for the Advancement of Women, 'Women 2000: women and decision-making', October 1997.

26. UNDP, *Human Development Report 1998*, and 'Women in government' (January 1996, United Nations, Division for the Advancement of Women).

27. United Nations, Division for the Advancement of Women, 'Women 2000'.

28. UNDP, *Human Development Report 1998*, classification of countries according to SHDI.

29. Rape in times of war or political violence is a particular problem. Women in Chile, Bosnia, Rwanda, Cambodia, Liberia and Somalia attested to this fact at the 1995 Beijing conference. Those acts are sometimes orchestrated for purposes of ethnic cleansing. It was in Beijing in September 1995 that, for the first time, an international text recognized rape as a war crime.

30. 'Dowry bride-burning in India, Part I', 3 February 1999, United Nations Radio Programmes – Women.

31. According to a demographer from Princeton University in the USA, Ansley Coale, 60 million girls and women in Eastern and Southern Asia are allegedly 'missing'. They would be alive today if there had not been any prenatal selection, infanticide or deaths caused by negligence.

32. *The Economist*, 5 August 1995.

33. Jodi Jacobson, 'Closing the gender gap in development', *State of the World 1993*, Worldwatch Institute.

34. UNDP, *Human Development Report 1995*.

35. World Bank, quoted in *Le Monde*, 31 August 1995.

36. Jacobson, 'Closing the gender gap'.

37. Ibid.

38. UNDP, quoted by G. Herzlich, *Le Monde*, 18 August 1995.

39. Jacobson, 'Closing the gender gap'.

40. Article 2 of the Universal Declaration of Human Rights.

41. Statement at the eighth meeting of the '21st Century Talks', organized by UNESCO, 8 June 1999. See Jérôme Bindé (ed.), *Les Clés du XXIe siècle*, Editions UNESCO/Seuil, Paris, 2000.

42. World Bank, study quoted in *Le Monde*, 31 August 1995.

43. *Courrier International*, special edition No. 10, October 1994.

44. Ibid. See also Muhammad Yunus, *Vers un Monde sans pauvreté*, J.C. Lattès, Paris, 1997.

45. Women Watch, an Internet information and chat space on the promotion of the status of women, was created on 8 March 1997 (International Women's Day) and brings together the Division for the Advancement of Women (DAW), the United Nations Development Fund for Women (UNIFEM) and the International Research and Training Institute for the Advancement of Women (INSTRAW).

46. UNDP, *Human Development Report 1995*.

47. Jack Lang, *Demain les Femmes*, Grasset, Paris, 1995.

CHAPTER 6

Winning the Fight Against Drugs: Education, Development and Purpose

A Rapidly Expanding Market

While many economists are rejoicing at the sustained growth of the world economy, there is one market in particular that is undergoing uninterrupted expansion throughout the world: the drug market, the cause of the most radical marginalization of human beings, since drugs abolish all notions of self or of other human beings.[1] According to the United Nations, profits derived from drug trafficking amount to $400 billion annually, that is to say 8% of world trade or, at a rough estimate, the equivalent of international trade in textiles in 1994,[2] or 1% of world GNP, or the GNP of the whole of Africa.[3] The production and consumption of drugs are rising constantly. According to the 1996 report of the International Narcotics Control Board (INCB), 'in spite of increased repression, production of and trafficking in drugs, together with drug addiction, have now reached hitherto preserved regions of the world'. As emphasized by an expert, 'Narco-states and narco-democracies, narco-terrorism and narco-guerrilla activities, narco-tourism and narco-dollars, are all signs that drugs have penetrated every sphere of political, economic and social life. The expansion of drug trafficking now goes hand in hand with the globalization of the economy and free market democracy.'[4] The highly efficient organization of drug trafficking, through a worldwide network based on extremely flexible and constantly changing units, has rendered any control of narcotics particularly difficult.[5] Production as such is still highly concentrated, as 90% of the illicit production of narcotics derived from opium worldwide originates from two major areas: the 'Golden Crescent' (Afghanistan, Iran and Pakistan) and the 'Golden Triangle' (Laos, Burma and Thailand) and 98% of world supplies of cocaine come from the Andean countries (Peru, Colombia and Bolivia).[6] But new connections have developed, production and trafficking areas have expanded and new synthetic drugs have appeared on the market. Drug trafficking is the hidden face of globalization.

It also happens to be one of its main beneficiaries, owing to increasingly porous national frontiers, the volatile nature of financial operations and the contagion of lifestyles, and even what might be called 'death styles'. INTERPOL estimates that only 5% to 15% of banned drugs are actually seized, which means that at least 85% of narcotics escape repression and circulate freely in a clandestine market controlled by criminals.[7]

According to OECD estimations, $85 billion derived from profits from such trafficking are laundered every year on the financial markets – that sum is greater than the GNP of three-quarters of the 207 economies in the world, according to a group of G7 experts.[8] The wealth accumulated by drug traffickers over the last 10 to 15 years could amount to as much as 'several trillion dollars'.[9] The drugs trade first and foremost 'benefits' the industrialized countries, if we may venture to say so: 90% of these sums is thought to be reinvested in the Western countries.[10] Many experts are increasingly concerned at the growing expansion of 'grey areas' within the world economy, which enable major organized crime networks to penetrate the very heart of some strategic spheres of the international economy such as the major world financial exchanges.[11] As pointed out by an expert, 'in every country, the banking system is actively involved in recycling drugs revenue, particularly through subsidiaries and correspondents established in the worldwide constellation of tax havens', which means, sometimes, that 'laundered money from drugs enables debt instalments to be paid or funds structural adjustment plans'.[12] The growing sophistication of financial operations, the globalization of the banking system, which is no longer hampered by frontiers and is able to operate round the clock, and the rapid emergence of unrecorded 'cyber-payments' require increased vigilance on the part of regulatory bodies and the extension of their partnership to the whole range of world financial institutions. The USA, for its part, recently advocated regulation of the non-banking financial sector, ranging from currency exchange and brokerage houses to casinos, as well as express delivery services, insurance firms and the precious-metal trade.[13] Multinational corporations and transnational finance companies should abide by codes of conduct in order to prevent the laundering of money derived from crime, whether it comes from drug trafficking, arms dealing or any form of criminal trade or mafia activity (embezzlement of public funds, racketeering, prostitution, illicit gambling, etc.).

The influence, whether overt or covert, of major criminal organizations, seemingly on the increase in many countries in both North and South, means that serious dangers are threatening economic ethics and the rule of law. According to the UNDP, expenditure on consumption of narcotics in the USA alone exceeds the accumulated GDP of more than eighty developing countries. Furthermore, organized crime has considerably extended its geographical areas of influence thanks to globalization and the development of drug trafficking, which often occurs in symbiosis with other criminal activities (arms trafficking, prostitution and the slave trade, the embezzlement of public funds, illegal gambling and penetration of the casino network by the mafia, etc.). The gigantic scale of illicit profits from drugs, together with the 'penetration' of entire sectors of the legal economy now controlled through money-laundering, could ultimately lead, through the dynamics of accumulation and concentration observed during the last two decades, to an irreversible situation whereby no state or organized force would be in a position to react as, through the laundering process, a substantial part of the economy and of pressure groups, in both North and South, would fall under the influence of drug trafficking. Keeping quiet in this matter amounts to observing the very principle that underlies the power of criminal organizations, namely the law of silence.

In our opinion, drug trafficking and consumption constitute one of the most serious threats to our planet, with disastrous consequences for health, development and society. We are all the more sensitive to this problem as we know all too well what effects drug addiction has on the brain's receptors and how irreversible lesions are caused above a certain level of consumption.[14] To these evils are added the effects of the spread of AIDS among drug addicts who absorb drugs intravenously. Young people, education and human values are affected first but drug addiction makes life unbearable for the whole family of the addict and, sooner or later, it is democracy itself that is threatened and, with it, peace. As pointed out by a specialist in this field, 'there is virtually no local conflict today that is not linked to a greater or lesser extent to drug trafficking'.[15] Drugs have become a form of violence not only towards the individual but also towards the whole of society.

Drugs are a threat not only to the human environment, but also to nature itself. The massive invasion of illegal crops has, in many countries, become one of the main sources of deforestation, soil erosion, contamination of rivers and of the ground water table through herbicides and pesticides, loss of biodiversity and excessive crop mobility. According to the Colombian government, four hectares of woodland have been destroyed for every hectare used for cultivating the coca plant, and 1.5 hectares of woodland are destroyed for every hectare used for cultivating marijuana. According to a report by the US State Department, 'the cultivation of coca in Peru, Bolivia and Colombia is responsible for 90% of the total deforestation recorded in those three countries'. 'Drug trafficking', in the words of an American official, 'is the main enemy of the environment, the cause of deforestation and the criminal contamination of water resources by toxic substances used for producing drugs.' Furthermore, the environment is also suffering from the massive use of defoliants used for eradicating drug crops.[16] It should be stressed, however, that in the case of 'synthetic' drugs, such intervention has little effect. What matters is first to reduce demand and, subsequently, to eradicate it. Instead of blaming the 'producer' countries, the 'consumer' countries should invest in prevention and in treating addicts – whether it be in human, affective, scientific or 'medical' terms. Like any other sick person, an addict should be able to benefit from the care he or she needs, and as quickly as possible. What is required is another vision of 'defence', that of citizens and not merely of national borders. Otherwise, we shall be heading for the absurd situation in which major defence facilities are at our disposal to defend territories in which insecurity, injustice and suffering are the norm.

We are particularly sensitive to drug-related problems as they often reflect the failure of our development strategies and, according to Hugues de Jouvenel, 'our incapacity to provide every individual with a proper place in society'.[17] At the same time, the profitability of trafficking makes drugs a genuine alternative to development, however criminally illusory, which gives rise to new markets, including in the producing countries. While the consumption of narcotics, for instance, would seem to be stagnating in much of the North, where nevertheless the largest market in the world for illicit drugs is to be found, 'the largest numbers of consumers are now to be found in the South'.[18] According to the United Nations, 'the highest rates of heroin addiction are no longer to be found in the developed countries but in a number of developing countries in Asia such as Pakistan and the highest rates of heroin abuse have also been observed in certain parts of Africa'.[19] A pluridisciplinary study produced by the United Nations International Drug Control Programme (UNDCP) states that in Pakistan, for example, where there was virtually no heroin addiction in 1979,[20] the consequences of heroin traffic have created, in the space of 15 years, a market of 1,500,000 consumers,[21] providing profits of $1.2 billion per year; similar phenomena can be observed in many other producing countries where the low price of drugs is compensated for by the scale of the market for them.

The fall in the prices of agricultural and mining raw materials has had a considerable influence on this surge in demand. The profits that peasant farmers can derive from drugs now considerably exceed those they can expect from traditional crops. While the income generated by the production of basic plants accounts for only some 3% of the final value of the product sold to the consumer, it is nevertheless five times higher on average than income from traditional crops.[22] When it has not actually led to the replacement of crops, the fall in prices has encouraged population drift from the countryside, which contributes to expanding shanty towns around cities. In these new urban jungles, where all the symptoms of exclusion and marginalization combine, unemployment and underemployment are sizeable. Here, the younger sections of the community, lacking any prospects, are offered the illegal counter-models of force and violence. In both the South and the North, in the urban and peri-urban ghettos, favelas, shanty towns and 'problem neighbourhoods', drug trafficking, in spite of the risks involved, has become the most profitable economic activity, if not the only activity for people who are unskilled, educational drop-outs and who, into the bargain, are *de facto* victims of social or ethnic discrimination on the labour market.

The ever greater inequality between the rich countries of the North and the poor countries of the South is largely responsible for the development of drug cultivation and production. Similarly, the development of dual societies, particularly in the mega-cities of the North and South, has substantially increased the number of consumers and dealers. Another tragic fact is that most local conflicts and many terrorist organizations are now funded by the 'super-profits' of drug trafficking, which also is an indirect cause of major epidemics. In Afghanistan, the annual production of opium, which was approximately 300 tonnes, has increased tenfold since the beginning of the war.[23] Drugs are like a tangled and twisted rope, tying up evil and misfortune and potentializing the effects of all social evils. They threaten the very purpose of any educational process and human venture and undermine the very idea of progress by reducing the chances of future generations. All these factors point to the need for rapid, concerted action on an international scale.

Eliminate Supply or Dry up Demand?

If effective action is to be taken against drugs, we must first of all open our eyes wider and open those of others. We need to discuss the problem with greater scientific rigour and critical awareness within the institutions that disseminate knowledge, namely schools, universities and all the channels of mass communication. Our task must be to show both clearly and unceasingly the real damage caused by the various drugs, the moral and physical servitude and the destruction of mind and body, attitudes and values, of which they are the cause. We must shed light on the harm caused to both society – starting with the immense suffering inflicted on the addict's family – and the individual. We must cease to portray drugs as malevolent yet attractive, and thus avoid demonizing them, as is too often the case, unaware that, in so doing, we turn them into a symbol of the urge to transgress social rules. If we cry 'Wolf!' too often, we are more likely to push young people towards drugs than to put them off. A survey recently conducted by a French opinion poll agency showed that for 52% and 44% respectively of drug-takers, pleasure and curiosity were the prime motive.[24] What we need to do is to demystify drugs by explaining to children that they are first and foremost a denial of existence, as stressed by Rita Levi-Montalcini, Nobel prizewinner in medicine, in her fine essay dedicated to young people, aptly entitled 'Your future'. Drugs will stop attracting adolescents once they have understood that they constitute, above all, a 'lessening of the power to act', as Spinoza might have put it, when he defined sadness in such terms in his work *Ethics*.

Some people believe that drugs should no longer be banned. According to these liberal-minded opponents of prohibition, it is through re-establishing control of narcotics by the legal economy that we can best fight the plagues which are the result of the illegal nature of the market, namely the enrichment of dealers and middlemen (which stimulates expansion of this trade), crime, violence, the marginalization of addicts, arms trafficking, terrorism and the suspicion of corruption that in many countries weighs on wide areas of public and political life. Nevertheless, we are among those who believe that we must firmly oppose the legalization of the non-therapeutic use of drugs. In that regard, the report of the International Narcotics Control Board (INCB) for 1997 deplored the existence of 'an overall climate of acceptance that is favourable to or at least tolerant of drug abuse'.[25] We can no more play around with narcotics than we can with weapons or medicinal drugs. The risk of a real surge in consumption is far too great. That is why drugs cannot be left to market forces, whether legal or illegal. In this domain, we cannot afford to be sorcerers' apprentices.

Conversely, the idea that it is possible to eliminate the production and consumption of drugs, however commendable it may be, strikes us as being scarcely credible. Many commentators are now advocating the replacement of prohibition policies by measures to reduce the harmful effects of drugs, in the belief that 'drugs are here to stay and we have no choice but to learn to live with them so that they cause the least possible harm'.[26] The policy of all-round repression can fail because, by making drugs scarcer, it merely makes drug trafficking more lucrative for new networks that have replaced earlier ones. While we thought that we were fighting organized crime, we were actually strengthening its financial power and capacity to corrupt, and dragging down large sections of society into delinquency.

A recent report states that 'Despite regional successes supply suppression is not a prescription for solving the world's illicit-drug problem. It is a prescription for funding drug mafias, peasant growers, petty traffickers and smugglers.'[27] There is naturally a price to pay for such a policy: several tens of billions of dollars are spent every year on repression, with results that, to put it mildly, are hardly convincing: delinquency in a growing part of society (the inner cities, ghettos, minorities, the younger generation, the interaction between consumption and 'petty trafficking', etc.), and the corresponding excessive growth of the repressive and penitentiary system, which ultimately penalizes addicts rather than traffickers. Everything, therefore, needs to be changed. On the one hand, an efficient judicial and penitentiary system must be set up to deal with drug dealers. On the other hand, preventive and curative measures should be introduced on a large scale. We must stress that addicts need to be given treatment – and adequate funds should be allocated for that purpose – by bringing into play all the means required, whether they be medical, scientific or of another nature.

We must therefore learn how to deal with the problems of drug addiction in our societies while reducing this phenomenon to a minimum and avoiding the criminalization of addicts. In terms of public health alone, realistic public policies 'for reducing the harmful effects' are required to respond to the fact that the total absence of control over the drugs market is a powerful vector for the development of AIDS and other epidemics: the distribution of free syringes helped in several countries to lower the contamination of drug addicts by HIV. Moreover, we believe the time has come to contemplate an international agreement whereby it would be possible, under medical supervision, to distribute a limited quantity of drugs to addicts who are not able to break out of addiction.[28] Drug addicts should be treated as patients rather than delinquents. As such, patients have a right to benefit from medical supervision and social assistance in much the same way as any human being suffering from a curable pathology. What is more, such a measure could reduce violence and delinquency and contribute to dismantling the illegal drugs market and, therefore, the major source of profits for organized crime. The difficulty underlying such a policy can be summarized as follows: any agreement would have to be international, as policies for fighting against drugs can no longer be conceived in purely national terms. Harmonizing the policies of various states would be the key to effectiveness in this field where interdependence is particularly marked.[29]

Clearly, such a policy will have to be accompanied by an in-depth survey on the specific harmfulness of drugs by the scientific and medical community, in close cooperation with the relevant national and international authorities. Such concertation might, as suggested by a French consultative body, make it possible to establish regulations for each substance, 'taking account of its toxicity, the risks of dependence relating to its consumption, the danger of desocialization it might entail and the risks to which its consumption might expose other people'.[30]

Prevention by educating and informing the public would also be indispensable for this project. We need the help of the media, as well as municipal and local authorities, to foster appropriate awareness, commitment and participation and to ensure that drug addiction does not become commonplace, the lame excuse of a society that tolerates the degeneration and distress of those who symbolize its future, namely, its younger generations. The Youth Charter for a Twenty-first Century Free from Drugs (1997), which received the support of UNESCO and the United Nations Programme for International Narcotics Control (UNPINC), rightly states that 'the first experiences with drugs are often motivated by curiosity, idleness, lack of self-confidence, indifference and violence in our immediate surroundings, but also by the difficulties and trials of everyday life'.[31]

Many experts and institutions nevertheless continue to give priority to reducing the supply of drugs. One of the solutions for reducing the production and therefore the supply of drugs would be to develop sufficiently lucrative alternative crops and new markets for the peasant farmers whose livelihood depends on poppy and coca cultivation. To do that, the cooperation of the peasant farmers concerned is all the more important in the choice of new crops as the cultivation of toxic plants is often related to cultural traditions. They need to be made aware of the dangers of drugs for their health and for the life of their community, as well as for the well-being of the whole of humanity. Unfortunately, policies for the eradication of plantations and help for the substitution of illegal crops have often failed and have had adverse effects through ignorance of the cultural factors of development, the local social environment, the requirements of sustainable development, as well as through anthropocentric naivety.

In such circumstances, the establishment of a scheme for subsidies and guaranteed prices for new crops bringing into play national and international resources would seem indispensable. In this type of situation, the international community, by lending its financial support, could invest in the future with success, benefit and a sense of long-term vision.

In addition to these difficulties, replacing drugs with alternative crops, in the absence of accompanying structural measures and international support, would appear virtually condemned to failure for four main reasons. No government would seem ready to pay the very high price of replacing crops worldwide, if the operation had to be subsidized. No agricultural production, on the basis of market prices, would be competitive with the price of base plants. Furthermore, the economy of many producing countries, which are often very poor, is now increasingly based on drugs. It is no secret, as illustrated by various reports produced by the United Nations, that the drug industry accounts for as much as 20% of GNP for some countries.[32] Worse still, once crops have actually been eradicated in a particular country, the outcome is disappointing and deceptive as production moves elsewhere, often to a neighbouring country.[33]

A global threat requires a global solution. A large-scale threat calls for large-scale solutions. Many countries are members of major international alliances that guarantee their borders and security. If we wish to mark the advent of the new century by making a fresh start, we must then have comparable alliances at our disposal for combating drugs, as would be required for combating global catastrophes of all kinds. The drugs problem should not be confined to protracted, trivial discussions on the respective responsibility of the producer and consumer countries: such a dispute is all the more futile as the frontier between the former and the latter has become increasingly blurred since the explosion of consumption in the South. Let us endeavour instead to fight the causes of supply and demand by offering acceptable living conditions and a better future to the peasant farmers attracted by illicit but more profitable crops, to the middlemen who, in many underprivileged countries or communities, often have no alternative income and to the consumers who, through lack of education and information, are ignorant of the dangers of drugs or who feel excluded from a society in which they are not able to fashion their own lives. Let us give hope and a future to them all. The terrible effects of drug addiction on human dignity constitute a powerful illustration of the importance of preventive action, which involves educating young people as early as possible.

Let us recall that international action against drug trafficking began some 80 years ago when the opium trade came under international jurisdiction. Since then, the multilateral system has devised many conventions and plans of action for combating this traffic which, at the highest levels of responsibility, may be considered to be a crime against humanity. In fact, the United Nations General Assembly proclaimed the 1990s as the 'United Nations Decade against Drugs'.

The most efficient means of fighting against drug trafficking is, as stated by the Italian judge, Giovanni Falcone, shortly before he was assassinated by the Mafia, 'the destruction of the financial power of organized crime, which would presuppose powerful international collaboration'.[34] This alone can help to prevent the emergence of the 'chain of connivance' composed of obscure acts of corruption and unavowed links described by the great Sicilian writer, Leonardo Sciascia, in his novel *The Context*, published in 1971. It is that chain of connivance that undermines democratic institutions and threatens their legitimate representatives.[35]

Judge Falcone added that it was necessary, with that aim in mind, to encourage and coordinate 'efforts aimed at identifying and confiscating wealth of illegal origin', which requires 'adapting international laws and achieving constant international collaboration'. Giovanni Falcone advocated 'first and foremost, the elimination of tax havens which, up to now, have countered the most serious attempts of various countries to identify financial flows originating from illegal trafficking'. According to Judge Falcone, 'this is a fight that concerns all members of the international community because its outcome will determine whether organized crime is destroyed or at least limited in such a way as to be no longer a serious peril for society'. The advice and sacrifice of Judge Falcone would not seem to have been totally pointless: since then, the Italian magistracy has intensified the seizure of assets of illegal origin, while the profits of the four major Italian criminal organizations (estimated by the Italian Anti-Mafia Investigatory Department at 10 trillion lire, or 30% of a turnover estimated at 30 trillion in 1994), seem to have shrunk massively in the same year.[36]

Furthermore, the production of narcotics is by no means limited to substances of natural origin. In its 1996 and 1997 reports, the INCB highlighted the preoccupying expansion throughout the world of synthetic drugs, particularly amphetamines or by-products, such as ecstasy, produced in clandestine laboratories. They supply a very lucrative illicit market for dealers and meet with alarming success among young people. The US Department of State believes that amphetamines, on account of their simple manufacturing process and the sudden growth in demand, are about to become 'the drug-control nightmare of the next century'.[37] In the face of this growing threat, which, paradoxically, has benefited from progress achieved in the field of pharmaceutical research, new measures for control, information, research and education are required, particularly for the benefit of young people.

There is therefore no miracle solution to the drugs problem. As long as there is demand, there will be supply. As noted by the UNDP in a lucid report, the real solution requires tackling the causes of drug addiction and eliminating the poverty that leads farmers to become involved in producing narcotics.[38]

We are particularly concerned with the consequences of drug consumption on the fate of street children who, today, number more than 100 million and who are fighting every day to survive in conditions of total deprivation. These children are those who are most threatened by violence, sexual and economic exploitation, AIDS, hunger, solitude and the scourges of exclusion, illiteracy and drugs. They are the 'golden fish' referred to by the French novelist Le Clézio which the ill-intentioned fishermen in search of innocent prey attempt to catch in their nets. Everything must be done to ensure that these children are fully integrated into society, that they learn to live in it, that they have access to education and that they are no longer manipulated by criminals who make them serve their evil purposes. The latter deserve to be punished all the more severely as by destroying innocence, they attempt to eradicate faith and confidence in the future.

The fight against drug addiction – like that against AIDS or against the collective shame represented by street children and children who are sexually or professionally exploited – will not be truly effective unless it is based on a major alliance between all countries, translated practically into a political will not to abandon the cause, just as we defend our country when national sovereignty is in jeopardy. In fact, in all the cases we have just referred to, it is national dignity that is threatened, which cannot be defended simply through charity or by organizing tombolas and galas. The best way of celebrating human rights, the fiftieth anniversary of the declaration of which we celebrated in 1998, would be an internationally reached decision aimed at ensuring its effective exercise by all human beings. The rest is no more than ceremony and empty rhetoric. The United Nations International Drug Control Programme (UNDCP) should be one of the most powerful in the entire United Nations system, in terms both of its authority and of its resources. This should also be the case, in a different field, for the United Nations of Environment Programme (UNEP). The limited means available to these programmes reflect a lack of political will and of public awareness as to what is required for combating drugs or preserving the global environment. We are, to varying degrees, all responsible for this twofold deficiency.

To fight against drug-related problems, the causes of marginalization and exclusion have to be tackled by investing in the welfare of young people, particularly through sports and training activities. It is UNESCO's responsibility to fight against the demand for drugs through education, and more especially preventive education. While education may be the main victim of drugs, it is also its best antidote. In fact, it is thanks to education that young people can become aware of the real dangers of narcotics, that they can escape 'the blues' and find their true path in society, and that they can acquire the knowledge and ethical attitudes that will enable them to assert their own personality and take their destiny in hand. Instead of paying the price for war and over-investing in armed defence, let us invest in the peaceful defence of individuals and young people, in cultural security and in genuine spiritual freedom which access to the world of knowledge and freedom from any servitude, can provide. Once education is widely perceived as having the objective of 'ensuring that people have control over their lives', then it is through education that any form of dependency can be combated, such as dependency on alcohol, tobacco, drugs and sects, etc. Through education we can learn to be free and responsible.

More than ever before, the vital issue is the political will of governments to agree on effective solutions and on implementing them. More than ever, UNESCO has a major role to play in the context of its fields of competence: education and information against drug abuse, communication activities among the populations, and the contribution of the social sciences and scientific research in order to fine tune action plans and national and international strategies, and to assess the specific harmfulness of drugs, which are a subject of debate.[39]

To be perfectly frank, however, education and information alone cannot, even in the long term, be the only solutions in this field, nor can development if it is reduced to mere economic prosperity. Without referring to the great minds who succumbed to 'artificial paradises', it is striking to observe the number of people with a high level of education and a comfortable income, who consume drugs in a number of countries. Psychological malaise as reflected by drug addiction cannot be cured merely by knowledge as, to paraphrase Henri Michaux, the poet, knowledge itself may lead to an abyss. If the twenty-first century is to win the battle against drug addiction (which some experts in science fiction doubt, imagining, on the contrary, the expansion of a form of 'addiction to soft drugs' controlled by the neurosciences and pharmacology), it will have to win the battle against nihilism, consumerism, and the fruitless pursuit of intoxication and ecstasy. We shall have to bring about a 'global mobilization' of governments, parliaments, the media, industry and society as a whole against drugs and addiction. The next century will have to give a new meaning to life.

Education, economic development and material well-being will probably not suffice to eliminate drugs even if they are the major instruments of prevention. To think so would be to imagine that human beings can be prevented from walking along the edge of precipices, from seeking to experience ecstasy or trance or, quite simply, from wanting to poison themselves. What therefore has to be done is to construct humanity's defences in people's minds, all the more so as drugs tempt the minds as much as they do the body. Thus new forms of wisdom and ethics will have to develop. What must also be done is to build humanity's defences by investing in human dignity, by reducing dire poverty, racism and exclusion. Fighting against drugs, the source of destruction, suffering and war, also means responding to the aims of the founders of UNESCO. It simply means building peace and development on the basis of the intellectual and moral solidarity of humanity. Fighting against drugs, in a united effort, with human and financial means that correspond to the scale of the plague, means protecting young people, our children and our future. It also means speeding up the transition from a culture of violence, war and indignity to a culture of peace, non-violence and dignity for all.

Pointers and Recommendations

- Reduce the demand for drugs in consumer countries, particularly through education, prevention and treatment.
- Educate and inform children and young people about the risks of drug consumption.
- Mobilize the international community against the main causes of drug consumption which are marginalization and poverty, in both urban and rural environments.
- Develop specific machinery, on international, regional and national scales, for fighting against corruption, the laundering of money from drugs and organized crime. Encourage ratification and implementation of international treaties related to narcotics control and the conclusion of international agreements aimed at destroying the financial power of organized crime.
- Help drug addicts to overcome their dependency and to adopt a sustainable

lifestyle without drug consumption, through appropriate educational, rehabilitation and vocational training programmes.

- Reduce the perverse effects of drug trafficking and consumption (financial development of organized crime, criminalization, delinquency and social pathologies) by studying the feasibility, on an international scale, of an agreement that, under medical supervision, would allow addicts who are in need and incapable of giving up their habit a limited supply of drugs.
- Give serious consideration to the adoption of 'reduction of the harmful effects' policies implemented in various countries under the terms of a policy and a world programme for narcotics control.
- Encourage scientific and medical research on the specific harmfulness of drugs and scientific research on the environmental impact of drug cultivation.
- Plan for the convening of a world summit on drugs, organized by the United Nations (United Nations International Drug Control Programme and the World Health Organization), which would take account of all aspects, whether old or new, of the problem of drug consumption and trafficking. Strengthen the means and authority of the UNDCP.
- Bring about a 'global mobilization' of governments, parliaments, the media, industry and society against drugs and addiction.

Notes

1. The term 'drugs' refers to narcotics and psychotropic substances as defined by the relevant international conventions.

2. UNDCP, *1997 World Drug Report*, Oxford University Press, New York, 1997; *Le Monde*, 27 June 1997.

3. Eric de la Maisonneuve, *La Violence qui vient*, Éditions Arléa, Paris, 1997.

4. Christian de Brie, 'La drogue dopée par le marché', *Le Monde Diplomatique*, April 1996.

5. Hugues de Jouvenel, 'L'inextricable marché des drogues illicites', *Futuribles*, No. 185, March 1994 (special issue 'Géopolitique et économie politique de la drogue').

6. UNDCP, *1997 World Drug Report*.

7. Address by the director-general of UNESCO at the 58th session of the United Nations International Narcotics Control Board (INCB), Vienna, 9 May 1995.

8. Quoted in UNDP, *1994 World Report on Human Development*, UNDP, Economica, Paris, 1994, p. 37; *UN Chronicle*, No. 3, 1996.

9. Alain Labrousse, *Les Idées en mouvement*, No. 35, January 1996.

10. Alain Labrousse, interview in *Le Nouvel Observateur*, 19–25 September 1996.

11. See 'The Mob on Wall Street', *Business Week*, 16 December 1996; Laurent Zecchini, 'La "pieuvre" mafieuse prolifère à Wall Street', *Le Monde*, 3 January 1997; Brie, 'La drogue dopée par le marché'; LaMond Tullis, *Unintended Consequences: Illegal Drugs and Drug Policies in Nine Countries*, Studies on the Impact of the Illegal Drug Trade,

Vol. 4, series editor LaMond Tullis, United Nations University and United Nations Research Institute for Social Development, Lynne Rienner, Boulder, CO and London, 1995.

12. De Brie, *Monde Diplomatique* feature, *Le Monde Diplomatique*, February 1996.

13. US Department of State, *International Narcotics Control Strategy Report, 1996*, March 1997.

14. Address by the director-general of UNESCO at the 58th session of the United Nations International Narcotics Control Board (INCB), Vienna, 9 May 1995.

15. Labrousse, *Les Idées en mouvement*.

16. Data drawn from the study by Viviana Macias Vences, 'El control de drogas en la zona Andina: una propuesta ecologica', thesis dissertation, Universidad Iberoamericana, Mexico City, 1994.

17. De Jouvenel, 'L'inextricable marché'.

18. Pierre Kopp and Michel Schiray, 'Les sciences sociales face à la drogue', *Futuribles*, No. 185, March 1994, pp. 5–7.

19. Report by the United Nations secretary-general, 4 June 1996.

20. Alain Labrousse, 'Géopolitique de la drogue: les contraditions des politiques de "guerre à la drogue"', *Futuribles*, March 1994, pp. 9–22.

21. Alain Labrousse, in *Les Idées en mouvement*, No. 35, January 1996.

22. De Brie, 'La drogue dopée par le marché'; de Jouvenel, 'L'inextricable marché'.

23. Labrousse, *Les Idées en mouvement*.

24. Patrick Piro, *Les Idées en mouvement*, No. 35, January 1996.

25. Report of the International Narcotics Control Board, 1997, para. 20.

26. Ethan A. Nadelmann, 'Commonsense drug policy', *Foreign Affairs*, January/February 1998, p. 112; Anthony Lewis, 'The war on drugs is being lost', *International Herald Tribune*, 6 January 1998.

27. LaMond Tullis, *Unintended Consequences*, p. 183.

28. See address by the director-general of UNESCO at the 58th session of the United Nations International Narcotics Control Board (INCB), Vienna, 9 May 1995.

29. Kopp and Schiray, 'Les sciences sociales'.

30. Conclusions of the Comité consultatif national d'éthique (CCNE), November 1994, quoted in Observatoire géopolitique des drogues, *Géopolitique des Drogues 1995*, Paris, 1995.

31. Charter co-ordinated by the NGO Environnement sans frontière, with the support of UNESCO and the United Nations Programme for International Narcotics Control (UNPINC). The signatories also emphasized that 'drug trafficking and use are a threat to the development and progress of our societies, they invariably cause greater violence, crime, exploitation and other infringements of our rights' and that the fight against drugs hinges on guaranteeing 'peace, freedom, democracy, solidarity, justice, protection of the environment and access to employment'.

32. UNDP, *World Report on Human Development*, 1994.

33. Ibid.

34. Giovanni Falcone, 'What is the mafia?', lecture to the Bundeskriminalamt (Wiesbaden), 1990, *Frankfurter Allgemeine Zeitung*, 27 May 1992, reproduced in *Esprit*, No. 185, October 1992, pp. 111–18.

35. See *Le Monde*, 10 February 1998, 'Cadavres exquis'. 'Cadavres exquis' is the French title of Francesco Rosi's film *Cadaveri Eccellenti*, based on Leonardo Sciascia's novel *The Context*.

36. *Libération*, 13 September 1995.

37. US Department of State, *International Narcotics Control Strategy Report, 1996*, March 1997.

38. UNDP, *World Report on Human Development*, 1994.

39. See for example, 'Marijuana: special report', *New Scientist*, 21 February 1998.

PART TWO

Towards a Natural Contract: Science, Development and the Environment

. . . .

CHAPTER 7

Developing with the Earth

§ RECENT concern for the preservation of our environment is an indication of a profound change in attitudes: starting scarcely one or two generations ago, this cultural, scientific and social metamorphosis broke with a long tradition of indifference and even hostility. For many centuries, human beings regarded nature as an object and sought to subordinate it to their domination. By disenchanting the natural world and by making human beings the masters and owners of the universe, modernity carried to the extreme the grand design of 'dominating the Earth', which had for long been identified with progress and the great discourse of emancipation of the Age of Enlightenment and industrial society – liberalism, scientism, socialism, Marxism and technological determinism. The enslavement of nature to human desires and needs was regarded as the distinctive feature of an advanced society, evidence of economic growth and a prerequisite for the welfare of the population.

Since the end of the Second World War, however, the limits of this approach have become perceptible. The first to sound the alarm were scientists who, at the initiative of UNESCO, undertook in the post-war period the first international studies on arid zones and established the first major networks for studying and preserving the environment. Damage caused to the natural environment ceased to be anecdotal, especially since it appeared that the multiplication of points of impact was threatening the safety of ecosystems. Henceforth, the security of the environment is one of the essential components of national and international security: the Chernobyl disaster acted as an alarm signal in this regard. Collective attitudes have themselves profoundly changed. In less than fifty years, for example, the popular perception of the Amazon basin has evolved from that of a 'green hell' to that of an 'emerald forest'. Traditional representations of a 'hostile', untamed world have given way to the diametrically opposite view of a heritage to be respected and managed judiciously.[1] A few decades ago, a visionary such as Gregory Bateson[2] was indeed an isolated figure when he affirmed, against Darwinian tradition, that the unit of survival was not the reproductive individual, or the lineage, or species or sub-species, but a flexible entity: an organism in its environment, and that an ecology of the human mind should correspond to an ecology of nature. Little by little, these ideas have begun to gain ground.

In future, the economy and the environment can no longer be dealt with separately. More than ever before, we must anticipate what the consequences of human activities will be on the environment within the next 20 to 30 years. The world population is growing and adopting new methods of cultivation, production and consumption. Most of the developing countries are still experiencing rapid demographic growth while the rich ones continue to consume raw materials, space and energy. Consequently, the ecosystem is under a twofold threat: 'excessive pressure from consumption in the North and excessive pressure from population and basic needs in the South'.[3] What is more, the rapid spread of production methods and styles of consumption of the North to the emerging economies and sizeable parts of many developing countries is increasing this pressure and will do so even more in the coming decades.

As underlined by William Rees and Matthis Wackernagel, the 'ecological footprint' of the inhabitants of the USA, Germany or Japan is up to ten times greater than that of the populations of China or India.[4] If the latter were to catch up with the former, humanity would need three planets the size of the earth in order to meet the needs in natural resources of a world population of eight billion people. Therefore, the current development models of the most advanced countries of the North could not be reproduced as such either in space or in time, without threatening the survival of the biosphere. The North would therefore be well advised to convert to ecological frugality as quickly as possible in order to reduce its negative impact on the global environment and the mimetic contagion of its consumption patterns in the South.

New Threats on the Horizon

The dangers weighing on the planetary environment are of many kinds. Serge Antoine suggests that in the countries of the South alone – even without any rise in living standards – carbon monoxide emissions in the atmosphere will be multiplied by four or five during the next 40 years. On a planetary scale, if greenhouse gas emissions continue to increase by 10% to 20% every ten years, their concentration could quadruple during the next century: global warming would then progress at a pace 10 to 50 times that which the Earth has experienced in 10,000 years.[5] Likewise, a surface area comparable to that of France is desertified each year in the world.[6] If deforestation continues at the present pace, rainforests will have been eliminated from the surface of the globe by 2050.[7] According to the most recent estimates of the United Nations

Food and Agriculture Organization (FAO), some 9.9 billion hectares of forest disappeared annually between 1981 and 1990. According to the World Wide Fund for Nature (WWF), some 15 million hectares of rainforest are destroyed each year. The WWF has also worked out, on the basis of United Nations data, that from some 8 billion hectares of primary forests that existed 8,000 years ago, no more than 3 billion exist today.[8] Deforestation wrought by man not only has dramatic consequences for biological diversity; it is also the major cause of concentration of carbon monoxide in the atmosphere.[9]

Emissions of carbon monoxide and other greenhouse gases have brought about dramatic changes that we cannot yet measure with any accuracy. Nevertheless, careful consideration of data collected over the last 130 years on average temperatures throughout the world has shown that the ten hottest years have all occurred since 1980.[10] According to a recent report from the National Oceanic and Atmospheric Administration in the United States, '1997 was the hottest year ever recorded since a system of measurement was introduced in this field' and the first five months of 1998 confirmed the average temperature rise on a world scale.[11] According to forecasts from the Intergovernmental Panel on Climate Change (IPCC), if the current trend continues, global warming may reach 1 to 3.5 degrees Celsius by the end of the twenty-first century;[12] some scientists on the panel seriously contemplate a rise of as much as 5°.

If such warming were to occur, the consequences would be dramatic. It must be borne in mind that a difference of 5°C in relation to the current climate average would entail consequences on a scale similar to the major climatic upheavals in geological history.[13] In coastal regions, the rising sea level would be likely to engulf vast inhabited areas or even entire island states such as the Maldives, aggravate sea erosion problems and multiply the risks of disastrous flooding as in Bangladesh. Global warming could raise the level of the oceans by between 15 and 95 centimetres; we must bear in mind that 80% of the world population now live less than 180 kilometres away from a coastline, and 21% live less than 30 kilometres away. The Hadley Centre for Climate Prediction and Research has stated furthermore that the growth rate of populations living within 30 kilometres of a coastline is twice that of the rest of the world population. Satellite monitoring has indicated that, between 1992 and 1995, the sea level had already risen by 3 millimetres per year.

The rise in temperatures has already brought about a faster thaw of the glaciers, observed in the Alps and the Andes alike. Researchers at ORSTOM, a French institute of research on development, have calculated[14] that the glaciers in Peru receded three times more rapidly after 1980 than they had during the previous decade; in Bolivia, '[the phenomenon] has been five times faster than during the previous four decades'.[15] This discovery is all the more worrying as the Andean glaciers provide a vital source of freshwater supplies during the dry season. According to the forecasts of IPCC experts, if the thaw continues at the present rate, 'between a third and half of the overall mass of existing Alpine glaciers could disappear during the next 100 years'.[16] Some experts even believe that all the Alpine glaciers will have disappeared by the end of the twenty-first century.

The thaw of the icecap at the poles combined with a rise in average rainfall – two predictable consequences of climate warming – could in the long term have paradoxical repercussions on some regions such as Europe. The disruption of Atlantic currents, particularly the Gulf Stream, whose waters contribute to the warming of the European coastline, could lead to a sharp fall in temperatures and winters comparable with those of Canada.[17]

Other consequences could affect biodiversity and ecosystems and some animal and plant species could disappear, particularly in Northern Europe. Climatic warming could prove particularly harmful to agriculture, in Africa in particular, where yields could fall by 30%, as well as in Pakistan, Kazakhstan, Mexico and in several regions of Brazil and Chile.[18]

Climatic warming could also have serious consequences for public health. According to a group of medical experts, including Eric Chivian, director of the Centre for Health and the Environment at Harvard University, eight million people are likely to die by 2020 of diseases transmitted by mosquitoes and on account of water contamination if nothing is done to fight against global warming.[19] Worldwide spread of malaria is likely to be one of the more dangerous consequences of global warming unless a truly efficient vaccine is found for that disease.

In addition to the dangers related to climatic warming, other trends are particularly alarming. We should be more mindful of the fact that by neglecting the quality of soils, we are likely to jeopardize their future capacity to respond to population needs. Already more than one-quarter of the land area for cultivation and stockbreeding has been degraded, more or less seriously. Every year, some 10 million hectares become unusable as a result of overworking. This waste corresponds to an annual loss of approximately 0.2% of the world's agricultural productive capacity.

The consequences of water pollution are just as serious. In the developing countries where water treatment systems are often non-existent or deficient, hundreds of millions of people are likely to fall ill each day because they are forced to drink water unfit for human consumption. Most cases of infantile mortality can be accounted for by the consumption of polluted water. Furthermore, polluted water is largely discharged into the sea, which means that coastal regions – which are usually the most heavily populated – are faced with serious problems of public health and conservation of fish populations.

Increasingly frequent natural disasters are of particular concern. According to data gathered by the United Nations, the number of major natural disasters

– cyclones, droughts, floods, avalanches, forest fires, tidal waves and earth-quakes[20] – has increased fourfold[21] during the last 30 years. At this pace, some two million more people are likely to be displaced each year on account of natural catastrophes. A new category of refugees, 'ecological refugees', has already appeared and the United Nations system will undoubtedly have to study this problem in the next few years.

Ever scarcer natural resources and parallel population growth in the developing world are likely to give rise to fierce competition, or even trigger major conflicts, particularly when other factors stir up violence. Acting today to ensure that the environment can be preserved also means investing in the future of democracy. Conversely, if excessive degradation of our planet continues, we are likely, sooner or later, to see authoritarian or even neo-fascist regimes imposing draconian environmental policies.[22]

Shouldering Responsibility for the Future

Caution is required: precaution in regard to today's environmental problems and also as regards those that could arise tomorrow. The upheavals we have witnessed since the beginning of the twentieth century give some indication of the uncertainty that is a feature of our future and the scale of transformations we will undoubtedly have to cope with. As noted by François Ewald, the principle of precaution 'illustrates the inverted relationship with science, whereby it appeals to us less for the trust it procures than for the doubts and suspicions it can nurture as regards both what we know and what we do not know'.[23]

Henceforth, the principle of precaution laid down by the Earth Summit in Rio de Janeiro in 1992 should guide international and national policies as well as the action of society in the private sector. If we do not act 'in time', future generations will have no time in which to act at all: they are likely to become prisoners of processes that have become uncontrollable. If short-term economic interests prevail over scientific rigour and ecological considerations, it will be impossible to attain the objective of sustainable development. We must realize that we are all in the same boat: those who are already born, wherever they may be, and those who are yet to be born. We must combine forces, those of governments, scientific and technological communities and public and private sectors in order to face our common future. A future which, it is to be hoped, will be more sharing than the past.[24] As the pace of change increases, it is becoming increasingly difficult to define 'acceptable' risk thresholds precisely, which means that we must manage the environment on the basis of presuppositions rather than certitudes. All in all, this century leaves us no choice: we shall have to learn to prepare for the unforeseeable; hence the need to review and redefine the issue of the environment. So far, priority has been given to the treatment of 'flows' (pollution or exploitation of resources); in future we shall have to give much more attention to management and restoration of 'stocks', which will require both an effort to prevent irreversible phenomena and the rehabilitation of degraded environments.

More than ever, governing means being vigilant. Vigilance, however, cannot be the sole responsibility of public or private authorities. It must increasingly fall to citizens themselves if they do not wish to lose control of democracy – and they will have to establish this vigilance on a global scale.

When applied to the new technologies, the principle of precaution calls for the greatest vigilance. While new technologies offer frequently promising prospects for sustainable development, they can also generate a new range of risks. Globally speaking, technical progress is directed towards reducing consumption of resources per unit produced, but it also involves diversification and 'complexification' of risks: for example, more than 1,000 new chemical products are brought onto the market every year. Is there any country that has the time and the will to test them all? Caution is therefore required, as it is often impossible to forecast the long-term effects of certain innovations in

---

Box 7.1 Towards Further Major Disasters?

The G8 Ministerial Conference on the Environment – composed of ministers from the seven most industrialized countries and the Russian Federation – held at Leeds Castle, United Kingdom, on 5 April 1998, referred to climatic disruption as 'the greatest threat to worldwide sustainable development, public health and future prosperity'. In fact, the overall situation is hardly encouraging. The year 1997–98, which was particularly dramatic from this point of view, seemed to herald the return of major catastrophes. The hottest year in meteorological history witnessed a multiplication of these phenomena: persistent fires and drought in Indonesia, South-east Asia and the South Pacific, a delayed monsoon; outbreaks of fire in the Amazonian forests (where it rained five times more than usual); 11,000 uncontrolled outbreaks of fire in Mexico; floods, landslides and the appearance of vast artificial lakes in Peru, Ecuador, Colombia, Chile and Argentina; and the African continent affected from east to west by drought. Instead of bringing some respite, the year 1998–99 seems to have reproduced and amplified these disruptions: flooding in China, Korea, Japan and Bangladesh; the hurricane Mitch in Central America; an abnormally mild winter in Europe and in North America and forest fires that ravaged Greece and Italy during the summer of 1998.

The scientific community is divided as to how to account for the

the industrial field. Furthermore, in the environmental field, the prospect of rapid adaptation of supply to demand is virtually illusory. Ecology belongs to the realm of slow-moving systems. For example, an increase in the presence of mercury in Swedish lakes was recently observed, some 25 years after its use had been banned in the paper-making industry.[25]

Mixed Accomplishments

Over the last generation, the efforts of the international community have often proved useful, particularly when they anticipated the development of phenomena for which the certainty of harmful effects appeared only recently – which shows how essential the role of forecasting has become in national and international policies. Action to protect the ozone layer provides a good illustration. The Vienna Convention on the Protection of the Ozone Layer, signed in 1985 by 150 countries and supplemented, in 1987, by the Montreal Protocol on Substances that Deplete the Ozone Layer, has produced particularly interesting results. For the first time, the United Nations obtained

increase in climatic 'accidents'. Is it possible, however, to eschew responsability by arguing that such events are exceptional? Can we continue to talk about 'out of the ordinary' events when these recur to the point of becoming the norm?

We have military alliances on a sub-regional scale that have substantial technical means at their disposal for confronting potential enemies, but what have we done to face the numerous environmental threats? When forests burn, when hurricanes and natural disasters that have dramatic consequences on populations multiply, where are the subregional alliances to cope with the situation? Where are the planes and the sophisticated technical means for detecting such threats, for preventing disasters or for reducing their impact? The answer is obvious enough: for centuries we have made preparations for war but not for improving the environment, avoiding degradation and reducing the impact of phenomena such as earthquakes, flooding and fires. We shall be able to cope with these threats not by relying on courts of law that pronounce judgments in the wake of such phenomena, but rather through preventive measures, which alone can help to address efficiently such important issues for our common future.

Source: 'L'année de toutes les catastrophes', *Le Monde*, 6 August 1998; Federico Mayor, address given at the opening of the Intergovernmental Conference on Cultural Policies for Development, Stockholm, March 1998.

statistically backed commitments to protect the environment. Estimations dating from 1995 show that emissions of CFC gases decreased 76% in relation to their maximum level in 1988.[26] According to the Montreal Protocol, the production of CFCs was to have totally ceased in the industrialized countries by 1996 and in the developing countries by 2010. Fifty-eight developing countries have already stated that they would be in a position to put an end to the use of CFCs before 2010. This initiative taken by the industrialized countries seems exemplary.

Nevertheless, the battle is far from having been won: the latest observations by the World Meteorological Organization (WMO) have revealed that deterioration of the ozone layer over Antarctica has never been stronger and that in September 1998 the hole in the ozone layer covered a surface area two and a half times that of Europe.[27] Thanks, however, to efforts made so far, experts predict that measures to restrict the use of CFCs will begin to have an effect from 2004 onwards and if the provisions of the international protocols are observed, the ozone layer could be completely restored by 2050.[28]

Conversely, the four conventions dealing with biological diversity, climate change, the fight against desertification and the law of the sea have scarcely been applied and have hardly had any effect. We could also quote the Statement of Principles on Forests, which is not legally binding. However, the conclusion of the major conventions on the planetary environment does have the merit of having brought together the countries of the North and those of the South so that they might begin to tackle environmental problems together. Now that a preliminary international legal framework for global protection of the environment has been set up, we must ensure that, in the future, words are translated into deeds and that the treaties will help to solve the problems instead of evading them.

The commitments made by the international community at the United Nations Conference on the Environment and Development organized in 1992 in Rio have had few practical repercussions up to now; the situation in the field has continued to deteriorate. Since 1992, for example, annual emissions of carbon dioxide have increased by 100 million tonnes. As for total greenhouse gas emissions, they have increased, since 1990, by 17% in the USA, 20% in Brazil, 27% in China, 28% in India and 40% in Indonesia and, since 1992, 8% in Japan.[29] A report by the US Energy Department estimates that annual emissions of carbon dioxide will have increased in the USA, by comparison with their 1990 level, by 34% in 2010, by 40% in 2015 and by 45% in 2020.[30] Up to now, only six countries have created 'eco-taxes' to discourage deforestation, the misuse of water and energy and mining activities harmful to the environment. Since 1992, 86 million hectares of forests have disappeared worldwide and, with them, several thousand species.[31]

Furthermore, commitments regarding public development aid that, in the terms made by the international community and the industrialized countries themselves, were supposed to stand at 0.7% of GNP for the OECD countries, have not been fulfilled: such aid has now fallen to 0.22% of the average GNP of those countries. The external debt of the developing countries rose from $1.662 trillion in 1992 to $2 trillion in 1997.[32] As emphasized by James Wolfensohn, president of the World Bank, virtually no progress has been achieved in improving the quality of life of three billion people who still live on less than $2 a day.[33] When people live in dire poverty, how can they see environmental protection as anything else but an unaffordable luxury? When people lead a hand-to-mouth existence, how can they fail to sacrifice the welfare of future generations? But how too, when they are rich, can they consider protection of the environment as an unaffordable luxury? How can they live in daily opulence and sacrifice knowingly the welfare of future generations?

If this is truly a scandalous situation, it is because we now know that we are threatening the survival of the biosphere and of future generations, unlike our predecessors who acted in complete ignorance of the consequences of their actions. The inertia of current policies is all the more unacceptable in that it does not have the excuse of ignorance or doubt.

Let us not delude ourselves: the Rio summit has not led to any significant progress. The final document adopted by the extraordinary General Assembly at the closing of the 'Rio + 5' summit in New York in June 1997 expressed 'deep concern' and stressed that 'the overall trends are worse today than they were in 1992'. As for the Kyoto Summit on climate change, which brought together 159 states in December 1997, it led to the adoption of a protocol advocating the reduction of greenhouse gas emissions by 2012 (by 5.2% on average for the industrialized countries in relation to 1990). Since then, however, it has been ratified by only a few countries, principally small island states, and the discussions held in Bonn between 1,200 delegates from 150 countries did not lead to agreement on methods of implementing the protocol. The Buenos Aires Conference on Climate Change, which was to provide practical definitions of implementation of the Kyoto commitments, was concluded without any practical commitment.

Nor did the Kyoto summit define specific commitments for the developing countries, although their energy needs will increase substantially in the coming years. Today, almost two-thirds of the global volume of greenhouse gases are emitted by the OECD countries but by 2025 they will be emitted mainly by the developing countries. Christian Brodhag, chairman at the time of the French Commission on Sustainable Development, observed that 'China, for example, is now building heavy infrastructure that will determine its consumption patterns and therefore pollution for 50 years'.[34]

Furthermore, it is to be feared that the expansion of stockbreeding and intensive agriculture will lead to constantly greater emissions of methane and rising deforestation in the South, whereas forests are expanding today in the North. Food needs could, by 2020, become twice what the earth produces today. As tomorrow's problems take root in those of today, Brazil put forward a particularly innovative solution at Kyoto that is potentially very promising: the creation of a green fund financed by a system of fines paid by those states that would not meet the commitments of the Kyoto Protocol. Thanks to the fund, it would be possible to finance projects in the developing countries and thereby facilitate the transfer of low-energy-consumption technologies, while establishing a dialogue between the countries of the North and those of the South.[35] Let us hope that this proposal will soon be translated into action.

In spite of the limited progress achieved since they were devised, *Agenda 21,* adopted at the Rio summit in 1992, and its plan of action, continue to set benchmarks for sustainable development that could be attained, if the political will existed. But progress in the forthcoming years must be based on specific measures and on increased responsibility towards future generations. Scientists in this regard have a decisive part to play: they should strive to make their research, discoveries and knowledge more accessible to civil society so that the latter could exert greater influence on political decisions. Decisions taken in Rio and Kyoto will have to be rapidly implemented, but above all, much more energetic steps will have to be taken over the next ten years if we are not to jeopardize future generations' exercise of their freedoms and rights.

In this regard, we should not overlook the wide range of laws and regulations voted by many states or groups of states and which make up the greater part of environmental policies today. If we are to set ourselves further goals and achieve them more quickly, it will be necessary to bring into play the support of parliamentarians, mayors, schools, young people, the media, namely all those who, instead of anticipating inevitable wars, wish to take up the inescapable challenges of the future.

The Role of the Private Sector

A democratic state must, in this regard, establish the orientation and framework and lay down the rules of the game through foresight, legislation, regulation and implementation of laws and rules and, above all, through taxation. It cannot, however, act alone. No action aimed at protecting the environment or integrating it more judiciously into development can have a lasting impact without the help and participation of the private sector. As damage to nature is essentially linked to economic activities, it is vital to foster greater awareness of environmental issues among entrepreneurs. Governments can adopt incentives through taxation and subsidies. As commercial enterprises are geared to making profits, responsibility lies with governments to ensure that the most profitable investments are those which are ecologically viable.[36]

Even from a strictly economic standpoint, it is not sure that there is much to be gained from polluting. According to the World Wide Fund for Nature (WWF), by reducing carbon dioxide emissions by 21% by 2010, the USA could save $136 billion on energy.[37] It is possible to make considerable savings by adopting ecologically sound solutions in the fields of transport, housing and agriculture. Furthermore, the 'bill' for natural disasters is so high that some leading economic and financial actors are beginning to take an interest in environmental problems. Over the 1980s, insurance companies worldwide paid out almost $17 billion in compensation for damage related to natural disasters. From 1990 to 1996, the figures rose dramatically to $60 billion. In July 1996, 60 insurance companies attended a meeting in Geneva of the signatory states of the Convention on Climate Change. They adopted a declaration calling upon governments to make a significant reduction in greenhouse gas emissions.

There is already evidence of some encouraging signs. In all fields ranging from pisciculture to solar energy, new companies are being set up that are concerned with viable long-term development. The OECD estimates that the world market for environment-related goods and services, which amounted to almost $200 billion in 1990, will probably have increased by 50% by the year 2000. Protection of the environment has therefore become a genuine industry with one of the fastest growth rates in the world and is now expanding in the developing countries. The commercial success of 'green' goods and services points perhaps to the emergence of genuine public awareness to which all enterprises will have to adapt. Companies mindful of their image will have to take account of consumers who attach much more importance than in the past to respect for nature. Whereas environmental concern was formerly seen as 'pure fancy in relation to the real world of business', today it is perhaps becoming 'the driving force behind the next industrial revolution'.[38]

Nevertheless, some caution, based on scientific rigour, is called for in this field insofar as the 'green' label is often above all a commercial label that serves to sell the product.

According to Ernst Ulrich von Weizsäcker, the challenge to modern societies involves mastering technological progress while taking account of the strategic importance of natural resources, which have become factors of production that are as essential as labour, if not even more so.[39]

He therefore believes that we should concentrate our efforts on increasing the productivity of natural resources. At the present time, to produce $100 of income in the developed countries, some 300 kg of natural resources are required.[40] Jacques Theys, head of the Forecasting and Scientific Watch Centre at the French Ministry of Public Works, Transport and Housing, believes that the trend in our society towards service and information activities could reduce this proportion and enable recycling to be developed. Consequently, it would be possible to respond to the two concerns that lie at the source of sustainable development: the permanence or renewability of natural resources and the welfare of the present or future populations that derive or will derive their livelihood from those resources.

Nevertheless, more environment-friendly production methods are likely to be rapidly confronted with the rigours of competition, entailing risks of

---

Box 7.2 Eco-employment: A Greener Economy?

In the United Kingdom, a particularly instructive study was submitted to Members of Parliament by Friends of the Earth. The study revealed that over 700,000 jobs could be created by 2010 if the United Kingdom were to opt for a 'greener' economy. The quality of life of its citizens would be transformed. The authors of the report believe that by funding the 'greening' of industry, transport and agriculture, more than £3 billion of unemployment benefits could be saved. As regards transport, they advocate giving priority to railways rather than roads. Another sector that could well generate jobs is that of energy, on condition that forms of renewable energy are promoted and a large-scale energy-saving policy is implemented. Finally, recycling and organic farming and the development and adoption of new processes for depolluting land and water are also promising sectors. Another study, conducted by the Institute of Public Policy Research, has revealed that a fiscal policy that would penalize environmentally hostile activities could make some £10 billion per year available. By using the funds generated in this way to reduce social contributions paid by employers, it would be possible to create 250,000 new jobs. Ian Christie, a researcher at the Policy Studies Institute, estimates that industrialists will only adopt the 'green option' if the public authorities impose stricter pollution standards and shift the tax burden from incomes towards resources. 'In the short term, there will certainly be some losers. But if all goes well, we shall create jobs, save energy and make our country more pleasant to live in,' he says.

With regard to eco-employment, the UNESCO Chairs of Eco-technology aim at training environmental technicians at all levels. The purpose of these Chairs is to integrate human activities and environmental processes and to develop an interdisciplinary international network to train decision-makers whose task will be to manage the planet's resources in a long-term perspective for the benefit of future generations.

Sources: Polly Ghazi, *The Observer*, London, in *Courrier International*, No. 227, 9–15 March 1995. Nicholas Schoon, *The Independent*, London, in *Courrier International*, No. 341, 15–21 May 1997.

ecologically damaging dumping and technical barriers to trade. Furthermore, it will be necessary to learn to combine market regulation and public action, particularly by encouraging international cooperation for the benefit of the poorest countries. All too often, advertising and sales are the only visible dimensions of a market, whereas the production of goods is often provided in the developing countries by workers who are subjected to particularly hazardous working conditions for wages that are no more than a pittance. In the future, it should no longer be possible for the laws of the market to be implemented in complete indifference to existing inequalities and to the growing inequalities that the process nurtures. Linking market regulation with regulation by the state and the public sector will bear fruit only if priority is given to long-term solutions: bringing to an end subsidies granted to polluting activities and reducing the sponsoring of wastage; fixing much stricter pollution standards; developing 'zero emission industries' making intelligent use of waste products; encouraging preventive action, more systematic information and education policies and 'double dividend' strategies based on fiscal policies that are favourable to both employment and the environment.[41]

UNESCO's Role

Protection of the environment is one of the priority tasks of UNESCO, which has played a pilot role in this field since its creation at the end of the Second World War. The idea of creating an International Institute for the Amazonian Forest was put forward as early as 1947. In those days, it was a project ahead of its time and was regrettably abandoned. Today, it is widely acknowledged that the future of the rainforests is a major issue for the future of the planet. In 1951, UNESCO launched an international research project on arid zones. Once again, a particular feature of UNESCO's action is the fact that the organization attempts to situate the conservation of the environment in a wider focus centred on relationships between the human community, its ecosystem, and solutions provided by science and social codes. In the words of the French environmentalist Michel Batisse, 'the degradation of the environment is merely the long-neglected face of poorly conceived development, of a development that is not sustainable, of a misdevelopment'. The Rio Declaration in June 1992 in fact indirectly paid tribute to UNESCO's philosophy and forward-looking outlook which, some 20 years earlier, and in comparative isolation at the time, had advocated development centred on human beings: in its first principle, the declaration states that 'human beings are at the centre of concerns for sustainable development'.

If degradation of the environment is to be fought against effectively, it is not a matter of relying exclusively on scientific or technological solutions. Account must also be taken of economic, social and cultural factors, as well as political options which have a bearing on the environment. Degradation of the environment, abdication of political responsibility in regard to production and consumption patterns that are ecologically ruinous together with a lax attitude towards an economy based on the plundering of natural resources and consequent pollution are closely linked: such abdication and *laisser-faire* are the primary causes, in a political sense, of the long-term ecological catastrophe the premisses of which are already blatant. However, degradation of the environment and poverty are also closely linked: as pointed out by Indira Gandhi,[42] poverty is the most serious form of pollution. At the 'Rio + 5' Summit in New York in 1997, Razali Ismail, then president of the United Nations General Assembly, drew attention to the indissoluble link between protection of the environment and the fight against poverty while deploring that aid for sustainable development had fallen from $55 to $50 billion since 1992. Can industrialized countries justify the reduction in development aid in the name of budgetary difficulties when the sum they devote each year to research and development in the field of armaments amounts on average to $150 billion?

The United States administration announced in early 1999 its intention to increase by more than $100 billion the funds allocated to defence during the next six years. Who actually needs to be defended? And against whom? Recent increases in military research and development budgets in many industrialized countries are very worrying. I believe that, unfortunately, the 'advanced' countries have not yet really changed course. We continue to live in a culture of war and defence while we should be moving towards a culture of prevention, foresight and action focused on the most pressing problems of our times. We continue to invest – and this is the economic and budgetary reflection of a political will – in war, in fighter planes, in submarines, but where are the investments required for implementing *Agenda 21*?

And when we act, is it really for the most vital causes? Is it right to concentrate our efforts on banning the ivory trade while industrial air pollution so dramatically demonstrates the limits of our solidarity? It is very easy to speak out passionately for the protection of threatened species when we live in New York or in Paris! Even if the will to protect elephants is praiseworthy, we have to acknowledge that the elephant population is now over-abundant in countries such as Zimbabwe or Botswana and raises serious problems regarding the balance of ecosystems. Let us put an end to the scientific arrogance of the North and combine our endeavours with the excellent scientific communities of the South, not only to prevent the extinction of protected species but, more particularly, to avoid any action that can harm our most precious heritage, the human being.

By closing our eyes to the profound destitution of men, women and children who in increasing numbers have to endure in poverty in the South, we are accomplices to the destruction of resources they are condemned to use in order to survive and to which the unbridled development of inhumane conglomerations leads, the development of cities that are increasingly left to their own devices by the public authorities. By ignoring the rules of the physical, chemical and biological world that surrounds us, we become strangers in our own home and we destroy, rarely by necessity but often by negligence or greed, the very sources of our subsistence and well-being. By causing irreversible damage to the environment and squandering the heritage bequeathed to us by nature, we are jeopardizing the resources of future generations and neglecting their rights.[43]

Through its research programme on Man and the Biosphere (MAB), launched in 1968, UNESCO is endeavouring to strike a sustainable balance between the need to preserve biological diversity, to promote economic development and to safeguard cultural values. To attain that objective, biosphere reserves were created in 1974 with three complementary purposes: for conservation, to preserve genetic resources, species, ecosystems and landscapes; for development, to encourage sustainable economic development; and for logistical support, to sustain research, as well as activities related to education, training and continuous monitoring and to promote sustainable development activities on local, national and global scales. The biosphere reserves can contribute to implementation of international instruments such as conventions on biological diversity, climate change and desertification and the Declaration of Principles on Forests.

The Seville Strategy adopted in March 1995 provided an opportunity for redefining the role and purposes of the biosphere reserves: they were to reconcile humanity and nature and enable us to extend our knowledge of the environment through public awareness, information and educational programmes. Furthermore, the biosphere reserves as a whole make up a world network of cooperation and exchange. The aim of the new strategy is to include the various social actors in planning and decision-making processes on every aspect of the management and use of biosphere reserves. It also seeks to encourage private-sector initiatives aimed at creating enterprises sustainable in environmental and social terms. All these measures should make it possible to establish a real pact between the local community and society as a whole.[44] The involvement of local communities is a crucial factor in ensuring the success of initiatives the purpose of which is to protect the environment. In Papua New Guinea, for example, where 90 to 97% of the land belongs to communities, the rate of deforestation does not exceed 0.1% whereas in other Asian countries, the rate is between 10 and 20 times higher.[45]

UNESCO's role is not confined to its action on the biosphere. Through its work on behalf of education, the organization also encourages acceleration of the scientific and technological revolution whereby the productivity of natural resources could be increased. It encourages formal and non-formal educational activities at all levels, for all and at any stage in life, aimed at protecting the environment and at ensuring sustainable development. It encourages the development and use of renewable energy sources such as solar energy.[46] It provides a scientific contribution to intergovernmental negotiations on the environment (such as climate change, biological diversity or the means of fighting desertification). Through the programmes of its Intergovernmental Oceanographic Commission (IOC), it strives for a scientific evaluation of the state of the oceans, marine life and coastal environments, particularly through the creation of the Global Ocean Observing System (GOOS). It contributes to evaluating national freshwater resources and the definition of directives for water management in the context of the International Hydrological Programme (IHP), particularly through future-oriented studies such as the project for a World Water Vision in 2025.[47] UNESCO is therefore at the heart of new development policies that seek not to 'dominate' nature but to work for it and with it.[48]

We have contracted an ecological debt by funding our excessive consumption at the expense of our children.[49] New development strategies will have to be socially equitable, ecologically viable, economically effective and will have to redress the balance in North-South relations.[50] In Rio, the industrialized countries recognized their responsibility to the developing world: they must set an example and change their patterns of consumption and production. This should go hand-in-hand with acknowledgement of the decisive role played by education, information and communication, culture and scientific knowledge. Perhaps we will then stop equating the level of development with the destruction of natural resources and the hyper-consumption of fossil fuels. Perhaps, on the contrary, development could become synonymous with the harnessing of energy, ecological wisdom and scientific foresight. With more education, greater knowledge, more effective institutions, it would seem reasonable to hope that protection of the environment, in the next decades, will cease to be seen as a 'luxury for rich countries', a luxury many of them deny themselves, and will appear as the prerequisite for sustainable development. In the words of the vice-president of the USA, Al Gore, 'environmental protection is not a luxury, it is a necessity. We are all on spaceship Earth together.'[51]

Nevertheless, the environment lies at the heart of major conflicts which must be democratically regulated by law. The Vienna World Conference on Human Rights, by proclaiming the right to development[52] in 1993, established for the first time a link between the environment and human rights, coupling the right to development with respect of the environmental needs of future generations.[53] In order to allow the right to a natural environment to prevail, we shall have to overcome three major contradictions: first, the conflict between the economy and the environment, and we must express satisfaction in this regard at the growing efforts to nurture a 'green' economy which is beginning to take account of nature and the damage which has been inflicted on it by economic reasoning. Second, the opposition between North and South, since the countries of the South find it hard to accept that new constraints should be imposed on their development in the name of a requirement – respect for the environment – which is largely the result of damage inflicted for many decades by the countries of the North on the global natural environment. The 'polluter pays' principle can take full significance only over the longer term, and the historical responsibility of the industrialized countries in the degradation of the world environment implies that they should set an example by being the first to take the necessary measures to reduce the greenhouse effect and pollution and by funding implementation of *Agenda 21* on an international scale. The third area of conflict is the tension between present and future generations. We shall return to this aspect in Part IV.

In spite of these tensions and difficulties, the human right to a natural environment should be proclaimed with conviction, because it is an essential means of solving them in a peaceful manner. For the time being, this field of law, in its embryonic stages, is still very technical, complex and fragmented, its procedures are still incomplete and it is still insufficiently autonomous and conceptualized. Nevertheless, in the words of Michael Bothe, 'the environmentalization of human rights is an important factor in defence of the environment'.[54] The right to a natural environment should be recognized as inseparably collective and individual. It is necessarily collective insofar as it more often than not affects human communities and also maintains a link with the right of peoples to sovereignty over their natural resources, proclaimed under Article 1 of the 1966 International Covenants relating to human rights. It is equally individual insofar as it is a fundamental right of the human person and citizen that should be 'protected through an organization at international level which would, through its impartiality, enable conflicts focusing on the environment to be settled peacefully'.[55] For the time being, the right to a natural environment is still torn between arcane technical rules related to environmental law, in which things seem to lose their meaning, and general principles and statements that are beginning to be recognized as legally binding. I note a positive development in this regard as the French Conseil d'Etat, in its 'Greenpeace ruling' of 25 September 1998, granted the value of a principle of law to the precautionary principle.

As in other fields, it is vital that the 'globalization of law', of which Mireille Delmas-Marty, in a prophetic vision,[56] announced the advent, should universalize these initial steps forward through exemplary normative action on an international scale. Why not envisage in this regard the elaboration of a Declaration of Human Rights to a Natural Environment, as a preliminary step towards preparing a Convention on the Right to a Natural Environment?

Such a development would seem all the more necessary as, for the time being, no procedure exists, at international level, for penalizing violations by states of existing conventions on the environment. Trends in jurisprudence at the European Court of Human Rights, which is gradually focusing on protection of the right to a natural environment, do nevertheless represent a promising step forward that could gain widespread acceptance.

We have referred to the need to strengthen existing international organizations in order better to protect the nascent right to a natural environment and to improve the effectiveness and coordination of international policies in this field. If the dangers are transnational, so should be the solutions. France has just advocated the creation of a 'global monitoring authority' on the basis of existing structures. Jacques Chirac, president of the French Republic, recently stated that

> we should organize the planetary management of global risks. The primary obstacle stems from the desire of states to preserve, in this field, an obsolete concept of their sovereignty. Pollution knows no boundaries. Interdependence requires universal regulatory mechanisms and impartial, effective provisions for implementing and monitoring any commitments made. We must first of all establish, at world level, an impartial and indisputable centre for the evaluation of our environment ... We also need a single site to embody worldwide awareness of the environment. This task could be performed by the United Nations Environment Programme. Responsibility ... would also fall to that organization to create a world authority based on a general convention which would provide the international community with a homogeneous doctrine.[57]

Obviously, the necessary strengthening of a world authority in the field of the environment in no way involves the disappearance of the specialized or sectoral structures that have proved their effectiveness within the system, such as UNESCO's intergovernmental scientific programmes applied to the environment or those of the WMO or the FAO, but requires even more efficient cooperation from each of the actors concerned on the basis of their acknowledged competence. The various agencies in the United Nations system need to be strengthened and given the necessary means to fulfil their tasks. Coordination between UNEP and the Commission on Sustainable Development must be improved, as must also be the operating of these two bodies. On a world scale, we also have *Agenda 21* at our disposal. What is lacking now is the political will, which should serve not to punish but rather to prepare for, protect against and anticipate disasters.

Within the United Nations family, which is often criticized for its excessive compartmentalization, the management of environmental problems has provided proof that it is possible to work in a concerted and coordinated manner. The problem of the environment transcends all borders; there are so many interests at stake and still so many uncertainties that without concerted action on the part of states, it is society as a whole that will have to pay for the actions or the inertia of a few irresponsible parties. With that aim in mind, I referred a few years ago to the possibility that, as today the very notion of security is understood in a broad and global sense, the United Nations Security Council should not only have the economic and social competence which it lacks but also competence in the environmental field. It is not enough to have at our disposal a central body for evaluation of the global environment. What is necessary is the appropriate authority for taking decisions and ensuring that they are enforced. I also referred to the possibility of creating a force of 'green helmets' to protect the environment, based particularly on scientific competence. The proposal aroused considerable interest as well as some apprehension. Will that idea perhaps develop one day? Perhaps, after so many steps backwards, we shall take a few steps forwards. As René-Jean Dupuy reminds us, 'widespread pollution affects not only environmentalists but the environment itself and, through the environment, humanity as a whole. Will humanity agree to be one again with the universe? Its return to the Kingdom of Earth presupposes a conversion. The conversion of intelligence.'[58]

Pointers and Recommendations

- Implement *Agenda 21* through the promotion of practical political and budgetary measures and the mobilization of governments, parliamentarians and the media, to ensure that the environment becomes a national and international priority with firm, carefully targeted commitments, particularly in the major industrialized countries.
- Promote the adoption of much more ambitious commitments regarding the reduction of greenhouse gas emissions, through effective and responsible energy policies implemented in each country.
- Promote the adoption of much more binding international and national standards on pollution with the adoption, by the United Nations commissions, of the necessary corrective measures, which should concern not only states but also international organizations.
- Improve the prevention of irreversible phenomena of environmental degradation and ensure the rehabilitation of degraded areas, by encouraging public and private scientific research and by facilitating access to environmentally friendly technologies.
- Encourage, through education, information and the circulation of scientific knowledge and technical culture, the adoption of sustainable and responsible patterns of consumption, based on the ethics of the future and following the precautionary principle proclaimed in Rio in 1992, which should be recognized as a legal principle.

- Increase the productivity of natural resources through the development of recycling, the taxing of environmentally harmful activities, the promotion of renewable energy resources and a range of provisions (incentives and subsidies) aimed at encouraging cleaner industries from an ecological point of view.

- Pursue, particularly in the context of UNESCO's Man and the Biosphere Programme and the biosphere reserves, the rational organization of the relationship between human beings and their natural environment in order to reconcile economic development, the safeguarding of cultural values and the preservation of biological diversity.

- Encourage the development, which so far has been limited, of a right to a natural environment by contributing, for example, to the preparation of a Universal Declaration on the Human Right to a Natural Environment, followed by a General Convention on the Right to a Natural Environment.

- Encourage the emergence, on the basis of the United Nations Environment Programme and with the active support of the other competent organizations in the system, of a global authority for the monitoring of the environment, which could be supported by the existing intergovernmental institutions and cooperation machinery – IOC, MAB, IHP and IGCP in the case of UNESCO – and which would submit to the Security Council practical measures to be taken to ensure implementation by all states of the rules, laws and standards relating to protection of the environment.

- Encourage a worldwide debate in order to support the idea of extending the competence of the Security Council to economic, social and environmental issues and of establishing 'green helmets' for the protection of the environment by basing such protection on scientific expertise.

- Promote chairs of eco-technology and the presence in all municipalities of persons with the requisite technical competence to undertake scientific treatment of problems related to the environment such as the management of waste, the reduction of greenhouse gas emissions, the protection of soils and biological diversity.

- Encourage worldwide discussion on the need to adopt new patterns of development based on restraint and on a radical redefinition of the notion of progress, which would no longer be measured by material consumption indicators.

Notes

1. Alain Pavé, 'Environnement, développement et progrès – éléments d'un débat prospectif', paper prepared for the Analysis and Forecasting Office of UNESCO, 1997.

2. Gregory Bateson, *Steps to an Ecology of Mind; Collected Essays in Anthropology, Psychiatry, Evolution and Epistemology*, Chandler Publishing, New York, 1972.

3. Michel Batisse, 'Une seule terre entre toutes les mains', *Federico Mayor Amicorum Liber*, 1995.

4. William Rees and Matthis Wackernagel, 'Ecological footprints and appropriated carrying capacity: measuring the natural capital requirements of the human economy', in A. M. Jansson et al. (eds), *Investing in Natural Capital: The Ecological Economics Approach to Sustainability*, Island Press, Washington, DC, 1994.

5. Intergovernmental Panel on Climate Change, *Climate Change 1995: The Second Assessment Report*, Cambridge University Press, Cambridge, 1995.

6. Serge Antoine, 'De Stockholm à Rio', *Demain la Terre*, Le Nouvel Observateur, Collection Dossiers, No. 11, Paris, 1992.

7. Central Planning Bureau, *Scanning the Future: A Long-term Scenario Study of the World Economy 1990–2015*, The Hague, the Netherlands, 1992.

8. Leyla Boulton, 'WWF warns forests face extinction', *Financial Times*, 9 October 1997.

9. Central Planning Bureau, *Scanning the Future*.

10. Jean-Paul Besset, 'Sécheressses, inondations: le scénario de l'inacceptable', *Le Monde*, 25–26 August 1996.

11. Jean-Paul Dufour, '1997 a été l'année la plus chaude jamais enregistrée', *Le Monde*, 10 June 1998.

12. Intergovernmental Panel on Climate Change, *Climate Change 1995: The Second Assessment Report*, Cambridge University Press, Cambridge, 1995.

13. Jean-Paul Besset, 'La terre se réchauffe. Les mises en garde des scientifiques', *Le Monde*, 26 November 1997.

14. In a survey conducted between 1993 and 1996.

15. Nicole Bonnet, 'L'Amérique latine redoute le retour d'El Niño', *Le Monde*, 6–7 July 1997.

16. Quoted in an article by Pierre le Hir, 'La fonte des glaciers des Alpes inquiète les chercheurs', *Le Monde*, 23–24 February 1997.

17. Jean-Paul Dufour, 'Avec le réchauffement planétaire, l'hiver canadien pourrait envahir l'Europe', *Le Monde*, 2 January 1998.

18. Besset, 'Le terre se réchauffe'.

19. Philippe Pons, 'Des millions de vies en jeu', *Le Monde*, 5 December 1997.

20. This only includes earthquakes having caused damage exceeding 1% of GDP and having resulted in more than 100 deaths.

21. Jean-Paul Besset, 'Avis de gros temps sur la planète', *Le Monde*, 7 October 1995.

22. See Laurent Rebeaud, 'L'écofascisme, un risque réel', *Journal de Genève*, in *Courrier International*, No. 341, 15–21 May 1997.

23. François Ewald, 'Philosophie de la précaution', *L'Année sociologique*, Vol. 46, No. 2, 1996.

24. Federico Mayor, address given at the Conference of the Royal Society of Chemistry on 'Chemistry and developing countries', London, April 1991.

25. Jacques Theys, 'L'environnement au 21e siècle: continuité ou rupture?', paper prepared for the Analysis and Forecasting Office of UNESCO, 1997.

26. Hillary French, 'Forging a new global partnership', *State of the World 1995*, Worldwatch Institute, Washington, DC.

27. Alain Leauthier, 'Le trou refait des siennes depuis début septembre', *Libération*, 6 October 1998.

28. Jean-Paul Dufour, 'La dégradation de la couche d'ozone inquiète les Nations Unies', *Le Monde*, 16 September 1995.

29. Besset, 'La terre se réchauffe'.

30. Nicholas Timmins, 'US lifts carbon gas emissions forecast', *Financial Times*, 13 November 1997.

31. Tom Burke, 'The buck stops everywhere', *New Statesman*, 20 June 1997.

32. Ibid.

33. World Bank, *Environment Matters*, Winter/Spring 1997, p. 3.

34. Christian Brodhag, 'Kyoto et le retard français', *Le Monde*, 5 November 1997. According to the World Bank, pollution in China is already the cause of 289,000 deaths per year and costs society the equivalent of 7% to 8% of GDP. The main causes of ecological deterioration are thought to be energy consumption, 80% of which is based on coal, and toxic emissions related to transport in urban areas. If current trends continue, the World Bank estimates that sulphur dioxide emissions will increase by 60% by 2020 and that the number of deaths due to air pollution will rise to 600,000 per year; Frédéric Bobin, 'La Pollution en Chine inquiète la Banque mondiale', *Le Monde*, 27 September 1997.

35. Philippe Pons, 'A Kyoto, les points de vue se rapprochent entre les pays du Nord et ceux du Sud', *Le Monde*, 5 December 1997.

36. Christopher Flavin and John E. Young, 'Shaping the next industrial revolution', in *State of the World 1993*, Worldwatch Institute, Washington, DC, pp. 180–99.

37. Besset, 'La Terre se réchauffe'.

38. Ibid.

39. Ernst Ulrich von Weizsäcker, 'Environment 2020. A prospective policy brief', paper prepared for UNESCO, 1997.

40. Of which 10% are imported in the United States and 70% in the Netherlands.

41. The German government, under the leadership of Gerhard Schröder, recently decided on a 2.4% reduction in taxes on salaries and a corresponding increase on those on energy; Lester Brown and Christopher Flavin, 'It's getting late to switch to a viable economy', *International Herald Tribune*, 19 January 1999.

42. At the Stockholm Conference in 1972.

43. Address given by the director-general of UNESCO, Mr Federico Mayor, on the occasion of the twenty-fifth anniversary of the UNESCO Conference on the Resources of the Biosphere (September 1968), Paris, 1993.

44. Seville Strategy for Biosphere Reserves; see also *Nature & Resources*, Vol. 31, No. 2, 1995.

45. *UNESCO Courier*, January 1996.

46. See Chapter 12.

47. See Chapter 9.

48. See the joint declaration of the chairpersons of the Intergovernmental Oceanographic Commission (IOC), the Man and the Biosphere Programme (MAB), the International Hydrological Programme (IHP), the joint UNESCO–IUGS International Geological Correlation Programme (IGCP) and the Management of Social Trans-

formation programme (MOST), submitted at each session of the General Conference of UNESCO, which is a striking example of cooperation.

49. Lester Brown, 'The New World Order', *State of the World 1991*, Worldwatch Institute, Washington, DC.

50. Martine Barrère, 'La transition vers une nouvelle ère', *Une Terre en renaissance*, ORSTOM, *Le Monde Diplomatique*, Dossiers Savoirs no. 2, Paris, 1994.

51. Al Gore, quoted in *Environment Matters*, World Bank, Winter/Spring 1997, p. 1.

52. However, at a debate on the effective implementation of the right to development that took place at the United Nations General Assembly in December 1998, the USA voted against the draft resolution submitted by South Africa, while the countries of the European Union abstained.

53. *Les Droits de l'homme à l'aube du XXIe siècle*, Mission sur la célébration du 50e anniversaire de la Déclaration universelle des droits de l'Homme, La Documentation française, 1998. In this field, a distinction should be made between the environmental law (the corpus of legal doctrine on this issue), the right of human beings to a natural environment and the right of the environment to be respected, which is tantamount to the duty of humanity.

54. Ibid.

55. Ibid.

56. Mireille Delmas-Marty, *Pour un Droit commun*, Éditions du Seuil, Paris, 1994; *Trois Défis pour un droit mondial*, Éditions du Seuil, Paris, 1998.

57. Jacques Chirac, president of the French Republic, address to the IUCN, Fontaine-bleau, 3 November 1998.

58. René-Jean Dupuy, 'La nature méprisée', in *L'Humanité dans l'imaginaire des nations*, Conférences, essais et leçons du Collège de France, Julliard, Paris, 1991.

CHAPTER 8

. . . .

The Advancing Desert

A Fast-growing, Worldwide Phenomenon

Despite the international strategies that were put in place in the 1970s, desertification is proceeding apace on a global scale. Since 1977, when the first United Nations conference on this subject was held, nearly 105 million hectares of once-fertile land – an area almost twice the size of France – have been affected. The degradation that has occurred since the beginning of the 1990s has been worse than in the previous twenty years. Desertification today directly affects 250 million people and threatens nearly a billion people living on the drylands of some 110 countries.[1] This figure could double by 2050, bringing the number of people affected to two billion, or even more, if deserts continue to spread at the present rate.

According to experts' estimates, the arid and semi-arid zones at present cover nearly 40% of the land surface of the Earth, whereas less than 10% of the surface is cultivated.[2] Furthermore, nearly 70% of the drylands under cultivation are either degraded or in great danger of desertification.[3] This problem has major repercussions on people and on health, since these are precisely the areas where the majority of the world's present 800 million underfed people are concentrated.

The general public is still not informed of the facts about the curse of desertification, which is usually associated in the public mind with the conventional image of the inexorable advance of the Sahara. The truth is that it is not always such a visible process: it is both more complex and more insidious, a process that means more than shifting dunes or an advancing wall of sand,[4] nor should it be confused with drought.[5] Desertification is in point of fact a general process of degradation affecting the soil and the vegetation, resulting in a progressive decline in the productivity of hundreds of square kilometres of farmland.[6] It is not only the developing countries that are at risk: according to United Nations figures, 74% of the cultivable arid land in North America is in danger of desertification,[7] which also affects both the sub-humid zones, thousands of kilometres away from any deserts, and the arid borderlands, which suffer the effects of the cyclical contraction and expansion of deserts induced by climatic variations. Apart from the climatic factor, human activity has for millennia been central to the desertification process.[8] It is for this reason that the United Nations Convention on Combating Desertification, signed at UNESCO in October 1994 and ratified, at the end of 1998, by 145 states, defines the phenomenon of desertification as 'the land degradation in arid, sub-arid and dry sub-humid zones resulting from various factors, including climatic variations and human activities'.[9]

The region worst affected by desertification is Africa: 65% of its surface area consists of drylands, one-third of which are hyper-arid deserts and the remaining two-thirds are arid, semi-arid and sub-humid areas, where the lack of rainfall accelerates land degradation[10] and where 400 million Africans – two-thirds of the population of the continent – live.[11] In the last 50 years, Africa has lost 650,000 square kilometres of productive land.[12] Degradation affects one-third of all the land used in Africa for crops and grazing; only 25% of the surface is suitable for rainwater-reliant agriculture.[13] If the total area affected is taken as the criterion, then the Asia-Pacific region is the one that suffers most from desertification, since nearly half the degraded land in the world – 24% of the region's land surface – is concentrated there; 35% of the productive land in Asia has now become desert.[14] In China, in particular, 34% of the land is subject to erosion, and the possibility of its rehabilitation remains doubtful.[15] Latin America, where 73% of the drylands in agricultural use suffer from varying degrees of degradation, and the USA are also affected by desertification.[16] In fact, no continent is spared.

Desertification attacks the fertile layers of soil; every month, two million tons of topsoil disappear, whereas it takes 100 to 400 years for a single extra centimetre to be produced. Soil must therefore be regarded, on the scale of human societies, as a resource that can be renewed only with great difficulty. It is in fact much more cost-effective to prevent desertification than to restore land that has already become degraded: according to the UNEP report *Down to Earth*, rehabilitating arid lands could take twenty years at an estimated cost of US$10 to US$20 billion a year, while according to Klaus Töpfer, executive director of UNEP, the loss of income by the population of the desertified zones amounts to US$42 billion a year.[17]

The international community has sized up the risks connected with desertification. At Rio de Janeiro in June 1992, the United Nations Conference on Environment and Development decided to establish an international Convention on Desertification, finally acknowledging the universal scale of the problem and agreeing to tackle it not simply as an environmental question but, above all, as a matter of global development requiring an integrated approach at worldwide level.[18] As James D. Wolfensohn, president of the World Bank, has stressed, 'addressing desertification is essential for poverty reduction and food security in the developing countries'.[19] It is true that, in the places ravaged by desertification, living conditions are especially difficult, poverty is omnipresent, and tensions are accentuated, with the attendant risks of conflicts between farmers and nomad shepherds, sudden migrations involving millions of 'environmental' refugees taking to the roads, and struggles to secure control of water supplies. Seen from this angle, the fight against desertification represents a world security issue in its broadest sense. The Convention on Combating Desertification could, as the Swedish diplomat Bo Kjellén[20] has emphasized, contribute to the exercise of 'preventive diplomacy', giving priority to peaceful, negotiated solutions and based on a wider concept of 'security'.[21]

Desertification affects not only the natural environment but also the cultural heritage: certain noteworthy sites, such as the ancient settlements of Mauritania, are under threat and in some cases already under the sands. It is 15 years since UNESCO launched a campaign to save the historic Mauritanian towns of Oualala, Chinguitti, Tichitt and Ouadana, and in 1982 it therefore registered the Algerian Tassili N'Ajjer National Park in Algeria on the World Heritage List in order to ensure the preservation of its natural and cultural treasures and to improve the living conditions of the inhabitants. Desertification at the same time represents a threat to traditional ways of life. Many nomad groups managed to resist the threat of being made to adopt a sedentary lifestyle throughout the colonial period and after independence, and in order to adapt and sometimes to thrive in arid environments, they developed complex strategies for making use of the natural resources while retaining their previous forms of community organization.[22] Now, owing to desertification, they often find themselves obliged to adopt a sedentary lifestyle in the worst possible conditions – namely, conditions of urban destitution in shanty towns or displaced-persons' camps.

An Environmental Problem and a Developmental Issue

Controlling the effects of population growth and urbanization Population growth exerts a determining influence on the future prospects of areas affected by desertification, since 'over 50% of the world's drylands are in developing countries that have to meet the increasing food requirements of rapidly expanding populations'.[23] The Sahel remains the outstanding symbol of this situation, since its population will very likely double in the next 30 years.[24] The World Food Summit organized by the Food and Agriculture Organization (FAO) in 1996 reckoned that, in order to cope with world population growth, food production worldwide would need to be doubled[25] and, in Africa, increased fivefold. Furthermore, in order to limit the clearing of new land for cultivation and the overgrazing and deforestation that aggravate desertification, technologies to make marginal and fragile lands more productive will have to be developed. At the same time, it is necessary to promote education which, especially in the last ten years, has entailed a considerable reduction in population growth.

Population growth often goes hand-in-hand with rapid urbanization, the ecological repercussions of which have still not been properly evaluated. In the Sahel region, the urban population is increasing at the rate of 6% a year and that of the rural areas by 2%, and the rural migration is continuing at the rate of 1% per year.[26] Four hundred towns of over 100,000 inhabitants have mushroomed in the semi-arid regions in recent decades, with generally high growth rates of between 3% and 10% per year.[27] Thirsty towns guzzle enormous quantities of water, to the point where certain dry-climate regions could exhaust almost all of their water resources in the near future.[28] In the poorest countries, runaway urbanization also threatens the survival of woodlands. Wherever wood and charcoal are still the main sources of energy, urban consumption is creating deforested belts around the towns sometimes more than a hundred kilometres wide, as in the outskirts of Delhi.[29] If this trend were to continue, we should arrive at a situation where, in the dry regions, desertified (and partly depopulated) rural areas would rub shoulders with overpopulated and pauperized large towns and their suburbs. The campaign against desertification thus demands that thought be given, over and above the implementation of specific local projects, to the overall management of the regions concerned.

Getting the better of climate change The short-, medium- and long-term evolution of the climate is a determining factor in the desertification process. The greatest impact of all probably comes from natural climate changes.[30] Some regions have been subject to recurrent droughts for hundreds or even thousands of years. Africa, for instance, has experienced 10- to 20-year arid cycles, both in the Sahel region and in the eastern and southern parts of the continent. These cycles have an especially serious impact on the already degraded lands of Africa: some experts reckon the decline in soil fertility to be a real 'time-bomb', the effects of which on the forms of agriculture concerned cannot yet be fully appreciated.[31] In the mid-1980s, some three million people died from the effects of the drought in sub-Saharan Africa, and about 10 million were displaced.

Global warming has a significant influence on desertification, as the increased concentration of carbon dioxide and 'greenhouse' gases impede the replenishment of ground water.[32] Scientists have moreover established a link between climate change and soil acidification.[33] It has also been shown that the reduction in vegetation resulting from soil degradation contributes locally to the greenhouse effect.[34] This threatens the most vulnerable ecosystems:

Africa, Australia, Latin America and the western USA are probably the regions most affected by the temperature rise due to the greenhouse effect.[35]

On the basis of analysis of geological data, however, one scientist even considers that, as happened in prehistory, climate warming could in the long run be accompanied by increased humidity and rainfall, bringing about 'a reduction in the tropical arid areas, at a pace of a few centuries or, at the best several decades', thus making the tropical deserts green.[36] Several objections have been raised to this hypothesis, which overlooks population growth and the effects of human activities on soil degradation. Thus, many experts stress that climate warming will have the result that droughts will become more severe and lands bordering on dry regions will become more vulnerable.[37] They add that the impact of climate warming could vary greatly from one region to another: while rainfall might increase overall, it could decrease in the Mediterranean region, North Africa and the Sahel;[38] the Brazilian rainforest might even shrink.[39] Some analysts also predict a decline in agricultural yields in the tropical zones and increased famines, with Africa being the most affected continent.[40] Hence, while climate warming could, theoretically at least, shift the frontiers of the deserts, it would not put an end to desertification, which is very largely the result of human mismanagement of ecosystems.

The campaign against desertification thus calls for integrated action to break the vicious circle of global environmental degradation. For this purpose, action needs to be taken against the multiple causes of desertification, which is more than a climatic problem: it is first and foremost a human problem.

Fighting desertification means fighting poverty Desertification in the developing countries feeds on poverty: there is a level of poverty and insecurity below which concern for the environment can appear absurd or incongruous. In the absence of agrarian reforms that would give them access to the land or of the technical and financial resources that would enable them to undertake long-term investments, one billion people in the world are forced to make what precarious use they can of marginal agricultural zones such as forests, grazing lands and mountains, and often to practise an itinerant form of subsistence farming. The precarious nature of land tenure is worsened in most of the countries of the Sahel by the uncertainty of the legal status of grazing land, since livestock rearing is seldom regarded in those countries as a formal mode of land use.[41]

Although it is true that arid zones may in certain cases be havens of prosperity, thanks in particular to their mineral resources,[42] for most of the countries concerned, the deserts are unproductive areas, 'an additional burden to their considerable economic and demographic problems'.[43] Of the 99 countries affected, only 18 – either industrialized or oil-producing countries – seem in a position to combat desertification with their own resources. The challenge is all the greater as over one-third of the world's poor are already subjected to a high or fairly high level of water stress.[44] Women are the worst affected, since in traditional societies it is they who are usually responsible for fetching wood, fodder and water. People should also be encouraged to undertake long-term investments in the protection of the soil and vegetation, by means of legal reforms that aim at perpetuating, in the case of women especially, the rights of ownership of, and access to, land, water and biomass.

Prior to this, environmental education and technical training programmes should be provided to help the population of affected areas realize the harmful nature of certain farming practices and train them in production techniques of long-term viability. Introducing these populations to modern technologies is an essential step along the road to combating desertification. As Michel Batisse points out, this implies 'a rapid transition from a low level of education and technical skills to the ability to practise modern forms of irrigation and grazing. It takes time to turn traditional nomads into efficient farmers and such a transition calls for massive institutional, technical and financial backing.'[45]

Fighting for a better use of resources   The effects of climatic variations are an insufficient explanation of land degradation. As one commentator has remarked, 'deserts do not advance, they are created by human beings'.[46] Desertification is considerably worsened by practices such as deforestation, overgrazing, the collecting of ligneous plants for fuel, and poor irrigation methods. Such practices have 'resulted in further weakening of ecosystems, the lessening of their capacity for regeneration and a decrease in their production potential. In the most fragile zones, overexploitation of natural resources has made the land more prone to desertification, and led to almost irreversible forms of degradation.[47] Whether the purpose of deforestation is to extend the area of cultivable land or to provide fuel, it results in depriving the land of its vegetation and intensifies the process of wind and water erosion, thus contributing directly to desertification. Overgrazing makes plants more vulnerable to drought and flooding.[48]

The control and sharing of water resources are two essential aspects of the fight against desertification. The FAO estimates that by 2010 over half the world's agricultural production will come from irrigated land, but the intensification of food growing is often achieved at the price of excessive irrigation practices that lead to overuse of groundwater reserves and serious land degradation. In the opinion of experts, improper management of irrigation causes salinization and alkalinization of the land, resulting in a form of desertification that is even more harmful than that affecting non-irrigated land.[49] The leaching that affects 20% of the world's irrigated land causes a serious reduction in fertility and an irreversible deterioration of the structure of the soil.[50] Nearly three million hectares have been lost this way in Pakistan.

Box 8.1 *The Aral Sea: Anatomy of a Disaster*

Human irresponsibility is threatening many inland seas and lakes that have helped to create the prosperity of many civilizations. One such treasure, the Aral Sea in Central Asia, is in the process of being quite simply destroyed. The Aral Sea basin has, since the break-up of the Soviet Union, been shared among five republics (Kazakhstan, Kyrgyzstan, Uzbekistan, Tajikistan and Turkmenistan). Until 1960 the Aral Sea, with its 66,000 square kilometres, was the world's fourth largest lake, but it now ranks only sixth in size, its volume having been reduced by 60% between 1960 and 1995 and its surface area by half. The sea level has fallen by 19 metres and salinity has trebled. Fishing, which in 1962 was still landing 40,000 tonnes, is now almost impossible, and of the 24 species that used to be caught, only four survive. The fishing industry has closed down and, in 1994, catches comprised only 3,000 tonnes of fish of questionable quality. The Aral Sea's particularly rich flora and fauna, and especially the unique woodlands bordering it, known as *tugai*, are at their last gasp. The two ports of Munyak – once an island – and Aral'sk are now 40km inland: the old fishing fleet now lies beached and rusting in a ghost-ships' graveyard. The climate has become continental, and wind-borne salt pollutes air, soil and water for hundreds of kilometres. The desert is advancing.

The cause of this ecological disaster is to be found in senseless agricultural development policies aimed at short-term profit, whereby the waters of the Aral's two main tributaries, the rivers Amu-Darya and Syr-Darya, were used for industrial-scale irrigated cotton growing. Scientists thought at the time that the damage could be repaired when it became too worrying. The effects of this short-sightedness are now plain: not only has it resulted in an irreparable impoverishment of biodiversity, it is also having repercussions on human health. As Nikita Glazovsky, deputy director of the Russian Academy of Sciences' Institute of Geography, says: 'For the first time in human history, a lake bigger than the surface area of some states is disappearing as a result of human activities. The damage done to the environment is causing an increase in sickness and infant mortality, and is also having profound repercussions on the region's economic development.' The drying up of more than half of the sea indeed poses a threat to the health, and ultimately the survival, of 3.5 million people. The situation in Karakalpakia, an autonomous republic within Uzbekistan with an ethnic minority population of 1.2 million, gives cause for particular concern. 'Our people are dying like flies,' explains Dr Oral Ataniyazova, a gynaecologist in the capital, Nukus, where she heads the autonomous republic's only centre for human reproduction and family planning. 'Karakalpakia has the former Soviet Union's highest death rates for mothers and children.'

According to the magazine *People and the Planet* (sponsored by the United Nations Population Fund, the World Wide Fund for Nature, the International Planned Parenthood Federation and the Swedish International Development Cooperation Agency), the countries bordering on the Amu Darya and Syr-Darya rivers are continuing to step up pumping in order to develop irrigation and sustain an export-oriented cotton industry. Irrigated land now comprises seven million hectares. No unified overall strategy has been put in place for the Aral, the regional environment and the local populations. 'The situation is getting worse month by month. It will be perhaps at best ten years before the sea is totally done for and the whole region becomes a desert,' reckons Dr Akhmed Khametyllaevich, director of the Nukus Institute of Bioecology. Dr Ataniyazova's predictions are even gloomier: 'Since 99% of Karakalpakians live within their own frontiers, we may very well be witnessing the death of a nation caused by human stupidity.' Is it already too late to save the Aral?

Experts now agree that it is no longer possible to repair all the damage done over the last 30 years, which is why partial solutions are now being considered. UNESCO should bring all its weight to bear to ensure that such initiatives are not limited to symbolic measures. It has already begun to do so by setting up a Workshop for Water and Peace in the Aral Sea Basin, whereby it provides assistance to the scientific community while encouraging politicians to take serious measures. In January 1998 it also set up a Consultative Council for the Aral Sea Basin, which held its first meeting in September 1998. Through its various programmes (International Hydrological Programme, Man and the Biosphere Programme, and Management of Social Transformations Programme), UNESCO can also promote a transdisciplinary approach to the region's problems, combining the ecological, sanitary and socio-economic viewpoints. This long-term regional outlook should, finally, be given its place within the wider context of the second World Water Forum, which is planned for the year 2000 and in which UNESCO is involved.

Challenges on a large scale call for solutions on a large scale, and it is in activities of that nature that efforts must be invested. In the short term, however, so as to save what can still be saved, emergency measures requiring the commitment of considerable sums – several billion dollars – should be taken to improve water quality, and negotiations should be organized between the countries concerned so that effective water-sharing agreements can be implemented and water use improved. If these steps are taken without delay and if the political will is forthcoming, it may be possible to avoid the final demise of the Aral Sea, but let this tragic example be a lesson to us: it is a sad reflection of the inadequacy of 'nick-of-time' policies and the negative effect of short-termism on our planet's future.

Sources: France Bequette, 'Saving the Aral Sea: the drama of Central Asia's great lake?', *UNESCO Courier*, October 1994. Don Hinrichsen, 'Requiem for a dying sea', *People and the Planet*, Vol. 4, No. 2, 1995. Peter Whitford and Lucy Hancock, 'The Aral Sea disaster: turning the tide?', *Environment Matters*, Winter/Spring 1997. 'UNESCO's initiative for the Aral Sea basin', *information document distributed during the 155th session of UNESCO's Executive Board*, Tashkent, 6 November 1998.

Control of water resources involves working out techniques for tapping, collecting, storing and using them. Some of these techniques are very ancient, such as the *kariz*, the underground canals used for centuries in the arid zones of Central Asia, the Middle East, North Africa and Spain.[51] These are 'true masterpieces of hydraulic engineering',[52] which supply water to fields and homes without using any external source of energy. Science and technology have made it possible to develop other particularly efficient techniques, such as the use of motor-driven pumps in the Gourara region of Algeria to bring disused underground galleries back into service.[53] These techniques enable more rational use to be made of that rare and precious resource, water.

Information and education should therefore be used to promote a genuine culture of 'water saving'. This entails the use of techniques that are both ecologically sound and efficient, and are based on traditional skills while embracing modern scientific and technological advances. Ultimately, it is the role of the state to arbitrate between the immediate aspirations of water users and the long-term public interest, keeping a watchful eye, in particular, on the preservation and fair sharing of water resources.

It would at the same time be wrong to overlook the biodiversity and phytogenetic resources of the drylands, which have given the world wheat, sorghum, millet, many pulses and cotton, among other crops.[54] Arid and semi-arid ecosystems have a varied fauna and flora, and they provide a natural habitat that is essential for the reproduction and migration of many mammals and birds. They also produce resins – from which incense, for example, is made – oils, waxes and the natural raw materials for potentially marketable pharmaceutical products. We therefore need, while pressing ahead with research, to improve our knowledge and control of these rich natural resources.

The restoration of degraded agro-ecosystems is all the more important in that it fulfils several objectives at the same time: the fight against desertification, the fight against the greenhouse effect (by storing part of the carbon fixed by photosynthesis), and the preservation of natural biodiversity or phytogenetic resources. As the executive director of UNEP has pointed out, 'The most effective actions for preventing dryland degradation are often the same actions needed to protect biological diversity or minimize the risk of climate change.'[55] The Global Environment Facility, set up in response to the decisions taken at the Earth Summit (UNCED, Rio, 1992), could lend its scientific and financial support to such ventures.

Scientific and technological progress also makes it possible to combat desertification. Climatic variations can now be forecast more efficiently, and techniques in this field are developing rapidly. A statistical relationship between regional rainfall and the quasi-periodic interannual oscillation of the general atmospheric and oceanic circulation (ENSO, *El Niño Southern Oscillation*) has, for instance, been recently identified.[56] Knowledge of this relationship makes it possible to forecast regional rainfall in quantitative terms three to six months in advance. Similarly, by combining high- and low-resolution satellite observations of the Earth with field observations and data from geographical information systems, it is possible to map areas of risk and assess the possibilities for the regeneration of arid lands, which allows the state of degradation of the environment to be ascertained and differentiated strategies to be suggested for combating desertification.[57] The Sahara and Sahel Observatory is thus conducting, in conjunction with UNESCO, various pioneering schemes of desertification observation, long-term ecological monitoring, and integration of information systems for the zones under threat.

Upgrading rural economies Unless timely measures are taken to adapt agricultural structures to climate changes, the estimated 640 million people of the world's population currently under threat of famine are due, according to the experts, to increase by about 300 million by 2060.[58] Conversely, a more rational use of soils and irrigated land, the development of adapted species and the application of new techniques would make it possible to cancel out most of the negative effects of climate change on production in the developing countries.

As emphasized in the UNESCO report on the arid zones, 'the rehabilitation and improvement of traditional systems and the development of new, better adapted systems can only be achieved in the context of an integrated, ecological approach to rural development, aimed at reconciling the objectives of socio-economic development with the imperatives of protection of the environment'.[59] An illustration of this general observation is provided by the changes that have taken place in the semi-arid Machakos region, Kenya. In this region, where the population increased fivefold between 1930 and 1990, per capita agricultural output has grown rapidly and new technologies have been introduced to meet the increased demand for food in both rural and urban areas.[60] Simple measures already make it possible to halt the advance of desertification: the systematic planting of trees erects natural barriers to wind erosion and stops livestock from straying on to ploughland.[61]

Agricultural policies, development cooperation policies and desertification prevention campaigns therefore need to be more closely interrelated and better coordinated. Agricultural production in most of the drylands is placed at a disadvantage by the absence of infrastructures and markets, the maintenance of agricultural prices at an artificially low level in order to meet urban food requirements, the preference given to cereal imports, and the aggressive marketing policies of the agricultural exporting countries.[62] The rural economy therefore has to be upgraded. In most of the areas experiencing desertification, this entails putting in place a sustainable form of intensive agriculture,[63] which makes it possible to limit the amount of new land cleared for cultivation and to make crop growing more profitable. Among the steps necessary to achieve this goal, the synergies between crop farming, livestock farming and sylviculture need to be strengthened, incorporating conservation activities into the production process and using local resources.[64] The 1994 Convention to Combat Desertification rightly attributes considerable importance to these lateral approaches. In areas subjected to high levels of water stress, it would also be desirable to encourage economic activity to move in the direction of high- added-value types of production, thus reducing dependence on activities that call for an intensive use of water.[65]

Desertification: A Global Challenge for the Twenty-first Century

The International Convention to Combat Desertification, signed in Paris at UNESCO Headquarters on 17 June 1994, marks a crucial stage in the battle against desertification. As pointed out by Ambassador Bo Kjellén, 'the Rio process with its strong emphasis on an integrated approach to sustainable development has put new tools into the hands of the designers and the practitioners of policies to combat desertification'.[66] The 1994 Convention, which is now an integral part of the 'three Rio conventions',[67] is based on five main points:

- the acknowledgement that desertification and land degradation represent worldwide problems with significant regional variations;
- the need for a joint approach to development, calling upon funding from many different sources;
- the implementation of a bottom-up approach based on local apportionment

of responsibilities (270 non-governmental organizations are currently participating in the process), and the parallel pursuit of the struggle for the
elimination of poverty;

- a 'horizontal' method of working, combining conservation with the sustainable management of water and soil resources; and
- interdisciplinary scientific and technical cooperation[68] involving research
and the exchange of information and technologies.

The drought situation, as we have seen, gets worse as the population
increases. Measures therefore need to be studied, in the framework of regional
and international co-operation agreements, for alleviating the human effects
of the most serious climatic crises, measures going beyond the simple context
of emergency food aid (cf. the chapter 'Will there be food for everybody?').[69]
In particular, steps need to be taken to ensure that communities can cope
with prolonged droughts while avoiding the phenomenon of large-scale rural
migration.

This placing of the desertification problem in its proper perspective represents a crucial step foward. It will make it possible to devise solutions to this
scourge on the basis of a multifactorial analysis of its causes. It will also make
it possible to launch a further stage in international cooperation, which will
make water an instrumental factor in sustainable development on a regional
and global scale, since countries subject to desertification and drought, and,
more generally, to land degradation, are vulnerable not only as regards their
soils but also, very often, in other ways connected with their overall economic
and political situation.[70] Participation in any policy by the people who live in
areas subject to desertification is thus essential if we wish to combat it
effectively, but we should also re-situate this issue within an overall view of
worldwide development. Drawing vital lessons from his experience of deserts,
Théodore Monod stresses: 'The world is indivisible, so let us take a global
view of it. As an English poet expresses it so well, "who picks a flower
disturbs the stars". That to me contains a true concept, that of the oneness of
the cosmos and hence of solidarity among living beings.'[71] As he goes on to
remark, 'deserts stir our emotions because they represent nature. They also
show us what it may be like after we have disappeared.'[72]

Desertification is largely the work of human beings, but it is also they who
can limit its effects and who must do so if they want to survive. Desertification
must give rise to solidarity and cooperation on the regional and international
levels. UNESCO was, half a century ago, one of the first intergovernmental
organizations to show interest in the problems of the arid zones. It has helped
greatly to mobilize the efforts of the scientific community to provide concrete
solutions; but only by continuing to enlist the participation of all concerned
will it be possible to keep the ravages of drought and desertification in check.

Box 8.2 UNESCO and the Fight against Desertification

UNESCO has been combating desertification almost since the day it was set up: following the 1948 General Conference, at which India proposed the establishment of an international arid zone institute, it helped to create the Indian Institute for Arid Zone Research and the Israeli Negev Desert Institute and gave its support to the Egyptian Desert Institute. It was the first agency to carry out, in 1951, an international study on arid zones, which marked the start of its scientific programmes in the field of the environment. An extension of this study, the arid lands project, launched in 1957, was not only one of the first attempts at North–South technical cooperation but also showed the value of a transdisciplinary approach combining the scientific and social dimensions of sustainable development. UNESCO was also one of the first institutions to highlight the fundamental role of water, as is demonstrated by the intergovernmental programmes drawn up at the time of the International Hydrological Decade (1965–74) and under the International Hydrological Programme, which has been in existence since 1975.

More recently, after lending its support to the establishment of the international Sahara and Sahel Observatory, UNESCO undertook, in collaboration with the International Union of Ecological Sciences, an analysis of the nature and scale of past climate variations, in order to anticipate probable future changes in the climate and the environment. UNESCO also promotes the use of remote sensing and of interactive geographical information systems to obtain better assessments of the effects of human activities on the environment. It advocates the use of solar energy in the arid zones instead of fuels such as wood, since the over-exploitation of wood resources is an important factor in desertification in such regions. Thanks to its Man and the Biosphere (MAB) programme, researchers in the fields of agronomy and sylviculture have been trained locally, and funding has been obtained for scientific installations in Africa, whereby, for instance, the selective breeding of tree and shrub species suitable for arid soils has been made possible.

In collaboration with the United Nations Environment Programme (UNEP) and in the framework of its environmental education activities, UNESCO also takes an interest in the socio-economic, political and historical aspects of desertification. The problems of drought and desertification are all the more important since the affected countries suffer from a lack of training and information; environmental degradation is often closely linked with poverty, malnutrition and disease, and with conflicts and migrations.

Here lies a challenge not only to those directly affected but also to the international community, which has undertaken to help them. It is not just the desert that is growing: we must also struggle to halt the advance of an ethical wilderness, the wilderness created by the lack of solidarity, by hardness of heart. The fight against desertification will be a living testimony to the fact that the human race is not doomed to moral desertification and to the gradual loss of that which makes it human.

Pointers and Recommendations

- Put into effect the recommendations of the 1994 United Nations Convention on Desertification and incorporate desertification issues into sustainable development strategies; devise indicators for monitoring the progress of desertification and evaluating the progress of measures to combat it.
- Make full use of techniques for the management of natural resources (water and soil conservation, farming techniques), with emphasis on a participatory approach.
- Encourage joint management of water resources, particularly at regional level, by setting up 'basin observatories' to monitor and manage water resources; draw up legislation and establish co-operation mechanisms encouraging the replenishment and fair sharing of water resources on the local, national and regional scales.
- Establish a plan of action in the field of science and technology, involving, among other things, the devising of appropriate systems of information and dynamic monitoring (using satellite observation in particular) and the setting up of a worldwide monitoring system for anticipating and forestalling desertification.
- Intensify current research in the fields of water, energy, and crop and livestock farming techniques, so as to increase science's contribution to the implementation of the Rio Conventions; set up intensive sustainable agriculture: strengthen the synergies between agriculture, stock farming and sylviculture.
- Organize awareness and training campaigns relating to the struggle against desertification; improve agricultural education and technical training.
- Encourage the wealthy countries and the bilateral and multilateral aid agencies to incorporate ecological questions into strategies for assistance to countries stricken by desertification, and provide for the agricultural development of arid lands and the maintenance of their productivity.
- Promote the use of solar energy in desertification-prone areas.
- Encourage a change in patterns of consumption towards greater moderation, solidarity and responsibility.
- Promote the adoption of agrarian reforms and land legislation adapted to

suit local contexts, in order to ensure access, in particular for women, to land ownership.

Notes

1. United Nations Environment Programme (UNEP) data, from *Global Environment Outlook*, Oxford University Press, New York, 1997; *Le Monde*, 2 December 1998, inaugural address by Abdou Diouf, president of the Republic of Senegal, to the second session of the Conference of Parties to the United Nations Convention on Combating Desertification, Dakar, 30 November 1998. See also UNEP, *Status of Desertification and Implementation of the United Nations Plans of Action to Combat Desertification*, Report by the Executive Director, UNEP/GCSS.III/3, 1991.

2. Godwin O. P. Obasi, secretary-general of the World Meteorological Organization (WMO), June 1998. World Bank, 1998; *Le Monde*, 25–26 August 1996 (meeting of 120 experts in Lisbon in June 1996).

3. *Connect*, UNESCO–UNEP environmental education newsletter, September 1994.

4. UNEP, *Global Environment Outlook*; see also Monique Mainguet, *Desertification: Natural Background and Human Mismanagement*, Springer Verlag, Berlin, 1994, Chapter 1; *L'Homme et la sécheresse*, Masson, Paris, 1995, Chapter 17.

5. As stated in a recent study by the French Ministry of Overseas Development, 'desertification is distinct from drought, which refers to the consequences of a relatively prolonged lack of water, although the latter is itself an aggravating factor of desertification' (*La Lutte contre la désertification*, Ministère de la Coopération, October 1994).

6. UNEP, 1991, *Status of Desertification*, Part 1.A.

7. Ibid., Annex.

8. P. Beaumont, *Drylands. Environmental Management and Development*, Routledge, London, 1989. Beginning in the late Neolithic period, the exploitation of fragile lands impoverished vast tracts both in the Near East and in China. It is even believed that upstream erosion in the Tigris and Euphrates basins caused the collapse of the Mesopotamian civilizations: the huge quantities of sediments brought down silted up the vast network of canals created by the Sumerians 4,000 years before the present era. Some of the traditional irrigation networks, such as the one in the Varamin plain in Iran, have survived, but for the most part the great irrigation networks collapsed as a result of invasions, like that of Genghis Khan in the eleventh century, which opened the Tigris–Euphrates valley to the desert.

9. *UNESCOPRESS*, 30 June 1995.

10. UNEP, *Global Environment Outlook*; Mohammed Skouri, in *UNESCO Courier*, January 1994.

11. UNEP, *Global Environment Outlook*, Chapter 2. According to UNEP, 36 African countries suffer drought or desertification (figure for 1994).

12. French Ministry of Overseas Development, *La Lutte contre la désertification*.

13. Figure quoted by Monique Mainguet, *Aridity, Droughts and Human Development*, Springer Verlag, Berlin, 1999. UNEP, *Global Environment Outlook*.

14. Including China, India, Pakistan, Afghanistan and Mongolia. UNEP, *Global Environment Outlook*, pp. 42–3. In Central Asia, the situation in the Republics of Kazakhstan and Uzbekistan is also disturbing, especially around the Aral Sea, which has now

been reduced to half its original surface area (see Box 8.1). What is less widely known is that the Russian Federation's borderlands are facing serious problems of desertification, particularly in the Kalmyk Republic. Since two-thirds of Latin America consists of arid or semi-arid lands, that region too is affected by desertification, as indeed is the USA.

15. F. Ramade, *Ecologie des Ressources naturelles, 4. Ecologie appliquée et sciences de l'environnement*, Masson, Paris, 1981. Proportionally, Australia is the world's driest continent, nearly three-quarters of it consisting of arid or semi-arid zones.

16. UNEP, *Global Environment Outlook*, Chapter 2.

17. Klaus Töpfer, executive director of UNEP, message to the second session of the Conference of Parties to the United Nations Convention on Combating Desertification (Dakar, 9 December 1998).

18. See Chapter 19.

19. Speech to the Special Session of the United Nations, 'Towards global sustainability', 25 June 1997.

20. Bo Kjellén, ambassador of Sweden, chairman of the Negotiating Committee of the International Convention on Combating Desertification, former chairman of Working Group I of the UNCED Preparatory Committee, responsible for negotiations on *Agenda 21*, Chapter 12, of the 1992 Rio Convention on Desertification and Drought. Personal contribution to the work of the Analysis and Forecasting Office.

21. The question of the sharing of water resources has already resulted in some important agreements, such as the 1995 Protocol of the Southern African Development Community (SADC) relating to shared regional watercourses. See also Katherine Waser, 'Water as source of life, water as source of cooperation?', *Aridlands Newsletter*, No. 44, Fall/Winter 1998.

22. S. Jodha, *Lutte contre la sécheresse. Les stratégies paysannes et leurs répercussions politiques*, IIED, Dossier No. 21, 1990.

23. *Connect*, September 1994.

24. In this respect, see Chapter 1 and A. Shaikh and S. Snrech, *Options pour un Développement durable: environnement et développement au Sahel*, Paris, Club du Sahel, 1993.

25. See Chapter 10.

26. Shaikh and Snrech, *Options pour un Développement durable*.

27. Beaumont, *Drylands*.

28. See Chapters 3 and 9. In Crete, for example, the tourism-related demand for water is set to increase exponentially in the next 20 years. Analyses carried out in the context of the European MEDALUS project show that the likelihood of water scarcity would then increase from 20% in 1980 to 85% in 2010.

29. *The State of India's Environment*, CSE, New Delhi, 1987.

30. See Mike Hulme's submission to the conference 'The African Sahel 25 years after the Great Drought', held at the Royal Geographical Society (London) on 13 and 14 March 1998.

31. Submission by Rob Groot, Henk Brukman and Herman van Keulen to the conference 'The African Sahel'.

32. Commonwealth of Australia, *Future Change in Australian Rangelands*, 1994, p. 20.

33. UNEP, *Global Environment Outlook*, Chapter 4.

34. Mick Kelly and Mike Hulme, 'Desertification and climate change', Tiempo Climate Cyberlibrary.

35. J. F. B. Mitchell, F. C. Johns, J. M. Gregory and S. F. B. Telt, 'Climate response to increasing levels of greenhouse gases and sulphate aerosol', *Nature*, 1995, No. 376, pp. 501–4.

36. N. Petit-Maire, 'Will greenhouse gasses green the tropical deserts?', *Geological Correlation*, No. 25, Paris, IGCP–UNESCO–IUGS, June 1997 (activity report of the International Geological Correlation Programme, IGCP).

37. Dave Thompson, Robert C. Balling, Martin A. J. Williams et al., *Interactions of Desertification and Climate*, John Wiley & Sons, New York, 1996.

38. Kelly and Hulme, 'Desertification and climate change'.

39. Hadley Center, 'Climate change and its impact (Buenos Aires, 1998)' (online on the Internet).

40. Ibid.

41. B. Thébaud, *Courrier de la Planète*, 1994, No. 20, pp. 23–4.

42. Michel Batisse cites the case of the oil-rich Middle Eastern countries whose income enables them to finance seawater desalination or to subsidize irrigation using groundwater, the latter solution incidentally not being without risks. On this topic, see Chapter 9.

43. Michel Batisse, *UNESCO Courier*, January 1994.

44. United Nations, 'Comprehensive assessment of the freshwater resources of the world: Report of the Secretary-General' (April 1997).

45. Batisse, *UNESCO Courier*.

46. *Courrier international*, No. 427, 7–13 January 1999 (article by Anton Vos from *Le Temps*, Lausanne).

47. UNESCO, *Arid Zones in UNESCO's Programmes*, UNESCO, 1995.

48. *Connexion*, September 1994.

49. UNESCO, *Arid Zones*.

50. United Nations, 'Comprehensive assessment'.

51. Daniel Balland, *UNESCO Courier*, January 1994.

52. Ibid.

53. In Tunisia, encouragement has been given to 'an agricultural development of semi-intensive type, based on judicious use of run-off water obtained, in particular, by the building of a multiplicity of small dams to hold back the water and combat wind and water erosion' (UNESCO, *Arid Zones*).

54. CIND, *Diversité biologique dans les zones arides du monde*, CIND, June 1994. *Gestion participative des ressources génétiques des plantes dans les parcours et les oasis au nord du Sahara*, FEM pre-project, October 1996.

55. Klaus Töpfer, 9 December 1998, press release.

56. R. C. Stone, G. L. Hammer and T. Marcussen, *Nature*, 1996, No. 384, pp. 252–5.

57. The regional approach recently adopted for the impact studies drawn up by the IPCC (Intergovernmental Panel on Climate Change) should enable closer analyses to be made of the interactions between climate change and desertification.

58. C. Rosenzweig and M. L. Parry, 'Potential impact of climate change on world food supply', *Nature*, No. 367, 1994, pp. 133–8.

59. Ibid. For an example of this approach, see *Preserving Resources. The Fight Against Desertification: A Priority of German Development Co-operation*, German Ministry of Co-operation and Development, Bonn, August 1996. See also *L'Eau: la coopération française et l'eau en Afrique*, Ministère de la Coopération, Paris, October 1994.

60. M. Tiften, M. Mortimore and F. Gichuki, *More People, Less Erosion*, Wiley, Chichester, 1994.

61. *UNESCOPRESS*, 30 June 1995.

62. Y. Jadot and J. P. Rolland, *Les Contradictions des politiques européennes à l'égard des pays en développement*, Solagral, Paris, 1996.

63. Also known as LEISA (low external input sustainable agriculture).

64. 'Sustainable land use', sectoral policy document No. 2, Development Cooperation, Ministry of Foreign Affairs, the Netherlands. This kind of local management of land, involving participation by the communities concerned, the mobilizing of civil society and environmental education are recommended, for instance, within the CILSS (Permanent Interstate Committee for Drought Control in the Sahel).

65. United Nations, 'Comprehensive assessment'.

66. Kjellén, personal contribution to the work of the Analysis and Forecasting Unit.

67. The other two being the Framework Convention on Climate Change and the Convention on Biological Diversity.

68. Exemplary work is being done on this by the University of Linköping, Sweden.

69. L. Tubiana, introductory note to the seminar 'Politiques et sécurité alimentaire: prospective à long terme', European Commission-Solagral, 1996.

70. Kjellén, personal contribution to the work of the Analysis and Forecasting Unit.

71. Théodore Monod, interview given to Michel Batisse, *UNESCO Courier*.

72. Ibid.

CHAPTER 9

. . . .

Is Water Running Out?

§ IN a nightmare vision, Coleridge's Ancient Mariner exclaimed: 'Water, water, everywhere, Nor any drop to drink'.[1] Will this sombre prophecy be fulfilled in the twenty-first century? At first glance, water is the natural resource our planet is least short of. The abundance of water has earned the Earth the nickname of the 'Blue Planet'. Nevertheless, out of a total of 1.4 billion km^3 of water, fresh water only accounts for approximately 2.5% of that quantity. Fresh water is mostly to be found in deep-lying aquifers, glaciers and polar ice caps which are all relatively inaccessible; only 0.3% of fresh water is renewable and available for human use and consumption.[2] Watercourses, which account for most of our renewable resources, represent only approximately 41,000 km^3 per year for continental water sources, and only approximately 9,000 km^3 are actually accessible and can be used for human consumption.[3]

Water, like air, is an essential natural resource for human populations, in terms of their health, economic activity and cultural well-being.[4] Water shares with air the predominant feature of being renewable, at least in appearance, though only in part. This means that the various uses of water do not destroy it but merely consume its qualities or transform its state. Both upstream and downstream, the uses of water for a particular purpose affect uses which could be made of it for other purposes and in other contexts (to borrow the language of economists, its uses determine significant 'external features'). Water is the only 'raw material' the use of which has repercussions on reserves. Nevertheless, one feature that makes water different from air is that it is not equitably distributed: water is perhaps abundant, it may be readily available, but not everywhere nor for everyone.

Today, almost one-quarter of humanity, i.e. 1.4 billion people, does not have direct access to drinking water[5] and more than half of humanity does not have satisfactory water purification plants, as efforts to facilitate access to clean water since the 1980s have, in fact, merely kept pace with population growth. One of the main problems facing the developing countries is that of ever faster urbanization, the result of which is that increasing numbers of people have to live in urban fringe areas or shanty towns where it is extremely difficult to provide an adequate supply of clean water.[6]

According to the World Health Organization (WHO), some 30 million deaths every year are thought to be attributable to water pollution, in the form of cholera, various types of hepatitis, dengue fever, malaria and other parasitic diseases, the effects of which are particularly devastating in the developing countries. It is estimated that four million children die every year from illnesses transmitted by water unfit for drinking, that is, one child every eight seconds. Out of the population of the developing countries 66% have no toilets, nor even latrines. According to the WHO, reducing the incidence of diarrhoeal infections would make it possible to save 1.25 million children annually. What is more, illnesses related to contaminated water hamper the economic development of the countries of the South for, when they are not fatal, they disable hundreds of millions of people.

The Dublin conference held in January 1992 acknowledged this terrible injustice and adopted a Statement on Water and Sustainable Development asserting the principle of equity which would lead to recognition of the fundamental right for every human being to have access to drinking water and purification plants. At a time when urban populations are continuing to increase and population growth is bringing additional pressure to bear on irrigated land, more judicious management of the planet's water resources has become a major challenge. In the words of Benjamin Franklin, 'When the well is dry, we know the worth of water.'[7]

Uncontrollable Demand?

For a long time, human consumption of water, which, like populations, was growing comparatively slowly, had only a negligible impact, compatible with the needs of other living beings in the biosphere and with the potential of natural reproduction. Those times are now over. In the last few decades, world consumption of water has continued to increase at a particularly fast rate, more rapidly, in fact, than population growth. It has increased sevenfold since the beginning of the century and threefold since 1950, with water consumption per inhabitant reaching a level 50% higher than that of 1950 on account, in particular, of improved living standards and the extension of irrigation.

Today, the quantity of water used for all purposes exceeds 3,700 billion m^3 per year (ten times more than at the beginning of the twentieth century), which represents approximately one-tenth of the total flow of rivers through-out the world.[8] Population growth, with almost two billion more people since 1970, has resulted in reducing the quantity of water available per inhabitant by one-third as the quantity available is virtually constant. For the period from 1995 to 2025, the increase in world demand for water is likely to reach 38% and that for drinking water 82%.[9] Obviously, these figures conceal enormous national and local disparities.

It should be noted, however, that there is nothing inevitable about those trends, since totally erroneous forecasts have often been made in the past, because of projections based on unchanged growth rates, as though the future could only replicate the past or present. In the USA, for example, after a rapid growth in the mid-twentieth century, the trend was interrupted in the 1970s and consumption patterns since 1980 have stabilized at levels quite different from earlier 'forecasts'. There is evidence today of a decelerating trend in many industrialized countries: most of the earlier forecasts seem to have been overestimated, often deliberately, in order to exert greater influence on investment policy decisions.[10]

Controlling demand, particularly for irrigation, is one of the most promising prospects for countries with limited water resources, and all the more so as it is difficult to increase supply with new dams, for example.[11] What matters above all is the integrated management of water resources. This idea would be part of a global approach to interaction between water and what is customarily called civilization, that is to say, the beliefs, values, types of behaviour and cultural customs that shape a particular society. Issues affecting water resources are in fact completely intertwined and that is why they are not easily understood. The management of water resources lies among UNESCO's fields of competence. From 1964 to 1973, the International Hydrological Decade highlighted – in prophetic terms – the need for coordinated action and collective research in the field of water. The International Hydrological Programme, with its 158 National Committee has, since 1974, been our main instrument in this field.

The Threat of Water Shortage

A particularly striking indication of the growing scarcity of water is the number of countries whose population has exceeded the numbers that could be easily provided for with existing water resources.[12] Once theoretical natural water resources (a level that takes account of the fact that one cannot economically and practically exploit all the water resources in a country) fall below 1,000 m³ per inhabitant in an average year, water is considered to be a scarce resource which hampers a country's development.[13] The Water Resources Institute estimates today that some 26 countries, including eleven in Africa, belong to that category and some 232 million people are affected. By 2010, this list will include six other countries and the number of Africans living in countries where water is scarce will rise to 400 million, which represents 37% of the estimated population for that continent. The situation is also critical in the Middle East as it is a region which must cope not only with water scarcity (nine out of 14 countries are short of water) but also with a very high population growth rate. In the region, geopolitical tension related to the use of water is likely to grow,[14] as competition for 'blue gold' intensifies.

It must be borne in mind, as regards water, that the problem is not so much water shortage on a world scale as the inequality of its distribution. Hydrologists estimate that even if population growth were to increase substantially and the world population were to reach between 10 and 12 billion people, theoretical natural water resources per capita would on average remain above the 1,000 m^3 per year per inhabitant required to avoid heightening tension and jeopardizing food production. Consequently, the fundamental problem is distribution and accessibility of water resources.

For example, Brazil, Russia, Canada, the USA, China, Indonesia, India, Colombia and the 15 member states of the European Union share between them almost two-thirds of the world's water resources.[15] According to other estimates, ten countries alone share approximately 65% of world water resources.[16] In an average year, water resources vary per inhabitant from 23 m^3 in Djibouti to almost 700,000 in Iceland.[17] While an American uses 425 litres of water per day for private and domestic needs, a Frenchman uses 150 litres and a Malagasy living in a rural area makes do with only ten.[18] An Israeli uses four times more water than a Palestinian.[19] What is more, the situation in the countries that have a deficit in water is likely to worsen over time, as the population of those countries increases: the number of people who are short of water in the Mediterranean area today amounts to 113 million, but this figure is likely to exceed 200 million by 2010.[20]

While the major concern is one of inequitable access to resources, the excessive, unregulated exploitation of ground water is also worrying. Intensive pumping methods draw enormous quantities of water and irremediably deplete this supply. This is already the case in China, India, Mexico, Thailand, the USA, North Africa and the Middle East. Furthermore, intensive pumping can deteriorate the quality of ground water by attracting salt water, particularly sea water in coastal areas. Boring for fossil ground water resources as practised in Libya can only be a temporary measure, even if it can continue for several decades.

The endless recurrence of the water cycle makes water resources renewable but not inexhaustible. In fact, renewable water resources can be exhausted when human beings have the power and means of using all the water flow in a given water system, and even of exceeding that limit in some instances by drawing on regulating reserves. This has already occurred in various countries such as the USA in the High Plains of Colorado and California, in Spain and in Israel. That is precisely why varied strategies are called for. It is obvious, nevertheless, that water can no longer be considered as an inexhaustible resource which every human being can use and misuse as he or she pleases.

What are the Prospects Between Now and 2025?

Among contemporary futurological exercises in this field, the most recent is that of the Russian hydrologist, Igor Shiklomanov.[21] According to his forecasts, the total quantity of water used on a worldwide scale in all sectors of activity, including the cooling of thermo-electric power stations and the evaporation of reservoirs, will increase from 3,760 km³ per annum drawn in 1995 (including 2,285 consumed) to 5,187 km³ per annum in 2025 (including 2,879 consumed), namely, an increase over 30 years of 38% in the exploitation of water resources and of 26% in consumption.

Igor Shiklomanov observes that the essential indicator is the ratio between renewable water resources and water consumption, that is to say, the percentage of available water used. According to this approach, four categories can be highlighted:

- when the ratio is below 10%, pressure on water resources is slight;
- when it is between 10% and 20%, pressure is medium;
- when it is between 20% and 40%, pressure is high; and
- when it exceeds 40%, pressure is extremely high, and when it exceeds 60%, it amounts to a catastrophic scenario.

According to Shiklomanov's estimations, 80% of the world's population in 2025 will find itself somewhere between the third and fourth categories, corresponding to high pressure on water resources. In the industrialized countries, in Europe and in the USA, the decrease in the availability of water will be relatively slight, insofar as the coefficient of reduction between 1950 and 2025 should be approximately 1.8. But in developing countries located in a temperate or tropical climate and blessed with adequate water resources, as in Asia and Latin America, the coefficient of reduction should reach 4.5. As for countries in arid regions, as in Africa and the Middle East, which will have to face the most dramatic circumstances, the coefficient should be approximately 8.5.

Another recent forecasting exercise, coordinated by the French hydrologist Jean Margat, posits two hypotheses, the lower projection that minimizes all the factors regarding water needs being more compatible with 'sustainable development'. This forecasting process has also enabled estimates to be made of net water extraction and consumption by 2025. According to the lower estimate, extraction of water (excluding hydroelectric power stations, which restore water after use) is expected to increase from an initial volume of

3,024 km² per annum in 1990 to 3,073 km³ per annum in 2025, while consumption will increase from 1,872 to 1,955 km³ per annum. According to the higher estimate, exploitation (excluding power stations) would reach 4,416 km³ per annum and consumption 2,950 km³ per annum.[22]

According to the higher estimate, the sharpest increase in exploitation would occur in Africa, where it would more than double in 35 years, compared with an increase of 70% in South America, 57% in North America (doubling in Mexico) and a reduction in Europe (−17%). In absolute terms, however, it is in Asia that there would be the sharpest increase (+1,087 km³ per annum). In 2025, more than two-thirds of world water use is expected to occur in Asia. According to the lower estimate, relative growth would be very limited almost everywhere, except in Africa (+45%), and sometimes nil or negative (−27% in Europe, −2% in the USA).

Average demand for water per capita is generally expected to decrease in all circumstances, but particularly according to the lower estimate, whereby the world average would fall from 575 m³ per annum at present to 395 or 490 m³ per annum. This trend could be observed virtually everywhere except in a few regions where current demand is very low, such as Africa and South America. This means that demand for water worldwide, in most regions, will cease to grow faster than populations in the twenty-first century, unlike the increase generally observed during the second half of the twentieth century.

Future water crises will therefore be linked less to growth in demand as such than to high consumption rates per capita, even when they are stabilized, of natural water resources and to the economic incapacity of meeting such demand, even when it is not growing. Two sorts of water shortages can and should be highlighted:

- Structural shortages due to the exhausting of conventional resources, worsened by cyclical shortages in times of drought, will affect an increasing number of countries.
- Shortages due to poverty will affect the least developed countries, which are unable to invest to meet demand, particularly that of major conurbations, or to modernize irrigation systems by increasing their efficiency and by reducing their consumption of water in arid areas.

Controlling Irrigation

One of the major problems that any policy for the efficient use of water resources absolutely must solve first and foremost is the excessive consumption of water in irrigated farming. Furthermore, water is not only drawn but largely 'consumed', in other words, it is returned directly into the atmosphere and not restored for local use. At present, agriculture worldwide consumes almost two-thirds of all water drawn from rivers, lakes and the water table. Since 1960, the quantity of water used for crop irrigation has risen by over 60%.[23] Enormous quantities of water are wasted on very low-value crops while needs, particularly those of major cities, continue to grow. In many developing countries, farmers use twice as much water per hectare, on average, as in the industrialized countries, for yields that are three times lower, and these low yields mostly affect semi-arid or arid areas.[24] Experts generally consider that only one-third of all the water used in agriculture actually contributes to making crops grow.

As noted by Sandra Postel, numerous techniques already exist that enable us to use waters more rationally, such as drip irrigation, small-scale projects such as mini-dams, relatively shallow wells and cheap pumps.[25] Very simple techniques aimed at increasing soil humidity around the roots of crops make for distinctly higher yields and make production less uncertain. Even with relatively low rainfall, some cultivation methods based on good water collection have proved to be very efficient. An original example is that of the use made in India of the vetiver, whereby yields of certain hillside crops can be doubled by creating barriers of vegetation that retain rainwater and preserve soil humidity.[26] A number of experts believe that it is possible to provide 50 litres of water per day per person for 54 people on the basis of a surface area of one hectare with an annual rainfall of 100 mm.[27]

The Israeli expert Uri Shamir also points out that modifications in the space around plants can improve the efficiency of water in producing crops in both rainfed and irrigated agriculture. This includes modifications in the micro-climate above the plants; shaping the land surface to minimize evaporation and run-off and maximize infiltration; ploughing and mulching to improve soil-water storage and distribution; and irrigation techniques designed and operated to deliver the water where and when it will be used efficiently by the plant for production of the desired crop.[28]

These solutions are by no means ideal and the advantages and efficiency of small-scale operations should not be exaggerated; nor should those of techniques that require major investments and profound change in attitudes and habits. Drip irrigation, which now extends over vast areas of cultivation, is usually relatively costly, small-scale dams often become silted up very quickly and shallow wells are often the least productive. That is why innovations of this kind should be part of a more global strategy. What matters is not only to encourage farmers to use water resources more efficiently but also to improve the quality of pipes that convey water to farms.

The reallocation to cities of a substantial proportion of water resources now used for irrigation should not result in a fall in farmers' income or in a rise in the prices of basic foodstuffs, which would have negative effects on the food security of the most impoverished populations.[29] To improve the agricultural use of water, farmers must be involved in the design, management and operating of hydraulic infrastructure. In the Philippines, for example, it has been observed that when farmers are involved in the planning and management of projects, irrigated areas increase in relation to initial estimates, the yield of rice paddies rises and the operating of infrastructures and piping systems improves.[30] Participation was in fact recognized as one of the essential principles of the Beijing Declaration, adopted by 50 countries in March 1996: 'Water development and management should be based on a participatory approach, involving users, planners and policy-makers at all levels.'[31]

Apart from reducing the quantity of water used and making it available for other purposes, more efficient use of water in agriculture would also have beneficial effects on the environment. Excessive irrigation and poor drainage accelerate the salinization of land. This is a particularly serious danger, even a 'time-bomb'. In Pakistan 25% of land under cultivation has been degraded in this way and some 200,000 hectares of farm land are lost each year throughout the world.[32] What is more, any attempt to recover land affected by salinization is extremely costly. To ensure that salinization does not destroy land irremediably, the quantity of water used by farmers must be reduced and drainage methods must be employed that enable water to be reused.

Two FAO experts, Wulf Klohn and Hans M. Walter, have made it plain that new computerized technologies applied to agronomy can help to irrigate crops in a more accurate and economical way, and that their relatively low cost should make it possible to adapt them without major difficulties to the needs of the rural communities in developing countries.[33] It might therefore be possible, in the future, for progress achieved in biotechnology to allow agricultural productivity to be increased while reducing the quantity of water required for production: it would be feasible, for example, to increase the resistance of plants to heat and drought, to transfer some of the properties of those cereals that require little water (such as sorghum and millet) to cereals that require more water (such as wheat and maize), or even to cultivate certain plant species in relatively saline water.[34] UNESCO sponsored a study on this subject at a research centre in Tunisia some 30 years ago.

Water Quality and the Environment

The problem of water pollution is one of the most preoccupying current developments and cannot be overlooked. Today, 90% of waste water in the developing countries is disposed of without having undergone any treatment,[35] and the situation is far from perfect in the industrialized countries.

River pollution is particularly threatening, whether it is caused by the lack of purification of waste water (predominantly intensive and localized pollution) or by the excessive use of fertilizers and pesticides (essentially extensive pollution). In the first case, the discharge of waste water may be such that it saturates the self-purification capacity of rivers. As for the second case, according to Nguyen Tien Duc, the concentration of nitrates in rivers in Western countries increased twofold and sometimes even fivefold in the 1970s and 1980s.[36] As emphasized by the International Conference on World Water Resources at the Beginning of the Twenty-first Century, held in June 1998 by UNESCO, the World Water Council and the International Association of Hydrological Sciences, degradation of the quality of water diminishes its use and increases its cost, particularly for human consumption. It also impoverishes the heritage we shall bequeath to future generations.[37]

It will be increasingly necessary to encourage projects promoting a reduction in the flow of nutrients and emissions of toxic substances of domestic, industrial or agricultural origin. Legislation for combating pollution has already had some impact in the industrialized countries by imposing compliance with specific standards regarding the quality of water before industries discharge their waste water into the environment. The most efficient and least costly way of abiding by such legislation consists more often than not in treating and recycling water, thereby reducing the volume of waste water. Such legislation therefore has two positive consequences: it contributes not only to purifying lakes and rivers but also to encouraging more economical and more rational use of water. Nevertheless, pollution of agricultural origin has not yet been adequately controlled in the industrialized countries, especially pollution caused by nitrates.

A promising example is that of the Rhine. The coordinated action of the states bordering on the Rhine has resulted in a marked improvement in the quality of the water of a river situated at the heart of an intensely industrialized region, which had earned itself the unfortunate nickname of the 'sewer of Europe'.[38] Among other encouraging examples, mention can be made of Japan, where the contribution to the gross domestic product of each cubic metre of water supplied to industry amounted to US$77 in 1989 as opposed to $21 in 1965. Mention should also be made of the USA, where the total quantity of water used for industrial purposes has decreased by almost 40% since 1950 while industrial production has been multiplied by 3.5 in real terms; or West Germany, where the total consumption of water by industry in 1995 did not exceed the level of 1975 although industrial production had increased during that period by 44%.[39]

Unfortunately, incentives to save water, treat it and recycle it are infrequent or not applied with enough rigour in the developing and industrialized countries, which fail to charge the proper price for the provision of water and neglect the treatment of waste water. Experience has shown, however, that these incentives can produce positive results. In Goa, India, a fertilizer plant has halved its water consumption in six years on account of high prices and

---

Box 9.1 Trees to Purify Water?

An interesting option, which would warrant closer examination and could play a significant role in water purification in the developing countries, especially in rural areas, involves the *Moringa oleifeira*. This is a tree from northern India whose seeds can be used to filter dirty water by attracting bacteria and viruses and by encysting them. This discovery was made by Geoff Folkard, a professor at the University of Leicester in Great Britain, whose studies have shown that by grinding these seeds and mixing them with muddy solutions derived from rivers, it is possible to obtain drinking water within a few hours, at a distinctly lower cost than that of the chemical products used today.

Source: Catherine Vincent, 'Les graines d'espoir du *"Moringa oleifeira"'*, *Le Monde*, 18 September 1995.

---

pressure from the government for it to reduce the quantities of effluents it discharges into the sea.[40] In the state of Jalisco, in Mexico, a sugar mill cut back its water consumption fivefold over four years, while reducing its production costs, thanks to a system combining water recycling and the setting up of closed circuits in which water circulates continuously through the various stages of production, thereby eliminating any wastage.[41]

Water: An Economic Asset?

Instead of seeking continually to satisfy growing demand for water, it will be necessary in the future to try to secure reliable water supplies through more judicious management of demand whereby resources could be saved and the environment better protected. This is not merely a problem of technology and expertise but, first and foremost, a question of political will. In this regard, undercharging for water often leads to wastage and the planting of crops that require too much water. A World Bank study that reviewed its plans for supplying water to towns showed that prices charged for the use of water account on average for only 35% of the cost of supply.[42] According to the same study, the water sector, among the major sectors of infrastructure, is the one where the return on production costs is the lowest. While the rate is 160% on average for the telecommunications sector and 60% for energy, it is only 20% for water.

This undercharging has several negative consequences. Firstly, it deprives governing bodies of funds that could be used for maintaining and improving

the mains network and other irrigation systems. Secondly, it hampers implementation of an effective policy for remedying water leakage largely due
to old pipes in poor repair; such a policy could nevertheless be of great
benefit. It is a recognized fact that almost half of the drinking water supply
is lost in Cairo, Jakarta, Lagos, Lima and Mexico City. Another major problem
is that the poor suffer most from inadequate water distribution; when they
are not connected to the mains, they have to buy water from hawkers who
charge them as much as $2 or $3 per cubic metre.[43] Buying water from
hawkers or through people connected to the mains network costs on average
ten times, and sometimes twenty times, more in most cities in the developing
countries. It is therefore a genuine culture of maintenance of the distribution
system that is called for today.

Greater saving in the use of water, made necessary by the growing needs
of an expanding world population, requires more rational use of this natural
resource thanks to recycling; the reduction of leakages; more efficient irrigation; the reuse of waste water; the promotion, in the appropriate context, of
unconventional water production techniques, such as desalinization; and the
integration of purification processes in the management of resources. However, the users themselves must become aware of their responsibility not only
to themselves but to future generations as well. This points to the importance
of education and information, as underlined in the eleventh recommendation
of the Beijing Declaration.

The World Bank has stated that between US$600 and US$800 billion would
have to be found by 2005 to meet the whole range of expenditure required
for ensuring water treatment, for funding supply infrastructure and for meeting the needs of irrigation and energy production, and that the greater part
of the sum will have to be raised in the countries themselves.[44] In many
developing countries whose resources are particularly limited, the financial
burden is likely, unfortunately, to grow faster than the gross national product.
An effort of solidarity on an international scale therefore seems indispensable.

Water is obviously an economic asset, but one of a very particular nature.
Its generally low trading value bears no relation to its usefulness. To consider
water purely as an economic asset would therefore be an oversimplification.
It is first and foremost a natural, ecological asset that plays a vital role in the
biosphere, whose usefulness to humanity cannot be reduced merely to that of
a raw material that humanity can exploit and consume as it pleases. It is also
an asset that belongs to society and to human heritage, whose uses are
governed by law. Water is a scarce resource, essential for life, and should be
seen as a natural treasure, a part of the common heritage of humanity. It is
not only a direct resource but indispensable for the health of ecosystems,
even in humid regions.

Realistic pricing should therefore not exclude differentiated tariffs according to the use made of water and the ability of users to pay for it. What matters above all is to democratize access to this vital resource, as recently undertaken by the South African parliament by enacting a law stipulating that the price of water would depend on its use and would be more favourable to the least fortunate categories of the population which rely on collective pumps.[45] Nevertheless, as rightly pointed out by Uri Shamir, 'Pricing for economic efficiency can be achieved only when use is closely monitored.' In most countries, however, the difficulty of arriving at such precision in measurement constitutes 'one of the biggest obstacles to the use of pricing as a demand management tool in the domestic sector'.[46] For the management of water resources it will be indispensable in the future to find intermediate solutions between a pure market approach and a fully public sector system. With that aim in mind, the World Commission on Water for the Twenty-first Century recently recommended a five per thousand increase in global investment in the water sector and recommended that this increase be allocated to expenditure on education, training, rehabilitation and counselling.[47]

The Future of Water

Water will undoubtedly be one of the major international issues in the next century. It is becoming scarcer as a result of over-exploitation of water resources by the very populous human race, which squanders and pollutes them.[48] Its strategic nature is undeniable: more than three hundred river basins and lakes straddle international borders and ten rivers in the world flow through six countries or more.[49] Many countries rely for their water supplies on resources outside their own territory: this is the case for Egypt for almost 100% of its supplies, Syria for 80% and Israel for 55%.[50] Some 40 countries in all could be affected by military tension on account of a shortage of water.[51] In the absence of genuine international legislation on water, the sharing of water resources is a question of balance of power rather than of cooperation or collective management.

'Many conflicts in this century have centred on oil,' observes Ismail Serageldin.[52] 'In the next century, *wars will be waged for water*,' he adds, sharing the fear already expressed by King Hussein of Jordan some years earlier when he asserted that 'if another war were to take place in the Middle East, it is water that would be at stake'.[53] Therefore, policies will have to be introduced as soon as possible in a serious effort to reduce the risks of war in hydro-conflictual areas. In the view of Mohamed Larbi Bouguerra, such confrontation is not inevitable. To prove this, he quotes the example of Lesotho, which makes use of revenue derived from water sold to South Africa in order to fund primary education for all the children in the kingdom.[54] In Valencia, Spain, the local population has made use for over a thousand years of the

Tribunal d'Aigües (Water Court),[55] in which elected judges ensure the equitable distribution of irrigation water from the Turia river and settle disputes between local farmers. Why not take this court as a model for settling disputes between countries?

As pointed out by Joseph Dellapenna, professor of international law at Villanova University in the USA, the international community has already taken a significant step forward by approving in 1997, by 104 votes to 3, the United Nations Convention on the Law on the Non-navigational Uses of International Watercourses.[56] Once it has been ratified by 35 countries, this outline agreement will come into force and will help to regulate the international sharing of freshwater sources on the basis of equitable use. It will enable states to refer disputes to a judge and thereby facilitate endeavours to find a negotiated solution rather than resort to arms.

Leaving aside the need to control demand, which must not be neglected, can supply be increased where resources are inadequate? It should be borne in mind that water is a renewable resource which can be used several times in succession provided that the problems of pollution, evaporation, treatment

---

Box 9.2 Water: Solutions for the Future

An interesting desalinization technique is based on the inverted osmosis process. This process consists of compressing water through a semi-permeable membrane that allows molecules of water to go through and filters out salts. The Canary Islands writer Alberto Vazquez Figueroa proposes to exploit the energy of pressures obtained at the base of wells at a depth of 700 metres, which could amount to 70 atmospheres. This system could replace conventional turbo-pumps used for desalinization, which are very costly and consume large quantities of energy. According to Vazquez Figueroa, it would be possible, with this process, to save 72% of costs related to desalination techniques used up to now, while substantially reducing the initial investment (installation costs of 370 million francs as opposed to 580 million francs for a conventional desalinization plant). The total production cost would be 32 pesetas per cubic metre of drinking water, which amounts to less than one-third of the normal price of desalinated water. Vazquez Figueroa's project is being tested in thermal energy power stations and has already benefited from the support of investors such as Obras Subterraneas, a Spanish mining engineering company, and the financial group SBC Warburg. Experts, including Rafael Mujeriego of the Polytechnical University of Catalonia, nevertheless believe that a complete assessment of the process is called for, particularly insofar as it requires the construction of under-

and recycling are adequately addressed. When viewed from that angle, it can be estimated that the availability of water per inhabitant will not necessarily be reduced as the world population increases. Solutions have been implemented to ensure that urban waste water could be used for irrigation once it has been treated. We must nevertheless be realistic when speaking of recycling waste water. Even if it is technically possible to return water after use to its initial state before use, the process usually entails the use of energy and raw materials, which may have an effect on the environment as well as a cost that can be met only by industry and some large cities.

Furthermore, the option of desalinization of sea water should be contemplated seriously. It is already widely used in some rich countries such as Saudi Arabia and Kuwait, or in some island states such as Malta. It has been developed for local domestic or industrial purposes and the production cost – at almost one dollar per cubic metre – is still much too high for large-scale use such as irrigation. Nevertheless, evidence suggests that new, more efficient technologies linked particularly to solar energy or to the inverted osmosis process (see Box 9.2) can help to achieve productivity gains that, when com-

ground galleries, the cost and construction problems of which may vary considerably.

Long aqueducts could be built whereby water could be transferred between river basins. This solution has already been chosen by France and Spain. Transferring water from the Rhone (approx. 10 m³/sec) could help to make up for the lack of water affecting more than 8 million people in the Barcelona area. While the construction of this 'aquaroute' requires major infrastructure (underground pipes and pumping stations), the technical obstacles can be overcome.

Also with a view to the transfer of resources, Norwegian, British and American experts have devised large-capacity plastic bags that, when towed by tugboats, could transport water from one country or continent to another. This solution would be much less onerous than the transport of water by tanker vessels, for example. Experiments carried out so far have shown that these bags (which float because fresh water is lighter than sea water) can resist storm conditions.

Sources: Courrier International, 'Un écrivain trouve un remède à la sécheresse', No. 338, 24–30 April 1997; *Financial Times*, 'Uncharted waters', 20 February 1997; Antoni, Ventura, 'Administering the integral water cycle, trends in Catalonia for 2005', *Prospectiva 5*, 1996; 'Les outres à eau font leur chemin', *La Recherche*, No. 295, February 1997.

bined with an increase in the cost of traditional sources of supply, could make this option competitive sooner than predicted, at least for drinking water.[57] Moreover, it should be noted that the desalinization of water that is merely brackish can be carried out at much lower cost and is of interest to quite a number of countries.

Any solution to the water problem will lie not only in greater productivity of water resources and more efficient use of water in the various sectors – principally agriculture – whereby exploitation of water resources can be stabilized or possibly reduced, but, above all, in new consumption patterns, both individual and collective, through the promotion of an authentic water ethic that, based on the principles of sustainability and solidarity, would prevent absurd conflicts from arising. Up to now, attempts at solving the problem of water have essentially focused on supply. It has now become increasingly clear that in parts of the world where there is a potential water shortage, attention will have to focus on modifying demand. Consequently, changes of an ethical nature are going to be indispensable.

Technology and the market will be vital allies in this task but the right solution must first of all be found in the local culture and therefore in patterns of behaviour. The water ethic should rest on four principles: moderation, daring, caring for others and sharing. Moderation, because water resources must be carefully managed, recycled, treated and their consumption restrained. Daring, because putting off courageous measures, on the grounds of some still unknown factors in this field, would lead to the worst scenario, that is to say, allowing the crisis to degenerate beyond the point where anything could be done to solve it. Care for others, because more than 1.4 billion people are still without access to safe drinking water. Sharing, because the only alternative to worsening conflicts lies in solidarity, the will to act jointly, and equity.[58]

Of the two features of town planning that Rome bequeathed to the West, namely the viaduct and the aqueduct, we have developed only the former. We have built millions of kilometres of roads that facilitate land transport at the cost of excessive oil consumption and high rates of atmospheric pollution. We should not only clean up and decontaminate our means of transport, but should also develop the second term of the Roman equation. To transport water, aqueducts and aquaroutes need to be built that are as efficient as gas and oil pipelines. In addition to these pipelines, large-scale hydrological reserves must be created in order to avoid or limit the consequences of both drought and flooding. Let us just imagine: one day, water from Northern Europe could flow as far as North Africa; one day, the Water Tribunal that used to convene at the portal of Valencia Cathedral could act with the same wisdom on an international scale.[59]

If access to water is now regarded as a fundamental right, it falls to us to reflect on the responsibilities involved in the exercise of that right. Such reflection was initiated at the first World Water Forum held in Marrakesh, Morocco, in March 1997. It must now be pursued and lead to genuinely integrated management of water resources, ensuring the well-being of both present and future populations, as well as respect for the natural environment. As pointed out by Jean Margat, 'We cannot expect nature to provide us with conflicting services: on the one hand, supplying us with water, while on the other, eliminating and absorbing our waste.' The priority should now be to reconcile 'planning of water use and the management of water resources'.[60]

An adequate response to the world water crisis rests on a sounder grasp of the interdependence between water resources and human behaviour and on adequate measures at the national as well as transnational level. By setting up the International Hydrological Programme 25 years ago, UNESCO gave the water issue the priority it deserves. This programme now comprises a vast network of collaborators in over 150 countries, and coordinates an enormous number of activities ranging from the monitoring and evaluation of the degradation of ground water to the publication of educational books for young people and teachers. More recently, within the framework of follow-up action to the first forum in Marrakesh, the IHP contributed to launching the project for a World Vision of Water in 2025, which will seek to strengthen awareness of the water problem among all populations and to identify the measures to be taken to respond to it adequately.

Today, we can no longer provide exclusively national answers to problems that extend beyond the boundaries of states. Just as pollution, drug trafficking and the illicit arms trade call for responses from the international community as a whole, the prospect of a water crisis requires all countries to cooperate in the quest for solutions.[61] Throughout the course of history, human beings have acknowledged the need to pool their efforts and share resources in order to preserve their common safety. Water, in particular, provides them with many opportunities of learning to live together. It is fundamental today that we see water as a potential source not of conflict but of peace and prosperity for humanity as a whole.[62]

Pointers and Recommendations

- Renew and promote widespread effort to conduct forecasting exercises concerning water needs and resources, and crisis situations concerning water supplies (tension between demand and resources) in the various regions of the world.
- Increase considerably the aid provided by industrialized countries to developing countries with the scarcest water resources, particularly in three fields: adaptation to local socio-economic conditions and implementation of effective, water-saving irrigation techniques; development of the reuse

of waste water and of recycling; research and development work on cultivated plants which require the least water and are most resistant to saline
water, as well as on improved productivity of irrigated agriculture.

- Improve evaluation of the effects on the environment of various uses of
water by means of the appropriate indicators.
- Heighten public awareness of the value of water used for producing goods,
particularly agricultural, through price-fixing policies which would penalize
production that most required water and through fiscal or other measures
for saving water.
- Encourage, at government and local authority level, investment aimed at
ensuring adequate treatment facilities and at avoiding loss of drinking water
due to old and/or badly maintained mains systems.
- Promote the preparation, recognition and implementation of international
legislation on water, which, in particular, would facilitate the management
of water resources common to several countries.
- Promote, where appropriate, the construction of infrastructure for the
transport of water comparable to that used for the transport of oil and
gas.
- Increase the number of initiatives in education, information and public
awareness, which should be appropiate to each country and to each
category of actors involved, making intensive use of modern information
and communication techniques, so as to encourage the development of a
water culture and ethic based on four principles: moderation, daring, caring
for others and sharing.

Notes

1. S. T. Coleridge, *The Rime of the Ancient Mariner*, 1798, part 2.

2. Robert Engelman and Pamela Le Roy: *Sustaining Water: Population and the Future of Renewable Water Supplies*, Population and Environment Programme, Population Action International, 1993.

3. Mostafa K. Tolba, 'Fresh water: a major problem of the 21st century', International Conference on World Water Resources at the Beginning of the 21st Century, UNESCO, Paris, 3–6 June 1998.

4. Guy Marblat, 'Qui paiera le prix de l'eau?', *Une Terre en renaissance*, Le Monde Diplomatique, Dossiers Savoirs No. 2, 1994.

5. Source: UNEP, United Nations University, World Day for Water, 11 March 1999.

6. Dr Dennis B. Warner, WHO, *Drinking Water Supply and Environmental Sanitation for Health*, International Conference on Water and Sustainable Development, Paris, 19–21 March 1998.

7. Quoted in Sandra Postel, 'Facing water scarcity', *State of the World 1993*, Worldwatch Institute, Washington, DC, 1993.

8. I. A. Shiklomanov et al., *Assessment of Water Resources and Availability in the World*, State Hydrological Institute, St Petersburg, Russia, 1996.

9. Rémi Sadoux, *L'Or bleu de l'an 2000*, Jeune Afrique, 6–12 March 1996.

10. Jean Margat, 'L'eau et l'humanité au XXIe siècle', note prepared for UNESCO, 1997.

11. Michel Batisse, 'Eau et sociétés', *Ena mensuel*, No. 198.

12. Postel, 'Facing water scarcity'.

13. Malin Falkenmark, 'The massive water scarcity now threatening Africa – why isn't it being addressed?', *Ambio*, Vol. XVII, No. 2, 1989, pp. 112–18.

14. Postel, 'Facing water scarcity'.

15. Jean-Paul Besset, 'L'eau, enjeu de la paix et de la prospérité du XXIe siècle', *Le Monde*, 20 March 1998.

16. Yves Mamou, 'Pression démographique oblige, la pénurie d'eau est pour demain', *Le Monde*, 2 February 1999.

17. Roger Cans, *La Bataille de l'eau*, Le Monde-Editions, Paris, 1994.

18. Houria Tazi Sadeq, 'A rare and precious resource', *UNESCO Courier*, February 1999.

19. Mohamed Larbi Bouguerra, 'Bataille planétaire pour l'"or bleu"', *Le Monde Diplomatique*, November 1997.

20. Plan Bleu, *L'eau en région méditerranéenne*, Fascicules du Plan Bleu, Valbonne, France, 1997.

21. Shiklomanov et al., *Assessment of Water Resources*.

22. Vazken Andreassian and Jean Margat, *Prospective des besoins en eau mondiaux à l'horizon 2025*, Colloque International 'Quel environnement au XXIème siècle? Environnement, maîtrise du long terme et démocratie', 8–11 September 1996, Abbaye de Fontevraud, France.

23. United Nations Commission on Sustainable Development, *Comprehensive Assessment of the Freshwater Resources of the World*, Report of the Secretary-General, E/CN.17/1997/9, 4 February 1997.

24. Rémi Sadoux, *L'Or bleu de l'an 2000*, Jeune Afrique, 6–12 March 1996.

25. Postel, 'Facing water scarcity'.

26. Sandra Postel, 'Saving water for agriculture', *State of the World*, Worldwatch Institute, Washington, DC, 1990.

27. Ismaïl Serageldin, 'Water in the 21st century: a dialogue', *Water Policy*, No. 1, 1998.

28. Uri Shamir, 'Science and the management of water', *1998 World Science Report*, UNESCO Publishing, Elsevier, 1998.

29. Wulf Klohn and Hans M. Walter, *Perspectives on Food and Water*, FAO, International Conference on Water and Sustainable Development, Paris, 19–21 March 1998.

30. Postel, 'Saving water'.

31. Beijing Declaration, Habitat II International Conference on Managing Water Resources for Large Cities and Towns, 18–21 March 1996, Beijing.

32. International Hydrological Programme, *Water in our Common Future*, UNESCO, Paris, 1993. See also Chapter 8.

33. Klohn and Walter, FAO, *Perspectives on Food and Water*.

34. Serageldin, 'Water in the 21st century'.

35. United Nations Commission on Sustainable Development, *Comprehensive Assessment of the Freshwater Resources of the World*.

36. Nguyen Tien Duc, 'Les besoins en eau douce', *Futuribles*, June 1994.

37. *Summary and Recommendations of the International Conference on World Water Resources at the Beginning of the 21st Century, Water: A Looming Crisis?*, UNESCO, IAHS, WWC, Paris, 3–6 June 1998.

38. Roger Cans, 'L'état de santé écologique du Rhin est en constante amélioration', *Le Monde*, 13 March 1996.

39. Postel, 'Facing water scarcity'.

40. Ibid.

41. Juan Carlos Núñez, 'Mexico, the sweet smell of success', *UNESCO Courier*, February 1999.

42. *FY94 Sector Review Water Supply and Sanitation*, World Bank, 1994, in Ismail Serageldin, *Toward the Sustainable Management of Water Resources*, World Bank, Washington, DC, 1995.

43. Roger Cans, 'Devenue rare, l'eau risque d'être l'enjeu de conflits futurs entre nations', *Le Monde*, 16 August 1995.

44. Serageldin, *Toward the Sustainable Management of Water Resources*.

45. Ferial Haffajee, 'South Africa: water for everyone', *UNESCO Courier*, February 1999.

46. Shamir, 'Science and water management'.

47. 'Réunion pour une charte sociale mondiale de l'eau', *Le Monde*, 24 March 1999.

48. In fact, about 9,400 litres of water are used to make four car tyres and about 1.4 billion litres of water are needed to produce a day's supply of the world's newsprint; 'What price water?', *UNESCO Courier*, February 1999.

49. Philippe Collomb, *L'Homme et l'eau*, Population & Sociétés, February 1995, No. 298.

50. Michel Batisse, *Eau et Développement dans le bassin méditerranéen*, International Conference on Water and Sustainable Development, Paris, 19–21 March 1998.

51. Virginie Fauroux, 'Vers un tribunal mondial de l'eau', *Le Figaro*, 22 December 1997.

52. World Bank, *The Water Crisis*, World Bank, Washington, DC, 1995.

53. Françoise Chipaux, 'Jordanie: l'eau vitale pour la paix', *Le Monde*, 21 April 1994.

54. Mohamed Larbi Bouguerra, 'Bataille planétaire pour l'"or bleu"', *Le Monde Diplomatique*, November 1997; *The Economist*, 20 June 1992.

55. 'Valencia: a thousand years of calm waters', *UNESCO Courier*, February 1999.

56. Joseph W. Dellapenna, 'Custom-built solutions for international disputes', *UNESCO Courier*, February 1999.

57. Sadoux, *L'Or bleu de l'an 2000*.

58. See Federico Mayor, 'Daring, caring and sharing', *UNESCO Courier*, February 1999.

59. F. Mayor, address given at the 21st Congress of the International Water Services Association, Madrid, 22 September 1997.

60. Jean Margat, 'Vers une nouvelle culture de l'eau', *Twenty-first Century Dialogues*,

UNESCO, Paris, 16–19 September 1998. See Jérôme Bindé (ed.), *Les Clés du XXIe siècle*, Editions UNESCO/Seuil, Paris, 2000.

61. F. Mayor, Address given at the 21st Congress of the International Water Services Asociation.

62. F. Mayor, 'Water and civilization', address given at the first World Water Forum, Marrakesh, 22 March 1997.

. . . .

CHAPTER 10

Will There be Food for Everybody?

§ FOOD security will be a key issue in the twenty-first century. 'Our only salvation is to win the race between food production and population growth in the developing countries ... particularly in the least privileged ones,' stresses Jacques Diouf, director-general of the United Nations Food and Agriculture Organization (FAO).

On 16 October 1945, 44 countries created the FAO, with the ambitious objective of 'feeding the planet'. Food security, defined as the permanent access to basic foodstuffs for everybody, is far from assured today. It was expected that decisive action would be taken by the international community to guarantee world food security at the World Food Conference in 1974 and at the World Food Summit in November 1996. Yet, according to FAO estimates, there are still over 840 million people either starving or under-nourished in the world, that is, one in every five people in developing countries, as well as 2 billion people suffering from nutritional deficiency. Each year, millions of children continue to die of starvation or of illnesses related to nutritional insufficiency. Today, FAO records show that nearly 190 million children are underweight, another 230 million suffer from rickets, while a further 50 million are emaciated.[1] According to the World Health Organization (WHO), each year 2.7 million children suffer from eye injuries owing to a lack of vitamin A, and a further 350,000 go blind, of whom 60% die within a few months of going blind.[2] Furthermore, UNICEF emphasizes that women suffering from malnutrition give birth to children whose IQ is on average five points lower than that of children born to healthy women.[3] As long as this remains the case, can we be satisfied with the modest objective that member states adopted in the Rome Declaration on World Food Security, namely, to reduce merely by half the number of under-nourished people by 2015? I protested vigorously against this Declaration, which I believe to be a reflection of short-sightedness and lack of solidarity: attention is focused on the globalization of markets when it is the world's stability that is threatened in the medium term; the gradual globalization of poverty is neglected when we should be concentrating on reducing social imbalances. We continue to invest billions of dollars in weapons and in what is superfluous, while failing to take account of the millions of human beings who, each day, suffer in silence.

If we are to understand the issues, successes and failures involved in food security and to perceive more clearly the importance of education and other social parameters, we must bear in mind that the situation may be explained for the most part by the demographic evolution of the world population – from one billion people in 1830, to 2 billion in 1930, 3 billion in 1960, 4 billion in 1975, 5 billion around 1990, to 6 billion today, about 7 billion in 2010, and to between 7.7 and 11.2 billion in 2050, according to the most likely estimates, which obviously imply a considerable degree of uncertainty. How can we thus be certain that the planet's natural resources will suffice for the needs of the population in 2050? Since 1991, the United Nations Population Fund (UNFPA) has set the alarm bells ringing in the following terms: 'As the 20th century draws to its close, the world is confronted by a daunting challenge: to bring growing human numbers and their growing needs into balance with the natural resource base that underpins much development … The collision between human numbers and the resources needed to sustain them will become more acute in the remaining years of this century and beyond.'[4]

Lester Brown, president of the Worldwatch Institute, argued before the Rio Earth Summit that the world could not sustain a population exceeding 8 billion individuals.[5] This pessimistic prediction, subsequently reiterated by Lester Brown although it is disputed by a number of experts, is based on the following argument: the fall in the growth rate of agricultural production observed since the middle of the 1980s increases the uncertainty surrounding humanity's ability to feed an ever-growing population.[6] Since world prices remain too high and the stocks of principal export countries are at their lowest level ever, the threat of world food shortage becomes ever more imminent.

Population growth and the availability of natural resources would thus appear to be antagonistic. However, other experts proffer a more optimistic vision. For example, according to the demographer Hervé Le Bras, population explosion slows down rapidly, as states develop economically and as access to education becomes more widespread.[7] Another element of uncertainty reduces the reliability of food security forecasts: while it is possible to estimate the number of inhabitants on the planet through censuses and to anticipate population growth, albeit with a considerable degree of uncertainty, as well as to calculate or predict the value of production, we still have not carried out the 'natural heritage survey' recommended by the programme of action (*Agenda 21*) adopted by the Rio conference in 1992,[8] as well as by the World Bank.[9] This failure prevents a precise assessment of the gravity of the situation. Prospective work is currently being carried out without knowing the precise degree to which future risks may be ascribable to Southern population growth, or to trends in production and consumption in Northern countries. Expert opinion is similarly divided on an equally critical issue, namely, what type of adaptation and innovation capabilities human societies will display. The question 'will there be food for everybody?'[10] thus deserves to be tackled with precise knowledge of the facts and a close analysis of the 'possible futures' already taking root in the present. This question begs a further one, no longer exploratory, but normative and strategic: what should we do to eradicate hunger and under-nourishment? How should we proceed to ensure that there will be food for everybody and that this food will be both sufficient and appropriate?

Improvements in the Food Situation Since the Second World War

Over centuries, cereal yields remained relatively low. Thus, in 1660, the average wheat yields in France did not exceed 10 quintals per hectare. The practice of letting land lie fallow disappeared in Europe only in the twentieth century, with the advent of widespread use of green manure. In France, at the end of the eighteenth century, 40% of arable land still lay fallow. Thanks to recent technical advances, wheat, paddy rice and maize yields, as well as the acreage dedicated to their cultivation, have doubled, or even tripled. Advances in cultivation have greatly exceeded population growth. In most of the world's high-density zones, the history of the progress made in rice, wheat and maize cultivation derives from soil improvement achieved through working the land and through hydraulic engineering. However, numerous examples also exist of vegetal or animal over-exploitation leading to desertification and the collapse of certain societies. Thus any prospective research must be carried out with the aid of a balance sheet of resources.

When confronted, between 1965 and 1970, with the most rapid population growth ever witnessed by humanity, the FAO initiated the most ambitious exercise in agro-demographic forecasting undertaken to date.[11] Two key questions lay at the core of this study: could growth in food production continue at a pace equivalent to that of population growth? What would be the maximal population of each country by the year 2000, according to regional context? This analysis was carried out according to investment estimates corresponding to the three fundamental stages of land development:

- Low estimate: human labour is the sole method of production. No fertilizer or insecticides used.
- Medium estimate: human labour is completed by the work of draught animals. Some chemical fertilizers used to complement natural fertilizers

supplied by animal rearing. Elementary practice of soil conservation measures.

• High estimate: human labour is enhanced by a total mechanization of agriculture, the expansion of which depends both on the exploitation of very high return genetic material and on the use of any chemical products considered to be indispensable. A vigilant policy of soil protection is implemented.

The FAO study underlined the fact that in progressing from the first to the third technological stage, production capacity could be increased tenfold thanks to new infrastructure, land and water development, animal and plant genetic research, investments in livestock and in farm implements, but also, and more particularly, thanks to human resourcefulness and skills. The final report also signalled that the number of countries in a critical situation would rise sharply in the run-up to the year 2000.

At present, the planet's nutritional requirements are, nevertheless, better and better assured. On a global scale, the ratio of food availability to nutritional requirements has increased from 1.05 in 1962, to 1.12 in 1970, and to 1.18 in 1990, despite the exceptional population growth witnessed over this same period. However, the situation varies from one country to another. Having experienced serious average food shortage per capita until 1962, Asia has made a distinct and continuous improvement in its food situation. Today, Asia is catching up with Latin America where, after a period of improvement in the rate of coverage, a degree of stabilization is apparent. In contrast, Africa has not managed to improve its food supply situation and on average the situation has deteriorated in countries which principally consume cassava, yams or taro (rate of coverage: 0. 98 in 1990).[12]

The average availability of food supplies per capita has risen more sharply than expected in a good number of countries and particularly in Asia. The dreaded critical situations of 2000 have turned out to be fewer in number and less serious than predicted in the period preceding this date. In retrospect, the FAO's predictions have been borne out in those countries where agriculture is the dominant national activity and where economic development and technological progress have remained modest. This is especially the case in Africa. Insolvency has prevented the importation of grains necessary to feed the population, irrespective of the population growth rate. Moreover, the extremely uneven distribution of agricultural production supplies and factors has been responsible for much of the chronic under-nourishment during this period. The slowing down of the growth in agricultural production observed since the middle of the 1980s and the reduction in cereal production per capita since 1984 in particular can be accounted for by technical adjustment methods, such as the practice of 'freezing' land, in the principal cereal-exporting countries (USA, Canada, European Union) with a view to reducing stocks and bringing about an increase in prices which had been kept artificially low.[13]

While in 1960, 80% of the world's population lived in countries where food supplies were generally recognized as being insufficient (less than 2,100 calories per day per capita), today, less than 10% of the world's population is in this position. In most countries of the world, productivity still remains distinctly lower than the level that could be attained through the use of scientific knowledge and existing techniques. Considerable increases in productivity could be achieved with a modest investment through the use of simple techniques. For proof, it suffices to compare, region by region, current yields with those obtained in optimal conditions. The latter are still five to nine times greater than the average yields observable in both industrialized and developing countries.[14] Therefore, it appears that food insecurity is more the result of failing to apply known techniques – due to inequality of access to the means of production, or to knowledge and skills – than of a general lack of knowledge and techniques.

Is it, therefore, possible to refer to a lack of food resources on a global scale? The real problem is the inadequate distribution of these resources over the world's surface and the food shortages that particularly affect certain regions and certain disadvantaged population categories. As Edgard Pisani so accurately notes, 'producing sufficient food does not mean that everyone has a sufficiency of food, nor that global food security is assured'.[15] The problem of world hunger is not – or at least not yet – the result of a planetary incapacity to produce: it is rather a problem of unequal access.

The question of distribution of food resources, from both geographical and social perspectives, is indeed the key question. The FAO estimates that where food availability per capita totals 2,700 calories, the proportion of the population that is under-nourished stands at 10%. This proportion reaches between 15% and 35% where the level of national average food availability totals between 2,200 and 2,500 kilocalories. In fact, 'true food security cannot be achieved unless the national average food availability levels exceed at least 30% of needs'.[16] In order to achieve such an objective by 2050, food availability would have to increase by 14% on a global scale, with an increase of 8% in Latin America, 14% in Asia, 33% in Africa and 50% in East Africa.

From this point of view, the current policy of reducing food stocks is a dangerous one, because it pushes agricultural sector companies into taking the same risks as companies that follow a 'just-in-time' policy and which aim at responding to increased demand only when it occurs. According to Professor Ray A. Goldberg of Harvard University, this 'just-in-time' policy only aggravates the problem in times of real food crises.[17] The hundreds of millions of individuals suffering from hunger or from malnutrition should not have to pay the price of policies that sacrifice food security to an alleged economic rationale but, in reality, to the law of maximum profit. Kevin Watkins, head of the British charitable organization Oxfam, underlines in this respect that 'food security depends not on the availability of supplies but on the control of resources and on a balance of power'. He notes that in the Sahel, 'the production of sorghum, millet and cassava has declined by 1% per annum for the last twenty years, while, simultaneously, wheat importation has increased at an annual rate of 8%'. Kevin Watkins emphasizes the necessity of reversing this trend, 'because no country can afford either to allow its own food security to depend on fluctuations on the world market, or to witness the destruction, due to low-cost importation, of those small farms which constitute the very foundations of society'.[18]

Within individual states, the unequal distribution of wealth may often radically affect the nutritional situation of disadvantaged populations. For example, in a number of Latin American countries land ownership is monopolized, for the large part, by *latifundia*, vast domains possessed by a small number of families or, increasingly, by giant national or multinational companies. Here, the extreme concentration of land jeopardizes the future of poor peasants, thus encouraging the continuation of the social practices of a former age and frequently placing obstacles in the way of the development of modern agricultural practices. A more just distribution of land must be encouraged for both social and economic reasons, by means of efficient and wide-scale agrarian reforms. These must favour large-scale access to private property, the development of family farming as a business and the establishment of farming cooperatives where these may be adapted to the local context or to community practices. Nor must these reforms be implemented without active recognition of the rights of indigenous populations. In this respect, the Catholic Church's courageous stand in favour of agrarian reform is welcome.[19]

The under-nourishment of a region or of a category of the population is, in practice, nothing but another aspect of poverty – more often as a result of lack of revenue than of actual food shortage. In these circumstances, effective action to resolve the problem of world hunger requires not only technical solutions but, especially, political will. The Nobel prizewinner in economics, Amartya Sen, has, moreover, underlined the importance of democracy, of freedom of the press and of free access to information (and, by extension, to education) as primary factors in the fight against famine and in the creation of this political will. In order to explain famine, Sen tells us, our first consideration must not be for the totality of food provisions, but instead, for the 'rights' of vulnerable parties, that is, the appropriation 'rights' to food that these people could assert.[20] In reality, the assertion of such rights may take place only where there exists both public democratic space and public opinion,

222 · *Towards a Natural Contract*

that is, free and independent media. Since the infamous famine in Bengal in 1943, in which 3 million people died of starvation despite the existence of adequate food supplies in the province, the elimination of famine in the new, independent and democratic India was in large part the result of a programme of systematic public intervention.[21] Conversely, the existence today of serious famine in countries where neither freedom of the press nor democratic plurality or political liberty exist, proves the validity of Sen's thesis.

Human Nutritional Requirements in 2050

Population growth by 2050 will be the principal cause of an increase in demand for energy-giving food in developing countries. According to a prospective food study carried out for the FAO and the UNFPA, these energy demands could increase by 95% in the developing countries as a whole, by 215% in Africa, and by 250% in those African countries whose staple diet is cassava, yams or taro.[22] In fact, a fall in fertility by 2050 will have little effect on the population growth of the poorest countries, owing to their young population and to the phenomenon of demographic inertia.

Moreover, developing countries will have to complete and enrich their food diet if they wish to eliminate chronic undernourishment of one segment of their population. In order to achieve this, food availability in developing countries will have to increase by 18% by 2050. To provide a balanced diet (amino acids, vitamins and nutritious elements), this food will also have to be varied, requiring a further 19% increase in food availability in developing countries by 2050.

In total, developing countries will have to increase their provisions of energy-giving crops by 175% by 2050. However, the projected growth rates for plant-derived energy in Asia and in Latin America are significantly lower than the growth rates of agricultural production facilitated by the Green Revolution in those continents in the 1975–90 period. To meet their food requirements up to 2050, Latin American and Asian countries will have to double their food availability while Africa will have to multiply its plant-derived energy extraction levels by a factor of five (by seven in the case of countries whose staple diet consists of roots and tubers). It is among the populations who principally live on cassava, yams, taro or plantain that extraction of plant-derived energy must expand most rapidly, with an increase of 600% by 2050. Nearly twenty-five countries will need to increase by over 4% per annum their output of plant-derived energy from their own natural resources, which amounts to an eightfold, tenfold or even fifteenfold incease in extraction levels in 55 years.

Countries currently affected by the most severe chronic under-nourishment (fewer than 2,100 calories per day) are those that will have to bring about the most rapid increase in their extraction levels of plant-derived energy. They will have to do this by drawing on their own resources or, if they have the financial means, by relying on imports. This dramatic increase in extraction levels is not solely linked to the necessity to complete the current population's food rations but is also connected with the aim of providing for the needs of future populations up until 2050. This concerns in particular a great number of African countries with a large rural population (60–75% of the total population).

To cater to its population requirements, development in African countries should come close to that observed in East Asia between 1975 and 1990, that is, it should correspond to the highest growth rate for agricultural production recorded in this region. However, at the time, general economic growth in Asia provided an environment conducive to rural development. Current economic development in sub-Saharan Africa is far from being as favourable and the most rapid growth rate recorded in this region over a period of more than fifteen years was 2.4% per annum between 1971 and 1990.[23] Therefore, in countries where there is chronic under-nourishment, the performance levels that must be attained in order to ensure food security require a substantial change in their scale of development.

The annual growth rate for Asian agricultural production will probably be lower than that in recent decades (4.3% per annum from 1975 to 1990). This will also be the case for Latin America. In Africa, the growth rate for agricultural production should largely surpass that of the last 15 years. Owing to lack of land, seven countries (Ethiopia, Mauritania, Namibia, Niger, Nigeria, Uganda and Senegal) are unlikely to achieve food security unless they employ to the full the most advanced techniques available. Ten countries (Algeria, Burundi, Egypt, Kenya, Lesotho, Libya, Morocco, Rwanda, Somalia and Tunisia) will be incapable of feeding their populations adequately, even if they use the most advanced techniques available, and will be obliged to engage in large-scale cereal importation. Finally, 15 countries, including the ten just listed, will be faced with serious shortages of drinking water. Of these, five countries (Burundi, Kenya, Malawi, Rwanda and Tunisia) may have to import massive quantities of water or, for those countries where it proves feasible, to desalinate large volumes of sea water.[24]

The main prospective work carried out worldwide concurs in the estimation that critical situations will arise in a group of countries which account for 5 to 10% of the world's population. The countries in question are those that currently experience the greatest degree of under-nourishment. According to the FAO's predictions, the increase in food insecurity in Africa could eventually lead to political, social and economic destabilization across the entire continent.[25] Furthermore, such a situation could maintain a climate of perpetual international crisis.

Increased yields, combined with the growth of arable acreage and of irrigated zones, will provide a response to growth in sustainable demand on a global scale until 2010, or even until 2025. If current trends continue, chronic under-nourishment is expected to decrease worldwide. The number of under-nourished people should fall from 800 million in 1988–90 to 650 million in 2010. This development may be primarily explained by the impetus provided by Asia, whose under-nourished population should decrease by half, from 520 to 270 million people (however, these estimates do not take into account the world economic crisis, which has severely affected Asian countries since 1997). In contrast, under-nourishment will increase in Africa, with the number of people affected rising from 175 to 300 million.[26]

Industrialized countries should not encounter any difficulties in providing the cereals necessary to make up for the developing countries' deficit up until 2010, and even until 2025.[27] The reduction in agricultural production recorded since the middle of the 1980s is due to a global decrease in net cereal production by the principal exporting countries. This reduction has not been accompanied by a corresponding worldwide increase in prices, which in fact, until recently, have been falling. The aim of this deliberate decrease in cereal production by the principal exporting countries was to avoid a drop in prices that could have resulted from difficulties in clearing the accumulated surplus. The principal problem is that of the weak progress of affordable demand or, in other words, that of poverty, which halts demand and thus food production. The slowing in growth of agricultural production since the middle of the 1980s cannot be interpreted either as foreshadowing a shortage of food supplies or as reflecting that an upper limit of production imposed by environmental conditions has been reached. If there were to be an appreciable improvement in the distribution of the means of agricultural production and the spread of knowledge, it would not seem impossible to provide for humanity until 2050, on condition that we are guided by the quest for political stability on a world scale rather than by purely economic interests. Instead of wasting resources on instruments of destruction, we should be investing in the human aspects of security as this is the best means of preventing massive migrations, tension and conflicts related to food insecurity. The prevailing world situation reveals the failure of force as well as an economic system based on loans, which widens the gap between the developed and the developing countries instead of narrowing it.

Eight Proposals for the Elimination of Food Insecurity

'The demographic transition' Current demographic change could help progress towards attaining food security in the developing world, eventually leading to a decrease in population growth in developing countries. Voluntary

restriction of the number of pregnancies, an important factor in the fight against poverty, would play a major role in this evolution.[28] If this demographic change is confirmed, a 1.8% increase in the annual growth rate of available plant-derived energy will be sufficient to feed the populations of developing countries until 2050. The faster the demographic change, the sooner it will be possible to assure long-term development and food security worldwide.

However, the role of voluntary limitation of pregnancies must not be overestimated. The stabilization of fertility rates at 1.6 (UN low estimate), 2.1 (medium estimate), or 2.6 children per woman (high estimate) requires that Africa multiply its consumption of plant-derived energy by 4, 5, or 6 before 2050. As for the populations whose staple diet is composed of cassava or other roots or tubers, according to each individual case, they will have to multiply energy consumption by 6, by 7.2 or by 8.4. Thus, depending on whether one envisages a slow, medium or rapid fall in fertility levels, these countries will have to increase their respective extraction levels of plant-derived energy by 3.9%, 3.6% or 3.4% per annum between 1975 and 2050, figures that correspond to annual increases that vary little, regardless of the rate of decrease in fertility. Whatever the degree of increase, such growth rates seem out of reach in the absence of an adequate socio-economic context or adequate infrastructure and, thus, of deep-reaching political, economic, social, cultural and technical transformation.

New methods of land capitalization An increase in cultivated terrain could provide another response to food insecurity. According to the FAO, one billion eight hundred million hectares suitable for rain-fed farming remain, as yet unexploited, on the earth's surface, without counting the land in China.[29] Of those 1,800 million hectares, 94 are occupied by human establishments, 770 are covered by forests and 200 form part of legally protected zones (national parks, conservation forests, natural reserves).[30] Therefore, over 700 million cultivable hectares remain, or a surface area approximately equal to the size of that currently exploited. Most of the cultivable land not yet exploited is situated in Africa (500 million hectares in sub-Saharan Africa), in Latin America (220 million hectares), which has a vast reserve of forests, and to a lesser extent, in East Asia (45 million, not counting China), or in Southern Asia (10 millions). For the most part, these are lands that have low natural fertility. This could partly explain why the land colonization programmes put in place in recent decades have never managed to absorb sizeable proportions of excess rural populations.[31]

In other respects, the use made of these lands has often proved to be in opposition to long-term planetary food security requirements. Indeed, the techniques employed since the 1960s to improve agricultural exploitation yields have often had harmful effects on the soil and on crops, with excessive irrigation causing salinization of the terrain or, conversely, an increase in waterlogging. A recent report by the International Food Policy Research Institute (IFPRI) estimates that, of 8.7 billion hectares of pasture, forests and lands used for agriculture all over the world, 2 billion hectares have already been damaged by erosion, desertification and salinization. It is in Asia that forests have suffered most while, in Africa, pasture and cultivated lands have suffered major damage.[32] Guy Paillotin, president of the National Agronomics Research Institute of France, estimates that six million hectares of cultivated lands disappear each year because of soil deterioration. When combined with urbanization, these trends could result in the loss of 16 million hectares of agricultural land per annum over the course of the next few decades.[33] It would therefore be very risky to count on the opening up of new lands for cultivation as a decisive guarantee of food security in coming decades.

In this respect, Professor Swaminathan has recently put forward the concept of an 'evergreen revolution' distinguished by long-term agriculture, 'rooted in the principles of ecology, economics, social and gender equity and the generation of employment'.[34] This 'evergreen revolution' would be based on the following seven factors:

- soil maintenance, which is indispensable for any lasting intensification;
- the most efficient use possible of water designated for agricultural purposes, especially through rainwater conservation;
- crop management and pest control campaigns;
- more efficient energy management, with greater use of biogas, biomass, solar energy and wind power energy;
- investment in sanitary and phyto-sanitary measures to produce quality food products;
- close study of the composition of the agricultural system; and
- efficient information and training systems allowing for precision agriculture.

Another particularly important factor is facilitating the storage and conservation of food products, particularly through simple transformation processes that can be undertaken in rural 'micro-industries'. With this in mind, UNESCO established in 1992 a university chair on simple technologies to be implemented after harvest at Makerere University in Kampala, Uganda. It is also essential for the developing countries to have ready access to technical skills to ensure that harvesting is not conducted by specialized labour coming from more advanced countries.

Growth in productivity of factors and biotechnological support According to the FAO, cereal production yields could rise by 37% between 1988–90 and 2010 in developing countries. This means that growth in cereal production (by approximately 58%) would be due more to an increase in productivity than to an increase in cultivated lands (17%). The average yields of the three main cereals (rice, wheat, maize) seem likely to increase by 36%, 42% and 39% respectively. Therefore, an annual increase of 1.5% may be expected from cereal yields. These increased yields will especially be the result of improvement of cultivars[35] and progress in research, which will make a reduction possible in the gap between the yields obtained during trials and actual crop yields and will favour the expansion of biotechnology as well as permitting the selection of new, more productive varieties of cassava, yams and taro. These improvements in agronomic research could contribute to reducing food insecurity on a larger scale where selected roots and tubers could survive in unfavourable conditions and develop greater resistance to pathogenic agents. Research into improved varieties of dry cereals (millet) and of sorghum should also be relevant to those varieties cultivated in unfavourable climatic zones. As yet, not enough research is concentrating on improved cultivars.

Potential research progress must not lead to regarding genetic improvements as a solution to all problems. Needs and solutions vary according to the nutritional habits of different countries. Rwanda and Burundi derive a large part of their nutritional energy from roots or tubers, while completing their diet in a traditional fashion with pulses, rich in protein. These countries, which have high population density, need to develop the productivity levels of each factor of production (labour, land and water). Many other countries, however, whose primary consumption consists of roots or tubers, possess important reserves of wet land, which could be converted into a sizeable extension of cultivable lands. Some of these countries are densely populated. In such conditions, the extension of root and tuber cultivation provides effective solutions to the food problem.[36] Moreover, growing cassava requires no particular technical skill, in contrast to growing yams, which requires a particular know-how, used particularly in Nigeria. On the other hand, land reserves in countries such as Cameroon, Gabon, Côte d'Ivoire and Togo are limited, thus rendering increased yields an absolute necessity. From this perspective, Professor Marc Dufumier, of the French National Agronomics Research Institute (Paris-Grignon), reports that systems connecting trees, cultivation and animal rearing could allow increased yields to be obtained in densely populated regions. He quotes the example in the Sahel of *Acacia albida*, 'a deep-rooted tree which fixes nitrogen, seeks water from the depths and loses its leaves in the rainy season, during which it becomes possible to cultivate the land beneath its branches'.[37] Some experts underline the importance of developing cultivation practices in Africa that, while remaining in harmony with local food habits, would make for a better balanced diet: the cultivation of mushrooms should receive priority attention in this context, as they are rich in protein and may be developed even in conditions of poor soil or scanty light.

Importing food supplies Another method of assuring food security involves the importing of cereals. Many developing countries have, to different degrees, increased levels of cereal imports over the past decade. The large net cereal exporters have experienced no difficulties in dealing with this increased demand. The subsidization of agriculture, which exporting countries benefit from, combined with exceptional expansion in productivity in the North, are the factors that explain the low prices, as well as an increased volume, of cereal imports into developing countries. As national produce gradually proves less capable of providing for the nutritional requirements of the population, cereal importation has become increasingly indispensable for poor countries. However, the volume imported depends entirely on the solvency of the country.

In this regard, African countries stand out for two reasons. Imports are less voluminous wherever population growth is greatest, a fact explained by the lack of solvency in countries with high fertility rates. Moreover, in countries where cassava, yam and taro consumption is particularly high, the higher the population relative to agricultural terrain, the lower the volume of cereal imports per inhabitant, which reveals the degree of food insecurity in these countries. The more precarious the economic and political situation, the sooner these states find themselves unable to import the cereals necessary to feed their population.[38] For this reason, it is particularly important to break the vicious circle of loans and indebtedness. For the sake of worldwide stability, it will soon be essential to work out modes of financing that would enable the different countries to fit better into a more balanced world, by reducing the present imbalances that threaten international security.

Population redistribution Food insecurity brings about migrations towards neighbouring countries. It is also a prime reason for refugees settling in neighbouring countries, and can therefore cause social unrest and major conflicts regarding ownership of natural resources such as water and land. The foreseeable level of migration flows, even if it were to remain limited, is likely to cause political instability in the arrival zones. International migration, generally tightly controlled by the potential host countries, will not help to reduce the disparities in geographic distribution of populations and that of natural resources. It can, however, be the cause of social unrest of great intensity and a probable upsurge in xenophobia, which can result in violence.

Investment in infrastructure The permanent nature of food insecurity stems largely from insufficient infrastructure and basic investment in the rural world and from a lack of endogenous capacities, which could not be offset by development focussed on loans and external aid. This deficiency affects most areas, from irrigation and management of water supplies, to the road network, means of transport, the circulation of information, the banking system, marketing structures and access to agricultural suppliers. What are the consequences of such shortages in infrastructure and investment? The absence of, or distance from, markets, the lack of community, cooperative or mutual benefit organizations, the lack of veterinary supervision of herds, the genetic ageing of plants, and a slow-down in the development of agricultural techniques and training. To this list must also be added the deficiencies in agricultural policy that threaten to slow down rural development. Such policy is often badly adjusted to market regulation, often lacking a credit policy, long-term bonus loans or legislation appropriate to dealing with situations in which land ownership is disputed or uncertain. For all these reasons, it is essential to carry out audio-visual programmes for intensive training for the benefit of illiterate populations, in order to strengthen the capacities of rural communities.

The involvement of the North   Agriculture in developed countries grew over a long period of time, because of low profits from the invested capital. It took centuries to form the soil used for large-scale cereal cultivation, in particular of rice or wheat. We can therefore measure the financial flow from the North that would be necessary to strengthen the rural economies of the South and to contribute towards the elimination of poverty and food insecurity there. Yet such investments or aid would probably only constitute a very small repayment of the profits earned on the flow of foodstuffs which, from the colonial period until the present day, have made their way from the South to the North, and which helped to achieve the financial, technical, scientific and cultural capitalization of the West. However, laws concerning capital profitability are only distantly related to the history of civilization. Only an awareness of its own interests could ever convince the North to participate seriously in the South's development. From this point of view, Southern countries represent a potentially huge market, the expansion of which would be enormously advantageous to the interests of these countries and the Northern countries alike. All the same, it seems unlikely that the solution to food insecurity will take place through rapid and unhindered capital investments in the South by the North.

A necessary increase in affordable demand   As long as dependence on agriculture remains strong in developing countries, the fight against poverty will take place through expansion of food production and agricultural productivity. Therefore, it is necessary actively to encourage large growth in agricultural production in the least developed countries in order to fight against food insecurity. This demands growth in domestic consumption and, thus, a continued fall in prices, supported both by governments and by the international community, in order to promote sustainable agricultural development. This effort must be accompanied not only by a stimulation of the productivity of the different production factors capable of generating increased revenue (labour, land and water), but also by policies promoting basic health and education. In the context of malnutrition referred to above, such investments are guaranteed to produce a large return.[39]

Education and Training as the Basis for Development

Policies promoting education are particularly important in countries where the population suffers from chronic under-nourishment and where there is a large proportion of country-dwellers. The failures of the Green Revolution are largely due to the lack of basic education. The countries that suffer from chronic under-nourishment are also the countries with the lowest levels of attendance in primary education. In most of these countries, children who attend primary school represent less than 80% of the age range of six- to eleven-year-olds. In reality, the proportion is lower still, because, along with children aged six to eleven, schools also include adolescents who left primary school early, as well as illiterate adults. Basic education and intensive training for adults are the key to agricultural development. It is this that guarantees the adoption of more sophisticated techniques of natural resource management.[40] It facilitates increased productivity linked to the use of new crops or of high-performance cultivars. The diffusion of economic information and of technological innovation renders professional training and popularization imperative.

The priority given to women and to young girls – who represent 65% of the total illiterate population – is particularly important in terms of food insecurity, owing to the essential role played by women in agriculture in developing countries and to the proven link between education and a drop in fertility rates. Indeed, increased literacy among young girls and women brings about a fall in fertility rates, which also permits a reduction in family sizes and in the pressure on the 'carrying capacity' of land. However, this basic education must be accompanied by an improvement in women's health, and especially their nutrition. All this presupposes a mobilization of forces that goes beyond the competence of education ministries alone.

If there is not a rapid upswing in international cooperation, it will take at least two generations to attain a new scale of development and for educational progress to have visible results. Technical prowess and material success will not suffice to assure global food security. The ultimate key to security is to be found in the immaterial sphere. That key lies in the domain of knowledge and democratic autonomy, in the establishment of transparent government and in the emergence of a society whose solidarity is based upon the sharing of common values. World food security, in this sense, is increasingly dependent on global economic and political security and on 'ethical security', which stems from the alliance between social justice and the rule of democratic law. In a situation where we are witnessing rapid urbanization in the South and an increase in urban poverty, the stakes are considerable, as is emphasized by Michel Griffon, from the Centre for International Cooperation in Agronomic Research for Development (Cirad). He declares that, nowadays, 'poverty and famine do not constitute a geopolitical threat. But, if they were to become one in the first ten years of the twenty-first century, countries would perhaps then decide to carry out a gigantic Marshall Plan against poverty.'[41]

Pointers and Recommendations

- View the question of food security in a wider context, with relation to the evolution of demographic factors, health and educational policies. Within this framework, give priority to promoting basic education for all, intensive training for adults, and agricultural instruction.
- Create or improve the infrastructure necessary for sustained expansion of agriculture in developing countries. This concerns in particular irrigation systems, means of transport, marketing structures, banking networks and systems for loans.
- Anticipate with greater accuracy the risks which might affect world food security through the permanent updating of prospective research and through the systematic evaluation of development operations for the use of land and natural resources.
- Prevent the increase in surface area of cultivated land as well as research on achieving higher yields from impairing sustainable development. Encourage natural agricultural resource management that is both efficient and sustainable in the long term, particularly with regard to arable lands and water resources.
- Energize agronomic research and the transfer of technologies and of know-how. Use the contribution made by research, particularly in biotechnology, to improve yields and to obtain more resistant crop strains, while taking into account the risks that could be incurred, in the long term, for both the environment and consumers.
- Strengthen international cooperation so that migration flows in connection with food insecurity do not become a further source of poverty, instability and violence.
- Give greater importance to better land distribution, especially by means of large-scale agrarian reform, in order to avoid situations of flagrant injustice.

With this aim in mind, establish an appropriate legal framework, including a better definition of rights of land ownership and usufruct.
* Direct the assistance of rich countries towards preventive measures rather than solely towards crisis management.

Notes

1. FAO, *Synthesis of Technical Background Documents*, World Food Summit, Rome, November 1996.

2. Stéphanie Debruyne, 'Le défi alimentaire', in 'L'an 2000, et après ...', special issue of *Futuribles* review, January 1999.

3. Michèle Aulagnon, 'La malnutrition tue plus que n'importe quelle autre épid-émie. Le rapport annuel de l'UNICEF estime que sept millions d'enfants meurent chaque année', *Le Monde*, 18 December 1997.

4. UNFPA, *Population, Resources and the Environment: the Critical Challenge*, UNFPA, New York, 1991.

5. Lester Brown, 'Il faut des taxes de pollution de plus en plus lourdes pour augmenter le prix des énergies classiques', interview by Marc-Ambroise Rendu, *Le Monde*, 4 March 1992.

6. Lester Brown, 'La guerre entre l'homme et la Terre est d'ores et déja engagée', remarks recorded by Jean-Paul Besset, *Le Monde*, 27 February 1996.

7. Hervé Le Bras, *Les Limites de la planète. Mythes de la nature et de la population*, Flammarion, Paris, 1994.

8. United Nations, *Agenda 21*, UN Conference on Environment and Development, New York, 1992.

9. *World Development 1992 – Development and the Environment*, World Bank, Washington, DC, 1992.

10. T. Gaudin, *2100, Odyssée de l'espèce*, Editions Payot, Paris, 1993.

11. FAO, *Potential Population Supporting Capacities of Lands in the Developing World*, ed. G. M. Higgins et al., Technical Report of Project-Land Resources for Populations of the Future, Food and Agricultural Organisation of the United Nations, United Nations Fund for Populations activities, International Institute for Applied Systems Analysis, Rome, 1982.

12. Philippe Collomb, *Food Requirement and Population Growth*, technical background document commissioned by the FAO and the UNFPA for the World Food Summit in November 1996, CICRED Documentation Centre, December 1995.

13. Nikos Alexandratos, *World Agriculture: Towards 2010, an FAO Study*, FAO/John Willey, Chichester, 1995.

14. Central Planning Bureau of the Netherlands, *Scanning the Future: A Long Term Scenario Study of the World Economy 1990–2015*, 1990.

15. Edgard Pisani, *Le Monde Diplomatique*, April 1995.

16. Philippe Collomb, 'L'alimentation de la population mondiale en 2050', *Population et Société*, Paris, April 1996, No. 312.

17. *Business Week*, 20 May 1996.

18. *Courrier International*, No. 315, 14–20 November 1996.

19. Pontifical Council for Justice and Peace, *Towards a Better Distribution of Land. The Challenge of Agrarian Reform*, Libreria Editrice Vaticana, the Vatican, 1997.

20. A. Sen, *Poverty and Famines*, 1981, Clarendon Press, Oxford.

21. A. Sen, 'La liberté individuelle: une responsabilité sociale', *Esprit*, Paris, March–April 1991.

22. Collomb, *Food Requirement and Population Growth*.

23. Alexandratos, *World Agriculture: Towards 2010*.

24. P. Collomb, 'Food security for humanity at the beginning of the XXIst century', note prepared for the Analysis and Forecasting Office, UNESCO, 1997.

25. According to the World Food Programme, in 1994, urgent food aid to Rwanda cost US$1.4 billion, or 20% of total world aid for that year; *Le Figaro*, 6 March 1996.

26. Alexandratos, *World Agriculture: Towards 2010*.

27. Ibid.

28. *Population and Development – Programme of Action Adopted at the International Conference for Population and Development, United Nations*, Cairo, 5–13 September 1994, Vol. I, ST/ESA/SER.A/149, New York, 1995.

29. Alexandratos, *World Agriculture: Towards 2010*.

30. As the FAO clarifies, there could be overlapping between zones occupied by human establishments, forests and protected zones.

31. R. E. Lee, W. B. Arthur, A. C. Kelley, G. Rodgers and T. N. Srinivasan, *Population, Food and Development*, IUSSP, Liège, 1988.

32. IFPRI, *People and the Planet*, Vol. 4, No. 4, 1995.

33. Debruyne, 'Le défi alimentaire'.

34. M. S. Swaminathan, 'Science and food security', *World Science Report 1998*, Editions UNESCO/Elsevier, 1998.

35. Cultivar: botanical term used to designate a variety of a plant species artificially obtained and cultivated.

36. S. Trèche, 'The importance of cassava as human food in the different regions of the world', in T. Agbor Egbe, A. Brauman, D. Griffon and S. Trèche (eds), *Cassava Food Processing*, ORSTOM, Paris, 1995.

37. Hervé Kempf, 'Le génie génétique est mal adapté aux besoins agricoles du tiers-monde', *Le Monde*, 20–21 December 1998.

38. P. Collomb, 'Transition démographique, transition alimentaire: I – La logique économique', *Population*, 3, 1989, pp. 583–612; 'II – De la logique démographique à la logique alimentaire', *Population*, 4–5, 1989, pp. 777–807, INED, Paris.

39. M. W. Rosegrant, M. Agacaoili-Sombilla and N. D. Perez, 'Global food supply, demand and trade to 2050: projections and implications for policy and investment', paper prepared for the workshops on 'A 2020 Vision for Food, Agriculture and Nutrition: Issues Facing South Asia', 27–29 March 1995, Kathmandu, Nepal; and *Long-Term Projections for 2020*, 11–12 April, International Food Policy Research Institute (IFPRI) Washington, DC, 1995.

40. Lester Brown, 'Facing food insecurity', *State of the World 1994*, Worldwatch Institute, Washington, DC.

41. Christiane Galus, 'Seul un gigantesque "Plan Marshall" pourrait vaincre la malnutrition', *Le Monde*, 20–21 December 1998.

CHAPTER II

Feeding the World: Are Biotechnologies the Answer?

Thirty Years on from the Start of the Green Revolution

As we enter the twenty-first century, we need to learn all the necessary lessons from the 'Green Revolution' that has been under way in Asia since 1965: it has been proved that international cooperation in biotechnology can double production in 20 years, as was the case between 1965 and 1985, with new strains of rice in particular. Growing the 2,000 varieties that already existed, selecting the most interesting, crossing them to bring together the required traits and eliminate the undesirable ones, these were the main stages in the Revolution that, by virtue of its unforeseeable and remarkable results, has to some extent disproved the forecasts established by the FAO at the end of the 1970s.[1]

In parallel with the improvement of existing systems of food production and distribution, new alternatives are being explored that will, it is hoped, make it possible to put an end to famine and malnutrition and to meet the food requirements of every human being. The many examples available in this domain are not drawn from the realms of science fiction, nor are they utopian. Scientists have, for instance, recently developed new plant varieties that can be grown in the acid lands of the *cerrado*, which cover 200 million hectares of Latin America.[2] Collaboration between three research centres, in Nigeria, Colombia and Brazil, has led to the identification of a biological method of dealing with one of the main enemies of the cassava grower, the green mite, which is responsible for the loss of over one-third of the crop in Africa.[3] The discovery of a banana resistant to the black Sigatoka disease could also have very swift beneficial consequences for the African countries where bananas are a diet staple. The International Laboratory for Tropical Agricultural Biotechnology has developed a variety of transgenic rice resistant to bacteriosis, a disease that destroys 5% to 10% of the world's rice crop and perhaps as much as half the crop in some regions of Africa or Asia.[4] Canadian researchers are currently working on 'biorestoration', a process that consists of using bacteria present in the soil to eliminate industrial pollutants from it.[5] Similarly, studies are at present being carried out, at the International Rice Research Institute in the Philippines in particular, to create a new strain of rice over the next ten years that will make it possible to obtain yields approaching 13 to 15 tonnes per hectare, as against the 8 to 9 tonnes obtainable with existing varieties.[6] According to some fairly conservative estimates, plant biotechnology should allow an increase in agricultural food production of 10% to 15% in the coming quarter of a century.[7]

It is theoretically possible for biotechnologies to be employed at each stage of a plant's development – its creation, growth, harvesting, conservation, use, processing and marketing and the processing of waste[8] – and to introduce improvements, at each of these stages, that could have a beneficial effect on the environment, by promoting agricultural techniques that are more efficient, less polluting and consume fewer resources. Spectacular progress should likewise be achieved, judging from current research, by means of new methods of genetic modification aimed at increasing plant resistance to viruses and disease, to drought, salt, cold and heat.

Considerable progress will also be within our grasp when research has been completed on the replacement of nitrogen-fixing chemical fertilizers, a major source of pollution, by direct atmospheric fixing of nitrogen within the plant itself. Such an achievement would reduce the harmful effects of chemical fertilizers, the accumulation of phosphates and heavy metals in soils, the infiltration of nitrates into groundwater and the pollution of lakes and coastal zones. This method could, moreover, prove much more cost effective and practicable for many developing countries, where chemical fertilizers are either too expensive or difficult to obtain. UNESCO's Science Sector, in cooperation with the FAO, is closely following all these new developments.

Biotechnology is bound to be one of the keys to the future of developing countries, since it should make it possible to narrow the gap between food production and population, increase individual calorie consumption and clear for cultivation land at present unsuitable for that purpose, and at the same time promote greater respect for the environment.

Some Expected Effects of Biotechnological Progress on Agricultural Products

Speeding up biotechnology research procedures Biotechnology now makes it possible to reduce by a factor of ten, twenty, or maybe more, the time needed to obtain higher-yielding varieties, as compared with the decades that it would probably have taken hitherto to obtain comparable results.[9] This is quite an achievement: the race is now on between population growth and higher yields.[10] The area of land farmed per capita should therefore decrease at a rate close to that of population growth, or even faster, as a result of soil erosion, desertification and urbanization. Hence it is essential to use all available technical resources, including those of biotechnology, to increase yields.

Adaptation to local climatic conditions In order to guarantee food security for a world population that could reach ten billion by 2050, there will need to be an increase by a factor of 2.25 in the nutritional energy derived from vegetable resources.[11] Better use must therefore be made of existing climatic conditions, while unused land, in particular land that is as yet unsuitable for growing crops, must be made suitable for cultivation. Biotechnology could, for example, make it possible to cut the cost of water desalination, thus increasing the area of land suitable for cultivation. Similarly, it could make some species more resistant to cold, drought and heat, which would in turn increase the area of cultivable land, while prolonging the vegetative period of certain fodder plants such as sorghum would increase their livestock-supporting capacities.

Improving agricultural yields The promise of increased yields through bio-technology may have very substantial direct effects on food production and markets. This concerns in particular the morphological modifications of plants and animals, generating increased productivity of such basic input factors as labour, land area or volume of water. Experiments are being carried out to shorten plant and animal growth cycles so as to reduce the time needed for a harvest or a litter of young.

Reducing yield variability of crops Farmers are often faced with a drop in yields in relation to the levels reached during trials. Here again, biotechnology offers solutions that are of great economic significance.[12] Much of the effort in biotechnological research is directed towards reducing the vulnerability of plants and animals to their environment, by increasing their resistance to pathogens, viral diseases and pests. This research has many applications to rice, maize, cassava, potatoes and other crops. Attempts to improve resistance to herbicides and tolerance of unfavourable weather conditions or hostile pedological[13] conditions (salinization, for example) can also have a strong influence on produce markets.

Improving conditions for the marketing of agricultural products Any reduction in production costs is valuable where food security is at stake. The transfer to certain basic food-producing plants of characteristics that enable substantial savings to be made in terms of inputs or that confer on agricultural produce desirable properties in terms of cost or length of conservation therefore constitutes another promising perspective for research and improvement.

Biotechnology will therefore probably be used to modify the physical character-istics of agricultural products in order to reduce foodstuff losses prior to the retailing stage; it also serves to cut losses during conservation and processing, between retail marketing and domestic consumption. Given the level of losses observed, in the developing countries in particular, losses that increase with the length of storage, such improvements would also be of great economic significance.

Creating new agricultural products in competition with those already exist-ing Biotechnology now makes it possible to do without certain relatively expensive agricultural products, often produced in the developing countries. It is, for instance, possible to manufacture fructose-rich syrups without using sugar cane. Microbial biotechnology allows isoglucose to be obtained and tetraloses to be produced using yeasts. New methods applied to existing products lead to new uses that can compete with other products: oils rich in lauric acid can replace the products of the coconut and palm trees, and oils rich in stearic acid can take the place of cocoa butter. All such technical advances (and not only those in the field of biotechnology) will have a global impact and must therefore be subject to a greater degree of regulation as well as to codes of conduct agreed upon worldwide, if they are not to have sudden and potentially devastating effects upon the economies of developing countries, which, as it is, are very dependent upon external technologies.

Finding new uses for existing agricultural products Biotechnology uses exist-ing products to make new ones. Some of these are used for purposes other than food: China and India, for example, are well advanced in making use of biomass, in particular the biogas produced for energy. Biotechnology is also making headway in the pharmaceutical industry. To take only the most com-mon and most important applications, we may cite the case of flax and sunflowers. Linseed oil may be made suitable for consumption if its lineolic acid content is reduced. Linseed-based products would have a longer shelf-life, and the seeds themselves would have valuable health properties because of their high fibre content. Using enzymes, it is possible to replace cocoa butter with products derived from the sunflower. Other future possibilities with significant implications for human health include that of producing human growth hormones, blood proteins and insulin from the leaves of the tobacco plant.

There are thus good grounds for all kinds of hopes, including hopes for the developing countries, but the progress now being made gives rise to many apprehensions, of which far from all are irrational. In many respects, the further development of biotechnology presupposes the emergence of 'bio-vigilance' based upon an ethics of the future and on the precautionary principle, and of genuine international cooperation from which solidarity may spring. In this respect, biotechnology will perhaps require the emergence of a new human being, capable of putting into practical application Rabelais' dictum that 'science without conscience is but ruination of the soul'.

The Effects of Biotechnology on Future Food Security

There are three factors that mean there will be a large increase in demand for nutritional energy derived from vegetable resources between now and the year 2050: population growth, the supplementing of the food intake of the chronically under-fed, and the enrichment of their diets with essential amino acids, vitamins and trace elements. The combined effects of these three factors will entail an increase in average demand in the developing countries by a factor of 2.7, a fivefold increase in Africa, and a sevenfold increase in those African countries that mainly consume roots and tubers (cassava, yam, taro). The increase could in certain cases be tenfold or even fifteenfold. Twenty-five countries will thus be facing a gigantic challenge: a 4% to 8% annual increase in their needs over the next 50 years.[14]

Increasing trade between the countries of North and South could, it is true, improve food security in the developing countries, but it will not necessarily reduce the level of poverty or the food insecurity of the most disadvantaged sections of the population. Most observers therefore advocate a large increase in agricultural production in the least developed countries, specifically in order to combat food insecurity. Unless the progress in productivity is sufficient to feed the populations of these countries, they are likely to try to increase the area of arable land at the expense of forest resources, in certain cases in breach of regulations for the preservation of sites. This prospect pleads strongly in favour of the use of biotechnology. It is thus important to look very closely at the ability of such technology to ensure the food supplies of future generations in these vulnerable parts of the world.

Generally speaking, we should look to biotechnology to facilitate a definite, swift decrease in the average area of land farmed per capita, and to alleviate the pressure on so-called marginal land, which could be achieved by means of greatly and rapidly improved productivity, especially in the developing countries. What are the future prospects in this respect?

Biotechnological breakthroughs are more than likely to occur initially in those places where the economic returns will be highest: whether one looks at improving seeds or devising techniques for the direct application of biotechnology to living organisms, the procedures involved require prior investments in various fields of competence (biology and microbiology, chemistry and biochemistry, physics and biophysics, etc.) and the availability of funds for short-, medium- and long-term investments. Only the developed countries, especially those that can commit themselves to very long-term investments, in other words the richest among them, meet all the above requirements; they will therefore be very likely to play the lead in the biotechnological revolution in the course of the next generation.

These countries are already giving priority to improving the resistance and tolerance of species cultivated in the developed world. Biotechnological applications are mostly concentrated on reducing the variability of yields, the objective being to bring the output of the production process close to optimum level, bearing in mind the genetic material used, and to make it less dependent on climatic, ecological or human factors. The aim of these applications is to transfer to these plants resistance to pathogens, pests, herbicides and pesticides and also tolerance of certain ecological conditions unfavourable to the vegetative cycle or to reproduction.

As regards cultivars[15] for the developing countries, research has so far made little progress and seems unlikely to make rapid headway unless it is decided to undertake and finance without delay large-scale international cooperative action. The potential benefits of biotechnology for the populations of these countries are, however, very great, as demonstrated by the above-mentioned examples of the breeding of a transgenic rice and a hybrid banana that would be more resistant to disease. On the basis of current research and the commercial applications that may reasonably be expected to result from it, it is probable that genetically improved varieties of rice, maize, cassava, soya beans, citrus fruits, bananas, coffee, rapeseed and cotton will be on the market in the next 10–15 years.[16] Research should in future be concentrated on new cultivars adapted to suit the contexts of the developing countries, their know-how and their patterns of food consumption. While food insecurity will probably be reduced in Asia, it is in danger of spreading in Africa, especially in those countries where the staple diet consist of roots and tubers. It will probably be through improved plants that biotechnology will help to meet the challenge of increased demand and the combat against food insecurity.

The rationalization of budgetary options and the priority given to markets where there is urgency in regard to food security explain why heavy investments in cultivar research have been mainly focused on the types of farming practised by the largest populations, the growing of rice, wheat and maize in particular. The need now is to encourage types of farming that have not appeared in the major research programmes and need investment in research all the more urgently as they provide most of the food for rapidly growing populations (the Democratic Republic of Congo consumes over 400 kilos of cassava per head of the population per year), who already constitute the greater part of the world's poor. This investment should go into cultivars of root and tuber crops (e.g. cassava, sweet potatoes, potatoes, yams, taro),[17] but also plantains, pulses, dry cereals (e.g. millet) and sorghum.

Implementing the applications of biotechnology will call for the adaptation of basic education and training and represents another crucial challenge. The Green Revolution was the result of technological programmes combining in particular high-yielding strains of rice and wheat, control of water supplies, inputs of fertilizers and pesticides, and a public-awareness campaign. The success of these programmes in fact depended on a whole set of contextual preconditions – educational, social, economic, infrastructural, commercial and institutional – and in particular on popular support and individuals' acceptance of the new methods and new tools. Foremost among those preconditions was basic education. Three- or four-year basic education – which should be open not only to children but also to teenagers who left primary school too early and to illiterate adults – is indeed one of the keys to agricultural and rural development. Farmers need to be able to read instructions, write out orders and invoices, and explain problems. The setbacks in the Green Revolution were due in large part to a lack of basic education. Such a favourable combination of preconditions for putting biotechnology into effect is as yet far from being achieved in the countries of the South, this still being the subject of intense international controversy over problems of safety, matters of intellectual property rights, and ethical issues. Most of the developing countries are also short of researchers, laboratories and research facilities, patents and patented information, and supply systems, while various economic constraints still prevent the poor countries from benefiting from these improvements. For all these reasons, the benefits of biotechnology will be fully and concretely felt in the developing countries only in ten or twenty years. Biotechnology must therefore not be expected to provide a short-term solution to the problem of food insecurity in the countries of the South.

Any overall, sustainable solution to this problem depends primarily on policies for tackling the lack of education, information, public health services and democracy, as well as the problem of poverty, all of which are deep-seated causes of chronic under-nourishment. Biotechnology nevertheless probably offers, albeit not immediately, the beginnings of an answer to food insecurity. The possibilities are many: one need only mention the discovery of new strains, more productive and more resistant to the different factors that limit yields, more tolerant of climatic variability and poor soil conditions, or the cultivation of land once unsuitable for traditional farming methods, such as arid lands and those saturated with salts or other chemical residues. It is even well within the bounds of possibility that, if the necessary national and international political will manifests itself in the form of adequate funding, research procedures can be speeded up to such an extent that new marketable varieties can provide solutions to the different cultural, social and ecological contexts, and thereby make it possible to eliminate food insecurity in one or two decades.

Risks Arising from the Use or Non-use of Biotechnology and Responses to Those Risks

Transgenic plants are now being grown on a large scale in the USA, Canada and China. According to a recent study, genetically modified organisms (GMOs) account for 32% of maize production and 38% of soya bean production in the USA – barely four years after Congress authorized the sale of genetically modified foods.[18] The number of such food varieties on sale is rapidly increasing. International trade is bringing products derived from genetically modified plants on to the world market, arousing much apprehension and raising many questions, often backed up by scientific or ethical arguments. The question is therefore to ascertain the risks incurred. As we shall see, most of the risks involved in the use or non-use of biotechnology are not of a new nature, but the previous risks seem to be greatly increased. The new risks are, for their part, very difficult to assess; not all of them are known, and many of them cannot even be ascertained yet. Furthermore, most of the biotechnology-related risks are probably unforeseeable simply because of the sheer number of factors involved in ecology. It is nevertheless already possible to mention some major risks that underscore the importance of scientific rigour and of respecting the precautionary principle as well as the need for a forward-looking, preventive approach.

Loss of genetic heritage The world's genetic heritage is rapidly shrinking. According to the FAO, 75% of the genetic diversity of agricultural crops has been lost since 1900. The explanation lies largely in the increase in human activities, which impoverishes natural ecosystems for many reasons – expanding agro-ecological systems, especially monocultures, transportation networks and industrial production units – but also because of modifications in rural and urban landscapes, the spaces we use for living and travelling, not to mention all the pollution for which we are responsible. The decline in agricultural biodiversity is especially serious, fraught as it is with the risk of depriving plant-breeders – who are constantly on the lookout for genes that are vectors of resistance or tolerance – of genetic material to draw upon. The risk may become a major one in the event of the disappearance of plant species that could ultimately prove vital for food security.

The fact is that food security is under threat from the intensive cultivation of certain species on a huge scale, which means that the whole crop could be rapidly destroyed if disaster strikes. This was what happened in the USA in 1995, when a laboratory-developed maize seed, Pioneer 3394, previously used successfully by growers, turned out to be particularly vulnerable to a disease known as grey leaf spot. In the summer of that year, this disease reached epidemic proportions. Experts have so far been unable to determine precisely what the respective roles played by this epidemic and by the bad weather were; be that as it may, the fact of using a single seed variety and the fact – which, incidentally, was already known – of that seed's vulnerability to disease led to massive losses.[19] This underlines the importance of conserving apparently 'uneconomical' plant and animal species that may turn out, in the very near future or two or three generations down the line, to be vital to food security. From this point of view, the useful and irreplaceable nature of the biosphere reserves set up on UNESCO's initiative needs to be stressed: they are not only an ecological treasure-house but also, and perhaps primarily, a unique instrument for long-term security, inasmuch as they make it possible to keep in reserve possibilities for remedial action in the event of major agro-ecological disasters.[20]

It is thus essential to take all necessary steps to ensure the proper management of these biosphere reserves and, wherever appropriate, their extension. The FAO indeed stressed at the World Food Summit in November 1996 that 'the maintenance of large gene pools, *in situ* and *ex situ*, for important crops will remain high on the agenda of the green revolution'.[21] Biotechnology will be needing more and more genetic material as the development expected from it is stepped up, so as to prevent some of the world's poorest countries from falling into the 'Malthusian trap'.

These countries cannot remain in isolation, for their problems are those of humanity as a whole. Thus it is necessary to make a genuine effort to collaborate at an international level, otherwise humanity as a whole will suffer for its lack of solidarity. We should be building up, as of now, the gene collections that will enable us to preserve what remains of the world's genetic heritage and ensure that it is accessible to all countries.

The standardization of cultivated species Many experts also warn of the danger of increasing uniformity in the plants that are being farmed. Traditional farmers grew thousands of types of fodder crops and hundreds of different types of potatoes. Although 50,000 different species of edible plants are known, 15 species now account for 90% of the world's food production, two-thirds of which is in the form of rice, wheat and maize.[22] The greater the reliance on a limited range of widely consumed varieties of grain crop, usually because of their high productivity, the greater the risk that their vulnerability to pathogens may lead to massive, possibly catastrophic, crop failures. The very large-scale farming of ultra-productive transgenic plants, such as is beginning in the USA, will constitute a major risk when and if applied to the staple foods of huge populations in the developing countries. While very few such plants are at present being marketed, numerous field trials are being carried out, as Sylvie Bonny points out.[23] More than one thousand such trials are reckoned to have been conducted between 1986 and 1993 in 32 countries.[24]

Maintaining a minimum level of biodiversity of cultivars is thus a vital prerequisite of food security.

Ecological risks The higher productivity made possible by biotechnology should in principle have a favourable influence on the environment, as it should make it possible to limit the extension of farmland at the expense of ecozones, forests in particular, and to alleviate pressure on marginal land. Biotechnology is, however, accompanied by its own share of ecological risks: the proliferation of transgenic plants (because of their increased vigour, greater fecundity, shorter intervals between one flowering time and the next, resistance to weedkillers, etc.), modifications in the structure and size of insect populations, or the evolution of new pathogens in response to resistant plants. These risks, combined with that of toxicity to humans,[25] explain the public's great mistrust of modern biotechnology, even though the results of the experiments carried out to date tend to show that it is without danger. This mistrust is aggravated by the extreme industrial secrecy surrounding research in this field, and by the suspicion that many experts and officials are not impartial in their judgements, owing to their dependence on economic pressure groups.

Of all the new dangers, the one that attracts the most attention is the spreading of transgenic characteristics, since this may go well beyond simple transmission to plants of the original variety, operating as it does with all varieties of the same species by virtue of the fact that cross-fertilization is possible between all strains of one and the same species and can also occur with other species that have a certain 'inter-fertility' with that of the transgenic plant. Spontaneously generated populations of plants resistant to various herbicides could thus multiply, and weeds against which weedkillers are ineffective could proliferate. Transgenic rapeseed, for instance, has passed on its weed-resistance gene, scattering its pollen over several kilometres and thus fertilizing wild varieties, although experts had reckoned that the risk of transmission was practically nil beyond 500 metres.[26] Referring to unprecedented 'blindfold' experiments, Jeremy Rifkin opines in a recent work that

> many of the transgenic genes being inserted into crops and readied for commercial introduction in countries around the world contain just the traits that are likely to provide a competitive advantage, if transferred to weeds in the wild ... The rapid globalization of commerce and the increased flow of international travel virtually guarantee that weeds contaminated with transgenes in one part of the world will eventually find their way to other regions, spreading genetic pollution over the planet.[27]

There will be fewer risks if the cultivated plants are geographically isolated from their wild relatives and cannot inter-fertilize with them. This is the case for most European plants, such as cereals, tobacco, etc., but not for certain species like rapeseed, sugar beet or endives in France, or for maize in Mexico, etc. It is therefore to be expected that, at the very least, transgenic resistance may be communicated to the wild relatives of genetically modified plants

---

Box 11.1 Bio-ethics: Participation and Supervision by Society

In May 1994, in the United Kingdom, 16 members of the general public were asked to assess the dangers and benefits of plant biotechnology and to draw up a report on this subject, with recommendations. Participants were chosen from among the 350 people who responded to a nationwide call for volunteers. Eight men and eight women supposedly representative of the diversity of British society were selected. The experiment aimed at encouraging the public at large to become more involved in the democratic functioning of society. This concept was born in the 1980s in Denmark, where it was adopted for the discussion of ethically controversial scientific and technological matters.

In its report, the group expressed opposition to the demands of professionals in this field who wanted to patent the new plants obtained in their laboratories. It also expressed concern about the possible breaking of the rules governing genetic experiments. Among its suggested solutions, the group recommended that the government appoint an independent mediator to oversee experiments, major commercial projects in particular, and to verify that neighbouring biotopes did not undergo any changes. The group also thought the government should subsidize research more, 'so as to develop to the maximum the advantages for the community, rather than leaving it up to the private sector, whose only motive is profit'.

A similar experiment was carried out recently in France, where, on the initiative of the chairman of the French Parliamentary Office for the Evaluation of Scientific and Technological Choices, Jean-Yves Le Déaut, a 'citizens' conference' was held in Paris on 20 and 21 July 1998 on the use of genetically modified organisms (GMOs) in agriculture and food. On this occasion, 14 members of the public debated with experts, some of whom spoke, in the name of prudence and the precautionary principle, in favour of a moratorium on the marketing of GMOs, while others urged the group to bear in mind the economic issues of genetic engineering. The opinions of members of the public and experts alike were taken into account in the preliminary report submitted to the government by the Parliamentary Office.

Sources: Susan Watts, *Independent*, London, in *Courrier International*, No. 227, 9–15 March 1995. Catherine Vincent, *Le Monde*, 23 June 1998.

when the latter are grown in places from which those relatives originate, so that proliferation is more or less inevitable.

The transmission of genes to microbial flora is also a possibility, so much so that it could well present serious ecological risks, especially in countries that are not financially in a position to mount a rapid response to such eventualities.[28] A recent study carried out by the Institut des sciences végétales (Institute of Plant Sciences) a body operating under France's Conseil national de la recherche scientifique (National Scientific Research Council), has indeed confirmed that the microbe population increases very greatly following the introduction of genetically modified crops, underlining the need for the marketing of such crops to be preceded by risk assessment and hedged about by as many precautions as possible.[29] The new risks created by genetic engineering make 'bio-vigilance' imperative, so that production may proceed in conditions of increased security, whatever the level of development of the country concerned. This presupposes national and international funding capacities and strategies tailored to the needs of different national situations.

Biotechnology also raises a fundamental environmental problem: by creating species that are increasingly adapted to an environment that is itself undergoing constant change, it represents a danger in that it allows the measures needed to preserve the environment to be avoided or deferred. The consequences of this need to be considered: the argument that laboratory substitutes need to be developed because wild plant ecosystems are disappearing so rapidly means a tacit acceptance of the murder of nature, amounting more or less to an endorsement of its replacement by artificial life. The more the forests and other plant habitats are reduced by the pressures of population growth, the argument goes, the more dependent the human race will become on synthetic products rather than those provided by nature. It should also be remembered that genetic engineering is not always the only way out, and that some of the developing countries still have enormous reserves of productivity. Jules Pretty, director of the Centre for the Environment and Society at the University of Essex, United Kingdom, who prepared a report on this subject for the United Nations, reckons that the use of organic farming methods can raise yields significantly in countries where traditional practices are still followed: yield increases of 300% for sorghum and millet have been recorded in Senegal, while Burkina Faso, Guatemala and India have achieved similar increases.[30]

While vigorous support needs to be given to the trend that lays down a scientific basis for human activities and decisions, a distinction should perhaps be drawn between that and an 'artificialization' of life, the soil and the planet, which, in the name of short-term economic imperatives, is advancing without a compass, without thinking about the ecological imbalances and the social harm it may cause. The considerable contribution that biotechnology has to offer should serve to increase the possibilities of every individual, rather than driving out human beings, living creatures and nature to make room for a world of techno-financial 'pipe-dreams'.

The presence of 'eco-technicians' in rural communities increasingly seems to be indispensable if the steady artificialization of the earth, and the unnecessary or dangerous use of all sorts of inadequately tested products, are to be avoided. At the same time, there needs to be more investment in research, so as to endow each society with people competent to make the difficult decisions confronting it concerning agricultural and biotechnological issues.

Economic and political risks For the developing countries themselves, the biotechnology revolution, like the two-faced god Janus, holds out many promises but also presents many drawbacks. Biotechnology indeed carries serious dangers for the countries of the South. First, it may entail a significant degree of financial and technological dependence on major firms from the industrialized countries, in whose hands advances in this field are concentrated, owing to the very high cost of DNA-related genetic research. In 1993, for instance, 71% of trials of transgenic plants were carried out by private-sector enterprises.[31] To give an idea of what is at stake, Jeremy Rifkin points out that there are at present in the USA 1,300 biotechnology enterprises, employing over 100,000 people and with an annual revenue of nearly US$13 billion.[32] The worldwide profits foreseen for the near future are colossal: according to Britain's Department of Trade and Industry, 'the global market for biotech products will reach $100 billion in another two years', and a study by the European Association for Bioindustries claims that 'the entire sector will be worth $285 billion by the year 2005' – enough to whet a lot of appetites![33] Sylvie Bonny thinks that one of the major issues for biotechnology arises from the fact that 'the private sector is in danger of catering only to solvable demand and not to the needs of the poorest'.[34] Unlike what happened at the time of Malthus, the keys to the agricultural revolutions of the future are not now in the hands of (possibly philanthropic) gentlemen farmers but in those of a few major agrochemical and biotechnological companies who are competing to offer new products backed by patents and intellectual property rights. Paul Kennedy, the eminent British historian and futurologist who teaches at Yale University, uses the notion of 'biological imperialism', adding:

> What if certain states or countries encourage new methods while others oppose them? One consequence, in the age of multinational corporations, will be that companies tranfer their research and development efforts – and the attendant flow of young scientific talent – to hospitable countries; already, for example, major German pharmaceutical firms have chosen to locate their DNA research in the United States because of restrictions in Germany itself.[35]

An out-and-out struggle is now going on between the major companies, which are trying to patent living material – whether plants, animals or even the human organism – and the developing countries, who are trying to preserve their genetic heritage, their indigenous resources and their traditional knowledge (though the latter is not patentable). According to one expert:

> the international effort to convert the genetic blueprints of millions of years of evolution to privately held intellectual property represents both the completion of a half-millennium of commercial history and the closing of the last remaining frontier of the natural world … At the very heart of the issue of patentability is the question of whether engineered genes, cells, tissues, organs, and whole organisms are truly human inventions or merely discoveries of nature that have been skillfully modified by human beings.[36]

Can they really be called human inventions? It seems not. The patenting of living matter is, on the contrary, in danger of becoming synonymous with the possibility for a few major industrial groups of controlling various aspects of the human organism, marketing its 'restoration' or 'repair', exercising monopolistic power over the main basic crops, hampering the flow of information on genetic material, and thus holding back medical advances and progress in food security. Many experts and members of the general public look upon the patenting of the genetic heritage as a legalized form of a downright economic and ecological hijacking operation, the appropriation of a resource that should, on the contrary, 'remain an open commons and continue to be used freely by present and future generations'.[37]

A second threat hanging over the economies of the developing world – mentioned earlier in this chapter – is that the *in vitro* production of substitutes for tropical products, manufactured in the laboratories of the countries of the North, may speed the decline in the proportion of farm workers in the workforce of those very countries where the conversion from agricultural to non-agricultural employment is incompatible with their level of development, owing to the inadequacy of the general level of education – which would mean the premature elimination of traditional forms of employment. Humanity would then experience in the coming years the pangs of an agricultural crisis of the kind that countries like France went through between 1950 and 1980, without having available to them the non-agricultural employment opportunities that the developed countries have been able to create for their generations of rural migrants.[38]

In this connection, Paul Kennedy cites some telling examples gathered by several authoritative researchers in the collective work *Plants, Power and Profit*.[39] Cane sugar, for example, which provides the livelihood of millions in the South, has already been largely replaced by isoglucose and other artificial sweeteners. Vanilla, an essential export for Madagascar, can now be manufactured by chemists. Coconut oil, the export of which provides at least part of the livelihood of a quarter of the population of the Philippines, is in danger of being replaced by substitutes obtained by the genetic manipulation of the soyabean and rape-seed, while the *in vitro* production of rubber, should it become a reality, could put nearly 16 million people out of work in the countries where the rubber tree is grown, Malaysia and Indonesia in particular.

The third risk, closely linked with the previous two, is therefore that in the long or very long term, according to the same experts, there could be a significant relocation of agricultural production (or the production of its substitutes) away from the developing countries, which would pose a threat to their trading position and could increase the burden of their debt and their general dependence on the industrialized countries. At a time when public opinion in the wealthiest countries is worried about the 'relocation' of industries and services – mistakenly so, in our opinion, since not only the development of the South but global development and world peace are at stake – a huge relocation-in-reverse of agricultural production from South to North is in the making, as food production moves to an ultra-scientific stage.

It should be added that even if the developing countries succeed, as multilateral and bilateral international cooperation should help them to do, in overcoming most of the obstacles to their entry into the 'biotech' age, and go ahead with *in vitro* production, their internal social stability could nevertheless be sorely tested, since millions of jobs would be threatened in the rural populations of the South, with immense social and cultural consequences, unless – before these major changes burst upon them – a forward-looking approach is adopted and courageous policy decisions are taken. All this makes the transition to a society of education, knowledge and culture even more necessary.

The cultural and social risks Owing to the growing demand for energy originating from plants and the increasing scarcity of available space for traditional farming, biotechnology appears to be an unavoidable transitional stage on the way towards supplying humanity's food requirements. The world's most disadvantaged populations will probably be unable to make the transition without a period of acculturation, which will necessitate some form of training in addition to their basic education. Conceptions of nature and the natural world, flora, fauna, the earth and its fertility, water and its properties, and the traditions and myths attaching to them, all these will undergo profound changes, and certain factors inherent in these changes may entail a destructuring – or indeed destruction – of traditional systems. As we have already pointed out, three-quarters of the genetic diversity of agricultural crops has been lost since 1900. In industrialized countries, the drastic reduction in agricultural labour following the intensive mechanization of farms is already a historical fact. After 2000, if present trends continue, hundreds of millions of those who work the land, especially in the countries of the South, will be doomed to undergo an agonizing conversion, and the stores of traditional knowledge built up by those who grew or reared those vanished species are in danger of vanishing in their turn.

That being the case, UNESCO's ethno-botanical functions need to be reinforced, so that, in cooperation with the FAO and the WHO, a storehouse of peasant lore about cultivated species and the customs related to agriculture, food and medicines native to the various cultures of the world can be established. If, as the Worldwatch Institute asserts, more than six thousand forest plants are traditionally used as natural medication, and over one hundred billion types of medication whose active principles are derived from forest plants are sold every year, humanity has much to gain from making an inventory of this heritage before it disappears. This memory bank could be part of the legacy bequeathed to the Earth's inhabitants of centuries to come.

It is time to give agriculture the human touch once more: the 'hi-tech' approach has its limits and should not result in our losing sight of the importance of having high-quality agriculture or of the need to enhance the quality of rural people's lives. This is of fundamental importance, with a view not only to preserving agricultural jobs but also to slowing down the exodus from the land of people who merely swell the numbers of the extremely poor in the outer suburbs of cities, that fertile soil for violence and social unrest.

Putting Biotechnology at the Service of All

The vigorous development of biotechnology will call for particularly vigilant combined efforts on the part of the international and the scientific communities, and of ethics committees. It should be noted in this regard that there is still no independent international authority with responsibility for monitoring and assessing developments in biotechnology. Perhaps it is high time that one was set up, within the FAO, for example. The use of genetic engineering does indeed make it necessary to establish national and international watchdog organizations, so that production may proceed in conditions of greater security, whatever the level of development of individual countries. Moreover, the public must be fully involved in this effort of bio-vigilance. Hitherto, as Beatrix Tappester of Germany's Eco-Institute claims, biotechnology companies 'operate on the "Après nous le déluge" principle'.

Given the present rate of population growth, there is such a need to increase food production, and the forces driving the biotechnological revolution are so strong, that it is hard to see how the movement could be stopped in its tracks – if, indeed, it even should be. 'If the genetic modification of plants were to be blocked for other than scientific reasons,' the French

Academy of Sciences stressed in 1993, 'the further development of agriculture in the twenty-first century might be jeopardized, at least in part.'[40]

The tool, however, should serve humankind, not humankind the tool. If international cooperation confines itself to unduly cautious action in response to industry's mighty vested interests, biotechnology is in danger of creating, to use Paul Kennedy's expression, a world of 'winners' and 'losers'. Jules Pretty considers that 'great improvements could result from genetic engineering, "particularly if research is publicly funded for the public good"'. Unless the political will for solidarity and active international cooperation, especially in science and technology, is forthcoming, the future 'horn of plenty' will not necessarily benefit those most in need of being fed, and millions of small farmers will be doomed to undergo an immense transition. As Philippe Collomb points out, genetic research in the field of agronomy should in future concentrate not only on wheat, maize and rice but also on the root and tuber crops, since these occupy a leading place in the diets of some of the countries most affected by malnutrition, in Africa in particular.[41]

The developing countries are, however, far from helpless in the face of biotechnology, to which they are making and can in the future make major contributions. As some experts in future-oriented studies have remarked in this regard, the developing countries at least have more chances of contributing to the development of biotechnology than they do to that of robotics or international finance. Many kinds of biotechnological research in fact require more brainpower than capital. Some developing countries have even invested heavily in such research: it will be recalled that China and India are among the leading countries in the use of biomass and biogas as sources of energy.

With the upheavals at present taking place, the outcome of the race between population growth (even if it slowed down) and agricultural production for all is still uncertain. But Cassandra may once more be given the lie by the new technologies of living matter. For our part, we remain confident of human beings' ability to combine freedom with ethical behaviour. We are therefore convinced that it is more than ever necessary to work together, while respecting democratic sovereignty: it is essential to enhance the role of international cooperation in a science that is still in its infancy and whose effects need to be more accurately gauged. Food security is a decisive issue in which human lives are at stake. As Edgard Pisani has noted, 'the South is wagering its survival on this; the North, world stability and peace'.[42] It is a fact that migrations brought on by famine are a threat to peace as well as to internal and external stability. We can no longer look on as helpless spectators at the paradoxical situation whereby the rich countries pour money into their agriculture and their farm surpluses while elsewhere in the world 840 million people are suffering hunger and malnutrition, and are far too concerned about their day-to-day survival to worry about their future.

There is no disguising the scale of the challenges the international community has to meet: by 2015, world food production will need to be increased by 75% to 100% and this substantial growth must be achieved by ecologically sustainable methods; at the same time, the scandalous paradox of 'hunger in the midst of plenty', to quote the Dutch authors of the report *Scanning the Future*, must be resolved.

Above and beyond the technical solutions we have outlined, any global, sustainable response to the problem of food security depends ultimately on policies that tackle the root causes of hunger, that is to say, inequalities, poverty, the lack of education and information, the unequal status of men and women, and the lack of democracy. It is thus essential that suitable educational policies and measures to facilitate access of all to knowledge, information and skills should accompany any form of green or biotechnological revolution and the necessary agrarian reform that many developing countries have still not carried out. One of the best ways of fighting the degradation of ecosystems on which agriculture is heavily dependent is to improve the security of those who live, and must be able to go on living, by working the land: to allow them to plan their future and bequeath a future to the generations of the twenty-first century, to feed our children tomorrow, the 'E' and the 'S' of UNESCO are clearly henceforward the best investments that can be made.

Pointers and Recommendations

- Continue, renew and strengthen UNESCO's 'Man and the Biosphere' Programme so as to promote the preservation of biodiversity.
- Promote the maintenance of vast genetic reserves, *in situ* and *ex situ*, not only for important crops but also for the conservation of many apparently uneconomical plant and animal species.
- Strengthen mechanisms for national and international bio-vigilance, in particular by the active promotion of public research and case studies of the effects of the production and use of transgenic plants, which should be entrusted to experts totally independent of vested economic interests.
- Ensure better public information and effective public participation in the democratic scientific and ethical debate on this subject.
- Promote rigorous labelling of genetically modified products.
- Support biological and biotechnological research capacities, through such initiatives as UNESCO's special project on 'biotechnologies for development in Africa'.
- Encourage public and private efforts to find cultivars that enable unused land unsuitable for farming to be developed and allow transgenic traits of

improved resistance to soil salinity and acidity to be transferred to certain cultivated species.

* Encourage public and private efforts to find new, more productive cultivars of cassava, yam and taro that tolerate unfavourable conditions of all kinds.
* Collect and disseminate traditional lore relating to cultivated species and the agricultural, food and medicinal uses of the world's various crops.
* Establish a moratorium on the patenting of genetic heritage.
* Introduce training in the requirements of modern agriculture, supplementing basic education in rural areas, so as to ensure the continuance of the Green Revolution, and an introductory training in biotechnology.

Notes

1. G. M. Higgins et al., 'Potential population-supporting capacities of lands in the developing world', Technical Report of Project – Land resources for populations of the future, FAO, UNFPA, International Institute for Applied Systems Analysis, Rome, 1982.

2. *The Economist*, 10 June 1995.

3. *Le Monde*, 22 May 1997.

4. Catherine Vincent, 'Les biotechnologies remportent une victoire contre une grave maladie du riz', *Le Monde*, 29 February 1996.

5. Vincent Tardieu, 'Des bactéries du sol pour dépolluer les friches industrielles', *Le Monde*, 20 December 1996.

6. Central Planning Bureau of the Netherlands, *Scanning the Future: A Long-term Scenario Study of the World Economy 1990–2015*, 1990.

7. Albert Sasson, 'Comment nourrir la planète au XXIème siècle?', *Une Terre en renaissance, les semences du développement durable, Dossiers savoirs, Le Monde diplomatique*, 1995.

8. The United Nations Convention on Biological Diversity employs the term 'biotechnology' to designate 'any technological application that uses the biological systems of living organisms or derived from them to make or modify products or processes for specific purposes'.

9. Philippe Collomb, 'La sécurité alimentaire de l'humanité au début du XXIe siècle', *Accroissement démographique, biotechnologies et sécurité alimentaire*, note prepared for UNESCO, 1997.

10. It is worth noting in this respect that the most recent demographic projections indicate that world population growth has decreased significantly over the last eight years, largely owing to the efforts made in the field of education. See Chapter 1.

11. Philippe Colomb, technical background document no. 4, commissioned by the FAO and the UNFPA for the World Food Summit of November 1996, CICRED Documentation Centre, December 1995.

12. FAO, 'Impact of biotechnology developments on trade of agricultural commodities', Committee on Commodity Problems, Sixty-first Session, FAO, Rome, 25–28 February 1997.

13. Pedology is the study of the chemical, physical and biological characteristics of soils, and their evolution and distribution.

14. Collomb, 'Croissance démographique'.

15. Term used in botany to designate an artificially obtained and cultivated variety of a species of plant.

16. FAO, 'Impact of biotechnology developments'.

17. D. Griffon, 'Orientations for research and development in tropical root and tuber crops', in T. Agbor Egbe, A. Brauman, D. Griffon and S. Trèche (eds), *Cassava Food Processing*, ORSTOM, Paris, 1995.

18. *Time*, 'Alien seed?' (cover story), 24 August 1998.

19. *Business Week*, 'The new economics of food', 20 May 1996.

20. UNESCO, 'Action plan for biosphere reserves', and 'Biosphere reserves' (map), Man and the Biosphere Programme Secretariat, UNESCO, Paris, 1985.

21. FAO, *Lessons from the Green Revolution: Towards a New Green Revolution*, technical backgound document No. 6, World Food Summit, Rome, November 1996.

22. *People and the Planet*, Vol. 4, No. 4, 1995 (IPPF, IUCN, WWF).

23. Sylvie Bonny, 'Les biotechnologies en agriculture. Perspectives et enjeux', *Futuribles*, July–August 1996.

24. P. Ahl Goy and J. H. Duesing, 'From pots to plots: genetically modified plants on trial', *Bio/Technology*, No. 13, May 1995.

25. These risks relate in particular to the toxicity of the products that may be synthesized by transgenic plants, to modifications in the plants' metabolism and composition, to the products of degradation by enzymes of the herbicides to which the plants are resistant, to the build-up of toxic substances by plants rendered genetically resistant to pathogens, etc.

26. Jacques Testart, 'Espèces transgéniques: ouvrir la boîte de Pandore?', *Manière de voir*, March–April 1998, *Le Monde diplomatique*.

27. Jeremy Rifkin, *The Biotech Century: Harnessing the Gene and Remaking the World*, Jeremy P. Tarcher/G.P. Putnam's Sons, New York, 1998, pp. 88–90.

28. Axel Kahn and John Libbey (eds), 'Les plantes transgéniques en agriculture – dix ans d'expériences de la Commission du Génie Biomoléculaire', Eurotext, Paris, 1996.

29. *Le Monde*, 7 January 1998.

30. *Time*, 'Alien seed?'.

31. Ahl Goy and Duesing, 'From pots to plots'.

32. Rifkin, *The Biotech Century*, p. 15.

33. *Time*, 'Alien seed?', 1998.

34. Bonny, 'Les biotechnologies en agriculture'.

35. Paul Kennedy, *Preparing for the Twenty-first Century*, Random House, New York 1993.

36. Rifkin, *The Biotech Century*, pp. 41, 45.

37. Ibid., p. 55.

38. Philippe Collomb, 'La mort de l'orme séculaire – crise agricole et migration dans l'Ouest audois des années cinquante', Travaux et Documents, Nos 105 and 106, INED, Presses Universitaires de France, 1984.

39. L. Busch et al., *Plants, Power and Profit: Social, Economic and Ethical Consequences of the New Biotechnologies*, Cambridge, MA/Oxford, 1991, pp. 172, 175, 181, 182.

40. 'Les manipulations génétiques au service du maïs américain', *Le Monde*, 19 August 1995.

41. Philippe Collomb, 'L'alimentation de la population mondiale en 2050', *Population et Sociétés*, April 1996, No. 312.

42. Edgard Pisani, *Le Monde diplomatique*, April 1995.

. . . .

CHAPTER 12

Towards the Revolution of 'Energy Efficiency'

§ FOR want of a forward-looking vision, the societies that emerged from the Industrial Revolution have been slow to recognize the impact of energy consumption on the environment and on health, so that, today, they are faced with an unprecedented build-up of greenhouse gases in the atmosphere and must address the challenge of extremely costly emission-reduction policies. Suddenly, it has been realized that the initial choices – which led to the development of huge conurbations in North America, for example – largely determine energy needs for decades. As a result, urban management of sparsely populated cities like Detroit or Phoenix (ten inhabitants per hectare) involve average annual urban population movements that are three to four times greater than in a city such as Paris: this makes for an average energy consumption in transport that is six times higher for a resident of Phoenix than it is for a Parisian. The immense technical progress in energy efficiency that is called for to offset the enormous difference in energy demand becomes immediately evident.

Furthermore, while the practical considerations of world energy supply are particularly complex, it is more important than ever to start reconsidering the way in which energy challenges are conceived. No longer can the organization of energy systems be viewed solely from the angle of production and distribution; more attention must be paid to human factors. As Amory Lovins, director and co-founder of the Rocky Mountain Institute, points out, 'energy wastage is not just a minor error of development policies. An inefficient engine or lamp in fact uses up money that could be devoted to the water supply, inoculation of children or action to promote the equality of women.'[1] Our objective for the twenty-first century must be to master and diversify our sources of energy.

Future Energy Needs

Although expert estimates differ, there is no doubt that we shall witness major growth in the developing countries' energy demands in the years to come. According to the OECD's International Energy Agency (IEA), by 2010 the world's energy demand will have increased by approximately 40%, and the share of the developing countries will have risen from the current 27% to 40%.[2] The World Energy Council (WEC) considers that, in a high-growth scenario, world energy demand could double by 2020. The developing countries' energy consumption would then account for 60% of the world total: the consumption of a Chinese person would increase by 85% and that of an Indian by 145%. Energy consumption is one of the major sources of greenhouse gas emissions (with a 55% carbon dioxide content).[3] The IEA estimates that by 2010, carbon dioxide emissions will have increased worldwide by 33 or even 50%. But even the massive increase in the developing countries' energy consumption cannot erase the huge gap separating industrialized and developing countries in this area. The developing countries, which comprise over three-quarters of the world's population, are today responsible for only one-third of world energy consumption. On average, per capita consumption in the developing countries is less than one-eighth that of the industrialized countries: despite the enormous increases predicted for the developing world, a Chinese person will still consume only one-fifth as much energy as an American by 2020.

Aware of the inertia of energy systems, experts in this area are wont to look far ahead when anticipating the investment decisions of those involved. So it is that we have numerous scenarios forecasting the energy situation in 2020, 2050 and even 2100, prepared by the energy producers, by the World Energy Council and by teams of academics. They can be divided into two categories corresponding to widely differing views of development.

The first group of scenarios portrays a future based on a productivist model of 'energy-abundant development', which would ensure strong economic growth based on limitless energy supply and on a dynamic of rapid technological progress. This group of scenarios can be subdivided into two main variants: the continuation of current, market-oriented policies, tempered by the application of the Kyoto international agreements; and, if the latter were not applied and *laisser-faire* policies were to prevail, the aggravation of existing problems. In this type of scenario, based on the implicit idea of a strict correlation between economic growth and energy needs, the various risks, which accumulate at a high level for the economy, for the environment and for society, are somehow accepted as the price to pay for technological progress. The scenarios differ only in the reduction or increase of one of the risks in relation to the others. They very soon run up against many contradictions: how can one guarantee easy access to fossil fuels if their consumption increases very rapidly, in a context of increased economic inequalities that are unfavourable at first sight to the development of world trade? How can one cope with the environmental pressures, especially climate change, that will surely result from large-scale use of fossil-fuelled power or from large-scale production of nuclear wastes?

On the other hand, some scenarios propose development based on energy restraint, in an attempt to restore balance to energy policies, giving high priority to control of the development of energy demand and minimizing the long-term risks. Starting from a detailed analysis of energy needs for development at a particular juncture, they advocate promoting development in the countries of the South by reducing capital needs that would be necessary to develop energy systems. Contrary to the scenarios of energy-abundant development, which rely on a common conception of energy policies designed, first and foremost, to organize an industrial matrix (oil, gas, electricity industries and others), the energy-restraint development scenarios call for a profound cultural evolution, since they aim at separating economic growth from energy consumption, which presupposes expanding the sphere of energy policy intervention to all sectors of activity that structure demand (transport, construction, urban management, capital goods, etc.). Indeed, the main determinants of energy demand are often closely linked on a long-term basis to major infrastructures and to options relating to urban planning, transport and fluid distribution networks (energy, water, etc.). In the long term, it is primarily in the volume, nature and regional distribution of energy demand that the scenarios reviewed differ, rather than in supply options.

Energy Consumption and Climate Change

Greenhouse gases – especially carbon dioxide – entail global warming: according to the evaluation report of the Intergovernmental Panel on Climate Change (IPCC), by the end of the twenty-first century we may expect a rise in global temperature of between 1° and 3.5°C.[4] Indeed, some of its scientists do not hesitate to forecast a 5°C increase. Climate warming would seem to be already under way: temperatures have, in fact, risen by between 0.3° and 0.6°C since the late nineteenth century.[5] The hottest year of this century was 1997, and the highest average temperatures since the beginning of meteorological monitoring on earth were recorded in July 1998. In May 1997, NASA published data showing that Greenland's icecap is melting three and a half times as fast as it is regenerating itself. This warming could raise ocean levels by 15 to 95 centimetres. Even if humanity succeeded in stabilizing its emissions at their current level, it is inevitable that greenhouse gas concentrations will double. It is on the basis of that hypothesis, and that hypothesis alone, that the IPCC has placed its temperature-increase forecast at between 1° and 3.5°C, with an average scenario at +2°C. However, the IPCC stresses that gas concentrations will be greater (by three or four times) and the consequences all the more catastrophic if these emissions continue at their current pace.[6]

Admittedly, the scientific community is divided when it comes to an accurate assessment of the consequences, scope and foreseeable evolution of climate warming. For the economist Jean-Claude Hourcade, 'warming poses the question of the rationality of political decisions in the face of major risks of uncertain or unknown probability'. Faced with that doubt, what should we do? Can we afford the luxury of waiting even longer? As Mohamed El-Ashry, of the Global Environmental Facility, remarks, even in the (highly unlikely) event that global warming does not occur, any investment designed to improve energy efficiency will have positive consequences on the economy and on health.[7] Our duty is therefore to take the long view and act without delay, if we wish to prevent today's procrastinating from translating into irreparable damage.

Courageous policies would reduce greenhouse gas emissions. However, subsidies continue to be granted, often at a total loss, to energy industries that damage the environment: this is the case, in particular, with the coal industry. The WEC points out that world coal consumption could double by 2020, a prospect all the more alarming as coal-fired power stations are much less efficient than those that operate on gas. Logic therefore dictates that coal subsidies should be progressively abolished. A coherent energy-saving policy also calls for a reasonable increase in the price of electricity and for intelligent urban transport planning. Abolition of the subsidies granted for the exploitation and use of fossil fuels would encourage consumers to economize on energy and turn to alternative sources: such a policy would cut greenhouse gas emissions by between 4% and 18%.[8] The WEC further estimates that the efficiency of energy use could be increased by between 25% and 30% in the developing countries, without even resorting to new technologies. José Goldemberg stresses nevertheless how important it is for the developing countries to have access as of now to 'clean' technologies, taking as an example the practically unavoidable expansion of the automobile industry in those countries, which risks thwarting the long-term aims of reducing greenhouse gas emissions if urgent action is not taken.[9]

However, it is up to the industrialized countries to set an example, since they account, directly or indirectly, for 73% of total energy consumption and have for decades been traditionally responsible for the build-up of greenhouse gases in the atmosphere. At the Earth Summit held in Rio in 1992, they accepted the notion of 'differentiated responsibility', which commits them to imposing stricter measures. At the same time, the developing countries have agreed to participate in the conservation effort, in exchange for financial and technological rewards. Unfortunately, despite the commitments made in Rio, the industrialized countries have not adopted the measures that would attest to a genuine 'effort to bring all greenhouse gas emissions down to 1990 levels by the year 2000'.

The USA, Canada and the countries of the European Union have already admitted that they would not be able to attain the objectives set. The American Energy Department predicts a 34% increase for the United States by 2010.[10] According to the IEA, only Switzerland, Luxembourg, Germany and the Netherlands will be in a position to control their gas emissions in the year 2000. Current trends are hardly more encouraging in the developing countries: if they persist, the emissions for the Asia and Pacific area could be two and a half times higher in 2025 than they were in 1990. Between 1990 and 1995, China's gas emissions increased by 27% and Indonesia's by 40%, chiefly as a result of strong growth of their GDP. Moreover, contributions paid to the Global Environment Facility (GEF) are still clearly inadequate; for the 1994–97 period it collected only US$4 billion in donations and co-financing, while the financing of the measures recommended in *Agenda 21* adopted in Rio was set at US$125 billion. In addition, it would be advisable to make a painstaking evaluation of the projects conducted so far under the GEF and of their relevance to *Agenda 21*.

So far, it has been possible to reduce pollution growth through voluntary measures, but carbon dioxide emissions, for example, continue to increase.[11] At the Kyoto Conference on Climate Change held in December 1997, the major industrialized countries finally undertook to adopt measures to reduce the level of greenhouse gas emissions by 2012 by 6% to 8% in relation to 1990. Given the magnitude of the problem and challenges, these advances, albeit positive, are still very timid and largely inadequate. They are all the more unsatisfactory as considerable uncertainty remains as to the mechanisms that will have to be instituted at international level to realize these modest aims. The Buenos Aires Conference on Climate Change, held in November 1998 – the chief merit of which was that it gave developing countries the chance to take a more active part in the discussions than in the past – set 2000 as the deadline for finalizing the negotiations on the reduction of greenhouse gas emissions.

However, attention should be called to some interesting initiatives. We refer in particular to the proposal that businesses or governments in the industrialized countries could include the results of investments abroad for technological transfer and reduction of greenhouse gas emissions in the fulfilling of their national anti-pollution objectives. It offers the developing countries the opportunity to equip themselves with cleaner, more effective technologies. For the rich countries, it would be a way of fulfilling their commitments and reducing gas emissions at lower cost: reduction of carbon dioxide emissions in Norway costs a Norwegian business $112 per tonne of carbon dioxide, while in Mexico it could cost as little as US$35 per tonne.[12] While such initiatives should be encouraged, we must beware lest they become for the industrialized countries a cheap means of release from their domestic responsibilities. We must also ensure that the international attribution of pollution quotas authorized by a permit system does not lead to a pollution-rights market, which would inevitably be detrimental to the populations of the poorer countries.

Box 12.1 Risks Involved in the Development of Energy Systems

Four major risks are linked to the development of energy systems: climate risk due to increased greenhouse effect, depletion and exhaustion of fossil and fissile energies, risks linked to the development of the civil nuclear industry and dangers connected with degradation of soils and competition for their use.

These risks have certain characteristics in common. Populations do not immediately feel their consequences and scientists cannot accurately quantify them. Furthermore, these risks are highly interdependent: the likelihood of the occurrence of one may either delay the occurrence of another or, on the contrary, hasten it. Their synergy must therefore be taken into account in any effective prevention strategy, while bearing in mind that their terms, their likelihood and their consequences on the future of humanity are all different. Finally, the consequences may manifest themselves in the form of radically new and harmful situations: if the depletion of fossil fuels is a continuous phenomenon, grave difficulties will arise well before their foreseeable long-term exhaustion because of sudden pressures on the oil market, if not regional conflicts. By the same token, global warming, bringing in its wake excessive rainfall and the melting of the polar icecaps, would most probably provoke violent alterations in salinity and circulation of ocean waters and make for paradoxical and brutal regional evolutions, such as the appearance of a Quebec-like climate in a Europe no longer warmed by the Gulf Stream.

Sources: Benjamin Dessus, 'Energy for 2020 and beyond', note prepared for UNESCO, 1998. Jean-Paul Dufour, 'Avec le réchauffement planétaire, l'hiver canadien pourrait envahir l'Europe', *Le Monde*, 2 January 1998.

Use of Fossil Energies will Continue

Some experts consider it unlikely that energy consumption patterns will change radically during the first quarter of the twenty-first century. It will be several decades before the major organizations responsible for energy distribution incorporate the technologies related to renewable energies into their infrastructure. According to the WEC's scenario of reference, fossil energies would continue to provide 75% of world energy consumption until 2020 (as against 80% today), while renewable energies would only provide for 4% of total consumption.[13] However, other scenarios – to which we shall return in a moment – suggest very strong growth of renewable energies in global energy consumption by 2050.

All forecasts suggest enormous growth in transport and the automotive industry, with the appearance of new markets in China and India, for instance. The number of vehicles on the world's roads could double by 2020. Oil demand would then increase from today's 66 million barrels per day to 94 million per day in 2010, unless the increase in the number of vehicles were at least partially offset by energy savings and efficiency.

According to the WEC, the earth's oil reserves are sufficient to maintain consumption at today's level for 60 years or even 175 years if 'non-conventional' sources are used. At present, however, the cost of this non-conventional oil is very high and there is no guarantee that it will fall appreciably in the foreseeable future. Moreover, it would be a catastrophe if conventional oil resources were to be exhausted: oil is a precious jewel, one of nature's wonders, constituting as it does the basis of all organic chemistry. The problem will arise later on, for to persist in reckless consumption of oil is to risk substantial swings in prices and severe repercussions on the climate, the world economy, the level of atmospheric pollution and human health. From that viewpoint, the developing countries' increasing energy needs and the prolonged use of coal in a number of countries (reserves are sufficient to maintain current production levels for 235 years) will inevitably bring an increase in emissions and atmospheric concentration of greenhouse gases. According to some surveys, public policies begin to address air quality issues only when per capita GDP approaches US$5,000.[14] By then, there is a risk of much more damage to the global environment and the natural environment of the developing countries unless serious efforts are made to give the lie to the experts' predictions.

Energy Efficiency

However, some experts doubt that energy consumption is doomed to intensify in the years to come. They accuse the WEC scenarios of concealing an important parameter – the distribution of market shares between fossil energies and nuclear energy – and of relying on two very pessimistic and unproved implicit hypotheses, namely, that energy productivity gains would reach saturation point in the countries of the North, while the countries of the South would be incapable of improving their energy performance to any great extent.[15]

There is really no firm correlation between GDP growth and increased energy consumption. Such a correlation was indeed observed during the economic boom between the beginning of the 1950s and 1973, but between 1973 and 1986, the GDP of the OECD countries increased by 35% while energy consumption increased by only 5%. On the contrary, we should observe a decrease in energy intensity as industrialization progresses and a country evolves on the energy learning curve.[16] A recent study reveals that since the 1860s, energy intensity per unit of value added has decreased by 1% per year, and by 2% per year since the 1970s, while carbon dioxide emissions per unit of power have decreased at a rate of 0.3% per year.[17]

The link between energy consumption, economic growth and standard of living is therefore not as obvious as one might think. Hence a Frenchman does not consume more energy than a Pole, while his standard of living is twice as high; conversely, an American consumes 2.3 times more energy than a Frenchman, even though his purchasing power is only about one-third greater. While energy use increases, commensurate technological progress often makes it possible to offset growing needs. In the 1920s, incandescent bulbs consumed five times more electricity than they do today. Likewise, in the 1950s, the countries of the North used four times as much energy for keeping warm as they do today.[18]

According to some studies, as soon as per capita GDP approaches US$2,000 per year, consumption of high-energy basic materials ceases to increase.[19] This tendency towards dematerialization is reflected in decreased use of materials designed for energy production as a society's technological level rises. Production therefore has a tendency to veer towards goods that incorporate more added value per 'kilo of material'; such goods are easier to recycle and use more sophisticated, information-rich materials: for instance, optical fibre cables replace copper cables.[20]

Seen from that perspective, the idea of sustainable development that combines efficiency and respect for the environment is no longer a pipedream. According to Benjamin Dessus, 'for the North as for the South, energy efficiency is no longer considered to conflict with development but, rather, to be one of the major conditions of such development'. As Oliviero Bernardini and Riccardo Galli point out, there is particular latitude for such a policy in the developing countries, where the relative dearth of infrastructure would enable them to move directly to more efficient technologies, provided, of course, that the industrialized countries supply the poorest countries with the scientific knowledge and financial resources needed for investing in the technologies of the future.

The phenomenon of a fall in energy intensity is undeniable in the industrialized countries but this trend has not yet been observed in the developing countries. A study covering the period 1962–91 confirms the diminution hypothesis in a handful of rich countries since the 1970s; it notes, on the contrary, an intensification in carbon dioxide emissions per unit of additional GDP in low- and middle-revenue countries. The authors are concerned for the future. They particularly fear that businesses in the industrialized countries will transfer their more polluting activities to the developing countries in order to escape the regulations in their own countries.[21] Moreover, even in the developed countries, the transport sector is still a marked exception to the trend towards lower energy demand.

Finally, even though energy intensity is tending to decrease as time goes by, global economic growth reduces its effects. While the intensity of carbon dioxide emissions per unit of added value has decreased by 1.3% per year since 1860, world economic growth stands at around three per cent per year. Consequently, carbon dioxide emissions worldwide have increased by about 1.7% per year since 1860.[22] Active policies are therefore called for if we wish to exploit and intensify the efficiency gains that are within our reach.

More optimistic scenarios suggest that the pursuit of economic growth can go hand in hand with a reduction in annual per capita energy consumption. As long ago as 1987, José Goldemberg, Thomas Johansson, Amulya Reddy and Robert Williams established a scenario based on increased energy efficiency and recourse to more environment-friendly forms of energy.

More recently, France's National Centre for Scientific Research refined the NOÉ (New Energy Options) scenario, based 'on pursuing efforts concerning energy efficiency in the industrialized countries and accelerating the energy learning of the countries of the South'.[23] The aim of this scenario is to stabilize greenhouse gas concentration and the world stock of the most dangerous nuclear waste, 'by attaining energy supply that suffices to ensure the development of humanity, which will consist of 11 billion people by the year 2100'.[24] All in all, in this scenario, world energy consumption would increase to 10.1 billion TOE per year by 2010.

According to Benjamin Dessus, technological development should make it possible in the year 2000 to mobilize a renewable energy potential equivalent to 3.3 billion TOE, which represents two and a half times the potential effectively mobilized in 1990. By 2020, that potential could be as high as five billion TOE, which corresponds to cumulative oil, coal and nuclear production in 1994. While renewable energies currently do not account for more than 17% of energy equipment, Dessus considers that 'A goal of 30% would make it possible to exploit three-quarters of the reasonably mobilizable potential', and that the additional costs linked to the installation of new plants would be rapidly set off through energy savings. Furthermore, compared with the WEC scenario, the NOÉ scenario would enable savings of 6 trillion French francs to be made for the period 1985–2020, linked to the reprocessing of nuclear fuel and environmental protection.

Measures to be Taken

The latest IPCC evaluation report proposes a number of measures that could considerably reduce greenhouse gas emissions. More rational use of arable land would, for instance, contribute to the development of carbon dioxide-absorbent plants and, consequently, the stocking of an appreciable amount of carbon.[25] In transport, one could obtain a reduction of 40% in carbon dioxide emissions through better land-use management and public transport, by developing more efficient engines and by the use of alternative fuels. Industry could reduce its emissions by 25% by intensifying its recycling measures and improving equipment performance.

Even more ambitious proposals are contained in two reports presented to the Club of Rome, *Taking Nature into Account*[26] and *Factor Four*.[27] They stress that only a real 'energy efficiency revolution' would respond to the cumulative challenges of energy, technology, employment and ecology. Wouter van Dieren, the Dutch coordinator of the first of these reports, considers it necessary to quadruple energy productivity in order to fill the gap between the increasing energy demand and the necessary reduction in greenhouse gas emissions. There is nothing Utopian about it. An annual 3% increase in energy productivity would attain the objective in a little over 40 years. It is quite possible to double the performance of many processes that consume large amounts of energy, even with existing technologies, without significant changes in habits or in infrastructure. However, other experts consider it necessary to go much further and to increase energy productivity tenfold.

Amory Lovins, co-author of the *Factor Four* report, has elaborated the concept of 'negawatts' to signify that investments linked to energy savings are more viable than investments in new power plants. The report makes a precise inventory of numerous technologies of the future already in existence, which, from the practical point of view, make this megawatt revolution feasible. Amory Lovins thinks that, with the technologies already at their disposal, the industrialized countries should be in a position to save three-quarters of the energy they consume. For the USA alone, that would represent a saving of over $300 billion per year.[28] Those gains could be even greater, on condition that 'green' accounting techniques are used, as well as taxes and subsidies to determine the real long-term costs of energy consumption. To that end, comprehensive tax reform must be envisaged, so that the state could draw an increasing share of its revenue from taxing activities that damage the environment.

Energy Alternatives: What is the Future of Nuclear Energy, Hydroelectricity, Gas and Hydrogen?

So far, the only energy alternatives to fossil fuels to have experienced a genuine expansion are nuclear and hydroelectric energy, which provide 17% and 18% of the world's electric power respectively.[29] Many research studies have dealt with ways of making nuclear energy safer and cleaner. A case in point: Professor Carlo Rubbia, Nobel laureate for physics, is working on an incinerator reactor that could combine electricity production and incineration of nuclear waste. This process, which is still in its embryonic stage, should make for better control of fission reactions and better combustion of nuclear matter.[30] Carlo Rubbia also envisages the possibility of using thorium in place of uranium, which would make it possible to produce nuclear energy without the simultaneous production of radioactive wastes. Other researchers are working on thermonuclear fusion, which could constitute a virtually limitless source of energy, safer and less polluting than nuclear fission.[31] However, the technical obstacles are still enormous and most experts doubt whether nuclear fusion will be a commercially viable solution by 2030.

Nuclear energy still provokes contradictory reactions. In the collective imagination it arouses hopes and fears that have sometimes tragically become reality. Despite the objections that continue to be raised, it must be recognized that, today, it represents a less polluting form of energy than fossil fuels, at least from the viewpoint of the goals set forth by the Kyoto Summit Conference. Accordingly, in the European Union alone, the use of nuclear energy makes it possible to avoid the emission of some 700 million additional tonnes of carbon dioxide each year.[32] Nevertheless, the environmental risks linked to poor maintenance of certain nuclear power plants and the anxiety caused by the question of the recycling of nuclear waste (some of which has a lifespan of 300,000 years) lead a number of experts to question the long-term viability of nuclear energy as a real option. World Bank economists are of the opinion that once the costs of closing down old reactors, treating and stocking wastes have been taken into account, nuclear energy is no longer a commercially viable alternative to fossil fuels.[33] Realization of these risks and drawbacks, combined with active anti-nuclear political movements, has induced some countries (including Sweden and Germany) to opt for a more or less rapid 'exit' from the nuclear power scene.

However, some experts consider that it would be irresponsible to abandon nuclear energy altogether – especially research into revolutionary processes such as those envisaged by Carlo Rubbia – since the threat to the climate is such that no form of energy reducing greenhouse gas emissions can be rejected so easily. In Philippe Roqueplo's opinion, this kind of research is justified, as long as the precautionary principle is observed and provided that it leads to a different nuclear energy, a safe and clean nuclear energy resulting from new developments in science and technology. In that context, he considers that a major strategic question will be 'the comparison between the harm (real and/or perceived) caused by nuclear waste and that caused by climate changes attributable to the concentration of greenhouse gas in the atmosphere'.[34]

In the case of hydroelectric energy, the growing unavailability of locations for large new dams necessarily limits its future development. Moreover, where installed, large hydroelectric dams can have negative consequences for populations and ecosystems. According to some estimates, construction of the Three Gorges project in China means that one million people will be displaced.[35] A number of projects for large dams have been abandoned because of the dramatic repercussions they could have had on indigenous ethnic groups and local populations, as well as on the natural environment.

Christopher Flavin and Nicholas Lenssen, from the Worldwatch Institute, stress the numerous advantages of natural gas that would justify the option of substituting gas for oil and coal, even though it is a fossil fuel:

- Thanks to its low carbon content, it produces 30% less carbon dioxide than oil per unit of energy produced and 43% less than coal.
- Its combustion does not produce ashes and releases less carbon monoxide and nitrogen oxide.
- Unlike coal, natural gas contains no heavy metal.
- It is easier to convert than oil and cheaper to transport than coal.[36]

The use of natural gas has increased by 30% since the mid-1980s; its price fell as new deposits were discovered and exploitation technologies improved. According to Flavin and Lenssen, the replacement of traditional oil- or coal-fired plants with gas-turbine electric plants would make it possible to reduce nitrogen oxide emissions by as much as 90% and carbon dioxide emissions by as much as 60%. They also stress the high potential of the use of natural gas in transport, once a way has been found to reduce the size of fuel tanks and increase the time between two refuelling stops of private cars.

When natural gas resources diminish and must be replaced, according to the authors, hydrogen could be a particularly promising and environment-friendly alternative, once the appropriate technologies have been perfected. The visionary writer Jules Verne has already forecast its potential. 'Water is the coal of the future,' he wrote in *The Mysterious Island*.[37] 'The hydrogen and oxygen that are its components, used separately or simultaneously, will provide an inexhaustible source of heat and light, and an intensity that coal could never have.' Flavin and Lenssen also think that hydrogen could play a funda-mental role in the transport of energy obtained from renewable energies. It would thus make for cleaner and more efficient production and distribution of energy. It must also be borne in mind that, while hydrogen is an excellent fuel, it does not exist as a natural resource – it must be manufactured, and this entails using energy. In this respect, it is solar energy that enables plants, thanks to their chlorophyll, to carry out the hydrolysis of water, which releases hydrogen and oxygen. In that context, solar energy could be used to carry out this breaking down of water. Research is also currently under way to perfect fuel cells that would convert hydrogen into electricity and to find safe storage systems.

Another innovative solution has been proposed by David FitzHerbert. He hopes to set up 'ethical' investment funds to finance the development of factories producing electricity from methane emissions emanating from public underground landfills.[38] Methane is one of the main greenhouse gases and the landfills we have inherited will keep producing it for a further 30 years. The technique conceived by FitzHerbert would make it possible both to produce energy at a reasonable cost and to remedy some of the abuses of the past. At the European level, this technique represents a potential electricity production estimated at 4,000 megawatts.

What is the Future for Renewable Energies?

The renewable energy currently most used comes from biomass drawn from organic matter, in particular from wood. It accounts for 15% of the world's energy consumption and 38% that of the developing countries; it is the main source of energy for nearly half the world population. Major pro-gress can be achieved in more effective exploitation of this form of energy, particularly through plantations of fast-growing trees. However, constraints on available water and land, which will necessarily be exacerbated in the future,[39] will *de facto* constitute a brake on future biomass exploitation. In addition, estimates are cautious concerning the capacity of photosynthesis to limit carbon dioxide in the event of climate warming.

Only a minute quantity of modern renewable energies is used: solar and wind energy provide only 1% of the electricity consumed in the world. However, wind-powered energy is at present the fastest-growing energy source. Since 1990, its production capacity has tripled, representing an annual growth of over 20%. The progress achieved in the last 20 years has made it so much cheaper to produce that it can sometimes compete with fossil energies. In Denmark, wind-powered energy today provides between 2% and 3% of electric power;[40] in the German *Land* of Schleswig-Holstein, wind-powered energy accounts for 10% of the electricity consumed. In 1996, the main markets for wind energy were Germany, followed by India, Denmark and Spain. According to Christopher Flavin, wind energy should be able to supply 20% of the world's electricity consumption in 30 years' time.[41]

Use of solar energy could be considerably increased. The annual solar energy received by the planet potentially represents 10,000 times the quantity of energy we use. The main difficulty is the cost of exploiting it, which is appreciably higher than the cost of exploiting fossil fuels. Research on the subject is far behind; it took the oil crisis of the 1970s for solar energy really to be considered a serious option. As use of this energy is encouraged and expanded, production and exploitation techniques will progress and prices will fall. As a general rule, the learning curve indicates that any doubling of cumulative production of a new technology brings about a 20% to 30% reduction in the average unit price. The current cost of photovoltaic cells is already only one-fiftieth of the cost in 1970.[42]

Solar energy is especially practical for isolated rural areas in the developing countries, that is, for the two to three billion people who are not and cannot be linked to an electricity network. In dozens of countries in the world, electricity, whatever its origin – fossil or nuclear – will never be available in sufficient quantities: the infrastructure conceived for central production and distribution through a network is unattainable for many regions, for at least several generations. China itself estimates that some 200 million of its inhabitants will never be linked to an electricity network.[43] With photovoltaic cells, it is now possible to convert the sun's rays directly into electricity without using a generator, making this system technically and financially more viable than connection to a central network. For the small-scale energy needs of a village of 500 inhabitants, solar energy is already rivalling generators.[44]

At the regional level, it has an advantage over dams or thermal power-plants in that it can be installed more rapidly, with a much smaller initial investment, and of being more environment-friendly. World Bank studies have shown that solar energy could cover five to ten times the developing countries' electricity demand, while occupying a smaller area than existing hydroelectric plants.[45]

After years of scepticism that have held back its development, photovoltaic energy for domestic use is now gaining ground in most rural areas. In the course of the last decade, over 200,000 homes in Brazil, Mexico, South Africa, Kenya, Indonesia, Sri Lanka and other developing countries have had solar energy equipment installed on their roofs. Thousands of villages have abandoned their diesel generators and now use photovoltaic cells for lighting as well as for televisions, refrigerators and water pumps.[46] In Kenya, there are now more houses equipped with photovoltaic cells than there are homes connected to the central electricity network.

This solution is also valid for the industrialized countries, particularly country homes that would be too costly to connect to a network, or isolated sunny regions such as the Greek islands. In Norway, 50,000 country homes are powered by photovoltaic cells and 8,000 additional homes are 'solarized' every year.[47] Japan, for its part, plans to install solar panels on the roofs of 70,000 homes by 2002.

However, persistent mistrust is delaying systematic use of solar energy. In the developing countries, governments continue to pay huge subsidies for expanding electricity networks in rural areas or for installation of diesel-fired water pumps. According to the IEA, of the US$8 billion that the rich countries devote annually to energy research, 50% is spent on nuclear programmes and less than 10% on renewable energies. By remedying those disparities and redefining priorities, solar energy could constitute an economically viable option and receive serious attention in energy policies. A recent European Commission study recommends that electricity production from renewable energies be tripled by the year 2010.[48] Michael Grub, in a report prepared for the British Royal Institute for International Affairs, estimates that half of the electricity consumed in Europe could be obtained from renewable energies by 2030.[49]

The use of photovoltaic cells for electricity networks in suitable regions will become economically viable on a larger scale, however, only if the price of solar technologies is further cut by three or even five times. Associated research by universities, laboratories and industry, with public-sector support, needs to be encouraged so that those technologies can advance. This progress will itself be accelerated by larger-scale production and by cuts in distribution costs.

In a scenario formulated by the Shell company, it appears that renewable energies, including solar energy, could meet half of the world energy requirements by 2050. Recognizing the strategic importance of these new forms of energy, Shell has decided to invest US$500 million in developing them over five years and hopes to capture 10% of the world photovoltaic cell market by 2005.[50] Another oil company, British Petroleum, is also backing solar energy and already controls 10% of a market that is growing at a rate of 14% a year. It expects to increase its photovoltaic cell sales tenfold by 2010.

On 16 and 17 September 1996, UNESCO organized in Harare the World Solar Summit, presided over by the president of Zimbabwe, Robert Mugabe. The World Solar Programme 1996–2005, adopted at that conference, set rapid development of renewable energies as its objective. The first phase of the programme aims at 'solarizing' 1,000 villages on the African continent and as many again in South America and Asia. In order ultimately to reach the two billion people who are not linked to an electricity network, the programme will have to implement 20 programmes for 1,000 villages every year for 50 years. It is now time to act: not only in order to respond to the energy challenge that is at stake here, but also to create the conditions of sustainable development.

Box 12.2 *Solar Energy in the Service of Development*

While solar energy may not yet be capable of providing the developing countries with resources comparable to those enjoyed by the countries of the North, it can help boost development in remote regions. Solar energy generates a benign cycle that benefits the entire village community. According to Yaya Sidibe, director of the National Centre for Solar Energy in Mali, 'solar energy helps develop farming activities, thanks to water-pump irrigation, and through conservation by refrigeration or by drying. It goes beyond subsistence economy; our villages enter into an economy of trade that brings in revenue; with street lighting and electricity in homes, access to television and telephones, communications get through, isolation recedes, the community is strengthened, and living conditions improve: there is hot water, refrigerators, air conditioning for schools and clinics. In the long run, it helps people remain in the village; it keeps them on the land of their ancestors instead of obliging them to leave for towns rendered unmanageable by growth, or even seeking exile in Europe, where they are no longer welcome. By staying put, they also help combat desertification.'

Also in Mali, the hospital in the Ouelessebougou region – which has 15,000 inhabitants but is not linked to the rest of the world by any electricity network, although it is only 80 km from the capital – now functions day and night, thanks to solar-panel energy. A five-million-CFA-franc (50,000 French francs) installation has sufficed to provide a permanent supply for 24 lamps, a large refrigerator for storing medicines and vaccines and two water heaters for washing newborn babies. The staff maintain the panels and batteries themselves. 'It is simple, it works and it costs nothing,' says the doctor.

But for Assetou Kone, coordinator of the Women-Energy project, the real advantage of solar energy is that it 'fits in with the culture of village communities. Decentralized electricity production gives autonomy to those who operate it. The villagers themselves – especially women – manage and maintain it without any outside intervention, obviating the need for sophisticated imported technologies and outbuildings. The village looks after its own lighting and organizes the distribution of energy in accordance with its own economic and social choices.'

Source: Jean-Paul Besset, 'L'autre fée électricité', *Le Monde*, 15 August 1998.

In the years to come, we shall have to face a very significant increase in world energy demand. We may remain passive, claiming that energy resources are adequate, that the adverse effects of greenhouse gas emissions have not yet been definitively proved and that economic growth alone will increase populations' standard of living, while making them more sensitive to environmental quality. However, in the long term, we would be heading towards a disaster scenario. But we can also, here and now, adopt the measures that, together with growth, will reduce the degradation of our environment and guarantee more universal access to sources of energy. We can here and now, with the technologies already at our disposal, learn to make more effective and rational use of our energy resources. The richer countries must accelerate the transfer of knowledge that would enable the least developed countries to make better use of available energies. We can also stop paying massive subsidies to the sources of energy that do most harm to our environment. Finally, official energy initiatives must be redirected and progressively replace centralized use of fossil energies with local control of renewable energies. Such action would be a token of responsibility for the future; it would provide the means of ensuring the continuity of the planet and its species.

It is a question not merely of humankind's ecological safety, but of safety plain and simple. The energy-restraint scenarios are in fact all the more vital since they reduce the risks of war that would result from new energy shortages, which are always possible in energy-abundance scenarios. This point has not been clearly grasped as yet because the present abundance of fossil energy resources, particularly oil, seems to postpone the risks of shortages. But those risks may occur during the twenty-first century and, with them, we would be confronted with further oil wars. It is therefore vital, in the interest of world peace, to use voluntary policies to promote energy restraint.

We cannot, however, pass over in silence the apparent contradiction, especially in the poorer countries, between the imperative need for long-term energy strategies and the urgency of development. If the disparity in the initial situations were to be ignored, the concern to preserve the global environment and its expression in terms of energy would perforce be seen as a whim of the already developed societies eager to preserve their acquired advantages. We must acknowledge, here and now, the legitimate aspirations of the peoples of the developing countries, who yearn for a better life. There can be no worldwide ecological solidarity in a context of economic war, no participatory citizenship in a world of exclusion.

It is therefore essential to seek some degree of synergy between the legitimate short-term concerns of the populations and the long-term objectives of development. At a time when economic stakes often take precedence over political wisdom, the challenges of energy development confer renewed legitimacy on public action. What is needed is a resolute political commitment involving new decisions that would make for effective inclusion of long-term issues in development options.

Protection of the environment is not synonymous with economic recession and there is no systemic contradiction between development and sustainability of development; there is, rather, a profound synergy. Low-key energy strategies bring profits on two fronts: the economic and the environmental. We must challenge the still widespread view of a contradiction between development and respect for the environment that can still be glimpsed in the concept of 'incremental cost' employed by economists to explain that protection of the natural environment would incur recurrent costs and systematically add to the costs of development. Analysis of the energy-restraint scenarios studied under the NOÉ project suggests that this additional cost is only transitory and corresponds in fact to a period of dynamic learning of more environment-friendly development. What we really need to know is what strategies to adopt in order to take the path suggested by the energy-restraint scenarios. The key-words of our action – if such is our ambition – are obviously equity and solidarity, between industrialized and developing societies on the one hand, but also within each society and among generations, which implies a long-term vision and the development of an ethic of the future. For it is surely cultural, institutional and political – rather than technical – obstacles that impede the transition to equitable and sustainable world development. We already possess a certain number of technical and economic means (which, drawing on the new, improved technologies, will have to be increased) to start the necessary transition towards energy development that is capable of meeting long-term challenges. It is up to us to establish the cultural, political and constitutional conditions.

Pointers and Recommendations

- Encourage measures aimed at energy-saving and management, which are often less costly than the production of energy.
- Promote the use of renewable energies, particularly by subsidizing research, in order to make them more rapidly competitive with fossil fuels.
- Encourage the use of solar energy and other renewable energies, especially in isolated rural areas that are not linked to electricity networks.
- Invest to a greater extent in research in nuclear fusion, in new, 'clean' methods of nuclear fission, and in producing energy from hydrogen.
- Change, through education and public information, as well as by incentive measures such as taxation and negative tax, the modes of energy con-sumption, particularly with regard to materials that most contribute to air-pollution and climate warming.
- Adopt even more ambitious objectives than those set at the Kyoto Con-

ference in December 1997 for an appreciable reduction of greenhouse gas emissions; institute in this field an international monitoring mechanism, and honour international commitments at the national level.

- Encourage, through international scientific co-operation, energy learning and transfers of technology that will enable the developing countries to improve their energy efficiency.
- Combat the transfer of the more polluting activities to the developing countries.
- Impose taxes on activities that are harmful to the environment in order to determine the real long-term costs of energy consumption, and influence the price of energy by levying taxes on its use.
- Implement new development policies that are much more forward-looking with regard to choice of infrastructure (town planning, transport, energy distribution networks, water, industry, etc.), that are socially much more equitable and that show greater solidarity.
- Establish balanced energy policies at the national level, which should include renewable energies and set measurable objectives as well as a clear timeframe.

Notes

1. Amory B. Lovins, quoted in Benjamin Dessus, *L'énergie à l'horizon 2020 et au-delà*, note prepared for UNESCO, 1998.

2. International Energy Agency, 1996 issue of *World Energy Outlook*, cited in *Futuribles*, May 1996.

3. Xiaoli Han, Lata Chatterjee, 'Impacts of growth and structural change on carbon dioxide emissions of developing countries', *World Development*, Vol. 25, No. 3, 1997.

4. Jean-Paul Besset, 'La terre se réchauffe – les mises en garde des scientifiques', *Le Monde*, 26 November 1997; Intergovernmental Panel on Climate Change, *Climate Change 1995: The Second Assessment Report*, Cambridge University Press, Cambridge, 1995.

5. Leyla Boulton, 'Factoring in the human influence', *Financial Times*, 28 November 1997.

6. Besset, 'La terre se réchauffe'.

7. Cited in Leyla Boulton, 'Pollution threat is the driving force', *Financial Times*, 5 December 1996.

8. *The Economist*, 20 July 1996.

9. José Goldemberg, 'Reduce subsidies and leapfrog old technologies', *Valuing the Global Environment, Actions & Investments for a 21st Century*, Global Environment Facility, 1998.

10. Besset, 'La terre se réchauffe'.

11. John H. Cushman, Jr., 'Washington targets global warming', *International Herald Tribune*, 18 July 1996.

12. Leyla Boulton, 'Exercise in international mutual aid', *Financial Times*, 5 December 1995.

13. Dominique Gallois, 'La consommation mondiale d'énergie devrait augmenter de moitié d'ici à 2020', *Le Monde*, 10 October 1995.

14. *The Economist*, 18 June 1994.

15. Benjamin Dessus, *Energie, un Défi planétaire*, Editions Belin, Paris, 1996.

16. Benjamin Dessus, 'Pas de panique en 2100. Assurer les besoins énergétiques de onze milliards d'hommes sans détruire la planète', *Futuribles*, July–August 1994.

17. Nebojsa Nakicenovic, 'Decarbonization: doing more with less', *Technological Forecasting*, No. 51, January 1996.

18. Benjamin Dessus, 'Les moyens d'éviter l'impasse énergétique', *Une terre en rennaissance, Le Monde Diplomatique*, Dossiers Savoirs, No. 2, 1994.

19. José Goldemberg et al., *Energy for a Sustainable World*, Wiley, New York, 1988.

20. Oliviero Bernardini and Riccardo Galli, 'Dematerialization: long-term trends in the intensity of use of materials and energy', *Futures*, May 1993.

21. J. Timmons Roberts and Peter E. Grimes, 'Carbon intensity and economic development 1962–91: a brief exploration of the environmental Kuznets curve', *World Development*, Vol. 25, No. 2, 1997.

22. Nakicenovic, 'Decarbonization'.

23. Dessus, *Energie, un Défi planétaire*.

24. Ibid.

25. Jean-Paul Dufour, 'Les scénarios du réchauffement climatique prévisible restent flous', *Le Monde*, 23 September 1995.

26. Wouter van Dieren, editor, *Taking Nature into Account. Towards a Sustainable National Income*, Copernicus, Springer Verlag, New York, 1995.

27. Ernst Ulrich von Weizsäcker, Amory B. Lovins and L. Hunter Lovins, *Factor Four: Doubling Wealth, Halving Resource Use*, Earthscan, London, 1997.

28. *The Economist*, 22 February 1997.

29. *The Economist*, 'The future of energy. The battle for world power', 7 October 1995.

30. Hervé Morin, 'Carlo Rubbia défend son projet de réacteur nucléaire "sans risque"', *Le Monde*, 4 December 1996.

31. Pierre Le Hir, 'Un nouveau record européen en fusion thermonucléaire', *Le Monde*, 16 October 1997.

32. Simon Hoberton, 'Future calls for power to persuade', *Financial Times*, 14 November 1997.

33. *The Economist*, 'The future of energy'.

34. Philippe Roqueplo, 'Long terme et nucléaire', *Les Cahiers de Global Chance*, No. 11, April 1999.

35. Ibid.

36. Nicholas Lenssen and Christopher Flavin, 'The unexpected rise of natural gas', *The Futurist*, May–June 1995.

37. Quoted in Christiane Calus, 'L'hydrogène est loin de pouvoir replacer l'essence', *Le Monde*, 30 January 1997.

38. Leyla Boulton, 'Gathering gas from rubbish dumps', *Financial Times*, 28 November 1997.

39. See Chapters 7, 8, 9, 10 and 11.

40. André Larané, 'L'aérogénérateur de Dunkerque redonnera du souffle aux éoliennes', *Le Monde*, 19 June 1996.

41. Christopher Flavin, *Energy in the Next 20–25 Years*, note prepared for UNESCO, 1997.

42. *The Economist*, 'The future of energy'.

43. Jean-Paul Besset, 'L'autre fée électricité', *Le Monde*, 15 August 1998.

44. Ibid.

45. Hervé Morin, 'L'électricité solaire pourrait connaître un nouvel essor', *Le Monde*, 18 April 1997.

46. Flavin, *Energy in the Next 20–25 Years*.

47. Ibid.

48. Angela Bleasdale, 'Here comes the sun', *Financial Times*, 5 June 1996.

49. Michael Grub, *Renewable Energy Strategies for Europe*, Vol. II, Royal Institute for International Affairs and Earthscan, London, May 1997, cited in an article by Caspar Henderson, 'Highly charged debate', *Financial Times*, 4 June 1997.

50. Nicholas Schoon, 'Le soleil est le pétrole du futur, Shell y croit', *Courrier International*, No. 371, 11–17 December 1997; Robert Corzine, 'Altruism is not the only driving force', *Financial Times*, 28 November 1997.

. . . .

PART THREE

Towards a Cultural Contract: From the Information Society to the Knowledge Society?

CHAPTER 13

The New Technology Revolution: Information, Communication and Knowledge

§ ACCORDING to most experts, the sudden growth of new information and communication technology is a real revolution. However, opinions differ as to the deeper nature of this phenomenon. For some, it is simply a technological upheaval that, for all its obvious economic and social repercussions, requires no more than an updating of political, legislative and regulatory structures. For others, it is a major watershed in civilization, as important as the development of the alphabet, the invention of the printing press, or the Industrial Revolution. In time, a new model of society could emerge from this social, cultural and political maelstrom in which we are already caught up.

However, everyone agrees on one thing: the information revolution produces unprecedented economic, social and cultural upheavals, which we are only beginning to perceive in their full extent. According to the economist Daniel Cohen, this revolution is the driving force behind a 'third industrial revolution' that will affect not only the nature and organization of work but also the terms of the social contract and existing disparities in development.[1] Is this new industrial revolution the prelude to a 'new age of inequalities'[2] and a 'new segregation'?[3] On a global scale, will it widen the gap between rich countries and developing ones? Will it increase the divisions within society itself and within each socio-professional group, because of 'assortative matching'?[4] The challenge is not only economic or commercial: it probably requires a redefinition of the social contract on a global scale. It calls, as Ethan Kapstein has pointed out, for a rethinking of the role of the welfare state, and also for a rethinking of basic social institutions, including school.[5] The 'third industrial revolution', driving the ongoing process of 'globalization', must work to the common good: its success depends on our ability to reduce inequalities both between nations and within them. It requires not only major economic efforts, but also considerable investments in education and training.[6] These efforts and investments, in the medium and long terms, will enable us to reduce disparities and to remove the divides that currently pose a very serious threat to international peace and security.

Digitization, Interaction, Simulation, Virtual Reality

The data processing, telecommunications and broadcasting industries are in the process of converging. Data, sound and images can now travel very quickly using the same processes for digital encoding of transmissions. We should therefore expect tremendous growth in storage and broadcasting capacity, which will multiply twentyfold over the next few years, thanks to the digital compression of information. Culture, in all its manifestations, will be available at home, on an individual basis, thanks to a single multifunctional appliance with the functions of a telephone, fax machine, television, video recorder, CD player and computer. Convergence of coding procedures for information, communication and data processing is perhaps the ultimate cultural event of the late twentieth century. Javier Pérez de Cuéllar was right when he said, 'When a society focuses more on images than on the material means of production, on the fashioning of symbols than on the fashioning of things, it is acting directly in the cultural sphere – using industrial means.'[7]

The communication and information revolution is characterized first of all by the development of a universal language: digitization. Digital representation has decisive advantages over other systems of representation: digital code is universal; it can be reproduced infinitely at a marginal cost of next to nothing; it is instantly available anywhere. From now on, all texts, images and sounds, can be represented in the same universal form of series of numbers. Digitization confers specific advantages: durability of recordings, new methods of archival storage and consultation, removal of the boundaries between different types of data and media, instant access from any point in space, and powerful indexing thanks to 'smart agents'. All this raises the possibility of putting 'all the memory in the world' into digital form.

With the development of new interfaces, new patterns of interaction are also appearing. Certain postures favour various kinds of 'interaction' between human being and machine, and also facilitate the handling of large quantities of information, navigating 'in' it, and, in so doing, uncovering previously unknown connections. As well as this new body language, we must not forget the psychological transformations produced by cyberculture and the spread of intimate Internet customs.[8] The variety of simulation techniques (known as 'thought experiments') is leading to the emergence of a new heuristic, a science of discovery that makes the most of the 'small worlds' that mathematical and computer modelling enable us to create. Thus the communication revolution could lead to a revolution in understanding, and the information revolution could, provided we take the time to reflect on it, lead to an intelligence revolution.

However, there is a price to be paid for the digitization and mathematization of reality: a weakening of the ontological connection to reality permits much excess, some impression of which can be gained from image manipulation and electronic special effects. Most of all, however, the prevalence of digital representations encourages a certain confusion of truth and fiction, nature and artifice, reality and the representation of what we believe to be reality. It encourages the manipulation of codes, images and symbols.

The irresistible rise of 'real-time' technology, the development of virtual reality and 'augmented reality', 'televirtuality' and 'telepresence' create the necessary conditions for the emergence of what one might call a new state of reality: the virtual state. This phenomenon brings with it a new danger: what if technology is the 'new artificial paradise of intelligence', to quote Jean Baudrillard? What if it were the secret weapon of a 'perfect crime'[9] – the disappearance of reality in a cyberworld of simulacra? Is the human spirit in danger of being swallowed up by addiction to the virtual, by the hallucinatory dizziness provoked by a '3D' universe replicating the real world?

The new 'virtual' world must never make us forget that our first and most important duty is to acknowledge and understand the complex nature of reality in order to transform it, and to take account of the global and irreversible nature of events. Those who know only a 'perception' of reality are condemned to transform only that perception, but not the reality that underlies it.

However, 'virtual reality' is not the same as unreality:[10] it is a representation that enables us to act with greater or lesser effect upon reality. Virtual worlds and virtual communities of people have a kind of reality of their own, a certain effectiveness, an operational capacity. They tend to erase the boundaries between different levels of reality. A new culture based on images and simulations is becoming essential for finding one's way among the labyrinths of digital representation. The need for this is all the more urgent as the network explosion has made this culture into a real *lingua franca*.

To balance this, the cultural policies of the future must encourage a revival of autonomous cultural activity, both individual and collective, to prevent the civilization of virtual reality from producing a society of generalized simulation, based on the hyperconsumption of standardized cultural products. Each human being, at each moment, is unique. This infinite diversity and this uniqueness constitutes humanity's treasure. To become uniform would be a backward step with terrible consequences for humanity.

From Cyberculture to Cyberethics

The proliferation of new technology raises high hopes because it gives rise to a new generation of machines capable of furthering development, education and the transmission of knowledge, democracy and pluralism. The ongoing revolution also raises vital questions about the consequences of 'globalization', which is characterized, according to José Joaquín Brunner, by 'a reorganization of time and space'.[11] Beyond the industrial innovation that accompanies the new information and communication technologies, we can already see major social choices in the making. What will be the effect of the Internet on business and financial markets, on fiduciary forms of exchange (the creation of a 'cyber-money'), on work, on commerce and consumption, but also on the creative and information media, on education, and on the transmission of knowledge? In the global information society, what part will be given over to the public Internet, and what part will be reserved for private Intranets? How can we further 'maintain, increase and diffuse knowledge' in this radically new environment?[12]

Most of all, what system of ethics will govern this world of interdependence and interconnection, dominated by information understood as an exchange value and a commodity, and by immediacy as the central global experience? What will be the prevailing aesthetic and cultural perceptions in a world where the experience of culture is multiple and no longer territorial, and in which the most distant events can enter into new and unexpected relationships with near and familiar ones? Finding the answers to these questions will be one of the greatest challenges of the coming years. The cultural globalization brought about by new information technology brings with it radically new forms of knowledge and new modes of representation. In particular, it has implications for the rights and dignity of human beings as individuals. As José Joaquín Brunner puts it:

> the world we live in is increasingly artificial and constructed; it is increasingly rich in knowledge, and yet ... increasingly opaque and incomprehensible ... The available technology ... has forever changed the way we see the world and the way we exist in it, but the price has been the destruction of our certainties and the growth of our perplexity. Paradoxically, knowledge has made us more uncertain.[13]

Nevertheless, the third industrial revolution has brought with it a confusion between two terms: the most reputable institutions, the organizations that trade in globalization, and sometimes the experts themselves talk interchangeably about 'information society' and 'knowledge society'. We must stop confusing 'knowledge' with 'information'. We live today in a global information society where technology has increased the quantity of information available and its speed of transmission beyond anything we might have thought possible a few years ago. As long as people all over the world are unable to approach all this information critically, as long as they cannot analyse it, sort it, and incorporate the elements which interest them into their existing knowledge base, this information will remain a mass of undefined data. Rather than mastering information, many people will realize that it has mastered them.

The Internet: A New Social Architecture?

> The Internet is one of the most interesting manifestations of the new [informa-tion technology] revolution ... This global network displays three characteristics of a new social architecture, which may, perhaps, in time, come to predominate on this planet. First it is a *self-organizing* system. It originated and has developed with no central driving force, no central planning, and no control from above. Its architecture is *horizontal and anti-hierarchical* (the complete opposite of the bureaucratic models of organization to which we are accustomed). Second, it is a network open to everyone who wants to be connected. Participation requires no special permit or membership of any group. Once inside the network you can take or leave what you choose. It offers multiple possibilities. Finally, it is an *interactive* architecture. When you enter it, you are in contact: 'on the net'. Every new member enjoys the entire available space for com-munication. The more people join it, the greater the value of the network as a whole.[14]

This is more than simply a revolution in equipment: it is first and foremost a scriptural revolution, a revolution in representation. Information and com-munication technologies favour the informed person rather than the conscious person, information rather than reflection, knowledge rather than wisdom. They allow the expansion of new ways of teaching, learning and carrying out research; they facilitate the development of new forms of culture and pre-viously unknown social roles; they make it possible to express new forms of individualism and solidarity; they enable the emergence of new kinds of human 'communities'. This, then, amounts to a genuine communication revolution, which could affect even the way we think, making it, perhaps, more dependent on external influences and representations, and perhaps less autonomous.

To the general public, the Internet is the paradigm of the new technologies. Granted, it is not yet fully 'global' in the sense of its geographical accessibility, but it nevertheless offers a new, potentially worldwide, form of expression. First, the Internet is continuously being enriched from within by the ever more varied uses to which it is put. The proliferation of public user networks with common interests gives rise to a growing number of activities and exchanges, which connect increasingly varied and distant geographical, social and cultural areas. The Internet enables scientists to work in a global context by putting together 'virtual' laboratories and research teams; it enables musicians to form virtual groups; young designers can enter electronic competitions to create images in three dimensions; lonely or elderly people can use it to escape loneliness. These international 'virtual diasporas' are certain to multiply and will, in the future, have an influence on both human creativity and sociability[15] as well as on the future of democracy on a national and international scale.

However, when we champion this new form of expression, communication, and creation, we incur special responsibilities towards those who are currently excluded from it for economic reasons, and towards its potential victims. The proliferation in cyberspace of networks for paedophiles or child prostitution,[16] copyright violation and incitement to racial hatred, for example, are new forms of crime, which should spur national governments and parliaments, along with criminal justice and the police, towards greater vigilance and cooperation. Cyberspace exists not outside the world, but within it: it is the duty of sovereign, democratic institutions to encourage the use of this medium to bring us closer to one another, not to create enmity and distance between us. Cyberculture must go hand in hand with the invention of a system of cyberethics. We hope that democracies will have the courage to set down this system first in national law, and that they will be able to agree on its principles in coordination and in cooperation with their partners at the international level.[17]

The Internet and Development: Including the Information Highway's Excluded

The current revolution brings us what amounts to a new way of transmitting writing and a new printing press. But it is entirely justifiable to fear the establishment of deep divisions between the new scribes, with their mastery of the new tools, and the new digital illiterates, who will find themselves cast out of the circle of initiate members. While the former cruise easily on global oceans of knowledge and networks of networks, the latter will seek refuge in dream universes of virtual drugs and in the artificial play paradises of 'reality parks', or will be utterly excluded from the new technology. Is there anyone, nowadays, who does not sing the praises of the amazing Internet boom? And yet, for a long time to come, we shall be living in a world of information highways and information subways.[18]

Participation in the 'civilization of the immaterial' is indeed very unevenly divided between different parts of the world. According to T. L. Jacobson, 'the inequalities between rich and poor countries with regard to health, education and earnings are reproduced for information services'.[19] Two primary indicators provide a measure of this inequality: access to basic telecommunication infrastructure, and access to the Internet. Access to traditional means of telecommunication is the determining factor since, without it, there can be little or no access to the 'information highway'. Yet, as Michel Elie notes, 'at least 80% of the world's population has no basic telecommunication facilities'.[20] In 1995, according to the World Bank, the rich countries had an average of more than one main telephone line for every two inhabitants; by contrast, South Asia must make do with 13 lines per 1,000, and sub-Saharan Africa with 11 per 1,000.[21] How, for example, can we provide competitive access to the 'information highway' for Africa when, as Thabo Mbeki notes, 'there are more telephone lines in Manhattan than in the whole of sub-Saharan Africa' and 'half the human race has never used a telephone'? As we have said before, what can the 'information highway' possibly mean to the 600,000 towns and villages still without electricity, and their two billion inhabitants?

True, the Internet is growing exponentially, with the number of servers doubling about every six months: the total rose from 1,313,000 in January 1993 to 43,230,000 in January 1999.[22] Some, perhaps very optimistic, predictions even propose a figure of 187 million connections globally, two million networks outside the USA and 2.5 billion users by the year 2000.[23] However, the extent of Internet penetration in different countries 'seems strongly correlated with their level of development'.[24] The relationship between the Internet and the GDP is comparable to the long-observed relationship between the telephone and the GDP. Only six African countries have more than ten servers per million inhabitants, whereas ten countries (six in Europe, two in the Pacific, one in Asia, and one in America) have more than one server per hundred inhabitants. According to the most recent report from the International Tele-communication Union, there are more Internet users in Iceland than in the whole of sub-Saharan Africa, while investment in telecommunications in 1996 ranged from US$6.9 per capita for the low-revenue countries to US$135.3 per capita for the high-revenue countries (in other words, a factor of 23).[25] Clearly, the global village and the electronic village do not coincide.[26] The outline of an up-to-date map of the spread of the Internet broadly reproduces the geography of development. Professor Dan Schiller writes:

> In January 1996, it was estimated that 60% of the nine and a half million computers connected to the Internet belonged to Americans ... The number of Internet sites per thousand people was between 10 and 18 in the United States, Australia, and Scandinavia; between 5 and 10 in Canada and parts of Western Europe. On the other hand there was hardly a single site to be found in Latin America or Africa (with the exception of South Africa), in the Near East, or in Asia (including the countries of the former Soviet Union).[27]

The Internet is currently a phenomenon characteristic of rich countries, as can also be seen from the distribution by country of electronic addresses.[28]

There is also a strong correlation between the number of Internet servers and the United Nations Development Programme's (UNDP) Human Development Index (HDI). However, the correlation is not absolute: even with comparable HDIs, some countries are better equipped than others (as is the case for South Africa, Turkey, Lebanon or Singapore). In contrast, 'some countries with a high HDI (Spain or France), or with an average or poor HDI (China, Saudi Arabia or Sri Lanka) are under-equipped'.[29] Where the country concerned has a very high HDI, this under-equipment results not from technical backwardness, whatever the media sometimes suggest, but from particular cultural and institutional factors. In the case of France, ranked second in the HDI in the *Human Development Report 1998*, it was the early development of Minitel, through the impetus given by the state, and its extraordinary technological and commercial success that, for a long time, obstructed the growth of the Internet. However, the Internet in France has been growing fast since 1997–98. There is thus no curse of the Internet that dooms the poor, or nations with marked cultural singularities, to remain exiled from the 'civilization of the immaterial', and permanently blocks their access to the new development opportunities created by the 'information superhighways'. The regional variations observed suggest that the Internet in particular, and the new information and communication technologies in general, have introduced a new, and in part unpredictable, element into the development process, an element that is also a sign of hope.

Technological and economical 'leapfrogging' by less advanced countries, made possible by these new technologies, requires a substantial investment in telecommunication infrastructure and equipment. The rapid evolution in technology therefore implies that experts, public, private and corporate partners, consumers and citizens will have to consider jointly the future of electronic space (on which development will largely depend from now on) taken as a whole, including equipment, infrastructure and telecommunications costs. They must also make a commitment to reducing inequality, based on the notion of 'universal access' and lifelong education for all.

Reducing the cost of telecommunication is essential. This applies just as much to industrialized nations. The OECD indicated in a recent study that in Europe the cost of Internet access is still markedly higher than in North America.[30] As Nobel prizewinner Arno Penzias states, 'a computer is only economical if the cost of communication is low'.[31] Hopes are high for a rapid fall in costs. According to Jean-François Rischard, vice-president of the World Bank, 'the cost of telecommunications is going to drop (even further) to the point where it will be practically zero. The cost of a one-hour transatlantic call could be less than 15 centimes by the year 2010.'[32] On this point it should be noted that computer communication works out even cheaper than point-to-point communication, and that it transforms the user into a 'potential publisher'. The rate of output of information supplied by a modem (20 or 30 pages a minute) is far greater than that of a fax machine, and is far less costly, because it may often be sent at the cost of a local telephone call.

Deliberation on the global information society is already under way. The G7 ministerial conference (the summit of the seven most industrialized countries), which was held on this subject in February 1995 in Brussels, emphasized the need for all countries, particularly developing countries and those in transition, to be integrated into the information society. The conference held at Midrand, South Africa, on the information society and development (ISAD, 13–15 May 1996), pursued this theme, emphasizing that 'there is clearly an unsatisfactory level of investment in information infrastructure development in the less industrialized countries', and calling for the requisite mobilization of investment in order to create a global information society.[33] 'No single model is universal', concluded the Midrand conference, justifiably.[34] We need to translate impressive declarations of intent into action, by increasing public aid for development in this field considerably, rather than decreasing it, in the many countries where private investment is manifestly inadequate.

Investment in education is equally urgent, so that *all* humans are able to make use of the information networks available. This means education for all, beginning with those who think that all problems are already solved by the computer. It also means that education must explore self-mastery, critical thought and creativity – which calls for the involvement of parents and teachers, over and above the computer. Our capacity for thought is what sets human beings apart. As Hans Krebs, director of my laboratory research into metabolism at Trinity College, Oxford, taught me, scientific equipment is important and resources are essential, but in the end, true research is seeing what no one has seen and thinking what no one has ever thought before. So let us remember that creativity is our greatest asset and our hope: every human being must be able to make use of this marvellous potential.

The struggle against under-equipment in communication technologies is becoming a global priority: this is the only thing that will allow fairer access to the information society for developing countries and for those excluded from it, and will contribute to making the 'global market' a catalyst for world development. Carlos-Alberto Alfonso, head of the Brazilian Institute for Social and Economic Analysis, states that data communication networks being set up in certain developing countries will allow civil society to exchange information and to participate in the debate on relevant subjects, whereas in the past, information reached them only once the debate was already over. For participation in an electronic debate, he notes, has a deeply democratic character: 'the point of view of a great "global" institution carries the same weight, from the visual presentation perspective, as that of a small popular group working on a village scale'.[35] From now on, organizations working for the defence of human rights can send their demands directly to the relevant United Nations services, researchers can update their bibliographies instantly, and schoolchildren can communicate with other countries on a daily basis.

Yet unless there is a rapid evolution and an appreciable strengthening of development aid policies, the expansion of the 'information superhighway' is in great danger of increasing existing inequalities in development and of leaving millions of people standing by the roadside. Those responsible for development must therefore, in the spirit of the Midrand conference, lay firm foundations for proper information development, based on new strategies and on lasting funding plans sufficient to meet the challenge of the latest technology. According to Jean-Louis Guigou, information development should therefore be the first priority of regional planning projects in the future,[36] and justify a new policy of infrastructure building in the greatest number of countries during the next 20 years.

Such a choice is above all a political one, and cannot rest on purely economic considerations. As Al Gore, vice-president of the USA, has stressed, it should be recognized that 'marketplace economics should not be the sole determinant of the reach of the information infrastructure'; it is, moreover, in this spirit that the USA has called for the extension of the 'National Information Infrastructure' to all schools, libraries, hospitals and clinics by the end of the century.[37] This becomes all the more necessary at global level, since, as the G7 member countries emphasized, 'globalization ... may accentuate inequality and certain parts of the world could become marginalized'.[38] I would add that personally, I am puzzled by the results of *laisser-faire* policies in this context. I have always considered, and do so increasingly, that the market must be led towards a sustainable development economy by values of justice and sharing. I also believe that the great problems of education, including the problem of violence within schools, in the USA and elsewhere, must be solved not by computers, but by good teachers and high-quality school courses. Human beings must first learn to master themselves before they can attempt to master their tools.

We need to invest in education *for all*. There would be no point in having an 'information highway' at our disposal if there were only a few drivers using it. At the dawn of the twenty-first century, we must take up the challenge: we must make a great effort in education to train the drivers of the future. And we must also construct 'information highways' that link up the *entire* planet, and not merely the most prosperous regions or countries, without letting ourselves be governed by tempting short-term economic interests. As Marc Guillaume suggests, 'we are still thinking in terms of "highways" when it is the junctions that are becoming important ... now hypertext and switching devices are transforming modes of production, consumption and information'.[39] The Universal Declaration of Human Rights recognizes the right of each individual 'to seek, receive and impart information and ideas regardless of frontiers through any media' (Article 19). Does this article not make it our duty to ensure *universal access* to the Internet?

At the same time as guaranteeing the globalization of lifelong education for all, why not also suggest that nations make a commitment to linking up the world's schools, universities and museums by the Internet within the next generation? This would give a decisive boost to the 'co-operation among the nations in all branches of intellectual activity' recommended by UNESCO's Constitution.[40] Should we not start thinking about setting up a global digital library, a subject we shall return to in the following chapter? Why not consider a joint special initiative between UNESCO and the United Nations devoted to establishing new information and communications technology in developing countries, particularly in Africa? Unless such mobilization takes place, we could well witness, as we already have in the sphere of education, the marginalization of many countries and millions of people, and the growth of a form of 'techno-apartheid' that may well increase the effects of economic exclusion tenfold and create even greater world division.

Just as, in the nineteenth century, compulsory schooling would, had it been truly universal, have prepared new generations to meet the challenge of the Industrial Revolution by offering a type of 'mass cultural adjustment',[41] it should in future attempt to bring about the widest possible dissemination of rudiments, codes and rhetoric related to this new method of transmitting text. Unless a concerted effort is made to achieve computer literacy and knowledge of 'virtual' languages, our society will be deeply divided between those with access to the new culture, and those left standing at the side of the information highway.[42]

Communication and information techniques actually open the way for a better grasp of the basics and rudiments of knowledge, and to a deeper understanding of their relationships. They produce a very positive catalytic effect, therefore, on those mastering them, who consequently possess powerful tools, of knowledge and action. On the other hand, those who do not possess the new tools or fail to master them adequately, will find the cultural, methodological and cognitive abyss growing ever wider, as the catalytic effect works against them.

The key question is this: how far are populations in a position to participate? Now that many are preparing to build information highways, how many people are left standing on the verge, or worse still, in the subterranean passages of the 'information civilization'? At first, creating the infrastructure of the information civilization will lead to increased cultural exclusion and dualism. The double handicap of poverty and lack of education instantly denies access to the information society to its victims, the poor and the uneducated. In a world where 25% to 30% of the labour force are under-employed, and where at least 140 million workers are unemployed,[43] largely owing to the supplanting of humans by machine-power, training in the use of new technology is a significant concern.

The growing gulf opened by the information civilization cannot be reduced to a purely economic phenomenon. The exclusion is deep-rooted in social and economic factors, and also has a significant cultural dimension. By denying certain populations access to knowledge, to forms of culture provided by education, and to new technology, exclusion not only deprives them of the main asset of development, but also destroys human solidarity by nourishing what Jan Pronk calls a 'culture of disdain'.[44] Cultural exclusion is one of the major scourges that needs to be overcome in the next few decades, since such a phenomenon could, if we are not careful, result in cultural deprivation, and in the tragic expansion of a culture of violence and oppression. We need to ensure that access to the civilization and information infrastructure is made easier by concrete policies, as part of a long-term plan, nationally and inter-nationally. Why not take the bold step of setting up 'cultural security systems' (financed by the 'dividends of peace', for example), along the lines of social security systems already set up at least partially in several countries? These cultural security systems would aim at providing easy access for all to lifelong continuous education, to the information civilization, and to types of culture dependent on technology. They would facilitate the 'inclusion' of excluded or marginalized populations, notably by providing access to the essential infra-structure of the information society (access to e-mail, to electronic forums, and to online data bases; distribution of products and scientific and technological information services, distance education,[45] cooperation between universities and major research institutions).

An Economy of the Immaterial

The economic and commercial applications of the Internet continue to grow. Seventy-three per cent of Internet users use the Web for shopping every month.[46] As well as the creation of 'intranets', technological innovation now allows 'made-to-measure' use of the Internet network.[47] Personalized searching on the Web, dubbed 'Webcasting', is already used by over a million people, who are thus not only able to sift automatically through the mass of available information, but also to be updated constantly in their selected domains. It was predicted that in 2000, webcasting would account for one-third of the US$14 billion market created by the Internet.[48] Webcasting in particular promises to become a very useful tool for the management and transmission of in-formation and transactions within private financial, commercial and industrial 'intranets'.[49]

Are the very foundations of traditional socio-economic organization being radically challenged? Concepts such as 'cost'[50] or 'work' seem to be losing weight, or to be changing their meaning significantly. Are we about to witness a gradual shift from a civilization built on transformation of materials and on consumption of energy and raw materials, towards a civilization based increasingly on communication and knowledge? We are convinced that such a civilization should be primarily based on intelligence and wisdom.

The advent of the paradigm of the 'immaterial' brings into play elements that could well transform global society, and profoundly change the self-image of *Homo sapiens*, and his image of his role in the world, with the speed of change varying according to geocultural location and state of humanistic, technological and human advancement. Machines are replacing humans in the field of industrial mass production, and will continue to replace them increasingly: they force us to rethink our role and to invent other functions for ourselves. Automation and rationalization of production enable companies to meet increasing consumer needs using ever-decreasing numbers of employees. This is the well-known phenomenon of 'growth without job creation'. As new technology grows more and more 'intelligent' and 'communicative', it is putting an increasing number of 'intelligent' and 'communicative' people out of work, as a result of the astonishing advances in productivity which it permits. It forces us in this way to expand our notions of 'intelligence' and 'communication' and also to determine what is specifically human about our activity, for fear of being definitively rendered obsolete, or being supplanted by machines we have created.

The expansion of modern technology favours a transnational, nomadic form of capitalism, quick to exploit on-the-spot differences in legislation and productivity between different 'global regions', which in the current economic order are gradually replacing nation-states and their eroded authority. The globalization of networks and the constant decline in cost of transport and communication are accompanied by a breaking up of regional zones and a fragmentation of nations, allowing virtual and ephemeral regroupings through global short-circuits.

While the market economy is interested only in profitable sectors, certain human needs, which are vital but not 'profitable', continue to grow. In this world of selective excess, a large proportion of the human population is still unable to find enough food. In the fields of education, scientific research, culture, health and environment, huge latent needs remain unfulfilled. Traditional economic concepts, such as 'the market', 'supply' and 'consumption', fail to account adequately for the complexity and diversity of these needs. These same concepts allow only a superficial understanding of the logic of the economy of the immaterial, particularly the underlying machinery of creation and distribution of 'value'.

The revolution in communication and intelligence establishes a new relationship between the real and the virtual. Production of real goods is of diminishing economic importance as compared to production of immaterial goods all based on information. The economy of the immaterial and of the virtual obeys very different laws from the economy of the material. While the material economy is affected by diminishing returns, the virtual economy is an economy of growing returns. 'Value' increases at the same time as a software program spreads, as a norm or standard becomes generally applied, as a network is globalized, or as an 'image' becomes universal. This value is not merely economic. It is of another order, located somewhere between the symbolic and the imaginary. It is an inherited, invisible, elusive value, which increases the more it is shared: it is rather like the subversive, seminal value of ideas, whirling about at lightning speed, materializing in myriad forms, and belonging to everyone yet no one.

This virtual economy tends to distribute increasingly widely, and at smaller and smaller cost, the fruits of an increasingly immaterial production. In so doing, it also tends to favour the constitutions of oligopolies, or even monopolies with global aspirations, especially in sectors that create powerful economies of scale, as found in the software industry, in information processing and distribution, and in the networked infrastructure industries such as transport and energy.

The virtual economy is particularly sensitive to speculation. Of the US$3 trillion turned over daily in the financial networks, 99% are purely speculative transactions and only 1% 'real' economic operations. As Paul Kennedy notes, the daily volume of stock exchange trading is now several hundred times greater than the value of goods exchanged.[51] Capital has become 'global' but even more than this, it has become 'virtual', that is, completely unreal or surreal in many ways. Many experts speak of the creation of a worldwide 'casino economy', the price of which has been the succession of financial crashes over the last twelve or so years.

We are not only living through an economic and social crisis. We are also witnessing a fundamental crisis of representation. It is a matter of a radical upheaval, which affects the very way we understand the world and society, and therefore the picture we create of our own place in the world, of the real purpose of humanity. A fitting response to this crisis of representation is needed: humanity must in future be able to provide a more adequate representation of the world. Some experts believe that a new kind of writing should be established, just as long ago in the Near East, the alphabet used by Phoenician merchants replaced the hieroglyphs of sacred texts, which led at the same time to a certain democratization of memory and knowledge. Indeed, they stress that each time a change in writing system is established within a society, the system of representing the world – the *Weltanschauung* – also changes.[52]

The appropriate response to this new challenge is simply the same as each individual would bring to essential *internal* questions. For, accustomed as we are to looking at the outside world through a screen, we have forgotten to look within ourselves. And we cannot be enlightened through external information, but only through thought and wisdom.

On the other hand, the current revolution seems rather to be introducing a new mode of transmitting text than establishing a new type of writing. In this sense, it can be compared less with the beginnings of the alphabet than with the sudden rise of the printing press. Everyone knows that the Chinese invention of the printing press with moveable characters found its second vocation in Europe, where it played a crucial role in the rise of Humanism, in the Enlightenment, in the spread of both the Reformation and the Counter-reformation, in the widening of commercial exchange, in the circulation of new technologies and science, and in the birth of industry. By individualizing access to knowledge and to sacred texts and making access more democratic, the book became the vector of a new civilization. Half a millennium later, we are still living on the foundations of that civilization. With digitization and the communication and information networks, are we witnessing a revolution of 'representation' on a similar scale, which could bring about equally great changes? If the experts are still far from unanimous on this subject, most recognize that we have embarked on a new age of discovery: the exploration of virtual worlds. We are definitely all going to have to learn to navigate the sea of knowledge. At the close of the twentieth century the world is swimming in culture: it has both too much and not enough. Since the information society is building, far beyond all our concrete towns, 'cross-border, invisible towns'[53] that extend throughout the whole planet, it seems to be putting into practice the dream of the blind Argentinian genius, Jorge Luis Borges: it is transforming the world into an infinite and immaterial library, which cannot be assimilated. While no one can claim to hold all the keys to it, only a small minority has access to it for the time being.

A New Frontier for Research and Education

The importance of new technology for education leaps to mind: one only has to mention the advantages in the field of distance education, as much for industrialized countries as for developing ones. The specific issue of distance education will be examined in Chapter 16. But we must emphasize at this point the upheaval caused by new technology in the field of knowledge production, and the development of research.

Scientific research did not, of course, wait for the Internet to use networks. The reverse is true: it is because scientific research already used networks that it lies at the origin of the Internet and its incredible 'boom'. Since the 1980s, new modes of production of knowledge have been developed,[54] supported by several parallel movements: diversification of research location, development of cooperation between institutions, the supremacy of multidisciplinary approaches over single disciplines.[55] This development benefited considerably from the growing role of information technology – and particularly the Internet – in research: 'the Internet phenomenon' encourages the networking of laboratories and is beginning to change considerably the system of publishing research results.[56] The potential of a free flow of information available in real time is a stroke of luck for the future of knowledge, expression and communication (700 online journals already exist on the Internet;[57] a growing number of libraries, universities, and museums supply services on the Net). One hundred years after opening to the public, the Library of Congress in the USA embarked on a project to put 5 million documents on the Internet by 2000 (see also Chapter 14).[58] Although it should not be confused with the universal civilization of knowledge, the global information society is a necessary gateway to it, suggesting solutions to the central problem of the distribution of knowledge.[59] The Internet is not an archive of worldwide science, but it is now an indispensable research vehicle.

In the USA, four-fifths of colleges and universities have increased their outlay on information technology significantly since 1996. These investments, and accompanying important changes in pedagogical methods, are radically transforming education and the whole educational experience, by 'dematerializing' the traditional campus. The consequences of this development are difficult to evaluate, but we believe that tools cannot replace teachers: teaching cannot be confused with teaching methods. In the end there is only one truly valid teaching skill: the one founded on humanity, example and love.

The networking of knowledge encompasses two challenges. The first is distribution and access, the importance of which has already been emphasized. 'Economic globalization goes together with a very unequal development of research and technology worldwide: the "triad" of the United States, the European Union and Japan represents 83% of global expenditure on research and development, and 80% of world scientific production of patents.'[60] The second challenge is the breaking down of knowledge into individual operations, which results from the fragmentation of its mode of production. 'We could, if we are not careful, end up increasing the Balkanization of research into sub-disciplines, thus making the development of joint operations and inter-disciplinary approaches more difficult.[61] A strategic vision and a long-term forecast governing production and distribution of knowledge are therefore necessary, in a context which new technology has distinctly altered. All too often the tool drives the thought, rather than the other way round. New technology, as has been observed, has made a clear contribution to the acceleration in 'global time' and to the triumph of short-term logic. So what about the long term, so essential to research? And what about the link between research and the central public concerns of education, health and management of natural resources? The state and regional and local communities have an innovative and imaginative role to play here, as efficient 'strategists' for a project bringing together research and technology. These bodies will therefore have to change quickly and radically to be capable of playing a role that will otherwise be monopolized by the private sector alone.

The availability of cultural goods on the Web could well benefit in future from the participation of key public services such as libraries, museums and audio-libraries, which will offer their services as 'multimedia libraries'. These could revolutionize public access to knowledge: in France, six million people are already members of such a multimedia facility, nearly three times more than those who are members of libraries, and such institutions allow a substantial number of new readers access to books, which they also lend.[62] Policies concerned with development of multimedia libraries for the general public, drawing on the potential created by multimedia, could in the long term form an important element of knowledge sharing, without rejecting the traditional and essential functions of cultural institutions. What a devastating loss for every one of us, and what a disaster it would be if it turned out that 'cybernauts' no longer read Heraclitus, Shakespeare or Cervantes.[63]

Education should therefore reconcile information with reflection at all levels. The instrument (the Internet and new technology) should be inseparable from its contents (books, knowledge), its contents from its functions (education, knowledge acquisition), and its functions from its missions (promoting world peace, human rights and democracy). There is a constant interaction and iteration from one to the next: in particular, education cannot be based merely on the pedagogical tool, whether it be the Internet, the textbook or the blackboard.

From Networks to Information Highways: Different Strategies

The 'miracle' of the Internet rested on the establishment of a particularly robust and efficient standard (TCP-IP) that allows a low running cost (the experts' jargon for this is the 'charter' effect of packet switching). This reduction in cost has led to highly attractive fixed costs, encouraging individual exploration and remote learning, community information sharing, creation of reference centres, consultation of public information put online by governments and public services. The Internet standard makes all networks and terminals compatible with each other, in theory. A telephone line and a personal computer are the only things required to create a central server and a redistribution node for Internet traffic. Entire countries can thus be opened up, and linked up to the global community of research, information and culture.

The information highways are at the heart of the global mechanism required to affirm the distribution of images, sounds and data in the best manner possible, while providing access to innovative functions such as real-time interaction with shared virtual worlds, participation in 'distributed' virtual communities, or navigation around virtual multimedia libraries available online. The networks that distribute and route information form the backbone of the virtual society. Although these networks are racing towards technological convergence, they are nevertheless still very varied. Geostationary or moving satellite networks, radio-relay systems, mobile communication networks (cellular phones), cable networks, fibre-optic networks, but also new sorts of terminals,[64] offer numerous possible combinations, with very varied relationships between investment and performance.

In spite of 'convergence', investment schemes may vary considerably. Only a careful study of political priorities and national and regional contexts will enable us to choose the correct balance between these various media. The central issue is to assess whether the current networks and techniques can from now on be put to use for priority development targets (education, research, environment, culture, health) to benefit developing countries, or whether we need to make huge investments, following the example of certain industrialized countries, which advocate the universal provision of fibre optics, for example.

On the same subject, it should be stressed that it is not in the objective interest of developing countries to wait for the next technological wave: they must grasp the potential offered by the present. For example, for developing countries, the rise of the Internet with its millions of users, its tens of thousands of servers, its thousands of data bases and freely available software packages, represents an extraordinary opportunity for linking up at a low cost to a global flow of data and images for educational, scientific and cultural use. The main problem is access to technology, as Roberto Bissio, director of the Third World Institute (Uruguay), underlines, saying that, in this domain, the gulf between North and South is even greater than for the distribution of other resources, and that this divide is in danger of widening. He also states that to meet the challenge, the South needs a cheap and pragmatic approach, 'based on the lowest common denominator, the e-mail message, and the interaction of "information brokers" within a decentralized network'.[65]

We should also remember that the race for better technological performance, which results in rapid obsolescence and permanent overbidding, is far from being always justified. Thus, in Europe, the currently available networks (telephone, cable, and even satellite networks) are in fact under-used, both quantitatively and qualitatively, and consequently are still vastly over-priced: in Europe, line rentals are ten to thirty times more expensive than in the USA. Instead of simply waiting for a new, costly, heavy-duty infrastructure to be established, it would make better sense to develop first and foremost an inventive industry, centred on the information and communication services, and on the creation of new 'contents'. Most of the latest applications of the 'electronic highways' are probably not financially viable. Who, apart from professionals, really needs .500 commercial television channels or even 150 specialized channels?

On the other hand, there is a considerable need for prompt and personalized access to precise, high-quality, cheap information within the spheres of education, research, and rationalization of work within administrations and businesses (particularly small and medium-sized businesses, so vital to the development of the North, and even more so to the South). For these applications, the telephone and cable networks currently in use are adequate for the time being. The most pressing problem is not to create an over-capacity of information highways for a consumer and leisure user-base, but rather to use current networks to their best effect so as to facilitate the emergence of a society equipped with abundant information, a free flow of knowledge, which is able to perform virtual navigation in the 'global memory'.

Just as not all global transport services use freeways and highways, virtual civilization will not revolve solely around the information superhighway. It is more probable that online and offline techniques will establish a distinctly complementary relationship. For example, applications for navigation and browsing such as those used on the Internet (Mosaic, Netscape, World Wide Web, VRML, Java, etc.) may easily coexist with a system of image distribution in the form of video cassettes or CD-ROMs sent by post. The transmission of images using fibre-optics will, moreover, eventually prove to be financially more viable than seemingly more rudimentary forms of image distribution, but the latter can be more useful and better adapted to the financial means of most developing countries.

The major projects for the development of the 'information highway' must not lead us to forget that with tried and tested technology it is already possible to build main roads, secondary roads, country lanes, tracks and paths. As for the 'highway' itself, many policies are possible. Moreover, while industrialized countries may be unanimous on the central issues, they differ substantially on investment strategies to be used, the speed of change, priorities, and particularly on the scale of desired deregulation and on the role of nation-states in networks and in international services. A review of these strategies would be useful, but it is beyond the scope of the present work.

The Limits of Deregulation

The 'information highways' are not, as we know, confined to the Internet network. The Internet is just one component of the technological revolution in progress. The 'network of networks' is enriched every day by new networks, new functions, new users and new interfaces. The Internet comprises 12,000 public access networks. Open networks such as these, Saskia Sassen underlines, are combined with 28,000 private, closed networks connected to the Internet, which are called 'Intranets'.[66] Thus cyberspace is made up of two-thirds of private digital space, comprising highly hierarchical networks, which function like exclusive clubs where not everyone is admitted. There is nothing surprising in this: the revolution in technology brings with it a revolution in communication and information management, especially within companies and administrations. In 2000, 1.6 million public and private networks should exist around the world. An enormous volume of financial transactions will operate in future in private digital space, thus bypassing the rules and regulations of traditional stock-exchange mechanisms, and raising new and difficult questions: whatever we gain in efficiency, we lose in transparency. What logic will govern this digital world: will it be in favour of open or closed networks? We cannot avoid noting that, behind the ideological façade of openness and of limitless communication everywhere, which more or less describes the ideology of cyberspace, the discreet logic of privatization and the closing-off of networks is set to dominate increasingly from now on.

We know, for example, that the traditional Internet is being outdistanced by a second-generation Internet (or 'Internet 2'), set up by the US National Science Foundation, using telephonic fibre-optic networks. Since the end of 1996, over one hundred university institutions and research centres in the USA have signed up, at their own expense and at the expense of their sponsors and patrons, to this super-network which links five supercomputers at American universities, and can transport 622 megabytes of information per second – that is, over ten times the speed of the traditional Internet and over 20,000 times the capacity of 28,000-byte modems. This new network means extremely complex calculations, up to a terabyte (a trillion bytes) per operation, can be executed very quickly, and the user can also visualize three-dimensional simulations of molecules or turbulence in real time. One of the great advantages of the new network is its capacity to gain time as compared to the 'classic' Internet, which is often congested and unable to perform such powerful applications, partly because of inadequate application software, a problem currently being addressed.[67] It is to be hoped that this super-network will be open to cooperation between the countries of the North and the South, in the field of scientific research.

The various policies for the establishment of 'information highways' are unanimous in stressing the urgency for necessary investment and its scale, as well as the importance of deregulation. The reason for deregulation is to leave a free rein for the private sector as far as possible, even if this freedom needs to be tempered by a reminder of the principle of free universal access to this 'universal service'. However, this crucial concept has never been very precisely defined. At best, it remains to be 'constantly redefined', and amended as new needs and demands arise in a constantly evolving information society.

Several problems remain unanswered in this respect: how can the financing of the 'universal service' be secured? Who should provide it? Who decides the costs? How does one guarantee freedom of expression, privacy for users and security of information effectively? How does one avoid letting deregulation become a quest for maximum profit, as it leaves the path open to *laisser-faire* economics? How can one prevent private operators, taking over from 'common carriers', from simply skimming off the most profitable clients by putting together personal consumer profiles, for example? Shades of Big Brother in marketing! Do the information highways need to be decentralized, cheap, and open to all, or should we encourage oligopolies and market fragmentation? Should we favour production and distribution of information by private individuals, which could lead to various forms of 'electronic democracy' already pointed out by many forecasting experts, or on the contrary, should we encourage commercial applications such as 'pay-per-view' films and electronic trade? Technological choices and engineering strategies depend on the answers to these questions, since they can in turn either promote or impede democratic life and social justice. We still need first of all to clarify the stakes, trends, risks, assets and foreseeable scenarios. New technology must be at the service of general policies, and these must still be clarified.

In the meantime, the principal steps have already been taken. The effect of deregulation is the accelerated convergence of technologies and services, the liberalization of markets, and the strengthening of a few global oligopolies, which are now replacing national monopolies. It is now no longer a question of wondering whether the revolution will actually take place: it has already crashed headlong into the old order. We therefore need to embark straight away on an ambitious campaign to establish a new type of 'information literacy', and to train society in new cultural and conceptual paradigms, if we wish to avoid creating an unbridgeable gulf between the new scribes and the computer illiterate, between 'info-rich' and 'info-poor'.

Ensuring the success of this policy certainly requires a confident, measured and well-advised form of 're-regulation'. This must be based on inalienable principles such as the right of people to access information and knowledge. In the name of this right, in June 1996 an American court compared the digital networks to an 'uninterrupted global conversation', thus protected by the first amendment of the American Constitution on freedom of speech.[68] Clear, international ethical principles should therefore be decreed, and respect for these ensured within the framework of the rule of law. National legal and judicial systems should be harmonized, taking universal principles into account. Several problems require urgent solution: intellectual property rights, respect for privacy, the right to access information, and freedom of expression.

Intellectual Property, the Common Good and Information in the Public Domain

The new technologies must contribute to 'maintain, increase and diffuse knowledge',[69] to the free circulation of ideas and information, and to lifelong education for all. Careful management of the public domain and of the laws regulating intellectual property must therefore accompany them. What is at stake is not in fact simply legal or commercial, but also ethical and political. In the USA, the notion of public access to information goes back to the founding fathers and in particular to Thomas Jefferson, who promoted the concept of the 'public library' and the doctrine of 'fair use' allowing academics to use protected texts for quotation and educational purposes.[70] Jefferson wrote:

> He who receives an idea from me, receives instruction himself without lessening mine; as he who lights his taper at mine, receives light without darkening me. That ideas should freely spread from one to another over the globe, for the moral and mutual instruction of man, and improvement of his condition, seems to have been peculiarly and benevolently designed by nature, when she made them, like fire, expansible over all space, without lessening their density at any point, and like the air in which we breathe and move and have our physical being, incapable of confinement or exclusive appropriation. Inventions then cannot, in nature, be a subject of property.

Some aspects of the present evolution point towards an extension of the length of the 'copyright' period to the detriment of the public domain.[71] Does this extension of protection, providing no counterbalance in favour of the 'common good', represent the first step towards the complete disappearance of the public domain? Is it compatible with the development of universal access to information, and with the true spirit of intellectual property law, which promises the return of work to the public after a certain period? The problem of databases and public sector data thus remains the focus of an unfinished debate.

The problem of intellectual property cannot be given a unilateral solution. Creation and innovation are certainly favoured by adequate rights protection. But too much protection works against the interest of rights-holders and users. Over-restrictive intellectual property rights lead to secure incomes, which are all the more unacceptable in that they foster the creation of monopolies without benefiting public interest in any way. Such monopolies could therefore stem from the need, inherent in the 'virtual civilization', for norms and standards in software and networks. In other cases, the problem is the very nature of the 'invention', and of its 'originality'. In this case, far from 'encouraging creativity', the law benefits only those who are already strong, and the international community of users finds itself obliged to admit defeat against a small number of ultra-powerful oligopolies. To combat this risk, we need to broaden the notion of public domain and bring down the norms and standards currently involved, so as to foster free competition, free circulation of ideas, and creativity in all cultures and actors. We must see to it, however, if we embark on this course, that the rich (who with access to networks will increasingly be spared the payment of intellectual property rights) are not given an unfair advantage and the poor made to pay. The poor, being largely excluded from these networks, would still be forced to pay rights, as they would remain dependent on traditional means of distribution, such as books.

Intervention should start in the key field of news documentation and other works that are spared all the problems of copyright, either because they are already in the public domain owing to the date of publication, or because they were produced by public or academic organizations whose chief concern is the cheap distribution of material of general interest. A growing number of authors are ready to let their own works be distributed free of charge, provided their names remain associated with the document and the integrity of the text is safeguarded. This conforms with the concept of 'copyleft' (where the author's rights are reduced to a moral right). UNESCO is particularly concerned with promoting the wider establishment of public document and information archives within member states to make material accessible online, in accordance with the principle of completely free access to publicly funded information, at a cost no greater than the marginal cost of reproduction and dissemination.

The upheavals currently taking place are not without consequence for the concept of copyright and the moral right of the author. Digitization allows several different media forms (text, sound and images) to be combined and processed. Information can be duplicated an infinite number of times, easily edited, and instantly distributed on the networks. A certain legal balance must be found, taking this into account, between protecting authors and the user's need to process and manipulate multimedia information. The important Anglo-Saxon notion of 'fair use' should be given greater standing. This is particularly important for the future of public libraries, archives and public systems of documentation. But it is also important because it becomes a matter of guaranteeing access to information and knowledge to disadvantaged social groups and to developing countries.

Whatever the case, international harmonization will become essential. It should be noted that critical legal problems will in the future be centred not on traditional modes of expression using new media, such as CD-ROMs showing photographs and audio-visual sequences, but on new creative means that are far more complex: distributed systems, network software and dynamic documents, for example.

The Struggle against Cultural Desertification

Because of its impact on cultural industries, new technology cannot be contemplated without regard for cultural policies, nor can it remain isolated from development strategies and economic constraints.

In the future, as a result of the unprecedented growth in the circulation of images, data and sound, the cultural industries will be eager for new programmes. In the USA, the entertainment and recreation industry is already the second largest export industry after aerospace. It is therefore essential that cultural policies, on the eve of the twenty-first century, should favour not only the digitization of the whole cultural heritage, both material and immaterial, but also much greater production capacity, both regionally and nationally, in accordance with actual situations and available potential. In certain industrialized countries, such as France,[72] officials estimate that to meet demand, it would be necessary to increase that capacity twentyfold. Failing that, supply will essentially be monopolized by one or two countries.

The effects of this revolution cannot, of course, be predicted yet with any certainty. Will it allow us to draw nearer to one another culturally? If so, 'distance culture' would be a culture in which distance is irrelevant. But what sort of culture would be at stake? A culture of 'globalizers' sold to the 'globalized'? Will such a form of culture lead to cultural erosion, or to cultural desertification, by the expansion of a standardized culture, which will become nothing more than a commodity? In other words, what will become of the rich diversity of culture in a world that is increasingly global, linked up by networks and interconnected? We worry about the threat to biological diversity. Can we manage to protect cultural identity, which seems to be threatened just as much by the uniformity of messages as by the 'monoculture' of development and of technocratic reasoning? What will our future look like? Cultural conformity, or cultural conviviality?

The introduction of this report addressed the issue of globalization. And it is a fact that most cultures, in spite of their differences, now live in the same global time, they travel the networks 'in real time' and are in a sense 'delocalized'. In this sense, the world has never been so up to date. The impact of this phenomenon has been greatest and most direct on the individual. In one sense, the individual's autonomy has been heightened, since culture is no longer dependent on a single location or group. This is what Marshall McLuhan understood when he spoke of the 'global village', designating thus not so much the global communication network itself, as the network as an extension of each individual's spirit and sensibility. 'Diaspora communities' also benefit from the positive impact of cultural 'delocalization', as the bonds between members are reinforced by network expansion. On the other hand, communities that are strongly territorial risk seeing their cohesion diminish, in the face of the growth of an 'à la carte' global form of individualism and of numerous transnational cultures.

Not all aspects of globalization are negative. Is there anyone who does not hope to see human rights respected everywhere without exception, science and medicine made universal, and modern communication methods breaking the isolation of 40% of the global population?[73] Who could complain if, by worldwide diffusion, new technology transformed everyone into a citizen of the world? Who could protest if it contributed, as noted by the UNDP, to the decline of certain oppressive cultural practices, such as serfdom, slavery, the traditional exclusion of certain groups and the cruel treatment of women?[74]

Yet the risk of cultural erosion must not be played down. Ancestral languages and cultures are dying out. Approximately six thousand languages are still spoken in the world, but only about twenty have a global audience. A few die every year. Are we going to let the diversity of language disappear forever? Will their richness (approximately 360 million words, estimating that each language consists of an average of 60,000 words) be left to dwindle to a single *lingua franca* derived from a single culture? This vital question is broached in Chapter 15.

The globalization of messages must not lead to a single unilingual culture dominated by technology. As Gandhi said, 'leave the windows of your house open and let the breezes blow through in all directions, but let the foundations of your house be solid and unshakeable'. Cultural conformism cannot be a global solution: because of the extreme reactions it has already provoked, it can lead only to violence and cultural conflagration.

The explosion of conflicts between minorities and the majority and, indeed, between different minorities, gives a foretaste of this violence. We noted in the introduction to this work that the twenty-first century has already begun, in the paradox of globalization, which is provoking a backlash of enormous fragmentation and violence. The very survival of many human groups is now threatened, as witnessed by the constant vulnerability affecting the 300 million indigenous people living in 70 different countries. In one country, which is very advanced in terms of development, the suicide rate within native communities reached 40 out of 100,000 in 1988, that is, three times the national average. In 1986 the Yanomani Indians living in the Amazonian forest numbered 10,000. Today their chances of survival seem very limited. Depression, despair and the prospect of the destruction of their culture and even of their descendants make up the tragic lot of many indigenous societies. How can 'distance culture' make up for the annihilation of the culture closest to us, that residing in our hearts?

Signs of evolution are noted, however, that indicate that technological progress and cultural diversity need not necessarily contradict each other. This is particularly true of language. Admittedly, the Internet, originally conceived in North America, uses English as its principal linguistic vehicle. But while English until only recently still made up 90% of Internet sites, it was down to 70% of sites in January 1997, with Germanic and Romance languages and Japanese sharing 25% of the rest.[75] In Chapter 15, we consider the future of languages, and the importance of establishing global standards allowing the interaction of all modern systems of writing (including the principal Chinese characters).[76] The growth of the multilingual Internet is justified not purely by reasons of access and communication but by cultural factors. We must take pains to ensure that this new means of communication serves as a true educational vehicle, a carrier of knowledge, training, exchange, communication and spreading of culture. The Internet must by rights be a principal player in the protection of diversity within the cultural heritage of humanity.

It is essential, given the risk of 'cultural desertification', to revive heritage, to protect the cultural environment and to encourage continuity in cultural legacy. Digitization of heritage could in the future make a decisive contribution to this. Active policies in favour of languages, based on the principle of 'linguistic decentralization' could bring about a renaissance of cultural diversity where it is threatened, within the framework of a pluralistic education in tolerance and conviviality.[77]

Heritage must be conserved, but it must also be revitalized. An effective struggle against 'cultural desertification' could involve far-reaching projects to link quality cultural tourism with cultural development, based, for example, on reviving the craft industry and protecting the cultural and the natural environment. It is time to think about creating national parks of cultural and natural heritage,[78] which would form real archipelagos of development. Such policies could encourage the rebirth of traditional architecture, for example the mud-brick buildings beloved of Hassan Fathy, in regions of particular heritage interest, with the participation of the populations concerned and using modern technology. The aim would be to promote development with culture, not development against culture. Such actions would offer a very convincing alternative to the unsuitable, imitative town planning and housing schemes used increasingly frequently in the South, as well as in many traditional environments in the North. Creativity and the art of straying from the beaten track lie at the heart of human adventure: these are the secret, peaceful weapons of development.

But we must go further. There are two types of cultural diversity, and therefore of 'multiculturalism', as Néstor García Canclini points out,[79] multiethnicity and multilingualism, which are the fruits of history, and multiculturalism born of modern forms of cultural fragmentation and organization in industrialized society. With regard to the second sense of the word, globalization and the new revolution in information and communications technology are not at all synonymous with cultural conformism. On the contrary, they give rise to an enormous hybridization of culture, simultaneously with the comparative erosion of national cultures, with free-trade agreements, and with the most varied sorts of encounters, through the media, but also through tourism or migration. Nowadays cultural cross-breeding has taken on global proportions, as witnessed by the spread of 'world music' or even the ever more frequent exchanges in culinary repertoires.

The next century will doubtless see the spread of something already perceived in our 'global village': a flood of new cultural syntheses, hybrid forms and 'cultural mutations'. The revolution of the virtual is set to make this happen even more quickly. In this sense, I am convinced that the struggle for diversity has not been lost. As Carlos Fuentes so elegantly said, 'culture is a sea-shell in which we can hear the murmurs of what we are, what we were, of what we have forgotten and of what we may become'. The only cultural diversity under threat, which we must protect with active policies, is the one that, inherited from the past, resides in the linguistic component and in the 'ethos' of each culture.

All these various developments taken as a whole will, in time, interact with another perceptibly imminent phenomenon: the twilight of the mass media. Many commentators hold that the mass media are powerful agents of cultural standardization. According to Gerald Levin, director-general of the Time Warner group, 'As television viewers begin to use their television sets for amusement and educational and cultural purposes in equal quantities, the demand for quality programmes will increase.'[80] This logic is already at work in the skyrocketing number of specialized channels in industrialized countries and in the decline of large general networks in the USA. As Gerald Levin states, 'interactivity is moving the consumer from the periphery of the electronic universe to its centre. [It] individualizes each person by giving them an infinite number of choices.' At the dawn of the twenty-first century, we shall undoubtedly witness a cultural segmentation of supply and demand that should increase diversity. The question will no longer be to attract the greatest number of people by offering a restricted number of programmes (the logic of prime time), but to tailor supply to increasingly wide-ranging cultural tastes and demands.

New Technology: Opportunity or Risk?

'Can we survive new technology?' John von Neumann, the father of the digital computer, asked himself.[81] Are the new information and communication networks a risk or an opportunity for our societies?

An opportunity, certainly. If the Internet is destined to alter the forms of power and conditions of exchange, this is primarily because, under hitherto unattained optimum conditions, it can function as an open system where the user's identity and status in the hierarchy could be less important than the value of his or her participation; where the effects of geography could be temporarily irrelevant; where all previously isolated forms of information (numerical, visual, audio) could be brought together in a common vehicle; and where an almost infinite number of participants could take part in a single process. Furthermore, the exchange of knowledge surely implies recognition of the Other, not as a subject of domination, but as a source of creativity and wealth. Thus the new technologies, at least in theory, encourage open, consensual and non-hierarchical relations between individuals and groups.

This vision, as we have seen, is far from being realized. There is a geography of the Internet, and limits on its capacity and access to it. Behind the separation of public Internet and private Intranets, we can already see the beginnings of a specialization of functions, of 'filters', 'locks' and 'frontiers'. What is more, the breakneck race for taking private possession of information and knowledge, seen simply as super-profitable goods, is rapidly taking us further away from the Utopia of an open, friendly, idyllic cyberculture. The globalization of information also carries risks of violations of privacy, isolation of individuals, loss of a sense of society and virtualization of reality. These are risks to the future of societies and democracy.

It is very tempting for the states that enjoy a significant technological advantage in this domain to treat the new technologies coercively as a tool to project their power. Is it not likely that the current unequal sharing of new technology will soon lead to the emergence of new forms of violence, domination and exclusion? What will be the extent of the cultural effects of mastery of the Internet: won't those who control the medium be tempted to control the message as well? 'Knowledge, more than at any other period of history, is power,' as two American experts recently summed it up.[82] Could it be, however, as the same authors suggest, that the same new technologies open up a new era in the practice of world diplomacy, in which the lure of technology could replace economic and military coercion and encourage the exercise of what the authors term 'soft power'?

'Ladies and gentlemen, my answer is technology. Now, what was the question?' Sir John Daniel, vice-chancellor of the Open University, announced ironically at the inaugural session of a conference. It must be said that the answer is the content, and especially, widespread access to knowledge through universal, lifelong education.

We are still a long way from achieving the combination of equality of access and freedom of use. As a result, the growth of information technology requires, on the international level, a renewed commitment to the very concrete promotion of 'the free flow of ideas, by words and by images';[83] it requires solidarity and sharing, because 'the market will not be enough ...

Left to itself, the market will, in all probability, continue to exert a profoundly unequal effect on the Internet.'[84]

It might be argued that the growth of any new technology, be it the printing press or the new networks, presents both an opportunity and a risk, an agent of turbulence and uncertainty:

> In itself, virtualization is not good, bad, or neutral. It appears as the very action of human beings' 'becoming other', or heterogenesis. Rather than fearing it, condemning it, or throwing ourselves bodily into it, I propose that we take the time to get a grasp of it, to think, and to understand the full scope of virtualization ... The virtual is not the opposite of the real at all. On the contrary, it is a means of being fertile and powerful. It frees the creative processes, opens up the future, and opens up wells of meaning below the dull plains of immediate physical presence.[85]

Starting from these new meanings and new ways of being together (virtual communities, virtual exchanges, virtual companies, etc.), the information society in the twenty-first century will have to build a new public space to correspond to the immaterial society. Cybernetics implies a redefinition of society's guiding principles. As a round table of Canadian experts highlighted, the term 'governance' derives from the Greek *kybernan* and *kybernetes*, meaning 'to guide' and 'pilot' or 'helmsman' respectively. 'The process of governance is the process by which an organization or a society steers itself, and the dynamics of communication and control are essential to this process.'[86] Just as Greek democracy was conceived according to the scientific and technological paradigms of antiquity, notably Euclidean geometry, twenty-first-century democracy will certainly have to be reconsidered in the light of the new paradigms: especially the science of complexity and cybernetics.

From this perspective, UNESCO's action should be essential. In the 'global village' we must build up each individual's means of cultural expression by developing communication infrastructure and renewing the concepts, paradigms and blueprints of knowledge and reflection. But the communication 'pipelines' are not everything. The contents must also be rethought, because they are often long obsolete: to communicate is also to reflect, and to anticipate. UNESCO strategy gives priority to strengthening anticipation and forecasting, in order to explore new pathways of reflection and action that will enable us to enter the twenty-first century well prepared. UNESCO is helping to build up the capabilities of the South in this field through the International Programme for the Development of Communication (IPDC). To achieve this aim, the creation of UNESCO university chairs of communication can also be a useful mode of action. Intercultural dialogue cannot take place unless the cultures involved possess the essential means of expression. For communication is participation. This is why, in accordance with the first article of its Constitution, UNESCO aims, in the field of communication, at guaranteeing the free circulation of information at national and international levels, as well as a wider and more even distribution of information with no obstacle to freedom of expression.

Pointers and Recommendations

- Promote lifelong education for all and 'cultural security' systems in order to train the users of the information highways; teaching founded upon example, reflection and the transformation of information into knowledge.
- Promote universal access to the new information and communication technologies in order to guarantee the right of every individual 'to seek, receive, and to impart information and ideas, through any media and regardless of frontiers' (Universal Declaration of Human Rights, Article 19).
- Encourage 'cooperation among the nations in all branches of intellectual activity' (UNESCO Constitution) by linking up schools, universities, libraries and museums of the whole world by means of the Internet, within one generation.
- Prepare societies for mastery of the multimedia environment by spreading the knowledge and skills needed to make use of digital information.
- Combat 'techno-apartheid', particularly by developing North–South cooperative projects in the field of information technology.
- Consider the setting up of a special UNESCO and United Nations joint initiative devoted to active encouragement of the new information and communication technologies in developing countries, especially Africa.
- Give priority, in national and regional planning, to information-related development and policies for large-scale public works in this area, in as many countries as possible.
- Promote the expression of cultural and linguistic diversity and of pluralism on the Internet.
- Ensure the development of 'public services' on the Internet (multimedia libraries, access to data bases, etc.)
- Continue international discussion with the aim of ensuring the best balance between fair use and the rights of authors and distributors of information.
- Pursue research work on the preservation and archiving of digital information.
- Ensure the development of legislative and judicial structures at national and international levels: 'cyberlaws' to deal with 'cybercrimes' (especially the sexual exploitation of children via the Internet).

Notes

1. Daniel Cohen, *The Wealth of the World and the Poverty of Nations*, trans. Jacqueline Lindenfeld, MIT Press, Cambridge, MA, 1998.

2. See Jean-Paul Fitoussi and Pierre Rosanvallon, *Le Nouvel Age des inégalités*, Paris, Le Seuil, 1996.

3. Cohen, *The Wealth of the World*, pp. 63ff.

4. On the concept of 'assortative matching' see Cohen, *The Wealth of the World*, Chapter V. As Cohen emphasizes, 'slight differences in individual performance can consequently result in considerable differences' (p. 77). This concept is related to the 'O-ring' theory of development described by Michael Kremer in 'The O-ring theory of economic development', *Quarterly Journal of Economics*, August 1993.

5. Ethan B. Kapstein, 'Workers and the world economy', *Foreign Affairs*, Vol. 75, No. 3, May–June 1996.

6. See Chapter 16.

7. Javier Pérez de Cuéllar, 'Presentation of work', address by the president at the inaugural meeting, reproduced in UNESCO, *Director General's Report on the World Commission on Culture and Development*, October 1993 (27C/INF.11).

8. On this subject see Sherry Turkle, *Life on the Screen: Identity in the Age of the Internet* (Simon and Schuster, New York, 1995; Touchstone paperback, 1997) and Ana Maria Nicolaci da Costa, *Na malha da Rede: Os impactos intimos da Internet*, Editora Campus, Rio de Janeiro, 1998.

9. Jean Baudrillard, *Le Crime Parfait*, Éditions Gallilée, Paris, 1995.

10. On this subject see Pierre Lévy, *Qu'est-ce que le Virtuel?*, La Découverte, Paris, 1998.

11. José Joaquín Brunner, 'Postmodernidad y globalización', Faculdad Latino Americana de Ciencias Sociales, Santiago, Chile, May 1996, p. 51.

12. UNESCO Constitution, Article I, paragraph 2 (c).

13. Brunner, 'Postmodernidad y globalización', p. 6.

14. Ibid., p. 35.

15. This hypothesis is maintained by most observers. See Joseph Coates, 'L'avenir hautement probable. 83 hypothèses sur l'année 2025', *Futuribles*, April 1996, No. 208, p. 30.

16. On this topic see the conclusions of the Expert Meeting on the sexual abuse of children, child pornography and paedophilia on the Internet, organized by UNESCO, 18 January 1999.

17. See especially the proceedings of the International Conference on Screen Violence and the Rights of the Child (Lund, Sweden, September 1995) and the INFO-DROITS and INFOETHIQUE (Info-Rights and Info-Ethics) conferences organized by UNESCO (Monaco, 10–12 March 1997 and 1–3 October 1998).

18. Jérôme Bindé, 'Prêts pour le XXIe siècle?', *Le Monde*, 29 July 1998.

19. Thomas L. Jacobson, 'Les messageries électroniques et les services dans les pays du tiers monde', *Revue Tiers Monde*, Vol. XXXV, No. 138, April–June 1994, pp. 343–55.

20. See Michel Elie, 'Internet et le développement: un accès à l'information plus équitable?', *Futuribles*, No. 214, November 1996, pp. 43–64.

21. Figures taken from *The Economist*, 24 May 1997, p. 114.

22. Source: Network Wizards, June 1999.

23. *1997 State of the Future*, American Council for the United Nations University, 'The Millennium Project', co-directors Jerome C. Glenn and Theodore J. Gordon, p. 6.

24. Elie, 'Internet et le développement', pp. 55–6. According to an estimate provided by Nua (Nua Internet Surveys), the total number of Internet users divides as follows: 171.25 million (world total), of which 1.14 million are in Africa, 26.97 million in Asia/Pacific, 40.09 million in Europe, 0.88 million in the Middle East, 97.03 million in Canada/USA and 5.29 million in Latin America. According to the same estimate, the world total of Internet users should reach 350 million in the year 2005 (figures for June 1999).

25. Forty thousand in Iceland compared to 35,620 in the whole of sub-Saharan Africa. International Telecommunication Union, *World Telecommunication Development Report 1998*, and *African Telecommunication Indicators, 1998*, ITU, Geneva, 1998. Investments in telecommunications in real terms further underline the existing differences: they stand at US$2.9 billion for the whole of Africa in 1996. At the same date, Japan had invested US$37.9 billion, and the USA US$23.6 billion.

26. Federico Mayor, 'Higher education and new technologies', Commentary, *UNESCO Courier*, December 1996.

27. The European Commission Report *Europe and the Global Information Society* (Bangemann Report, 1994) stresses this major risk.

28. *Bilan du Monde 1997*, p. 23.

29. Elie, 'Internet et le développement'.

30. 'Internet: l'information sur un plateau', *Les Echos*, 14–15 March 1997.

31. Interview for *Le Monde*, 1 February 1997.

32. 'Le savoir va-t-il détrôner le travail et le capital?' *Bilan du Monde*, 1996 edition, published by *Le Monde*, Paris, p. 176. The global agreement of 15 February 1997 on telecommunication, signed by 68 countries within the World Trade Organization, should lead to an 80% reduction in the cost of international calls, and facilitate the provision of networks in countries where local operators cannot set them up (see *Le Monde*, 18 February 1997).

33. Midrand conference on the Information Society and Development (ISAD, Midrand, South Africa 3–15 May 1996), 'Chair's conclusion'.

34. Ibid.

35. Carlos-Alberto Alfonso, *Le Monde diplomatique*, July 1994.

36. See Jean-Louis Guigou, 'Le mythe des grands travaux. Des infrastructures de transport à la société de l'information', *Futuribles*, 225, November 1997.

37. Vice-President Al Gore, remarks before the International Telecommunications Union, 21 March 1994.

38. Lyons Summit, economic communiqué, 'Making a success of globalization for the benefit of all' (Lyons, 28 June 1996).

39. Marc Guillaume, 'Une société commutative', *Quintesciences*, 10, May 1997.

40. UNESCO Constitution, Article I, paragraph 2 (c).

41. See 'Preliminary Outline of the World Report on Culture and Development', World Commission on Culture and Development, document CCD-III/94/DOC.2, UNESCO, February 1994, and Thierry Gaudin (ed.), *2100: Récit du prochain siècle*, Payot, Paris, 1990, particularly Chapter 20; see also Thierry Gaudin, *2100, Odyssée de l'Espèce*, Payot, Paris, 1993.

42. The European Commission Report *Europe and the Global Information Society* (Bangemann Report, 1994) stresses this major risk.

43. Figures taken from the World Employment Bureau (*World Employment Report, 1998–99*, Geneva, 1998).

44. Jan Pronk, *Culture as a Mainstream*, Voorlichtingsdienst Ontwikkelingssamenwerking van het ministerie van Buitenlandse Zaken, the Netherlands, 9 June 1994.

45. On this subject see Chapter 16.

46. See for example *The Economist*, 10 May 1997, 'Survey: electronic commerce'.

47. Web browsers are now accompanied by software for specific searches ('tuners' and 'transmitters') that responds to specifications defined by individual users.

48. Amy Cortese, 'A way out of the web maze', *Business Week*, 24 February 1997, p. 44. See also *Le Monde*, 16 September 1997, 'Internet, le grand supermarché'.

49. By means of new technology new players are 'assembling a demand rather than a supply and creating a "community" by taking over consumers', paid for by the content supplied to users. See interview with Xavier Dalloz, *Les Echos*, April 1997. The favouring of content is crucial: it indicates a favouring of education and culture.

50. 'It would be wrong to confuse value with cost' (*Es de necio confundir valor y precio*), wrote the great Spanish poet Antonio Machado.

51. Paul Kennedy, *Preparing for the 21st Century*, Vintage Books, New York, 1994.

52. Even if alphabetical writing systems have not supplanted all other types of script, for example ideograms or characters, they have certainly come to dominate the scientific world, together with mathematical language, and they have contributed to generalizing a democratic model of universal knowledge distribution, which has itself changed the use of ideographic writing.

53. The expression 'invisible towns' is taken from the Italian writer Italo Calvino.

54. Michael Gibbons, *The New Production of Knowledge*, Sage, London, 1994.

55. Yoshiko Okubo notes that for the USA, Germany, Great Britain and Japan, 'the relative weight of cooperation in scientific work ... doubled at least between 1976 and 1986, and continues to grow in the 1990s' ('L'internationalisation de la science. Une analyse bibliométrique', *Futuribles*, 210, June 1996, p. 45).

56. See Pierre Papon, 'Un New Deal pour la recherche et la technologie', *Futuribles*, 217, February 1997, pp. 33–52.

57. Iver Peterson, '700 on-line newspapers, but only one charge for everything', *International Herald Tribune*, 11 February 1997.

58. R. W. Apple, Jr., 'Everyman's Internet', *International Herald Tribune*, 21 February 1997.

59. See Jérôme Bindé, 'Communication et intelligence: l'éducation et la culture à distance?', paper given at the conference on 'The Information Society: Technical, Economic, Legal and Cultural Approaches to the Information Superhighway', 22 February 1996, published in *Les Petites Affiches*, 134, 6 November 1996, Paris. English translation in *Futures*, Vol. 30, No. 8, 1998.

60. Papon, 'Un New Deal', p. 36.

61. Ibid., p. 45.

62. *Le Monde*, 24 October 1996.

63. See Chapter 14.

64. 'The scramble to set up satellite phone services', *International Herald Tribune*, 9 June 1997.

65. Roberto Bissio, *Le Monde diplomatique*, July 1994.

66. See in particular: Saskia Sassen, *The Global City: New York, London, Tokyo*, Princeton University Press, Princeton, 1991. According to Dan Schiller, of the communications department at the University of California, San Diego (USA), the figure is even higher: 'Well-informed sources say there four times as many "hidden networks" connected to the Internet as there are networks with open connections' ('Les marchands du "village global"', *Le Monde diplomatique*, May 1996).

67. *International Herald Tribune*, 28 January 1997.

68. 'Free cyber-speech', *International Herald Tribune*, 15–16 June 1996; 'An Unfettered Internet', *International Herald Tribune*, 28–29 June 1996.

69. UNESCO Constitution, Article 1.

70. In France, the Le Chapelier law two hundred years ago established the fundamental principle of 'freedom to copy', to foster freedom of trade and business, to encourage competition and to avoid monopolies linked to 'privileges' of an exclusive right to intellectual property.

71. In 1998, the United States Congress voted in a new law extending the copyright period from 75 to 95 years after the author's death.

72. Speech to the Senate by Jacques Toubon, then minister of culture, 6 December 1993.

73. Federico Mayor, *Cultures in the Global Village*, UNESCO, New Delhi, May 1995.

74. UNDP, *Human Development Report 1994*.

75. *Le Monde*, 10 May 1997.

76. See Chapters 14 and 15.

77. This is why UNESCO's Language Division ('Linguapax') is now integrated into the Department of Education in Peace Culture, with education for peace, human rights, international understanding and tolerance.

78. See on this subject the Preliminary Outline of the World Report on Culture and Development, World Commission on Culture and Development (WCCD), document CCD-III/94/DOC.2, UNESCO, February 1994, presented by Javier Pérez de Cuéllar (paragraph 274). Much of the analysis contained in this chapter was partly inspired by this text.

79. Néstor García Canclini, 'The future of multicultural societies', UNESCO, World Commission on Culture and Development, regional consultation for Latin America and the Caribbean, 1994.

80. Statement to the 31st meeting of the National Association of Television Program Executives (NATPE), 24–28 January 1994, Miami, Florida, USA.

81. Quoted in Jacques Robin, 'Les dangers d'une société de l'information planétaire', *Le Monde diplomatique*, February 1995.

82. Joseph S. Nye, Jr. and William A. Owens, 'America's information edge', *Foreign Affairs*, March–April 1996, pp. 20–36.

83. UNESCO Constitution, Article I, paragraph 1.

84. Nye and Owens, 'America's information edge', p. 34.

85. Lévy, *Qu'est-ce que le Virtuel?*, p. 10.

86. Steven A. Rossel, 'Changing maps: scenarios for Canada in an Information Age', *International Affairs*, Vol. 72, No. 4, 1996, pp. 675–90.

CHAPTER 14

. . . .

What Future for Books and Reading?

§ IN 1972 UNESCO was entrusted with the task of coordinating the events to be held during the International Book Year. These brought the future of books and reading to public attention. Almost a generation later, the cybernetic revolution has drawn up the blueprint of a new information society and the status of books seems to have altered radically. Against this rapidly changing background, and despite prophecies announcing the end of the Gutenberg era and the imminent obsolescence of the printed word, we are convinced that books are still, and will remain, an essential tool for educating future generations, for the advancement of knowledge and for circulating ideas freely. The fact is that books continue to constitute an irreplaceable vehicle – one unrivalled throughout most of the world – for information and knowledge, for dreams and escape, which appears most unlikely to disappear in the near future.

The new audio-visual and multimedia communication technologies will, admittedly, modify the conditions in which information and the written word are produced, circulated and received. Because of this prospect we must take a fresh look at how knowledge is circulated and shared. But it is to our mind important to resist the false and historically incorrect idea that a new mode of communication is predestined to replace previous modes and make them obsolete: the invention of printing has not ousted oral communication and transmission. The various modes of communication must therefore be regarded as complementary rather than competing.

The current technological revolution should thus not cause us to play down the role of books; rather should it spur us on to redefine the function of the written word in our societies and in the communication media in their new forms. This exercise in projection is particularly necessary because books remain the preferred medium for all critical and creative thought. Without a reader there is no book: to play its full part, a book requires an infinite diversity of readers who, in the very act of reading, give it not only its full meaning but also a multiplicity of meanings. As Plato wrote in *Protagoras*, books 'can neither reply nor question'. That is the privilege of human beings; reading is that act in which, in confrontation with the Other, the start of a silent dialogue, the sign of intellectual solidarity, the beginnings of respect for others and the gesture initiating a culture of peace and tolerance all come together. Totalitarian systems never mistake their enemy: as soon as they have ensured their dominance their immediate concern is to burn books and impose an unremitting censorship of the written word.

Books: Instrument of Freedom and Bearer of the Universal Cultural Heritage

Reading is also an act of freedom that opens the doors of knowledge and gives everyone the additional power to influence the world. A study of functional illiterates by the linguist Alain Bentolila reveals that the conversation of young functional illiterates contains scarcely 0.5% of abstract words – 'a shortcoming which leaves them terribly helpless against the imposition of any concept presented as a unique and universal explanatory principle'.[1] Reading, on the other hand, constitutes one of the surest guarantees of 'the unrestricted pursuit of objective truth' and of the 'free exchange of ideas and knowledge', which UNESCO is responsible for promoting under its Constitution. It is therefore essential to step up even further the fight against illiteracy which, although it has fallen in relative terms, still affects 880 million people. Fresh impetus must also be given to the campaign against functional illiteracy, a particular form of radical exclusion that often accompanies and nourishes other forms of segregation. Universal lifelong access to books and reading must be one of our priorities for the twenty-first century.

Books, we are convinced, are quintessentially a tool for emancipation. Yet, in practice, they can be diverted from their objective and exploited for oppression, discrimination and violence. When respect for books is exclusive it can lead to intolerance and to a rejection of any other form of knowledge since it perverts tradition by turning it into an ideology of exclusion. As the Spanish philosopher Fernando Savater writes, 'The Caliph burnt [the library at Alexandria] not because he hated all books but because he loved only one.'[2] Here we must look particularly at school textbooks. These are too often diverted from their objectives and help to glorify a culture of war and isolation; they erect impassable barriers between cultures instead of bringing them together and conceal the role played in history by the people, by women, by minorities and by the humble in favour of celebrating more often than not the doings of princes, the powerful and conquerors alone. That is why the revision of school textbooks constitutes the first step towards the culture of peace that UNESCO so earnestly desires: a culture that, without denying national history, will make knowledge serve humans rather than humans serving ideology. This overhaul of school textbooks must be dealt with through bilateral negotiations between nations which history has often placed in opposition to each other, or by integrated regional procedures where these are possible through advances in cooperation. This is the immense task facing us: to encourage on all sides the burgeoning of multiple forms of reading, writing and speaking that reflect the world's complexity, richness and plurality.

This plurality is expressed in the first place by the diversity of languages, which gives rise to determine a multiplicity of world views. Conversely, as stressed by Jacques Derrida, 'with a single language, one philosophy and one set of axioms governing philosophical discourse and communication always dominates, without possible discussion'.[3] Today, however, numerous languages are disappearing at a probably unprecedented rate.[4] As this happens, the world's cultural diversity comes increasingly under threat. UNESCO must act in this field, and the safeguarding of linguistic diversity must be one of its priorities: the circulation of books and the promotion of reading in the greatest possible number of languages are thus two basic policy thrusts which we must continue to develop.

However, an effective policy of supporting books must not just promote reading, which is but the last stage in a long process. It is also necessary, and we shall return to this point, to encourage the forerunner of reading, namely literary production and writing. The establishment of literary prizes at national but also regional and international levels can be useful in this respect; in particular, essay-writing must be practised from the earliest primary-education stages and throughout secondary education, while creative writing courses should be introduced at university level. The encouragement of oral expression (especially through the theatre) is part of the same logic. The challenge is considerable: languages constitute a unique and precious aspect of the human heritage. Only if we know how to protect them will words become, in the expression used by Camilo José Cela, 'more durable than stone'.

Satisfying the Hunger for Books: Towards Universal Access to the Written Word

We must not be dazzled by the rise of the Internet: in most countries, access to new technology is still the exception and books remain a rare privilege. While in numerous industrialized countries there is an abundance of books but a falling demand, the vast majority of developing countries find themselves in the opposite situation: there the 'hunger for books' is endemic and aggravated by population growth, while schoolbooks and technical textbooks and children's books are in short supply, library networks deficient and prices prohibitive. According to a UNESCO survey, in 22 of the 93 countries which returned the questionnaire nearly 60% of primary pupils had insufficient schoolbooks.[5]

Nearly 900,000 titles are published each year worldwide. However, production is distributed very unevenly: three-quarters (73.6%) of them are still published in the developed countries.[6] One might, of course, believe that this is an encouraging trend, since this proportion was 86.6% in 1970. But, in relation to population, the disparity between the number of titles published in the industrialized countries and in the developing countries is even more striking, about 10 to 1.[7] Certain regions are particularly disadvantaged: according to the latest available surveys, Africa published only 1.5% of the titles that appeared worldwide while it is home to 12.3% of the world population; Asia published 24.9% and has 58.9% of the world population. By contrast, Europe, with 9.3% of the world population, published 46.7% of titles and North America, with 5.2%, published 11.8%.[8] The distribution of national, non-specialized, public, university and school libraries worldwide confirms and even accentuates this general tendency, namely under-equipment in the poor countries and affluence in the rich ones. Likewise, the number of volumes available in public libraries varies considerably by country: 7 per 1,000 inhabitants in Benin and 7,226 per 1,000 in Finland.[9]

The volume of annual accessions by public libraries highlights even more accurately enormous regional discrepancies in access to books and indicates the geographical outlines of the 'hunger for books'. While acquisitions are counted in millions in the developed countries, they amount, at best, to some tens of thousands in the developing countries.[10] In the majority of countries worldwide, mainly in Africa, Latin and South America, South Asia and the Arab world, the number of books bought by public libraries is smaller than the number of children born. In other words, public investment in book purchases is below one volume per new inhabitant per year. This investment must be increased at least tenfold by 2010 if even the slightest inroads are to be made into the serious inequality that affects access to books according to a country's level of development. This type of investment is essential not only for development but also for peace and democracy. Unfortunately, the apathy witnessed in the drafting of national budgets and the level of military expenditures – which, in certain countries, is once again on the increase – hamper such investment, which would enable the populations of developing countries to make a fresh start, if the decision-makers in the richest countries realized the extent to which even modest support in this area could be decisive for progress in the countries concerned.

The issue is not just quantity. For example, the number of new titles published in 1995 under the history/geography heading varied strikingly by country, with gaps ranging from 1 to 11,493.[11] Set against population, these figures show the existence of a near monopoly by the developed countries over the production of history and geography books. Such imbalances (which, with variations, are found in all subjects) cannot fail to affect the relationship maintained by the peoples of the world with their own and other cultures and the ability of developing countries to preserve their cultural heritage.

It will be argued, not unreasonably, that oral tradition in traditional societies has long righted such imbalances by ensuring that essential knowledge and skills, such as the immaterial or symbolic cultural heritage, are handed down from generation to generation. The written word is certainly not the sole medium of knowledge or the only instrument for passing it on, but books last longer than words; in the celebrated phrase of Amadou Hampâté Bâ: 'In Africa, when an old man dies, a library burns!' In addition, books represent an important and inescapable way of gaining access to modern knowledge. It is therefore essential to circulate them widely in order that all persons may have the right guaranteed by Article 27 of the Universal Declaration of Human Rights 'to share in scientific advancement and its benefits'. How can education and training be developed without access to the written word? How can engineers and researchers be trained where university libraries are without the latest scientific and technical journals? This deficiency constitutes a major obstacle to development by encouraging a brain drain from poor to rich countries, where reference works are immediately accessible and scientific dialogue can take place immediately. Universal access to the written word is therefore a priority for development since, in addition to basic education, it allows a form of post-literacy training and constitutes a corridor to other types of knowledge. It is also a priority for UNESCO, one of whose chief missions is specifically to help disseminate knowledge 'by initiating methods of international co-operation calculated to give the peoples of all countries access to the printed and published materials produced by any of them'.[12]

Once mastered, reading permits a form of lifelong self-teaching that makes the reader the agent of his or her own training. A dialogue starts up between author and reader, with the reader becoming, as it were, the co-author. If reading is not encouraged, populations cannot be given lasting literacy or training. It is the irreplaceable instrument of 'lifelong learning for all' on which UNESCO has focused the strategy that it defined in 1995. This point should be stressed because reading is unfortunately not an ability that is acquired for life. Since the implementation of the Experimental World Literacy Programme launched in 1967, post-literacy has emerged as a genuine need. It is based on access by every individual to reading materials throughout life.[13] An authentic reading policy must thus be introduced at all educational levels and at all life stages of individuals, including in the professional context: staff libraries in firms and institutions can be very important here. It is also vital that access to the written word be made the centrepiece of any reform of education systems and that priority be given to children, women and the least advanced countries in national and international action plans.

However, what is the use of access to books if they are not read, i.e. if the literacy underpinning such access is absent? Considerable progress has admittedly been made in this field. UNESCO estimates that four out of five adults are now able to read and write.[14] Yet deep inequalities persist: around two-thirds of illiterate adults are women, a figure resulting from decades of neglecting the education of girls.[15] The level of functional illiteracy is another matter for serious concern that requires the official literacy statistics to be taken with a pinch of salt. The governments of certain industrialized countries report literacy levels of 99% for the adult population. Are these figures realistic? Education experts have their doubts and point to the persistence and even expansion of a functional illiteracy affecting both young people and adults. The magnitude of this phenomenon, which emerges only imperfectly from the statistics, now seems to be evaluated better: it is estimated that about 20% of the adult US population suffers from functional illiteracy; many experts are of the opinion that this phenomenon affects between one-tenth and one-fifth of the adult population in the majority of industrialized countries.

The campaign for literacy, a cornerstone of development, could benefit greatly from educational and cultural policies ensuring access by all to the written word, particularly to what is published in the reader's mother tongue. But what means should be employed to deal with the shortage of books and satisfy the hunger for reading and knowledge that torments young people in so many developing countries? Can the potential of the new technologies be used to boost books? Let us make one thing clear: it is out of the question to advocate a return to the educational methods of old-style academicism based on the dominance of the written and printed word. This is ruled out by the principle of cultural pluralism and by the relentless march of technology. It is also out of the question to encourage abandoning other forms of cultural expression, particularly oral and artistic, in the name of a monoculture of the written word. No more should we discourage the aid that should be provided for developing the new information technologies.

The goal is clear: the remaining gaps must be reduced, using all the means made available by existing networks and the new technologies. A first step must be to correct the major imbalances as regards quantity: the scale of book production in the developing countries must be changed and methods of distribution improved. Two practical approaches deserve examination. The first is to encourage the production and distribution of very cheap books and is based on one simple fact: book prices are still much too high for the poor or less well-off sectors of the population. Manufacturing costs for books largely determine how widely they are circulated. On the other hand, reference works can be given a much wider circulation by publishing them in very cheap paperback form, which technical innovations now have made possible. This approach, which is breathing fresh life into paperback publishing, is already very successful in the industrialized countries.[16] Another approach is to encourage the publication of works in serial form in the press, along the lines of the 'Periolibros' project launched with UNESCO assistance, which enables a network of major newspapers to circulate millions of copies of high-quality books throughout Latin America.[17]

From a more qualitative point of view, reading should be encouraged among children and young people. Periodical studies and surveys in the wealthy countries show a progressive decline in reading, accompanied by a growing enthusiasm for the new media, especially among the young. We must recognize that the advance of education and the increase in leisure time are not being reflected in an expansion of reading. For us, therefore, it is a matter of urgency, while encouraging the development of new technology, to give books and reading pride of place again and to point to the riches they hold: reading is at once an essential education instrument, a pleasure and a pastime, a source of general and specialized, political and practical information, an instrument of both vocational training and personal, artistic and spiritual fulfilment,[18] and a tool for lifelong learning about freedom, citizenship and critical thought – all of them cornerstones of democracy. I therefore salute the exemplary work of the NGOs that support the production of children's books or work more generally for the development of reading through rural or mobile library projects. It is UNESCO's natural function to support their efforts.

Transformations in Writing and Reading: Digitization, Hypertexts, Hyperdocuments

Is it not somewhat outdated to be defending books in an age of new communication technology? The paradox is only seemingly one. The history of humanity teaches us that old and new modes of communication are superimposed on, and supplement, one another, they combine without cancelling each other out and are even a source of mutual enrichment. The oral transmission of knowledge did not disappear after printing was invented, nor has television consigned daily newspapers to oblivion. Fax transmission and e-mail have not eliminated written (or printed) correspondence but are ushering it along new paths and in themselves are imparting fresh impetus to exchanges of letters, which are often even handwritten in the case of fax transmission and had declined with the increased use of the telephone.

What does the advent of the new communication technologies mean for books and reading? Will they lead to the gradual disappearance of books, to a decrease in the author's individual role, to a radical transformation in our modes of reading (and writing), information and communication? The new forms of book production and circulation depend less on traditional physical intermediaries such as books and libraries and more on computerized instruments, which open up new roads for the transmission and circulation of information and knowledge.

These revolutions offer as yet unexplored prospects for the progress of knowledge and its transmission. The campaign for reading, and thus for literacy and education, now extends to other areas in which UNESCO is called upon to play a leading part. Computerization does not supplant education but simply redefines its field of application. Nor does it abolish language, which simply turns towards other forms of expression and representation. However, these possibilities also have their risks: first, because access to these new media reveals worrying disparities, as we have shown in Chapter 13; second, a fundamental and perhaps irreconcilable difference exists between information consumption on the one hand and reading on the other.[19] In its most extreme form the modern technological Utopia could result only in an insatiable appetite for information from which critical thought, human judgement and memory would be excluded. It would eliminate forms of oral communication of knowledge and wisdom that are essential to human development, to the teacher–student relationship and to the preservation of cultural diversity.

The advent of the 'civilization of the immaterial' mentioned in the previous chapter has radically transformed our relationship with the written word and caused deep changes in production, distribution and consumption patterns. The increasing digitization of the written word and the appearance of new media (electronic data banks, electronic mail, publishing software, etc.) are already giving rise to new forms of writing and reading but also of printing and circulation. An increasing number of daily news sources are now available on the Internet even before being printed; written correspondence can now be drafted, sent and read instantly via e-mail; document dispatch costs are considerably reduced by transferring files or sending floppy disks; the production of publications is increasingly computerized; books are becoming raw material that can be infinitely manipulated.

Some experts are already predicting the 'dematerialization' of the book and announcing that it will soon be possible to access all libraries through a computerized world network. Computer-assisted reading is being successfully developed and promises researchers impressive possibilities of access to sources and of text location and manipulation.[20] The advent of the rewritable 'single book' is now being predicted: its pages, composed of microcells, will be capable of being deleted and rewritten at will. A reader with poor sight will even be able to decide to enlarge the letters; someone wanting to take notes will be able to expand the margin, even write on the page using a stylus and retrieve his or her notes by computer. Readers will become their own editors and will make books to measure, drawing on texts scattered throughout the Internet.[21]

Certain experts already see in the appearance of new reading modes, a 'new coupling' (between machine and thought rather than between book and thought) and the emergence of a 'reading system' linking human and network: a system that would be 'more socialized, more versatile, possessing greater storage and assuredly more political'.[22] Others firmly believe that the new technologies will lead to a real 'Copernican revolution' that will make books revolve round the reader and knowledge around people instead of the other way round as at present.

Through interactivity, readers will henceforth have an almost infinite range of choices with respect to a text. Reading will thus become truly plural and pluralistic. As visualized by Régis Debray, 'Hypertext will perhaps be the ultra-democratic text, without a parent or owner, without frontiers or customs officials, which can be manipulated by all and disseminated everywhere.'[23] The rise of the Internet will bring with it an increase in 'grey literature', those 'writings which do not yet have the status of publications', 'spontaneous works',[24] of which neither the origin nor the qualities of their author are known. On the horizon we can already discern new educational 'instruments' that link the text with diagrams or pictures, sounds or musical sequences and explain references to it or treat it more thoroughly. Ultimately, therefore, the nature, status and form of text will undergo drastic change.

The new technologies will also bring about appreciable changes in the constitution and communication of knowledge. By allowing dialogue between the different forms of expression and between fields of study, digitization should help to open up new approaches to scientific research and produce a mutual enrichment of the various forms of the cultural heritage, both tangible and intangible. Twenty-first-century schoolbooks, and educational works in general, will have to be designed with an eye to greater interactivity between the various fields of knowledge in order to satisfy pupils' needs and tastes and encourage the development of self-education. As regards virtual images, which are no longer reproduced but created entirely by users, they already have practical, personal and commercial uses. By a singular twist of postmodernity, the viewing of electronic books and interactive multimedia 'hyperdocuments' might seem to be reviving the pre-alphabetic tradition of the spoken word and dialogue and confirm the intuition of Paul Claudel when he wrote: 'The eye listens.'

At the same time, as stressed by Yannick Maignien, as the nature of the text changes, so

a new type of reader develops. He or she can explore at once the linearity of libraries and the virtual depths opened up by the multiple links to document content and structure. Without doubt, we are in the presence here of a new reading practice: depending on the interests shown or pursued (from computer games to encyclopaedic research, including in their path the on-screen monitoring of market trends), it is the reader who controls the course of consultations through interaction, all this within an imaginary space free from the physical constraints traditionally associated with the printed word.[25]

There thus appears a new manner of reading, the path of which is no longer linear but winding and which can be described as navigation, 'with all that this implies in the way of free ranging – whether random or guided – within a space requiring tools for location, for displaying perspectives and for memorizing spaces already covered'.[26]

But if reading modes change, reading institutions will change as well. Soon we shall see the development of 'multimedia' libraries based on a greater complementarity of the various available information systems and on the merging of traditionally isolated services (libraries and electronic networks). Traditional libraries will thus evolve into 'knowledge centres' open to all digital information and research sources. When assembled in networks, they will lead to improved planning of the cultural landscape. State involvement will be decisive in this respect, but it will also be the job of the major libraries in wealthy countries to help build up developing-country libraries through partnerships. They could, for example, devote a portion of their purchasing budget to donations of books, reading materials and systems for gaining access to the specialized electronic networks. It will also be necessary to work towards the setting up of a planetwide digital library. Technology now makes it possible to link up the major national libraries and to establish vast world collections on high-density optical disks.[27] Such a planetwide digital library would provide students and researchers throughout the world, and also whole nations, with access to the digital information sources vital to the progress of knowledge, education and democracy. International cooperation must therefore support this effort, and we must help developing countries which lack suitable premises and specialized training facilities to set up their own archive collections using the latest techniques for preserving ancient manuscripts and books. The preservation of written documents against damp, insects and acidification is expensive and requires ever more sophisticated techniques.[28]

Will the digitization of texts lead, on a deeper level, to a better dialogue between academic fields, to a recognition of the diversity of ways in which human thought can be expressed and to a better mutual appreciation of cultures? This optimistic scenario is by no means implausible. The written word would thus open the door to that 'reading of the world' referred to by Paulo Freire, in other words to an ever-renewed, ever-moving construction of knowledge. For knowledge is built not on certainty but on questioning, on what Ernesto Sábato calls 'the virtue of wonder'.[29] As an ancient Greek philosopher said, science is the daughter of surprise.

These revolutions open up as yet unexplored prospects for the development of knowledge and its improved dissemination. As a result of them, the campaign for reading, and thus for literacy and education, will extend to new fields to which UNESCO must now direct its activities. However, this promising outlook also entails very real risks. First, access to the new media coincides with, and even accentuates, the regional and socio-economic disparities already noted for books. Second, these new vehicles for information are disturbingly flawed. While books have preserved human knowledge intact for several centuries, it is estimated that the 'lifetime of optical media belonging to the CD-ROM family is at most 30 years'. In addition, 'existing procedures for the electronic capturing of fixed or moving images do not give a resolution comparable in quality to that of films or microfilms'.[30]

What, in particular, will be the implications of the various transformations of the written word for modes of thought and for cognitive activity itself? As Marshall McLuhan has shown, the reception and understanding of a message depend greatly on the medium conveying it. The apparently neutral medium in fact imposes its own value system and its framework of thought on the receiver, regardless of the content of the message. If the written word and its vehicle, books, disappeared, would there not be a very serious risk of seeing reasoned and structured reading replaced by a passive and unthinking form of information consumption?[31] Not a few intellectuals have already voiced disquiet about the possibility that the human memory, one of the essential foundations of reason and judgement, might atrophy in the multimedia age. They also fear that critical thought and logical judgement might be weakened as our dependence on computers increases: in its most extreme form, the modern machine Utopia might, if we fail to act, lead only to an insatiable appetite for data that would leave no room for critical reflection, human judgement and memory. We shall also have to ensure that progress in computer technology does not cause a decline in forms of oral communication of knowledge and wisdom, which are and will remain essential for the teacher/ student relationship and the preservation of cultural diversity.

Digitization of the Written Word: The Cultural Challenges

Future policies on books and reading will plainly have to be worked out as part of a process of overall reflection – currently still at an embryonic stage – concerning the cultural dimensions of globalization and the development of new technology. The rapid emergence of postmodern cultural identities of a trans-territorial nature constitutes an unprecedented challenge to all cultures, particularly oral cultures, particularly because access to the transmission of knowledge via the new media is very unevenly apportioned. At a time when more than half of the some 6,000 languages in the world are in danger of disappearing, such a process of reflection is indispensable and urgent. It will have to be based on the idea of the universal dissemination of knowledge and the participation of all in that knowledge.

Among the immediate technical challenges forced on us, the digitization of the written word implies the establishment of world standards permitting the use on the Internet of all world writing systems. The drawing up of a world code (Unicode) already represents a significant initial advance in allowing most of these writing systems (including Chinese ideograms) to be represented. This point is of strategic importance, for only when agreement exists on a common code will it be possible for all languages to be expressed unambiguously and with equal opportunities on the world network. If this were not so, minority writing systems would be compelled to invent local codes that could not be recognized elsewhere.

What applies to the writing system also applies to coding of the image (particularly colours), sounds and printing processes (postscript language). The same applies to inter-machine transmission, data storage and high-resolution television. All these questions are already the subject of immense battles regarding standards – in which the stakes can be counted in billions of dollars – between software designers and manufacturers. These conflicts delay public access to the new tools of culture and make it more expensive. It is therefore important to work to establish world standards determined by consensus in the context of wide-ranging negotiations.[32]

Publishing and Copyright

The new technologies have deeply shaken traditional book-circulation channels. They have led to the development of professional electronic publishing and to the digitization of images and text using static or dynamic media. The use of desk-top publishing, of the scanner (a digitizer linked to a computer), of computer-assisted colour treatment and of the control of typesetting stages by means of software has revolutionized printing and led to reduced book-production costs. This technological upheaval is opening up fresh economic prospects, for example, the development of telework in the publishing field.[33]

By the same token the book is in great peril if it loses its traditional form as a result of the latest technology such as automated data banks, interactive compact disks and multimedia applications. Some libraries are already offering the full text of certain works in addition to bibliographical references. Works can be consulted on screen or paper (using a printer) unless recording on floppy disk is preferred. In addition, as it is now easy for libraries to link themselves up in national and international networks, the number of titles available in computerized form is likely to increase considerably and rapidly. In these conditions, the book is liable to change in nature: formerly a finished product, it is now becoming a base product for data banks. Its industrial status is also threatened. The widespread use of photocopying has for a long time severely compromised the book trade by facilitating the illicit reproduction of texts and has diminished the ability to control the circulation of such photocopies. But the development of Internet capability is making these problems even more acute. A work whose publication is prohibited in a country can be reproduced electronically and circulated worldwide over the Internet; a source of written information hitherto difficult to reach is now available via a simple computer terminal. The United States Supreme Court has described the Internet as 'an uninterrupted world conversation'. For better or for worse, it also constitutes a new domain for uninterrupted world reading.

What then will become of the rights of authors and publishers? Before the 'hypertext', there is, of course, the text, and before the reader comes the author. UNESCO is making sustained efforts to protect literary and artistic property throughout the world in close cooperation with the World Intellectual Property Organization and other institutions and groups such as the International Literary and Artistic Association; these efforts have gone some way towards eliciting the different legal traditions governing copyright, towards adapting it better to the demands of contemporary social life and towards setting in train a significant legislative movement to protect copyright and related rights throughout the world.[34] UNESCO is examining the adaptation of these rights to the new requirements of digital technology so as to make sure that the legitimate rights of authors and other rights-holders are identified under the new production, storage and circulation conditions resulting from these technologies. One task is to clarify the rules governing the author's relations with his or her work and with the parties responsible for producing and circulating it. Copyright is both a human right and a factor of cultural development; for these two reasons it is included among the major concerns of UNESCO, which has a duty to create, in accordance with the new contemporary realities, the most favourable conditions for works of the mind to exert their widest possible influence. It is particularly important to safeguard the principle of 'fair use', which is essential if libraries and archive services are to be able to play their proper part and ensure that the public gains equitable access to information in a modern society, while steering clear of *laisser-faire* excesses that could result in the abolition of any idea of intellectual property rights in cyberspace. Protection of those rights is an important factor in the development of creativity, just as the free movement of information is vital to the emergence of a well-educated democratic society.[35] Innovative solutions will therefore have to be devised in order to reconcile copyright protection with universal access to information and culture in cyberspace: the World Wide Web, it should be recalled, was originally developed by Tim Berners-Lee to facilitate information and data exchange between researchers. This function must be strengthened; the availability on the Internet of all texts, documents and manuscripts belonging to the public domain must be facilitated. Through the creation of a public-service domain in cyberspace, this will gradually allow 'the people of all countries access to the printed and published materials produced by any of them' and 'the free flow of ideas by word and image' called for by UNESCO in its Constitution.

An Opportunity for the Written Press

There is an immense difference between the situation prevailing in the industrialized countries, where the sheer abundance of the periodical press (dailies, weeklies, monthlies) is an incentive to daily reading, and that of the developing countries, where the press is much less present in daily life. Judging by the circulation of daily newspapers per 1,000 inhabitants, a gap was recorded in 1994 of 1 to 6.5 between developed and developing countries, that is, the same ratio as in 1980.[36] If the yardstick were to be newsprint consumption, which is particularly large in the wealthy countries, the gap would be even wider: 1 to 14.4 in 1995 in favour of the developed countries, a gap which has undergone little change (1 to 20.3 in 1970).[37] It is true that reading patterns vary from one country to another: the reading of one newspaper by several persons, common practice in regions such as Africa, means that newspapers have a real circulation much greater than that implied by print-run figures. Nevertheless, individual access to the print media is an act of familiarization with the written word that it would be hard to replace. It is also the foundation of democratic life. Thomas Jefferson referred to it in these terms: 'The basis of our government being the opinion of the people, the very first object should be to keep that right; and were it left to me to decide whether we should have a government without newspapers or newspapers without a government, I should not hesitate a moment to prefer the latter.'

If the press is required to play this emancipatory role, we must then find the means to use the new communication media to ensure its wider circulation, particularly in the developing countries. The process would seem to have already started. As Gérard Théry stresses: 'The new electronic networks are an asset to the press.' The latter 'will make increasing use of the new networks as soon as it has completely digitized its production process, which will happen soon'.[38] New technology already, in fact, allows the national and international press to be accessed on the Internet, sometimes even before it is published at points of circulation. The range of newspapers available is expanding considerably and formerly isolated populations can now get to know new styles of news reporting and comment, obtain outside viewpoints concerning their country or continent and take an active part in discussions about current events. In this connection, certain original initiatives should be welcomed, such as the creation in 1977 of the Pan African News Agency, which started up in 1983 and has received UNESCO support; this agency gives access to most of the African reference press on its Internet site.

The End of Books or the Transformation of Writing?

How often have Jeremiahs prophesied the death of books over the past 150 years? Their inevitable wasting away was forecast when the major newspapers came on the scene; the same happened with the coming of the cinema, radio and television. But they have survived all those who predicted their demise. We are convinced that books as we know them will continue to exist throughout the twenty-first century. We are equally convinced, however, that the written word is on the verge of a genuine transformation: it will become hybrid, it will form a symbiotic relationship with audio-visual techniques and its distribution will ultimately be drastically changed by electronic publishing. A knock-on effect will be a complete reshaping of the structure of books, accompanied by changes in their content and in the very nature of reading.

Unless we want to cling to the past, we must keep resolutely in step with the diversification of media for the written word and make the best of the new communication technologies. In the era of the Internet and satellites, it is now technically possible to project the *local* printing or reprinting of newspapers or books produced at a distance and thus, eventually, to reduce considerably transport costs and times. The latter are still too long and lead to delays in the circulation of magazines and books, which increasingly suffer from rapid obsolescence of the knowledge and information they contain. Because it offers bright prospects for educational, economic and cultural development, rapid transmission of the written word will therefore have to occupy a leading place in government policy. As we have pointed out, the possibility of remote consultation of books and magazines through library networking offers new prospects for distance education and, on a wider scale, for exchanging knowledge between industrialized and developing countries. A new generation of cultural equipment is undoubtedly destined to replace our out-of-date libraries owing to the novel multimedia applications available and the new modes of consulting the written word: such equipment will be more versatile and formed into networks or grouped together in multi-disciplinary cultural activity centres. In the most deprived countries it can be light and mobile in order to serve the whole territory properly.[39] It would be useful here to take as a model the encouraging experiments in informal education currently taking place in several regions of the world: we refer particularly to the 'Escuela Nueva' programme in Colombia adopted by teachers in half the rural schools in that country.[40]

We have already stressed our particular duty to give an unprejudiced welcome to contemporary technological changes in order to derive the greatest advantage from them. But a spirit of openness must not become technomania; even less should it prevent us, in a fit of commercial euphoria, from perceiving the limits of cybernetic progress. At the moment, only a small minority benefits from it, and it is hard to see how the three billion poor people – half of humanity – who live on less than two dollars a day or the four and a half billion human beings who possess no basic telecommunication facilities can gain access to it in the short or medium term. Far-sightedness and political will, considerable in scope and long-term in approach – one or two generations – will be necessary in this field in order to make the advertising slogan 'a connected world' a universal reality.

Confronted with the new communication technologies, national and international institutions should therefore encourage populations to learn about the new gateways, complementarities and interactivities introduced by the new media. If the development of new technology were to result in the neglect of basic educational activity, the 'virtual' world would truly have triumphed over the 'real' world, and the 'civilization of the immaterial' would have become not only futile but absurd. Overcoming this potential contradiction will be one of the major challenges that all of us, together, will have to take up in the twenty-first century.

Yet we remain confident. If books, which for centuries have been the vehicle for ideas and knowledge, are now meeting competition among the younger generations from electronic writing, it is more often than one might think from praiseworthy motives. Alongside the abuses to which this new medium sometimes leads (sites calling for racial or religious hatred, xenophobia and anti-Semitism, paedophilia, etc.), which must be punished under the rule of law and existing legislation, we may evoke the image of those young Serbs and Croats who communicate with one another by e-mail and escape by this means from the sectarianism of the society surrounding them. We do not believe that there is really any competition between the two media (books and electronic writing) but think that there will be simultaneous use of these two forms of communication, with one being more suitable in certain circumstances for the free expression of thought than the other. Let us therefore welcome these new forms of expression as a further stage in the progress of human communication and an additional tool of knowledge and research. Technology is only what we make it and can be compared to a new language whose syntax, grammar and vocabulary must be discovered, or rather, invented.

Some say that we are living in the 'information age'. This 'information', however, coming at us from all sides, often as raw facts, is of no use to us if it is not transformed into knowledge. Books and reading are essential to intellectual development: knowledge is acquired 'book in hand' and through reading and re-reading, which make it possible for us to engage in a dialogue with the text and mentally to rewrite it. Books will never disappear. On the contrary, in a world where all the media are in a state of upheaval, books will be of ever more crucial importance. If we manage to master the new communication tools without being manipulated by them, they will help us to forge the culture of democracy, freedom, peace and tolerance that we so ardently desire for the twenty-first century. Investing in reading is investing in developing reflection and the civic spirit and, hence, investing in consolidating democracy in the twenty-first century. Communication will then be able to bring about the ideals of 'freedom of thought, conscience and religion' and of 'freedom of opinion and expression' proclaimed by the 1948 Universal Declaration and international pacts on human rights.

Pointers and Recommendations

- Ensure universal access to books and reading by developing basic education, fight functional illiteracy, promote the written and literary heritage.
- Encourage and raise the prestige of reading, particularly among children and young people, as an act of freedom, of introduction to critical thinking and of getting to know one another.
- Promote the production and dissemination of cheap books and 'periolibros' (in the form of serials in the written press); encourage the creation of mobile libraries and of reading centres adapted to the needs of rural or disadvantaged populations.
- Promote the use of the new communication technologies as a medium for the written word, and devote a portion of the development assistance for new technology to the preservation and utilization of the written heritage.
- Encourage the establishment of a worldwide digital library and bring about greater complementarity between all available information systems by merging traditionally separate services (libraries and electronic networks). Promote their use in educational and cultural systems.
- Convert libraries into 'knowledge centres' open to all digital information and research sources. Help developing countries to establish libraries and archive collections and to finance the training of competent personnel. Encourage protection, conservation and democratization of access to archive collections and libraries.
- Develop instruments of language knowledge and learning (dictionaries and grammars), research in the linguistic field, the collection of oral traditions in written form and historical-publishing projects that draw attention to the great interest of the world's written heritage.

- Encourage the revision of schoolbooks by means of bilateral negotiations between nations or by integrated regional procedures that take account of the latest findings of historical research and of studies in the social science field, in order to promote a culture of peace and tolerance and the eradication of prejudices based on 'race', sex, language or religion or too narrowly national views of history.
- Encourage the development of world standards determined by consensus and permitting, in particular, the use of all world languages on the Internet.
- Promote literary creation by the establishment of more competitions and prizes at national, regional and international level and by providing incentives to writing, from the primary-education to the higher-education stages; continue the efforts started as regards the protection of intellectual property rights, making allowance for the novel problems posed by the new communication technologies.

Notes

1. Alain Bentolila, *De l'Illettrisme en général et de l'école en particulier*, Plon, Paris, 1996, p. 66.

2. Fernando Savater, professor of philosophy at the Complutense University of Madrid, 'La vénération du livre est à la base de l'intolérance', *El País*, reproduced in *Courrier International*, No. 326, 30 January–5 February 1997.

3. Jacques Derrida, *Le Droit à la philosophie du point de vue cosmopolitique*, UNESCO Publishing, 1997.

4. See Chapter 15.

5. 'Special survey on primary education: school fees and school books in state schools', UNESCO, Statistics Division, November 1991.

6. UNESCO, *Statistical Yearbook 1995*. There were 863,000 titles published throughout the world in 1991 compared with 521,000 in 1970.

7. The world average in 1991 was 160 titles per 1 million inhabitants. At the same date this average was 513 in the developed countries, 55 in the developing countries, 20 in Africa and 802 in Europe. Source: ibid.

8. UNESCO, *Statistical Yearbook 1995*, 1991 figures.

9. *World Education Report 1998*, UNESCO, Paris, 1998, Table 2.

10. See UNESCO, *World Information Report 1997–1998*, UNESCO, Paris, 1997, pp. 78–90.

11. Source: UNESCO, *Statistical Yearbook 1998*.

12. Constitution of UNESCO, Article 1, paragraph 2, subparagraph c.

13. See in particular Ali Hamadache, *Savoir Lire, et après? Produire les Matériels de lecture pour la postalphabétisation: Guide pratique illustré*, in the collection 'La bibliothèque de formation professionnelle', UNESCO, Paris, 1996.

14. Projections for the year 2000. Source: UNESCO, *Statistics on Adult Illiteracy: Preliminary Results of the 1994 Estimations and Projections* (UNESCO Statistics Division, October 1994).

15. UNESCO, *World Education Report 1995*, UNESCO, Paris, 1995.

16. See 'Books for a buck', *Newsweek*, December 4, 1995. In Egypt, the 'Reading for All' programme, with the strong encouragement of Mrs Susan Mubarak, has made it possible to disseminate educational books at very low cost.

17. This initiative is now being followed throughout the Arab region through the 'Kitab fi Jarida' project in association with 21 leading daily newspapers, which publish the works of major Arab writers in the form of free monthly supplements.

18. See A. Hamadache, *Savoir Lire*; Alvaro Garzon, *National Book Policy: A Guide for the User in the Field*, The Vocational Training Library/UNESCO Publishing 1997; H. S. Bhola *A Source Book for Literacy Work – Perspective from the Grassroots*, Paris, UNESCO/Jessica Kingsley Publishers, 1994; Ralph C. Staiger, *Roads to Reading*, UNESCO, 1979. See also the *International Literacy and Education for All Watch* bulletin.

19. Yannick Maignien, 'Lector ex machina', *Le Débat*, September–October 1995, No. 86.

20. See André Zysberg, Yannick Maignien, Jean-Didier Wagneur and Bruno Blasselle, 'La lecture assistée par ordinateur', *Le Débat*, September–October 1995, No. 86, pp. 152–64. For instance, computer-assisted reading was introduced at the Bibliothèque de France in 1989 (ibid., pp. 152–5).

21. 'Le Livre Perpétuel', *Libération*, 15 July 1998.

22. Maignien, 'Lector ex machina'.

23. Pierre Lévy, *L'Espace du savoir, éléments de cartographie anthropologique*, Neuropelab, International Business Park, 1993; Michel Authler and Pierre Lévy, *Les Arbres de la connaissance*, La Découverte, Paris, 1992. Quotation from Régis Debray, 'Dématérialisation et désacralisation: le livre comme objet symbolique', *Le Débat*, September–October 1995, No. 86, p. 27.

24. Blaise Cronin and Geoffrey McKim, 'Internet', *World Communication Report 1997–1998*, UNESCO, Paris, 1997, p. 266.

25. Maignien, 'Lector ex machina', p. 156.

26. Ibid.

27. See *World Information Report 1997–1998*, UNESCO, Paris, 1997, pp. 236ff.

28. See *Le Monde*, 3 May 1998.

29. See Ernesto Sábato, *UNESCO Courier*, UNESCO, Paris, 1994, pp. 235–6 (reproduction of an interview published in the *UNESCO Courier* in October 1990).

30. UNESCO, *World Information Report 1997–1998*, UNESCO, Paris, 1997, pp. 235–6.

31. Maignien, 'Lector ex machina'.

32. See WCCD, 'Preliminary outline of the World Report on Culture and Development', World Commission on Culture and Development, document CCD-III/94/DOC.2, UNESCO, February 1994.

33. See Milagros del Corral and Alvaro Garzón, 'The future of books', World Commission on Culture and Development, document CCD-III/94/SEC.1, 1994.

34. This international effort has led to greater harmonization of national legislation and to an extension of the international consensus, which has been marked by the accession of numerous states to the Berne Convention and to the Universal Copyright Convention.

35. See in particular the conclusions of the International Congress on the Ethical, Legal and Societal Aspects of Digital Information (INFOETHICS), organized by UNESCO in Monte Carlo in March 1997.

36. 'Daily newspapers: number and and circulation', UNESCO, *Statistical Yearbook 1997*, UNESCO Publishing/Bernan Press. This proportion is more or less the same as that separating those countries in respect of radio broadcasting (gap for the number of sound broadcasting receivers: 1 to 5.4), 1993 figures.

37. Ibid., 'Newsprint production and consumption'.

38. Gérard Théry, *Les Autoroutes de l'information*, Report to the Prime Minister, La Documentation Française, Paris, 1994, pp. 61–5.

39. WCCD, 'Preliminary outline'.

40. Ernesto Schiefelbein, *Redefining Basic Education for Latin America: Lessons to be Learned from the Colombian Escuela Nueva*, UNESCO: International Institute for Educational Planning, Paris, 1992.

CHAPTER 15

. . . .

An Endangered Heritage: Languages

§ AT least half of the 5,000 to 6,700 languages spoken throughout the world today[1] are likely to disappear by the end of the twenty-first century. Nor will the extinction threatening these 3,000 languages – some more than others – be to any great extent counterbalanced by the emergence of new languages, the number of which is expected to be insignificant.[2] Every two weeks, a language somewhere in the world dies. In most cases, it is a non-written language and its death is accompanied by the death of its oral literature. Entire families of languages, such as the Khoisan languages of South Africa or the Aboriginal languages of Australia, will probably cease to exist. Our knowledge of the mechanisms and of the true extent of this immense cultural upheaval, comparable in scale to the massive extinction of animal and plant species currently affecting the biosphere, is still far from complete.[3] According to certain linguists, the process of extinction could assume much greater proportions than most specialists have been predicting: in the long run, it is not half but 95% of the languages now spoken that they regard as doomed.[4]

All the regions of the world will suffer, though not to the same extent, from this process, which affects above all minority groups and indigenous populations. Extinction rates are likely to be particularly high in regions possessing the greatest linguistic diversity. The fact is that the world's linguistic heritage is very unevenly distributed: according to a still imperfect approximation, 15% of the 6,703 languages still spoken in the world are located on the American continent (1,000 languages), 30% in Africa (2,011), 32% in Asia (2,165), 19% in the Pacific (1,302), and 3% in Europe (225); in other words, about half the languages still in use today are located in the Asia and Pacific region. These are obviously not the exact figures but rough estimates of the state of the world's linguistic heritage (see below our comments on some regional approximations).[5] The extinction process is more advanced in some regions than in others: it is, for example, more recent in North-east Asia than in Europe, the first region to suffer from language erosion. Moreover, the world language map does not coincide with that of the world population.

According to Osahito Miyaoka, professor at the University of Tokyo, 96% of languages are spoken by only 4% of the world population.[6] William F. Mackey observes that 'only 1 per cent of the world's languages are spoken by more than half a million people and only 10% by more than 100,000 persons, whereas some 20 to 30% are no longer spoken by the young and 10% are virtually extinct'.[7]

Current estimates also vary greatly depending on the methods of counting used, which in some cases are based on poor statistics and in others reflect the prejudices of their authors.[8] Rather than speaking of 'a' language (usually the 'first' language), it would doubtless be preferable in certain cases to speak of 'families' of languages that are not necessarily fully comprehensible to each other but belong to the same language group. At all events, and in spite of the differing estimates, about half the world's population express themselves in one of the eight most widely spoken languages (Chinese, English, Hindi, Spanish, Russian, Arabic, Portuguese and French).[9]

Language extinction is accelerated by a wide variety of factors related to globalization and the 'third industrial revolution': industrialization, urbanization, new forms of consumption, the influence of the audio-visual media. Faced with the speed and scale of the process, must we remain inactive? Can we, as certain specialists do, regard it as straightforwardly quasi-Darwinian, with only the 'fittest' languages being able to survive in a given context? Must globalization necessarily entail the crushing of the world's cultural and linguistic diversity as a result of the hegemony of one or two or three common languages? Or is it on the contrary compatible with a genuine linguistic pluralism, the only approach capable of giving a voice and a chance to all the cultures of the world? Do the new information and communication technologies represent a danger for language diversity or, on the contrary, a source of hope for their promotion and spreading? Will the twenty-first century see a vigorous and fruitful interbreeding of languages, a general creolization, and that freely assumed 'bastardization' mentioned by the writer Edouard Glissant? Will hybridization and cultural nomadism be accompanied, according to the hope expressed by the linguist Claude Hagège in his book *Le Souffle de la langue*, by linguistic hybridization and nomadism and the widespread adoption of multilingualism? What language policies are needed for the twenty-first century?[10] Above all, is there not, as UNESCO is convinced, an intimate link between language teaching, intercultural dialogue and the emergence of a culture of peace?

Endangered Languages

Most endangered languages have two traits in common: a small pool of speakers (from a few hundred to a few thousand) and a top-heavy age pyramid in which the youngest speakers are greatly under-represented. There is general agreement among linguists that one-tenth of the world's languages, which now have fewer than a hundred speakers each, are in an extremely precarious state and will probably soon cease to exist.[11] It is not easy to fix a definite figure for the number of speakers below which a language is in danger, for the threshold can vary from region to region: in the Pacific, a language spoken by 500–1,000 persons may be fairly stable but in Europe or in Africa the language of a population of similar size must certainly be considered at risk. It is important, however, to note that some 90% of the world's languages are each spoken by fewer than 10,000 individuals.[12]

This makes it possible to distinguish several stages or levels on the road to extinction. The authors of the *Red Book* (North-east Asia; Europe) distinguish five levels, from 'nearly extinct languages' (category 1) to 'not endangered languages' (category 5).[13] The current pace of extinction also varies: in North-east Asia, the proportion of endangered languages is very high (60% in categories 1 and 2); in Europe, the languages are more stable, with 70% in categories 3 to 5, though there are still a large number of nearly extinct languages.[14] The two regions are clearly going through different historical phases. In Europe, the extinction process started much earlier, there are few languages without a literature and many of them are backed by a state; as a result, a fairly large number of languages are in a position to hold their own. In North-east Asia, language erosion appears to be much more recent and to be directly attacking a zone in which a great many languages do not possess the necessary characteristics (existence of literature, status of national language) to withstand the changes arising from modernization. Is it then possible to say that the current situation in Europe foreshadows the future state of languages and that the language extinction process will stabilize, relatively, at some time in the future?

The current situation is highly contrasted. Although it is impossible here to give a precise general picture of developments at the regional level, certain major trends emerge clearly: Africa and Asia, which are currently the regions with the greatest linguistic diversity, should retain their positions up to around 2010 since a large proportion of foreseeable extinctions will affect the Pacific and the Americas. However, both Asia and Africa are likely to suffer from a considerable reduction in their linguistic diversity. The Americas will probably tend towards a situation similar to that of Europe, with only a small number of languages subsisting, each with quite a large number of speakers and an institutional base. It is also highly likely that ongoing changes will reinforce the dominant languages of today and the current *linguae francae*, which are spoken in a bilingual context over large areas of linguistic diversity. A few more precise details will give an idea of the diversity and scale of the challenges.[15]

In *Africa*, according to certain experts, 222 languages are threatened with extinction in the course of the twenty-first century (fewer than 500 speakers),[16] out of a total estimated variously at between 700 and 2,000. The whole of the continent is affected.[17] For southern Africa as a whole, some 48 languages are already totally or almost extinct, many of them languages of the Khoisan family (Bushmen-Hottentots), which are likely to disappear altogether in the next hundred years. Demographic and economic changes will exert a powerful impact on the process there, as elsewhere. In the event of significant economic progress in Africa, the number of extinctions could be much greater. Continued population growth, foreseeable for at least part of the twenty-first century, will initially favour the survival of endangered languages. But the acceleration of the demographic transition might well provoke a second wave of mass extinctions. Some experts think that it will be the African *linguae francae* such as Wolof and Swahili, together with languages that have a national or regional status, rather than the languages of the former colonial powers, that will be in a position to emerge as dominant languages by the end of the century.[18] However, this view is far from being unanimous since the area covered by these *linguae francae* is at best a subregion and the globalization process might well favour, in the African context of great linguistic fragmentation, the maintenance of the widely spread languages inherited from the colonial period.

In the *Americas*, the endangered languages, with only a few exceptions, are all native or Creole languages. In *South America*,[19] between one-third and one-half of the 470–500 existing Indian languages may be regarded as endangered owing to the small number of speakers, and particularly so in Brazil, where the 170 to 200 native languages are for the most part spoken by such tiny communities that they have hardly any chance of being passed on to future generations.[20] In that region, only some 150 to 200 native languages will survive until 2100 alongside Spanish, Portuguese, English, French and Dutch. The reduction in diversity is likely to be the most severe in Brazil. Mention should be made of current preservation efforts within the Latin America and the Caribbean region, where UNESCO is supporting programmes aimed at the compiling of dictionaries for languages including Nahuatl, Aymara, Maya and Guarani, and is lending its support to the 'House of the Native Writer' in Mexico. It is in the *United States of America* and in *Canada* that the decrease has been the most rapid: specialists have identified about 200 native languages[21] and are finding extinction rates that are disturbing. Ofelia Zepeda and Jane Hill report that the 51 languages identified in a 1962 survey as being spoken by between 1 and 10 persons[22] are now extinct. These two experts consider that *all* the native languages of North America are in danger, even the ones that are the most geographically remote (Inuit) or spoken by large numbers of people (Navajo), though the danger is not immediate in the latter case.[23]

A very small number of native languages in North America, including

Navajo, Cree and Ojibwa, are likely to survive alongside English, French and Spanish. This great loss of linguistic diversity will be only partly offset by immigrant languages (Chinese, Korean, etc.), and only provided that these are transmitted to future generations.

Some 600 to 700 languages have been identified in *South-east Asia* (including South China), over 40 of which are in danger.[24] The future of these languages will depend on national policies. If the policy of repression of minorities conducted in some of the countries concerned were to continue, the consequences for linguistic diversity would undoubtedly be serious. In view of the local population density and the relatively high average number of speakers per language, the survival of several hundred languages is foreseeable. The official languages of this subregion – Vietnamese, Laotian, Thai, Cambodian, Burmese, Chinese, etc. – will be among them and will strengthen their hold at the expense of less widely spoken languages and above all at the expense of their own dialects. Nevertheless a good many languages will disappear. In China, the Chinese 'dialects' – Cantonese, Wu, Min, Hakka, Xiang, etc. – which are in fact distinct languages whose diversity, concentrated in the south-east corner of the country, is comparable to that of the Romance languages, are more threatened with extinction than the languages of the national minorities because of the spread of the Chinese common language *P'ut'unghua*.

Out of 47 languages (excluding Russian) recorded in *North-east Asia*, 20 are dying, eight are close to extinction and 13 are endangered.[25] Tatar and Buriat are potentially endangered languages. Yakut, Mongol (at least its standard dialect), Tuva and Oirat are viable. Experts consider that only a small number of languages (possibly six) will hold their own alongside Russian, which is expected to confirm its status as the *lingua franca* of the region.

In *Europe*, one estimate asserts that, out of 123 languages in current use, nine are nearly extinct, 26 seriously endangered, 38 endangered and 50 either potentially endangered or not endangered.[26] The languages in danger are usually located in peripheral and insular areas of Europe: the Baltic languages, Frisian, the Gaelic languages of the British Isles, Breton, Basque, Sardinian and certain varieties of Croat. For some experts, 50–70 languages will survive to the end of the twenty-first century. All the national languages will strengthen their positions, together with a few languages of local importance, especially in southern Europe (Galician, Lombardic, Corsican), or with official status at the regional level (Catalan). It should be noted that the number of languages identified in Europe can vary by a factor of one to two (from 123 to 225), according to the definition criteria used.

In *India*, the number of languages spoken ranges from 200 to 381 according to the estimate.[27] The statistics still vary and it is not yet possible to say exactly which languages are in danger of extinction.[28]

South-east Asia and the *Pacific* are characterized by great linguistic diversity:

R. M. W. Dixon has counted 1,830 languages still spoken in the region (his survey identified 1,980 languages, including 150 Australian Aboriginal languages now extinct).[29] In the whole of New Guinea (the Indonesian territory of Irian Jaya and Papua New Guinea) alone, 960 languages are thought to exist – between one-sixth and a one-seventh of all the languages in the world. This diversity reflects the very ancient settlement of the island (70,000 to 50,000 BC according to the estimate) and the subsequent evolution of the languages *in situ* in an extremely mountainous terrain. In terms of variety, the languages of New Guinea represent the equivalent of 50–60 linguistic families of Europe.

Although the average number of speakers per language in the Philippines and Indonesia is quite high, this is not true in Oceania (including New Guinea) and in Australia, which is very sparsely populated. Everywhere the average number of speakers per native language is under 8,000 and nearly half the languages of the region have fewer than 1,000 speakers.[30] The consequence is an extremely high risk of extinction throughout the region.

In the case of *Australia*, where 100 Aboriginal languages are said to be spoken today (as against 250 when the Europeans arrived), the decrease has been spectacular. Dixon, in what he considers an optimistic forecast, says that 25 Aboriginal languages might still be in use at the end of the twenty-first century. He predicts that the process of language extinction will spread to the other territories of the *Pacific* (Oceania, New Guinea) with the same consequences as in Australia. Language extinction will be hastened by the small size of the communities, the development of trade and the propagation of *linguae francae* (Indonesian, Tagalog, Tok Pisin, English, French, etc.). In his view, by 2200 the number of languages still spoken in the Pacific region will lie between 20 or 30 and 200. The loss of diversity is likely to be more massive in the eastern than in the western part of the region (Indonesia and the Philippines). Even in the west, however, numerous languages will most probably disappear: in particular danger are the 'Negritos' of the Philippines and most of the aboriginal languages of Taiwan.

Languages and Globalization: The Extinction, Diversification and Survival of Languages

When a languages dies it is, in the immense majority of cases, dead for ever. Exceptions are rare: some languages with a written tradition have been reborn, as have some with an oral tradition that were mistakenly thought to be extinct (Latin America, New Guinea). The rebirth of an ancient language such as Hebrew is the most frequently cited example of language revival. But these remain isolated cases and it is more usual for a language to disappear with the death of its last speakers.

The particular reasons and the time taken for extinction processes to operate vary greatly: a language may disappear as a result of catastrophic changes in the environment of the linguistic communities concerned – genocide,[31] occupation of the territory of a language by the speakers of another language,[32] natural disaster[33] or epidemics. In the view of certain experts, the increase in the number of natural disasters caused by the global warming observed in recent years might contribute to the extinction of languages spoken by small populations exploiting particular ecosystems (languages of New Guinea, the Amazon, Asian languages in central Malaysia). In addition, emerging and re-emerging diseases probably constitute a direct threat to languages spoken by small traditional societies: the AIDS pandemic might in the future endanger a good many languages with few speakers in Africa and Asia.

However, language extinction is usually the consequence of gradual changes to a language's human, economic, cultural and political environment. The most common case occurs when two languages come into contact, often as a result of trade, cultural exchange or migration.[34] At the very least such a situation leads to bilingualism: thus Malay in Malaysia, Tok Pisin in New Guinea and Swahili in Africa have become the second language of a great many communities without supplanting the mother tongues. But when a situation of bilingualism is accompanied by powerful political and cultural pressure, as is often the case, the predictable outcome is the marginalization of the group's own language, which ends up being known only to its oldest members, and dies with them. This extremely widespread mechanism explains the decline of the French dialects, still vigorous at the beginning of the century, and of numerous minority languages in the former Soviet Union, continental China and Taiwan (despite a policy of encouragement). The same mechanism is contributing to the decline or disappearance of Aboriginal languages in Australia, of numerous native American languages, of Ainu in Japan, Manchu in north-east China and Gaelic in Scotland. The original language may survive to some extent in creolized form[35] (Caribbean Creoles, Aboriginal English in Australia, etc.) or through secondary bilingualism, in which the dominated group speaks its original language only in marginal circumstances or at particular moments of social life.[36] Furthermore, the dominant language often exerts a powerful influence on the vocabulary but also on the syntax and morphology of the original language.[37]

In contrast to the factors conducive to erosion or extinction are other factors that help maintain linguistic diversity, the most important being the tendency of languages to split into dialects. This basic trend lies behind the immense diversity of human languages and is most apparent when the geographical or political cohesion of a language community is weak, for example in mountainous regions where communications from one valley to another are difficult, or when a language community splits owing to the migration of a proportion of its speakers, or when a central political authority is lacking or is counterbalanced by influential political power at the local level. For this reason mountainous regions often display greater linguistic diversity than their adjoining plains (Caucasus, Pyrenees, Fujian, New Guinea, etc.); British English has diversified as a result of migration into a series of colonial dialects (USA, Australia, New Zealand, etc.) and American English has itself diversified into regional varieties that reflect the strength of distinctive local traits. This general trend, however, operates in the long term whereas the detrimental factors mentioned above often have a very rapid impact. This is partly why, in recent times, the balance of language creation and language extinction is largely negative and will continue to be negative during the twenty-first century.

The survival of endangered languages may be assisted by several other factors besides the trend towards dialect formation. The first of these is geographical isolation (islands, mountainous regions), which restricts contact with expanding languages and might offer some degree of protection for isolated regions (languages in the Caucasus, the Atlas, the Andes, the Himalayas, the Pacific, etc.), but which could in the none too distant future be largely offset by the expansion of telecommunications and tourism. A second factor is the existence of a writing system and varied literature that are taught in schools. This will protect languages with a substantial written tradition,[38] but probably not those for which a writing system has just been created and which do not possess a varied literature. A third asset for survival is national language status. Lastly, languages regarded by their speakers as a symbol of identity appear to stand up more effectively than others to contact with expanding languages (Maori in New Zealand). However, it must be admitted that very few languages display one or another of these characteristics: fewer than 15% of states have more than one official language and only a very few have more than two; these official languages, moreover, are few in number (about a hundred) and 125 sovereign states use as their official language one of just four languages – English (45), French (30), Spanish (30) and Arabic (20).[39]

Furthermore, languages are neither unchanging nor monolithic: they evolve ceaselessly and constantly adapt to their environments. Local dialects are usually embedded in a peasant society that is today undergoing profound change if not actually vanishing in many parts of the world. Any social or economic upheaval is quickly reflected in the language, one example being the almost total disappearance from the collective memory of words connected with professions no longer practised – in Europe, for instance, agricultural implements, the tools of wheelwrights or the techniques of clog-makers – and the emergence of new terms in multicultural contexts.

In various regions, hybrid languages often develop. Common oral languages, serving as instruments for interregional exchange, may function within a single grammar system, retaining only the base that is common to all the languages in the area: Kanjé, for example, is a simplified form of Mandingo (a West African language spoken in several countries – Senegal, Gambia, Burkina-Faso, Guinea Bissau, Ghana) understood by all speakers of the various Mandingo dialects, whatever the variety they speak as their mother tongue. A common language may also be a simplified form of the language of one of the peoples in a particular region and operate within societies with different mother tongues: Wolof, for example, is used throughout Senegal as an instrument of oral exchange and common Malay has spread from Malaysia to the Indonesian ports.[40]

Languages for Peace: The Challenges of Linguistic Pluralism

The importance of linguistic diversity is still a long way from receiving the same kind of recognition as biodiversity. It has suffered, and often continues to suffer, from a number of prejudices that have combined to belittle the importance of language teaching and the preservation of the world's linguistic heritage.

Linguistic diversity has long been associated with the negative idea of the *incommunicability* of cultures, an idea sublimated by the biblical image of the world after the Tower of Babel, punished by God with the confusion of tongues and incomprehension. This prejudice, exacerbated by the present vigour of globalization, has had serious consequences: through a paradoxical distortion, it was long thought necessary to eliminate linguistic diversity in order to facilitate communication and understanding between cultures and human beings. Some people have even suggested that the building of universal peace required the use of a single universal language. And yet all human experience pleads against this prejudice: true, language differences may lead to incomprehension between human groups speaking different tongues, but that problem can be resolved to a large extent by the development of inter-cultural communication and cooperation. In other words, it is not languages that are divisive but the lack of communication between cultures, which creates barriers between people. Those afraid of a linguistic 'Babel' in the twenty-first-century world should be made to understand that it is not incom-municability we should fear, but the failure to communicate. The existence of major common languages and the practice of bilingualism, found throughout the world, show that linguistic diversity by no means leads necessarily to incommunicability.

A second prejudice, to some extent connected with the first, has consisted in the *ranking* of languages: some languages (especially those with a written tradition) were deemed 'superior' and vehicles of 'civilization' while others (often those with an oral tradition) were regarded as inferior, 'primitive' and doomed to vanish with industrial and economic progress or with the expansion of the dominant religions. This prejudice, which was often based on the idea of the presumed superiority of certain cultures over others, sometimes in a colonial or missionary context,[41] greatly hastened the decline in the teaching and transmission of minority and regional languages, and of native languages in colonial times, often against a background of racial discrimination. This prejudice is far from dead but all experts now agree that the idea of a hierarchy of languages is fundamentally flawed: no language is inherently 'superior' to another; each performs its role in a specific cultural, economic, social, ecological and political context and each describes in its own particular way a different environment. The death of a language is not therefore linguistic in origin – it is caused not by the supposed linguistic inferiority of one language in relation to others but by other factors such as a sudden upheaval in the general environment in which the language is used, changes in the lifestyles with which the language is associated, or the absence of a written heritage to counterbalance the shortcomings of oral transmission. Languages with an oral tradition, many of them associated with a rural way of life, are currently the most likely to be abandoned.

A third and last prejudice, largely contemporaneous with the emergence of the nation-state, has been the policy of consolidating a unitary state through the promotion of a single official language. This policy has frequently led to the discouragement of cultural and linguistic pluralism and the encouragement of *monolingualism*, regarded as a guarantee of national unity and cohesion. The indivisibility of the national community was and still is invoked in many countries to call into question the existence and teaching of regional dialects and languages, which are sometimes even actively opposed by means of forced assimilation policies, with multilingualism regarded as an obstacle to development. This situation has long prevailed in the countries of Western Europe but also in several other regions of the world where language policies have tended to favour the predominance of a national language. In the colonial period, the teaching of colonial languages as common languages was often imposed at the expense of local languages. In many regions where plurilingualism[42] is the rule rather than the exception, such a policy hinders the learning process for young children and creates situations in which mother tongues, in some cases spoken by a majority of the population, are neither taught nor employed by the media.

This is an issue that in reality transcends the particular fate of an individual language: what is at stake is the constitution of societies whose cultures reflect, in the diversity of their expression, the values of pluralism, tolerance and respect for others that lie at the root of true democracy. It is, moreover, essential to recognize that the world's languages are not an ordinary consumer product that can be endlessly manufactured and replaced: language cannot be separated from society, like the two sides of a sheet of paper. The death of a language is therefore a loss for all of us since it is often the final act in the disappearance of a way of life, a culture and a particular view of the world for which it was the main vehicle; as nothing is done in most cases to preserve any trace of it, the historical knowledge and millennia-old experience it embodies are lost for ever. This has happened with the recipes of healers, with the names of plants and their properties, not to mention place names and the historical memories they indirectly call to mind. When in addition the extinction is imposed by others, it is the freedom and dignity of a community that perishes. In the words of the Sicilian poet Ignazio Buttitta, 'a people / becomes poor and enslaved / when robbed of the language / bequeathed by its ancestors: / it is lost for ever'.[43]

It is all too often forgotten that languages themselves contain a large proportion of the unwritten archives of humanity: in their vocabulary, in their morphology and in their syntax, they embody vestiges of their common origin with other languages, in some cases very remote, and traces of the cultural contacts of their speakers with the speakers of other languages. Deciphering this information is far from easy but, like archaeology and genetics, language is one of our windows onto the past,[44] as attested by Indo-European studies concerning the proto-history of people in Europe and south Asia. It is often the most marginal and the most divergent languages that are in danger. The death of Tasmanian, of which nobody took the trouble to make even a rough description, is as serious a loss as the destruction of a major archaeological site.

The cultural impoverishment resulting from the death of a language frequently reflects a broader and more complex situation: the underdevelopment, exclusion, dependence and marginalization of entire communities that find themselves refused 'the right to be different, to consider themselves as different and to be regarded as such' in the words of the UNESCO Declaration on Race and Racial Prejudice (1978).[45] 'Wherever violence reigns,' wrote the philosopher Hannah Arendt, 'not only are the laws silent, in the expression used at the time of the French Revolution, but each and every person must keep silent.'[46] The fight for linguistic diversity is a battle for freedom of expression and peace: 'You understand people by speaking to them,' as a Spanish proverb rightly reminds us in urging us to resolve our conflicts through dialogue. Speech permits contact with the Other on an equal footing, reaching beyond the tendencies towards uniformity on the one hand and isolation on the other. The fight against linguistic prejudices is also a fight against alienation and ignorance and in support of two concepts – peace and speech – so dear to the poet Blas de Otero. It calls for a multilingual education and the pursuit of active language and cultural policies geared to the local, national and regional context, policies which should be the subject of negotiated regional agreements along the lines of the European Charter for Regional and Minority Languages. This is the goal of UNESCO's Linguapax project.[47]

Box 15.1 Linguistic Rights

Several international instruments are concerned with linguistic rights: Article 27 of the International Covenant on Civil and Political Rights states that 'In those States in which ethnic, religious or linguistic minorities exist, persons belonging to such minorities shall not be denied the right, in community with the other members of their group, to enjoy their own culture, to profess and practise their own religion, or to use their own language'.

The Convention against Discrimination in Education, adopted by UNESCO in 1960, stresses that 'it is essential to recognize the right of members of national minorities to carry on their own educational activities, including the maintenance of schools and, depending on the educational policy of each State, the use or the teaching of their own language, provided however ... that this right is not exercised in a manner which prevents the members of these minorities from understanding the culture and language of the community as a whole and from participating in its activities, or which prejudices national sovereignty ... ' (Art. 5, 1[c]).

The main reference is still the Declaration on the Rights of Persons belonging to National or Ethnic, Religious and Linguistic Minorities, adopted by the United Nations General Assembly on 18 December 1992. Article 1 expands the scope of the Declaration by requiring that 'States shall protect the existence and the national or ethnic, cultural, religious and linguistic identity of minorities within their respective territories and shall encourage conditions for the promotion of that identity'. Various measures seek, not without some restrictions and hesitations, to promote cultural rights. '2. States shall take measures to create favourable conditions to enable persons belonging to minorities to express their characteristics and to develop their culture, language, religion, traditions and customs, except where specific practices are in violation of national law and contrary to international standards. 3. States should take appropriate measures so that, wherever possible, persons belonging to minorities may have adequate opportunities to learn their mother tongue or to have instruction in their mother tongue. 4. States should, where appropriate, take measures in the field of education, in order to encourage knowledge of the history, traditions, language and culture of the minorities existing within their territory.

Persons belonging to minorities should have adequate opportunities to gain knowledge of the society as a whole.'

The Universal Declaration of Linguistic Rights (Barcelona, 1996) stresses in its Preamble the impossibility 'for many languages to survive and develop unless the following basic goals are taken into account. In a political perspective, the goal of conceiving a way of organizing linguistic diversity so as to permit the effective participation of language communities in this new growth model. In a cultural perspective, the goal of rendering the worldwide communications space compatible with the equitable participation of all peoples, language communities and individuals in the development process. In an economic perspective, the goal of fostering sustainable development based on the participation of all and on respect for the ecological balance of societies and for equitable relationships between all languages and cultures.'

Towards Multilingual Cultures in the Twenty-first Century

Monolingualism is far from being the normal situation in the world: according to experts, bilingual individuals make up half the world's population,[48] and there hardly exists a country without some form of bilingualism. In many countries and continents, it is not so much monolingualism as bilingualism (and occasionally multilingualism) that is the norm (for example in Africa, in India, in the Southwest Pacific, in Indonesia, in the Philippines, in Switzerland, in Finland, in Paraguay, etc.). This bi- or multilingualism, which cultural contacts are making more and more common, may be acquired quite easily during early childhood and last throughout a person's life, with each language operating within its own social and functional context. Indeed, the reality of language use is changing at an increasing pace: taking just the centre of London, more than 175 mother tongues have been recorded in the schools run by the London City Council.[49]

Furthermore, all experts agree that 'bilingual persons are generally more adaptable and possess greater cognitive flexibility than monolingual persons'.[50] The same point was made in the Age of Enlightenment by the French humanist Charles Rollin, who observed that 'an understanding of languages serves as an introduction to all branches of knowledge'.[51] The linguist R. Jakobson considered bilingualism the most fundamental problem of linguistics.[52] In facing up to the linguistic and cultural challenges of the twenty-first century, school must henceforth foster the development, within what Roberto Carneiro called 'plural educational communities',[53] of a truly multilingual culture, token of a new conviviality between cultures, and of real democratic participation. To do so, school must adapt to the linguistic circumstances of each community and make a systematic effort to find points of convergence and coordination between the teaching of a 'mother' tongue and the teaching of several other languages.[54] The 'mother tongue', the repression of which is profoundly detrimental to the development of the child's cognitive faculties and is considered by all experts to be the most reliable vehicle for literacy training,[55] could thus play its full role as a springboard for the learning of other subjects.[56]

The teaching of two or three languages requires the coordination of curricula in an approach to teaching founded on complementarity.[57] The teaching of foreign languages must begin very early: on this subject the linguist Claude Hagège stresses that the eleventh year of a child marks the end of the 'critical period', when 'the ear, hitherto the normal organ of hearing, becomes national'.[58] Languages must be taught not as academic subjects like the others but as instruments of communication, expression, creativity and play. Use should be made of linguistic immersion, possibly facilitated by exchanges of primary teachers on a massive scale within or between particular regions of the world. It should permit the learning of minority languages or languages that are insufficiently taught. It should continue from the primary to the secondary level to ensure permanent upkeep of the knowledge gained and new knowledge.

It would seem in any case desirable to aim in the twenty-first century for a multilingual education – at least bilingual and, as far as possible, in all countries for which it is possible, trilingual – based on the mastery, by ways and means to be worked out locally, of several languages selected among those most likely to contribute to education and development (mother tongue, national language, neighbouring national language, international common language, etc.).[59] This multilingual education should begin at the primary level. The choice of languages and of teaching methods will necessarily vary according to the regional linguistic context. At the primary level, it would seem desirable to use languages with a wide international audience, which could be neighbouring regional languages; certain experts have pointed out that if the intention is to promote linguistic diversity, English is not vital at this stage and could be introduced, with other non-regional languages, at the secondary level or as the second foreign language in primary education.[60] Education in the twenty-first century should therefore be not only multilingual but founded on receptiveness to all the richness of the world's linguistic heritage.

The new information and communication technologies should also be more welcoming to linguistic diversity. Today, 60% of the computers linked up to the Internet are located in the USA; outside Europe and North America, use of the Internet is for the most part recent and limited (see Chapter 13). According to

Bernard Oudet,[61] the technical problems posed by the transmission of written language through the Internet are still serious.[62] Admittedly the Unicode standard, which permits the transcription of almost all the writing systems of the world, is steadily gaining ground. But, as Bernard Oudet stresses, there is still a long way to go before a truly multilingual Internet 'in which an author will be able to include a quotation in Greek in a Russian text that is readable on a computer in Latin America' becomes available. Computer-assisted translation, widely used in Japan, in Europe and in the USA, is developing rapidly but it cannot dispense with revision by a human hand and will never replace the desire for a faithful reflection of our thoughts and feelings – and the richer the vocabulary, the more fruitful that reflection will be.

Encouragement of Linguistic Research and Rescue of Endangered Languages

The majority of endangered languages are oral languages or languages with a writing system too recent for their literature to be expressed in written form. The death of these languages will therefore entail the death of their oral literature.

We need transdisciplinary theoretical reflection at the international level on the concept of language itself, and more specifically on the concept of 'endangered languages', on the complex processes threatening the survival of languages and on the linguistic rights of minorities. Such intellectual co-operation could be conducted through the holding of regional symposia for each continent and culminate in a world meeting of experienced specialists that would be expected to produce concrete recommendations on the teaching of languages and on their use in the media and in social and economic life.

As we move into the twenty-first century we need a rigorous analysis of the world's linguistic diversity that will make it possible to draw up a reliable world inventory of languages which, in the form of a periodical report on languages that could be published on a regular basis – say every eight to ten years – should also record cases of language-related persecution, a list of relevant laws and texts in that field and a report on the state of ongoing experiments for the defence and promotion of languages. It should foster awareness of the linguistic heritage, contribute to the monitoring of changes and recommend appropriate measures for the protection of languages in use today. This inventory should serve for the preparation of a regularly updated descriptive and explanatory world language map, which would have the practical purpose of defending and protecting present-day languages.[63] A scientific project along these lines is now being implemented by the Linguapax International Committee, appointed by UNESCO, which is preparing a report on the world's languages and a world language map for 2001.

The international community also needs legal instruments and specific provisions for the protection of the world's linguistic richness, which is often endangered by political or economic interests and by the phenomena of cultural hegemony. I think that an international convention on linguistic rights could help us not only to save many of the most endangered languages but also to encourage the growth of intercultural practices that prevent arrogant attitudes. Such a convention would facilitate the promotion of a multilingual culture and encourage states and regions to take the necessary step of reviewing their language policy criteria and developing appropriate educational instruments. Languages and cultures are, like individual human beings, equal in dignity. The right of the child to develop harmoniously in his or her mother tongue, whichever it is, must be recognized, as must the right of any individual to open out to others and participate in the universal culture by the learning of at least two other languages.[64] This convention could be based on earlier progress in this area, such as the Universal Declaration of Linguistic Rights (Barcelona, 1996),[65] and on regional initiatives such as the European Charter for Regional or Minority Languages (1992).

The preparation of a world inventory of languages could benefit from numerous studies in progress.[66] At the Fifteenth Congress of Linguists, held in Quebec in August 1992, the International Standing Committee of Linguists invited UNESCO 'to respond to this situation by promoting, and if possible sponsoring, programmes of linguistic organizations for the description of hitherto unstudied or inadequately documented endangered and dying languages, in the form of grammars, dictionaries and texts, including oral literature'. A programme entitled the Endangered Language Fund was adopted by the General Conference of UNESCO in November 1993. It provides support for the recording of endangered languages and their oral literature. In relation with this programme, an International Clearing House for Endangered Languages was founded at the University of Tokyo to conduct research on the endangered languages of Asia and the Pacific and to coordinate the efforts of local organizations.[67]

The most urgent need is to preserve for future generations as much information as possible on the languages and cultures that are doomed to disappear. It is a gigantic task that requires the setting of priorities. According to one expert, the study of endangered languages should 'take into account the imminence of their disappearance, their place in the genealogy of languages and their physical isolation'.[68] The political authorities should do all they can to promote the work of language description and foster the recording of literatures and the oral tradition. Wherever a particularly large number of languages are almost extinct, on the way to extinction or in great danger, as in North-east and South-east Asia, America or Africa, a local training programme for linguists could be envisaged. If the pace of extinction is too rapid to permit a full description of the languages concerned, sound recordings could be made, accompanied by translations. In digital form, such recordings could preserve the actual sounds of the languages and serve as 'Rosetta stones' for the linguists of future centuries. The authorities of countries possessing great linguistic diversity have special responsibility here but they should be able to count on the assistance of existing organizations concerned with the preservation of data and on the development of appropriate programmes of education.

Wherever rescue is possible, it should be supported by political authorities. One urgent task is to build up archives to permit conservation of the traces of vanishing languages and civilizations. This constitutes a duty to future generations. The saving of a language requires the establishment of a writing system (if one does not exist already), preferably without rare symbols, so as to facilitate the printing of texts in widely used fonts and their exploitation by computer. The language should be taught in schools, and if possible become a medium of instruction, which implies, unless the speakers are too few in number, the production of textbooks. If possible, a programme for the translation of major literary texts should be initiated.[69] Successful rescue will depend on a number of conditions: the language must have been properly described beforehand so as to permit the writing of textbooks; the age pyramid of speakers must not have deteriorated too much; the language must still be spoken in the home; and, finally, there must be a strong demand on the part of the language's speakers. When these conditions are satisfied, states should encourage appropriate action, firstly at the standard-setting level (the European Charter for Regional and Minority Languages offers an interesting example of this), and then at the practical level, with the aim of ensuring the survival of endangered languages in a context of bilingualism alongside the national languages. In most cases, the fear that such languages will supplant or even compete with the national language is groundless.

It is up to each one of us to strive for the preservation of languages, for each and every language contains a hidden treasure.

Pointers and Recommendations

- Establish by 2001 and regularly update a world report on languages and a linguistic map of the world, with a view to facilitating the practical safeguarding and protection of living languages (UNESCO's Linguapax project).
- Negotiate an international convention on linguistic rights as well as national and regional agreements for the protection of linguistic diversity by means of appropriate language, educational and cultural policies.
- Promote linguistic research through the training of linguists, the publication of grammars, dictionaries and texts, the preparation of textbooks, the

recording of endangered languages and of their oral literature, and the establishment of archives to keep a trace of vanishing languages and cultures.

• Encourage bilingualism and, as far as possible, trilingualism, from early childhood and from the primary level of education; actively promote multi-lingualism through the continuation of language training at the secondary level; use linguistic immersion methods, possibly through large-scale exchanges of teachers within a region of the world.

• Promote the teaching of minority languages or languages that are insufficiently taught.

• Encourage the dissemination of languages through printed and audio-visual media, as well as through the Internet, which must become truly multi-lingual.

Notes

1. Average estimates range from 5,000 (Stephen Wurm; see note 15) to 6,703 (*Ethnologue 1996*, International Academic Bookstore, Dallas, updated in February 1999). For a discussion of counting methods, see below.

2. Source: Endangered Language Fund. This figure should be regarded more as an estimate than as a scientific fact; however, it was established by professionals and constitutes a plausible approximation.

3. Although all present-day linguists agree about the scale on which languages are dying, there exists no common operational definition of the concept of endangered language. Nor does there exist any universally accepted list of the languages currently spoken in the world and of the number of persons speaking them. The word *language* covers very different realities, from a local vernacular speech to a common or regional language to a national language. A good many languages are, for some experts, simply dialects – hence the diverging estimates of the total number of languages spoken in the world.

4. Estimated by Professor Michael Krauss of the University of Alaska in Fairbanks.

5. Source: *Ethnologue 1996* (update of February 1999).

6. Statement to the symposium of the *Linguistic Society of Japan*, Seisen University, Tokyo, 3–4 October 1998, cited in the *Daily Yomiuri*, 10 October 1998.

7. William F. Mackey, 'Language policy, literacy and culture: contexts, contents and constraints', in *Language Policy, Literacy and Culture* (Round Table, International Conference on Education, 18 September 1992), Geneva, 1992, p. 11.

8. Thus certain linguists arbitrarily divide spoken Arabic into some 30 distinct languages, without any indication of their mutual comprehensibility and without allowing for the fact that Arabic is spoken by nearly 202 million persons, while others go as far as to assert that only 30 of the 58 million Italians speak 'Italian' as their first language, the rest of the population speaking another first language – Lombardic (8.7 million), Napolitan-Calabrian (7 million), etc. (See*Ethnologue 1996*.) These estimates raise many problems.

9. According to the *Millennium Family Encyclopedia* (Dorling Kindersley, London,

1997; *Encyclopédie Millénium*, Nathan, Paris, 1998), 'one person in two expresses him or herself in one of the eight most widely spoken languages in the world': Chinese (1.2 billion), English (478 million), Hindi (437 million), Spanish (392 million), Russian (284 million), Arabic (225 million), Portuguese (184 million) and French (125 million). *Ethnologue 1996* provides comparable data when 'mother tongue' and 'second-language' speakers are jointly taken account of.

10. On this subject, see WFMLA, *Language Policies for the World of the 21st Century: Report for UNESCO*, World Federation of Modern Language Associations (WFMLA), August 1993.

11. Throughout the world are found languages spoken only by the elderly: Krenak, in south-east Brazil, is now spoken only by a few persons over 70 years old.

12. Some 52% of languages are allegedly spoken by a population of between 1,000 and 10,000 persons, 28% by groups of between 100 and 1,000 persons and 10% by groups of under 100 persons (based on data collected by *Ethnologue* for its estimated total of 6,700 languages). Of these 6,700 languages 83% are spoken in a single country and therefore depend on the policy of a single government.

13. *UNESCO Red Book on Endangered Languages: Europe* and *Northeast Asia*. The levels are: (1) nearly extinct languages, with a few dozen speakers at the most, of all ages; these languages have almost no hope of surviving and will have disappeared in a generation or two, that is, in the next 25–50 years; (2) seriously endangered languages, with a larger pool of speakers but with no children using them; (3) endangered languages, with children among their speakers but in decreasing numbers; these languages are not threatened with immediate extinction but the demographic trends are disturbing; (4) potentially endangered languages, with a large number of children among their speakers but lacking prestige and official status; their future will depend on the attitude of governments and of the speakers themselves; and (5) not endangered languages, whose transmission from generation to generation is assured, at least for the moment. Unless rescue action is taken to revitalize certain endangered languages, the languages still alive at the end of the twenty-first century will probably be restricted to those in the present categories 3 to 5. Some of these languages, although not at present endangered – especially the ones not used for literary purposes, not taught in the schools, not national languages or not used for administration – will in turn become in danger of extinction by 2100.

14.

Levels	1	2	3	4–5	Total
North-east Asia	20	8	13	6	47
Europe	9	26	38	50	123
Total	29	34	51	56	170

Source: Ibid.

15. The subsequent details and references are drawn from the collective work entitled *Endangered Languages* (Robert H. Robins and Eugenius M. Uhlenbeck, eds, Berg, Oxford and New York, 1991) and from the *Atlas of the World's Languages in Danger of Disappearing* (Stephen Wurm, ed., maps by Theo Baumann, UNESCO/Pacific Linguistics, Paris, 1996).

16. Matthias Brenzinger, Bernd Heine and Gabriele Sommer, 'Language death in Africa', in Robins and Uhlenbeck, *Endangered Languages*, pp. 19–44. These figures are fairly similar to those presented by the *Atlas of Endangered Languages*, which gives a non-exhaustive list of about 150 endangered African languages.

17. The most seriously affected country is Nigeria (17), which is also the African

country with the greatest linguistic diversity. Next comes Tanzania (6) followed by Kenya (5).

18. Brenzinger et al., 'Language death in Africa', pp. 40–1.

19. Adelaar offers a country-by-country discussion (Willem F. H. Adelaar, 'The endangered languages problem: South America' in Robins and Uhlenbeck, *Endangered Languages*, pp. 45–91).

20. For Mexico, in Central America, Garza Cuaron and Lastra give the figure of 58 native languages, including 13 with fewer than 500 speakers (for the most part languages spoken near the US border) (Beatriz Garza Cuaron and Yolanda Lastra, 'Endangered languages in Mexico' in Robins and Uhlenbeck, *Endangered Languages*, pp. 93–134).

21. For the United States, Zepeda and Hill estimate the number of native languages at under 150 (see Ofelia Zepeda and Jane H. Hill, 'The condition of native languages in the United States' in Robins and Uhlenbeck, *Endangered Languages*, pp. 135–55). For Canada, Kinkade gives the figure of 50 languages, half of which will be extinct in 50 years, a further third having a reasonable chance of surviving and only four with long-term viability (M. Dale Kinkade, 'The decline of native languages in Canada' in Robins and Uhlenbeck, *Endangered Languages*, pp. 157–76).

22. For the United States and Canada as a whole, Chafe (Wallace L. Chafe, 'Estimates regarding the present speakers of North American Indian languages' in *International Journal of American Linguistics*, 1962, 28: 162–71) gives a distribution of languages by number of speakers:

Number of speakers	1–10	10–100	100–1,000	1,000–10,000	10,000+
Number of languages	51	35	75	43	9

23. For example, North Pomo, one of the 50 native languages in California, ceased to be transmitted when its last speaker died at the beginning of April 1995.

24. According to James A. Matisoff, 'Endangered languages of Southeast Asia', in Robins and Uhlenbeck, *Endangered Languages*, pp. 189–228.

25. Source: Tapi Salminen, *UNESCO Red Book on Endangered Languages: Europe.*

26. Ibid.

27. Sources: Mahapatra, 'An appraisal of Indian languages' in: Robins and Uhlenbeck, *Endangered Languages*, pp. 177–88, and *Ethnologue.*

28. Ibid.

29. R. M. W. Dixon, 'The endangered languages of Australia, Indonesia and Oceania' in Robins and Uhlenbeck, *Endangered Languages*, pp. 229–55.

30. Ibid., p. 253. See the figures given by Dixon (p. 230) excluding Australia: 260 languages spoken by 1 to 200 speakers, 750 by 1 to 1,000 speakers, 1,400 by 1 to 10,000 speakers and 430 by over 10,000 speakers.

31. Tasmanian, and a good many native American languages that suffered the impact of colonization, disappeared as a result of genocide or epidemics. In Europe, Judeo-Italian, Judeo-Greek and Judeo-Crimean are today nearly extinct owing to the Hitlerian genocide. Brenzinger et al. (Robins and Uhlenbeck, *Endangered Languages*, p. 21) have found no case of comparable extinctions in Africa.

32. Such occupation has in the past led generally to promotion of the victor's language. This was more or less the policy of the colonial powers in their colonies in Africa, Asia, Australia and America. However, such policies are not always successful –

the Mongols, and subsequently the Manchu, failed to impose their languages on the Chinese.

33. In the Sunda Islands, a language of Sumbawa, Tamboran, disappeared completely owing to a volcanic eruption in 1815.

34. Examples include the emigration of Chinese to Tibet and Qinghai, of English settlers to Wales, of French ones to New Caledonia and of Russians to Central Asia and Siberia.

35. A creole is a pidgin that has become the first language of its speakers.

36. Such is the case of Breton, Irish and a good many languages in China (Miao-yao, Tujia, She, etc.) and in the former USSR (Khanti and Mansi – Ugrian languages – Tungusic languages such as Nanay and Paleo-Siberian languages such as Itelmen).

37. Source: S. G. Thomason and T. Kaufman, *Language Contact, Creolization, and Genetic Linguistics*, University of California Press, Berkeley and Los Angeles, 1988. For example, Turkish, Persian and Swahili have been strongly influenced by Arabic; languages of South-east Asia such as Burmese, Thai, Khmer and Tibetan by Sanskrit; and, further back in the past, Vietnamese, Burmese and Tibetan by Chinese.

38. For example, the languages of South-east Asia, such as Burmese, Tibetan, Thai, Cambodian and Vietnamese.

39. Mackey, 'Language policy'.

40. These common languages are hardly ever written: accounts of the *lingua franca* long used in Mediterranean ports are rare despite the importance of this common language for trade. If such common languages acquire a written form it is a sign that they are changing in status and becoming a 'standard' language (as in the case of the pidgin of Melanesia, for instance) or even the norm (Bahasa-Indonesia has become the official language of Indonesia).

41. Certain experts emphasize the ambiguous impact of evangelism by missionary societies: on the one hand they recorded the native languages for the pupose of translating Christian texts (missionaries have bequeathed useful romanization systems, Bibles and catechisms in native languages as well as dictionaries and grammars for various languages in Asia, the Pacific, Africa and America, some of which no longer exist); but these results were often obtained at the price of occulting the religious beliefs and oral traditions of the peoples concerned, resulting in the destruction of the native cultures and their oral literature, which disrupted their social organization and paved the way for the eventual extinction of the languages. By facilitating the access of missionary societies to indigenous populations, or by giving them exclusive access, certain governments may in fact be contributing to the disintegration of the languages and cultures of such populations.

42. 'Plurilingualism' here designates the coexistence of a plurality of languages in a given geographical area or political unit; 'multilingualism' refers to an individual's familiarity with several languages (see Claude Hagège, *L'Enfant aux deux langues*, Odile Jacob, Paris, January 1996, p. 11).

43. 'A un populo / mittitulu a catina / spugghiatillu / attupatici a vucca, / é ancora libiru // Livatici u travagghiu / u passaportu / a tavula unni mancia / u lettu unni dormi / é ancora riccu. // Un populu, / diventa poviru e servu, / quannu ci arrobanu a lingua / addudata di patri: / é persu pi sempri.' ('Enchain / a people / despoil it, / muzzle it, / it is still free. // Rob its men of their work, / take their passport, / take away the table where they eat, / the bed where they sleep, / they are still rich. // A

people / becomes poor and enslaved / when robbed of the language / bequeathed by its ancestors; / it is lost for ever'). I. Buttitta, *Lingua e dialetu.*

44. Whether our species is of recent origin (100,000–150,000 years, as several linguists and anthropologists in favour of the 'African' theory, such as M. Ruhlen and A. Langaney, maintain) or more ancient, as the supporters of the regional evolution theory (such as Wolpoff) argue, it is not absurd to think that eventually more sophisticated methods of comparative linguistics will make it possible, with some confidence, to work back beyond the few thousand years that constituted the limits of the comparative methods of nineteenth-century Indo-Europeanists and that the systematic exploitation of the linguistic heritage of humanity will cast light on the prehistory of our species over several tens of thousands of years.

45. A text 'of general scope', as N. Rouland has stressed: N. Rouland (ed.), *Manuel de Droit des minorités et des peuples autochtones*, PUF, Paris, 1996.

46. See Hannah Arendt, *On Revolution*, Viking Press, New York, 1965.

47. See UNESCO, *Linguapax*, an international seminar on language policies, UNESCO ETXEA, Bilbao, 1997.

48. F. Grosjean, *Life with Two Languages: An Introduction to Bilingualism*, Harvard University Press, Cambridge, MA, 1982.

49. Mackey, 'Language policy'. Mackey adds that 'cities as different as Yaounde, New York, Rio de Janeiro or Los Angeles have recorded more than a hundred mother tongues in their primary schools'.

50. C. Hagège, *L'Enfant aux deux langues*, p. 10. On this point see Stephen Wurm, 'What future for minority and endangered languages?', a communication made to the *Twenty-First Century Dialogues* organized by the Analysis and Forecasting Office of UNESCO in Paris, 16–19 September 1998; B. Bain, 'Bilingualism and cognition: towards a general theory', in S. T. Carey, ed., *Bilingualism, Biculturalism and Education*, University of Alberta Press, Edmonton, 1974, pp. 119–28; J. Cummins, 'Metalinguistic development of children in bilingual education programmes: data from Irish and Ukrainian-English programmes', in M. Paradis, ed., *Aspects of Bilingualism*, Hornbeam Press, Columbia, SC, 1978, pp. 127–38.

51. In his *Traité des études* (1726–28), cited in Hagège, *L'Enfant aux deux langues*, p. 99.

52. Roman Jakobson, in *Results of the Conference of Anthropologists*, supplement to *International Journal of American Linguistics*, Vol. 19, No. 2, April 1953, Chapter II, 'From the point of view of linguistics'.

53. Roberto Carneiro, 'Revitalizing the community spirit: a glimpse of the socializing role of the school in the next century', in *Learning: the Treasure Within*, Report to UNESCO of the International Commission on Education for the Twenty-First Century, chaired by Jacques Delors, UNESCO Publishing, Paris, 1996, pp. 201–7.

54. The term 'mother tongue' is used in the broad sense; certain experts prefer concepts such as 'first language', 'native language' or 'family language', etc. (see Hagège, *L'Enfant aux deux langues*). See also Joseph Poth, *L'Enseignement d'une langue maternelle et d'une langue non maternelle*, Linguapax Guide No. 5, CIPA (International Centre for Applied Phonetics), Mons, 1997.

55. A good example is the Ethiopian Literacy Programme, which covered the use of 15 languages and reduced illiteracy from 93% in 1974 to 24% in 1989 (Ayo Bamgbose, 'Les options en matière d'éducation de base et leurs incidences sur la formulation de politiques linguistiques' in *Language Policy, Literacy and Culture*, pp. 20–7).

56. J. Poth, in R. Renard and D. Peraya, eds, *Langues africaines et langues d'enseignement*, CIPA, Mons, Paris, 1986.

57. Poth, *L'Enseignement d'une langue maternelle*, p. 11.

58. Hagège, *L'Enfant aux deux langues*, p. 34, See also Wurm, *Atlas*.

59. There have been numerous attempts to invent artificial languages in the course of history. Some of these languages, like Volapük, had an enormous success before being totally forgotten. Esperanto has not been as successful as its promoters hoped but it does play a certain role and there does exist a worldwide Esperanto community.

60. These recommendations are based in part on the ones proposed by Hagège, *L'Enfant aux deux langues*, Chapters V–IX.

61. Bernard Oudet, 'Multilingualism on the Internet', *Scientific American*, March 1997.

62. Even in the case of Latin characters, for which a standard authorizing the use of diacritical marks has gained acceptance (the Extended Simple Mail Transport Protocol [ESMTP], which accepts 256 characters as against the 128 of the Arpanet, ancestor of the Internet), communication with a computer equipped with unsuitable software for this standard makes communication difficult. See Oudet, 'Multilingualism on the Internet'.

63. See Poth, *L'Enseignement d'une langue maternelle*. See also Mackey, 'Language policy', p. 12, who recommends 'an exhaustive count of the languages represented within the political boundaries of the state, their geographical and social distribution, their mutual intelligibility, their degree of standardization in speech and writing, the divergence between local variants and the standard written form, and the proportion, type and degree of bilingualism of the speakers of each variant'.

64. Raymond Renard, 'Approche Linguapax de la politique linguistique', in UNESCO, *Linguapax*, pp. 143–53.

65. This Declaration was produced by the World Conference on Linguistic Rights (Barcelona, June 1996), organized with the support of UNESCO.

66. Major projects centred on the establishment of language atlases are under way: mention could be made of the Atlas Linguarum Europae, the Atlas Linguistique Roman (both published by the Istituto poligrafico dello Stato, in Rome) and of various national Atlases in different parts of the world. There exist many other resources, such as the Endangered Language Fund, the Foundation for Endangered Languages and several Internet sites.

67. Takeshi Nara, professor at the University of Seisen and chairman of the Committee on Endangered Languages of the Linguistic Society of Japan, has stressed that the majority of endangered languages are concentrated around the fringes of the Pacific, including Siberia and Alaska, and emphasized the decisive importance of research to combat the crisis (*Daily Yomiuri*, 10 October 1998).

68. Mackey, 'Language policy', p. 18.

69. Such texts should also be distributed in Braille for the blind, who number between 23 and 40 million persons in the world (source: *Ethnologue*, 1996).

CHAPTER 16

Education at the Horizon 2020: With or Without Distance?

An Education for All

Lifelong education for all will be the major challenge to be met in the twenty-first century. It is also the task that UNESCO had already set itself in the strategy it adopted as early as 1995. The prime objective will be to ensure the empowerment of individuals. With that goal in mind, education in the future should be aimed, first and foremost, at those who are most vulnerable and most impoverished – in a word, all those who, because of their limited means and unfavourable circumstances, were prevented from gaining access to knowledge. The objective is, quite simply, to include the excluded and reach those whom society has rejected.

Enabling everyone to acquire basic education and combating illiteracy and functional illiteracy continue, even today, to be fundamental priorities that require a constant mobilization of energies. On this front, the battle has yet to be won and it is in the light of this realization that new technologies warrant particular attention. Contrary to what is commonly thought, such technologies are not inventions reserved for the privileged but, on the contrary, a hope and a weapon in the service of education as a whole, be it basic or lifelong education. Distance education is the most emblematic illustration of such potential complementarity between technological progress and the need to provide basic education for all. By combining a pedagogical aim with modern tools, distance education can contribute to achieving the basic task of any educational process, namely, liberating the human being, wherever it is possible, from constraints and ignorance.

Obviously, this issue is an urgent one as the traditional systems and forms of education are no longer in tune with current economic and social reality. The major educational task the twentieth century set itself on a world scale – namely the eradication of illiteracy – had encouraging impact in terms of percentages but absolute figures remained high, due particularly to the increase in life expectancy. In 1999, it was estimated that there were 880 million illiterate people aged over 15 in the world, two-thirds of whom were women. Although illiteracy has therefore decreased substantially in relative terms, in the space of a generation it has continued to increase in absolute terms: for example, whereas the *percentage* of illiterates fell from 30.5% in 1980 to 22.7% in 1995, the *number* of illiterates rose from 877 million in 1980 to 884 million in 1995. Nevertheless, the most recent estimates and projections point to a reversal of trends. Accordingly, it is expected that the total number of illiterates in 2000 will have fallen to 876 million and by 2010, it will stand at 840 million. That would mean that the percentage of illiterate people would fall from 22.7% of the world population in 1995 to 16.8% in 2010.[1]

Whatever the case, it will be our responsibility, during the next generation, to take up the unresolved challenges of both the twentieth and the twenty-first centuries. The phenomena of functional illiteracy and the inadequacy of basic education in developing the capacities required for participation and social, economic and cultural integration are becoming increasingly wide-spread. Functional illiteracy, that is the inability to read or write with adequate understanding a simple, brief description of facts in relation to everyday life, is a much more common phenomenon than official statistics for education would suggest, including in the developed countries. In the United Kingdom, a survey prepared by the National Statistics Office reveals that approximately one British citizen in five has a very inadequate level of literacy and shows that 22% of 16 to 65-year-olds 'are incapable of comparing two written items of information, reading a newspaper, understanding a timetable or filling in a form'.[2] Most of the surveys conducted recently show that between one-tenth and one-fifth of the population is affected by the phenomenon of functional illiteracy in various industrialized countries.

This failure of traditional forms of education to match the requirements of adult education and literacy, or to meet the challenges inherent in the democratization of societies and in economic and technological development, is aggravated by the speed and scope of the change that has been brought about by the advent of new technologies and a variety of scientific innova-tions. In that respect, there is very probably a direct correlation between developments in economies, the metamorphosis of societies and the crisis pertaining to education systems. While the part played by information in the production of goods and services is growing constantly, and while the new information and communication technologies are used massively for reducing production costs, education has been seriously called into question. The crises experienced by national education systems indicate how difficult it is to reconcile the traditional task that falls to the school, namely the perpetuation and passing on of knowledge, and the new requirement it must meet, namely offering a framework and specific forms of training in response to new criteria and particularly to the new requirements of the job market.[3]

One of the major challenges facing education in the twenty-first century will be to ensure that the new information and communication technologies are readily available for the spreading of knowledge and skills. These technologies enable knowledge to be relocated, thanks to the setting up of networks. Consequently, knowledge in the future will no longer be necessarily concentrated in privileged, inaccessible places. The abolition of material obstacles to knowledge should also lead to a reduction in all symbolic distances, all barriers established by social structures and various processes of 'initiation' that govern access to knowledge. The issue at stake is to make distance education materially possible and ensure that it is the instrument of an education without distance, an education that is democratic and adapted to individuals, an education that can be provided everywhere and for everyone.

Faced with these challenges, UNESCO has emphasized the importance of universal access to education, within an open, worldwide educational system comprising 'the basis for open education without frontiers, universal, human, non-discriminatory and ethical in nature ... not necessarily based on a particular centre for disseminating knowledge but seeking to respond to the needs of all those who seek knowledge, science and technology'.[4] What is urgent in this field is to succeed in overcoming the inequality of access to technology caused by the cost of infrastructure as well as the heterogeneous nature of the cultural environments that do not encourage its utilization in comparable ways. Admittedly, providing every individual with the basic education to which he or she is entitled continues in many countries to be the top priority and an objective that is not only difficult to achieve but is constantly brought into question. Intensive audio-visual training in the commonly used language is a particularly effective method of overcoming illiteracy as it enables the student to progress rapidly while gaining self-respect. Closer cooperation between schools, libraries, museums and distance education establishments can be a decisive opportunity for the developing countries, which could thereby at one and the same time open up their system in pedagogical terms, while improving the quality of education and making it available to a larger number of students at a lower cost.

In this context, would it not be possible to adopt a new educational approach that would offer the possibility of reaching the largest possible number of students at a lower cost than traditional education? That is the idea advocated by the philosopher Michel Serres:

In rich or poor countries, at least in financial terms, solutions to problems created by unemployment, starvation, violence, disease, economic crises and the population explosion ... depend to a large extent on the scientific and cultural development of individuals or groups. In actual fact, the economy is guided by innovation. *In countries throughout the world, including the richest, the demand for training has therefore grown by at least 10% a year while the budget for education and training, both public and private, both central and regional, has become saturated and cannot grow ... Thanks to today's technologies, distance education costs less than conventional education, the massive cost of which is met everywhere with declining resources [emphasis added].*[5]

We should not forget that the teacher continues to be the cornerstone of education. Teachers have been, are and will continue to be the key to education at all levels. The new technologies are a tool, an instrument that, while providing solutions, can nevertheless aggravate inequalities. They are already contributing to the emergence of growing disparities between countries and even within each nation, between a small group of people who have mastered the necessary codes for participating in a broader, more diverse society without frontiers, and a mass of excluded individuals who do not have the key of access to these codes. The development of new technologies has given rise to a new form of illiteracy, 'computer illiteracy', which tends to produce as much discrimination as traditional illiteracy as it generates the same forms of maladjustment and exclusion. What is at stake in the third industrial revolution, which is driven by the 'computer revolution', essentially involves the type of work organization it will generate and the structure of society resulting from it. While skilled workers are more able to cope with innovation and can easily find employment in a changing job market, it is to be feared that in both developing and rich countries, groups of excluded, 'newly unskilled'[6] and disqualified people may gradually form, who will mistakenly be considered 'unemployable'.

This phenomenon has already been borne out by the facts. Whereas in many democratic countries, school seeks – or rather sought – to provide a place where children from different backgrounds can mix, where a common culture can be created, where basic knowledge and social advancement can be acquired, it is now witnessing the development of a process of 'assortative matching'[7] similar to that observed in the organization of work. In fact, the overall rise in the level of literacy and skills has, according to some analysts,[8] produced a perverse effect: the decrease in the number of unskilled workers, far from enabling them to find a job corresponding to their skills more easily, has on the contrary raised the demand for skills even in those sectors that hitherto were less demanding. We are therefore witnessing the definitive exclusion of unskilled workers and the regrouping of people possessing similar skills. Today, there is a very marked trend among upper-middle-class families towards strengthening the educational selection process by a deliberate choice of schools reputed for the excellence of their results – establishments from which the children who do not belong to the same socio-cultural background are increasingly excluded.

With the increasingly rapid disappearance of a socio-cultural mix and the appearance of more or less disguised forms of educational apartheid, education – which, according to the democratic concept, has the task of reducing inequalities – is likely, if we are not careful, not only to reproduce these inequalities to a large extent, as was the case in the past, but also to increase them. In fact, whether it be basic training, literacy, the mastery of foreign languages or computer science, the increasingly wide distribution of basic knowledge is tending to exclude a little more those who do not have access to it. In contrast, those students who do have access to it are increasingly likely to be separated, from a very early age onwards, and generally according to the socio-economic status of their parents, into educational strata destined for increasingly diverse academic and professional achievement. Far from requiring less education, we need more of it, of a higher standard and for all. In other words, we must restore to education the full meaning of its democratic design. Consequently, acquiring new skills, thanks to new forms of knowledge, should become a priority for all. Computer and technological skills should now be taught as codes and instruments for social integration and not merely as components of knowledge. Otherwise, we are likely to witness the emergence of a many-tiered education system that will not provide every individual with the same opportunities and will therefore generate greater inequality and social fragmentation.

To encourage the use of more modern educational tools, it is indispensable that teachers' skills be regularly updated. The traditional duties of passing on knowledge and values and the fashioning of positive attitudes and forms of behaviour must now be supplemented by a capacity to keep in touch with current developments and to react rapidly to the emergence of new needs.

Educational Challenges in 2020

Several issues will weigh heavily on the future of education in the next 20 years. The first issue will be that of the availability and the constant updating of teachers' skills at all levels. More than ever before, it is obvious today that the quality of education depends on the quality and commitment of the teacher and on his or her relationship with the student and family. The second issue will be that of the educational content of all disciplines, but special attention will have to be given to civic education and to the values required for shaping the attitudes of responsible citizens. A third issue will be that of introducing electronic networks as tools for assisting learning. The fourth issue will be that of devising educational contexts to take account of the contribution of new forms of knowledge – particularly in biology – to the study and mastery of the cognitive processes. A fifth issue will be that of the attentive observation, and translation into learning patterns, of evolving contemporary skills. Priority will have to be given to scientific knowledge and to historical and social awareness that can facilitate the construction of cultural and ethical points of reference and multiple forms of citizenship (local, national, regional and global). The sixth issue will be the management of the lifelong alternation between time devoted to education and learning and time devoted to work and leisure. The seventh issue will be the gradual development of educational institutions towards a flexible, non-hierarchical form of management that will transform them into more autonomous educational enterprises (whether public, private or non-profit) but share common educational standards in order to communicate and prepare for the knowledge and quality of citizenship of the future. The eighth issue is the intervention of public authorities, which must lay down strategies for the education systems, whether public or private, devise new methods of funding and establish partnerships or agreements with systems that are often private and closely related to education, such as communication and publishing. The ninth issue is the development of various educational institutions (formal, informal, distance and alternate education), which should take advantage of their diverse approaches for mutual enrichment and for taking up the challenge of growing inequality in access to resources and new technologies.

In its traditional forms, education has up until now made use largely of human resources and has not yet made much use of capital. In 1992, approximately 80% of expenditure on education in the OECD countries was allocated to staff.[9] The way scholastic institutions are organized rests almost entirely on the 'four ones' pattern, which is virtually identical everywhere: one teacher, one subject, one period, one class. Naturally there are variations on this pattern, such as that of primary education in which the teacher is responsible for teaching the whole range of subjects, grouped as basic learning skills. Admittedly, educational teams of a new nature and experimental schools emerged some time ago, but the general model has remained basically unchanged. Other forms of education are pursued in other contexts, such as informal education (an example of which is the interactive museum), distance education (as demonstrated by the Open University in the United Kingdom) or alternative education (at school and in the workplace). In each case, it is clear that the introduction of learning tools (manipulation in museums, communication tools and networks for distance education, working tools in alternate education), has led to changes in the basic 'four ones' pattern and to a degree of diversification in the educational process.

It is therefore probable that the development of networks will, in the twenty-first century, go hand in hand with reorganizing the way education is run and therefore the way learning skills are taught. In this regard, three other vital elements should be taken into account. The first of these is the economic factor, which has already reached its limits in most of the industrialized countries and will no doubt do so during the next generation in many develop-ing countries. Expenditure on education amounts to almost 6% of GDP, sometimes even more in the rich countries, and a number of developing countries have already gone beyond that point or will do so in the near future. It is difficult to imagine how this figure of 6% of GDP could be exceeded by much at a time when rising health expenditure, lengthening life expectancy and the cost of pensions systems will weigh very heavy on economies and where most industrialized countries are attempting to curb rising public expenditure in those fields. A second factor that will encourage the reorgan-ization of the way education and learning skills operate is the combination of the demand for education on the part of families and the third industrial revolution which, by increasing the intensity of economic competition, gives a comparative advantage to those countries that possess the best-trained labour force. The third factor is the management of educational institutions, which will have to evolve under the influence of the competition that has arisen between educational institutions and systems: it will probably involve a change from administrative forms of management towards managerial methods that will make educational institutions genuine training enterprises, whether public, private or non-profit-making, where results will be assessed according to the resources used.

The effect of these four parameters, namely the sudden emergence of high-potential networks in terms of learning skills and cognition, economic im-peratives, new methods of managing educational institutions and demand on the part of society for better results in relation to the requirements of the labour market and global economic competition, and the behaviour of students (violence and the lack of discipline in educational institutions are particularly preoccupying in the richest countries), must not be underestimated. In the long term – probably over a longer period than that of the next 20 years – the compounding of these factors is likely to lead to profound change in the way educational institutions are organized, change that will occur all the more rapidly in the richest countries on account of the economic revolution, the beginnings of which are clear to all, namely the increase in productivity of services.

Setting up Infrastructures

If education for all is to become a reality, teachers must first of all be given the social status and income they deserve. Investing in teachers is a prerequisite for any improvement in the educational process. At the same time, steps must be taken to ensure a minimum of facilities in the field of new technologies. The cost of investment in infrastructure is largely set off by the wealth of information such infrastructure can convey and by the very fact that new networks can distribute anywhere what up to now could be found only in privileged centres. Such investment is admittedly less spectacular, less visible than the funding of buildings or motorways, but its effect is more lasting and far reaching. In other words, investing in education means investing in development: it is investment of this kind, largely immaterial and invisible, which can create a sound foundation for any development policy.

Public centres bringing together technologies and competent personnel can play a very useful complementary role. Thanks to the setting up of networks, we can expect more effective redistribution from more prosperous centres towards less privileged areas. Experiments under way in this field have been encouraging. We need only take the practical example of possibilities offered by the new distance education technologies: at the University of California at Berkeley the Electronic Mentoring, Teaching and Information Resource Network Project is aimed at providing computer access to the university's resources for all teachers and students in California, by giving preference for admission to minorities, the disabled and disadvantaged students at all levels.[10] This project offers a variety of services ranging from academic guidance to tutoring by faculty members. Teachers also have the possibility of computer access to the whole range of educational material at the university and of obtaining information on lectures and seminars they can attend through the electronic media. The Berkeley astrophysicists have even planned to teach teachers how to transfer onto their computers the NASA pictures of the Earth and Mars for use in their teaching.

Autonomy, Responsibility, Decentralization: The 'Charter Schools' Movement

At the same time, it is important to ensure that the different cultures and communities are able to play an active role in the setting up of this worldwide educational system and that each community can make its voice heard as clearly as others. Education must therefore be adapted to the needs of individuals, cultures and social specificities by contemplating decentralized, flexible forms of management of educational structures. For example, the charter schools that are developing in the USA are financed through public funds but independently managed, financially and pedagogically. While catering first and foremost to disadvantaged sections of society, they allow much more scope for innovation, participation and autonomy of the individual and offer the advantage of adapting the teaching to the needs and demands of the students and of giving them more responsibility in the way the teaching is carried out. This initiative is undoubtedly a solution for the future insofar as it has up to now produced good scholastic results and diminished absenteeism, particularly in the most underprivileged areas. As emphasized by the com-

Box 16.1 The Charter Schools: An Experiment in Progress

The phenomenon of charter schools came into being in the USA. It appeared in the early 1990s and now includes some 1,000 primary and secondary schools attended by approximately 150,000 pupils. It claims to be a credible alternative both to the occasionally burdensome standardization of public education and to the selective elitism of private institutions. These schools enjoy a special status insofar as they benefit from virtually complete pedagogical autonomy (subject to satisfactory academic results) while receiving public funding that guarantees free schooling.

These features enable charter schools to provide an alternative form of teaching, outside the compass of national educational bodies, such as the influence of the teachers' unions. The usually limited size of the schools – 200 pupils on average – also affords greater pedagogical flexibility combined with the active participation of the pupils and their parents in their institutions' orientation. Each institution enjoys complete freedom in defining its pedagogical methods and curricula, which accounts for the number of different approaches: some schools stress the importance of technologies whereas others rely on creating a protected, reassuring environment. At the City on a Hill School in Boston, emphasis is put on the participation of the pupils in 'citizens' debates' in which they discuss subjects of public interest, ranging from a strictly local to a more general nature, and where each pupil learns to defend his or her point of view in front of an audience. At the Chavez School in Washington, the principal teaching objective is to prepare adolescents from disadvantaged districts for a career in public administration. At the Renaissance School, teaching is based on a wide use of new communication technologies as a complement to traditional classes. The pupils work partly at home, using computers linked to the school network, and thereby explore themes that have been introduced in class. Furthermore, this type of school lays special emphasis on promoting 'integrated' courses in which, for example, ballet lessons are taught in French and arts and sciences are constantly combined. The great diversity of these schools provides their pupils with a wider choice and makes it possible to respond to the specific expectations or sensitivities of certain categories of the population, be they ethnic, linguistic or socio-economic.

The charter schools provide a transition from a system governed by supply to a more flexible type of education in which the 'consumer' is involved in the choice and development of the teaching he or she will receive. The indirect result of this is that the most promising pedagogical experiments can serve as models for reform of public education and as a 'laboratory of ideas' for defining major orientations for education in the future.

President Bill Clinton has expressed the wish that these institutions should develop to reach 3,000 in number by the beginning of the twenty-first century.

Sources: The Economist, 22 February 1997; 17 October 1998; Center for Education Reform, *Charter Schools, Highlights and Statistics,* 1997.

mission chaired by Jacques Delors, 'administrative decentralization and the autonomy of establishments would seem, in most cases, to lead to the development and the generalization of innovation'.[11]

Another example of educational innovation is provided by the SHELCOM programme, developed by the National Center for Adult Literacy (NCAL), located at the University of Pennsylvania, which illustrates the social role new technologies can play in integrating disadvantaged populations by broadening access to education. The programme is geared primarily to the homeless and provides literacy courses for adults on a network linked to the Internet. The people involved can access this network using computers installed in special centres. A programme of this kind enables the homeless not only to acquire basic knowledge but also, quite frequently, to recover their self-esteem and to have a better chance of becoming integrated into society again.

The Development of Distance Education

In the industrialized countries, distance education has been developing steadily, thus contributing to the objective of lifelong education for all. For example, the Open University is now the largest educational institution in the United Kingdom. Its courses are followed by more than 200,000 people and the university makes ample use of new technologies: 'virtual courses' are offered, together with group discussions and the correction of homework via the Internet. In 1997, the students were able, on a daily basis, to read some 150,000 electronic messages on over 5,000 lectures provided by the Internet.

Nevertheless, the industrialized countries are not and should not be the only ones affected by the development of these programmes. New media forms should above all serve those countries that must provide for the education of a very large number of adults, provided they are combined with traditional – and still essential – methods of imparting knowledge. It entails not replacing traditional methods of training and of information transmission by new methods but seeing them in their complementary roles and enabling all countries to develop at their own pace. It is worth recalling that, according to a UNDP report for 1993, average access to traditional methods of communication in the developing countries in relation to their availability in the industrialized countries was 5% for the telephone, 25% for the postal service, 10% for books and television and 16% for newspapers and the radio. Substantial efforts will therefore have to be made as regards 'traditional' technologies, which are often less costly than new ones. Nevertheless, in contexts of economic and geographical isolation, the new information technologies can contribute, with the help of a sound tutoring system, to meeting needs in the fields of information, basic education and continuous education.

The many initiatives in the countries of the South already show how conscious they are of the advantages they could derive from distance education and a judicious use of modern communication infrastructure for educational purposes. Experiments of this kind deserve to be underlined as they highlight a vital point: it is for the poorest populations that the new technologies can prove to be of the greatest use and are particularly promising. In that regard, the Joint Initiative on Distance Education launched in 1993 by UNESCO at the Summit on Education for All in New Delhi was remarkable. It enabled nine highly populated countries from the South (Bangladesh, Brazil, China, Egypt, India, Indonesia, Mexico, Nigeria and Pakistan) to share their experience and to combine their efforts in the field of distance education. These countries, which account for 70% of the illiterate population of our planet and over half of all children without schooling in the world, have realized how much progress can be achieved in education without frontiers – particularly by using satellites spreading information even to the remotest villages.[12] This example of South–South cooperation now exists in addition to the multiple forms of North–South cooperation in the field of distance education, particularly between the countries of the Commonwealth and within the French-speaking world (in the latter, through the action of the Institut de recherche pour le développement en coopération – IRD, formerly ORSTOM).

Apart from two exceptions, the countries mentioned above have also developed distance education programmes by making use of more traditional resources (the distribution of printed teaching material or audio and video cassettes, radio and television programmes) or by combining the use of traditional and new media. In India, for instance, the National Open School has provided basic education and enabled over 250,000 students to obtain professional qualifications. In 1996, 35 traditional universities and five open universities offered distance education courses in India.[13] In China, Pakistan, Nigeria and Egypt, distance education is a particularly essential tool in teacher-training programmes. In Mexico, Telesecundaria broadcasts educational programmes throughout national territory thanks to the Solidaridad satellite system. Similarly, the educational programme in Brazil, Um Salto para o futuro (A leap towards the future), is aimed at training and providing support to teachers by combining satellite broadcasting and direct intervention by telephone. Furthermore, the Federal University of Para in Brazil has set up a distance-education programme for reaching the communities of the Amazonian region, who often live more than 1,000 kilometres from each other. What is remarkable is the fact that out of the eleven largest distance-education institutions in the world (those which in 1996 had over 100,000 students enrolled in diploma courses), eight were in the developing countries.[14]

Distance education is of special interest to the African countries. Thus, the Portuguese-speaking countries of Africa (Angola, Cape Verde, Guinea-Bissau, Mozambique and São Tome e Principe) have decided to develop a joint project entitled Interactive Instruction by Radio in order to improve the quality of teaching in schools. Similarly, the countries of Southern and East Africa have set up the Multi-Channel Learning Base (MCLB) in order to develop alternative solutions to traditional educational methods. South Africa is leading this trend with the Colisa project (Confederation of Open Learning Institutions in South Africa). This is an agreement concluded between three South African higher education institutions for the joint development of distance education and the creation of a technology centre that can be accessed from anywhere in the world. Together, the three institutions have approximately 250,000 students, which means that Colisa is one of the ten largest higher education institutions in the world. This constitutes an original response to the rising number of students and the need to promote universal access to education. Naturally, UNESCO lends its support to this movement by encouraging practical activities: it has, for example, recently proposed to set up learning networks for African teachers with a view to introducing them to the Internet and facilitating their access to that network. The project will link the teacher-training colleges of the African countries to the Internet in order to set up local, national and regional networks.

Lifelong Education for All

The assimilation of constantly evolving technologies and scientific knowledge requires a faculty of adaptation and a desire to learn, which educational systems must promote. Today, the accumulation of information is less important than the development of learning faculties. Admittedly, that has always been the fundamental purpose of education. Education must train individuals who are capable of learning by themselves, people who have learned how to learn. This is all the more essential as most forecasting experts predict considerable 'volatility' in the labour market; it is impossible to know precisely which professions will provide opportunities 10 or 20 years from now.

The education system must therefore strike a balance between theoretical knowledge accumulated and passed on by the community and the application of such knowledge by individuals in specific contexts. The inadequacy of traditional educational systems is largely due to the gap that exists between theoretical learning and practical applications. If they were to be harmonized, this could lead in the coming decades to the reorganization of time spent learning, of which a part could then be spent in a working environment. Admittedly, ending the traditional opposition between 'study time' and 'work time' will inevitably raise problems of management and organization. Making a distinction between the learning process and its professional application has become impossible in a society where scientific discoveries and the practical applications of those discoveries follow one another at an increasingly fast pace, distinctly shorter than a lifetime or an individual's career. That is why school should offer every individual not a specialization but rather the capacity to change specializations during his or her lifetime and to cope with economic and social change. That is also why education should be multidisciplinary, not only providing a vital minimum of literary and scientific knowledge, but also serving as a preparation for civic, cultural, social and family life. As Paul Valéry wrote in 1935 in *Bilan de l'intelligence*, 'the most forbidding machines are not material but composed of specialized individuals, they are built in imitation of a mind and of what is quite impersonal about it'.

Education should thus be seen no longer as a period of apprenticeship limited in time, but as a lifelong process. Strictly social solutions are not enough to cope with unemployment. We should use education as a remedy if we wish to compensate for skill losses which will be increasingly frequent in a constantly changing economy and technological sphere. Post-school training in all its alternative forms should become a priority, both for making up for the deficit in scholastic literacy and for preventing the spread of subsequent illiteracy and the devaluation of acquired skills. Encouragement should be given to academic experiments in the workplace or complementary to the workplace, in such a way that failure in preliminary schooling does not become a 'curse' that pursues the individual throughout his lifetime. In that context, governments should encourage adult education as underlined in 1997 at the Hamburg Conference organized by UNESCO on that theme. For example, distance education at the University of Phoenix, Arizona already reaches 32,000 adult students, most of whom attend evening classes on three dozen campuses located in eleven states and Puerto Rico.[15]

To ensure crucial access to lifelong training and education, Jacques Delors has proposed the creation of a study-time entitlement, a sort of 'training voucher' whereby everyone would be entitled to a certain number of years of education that he or she would use according to choice, life experience, academic background and convenience. This solution would enable individuals to decide on the nature and duration of their studies, as well as when they would be pursued, on the basis of their specific needs.

This vision of education means that the role of the university in particular should be redefined.[16] A university can no longer operate in isolation. It must break free from the image of either a diploma factory or an ivory tower in order to become, first, a local resource of development and, second, a cultural hub. As emphasized by Eduardo Portella, president of the General Conference of UNESCO, in his opening address to the World Conference on Higher Education, 'educating at a higher level means teaching the theory and practice of how to relate to others through the consolidation of cultural plurality'.[17] The university of the twenty-first century will inevitably be citizen-based and will need to play a decisive role in the consolidation of democracy. Universities should also open up to the professional world and take account of society's real needs. Many universities already offer courses in the framework of ongoing training, aimed at adults who wish to upgrade their skills or acquire new ones. Continuous training is the practical manifestation of lifelong education: today, education should be a lifelong experience. But this opportunity must be made available to all as Article 26.1 of the Universal Declaration of Human Rights stipulates, 'higher education shall be equally accessible to all on the basis of merit'. Will the twenty-first century revive the spirit of the Greek philosopher Socrates, who in antiquity put forward as a principle that education was a lifelong concern?

Individual Careers and Common Values

Regardless of the didactic and pedagogical methods used, education should never lose sight of its humanistic and pluralistic vocation. The Declaration of the International Conference on Education in Geneva in 1994 is eloquent enough: 'If we wish truly to protect diversity and stimulate our potential to become masters of our lives, in order to trace our own future, the educational system should not be uniform and rigid but, insofar as possible, should resort to a personalized approach. *We should have teachers who monitor the progress of every child and enhance the potential of every student because every one of them is unique* [emphasis added]'.[18] School should develop the particular abilities and talents of every individual, thereby breaking with the model of the standard-ized school, which imposes a virtually identical curriculum on all pupils on the basis of a one-dimensional view of intelligence. School should offer a wider variety of subjects and teaching styles as well as opportunities for training outside school. It could then optimize the potential of every individual by giving the possibility of cultivating the most distinct features of his or her personality.[19]

Education in the twenty-first century will therefore have to be adapted to the individual and must build the cultural values and ethical references of a citizens' society. The impetus of knowledge and technology that transforms the world should not lead to the fragmentation of knowledge and to an incapacity to provide peaceful solutions to conflicts through democracy and negotiation. It is vital that this store of knowledge that human beings are building up should not become a Tower of Babel in which every individual speaks a language that he or she alone could understand. Our societies must give constant and critical thought to defining a standard corpus of knowledge for all: in this regard the importance of philosophy and history conceived as scientific disciplines should be emphasized. From that point of view, the theoretical training provided by traditional educational systems plays an essential part in forming a collective imagination and common representations that guarantee the identity of cultural groups, as well as in learning critical reflection, without which democracy is but an empty word. What matters therefore, in the twenty-first century, is not to cut back on the teaching of philosophy and history but to extend and improve it. Philosophy should be introduced in the final year or, better still, in the last two years of secondary education in those countries where it is not yet taught. As for history, this subject should, without omitting national history, be opened up much more to regional and world history.

History and philosophy in fact reflect the essential values human beings pass on to their children through education. General knowledge is of great importance when it is seen not through an encyclopaedic approach but as an instrument for perceiving problems and viewing our relationship with others and as a basis for the rehabilitation of the long term and the ethics of the future. The universal access to knowledge should help the foundation of a human community on a national, continental and world scale. After all, the Delors Commission considered that one of the four pillars of education was that it should teach us not only to know, to do and to be, but also to live together. With that aim in mind, civics classes are a priority for school: one or two hours a week should be set aside for it as early as primary school and it should be taught throughout secondary education.

School plays an essential role in preparing for citizenship. It would be unthinkable to abandon this traditional task at a time when cultural values and landmarks are less and less transmitted by the family and by social structures. The concept of citizenship should therefore be renewed, taking into account the specificities of various groups and the changes affecting them: citizenship should be able to encompass local, national, regional and worldwide preoccupations. To that end, UNESCO emphasizes the need for reform in educational curricula so that they give more attention to the promotion of a culture of peace. They should no longer be exclusively concerned with national identities at a time when cultural interpenetration is growing:

without denationalizing education, the time has come to universalize it, in every sense of the term, in order to prepare young people to experience pluralism and cultural hybridization. Education should encourage all forms of dialogue in society or between societies so as to foster agreement on common learning objectives, in a world that is becoming more global, more diversified and better informed.

A New Relationship with Knowledge

Adopting a new approach to education means accepting the scope and diversity of knowledge, particularly of the knowledge linked to science and technology. New curricula should include new items of knowledge, such as developments in biology and astrophysics. Teaching and assessment methods are still frequently out of step with reality and people's aspirations, particularly in relation to developments in the job market, technology and society. Furthermore, they do not always take account of the difficulties the weakest students have to contend with. We shall therefore have to display imagination in the way we devise new programmes so that they may be open to new subjects and take account of the diversity of the students for whom they are intended.[20]

With that aim in mind, further consideration should be given to the way knowledge is built up, a process that could be termed 'meta-cognition'[21] or, more simply, reflexive knowledge, which helps us learn how to learn. If we are able to understand how knowledge is assimilated, we will be in a better position to control our own processes of assimilation consciously and deliberately, which may vary from one field or type of knowledge to another. This means being in a position to master our reasoning and the way our memory works and to enrich and diversify the ways in which we learn. The learning process and its practical applications, as well as the pursuit of knowledge as a lifelong process, largely depend on the ability to master the cognitive approach adapted to its object. That is one of the conditions for ridding ourselves of the fear of the new, a fear that is often responsible for mental blocks, particularly among adults. There are already models for effectively solving problems that highlight the importance of the initial approach to the issue and the way we view the initial data. They can help us to plan solutions by linking up the facts of the problem, the people who have the expertise and the unknown factors needing to be elucidated. This is an important step as, according to the cognitive approach, the path we follow often matters more than the goal we reach. It would be fair to say that the underlying meaning of the learning process is to absorb what has been taught and to assimilate it.

The principles that underlie the use of new technologies are the same as those that determine the learning process. On the one hand, this process establishes a person-to-person relationship, reciprocity between teacher and student, and, on the other hand, the learning process is all the more successful if it is pursued on the initiative of the student, guided by well-designed educational systems, and teachers who are familiar with new approaches and reliable assessment methods. And that is precisely what the great transformation that the new technologies are introducing into learning methods has to offer: networks are built on the principle of personal initiative and enable interactivity with ideas and data as much as with people. Not only do they leave it to the individual to explore, navigate, check and validate, they also encourage collaboration in the production of knowledge between teachers and students. Furthermore, they make possible representations of the cognitive approach through which knowledge can be assessed, compiled and retrieved as required. Henceforth, the coupling of the computer and the network provides – if adequate guidance is available – a very substantial capacity for supporting and extending cognitive approaches that, above and beyond the ability to access databases, offers the possibility of observation and above all conversation between pupil and teacher.

Nevertheless, the new relationship with knowledge that will gradually come into being in the twenty-first century will have to go beyond a mere technological and scientific *aggiornamento*. It supposes a more radical transformation or, to borrow Edgar Morin's expression, a genuine 'reform of the mind',[22] in which far greater emphasis would be laid on the complexity of problems, the globality and multidimensional aspect of events, whereby links could be established between various types of reality and various forms of knowledge. Such a 'reform' is necessary if we wish to define education otherwise than through strictly quantitative criteria. This does not mean that we may neglect material resources that are indispensable to ensure that the educational system operates satisfactorily; however, this is not enough. Efforts must also be made to promote new ideas, otherwise reforms will have to be made that, on every occasion, will have no more than a palliative role, without our being able to modify the fundamentals of the educational process. Edgar Morin provided a very accurate description of the vicious circle of educational reform when he wrote: 'We cannot reform the institution without having first of all reformed the minds, but we cannot reform the minds if we have not first of all reformed the institutions.' Educational reform, if based on a radical 'rethinking', should open the door to a reform to participation aimed at enabling every citizen to contribute to decision-making and to have a right to examine that process. In other words, reforming the way we think about problems is the key to participation in a cognitive democracy relying on access to lifelong education for all.[23]

A New Teacher–Pupil Relationship: Education as an Interactive Communication Link

It is sometimes said that the inertia of education systems results from their traditional function of reproducing and preserving rather than innovating. And yet, school should first and foremost be a place for innovation. It is on those terms that school will respond effectively to the discrepancy between the already emerging requirements and the absence of reform in structure and types of training. The gradual emergence of an education society provides an opportunity of going beyond the traditional image of the learning process concentrated in a particular period of time, youth, in a particular place, school, and entrusted to just one teacher or a successive or simultaneous series of individual teachers. The hybridization of methods of access to knowledge and the *diversification* of the players in education are essential for the creation of education without distance, guaranteeing a society without distance. Encouraging the combination and reciprocal borrowing of practices between formal, informal (for example with museums and other cultural institutions) and distance education, or work experience programmes, is a crucial issue for the coming decades.

School must, of course, preserve its role as a meeting place, a place of learning and of socialization with the twofold aim of imparting knowledge and fashioning citizenship. It is not merely the creation of a 'computer network', but also a social network, as schools can be linked to each other not only through a network but also through their immediate environment with parents, for example, thereby opening up to new sources of information, new communication resources and new areas of debate. Henceforth, school will be a hub for a vast range of information, communication and learning technologies. It will become the hub of such a network by giving access to local resources, guiding individual vocations and conducting constant assessment of results.

Nevertheless, incorporating new technologies in learning processes cannot be undertaken to the detriment of the interpersonal relationship between teacher and student. Education is still fundamentally an interaction between people, between their visions of the world, their skills and their values. New technologies can broaden and diversify that relationship. Their most enthusiastic advocates, such as those in charge of the Open University in the United Kingdom, acknowledge that distance education made possible thanks to the Internet is no substitute for books or a privileged relationship between teacher and student.[24] Quite simply, 'the computer can never replace a teacher surrounded by his students'.[25] At a time in history when inventions and innovations are appearing more and more rapidly, it is important that disciplines, particularly sciences, should be taught in a lively manner, both in school and out of it. Of greatest interest are the efforts of scientists such as the Czech astronomer Jiri Grygar or the astrophysicist Javant V. Narlikar, winners of UNESCO's Kalinga Prize for the Popularization of Science in 1996, who have brought science closer to a wider public, particularly the young, through works of popularization and radio and television programmes. Equally exemplary is the work of Robert Swann from the UK (UNESCO's special envoy for the environment and the first man to have reached both the North and South poles on foot), who led an expedition to the Antarctic with 35 explorers aged 16 to 24.

Changing schools and diversifying their functions also raises the question of the role and therefore the training of the fundamental figure of the teacher. Teachers will no longer be the sole dispensers of specialized knowledge. Their role could become more diversified and rewarding on condition that training and social recognition corresponding to their responsibilities, combined with adequate pay, give them the necessary capacity and will. Their main duty will be to impart knowledge to others but they will be required to clarify the objectives and purpose of the learning process, to guide their pupils in their development, to create collective dynamism in the classes entrusted to them, to assess pupils on a continuous basis but also to evaluate and inventory worthwhile and accessible sources of learning. A teacher's competence will then combine mastery of knowledge, familiarity with the students and a capacity to devise suitable learning conditions. More so than in the past, teaching cannot be limited to the mere passing on of knowledge.

Teacher training is decisive for the training of future generations. Major efforts must be planned in this field, particularly as regards new techniques for processing and disseminating information. Teaching is the profession for which permanent training is most vital. The time has come for greater recognition to be given to the growing responsibility that falls to teachers in the training of citizens, professionals and human beings in general at a time when social and family structures are less able to cope with these challenges.

The Transformation of Publishing Systems

Careful consideration needs to be given to methods for managing networks as sources of knowledge, that is to say, adapting publishing methods to network operations. Publishing systems play the strategic role of an ancillary system to the educational system, which, if the latter is to operate properly, has become indispensable and goes far beyond the scope of educational publications. Adaptation of publishing systems will naturally take the form of what is referred to as electronic publishing, with the development of CD-ROMs and shortly DVDs, whereby information can be recorded, stored and retrieved in a mixed form (pictures, sound and data), which is more diversified than that provided by books and, above all, more likely to be adaptable to use on the networks and easier to archive and reprocess.

But the true function of publishing is not so much to choose a medium as to select a content. Publishing means sorting, eliminating, drafting and re-drafting texts and information. Nevertheless, one of the major criticisms levelled at the Internet today is that it completely overlooks the editing function. There perhaps lies its limit. Only quality sites, whose content will have been the subject of careful appraisal, can stand out and outlast the current confusion surrounding the network. Particularly outstanding sites will be enhanced by functions relating to selection, identification (through hypertextual links whereby a particular quality site can easily refer to another quality site) and annotation. The emergence of quality sites already shows great diversity rather than uniformity through 'cloning', as had been feared. Encouragement must be given to this creativity and diversity in excellence, as a guarantee of genuine cultural pluralism without reference to any dominant model.

The development of education in the twenty-first century will require a network that is at least partly 'edited' – while the rest of the network will correspond to conversation functions that are complementary to those which concern data access. One of the obstacles to the introduction of publishing on the Internet is in fact one of its fundamental virtues and singularities: its prevailingly non-economic character. Massive publishing in this sector will occur only once 'non-economic' conditions have changed. In turn, such change will be made possible only once the telecommunications companies have offered rates which encourage traffic. One of the major issues in the next 20 years will be to manage the joint development of educational, publishing and telecommunications systems. Public policies could safeguard their educational dimension. It is therefore through partnerships between public and private sectors in the peripheral areas of education, which are none the less essential to society, that one of the keys can be found to the development of educational systems and therefore of learning procedures.

The Role of Public Authorities

What should be the role of the public authorities during the next 20 years? Given the scale of investments that will be required to tackle the issues referred to earlier, and considering that their profitability will remain very largely indirect and that education should continue to be a priority field of solidarity, public authorities will have to continue providing massive funding to the education sector – which is not in contradiction with the need for more flexible, devolved forms of management for educational enterprises. Guiding this reform of educational management will be one of the major challenges during the first two decades of the twenty-first century.

Public authorities will have to ensure the promulgation of educational standards, responsibility for which could be assigned to autonomous reference institutions that would be better able to monitor developments in the expertise, needs and aspirations of society and knowledge related to cognitive and learning processes.

Finally, public authorities should enter into strategic partnership with the publishing and telecommunications sectors. Joint action of this kind, while respecting the nature of such enterprises, which are usually profit-making, could help to devise safeguards against the excesses of networks (calls for violence, racism and paedophilia) and promote carefully targeted pricing policies likely to encourage the development of learning tools that would improve the quality and productivity of education. In this regard, the choice of judicious economic policies will be crucial for the success or failure of the transformation of educational systems. Those countries that make the right strategic choices, while taking account of their traditions, will find themselves in possession of distinct advantages in economic terms. They will be able to help not only their populations but also the least privileged sections of those populations to establish points of reference, strengthen their cohesion and embrace the various facets of citizenship that each and every one of us must increasingly refer to during the twenty-first century.

Will we succeed in creating an educational system that can abolish distance between peoples and within nations while managing to preserve certain points of reference, such as the meaning of education, a feeling of belonging and the values bestowed by it, without which any notion of ethical cohesion disappears? Humanity now possesses the instruments to reduce distances in this way. From now on, it must use them and share them out equitably. The diversification of forms of knowledge, the extension of the learning process to the whole human lifespan and the synthesis of all forms of education, whether formal or informal, should be supported by a culture of learning that considers knowledge not as an end in itself but as a stage in humanity's quest for knowing what it is, a quest in which the path is an end in itself. The culture of learning derives its substances from the cultural diversity of groups, nations and continents. It is a culture of questioning, of acting, of experimenting without fear, a culture of exploring and planning, a technical culture centred on the solving of problems. Such a culture, however, is fragile, and is likely to dry up, to become purely technical, to become fragmented into groups isolated by their own codes and their own rites of initiation. One of the major challenges in the decades to come will be to ensure the overall expansion of this culture of learning, to make it more dynamic and to sustain it in the long term. This will depend on the genius of peoples and the generosity of individuals.

Lifelong education for all will be the decisive issue in the twenty-first century because it is already the key to peace, growth and development, democracy and respect for the environment and cultures.

Pointers and Recommendations

- Promote lifelong education for all: give priority, in this regard, to adult education, particularly for women, through intensive technical and vocational training in their own language, the universalization of basic education and the inclusion of the excluded.
- Encourage continuous training for teachers and the upgrading of their skills in order to create an interactive context for a lifelong learning process at all levels.
- Devise all education systems along a dual axis: encourage all personal initiatives of knowledge acquisition and available methods and offer everyone a basic education that is a source of personal development, cultural and ethical identity and civil responsibility. Education must both build societies and train individuals; redefined civics classes should, to that end, be given priority in the whole range of curricula.
- Anchor local dimension in worldwide dimension and individual dimension in collective and civic dimension: accentuate the interpersonal relations in the exchange of information, provide scope for the expression of all local and regional specificities within the worldwide network, while preventing the creation of any hegemonic culture.
- Devise an education system in its plurality: plurality of methods, plurality of careers, plurality of traditional and new instruments, plurality of actors, plurality of contexts (schools, but also libraries, museums, local communities and governments, enterprises and family); plurality of time sequences (childhood learning stages, but also professional life and leisure and retirement).
- Enrich the concept of knowledge: moving from the idea of knowledge through accumulation to the concept of awareness of methods and objectives. Learning to learn rather than merely learning. The training of teachers who are completely familiar with the new technologies and the new requirements of society must be a priority.
- Encourage all initiatives aiming at universal access to the new information technologies, universal not only within countries but also between the industrialized and the developing countries, in order to reduce all forms of bipolarity. As regards education, the aim should be to establish a worldwide network of education accessible to all, without frontiers or distance of any kind.
- Develop at national and international levels policies for building communication infrastructure, whether traditional (libraries, audio-visual and

computer equipment) or related to new technologies (multimedia, CD-ROMs, connection to the Internet), by placing special emphasis on disadvantaged and isolated areas and by attending the interface of this infrastructure.

- Transform universities into centres which can provide lifelong education for all, in accordance with Article 26.1 of the Universal Declaration of Human Rights that stipulates that 'access to higher education shall be equally accessible to all on the basis of merit'.

- Grant to every individual a 'training voucher', providing access to a number of years of education which every individual can use according to choice, career, academic experience and time scale.

Notes

1. Estimates and forecasts regarding illiteracy, Division of Statistics, UNESCO, 1999.

2. *Le Monde*, 20 November 1997.

3. Jérôme Bindé, 'L'analphabète, Condorcet et l'ordinateur: formation, société d'information et transformation sociale. Tendances et problèmes de l'éducation dans les pays industrialisés', unpublished paper, UNESCO, 1988.

4. *Rapport du Forum de réflexion sur l'éducation à distance*, submitted to the Executive Board of UNESCO at its 142nd session, document 142 EX/37, 1993.

5. Michel Serres, *Atlas*, 1995, quoted by the author in an article in *Le Monde de l'éducation*, March 1997.

6. Daniel Cohen, *The Wealth of the World and the Poverty of Nations*, trans. Jacqueline Lindenfeld, MIT Press, Cambridge, MA, 1998.

7. There is a current trend in our societies towards the resurgence of inequalities within each socio-cultural category, within each age group, at each level of qualification and in every sector of the economy. This idea rests on the fact that in the world of work, minor differences in skills between two workers often lead to major differences in pay and production. The consequence is a matching of workers according to their level of skills and a disparity between the elite and the rest of the workforce at all levels in the production process. Similarly, differences in pay and productivity are very significant between countries where levels of skill differ considerably. Michael Kremer, 'The O-Ring theory of economic development', *Quarterly Journal of Economics*, Vol. 58, No. 3, August 1993; Daniel Cohen, *The Wealth of the World and the Poverty of Nations*.

8. Michael Kremer and Eric Maskin, *Segregation by Skill and the Rise of Inequality*, MIT Press, Cambridge, MA, 1996.

9. *OECD Observer*, No. 199, April–May 1996.

10. *The Futurist*, World Future Society, Bethesda, July–August 1995.

11. *Learning: The Treasure Within*, report to UNESCO by the International Commission on Education for the Twenty-first Century, chaired by Jacques Delors, UNESCO Publishing, Paris, 1996.

12. J. Visser, *Distance Education for the Nine High-Population Countries*, UNESCO, Paris, 1994.

13. S. Manjulika and V. Venugopal Reddy, *Distance Education in India: A Model for Developing Countries*, Vikas Publishing, New Delhi, 1996.

14. J. S. Daniel, *Mega-Universities and Knowledge Media: Technology Strategies for Higher Education*, Kogan Page, London, 1996.

15. Joseph Rosenbloom, 'On U.S. campuses, a rush to click on to computerized learning', *International Herald Tribune*, 11 February 1997.

16. See Declaration and Plan of Action of the World Conference on Higher Education, UNESCO, Paris, 5–9 October 1998.

17. Eduardo Portella, *La Troisième université*, World Conference on Higher Education, UNESCO, 5 October 1998.

18. Declaration at the 44th session of the International Conference on Education (1994).

19. See Howard Gardner: 'Fostering diversity through personalized education: implications of a new understanding of human', *Prospects*, Vol. 28, No. 3, September 1997.

20. See 'The curriculum redefined: schooling for the 21st century', OECD document, 1994 (particularly a paper by Roberto Carneiro, 'Curriculum for the 21st century).

21. See Goéry Delacôte, *Savoir Apprendre – les nouvelles méthodes*, Odile Jacob, Paris, 1996.

22. *Réforme de la pensée*.

23. Jérôme Bindé, 'Complexité et crise de la représentation', in *Représentation et Complexité*, second meeting of the Millennium Agenda, Educam/UNESCO/ISSC, Rio de Janeiro, 1997.

24. Barry James, 'Online lessons: defining limits – jury is still out on role of the new technology', *International Herald Tribune*, 11 February 1997.

25. Jacques Delors, address given at the 45th session of the International Conference on Education in Geneva (30 September–5 October 1996).

PART FOUR

Towards a New Ethical Contract

. . . .

CHAPTER 17

Will There be an 'African Miracle'?

§ WILL there be an 'African miracle', similar to the 'Asian miracle'? The Asian model has demonstrated, the recent financial crisis notwithstanding, that it is possible to sustain consistently strong economic growth for almost thirty years.[1] It should not be forgotten that the 'Asian tigers' were at the same level of socio-economic development in 1960 as sub-Saharan Africa is today. For example, South Korea was at the level of Nigeria today, but is now ranked 30th worldwide (Nigeria is 142nd); as for Thailand, which in 1960 was at the same level as the Democratic Republic of the Congo is today, the UNDP now places it 59th on the world list (the DRC is 143rd).[2]

However, such a 'miracle', which implies far more than economic growth alone, is possible only at the cost of radical changes which would impel Africa to development on a new scale. These changes would include major political and administrative reforms aimed at improving the management and quality of public services, a widespread adult education programme, fundamental reforms to education systems, the expansion of distance learning, a significant cut in arms spending, priority investment in health care, the effective use of agricultural resources and the adoption of sustainable farming techniques, a reassessment of the relationship between urban and rural areas in favour of the latter, the development of credit and micro-credit systems, adjustments in urban policy-making, programmes on behalf of women, the exploitation of renewable energy resources, the promotion of African cultures and the massive development of a telecommunications infrastructure. The international community will have to play its part in the 'miracle' by cancelling or converting the greater part of African debt to give the continent a chance to buy into growth industries.

Since the 1980s sub-Saharan Africa has been in deep crisis. In 1993 around 40% of the population survived on less than one dollar a day. On average, between 45% and 50% live below the absolute poverty line.[3] In 1997, fully 31 of the world's 48 'least developed countries' were in sub-Saharan Africa,[4] as were 31 of the 44 countries on the UNDP's list of those where human development was qualified as 'weak'.[5] Sub-Saharan Africa has the highest rates of overall and infant mortality on the planet, the shortest life expectancy, the lowest per capita income and the fastest rate of population increase.[6] Two-thirds of all Africans have inadequate access to clean drinking water, and more than half have no access to public health care. The region is at the mercy of a wide range of diseases, including malaria, sexually transmitted diseases, tuberculosis and the major childhood illnesses.[7] Two-thirds of all carriers of the HIV virus are to be found in sub-Saharan Africa (where around 21 million individuals are infected), and AIDS affects one-quarter of the adult population in some countries. As a cause of mortality, AIDS is on the point of overtaking malaria, which kills almost 2 million Africans every year (90% of the victims worldwide), most of whom are young children.[8] In several countries of the region, armed conflict, the AIDS pandemic and the burden of debt hinder and even reverse what little hard-won progress has been made. Sub-Saharan Africa has 46 countries with a total of 605 million inhabitants, or roughly 10% of the world's population; however, it makes up only 2% of world GDP.[9] Its share of world trade is just 2.5% – no more than that of Belgium.[10]

To make matters worse, the third industrial revolution and the accompanying phenomenon of globalization will probably remain of little benefit to Africa for some time to come. This is because they are the results of a dematerialization of the economy and the unusually rapid introduction of replacement sectors in the fields of science and technology, for which Africa as a whole is poorly prepared.[11] At the same time, however, they are based on a new economy of industries and services with a high 'value-added' cultural component whose market is a global one. In this way they open up new opportunities for Africa, provided the continent succeeds in exploiting its very rich potential for the development of culture-based industries, such as fashion, textile manufacture and design, the service sector, small and medium-sized businesses and craft industries, cultural tourism and eco-tourism.

Beyond all the worries, then, there are some real signs of hope for Africa which any forecasts must take into account. Demographic patterns show one of the welcome surprises of the present decade. Outside Uganda, Zambia and Zimbabwe, where it has been cut by the AIDS epidemic to under 50 years, life expectancy has shown a continuous increase, and the proportion of young people surviving childhood diseases is constantly increasing.[12] That the 'culture of extreme fertility' that formerly characterized the African continent is in retreat on all sides is evidenced, for example, by the rise in the age at marriage, the increase in contraception and the spacing out of childbirth rather than giving up the idea of having children. No 1980s demographer, surely, would have dared to predict what is taking place in front of our very eyes: not only is fertility declining, but this sharp decline is confirmed in the

'African fertility model' now emerging. Does this indicate, as several experts now believe, a demographic trend towards the end of 'the African exception'?[13]

Economically speaking, too, African countries are showing some encouraging signs of improvement.[14] Is this just a remission, or is full recovery on the way? In 1996–97, for the first time since 1979–80, per capita GDP in Africa rose for two years in succession, and growth exceeded 5% in eleven states.[15] In 1997, average GDP growth in sub-Saharan Africa stood at 4.6%. According to the World Bank, real annual GDP growth in the region for the period 2001–07 will reach around 4.1%.[16] However, the region would really need to grow by 8 to 10% every year[17] if it is to make the necessary qualitative advances (given that the rate of population growth is almost 3% per annum). The fact that global economic growth is currently benefiting sub-Saharan Africa less than other developing countries cannot be ignored.[18]

There is still a long way to go, and the overall situation in Africa remains very uneven. Yet the idea that 'Africa's fate' is to be condemned automatically to poverty and instability is absurd. On the contrary, we are convinced that Africa will manage on its own to find the way out of the crisis, as soon as attempts at imposing unsuitable and costly development models from abroad cease. We need first of all to do away with the defeatist doctrine of 'Afro-pessimism', which all too frequently colours our view of Africa. The international community and Africa itself must learn to exploit the continent's enormous potential and outstanding creative energy, both of which simply need to be given the opportunity to reach their full expression. Far from being the problem, Africa is the solution. Just consider the extraordinary vitality of African culture in such varied fields as literature, cinema, painting, sculpture, dancing, music, handicrafts and traditional popular art forms.[19] But it must seize its destiny with both hands. It must begin the process of 're-possessing' itself.

Peace in Africa: The Key to Development

At the dawn of the twenty-first century, the greatest threat facing Africa is the proliferation of conflict situations. In the words of Kofi Annan: 'Since 1970, more than 30 wars have been fought in Africa, the vast majority of them intra-State in origin. In 1996 alone, 14 of the 53 countries of Africa were afflicted by armed conflicts, accounting for more than half of all war-related deaths worlwide and resulting in more than 8 million refugees, returnees and displaced persons.'[20] The primary victims of these conflicts are civilians: according to General Amadou Toumani Touré, 92% of the victims of war and of the famine that so often accompanies war are women and children.[21] How can the international community go on closing its eyes to such undeniable war crimes, committed during recent and ongoing conflicts, as the recruitment of child soldiers, the barbaric employment of young boys in the task of mine-clearing or the systematic rape and forced prostitution of women? How can it continue to pass over the recurring genocide and massacre of civilians inflicted on the Great Lakes region?

The other main victim of these conflicts is the development of African countries. The African Development Bank estimates the cost of war between 1980 and 1993 at US$250 billion, or a sum equivalent to the total annual output of the continent. The extreme poverty of the people merely increases the severity of the successive crises. In Liberia and Sierra Leone, refugees account for 10% of the population, and in many countries there are ever greater numbers of street children.[22] During the Audience Africa, African leaders themselves meeting at UNESCO made the following statement:

> as long as the idea of peace is mistreated in Africa, efforts to promote develop-ment will never live up to expectations. Armed conflicts, civil wars, border disputes, tribalism and ethnic rivalries, political disputes and the exploitation of religion for partisan ends make it only realistic to regard political instability and war not as epiphenomena but as a serious and ongoing trend. We can reverse this trend, which has gone on for 50 years, but we shall need an inflexible political will.[23]

Strangely, the violence tearing Africa apart spares the interests of the major transnational firms and businesses, which, however extreme the conflict and killing, are in most cases continuing to exploit local natural resources in complete security. Let us be honest: in many cases war persists because it is profitable. As Kofi Annan has pointed out, the natural resources of Liberia, Angola, Sierra Leone and other countries feed internal conflict and profit international arms dealers.[24]

Despite their huge scale, these murderous conflicts do not receive the media attention they deserve; nor do they arouse the same degree of indignation as certain other wars. The international community and public opinion cannot go on being passive in the face of such slaughter, with its interminable procession of dead and wounded, its humiliations and destructiveness. The United Nations needs to be given the means of protecting the weak, civilians and refugees. It is my strong conviction that, when the very concept of statehood fails under the shock of civil war, or human rights are violated on a massive scale, the UN is duty-bound to take action under the responsibility of the Security Council.

However, in the case of Africa we must not satisfy ourselves with the logic of humanitarian action, which is concerned less with cause than with effect and all too frequently takes the place of long-term action and vision – that is, when it is not diverted and instrumentalized to the point of prolonging conflict rather than bringing it to a close. As Kofi Annan has said, of special concern is the fact that humanitarian assistance is sometimes treated as a substitute for political action rather than as a supplement.[25] Not only must peace be re-established, it must above all be solidly built on massive investment in sectors which will provide some hope for the future of the people: education, health care, communication, culture and sustainable development. At the dawn of the twenty-first century, particular priority must be given in Africa to education.

Massive Investment in Lifelong Education for All

Ever since independence, enormous advances have been made in Africa in the field of education. No other continent has progressed so quickly towards literacy in so little time: between 1980 and 1995, the proportion of people aged 15 upwards in sub-Saharan Africa who were unable to read or write fell from 59.8% to 43.2%, and school enrolment figures grew constantly (primary attendance rose by 4% during 1990–94, compared with 2% on average for the whole of the developing world).[26] Between 1990 and 1995, the number of pupils in primary education increased by 10.3 million.[27]

Yet despite all the efforts made by states and international organizations, schooling and formal education have far from fulfilled their objectives. School attendance is still far lower in sub-Saharan Africa than in other developing regions (overall attendance stands at 60%, compared with 90% in Latin America and East Asia). Secondary education, which is so crucial to development, is available to only 17% of children. A tiny proportion of young Africans (in 1996, just 2% of those finishing school)[28] go on to higher education. There is still a marked difference in attendance between boys and girls.[29] And then there is the unacceptable figure stating that 41% of African children aged between 5 and 14 are at work, and that the number of 6- to 11-year-olds not attending school has risen in sub-Saharan Africa by 12 million to 44 million – two-thirds of them girls.[30]

Africa is suffering a genuine decline in schooling, marked by the fall in school enrolment in almost fifteen countries since the early 1990s.[31] States often have no more money to spend on education, rich countries are less and less inclined to finance cooperation programmes, and enrolment is seriously hindered by the fact that war in particular displaces many families on a permanent basis. During the 1990s some international funding sources withdrew their funding for education in Africa.[32] When they finally began again, their loans were accompanied by unacceptable conditions (for example, an increase in financing for primary schooling had in certain cases to be offset by a fall in budget allocations to higher education and research).

The greatest problem is the tendency of all too many families, having lost confidence in the schools, to stop enrolling their children. This may be due to the poor performance of individual schools, the lack of infrastructural support and absenteeism of teachers, who are often poorly paid, but it is also due to the cost of education in very fragile economic circumstances. One particularly disquieting development is the deteriorating economic and working conditions of teachers, who are often the first victims of structural adjustment plans and who must work in overcrowded classrooms for too little pay. As a result, they are compelled to take additional jobs, mostly in the informal economy, and the rate of absenteeism is rising. A further worrying statistic relates to the shortage of books, libraries and teaching materials.[33]

The strongly felt conclusion of the politicians and academics who met at UNESCO for Audience Africa was that 'After a period of expansion of some 20 years, education and training had been marked in recent years by the emergence of wide disparities between rich and poor, urban and rural areas and girls and boys. That was being compounded by the inability of education systems to move with the times and adapt to the requirements of an ever-changing world.'[34] The task is immense. Primary education must be made universally available once again; an end must be put to gender imbalance; the quality, effectiveness and relevance of education need to be improved; secondary and higher education must be reformed and transformed into tools with which to establish a society based on learning; and technical and vocational training opportunities must be exploited to the full.[35]

African states will have to make education for all their number one priority, alongside much broader access to secondary, vocational and higher education. Special attention will need to be given to those groups of individuals that are most under-represented (girls and those from rural areas), and distance-learning techniques must be used where necessary to reach the most isolated regions. According to Amadou Toumani Touré, former Malian president, the education crisis will begin to recede thanks to virtual universities. It will no longer be necessary for students to go abroad or even to leave their village to benefit from the best teaching. The Internet and simulated experiments will mean quality instruction for all and put an end to the brain drain.[36] It was precisely in order to reduce the brain drain, which is depriving Africa of the priceless talent of its people, that UNESCO set up the UNITWIN programme combining inter-university networks, 'UNESCO Chairs' and short-term renewable scholarships for intensive courses of study.[37] It is our view that the most important parts of such a programme are its teachers and scientists, and the specific challenges encountered in each country must be met on the spot. 'Virtual' teaching has a vital supportive role, of course, but the principal challenge lies in ensuring that human creativity can develop despite the concrete everyday problems that individuals face in their home environment. Particular emphasis must be laid on mother-tongue instruction: Audience Africa rightly stressed how important it is to guarantee each child four years of uninterrupted elementary-level teaching in his or her native tongue or, where this is impossible, in a 'national' language.[38]

Yet it is not enough merely to ensure that there is access to teaching. Teaching also has to prove its usefulness. To that end, more emphasis should certainly be placed on technical training, and courses must be made more vocational. This can be done in particular by setting up technical colleges or managing them more effectively, so that they offer short vocational courses leading to rapid qualification in the skills necessary to carry out a trade.

Much also remains to be done by way of improving the quality of higher education, as was stressed by the UNESCO Conference of Ministers of Education of African Member States meeting in April 1998 in Durban. Africa must become able on its own account to train the top people it needs; it must learn how to develop research aims to reflect local circumstances, especially in the fields of food production, solar power and other forms of renewable energy, rural poverty, health care, hygiene and housing.[39] The development of higher education structures will also have to resolve the issue of the brain drain: today, more than 30,000 Africans with a doctorate live outside Africa, so that their services benefit the industrialized world (where they are likely to have attended university) rather than the African economy. Many experts believe that the most effective solution would be to develop higher education in Africa on a regional basis, namely, by establishing regional centres of excellence. When these are set up, it is vital that they should enjoy the latest communication links, including the Internet, both with each other and with the best universities around the world.

In the future, funding for education in Africa could come from a wide range of sources:

- The state must not shirk any of its responsibilities in education matters. It was proposed during Audience Africa that countries should spend at least 5% of their GDP on education. This would mean taking a number of bold decisions, especially where budgets are concerned, as other countries (e.g. India and Brazil) have already done. Countries could share the burden and cost of education, on a jointly negotiated and mutually acceptable basis, with regions, counties, municipalities, rural communities and families.

- Africa's internal and external political relations can be no excuse for such a high (and constantly increasing) level of military expenditure (3% of GDP in 1991, compared with 0.7% in 1960). I would echo Kofi Annan's call for African countries to reduce their spending on arms and ammunition to below 1.5% of GDP and make a commitment not to increase their defence budget for ten years.[40] The funds thus made available should be reinvested in the crucial sectors of education and health, whose share of GDP should be increased each year to remedy the fact that they have been the most seriously neglected areas of social spending in times of conflict.[41]

- The international community must encourage investment in education. An annual investment of US$2.5 billion would provide sufficient funds for universal primary education in sub-Saharan Africa. One proposal seems especially promising: that of conducting a 'debt swap' to increase investment in education, science, technology and health care.[42] Rather than require destitute countries to make unproductive repayments that in turn will make further aid necessary, why not propose that developing countries (and those in Africa in particular), convert some of their debt into domestic spending on educational needs – new school buildings, teacher training, the purchase of teaching materials and investment in the new technologies?
- A further solution might be to allocate one-quarter of all development aid to the education sector. Such a proposal was made by the UNESCO commission chaired by Jacques Delors.[43]
- In view of the substantial profits which they make in African countries, transnational companies could be asked to commit at least 1% of their turnover to improving education in the countries where they operate.[44]
- As regards scientific and technological development, it has already been proposed that African countries should increase investment in this field by 0.05% of GDP every year for six to eight years, up to a minimum figure of 0.3–0.4% of GDP per annum, a percentage that would permit scientific research gradually to gain momentum. In addition, 3% of funds from the UNDP should be allocated to research and development.
- Finally, the UN should oversee a system of 'codes of conduct' for multinational companies, the aim of which would be to avoid the excessive exploitation of Africa's natural resources. Over-exploitation and the effects of 'financial colonialism' combine to make the future of Africa appear bleak indeed.

Democracy, Human Rights and the Rule of Law: Meeting the Challenges of the Future

On its own, economic growth, which is a basic condition for improving human living conditions (and ensuring their survival), is an insufficient guarantee of peace and democracy. In the words of Nigerian economist Adebayo Adedeji, 'What we confront in Africa is primarily a political crisis, albeit with devastating economic consequences.'[45] More than ever, Africa needs 'good governance', i.e. the pursuit of the democratic process, the strengthening of institutions and legal framework, and respect for human rights and the rule of law. These must be our primary concerns for Africa, as Kofi Annan has pointed out.[46] The continent must also stop over-investing in a political approach that to all intents and purposes means the continuation of war by other means. Politics must henceforth aim at managing rather than dominating, and at providing quality services to the people rather than serving its own interests. One tool for achieving this transition is civics classes, which may be offered by the government, by NGOs, by the media or by some other group. Civics are of tremendous importance if a culture of democratic citizenship is to make any impact in Africa.[47]

The development of pluralism and free elections is a promising step on the path to the democratization of Africa. Democratic ideas are taking hold slowly, but they are taking hold nevertheless. In the early 1980s there were only three democracies, compared to 30 military or single-party regimes; 30 is now the number of sub-Saharan states (out of 46) that have recently held elections.[48] A decade ago, Africans still frequently perceived democracy as an imported commodity and almost an exotic curiosity. Now, as the peaceful change led by Nelson Mandela in South Africa has shown, it is increasingly experienced as an internal demand arising within local communities, born of their own history, conflicts and rich cultural heritage. African societies wish to build their future on the principles of the rule of law and participatory citizenship. This was stressed at UNESCO by the continent's representatives meeting at Audience Africa: any centralization of power or seizure of power by a minority operating throught a single party or a state-party is harmful. It is contrary to the process of development and represents a form of dictatorship. It must be opposed.[49]

They went on to say that Africa needed democracy as the missing link between development and peace. Democracy must be seen not as a model to be copied but as an attainable goal.[50] And it is only by means of the values particular to the African people that it will be possible to devise ways of organizing society and community life that, while remaining true to universal democratic principles, will correspond to everyday African realities.

It will not be possible to introduce democracy into Africa unless there is absolute freedom of expression. The 1991 Windhoek Declaration, adopted under UNESCO auspices, held that 'the establishment, maintenance and fostering of an independent, pluralistic and free press is essential to the development and maintenance of democracy'.[51] This presupposes a policy of support for the training of journalists, for independent media organizations (especially radio stations) and for the setting up of newspapers. UNESCO's International Programme for the Development of Communication (IPDC) is working actively towards this goal.

The strengthening of African institutional frameworks and the fight against corruption and for the rule of law require the training of a sufficiently large number of African specialists in key institutional areas, such as economics, administration, law and the judicial system. This will give institutional structures long-term stability, and ensure that law and justice are applied impartially and that policies are carried out on a rational basis. Whether in or outside

Africa, university grants should be made available to encourage study and research in these areas.

A Real Chance for African Women and Children

There is no sense in development unless it takes account of the aspirations and needs of the human beings whose living conditions it seeks to improve. It so happens that statistical data and political programmes often overlook the actual or potential contribution by certain categories of the population to social progress. This is strikingly true of the role of women and young people in Africa. They are a valuable asset and a breath of hope for the future.

The economist Daniel Cohen has written that the world's poorest person is 'a woman': an African woman.[52] The 1995 *Human Development Report*, which highlighted the importance of women's 'invisible', unpaid contribution to world production, stated that women's role in economic activity was greater in Africa than anywhere else. In commerce, they are responsible for 44% of total hours worked, largely because of their presence in agriculture and service industries. In contrast, they represented only 17% of total hours worked in the industrial sector. In rural areas of Kenya, women worked an average of 56 hours per week, as compared to 42 hours worked by men.[53] In agriculture, the female labour force is currently responsible for 70% of Africa's total food production.[54]

African women must be given their rightful place in the continent's development strategies. Their governments must encourage them to participate in all areas of social, economic, political and cultural life as well as in the media and in public life, facilitate their access to bank loans and micro-credit and guarantee them full social equality with men – especially in the sphere of property and inheritance rights. In 1995 only 52% of girls were enrolled in schools, as opposed to 61% of boys. The single most effective way of bringing about a lasting improvement in the status of African women will be to give girls the same educational opportunities as boys.

Young people represent one of Africa's greatest hopes. Never before has the population been so young, and it is highly unlikely that it will ever be so young again. At present, 40% to 50% of the population is aged under 15; in 2050 this proportion will have dropped to 19% to 28%, an ageing due principally to the decline in fertility.[55] The enormous challenges facing Africa in the twenty-first century will be resolved by its young people. True, they suffer from huge inequalities compared with the rest of the world (especially as regards income, education and life expectancy) and within Africa itself (the rural infant mortality rate is particularly high, owing to the poor educational level of mothers in country areas). Nevertheless the potential of African youth is enormous: no generation has ever been so well educated, so keen to play an active role in the continent's democratic future or so aware of the huge hazards that endanger the environment. Neither Africa nor the rest of the world can afford to let this chance go.

So what is being done to make the most of the present opportunity? The future of African young people is fraught with danger. In the vast majority of countries, basic education for all remains a distant hope (one-third of pupils abandon primary school before completing four years)[56]. Exposure to new technologies remains a dream, employment in the formal sector is still a privilege, and health care is a near-impossible ideal for people accustomed to battling for survival. A recent UNESCO report explains that urban African youth increasingly has no future in traditional employment and income patterns. Training opportunities are diminishing, and those who make it through find it hard, however good their qualifications, to make any progress in the employment market.[57] According to a recent study by the UNDP and the ILO, between now and 2010 a total of 8.7 million new jobs will have to be found for young Africans every year; official urban unemployment has doubled in the last 15 years, and 75% of jobs in sub-Saharan Africa are on the periphery of the formal economy, either in subsistence agriculture or in hand-to-mouth businesses.[58] Nor should the social effects of 'structural adjustments' be forgotten, not to mention those of the exploitation of Africa's natural resources by foreign multinationals.

A simultaneous trend is that of 'children without a childhood'. These include the 41% of children aged 5–14 who go out to work, a form of exploitation that often hides behind the mask of 'family solidarity'; they also include street children, who were thought to be confined to countries torn asunder by civil war (such as Mozambique, Angola, Somalia and Eritrea) but who, it is now realized, can be found in the majority of African cities, including the capitals of the least impoverished states.[59] Another category is that of 'war children': orphans, victims of anti-personnel landmines, child soldiers forcibly recruited into battle units during local conflicts (some 15,000 to 20,000 in Liberia alone), refugees and the malnourished.[60] Finally, there are the youthful victims of drugs, poverty and life on the edge, the victims of life in the merciless city environment, who are drawn into organized crime, drug trafficking and prostitution.

Given these circumstances, the intellectual and creative resurgence of African youth is all the more worth holding on to. We must not hesitate to take advantage of the present opportunity before it disappears, perhaps for ever, by giving young people sufficient means to live and express themselves. The new partnership I propose for Africa would make children and young people a priority group for action aimed at encouraging them to take their destiny in hand rather than remain passive observers. For there is no hope of building peaceful, democratic societies as long as unemployment, violence and the illegal economy are the only things that young Africans have to look forward to. If the developed world really wants to see zones of stability developing in Africa, it must begin to invest in education for the continent.

Humanizing the African City

The modern townscape has entered contemporary African culture in the form of the *'Cruel City'* – title of the famous 1954 novel by the Cameroonian writer Eza Boto (*Mongo Beti*). This is the perception not only of the intellectual and political elite: it is shared by the common people. In this respect considerable blame has to be placed on the popular songs that for so long have spread a negative image of the city, identifying it with sinister and unfamiliar practices. In this hostility towards the city, there is a mixture of nostalgia for the mythical concept of a 'village Africa',[61] which to a large extent is an idealized fabrication, and a painful awareness of the very real issues facing those living in the urban environment. The major challenge facing Africa in the twenty-first century will be that of humanizing its cities.

Sixty-six per cent of the population of Africa still live in rural areas. Agriculture produces around 35% of GDP and 40% of exports. And yet within 25 years Africa will bear little resemblance to the predominantly rural image that is still presented of the continent. Although the rate of urbanization is currently only 34% (compared with 14.7% in 1950), between 1990 and 1995 it grew by 4.6% per year, and the UN estimates that it will reach 54% in 2025.[62] By that date, there will probably be 36 cities of more than 4 million inhabitants in Africa, and more than one-third of the total population will live in them. What is more, only one-half of urban growth is now attributable to the rural exodus, the other half being due to the natural growth rate of the cities themselves. 'Africa is no longer rural basically,' says Anne de Lattre, the founder of the Club du Sahel. 'It has been urbanizing at high speed, above all since it was hit by drought in the Sahel. African towns are the location for political expression and the search for a new balance between government and society at large.' They are also the place where new forms of expression take shape.[63]

Predictions of urban growth have been generally wide of the mark. Huge discrepancies exist between forecasts and actual rates of growth, and planning estimates have all been greatly exceeded – sometimes by as much as ten times.[64] In the 1980s and 1990s, the rapid and often unauthorized urbanization of Africa has been accompanied by an 'urban crisis' consisting of three major components: a rise in unemployment in the official labour market and the subsequent expansion of 'informal' activities in many key areas of the urban economy, a deterioration in the quality and availability of basic services, and damage to the urban environment, both natural and built-up.[65] In addition to the spread of urban deprivation and insecurity (unemployment, prostitution,

crime, drug trafficking and the destruction of traditional community networks), there is a growing housing crisis and an almost total disappearance of
the 'natural environment' in towns, which is not compensated for by a policy
of providing parks – it is rare indeed to find African towns that, like 'Green
Brazzaville', can boast of such a policy. Population growth in cities is reflected
in the continuous outward expansion of urban areas (for example, Dakar has
grown by 20 km in 25 years, and Kinshasa by some 40 km in 30 years), the
accumulation of household and industrial waste, inadequate road-building
and outdated, overloaded transportation networks.[66] Water poses a particularly
acute problem for African cities, which suffer from inadequate supply and
purification systems.[67] The situation gives rise to drinking-water contamination, which in turn leads to diarrhoeal illnesses – the main cause of infant
mortality in Africa (some estimates make them responsible for one-quarter of
deaths among children under five)[68] – and a good number of other diseases
(cholera, typhoid fever, hepatitis B, etc.), which also primarily affect children.[69]
Needless to say, urban society is also the most fertile breeding ground for
AIDS.

However, there is no reason to give in to the philosophy of 'city pessimism',
which considers that the final goal of all town planning must be to reduce the
rate of urban growth and, if necessary, the number of city residents. It is
within the urban environment itself that the necessary solutions must be
implemented. Rather than trying to put a stop to the process of urban growth,
it should be anticipated and controlled through the provision of adequate
transport facilities and water and energy supplies, and without sacrificing vital
social services such as health care and education. Chapter 3 described the
various measures that must be taken to humanize cities. In addition to these,
steps must be taken to discourage the rural exodus by improving the quality
of village life. If the most advanced countries had honoured their commitment
to devote 0.7% of GDP to public development aid, domestic and international
people movements would be far less severe a phenomenon. The example of
UNESCO's 'solar villages' demonstrates that it is possible, with modest investment, to improve living conditions – education, health care and environment
protection – for rural populations.

To that end, African cities will need to draw more and more on national
and local cultural strengths. Suitable urban technologies will need to be
developed, especially as regards the construction of housing, so that traditional
building materials and styles are used as much as possible. It is absurd that
African cities should be built with concrete, when earth architecture could so
often provide far less costly solutions, which would also be far more appropriate to the local climate and cultural circumstances. Another possibility for
Africa would be the nurturing of 'urban sociability', a sphere in which African
cities are already far in advance of other cities in both the northern and

southern hemispheres.[70] Their rich inventiveness in the informal sector is evident, for example, in the success of *tontines* or systems of collective loans.[71] Such initiatives are no longer merely a way of reducing the employment and urban community crisis; they are a genuine strategy whereby city-dwellers can take over in running their towns and an effective urban means of social integration.

Improving Food Security in Africa

In Africa, urbanization is all too frequently accompanied by a lack of attention to rural areas and basic rural infrastructures, and too little interest in making the most of agricultural resources. This is a major cause of rural decline and poverty. A recent World Bank report acknowledges the inadequacy of national and international investment in the African rural economy.[72] For example, whereas in India there are over 500 metres of rural roads per square km, in Africa the equivalent figure is 34 metres, and 50% of rural roadways are in a serious state of disrepair.[73] According to Daniel Cohen, 'it would be misinterpreting history and theory to think that current "urban" policies such as those carried out in Africa could speed up the birth of an industrial society ... Cities cannot be helped by the pauperization of the countryside: sooner or later, famine will erupt as a consequence of a poorly controlled rural exodus.'[74] Adequate rural planning policies are therefore crucial, as is the move to a more balanced understanding of what is meant by development. To this end, the countryside must be recognized as the heart and lungs of economic progress. In previous centuries, it was in country areas that the first signs of industrialization were seen, well before the explosion of the 'industrial revolution'. Measures are needed to encourage the revival of the countryside, in particular by rationalizing the price of agricultural products. Again according to Daniel Cohen: 'by keeping the price of agricultural products artificially low, the urban elites ruin the most vulnerable farmers, forcing them into cities, where they depend on subsidization of the prices of the farm goods they now must buy'.[75]

The African countryside is currently incapable of meeting the population's food needs, and the number of under-nourished people in sub-Saharan Africa rose from 103 million in 1970 to 215 million in 1990.[76] This figure must give cause for concern, given that the population of Africa is doubling every 23 years, while its food production does so only every 30 years. Moreover, in 1960 Africa was able to meet 107% of its food needs; today, this figure has fallen to 78%.[77, 78] Some experts even predict that southern Africa in the twenty-first century could depend for food on countries situated north of the Zambezi, such as the Democratic Republic of the Congo and Zambia. An important factor in this situation is the growing infertility of the soil owing to inappropriate farming methods; other elements are rural poverty and the especially critical pressure of population needs in areas where fertile land is uncommon.[79] The quest for accelerated growth and short-term profit has led to a parallel trend towards the over-exploitation of natural resources, and forests in particular.[80]

It is therefore crucial to find ways of reconciling socio-economic development with environmental conservation, not only in the interest of food security but also for the sake of the tourist industry and associated activities – areas in which Africa has tremendous potential. It is vital that genuine agricultural policies should be introduced along with strategies for promoting rural activities and the development of agricultural research.[81] This means forming regional or sub-regional markets worthy of that name, that is to say pursuing a reasonably dynamic integration policy between states. Such a strategy would go hand in hand with an increase in the use of renewable energy sources: solar power is of particular interest, and many African countries have already taken steps towards exploiting it more fully (see Chapter 12).[82] Africa could benefit from improved water economy: only 8% of the continent's arable land is under irrigation. As Henri Konan Bédié, the president of Côte d'Ivoire, has stated: 'the continent will not achieve food security unless it can master its water supply. Without abundant water reserves, the introduction of new farming techniques, productivity gains and the use of high-yield varieties will have a quite insignificant effect.'[83] Finally, the positive effect of rural education on farming output should not be underestimated. According to James Wolfensohn, President of the World Bank, 'the production capacity of village communities can easily be doubled by means of simple farming methods and greater efforts to increase school attendance, especially among young girls'.[84]

The destruction of the African environment is not only caused by soil degradation or human mismanagement. It can also be explained in terms of rich countries' policies towards Africa. These consist in the destabilization of the local economy by the sale of agricultural surpluses from the developed world at low prices on African markets; the over-valuing of local currencies (which encourages imports and discourages local production); the imposition of inappropriate rural development projects on Africa that encourage single-crop farming and lead to dependence upon a market that is both uncontrollable and uncontrolled; and the wasteful use of arable land (potato-farming in the Sahel region, for example).[85] They also bring about the almost irreversible process of soil salinization as a result of extensive irrigation programmes carried out with no thought for traditional irrigation methods, and the pillaging of natural resources by private firms taking advantage of the absence of strict legislation.

Lack of interest in local knowledge, scorn for what are considered to be archaic methods of subsistence farming, economic authoritarianism, and policy-makers' fixation on production for export and macro-economic statistics – all have done much to impede the development of agriculture in Africa.[86] Given these circumstances, it is vital to favour a genuinely African style of farming, not only by calling for an African common agricultural policy, but also by guaranteeing that Africa has access to the markets of the developed world.

Meeting the Challenges of the Global Information Society[87]

To put the issue briefly: 'In a world where thought and knowledge are becoming essential to economic and social life, and where the demand for the rapid processing of enormous quantities of data makes brainpower the pre-eminent factor, Africa cannot and must not fail to take its place in the metamorphosis of society, the effects of which are likely to be considerable on the continent's development.'[88]

In reality, Africa has the lowest average telecommunications density in the world. In 1996 there were 0.52 telephone lines for every 100 people south of the Sahara.[89] As Thabo Mbeki, then South African vice-president, pointed out, there are more telephone lines in Manhattan than in all of sub-Saharan Africa.[90] 'Teledensity'[91] varies enormously at national level, from 0.80 in towns and cities to 0.04 in rural areas.[92] More familiar modes of communication are only slightly more widespread: just 3.5% of the population have access to television.[93] Nevertheless, the number of radio receivers exceeded 100 million for the first time during the present decade, and radio is now a well-established training and information tool, and consequently one that can be used to promote participation, cooperation, democracy and peace.

Internet connections are less numerous in Africa than anywhere else in the world. In 1997 there were 0.07 Internet servers for every 10,000 people living south of the Sahara (compared with 1.7 for the whole of Africa). This figure was 400 times less than the world average, and 2,500 times less than the average in high-income countries.[94] According to one expert, only South Africa, Mauritius and Senegal, of the countries offering full access, had installed lines on every part of their territory, although some smaller towns in Benin and Kenya had similar provisions.[95]

The Internet offers an unparalleled opportunity for obtaining and sharing information; as mentioned above, this includes opening up new horizons for distance learning. In view of what the new information and communication technologies have to offer, in political, economic, technological and cultural terms, it is crucial that the private sector and the state set up partnerships in this field, since only this level of cooperation will be sufficient to guarantee universal access to these technologies and their appropriate use to meet African needs. UNESCO has stated that the revolution cannot be left totally to market forces. Information highways must not simply provide new and more powerful electronic channels for consumption. They must provide large spaces for knowledge sharing and public debate.[96] The African nations have now begun to become aware of all that is at stake in this sector.[97]

Putting an End to the Scandal of the Debt

Every man, woman and child in sub-Saharan Africa is in debt to the tune of US$380.[98] Debt servicing is an increasingly heavy weight on African shoulders. Thirty-one of the 48 nations of sub-Saharan Africa are considered to be severely indebted low-income countries; the World Bank calculates that for seven of them the debt is unsustainable, while for another nine it is potentially difficult to sustain.[99] From 1990 to 1995, sub-Saharan Africa spent an annual figure of US$12 billion on average on debt servicing, while the outstanding debt itself rose by US$33 billion. As the UNDP points out, in some cases expenditure on debt repayments is worth nearly as much as the total amount of development aid received.[100] This debt burden is a true sword of Damocles threatening the balance of public finance and delaying urgent investment in crucial areas such as education, health care, communication and transport. A recent World Bank study estimated that it would take 70 years to double the daily income (one dollar) of every African.[101] Will it really take more than three generations to enable every African to earn the paltry sum of two dollars a day?

Let it be said again: human happiness cannot be achieved at the expense of the suffering of an entire continent. Not only that, the countries of the Western world also have a historical debt towards Africa, seeing that their power, wealth and dynamism were achieved in part thanks to the sacrifices forced on the Africans under the slave trade and colonialism. Given their responsibility towards Africa, Western states have no right to ignore the continent just when it is striving to overcome its difficulties.

Africa owes its marginalization chiefly to a fall in private and public investment. In 1996 less than 4% of the US$244 billion directly invested from abroad in developing countries went to sub-Saharan Africa.[102] Between 1990 and 1995, direct private investment in African states came to 1% of the total global figure.[103] Private investment, which in any case focuses on a small number of the region's countries, will never be sufficient, especially for developing education, health care and communication infrastructures. In the words of Henri Konan Bédié, the president of Côte d'Ivoire: 'We see certain countries going through budgetary difficulties that want to back away from offering development aid. They say everything ought to be referred to the private sector. If you wait until the private sector comes to build primary schools for children, I think you could wait a long time.'[104]

As a result of disinvestment from the private sector, an enormous increase in public development aid to Africa, from both multilateral and bilateral sources, is now necessary. However, official aid to sub-Saharan Africa fell from US$17 billion in 1990 to US$15.3 billion in 1996.[105] Many industrialized countries are just not pulling their weight. For example, the USA allocates only 6% of its total foreign aid budget to Africa, a figure equivalent to 0.5% of its overall budget and 0.09% of its GDP.[106] Every measure designed to reduce the debt of the poorest countries is an encouraging step in the right direction.[107] But more must be done: the debt of the poorest countries must be cancelled in 2000, and this measure should apply to as many countries as possible. At the Cologne Summit, the G8 made a resolution to reduce the debt of the poorest states; but this merely shows that the 1996 decision to do the same was not honoured. This time, all commitments must be implemented at once and unconditionally. In this regard, one measure which needs to be implemented very rapidly is the sale of part of the IMF's gold reserves.

Some observers in the industrialized world have evoked the phenomenon of 'aid fatigue'. It has been overlooked that this 'fatigue' is also felt in Africa, inasmuch as aid has been made conditional on some particularly strict measures of economic cooperation, budgetary and tax discipline and economic reorganization, all of which jeopardize state sovereignty and have an often negative impact on the recipient society and the local economy. As Eritrean president Issayas Afeworki recently stated: 'Permanent aid leaves you disabled.'[108]

The international community is duty-bound to work to support nascent African growth. The first step must be to relieve African countries of an inordinate burden by simply cancelling most of their foreign debt. This must be accompanied by reforms aimed at bringing Africa back into the global economy. Such reforms could form the basis of a 'new contract for Africa'.

Box 17.1 Audience Africa

Africa will never be built by foreigners, whatever emotional, cultural and personal bonds they have formed with the continent, and whatever the terms of the moral contract that might lay the basis for a new type of partnership between our continent and the international community. Incidentally, the end purpose of assistance is to make it possible for assistance to be phased out ... Only Africa can decide its destiny. Africans – and they above all – must take the initiative in solving their own problems. Africa is neither a 'lost continent' nor a 'continent in distress', inhabited by people incapable of raising themselves to the level of other peoples.

(Final Report, 'Audience Africa. Social development: Africa's priorities', UNESCO, 2 March 1995)

The long-term goal must be to free Africa from its debt-dependent state and help it to set in place the necessary infrastructures for restoring economic activity while revitalizing rural and urban development. To that end, it would be desirable, as the European Commission has proposed, to make structural adjustment programmes more flexible by 'internalizing' them – i.e. by adapting their format to the capabilities and constraints applying in each country.[109] These programmes, which are imposed by international financial institutions, have often proved inappropriate to the real situation and needs of Africa. Because the situation is perceived as urgent, too much is asked of Africa and too quickly. This is evident from a glance through the interminable list of reforms which structural adjustment plans impose on African states: one economist has counted 111 conditions introduced by the World Bank into its policy-framework paper for Kenya.[110] How many industrialized nations would stand up to such prescriptions?

Promoting Long-term Development Strategies

Unless it is sustainable, there is no sense in development. Consequently, any consideration of the working of development in Africa must be part of a long-term vision, and planning ahead must be part, at the highest level, of government policies in Africa. As far back as the Monrovia Colloquium in 1979, the Organization of African Unity (OAU) stressed the importance of forward planning and long-term development in the continent's future.

Another reason why planning for the future is so crucial in Africa is that past experience has revealed the consequences of collective blindness on the part of policy-makers. The facts need to be faced: the human catastrophes that have smitten Africa were just so many pending failures. Many of them were predictable, and a fair few had been predicted. Yet we are never ready in time. This lack of anticipation is nowhere as costly as in Africa, because nowhere else does the material vulnerability of the people put them so much at the mercy of conflict, however localized it may be.

It is time to move on from crisis management to working out long-term development strategies in Africa. The faculty of anticipation must be strengthened at all levels if the continent's future problems are to be resolved in time. In addition to preventing conflicts, anticipation and prospective analysis constitute a new approach to development. They lie beyond the traditional scope of short- and medium-term development plans, which generally do not exceed five years, as well as that of structural adjustment programmes (SAPs), which are designed solely to correct macro-economic imbalance in the short term. The economic and political measures introduced so far in response to the challenges which Africa faces, whether internally or externally, have not been up to the task. Most of the time they have been too specific and fragmentary, and have been lacking in coordination and sustained follow-up. Given such circumstances, it is small wonder they have failed so often.

Measures based on emergency thinking also impose a high cultural cost, since they tend to marginalize the contribution of culture to development. There is a need for a better understanding of the links between culture and development in Africa. If the continent is to make any progress, it is not enough just to ask which cultural factors can contribute to development; we must also ask which form of development to stimulate so as to take account of Africa's abundant energy, diversity and cultural heritage. In this respect, genuine cultural policies must be promoted and the 'museum and folklore' approach that has reigned for so long in Africa must be abandoned. Cultural policies must favour a dynamic vision grounded in the vibrant talent of artists and cultural 'entrepreneurs'.

Time for Concerted Action

So long as the drive towards division persists in Africa, the dream of building peace will remain a pious hope. Africa's wealth lies in its diversity, but its strength lies in unity. According to Kofi Annan, UN secretary-general, Africans are increasingly aware of their common destiny and understand that their future lies in solidarity. 'We are beginning to end the stereotype of Africa as a continent in crisis, a house divided against itself. African unity is the key. Africa does not command great arsenals. But African unity can be a strong moral force. When Africa speaks with one voice, the world listens. But

---

Box 17.2 Alpha Oumar Konaré: 'We Must Anticipate'

For a long time now, before daring to think, we waited for things to go irreparably wrong. From now on we must anticipate. We must anticipate because of all the last-minute solutions which have not worked; because of the criminal philosophy of procrastination which has weighted down our overpowering fatalism for more than 30 years; because of the propensity of the African State to exploit the intellectual resources of the continent for short-term projects alone, forgetting that the ever faster maelstrom of globalization is carrying where it will this Africa which, apparently lacking in resistance and defence, seems resigned to its fate. We need once again to seize the initiative; we need to keep the initiative and make it ours.

(Alpha Oumar Konaré, president of the Republic of Mali)[111]

if Africa speaks with a cacophony of confused messages, few will listen, and no one will hear.'[112] A Yombé proverb puts it in another way: 'one arm is not enough to cut up an elephant'. In the twenty-first century, one of Africa's priorities will be to relaunch campaigns for unity at regional level. The unity message, taken to heart and broadcast by the OAU, is the message of the future. For peace and development are not built in isolation but through sharing and talking, through respect for others, through solidarity and by overcoming artificial barriers, all of which form the basis of security in the widest sense of the term.[113] In the words of Gertrude Mongella:

> Africa has a distinct history. It has a rich variety of people, each with their own languages, cultures, values, ethics, and knowledge. Unfortunately, we lack our own politics. The politics that have emerged in Africa are above all a politics of survival ... Unfortunately, the economic policies implemented on the continent have only been a succession of attempts lacking a long-term vision. It is precisely this vision we need today and we must take the time to create it. The context of the previous centuries never gave us the opportunity to do so. Now is the time to act. We must take advantage of our marginalisation to develop a distinct identity of the continent.[114]

The urgent requirement for peace has already strengthened awareness of the shared responsibility of the region's nations in conflict prevention and resolution. The increasingly important role of African diplomacy in settling conflicts on the continent is an encouraging sign. Long silent for the sake of the 'non-interference' rule written into its Charter, the OAU is now striving to work out mechanisms for conflict resolution, and several African states regularly take part in operations to restore peace on the continent. Simultaneously, there has been an upsurge in integration projects at regional level, a process that is more or less advanced depending on the region concerned. It is particularly noticeable in West Africa, through the Economic Community of West African States (ECOWAS) and southern Africa, through the Southern African Development Community (SADC), which represents 180 million people in 14 countries.[115] These groupings, which were originally strictly economic in nature, are tending to expand into other areas, in particular those of security (ECOWAS), the fight against extreme forms of poverty and the promotion of culture (SADC).

Once again: the development of Africa is first and foremost a concern for Africans. Nevertheless, the challenges facing Africa are far too serious to be resolved without international intervention. It was on this understanding that the UN secretary-general and the president of the World Bank launched the UN System-wide Special Initiative on Africa on 15 March 1996. This unprecedented action programme will cost US$25 billion over a ten-year period. By far the greatest proportion of spending (around 85%) will go to improving basic education and primary health care.[116] The Special Initiative is both the most extensive UN operation to be carried out on behalf of the population of a continent and the largest collection of measures it has ever assembled.[117] UNESCO has a major role in the Initiative as the 'lead agency' in the following priority areas: communications for peace-building, harnessing information technology for development, and basic education. The last area alone will receive between US$12.5 and US$15 billion over ten years – or 50% of the resources committed to the Initiative. It is my ardent wish that the Initiative will not be another frustrated hope. Donor countries must all undertake steadfastly to resolve the all too real problems faced by this continent, which has already suffered and been exploited more than enough. And yet the pivotal role in the Initiative, let me reiterate, will fall to the African states and the African people themselves. Nothing has contributed to keeping Africa in a state of dependence so much as ignorance of its great potential and insistence on seeking to secure its well-being without the commitment of Africans themselves.

Pointers and Recommendations

- Encourage the developing of a culture of peace in Africa. Restore peace through international action, under the aegis of the UN Security Council, where state mechanisms have collapsed or when human rights are being violated on a huge scale.
- Cancel the debt of the poorest sub-Saharan countries, and considerably reduce the debt of the remaining countries. Convert as soon as possible the remainder into a debt swap for investment in education, science, technology and health care.
- African countries must invest at least 5% of their GDP in education. One-quarter of development aid should go towards funding education. Multinational companies should be made to contribute at least 1% of their turnover to improving education in the African nations in which they operate.
- Spending on arms and ammunition must be cut to below 1.5% of GDP, and African states must commit themselves not to increase their defence budgets during the coming ten years. The sums thus made available are to be reinvested in education and health.
- 0.05% of GDP must be invested at national level in research and development for a period of six to eight years, up to a minimum figure of 0.3–0.4% of GDP per annum. 3% of UNDP funds must be invested in this sector to allow Africa to gain momentum in the field of science and technology.
- Launch a 'new contract for Africa' so as to open up a new era in multilateral

aid for the continent, encourage better international regulation of the global economy in favour of Africa, guarantee greater market openness to Africa's exports and prepare the way for African reintegration into the global economy.

- International assistance must be given to regional development projects. Such assistance should primarily target education and health, transport, communications, energy and agriculture.
- Give priority support to disadvantaged groups, especially women, young people and children, who must be encouraged to participate in building the future of African society.
- Support independent, pluralistic and free media.
- Encourage universal access to the new information and communication technology resources.
- Upgrade the rural environment; exploit renewable energy sources, especially solar energy, more widely; improve water management.
- Give African cultures their proper status and draw on their inherent potential to promote new development strategies.
- Promote anticipation and prospective analysis as part of development strategies.

Notes

1. For example, between 1960 and 1994, GNP grew at an average annual rate of 5.2% in Thailand, 4.2% in Malaysia, 3.8% in Indonesia and 7.0% in South Korea. The Philippines were an exception, with only 1.1%. By comparison, during the same period France expanded by an average of 2.7% per annum, and the USA by 1.9%. The growth of the Asian states was due in part to massive investment in education. From 1970 to 1994 the literacy rate rose in Malaysia from 60% to 83%, in Thailand from 79% to 94%, in Indonesia from 54% to 83%, in South Korea from 88% to 98% and in the Philippines from 83% to 94%. The impact was most noticeable on secondary and higher education (between 1980 and 1996 the enrolment rate in secondary schools rose from 48% to 62% in Malaysia and from 29% to 57% in Thailand). Public health improved in much the same way. Life expectancy at birth is now 71 years in Malaysia, 69 years in Thailand, 63 years in Indonesia, 71 years in South Korea and 66 years in the Philippines – as compared to 77 years for France and 76 years for the USA (source: UN, 1995). The final focus for investment has been the provision of fresh water. According to the latest estimates, 78% of the Malaysian population had direct access to drinking water, while in Thailand the figure was 89%, in Indonesia it was 62%, in South Korea it was 93% and in the Philippines it was 86% (UNDP, figures for 1990–96).

2. Figures from UNDP *Human Development Report 1998*, UNDP, New York, 1998. In 1960, Malaysia (now 60th worldwide) was at the same level as Uganda (160th) is today. Indonesia (now 96th) was at the level of Burkina Faso (172nd) today.

3. World Bank, *Taking Action for Poverty Reduction in Sub-Saharan Africa*, 1996; World Bank, *A Continent in Transition – sub-Saharan Africa in the mid-1990s*, November 1995. On the topic of African poverty, see: *Poverty, A Global Review. Handbook on International*

Poverty Research, Else Øyen, S. M. Miller and Syed Abdus Samad (eds), Scandinavian University Press and UNESCO, 1996, Part Three. As the World Bank makes clear, the fall in the number of people living below the poverty line has been far too slow in this region, and past efforts to remedy the situation have been ineffective.

4. See in particular UNCTAD, *The Least Developed Countries Report, 1998*, UNCTAD, New York, 1998.

5. UNDP, *Human Development Report 1998*.

6. Audience Africa, Final Report, 6–10 February 1995.

7. *African Recovery*, March 1998.

8. 'A survey of sub-Saharan Africa: Africa for the Africans', *The Economist*, 7–13 September 1996. UNAIDS figures, December 1997. Four HIV-positive women out of every five are African, and 90% of contaminated infants are born to HIV-positive mothers in sub-Saharan Africa. Dr Pierre Piot, UNAIDS executive director, says that the figures for the transmission of HIV in sub-Saharan Africa are 'grossly under-estimated' (*African Recovery*, February 1998).

9. Philippe Hugon, 'Quinze ans d'ajustement en Afrique. Quelle évaluation?', *L'État du monde 1997*, Éditions La Découverte, Paris 1996, p. 121.

10. Jean-Pierre Tuquoi, 'Le sursaut de l'Afrique', *Le Monde*, 7 January 1997.

11. See Chapter 13.

12. Guy Herzlich, 'Trompeuse Afrique', *Le Monde*, 14 January 1997. UNDP, *Human Development Report 1998*, Chapter 1.

13. Thérèse Locoh and Yara Makdessi, *Baisse de la Fécondité: la fin de l'exception africaine*, La Chronique du CEPED, No. 18, June–September 1995, pp. 1–4; *Population Politics and Fertility Decline in sub-Saharan Africa*, CEPED Series, No. 2, December 1996. The African states made a collective undertaking in the 1993 Dakar/Ngor Declaration to bring the continent's natural growth rate down to 2.5% before the year 2000, and to 2% before 2010.

14. For example, following ten years of lethargic growth at 1.7% per year, the economy of sub-Saharan Africa grew by 5% in 1996, or faster than the rate of population growth. Three countries saw annual growth superior to 8%, eight achieved 6% to 8%, and a dozen more managed 3% to 6%.

15. James Gustave Speth, UNDP administrator, 'Bonnes nouvelles d'Afrique', *Jeune Afrique*, No. 1935, 10–16 February 1998. James Wolfensohn, World Bank president, declared in 1996 that 'hope seems to be back in Africa' (interview with *Le Monde*, 16 February 1996).

16. World Bank figures. See also World Bank, *Global Economic Prospects and the Developing Countries 1998/1999*, World Bank, Washington, DC.

17. James D. Wolfensohn, president of the World Bank, speech in Addis Ababa, 27 January 1998.

18. According to the UN, GDP in sub-Saharan Africa grew by 4.75% in 1997, compared with 6% for the developing world as a whole (*World Economic and Social Survey 1997*, United Nations, New York, 1997). Over the past 20 years, per capita income has risen by only US$70 in Africa, compared with a leap of $900 in East Asia. Stephen Buckley, 'Investors skip the sub-Sahara and its many flaws', *International Herald Tribune*, 2 January 1997. Daniel Cohen, *The Wealth of the World and the Poverty of Nations*, trans. Jacqueline Lindenfeld, MIT Press, Cambridge, MA, 1998.

19. On these topics, see UNESCO *Voix, Valeurs et développement: réinventer l'Afrique*

au sud du Sahara, UNESCO, Paris, 1997; E. M'Bokolo, *Afrique noire. Histoire et civilisations, XIXe–XXe siècles*, Hatier-AUPELF, Paris, 1993. See also 'Africa: issues, trends and prospects' and 'African towns: issues, trends and prospects' (contributions by the same author for UNESCO's Analysis and Forecasting Office).

20. Kofi Annan, 'The causes of conflict and the promotion of sustainable peace and development in Africa', report by the UN Secretary-General to the United Nations Security Council, 16 April 1998, para. 4.

21. General Amadou Toumani Touré, former Malian head of state, 'Africa: issues and threats', a speech to the international colloquy 'War and peace in the twenty-first century' organized by the Foundation for Defence Studies at UNESCO on 18 and 19 December 1995 (the figures relate to a study carried out in six countries during the period 1991–95).

22. Annan, 'The causes of conflict', para. 56.

23. UNESCO, 'Audience Africa. Social development: African priorities', extracts from the Final Report, UNESCO, Paris, 2 March 1995.

24. Annan, 'The causes of conflict', para. 14.

25. Ibid., para. 58.

26. Source: *UNESCO Statistical Yearbook 1996*, UNESCO Publishing & Bernan Press, Paris, 1997.

27. UNESCO, 'Education for all: achieving the goal', *Final Report of the Mid-Decade Meeting of the International Consultative Forum on Education for All*, Amman, Jordan, 16–19 June 1996, UNESCO, Paris, 1996, p. 15.

28. *UNESCO Statistical Yearbook 1998*, table 2.4.

29. In 1996 only 45% of all those in education were girls.

30. *Wasted Opportunities: When Schools Fail*, UNESCO, Education for All, Status and Trends 1998, pp. 11 and 20; UNESCO statistics.

31. See in particular *UNESCO Statistical Yearbook 1998*, table 3.2 (enrolment rates).

32. World Bank education loans to the African region fell steeply from 1995 to 1997, from US$291.9m in 1989–93, US$286.7m in 1994, US$156.6m in 1995, US$131.6m in 1996 and US$75.1m in 1997. They rose again to US$380.3m in 1998. On this topic, see World Bank, *Annual Report 1998*, Washington, DC, 1998, pp. 16–20.

33. See Chapter 14.

34. UNESCO, 'Audience Africa. Social development: African priorities', Final Report, UNESCO, BRX-95/CONF.006/7, p. 5.

35. See UNESCO, *Higher Education in Africa: Achievements, Challenges and Prospects*, UNESCO, regional Office for Education in Africa, Dakar, 1998. See also the conclusions of the 7th UNESCO Conference of Ministers of Education of African Member States (MINEDAF VII, Durban, South Africa, 20 April 1998).

36. Amadou Toumani Touré, presentation at '21st Century Dialogues', organized by UNESCO's Analysis and Forecasting Office (September 1998).

37. UNITWIN/UNESCO Programme.

38. Audience Africa also insisted that a mastery of reading, writing and arithmetic is an indispensable precondition for success on science and technology courses.

39. These were identified during Audience Africa as priority research fields.

40. Annan, 'The causes of conflict', para. 27.

41. Before the war in Liberia, there were 1,636 schools open in the country, with a

total of 276,320 pupils. By 1994 it was estimated that these figures had fallen to 398 and 75,000 respectively. UNESCO-BREDA, *Rapport sur l'État de l'éducation en Afrique, 1997: Innovations et refondation*, November 1997. See also UNDP, *Human Development Report 1994*, UNDP, Oxford University Press, New York, 1994.

42. Recommendation by delegates at the meeting in Amman of the International Consultative Forum on Education for All (16–19 June 1996), organized by UNESCO, the World Bank, UNICEF and the UNDP; also in the Delors Commission report entitled *Learning: The Treasure Within*, UNESCO Publications, Paris, 1996, Chapter 9.

43. Ibid.

44. Speech by Federico Mayor, UNESCO director-general, in Palermo (27 September 1997).

45. 'A survey of sub-Saharan Africa: Africa for the Africans', *The Economist*, 7–13 September 1996.

46. Kofi Annan, 26 March 1996 (Press Release SG/SM/6192).

47. Annan, 'The causes of conflict', para. 73.

48. Tuquoi, 'Le sursaut de l'Afrique'.

49. UNESCO, 'Audience Africa. Social development: African priorities', extract from the Final Report, UNESCO, Paris, 2 March 1995.

50. Ibid.

51. Windhoek Declaration on Promoting an Independent and Pluralistic African Press, 3 May 1991. See also Jean-Pierre Langellier, 'La solitude des journalistes africains', *Le Monde*, 9 March 1996.

52. Cohen, *The Wealth of the World*, p. 6.

53. UNDP, *Human Development Report 1995*. See also this report's definition of a gender-specific human development indicator, which uses a base index that is weighted to take account of gender inequality. On this basis, economist Daniel Cohen noted that 70% of domestic work and productive activity in Zaire (now the Democratic Republic of the Congo) was carried out by women (ibid., p. 6).

54. *The Economist*, 'A survey of sub-Saharan Africa'.

55. Francis Gendreau, *Démographies africaines*, Editions ESTEM, Paris, 1996.

56. For those who entered school in 1994, the drop-out rate was estimated at 32% (*UNESCO World Education Report 1998*).

57. UNESCO–BREDA, *Rapport sur l'État de l'éducation en Afrique, UNESCO, 1997: Innovations et refondation*, UNESCO, 1997, p. 75.

58. Speth, 'Bonnes nouvelles d'Afrique'.

59. Y. Marguerat and D. Poitou (eds), *A l'Écoute des enfants de la rue en Afrique noire*, Fayard, Paris, 1994.

60. UNESCO–BREDA, *Rapport sur l'État de l'éducation en Afrique*, chapter III, *passim*.

61. J.-M. Ela, *L'Afrique des villages*, Karthala, Paris, 1982; *La ville en Afrique noire*, Karthala, Paris, 1983.

62. Urbanization worldwide will have attained 61% by the same date. See Francis Gendreau, *Démographies africaines*. There are gaps in the African population statistics, since some countries have held no census since 1980. See UN Habitat, *An Urbanizing World: Global Report on Human Settlements 1996*, Oxford University Press, New York, 1996, pp. 84–99.

63. Quoted by Alain Frachon in 'L'Afrique n'est plus rurale, elle se modernise', *Le Monde*, 13 November 1996.

64. See on this topic: Lelo Nzuzi, *Urbanisation et aménagement en Afrique noire*, Sedes, Paris, 1989, p. 111.

65. UN Habitat, *An Urbanizing World*, pp. 89–93.

66. Internal World Bank report, African Region, 'A continent in transition – sub-Saharan African in the mid-1990s', November 1995, Chapter 2.

67. Population growth in urban Africa cancelled out any progress made during the International Decade for Drinking Water and Sanitation Improvement (1980–90): in 1990 fewer citizens had access to an adequate supply of acceptable drinking water than in 1980.

68. Gendreau, *Démographies africaines*, p. 45.

69. Nicholas D. Kristof, 'Dirty water seals fate of poor in the world', *International Herald Tribune*, 10 January 1997.

70. M'Bokolo, *Afrique noire*.

71. 'Urban fraternities'; economic solidarity, as illustrated by the *tontines* system; solutions to unemployment through the so-called 'informal' economy, which provides an enormous number of jobs in urban areas, with a spectacular annual growth rate (7% in West African big cities), and which no policy for tackling unemployment can afford to ignore; small businesses, often operated by women and children, that collect and recycle household waste.

72. World Bank, *Taking Action to Reduce Poverty in Sub-Saharan Africa*; see in particular pp. 96–8.

73. World Bank, 'A continent in transition', Chapter 2.

74. Cohen, *The Wealth of the World*, pp. 9 and 12.

75. Ibid., pp. 8–9.

76. UNDP, *Human Development Report 1998*, Chapter 3.

77. InterAction Council, 'Bringing Africa back to the mainstream of the international system', Recommendations and conclusions of the Cape Town meeting, 21–22 January 1993.

78. Between 1961 and 1995, while per capita food production in Asian developing countries rose, in Africa it dropped by 12%. Yet agricultural export income rose in Africa by 4.4% per year from 1988 to 1993. The World Bank estimated that food exports would continue to increase by 3.8% per annum until the end of the decade. The African rural migration might therefore be interpreted as indicating a relative rise in agricultural productivity in certain regions, accompanied by a significant rate of migration from the country to the towns.

79. See Chapter 8. In Africa, cultivable land is increasingly infertile, while in Europe and North America it has an excess of nutrients. Pedro Sanchez and Anne Marie Izac, 'Soil fertility replenishment in Africa: a concept note', International Centre for Research in Agroforestry, Accra. Quoted in World Bank, *Taking Action to Reduce Poverty in Sub-Saharan Africa*, World Bank, Washington, DC, 1997, p. 97.

80. For example, two-thirds of the habitat of African wildlife has already disappeared, causing numerous species to become extinct.

81. There is a great deal of potential in the use and improvement of native plant species (for example, with regard to the pharmaceutical applications of plants).

82. It was especially evident during UNESCO's World Solar Summit in Harare (September 1996) that recognition of this need was gaining ground; the summit highlighted the innovative role alternative energy sources can play in agricultural development, as well as the need for African regions genuinely to become less isolated economically. The 300 or so 'strategic projects' coming under the 1996–2005 World Solar Programme (rural electrification, rural schools running on solar energy, etc.) will mark an important step towards Africa's taking control of this form of renewable energy, which should be its principal source of power.

83. *Le Figaro*, 13 November 1996.

84. Interview with James Wolfensohn, *Le Monde*, 16 February 1996.

85. Example given in *The Economist*, 'A survey of sub-Saharan Africa', p. 8.

86. On this topic, see *The Economist*, 7 September 1996.

87. The new information and communication technologies (NICT) boom on the African continent raises specific problems (for an overview, see Chapter 13).

88. Edem Kodjo, 'Les enjeux politiques et économiques des nouvelles technologies pour l'Afrique', in *Afrique 2000: Revue africaine de politique internationale*, No. 25, October–December 1996, p. 8.

89. For Africa as a whole the figure was 1.85/100. The proportion varied from 0.09 in Chad to 19.56 in the Republic of the Seychelles. See ITU, *African Telecommunication Indicators*, ITU, Geneva, 1998. By comparison, the 1996 rate was 6.02 in Asia and 34.60 in Europe, and varied worldwide from 0.08 in Cambodia to 75.82 in Bermuda. High-income countries had an average of 54.06 telephone lines per 100 heads of population, and low-income nations an average of 2.45. The global figure was 12.88. See also World Bank, 'A continent in transition?', Chapter 2.

90. G7 meeting, Brussels, February 1996.

91. Defined as the number of lines per 100 inhabitants.

92. *African Telecommunication Indicators*, ITU, Geneva, 1998. In South Africa, for example, where teledensity averages 10, it varies internally from 20 in Gauteng Province (around Pretoria and Johannesburg) to only 2 in the poorest region, Northern Province. ITU, *African Telecommunication Indicators*, p. 20.

93. *World Telecommunication Development Report 1998*, ITU, Geneva, 1998.

94. 1996 figures were 28.14 worldwide and 171.92 in wealthy countries. ITU, *African Telecommunication Indicators* and *World Telecommunication Development Report 1998*.

95. Mike Jensen, rapporteur for the High-level Working Group on Information and Communication Technology, African Council of Economic and Social Development Ministers. 'L'Afrique toujours plus ouverte à l'Internet', *Afrique 2000*, No. 25, October–December 1996, pp. 27–31.

96. UNESCO, *The Challenges of the Information Highways: The Role of UNESCO*, 16 August 1996, UNESCO, doc. 150 EX/15. The 1996 Conference on the Information Society and Developing Countries (held in Johannesburg) also stressed the urgent need for developing countries to find a role in the global information society.

97. See in particular the declaration on 'Building Africa's information highway', adopted by the African states in May 1995, and the AEC project on 'African society in the information age' (May 1996).

98. Sub-Saharan Africa (population estimated in 1996 at 605 million) has a total debt burden of US$230 billion (*Financial Times*, London, 3 February 1999).

99. *Global Development Finance*, Vol. 1, p. 43.

100. UNDP, *Human Development Report 1998*, p. 41. Mozambique's external debt is nine times greater than the value of its annual exports, and it spends nearly half of its budget on debt servicing – four times more than on health care (ibid.).

101. 'Rigueur économique et souffrance sociale en Afrique', *Le Monde*, 31 October 1996.

102. Speth, 'Bonnes nouvelles d'Afrique'.

103. Hugon, 'Quinze ans d'ajustement'.

104. Buckley, 'Investors skip the sub-Sahara'.

105. World Bank, *Global Development Finance 1997*.

106. 'Why Africa matters: the case for continued US assistance to Africa', Summit of Africa Aid, 3 February 1995. OECD, 1998 Report of the Development Aid Committee, table 13.

107. On this topic, see Chapter 12.

108. Quoted in Tuquoi, 'Le sursaut de l'Afrique'.

109. Ibid.

110. Jeffrey Sachs, 'Growth in Africa: it can be done', *The Economist*, 29 June 1996.

111. Part of the opening speech of the Europe–Africa meeting on the theme: 'Africa and the new information technologies', Geneva, Switzerland, 17 October 1996: 'Africa in the wars of new information technology' (printed in *Africa 2000*, No. 25, October–December 1996, pp. 15–20).

112. Kofi Annan, 26 March 1997 (Press Release SG/SM/6192).

113. See Audience Africa, 'As compared with Europe, the Americas, and the countries of the Indian Ocean and the Pacific, which are forming economic blocs engaged in cut-throat competition, micro-States have no chance of becoming significant and credible forces unless they unite.' Audience Africa, 'Social development: African priorities', UNESCO, Paris, 2 March 1995.

114. Gertrude Mongella, presentation at '21st Century Dialogues', organized by UNESCO's Analysis and Forecasting Office (September 1998).

115. South Africa, Angola, Botswana, the Democratic Republic of the Congo, Lesotho, Malawi, Mauritius, Mozambique, Namibia, the Seychelles, Swaziland, Tanzania, Zambia and Zimbabwe.

116. UNESCO, 'The role and action of UNESCO within the context of the United Nations System-wide Special Initiative on Africa', UNESCO, DGE 96/5.

117. Press release announcing the launch of the Special Initiative.

CHAPTER 18

The Dividends of Peace and Global Security

§ THE end of the Cold War had given rise to the hope that it would at last be possible to make a significant reduction in defence budgets and to invest more in human development, particularly education. However, we must admit that the famous 'peace dividends' have still not appeared. Some countries, no doubt, have succeeded in taking advantage of an opportunity to reduce their military expenditure, but budgets for human development are far from having increased by the same proportions; on the contrary, the debt burden and the degradation of the terms of trade reflect the poorer nations' increasing contribution to funding the well-being of the richer ones.

Admittedly, as far as the figures are concerned, the 'disarmament race', which began in 1989 after the collapse of the Berlin Wall, would seem to have borne fruit.[1] Since 1989, defence expenditure had decreased by one-third worldwide[2] and, during the period 1990 to 1992, the volume of arms imports throughout the world decreased by half.[3] According to the United Nations, global defence expenditure decreased on average by 3.6% annually between 1987 and 1994.[4] The Bonn International Centre for Conversion (BICC) estimates that reduction at 4.5% annually between 1987 and 1996. According to the same institution, defence expenditure accounted for no more than 2.3% of world GNP in 1996.[5] In that year, the industrialized countries still accounted for some 75% of worldwide defence expenditure. The Stockholm International Peace Research Institute (SIPRI) estimates that worldwide defence expenditure accounted for 2.6% of world GNP in 1997 but that the rate of reduction had fallen in the same year to less than 1% in real terms.[6] Since then, unfortunately, investment in arms has increased once again and at a spectacular rate in some countries.

The first thing to note is that this reduction in defence budgets was attributable largely to budgetary cuts undertaken in Europe and the USA. According to one expert, 'while Europe easily ranked first with a reduction of more than

50% for the last decade, this spectacular fall must be ascribed primarily to reductions made in Russia as from 1992. In Western Europe the reduction … was far smaller, of the order of approximately 14%'.[7] In fact, the reduction in defence budgets was much greater in the countries that were members of the Warsaw Pact: between 1988 and 1993, expenditure fell by 22% on average. As regards Russia, defence expenditure in 1997 amounted to scarcely 10% of its 1988 level.[8] In the USA, between 1986 and 1997, defence expenditure fell from 6.2% to 3.2% of GDP, reaching its lowest level since the end of the Second World War.[9] For the USA, the annual saving amounted to approximately $100 billion; in 1999, however, the US administration decided to increase defence expenditure once again.

Worldwide, military expenditure remains considerable. Estimates vary according to sources, as it is extremely difficult to gather reliable and comprehensive data in this field. According to the United Nations Development Programme (UNDP), for example, expenditure amounted in 1995 to almost US$800 billion, representing the consolidated income of almost half – the poorer half – of the world population.[10] Other United Nations sources assessed world defence expenditure at US$797 billion in 1996, i.e. the equivalent of US$135 per inhabitant on earth.[11] According to the BICC, expenditure amounted in 1996 to US$688 billion whereas it represented US$1.03 trillion in 1987. SIPRI estimated that expenditure stood at US$740 billion[2] in 1997, or approximately US$2 billion per day and 2.6% of world GDP, against US$3 billion per day towards the end of the 1980s.

As emphasized by the UNDP, 'peace dividends' assessed at world level exceeded in all some US$900 billion in the mid-1990s but 'the greater part of the savings would seem to have helped to reduce budgetary deficits and expenditure unrelated to development'.[13] According to the Worldwatch Institute, peace dividends would seem to have largely vanished into some kind of gigantic 'fiscal Bermuda Triangle'.[14] Reductions in defence expenditure observed in recent years could therefore be considered not so much an authentic peace effort as a technical budgetary adjustment bringing defence spending, the level of which had been particularly high in 1987, back to a routine level.[15] Furthermore, the reduction in the OECD countries of spending on research and development in the defence sector was also accompanied by a reduction in budgets for public research focused on non-military activities.[16]

We should not therefore jump to the conclusion that any real progress has been achieved in this field on a world scale. What is more, since the end of the Cold War, world markets have been flooded with weapons that the Western countries and the countries in transition no longer need and are now being sold off very cheaply. 'Those States which produce and sell weapons have made up for the reduction in demand for defence equipment in the industrialized countries by exporting towards Third World countries, which happen to be the theatre of most present-day conflicts.'[17] The 'dumping' of weapons, a vast 'surplus store' of terror, creates a major risk as it can worsen many conflicts. For want of a concerted effort on an international scale, disarmament policies in some regions of the world have led to increased risk of conflict elsewhere. According to the BICC, stocks of conventional heavy weapons were reduced by 165,000 between 1990 and 1995, but over 18,000 weapons from this surplus were exported, mainly to the Middle East.[18]

The situation is even more catastrophic in the case of light weapons, which fuel internal conflicts. Their exact number is still a matter of great uncertainty but it could be between 100 and 500 million, that is, an average of one for every 12–60 people.[19] It is worth recalling that, for the price of a fighter plane, it is possible to buy 200,000 rifles. As secretary-general of the United Nations, Boutros Boutros-Ghali had already stressed the need for undertaking 'micro-disarmament' when implementing peace agreements by collecting and, where necessary, buying up weapons used by the warring factions. One solution contemplated by a growing number of experts would be to conclude a multilateral treaty, within the United Nations framework, on the control and limitation of transfers of conventional weapons, including light weapons. This proposal in fact corresponds to the thrust of the message expressed by Pope John Paul II on the occasion of celebrations to mark World Peace Day on 1 January 1999, when he stated that 'responsibility lies with governments to take appropriate measures to control the production, sale, import and export of instruments of death. This is the only way whereby it will be possible to take an effective stand against the overall problem of the enormous illicit arms trade.'[20]

The UNDP has observed, however, that 'few efforts have been made to devise a totally new security system'; furthermore, the regions of the world which have the largest number of poor – particularly sub-Saharan Africa and southern Asia – are far from having slowed down their defence expenditure. Two countries in southern Asia alone, which have been involved in a lengthy regional conflict that has recently flared up again, accounted in 1994, according to the *Human Development Report*, for more than 18% of worldwide arms imports, that is to say, practically twice as many as the main oil-producing weapons importer. Asia is the continent that has experienced the largest increase in military expenditure (+26% between 1988 and 1997). South America, however, has also succumbed to the temptation of rearmament as defence budgets there rose 14% over the same period. As for the subregion of North Africa, defence spending increased 45% between 1988 and 1997.[21] In the Middle East, a traditional market for arms exports, defence expenditure has also grown at a steady pace (+9%). Sub-Saharan Africa, although it reduced defence expenditure by 46% over the same period, which is welcome news, more than quadrupled the share of regional GDP allocated to such expenditure, which rose from 0.7% to 3%, between 1960 and 1991. In 1996, defence expenditure in Africa increased by 2.3% in relation to 1995.[22] According to SIPRI, countries with a low or middle income increased their defence expenditure by 19% and 12% respectively between 1988 and 1997.[23] What is more, the rapid economic development of a number of emerging countries has frequently enabled them to raise their military spending very substantially.

As emphasized by Vicenç Fisas, 'it is a sorry state of affairs but it is the countries which most need to invest in their development which spend most on military activities, all too often more than they devote to health and education'.[24] Nevertheless, Central America stands out as an exception: ravaged as it was for decades by armed conflicts, it succeeded in reducing defence expenditure by almost 40% between 1988 and 1997, thanks to the signing of peace agreements.

On average, defence budgets have remained as high as at the end of the 1970s, and in several regions of the world peace is far from having been established. A number of governments, believing that their security is under threat, are in fact currently increasing their military potential. According to the BICC, defence expenditure began to increase again in 1996, in Eastern Europe and in the countries of the Commonwealth of Independent States; in the developing countries, expenditure increased overall by 3.5% in relation to 1995. While it now seems certain that the effects of the financial recession that hit East and South-east Asia in 1997 will lead to a reduction in defence expenditure in the main countries concerned, it is to be feared that this reduction will be short-lived.

The USA has also decided – as stated earlier – to include in its budget a sizeable increase (of 4.2%) in funds devoted to defence, for the first time in 15 years. The increase of $12 billion in 2000 and $110 billion in all over the next six years will serve not only to increase the salaries and pensions of the military, but also to improve the equipment and state of preparation of the armed services.[25] Such an increase in defence expenditure unfortunately supports the thesis according to which the reduction in military budgets that occurred in recent years was perhaps only a passing phenomenon, more attributable to concern with balancing the budget than to a genuine commitment to peace and human development.

Reducing Weapons Means Increasing the Chances of Peace

Expenditure on weapons monopolizes resources that could be devoted to education, scientific and technical development, key infrastructure for development such as communications, conservation of the environment and cultural development. That is why it is vital that the competent international and regional institutions give new impetus to machinery for preventing and settling conflicts between states and also within nations themselves. In fact it is the latter conflicts that give more and more weight to the arguments of those who claim that expenditure on weapons is a priority.

We must therefore pursue and intensify the reduction in defence expenditure, which cannot merely be the outcome of short-term policies for budgetary austerity. This is a vital task but a difficult, complex and arduous one. What is called for is a special effort of reflection, analysis and communication. It must be clearly established, in response to the sceptics and 'realists', that a reduction in weapons and the conversion of the defence industries are a long-term investment process, the temporary social costs of which will be compensated for by much more tangible benefits in the future.

According to the United Nations report referred to earlier, econometric studies show that reductions in defence expenditure have clearly positive effects in the medium and long terms. Admittedly, cutting funds may initially lead to a reduction in the scale of economic activity and cause a temporary increase in unemployment, particularly in those areas where the defence industries are located. In the longer term, however, the resources made available in public budgets can be invested in more productive activities for society such as education.

Once the sums saved in this way are used judiciously, the reduction in defence expenditure and therefore in the debt of certain states can lead to a lowering of interest rates, which encourages private investment and job creation. According to Lawrence Klein, Nobel prizewinner for economics, a decrease in defence expenditure rapidly generates growth in investment and consumption and substantial gains in the economy as a whole. Another economist, Edward Yardeni, has pointed out that, over the last 150 years, bringing wars to an end made possible an overall lowering of prices as economic relations between states improved.[26]

In a recent article, three IMF economists made use of an econometric model analysing the impact of defence expenditure on economic growth in 79 countries between 1971 and 1985: their research established a clear correlation between a reduction in defence expenditure and the development of growth.[27] Accordingly, the reduction in defence expenditure observed in the industrialized countries since 1985 and up to 1990 should in the long term bring about an overall increase of 2% in absolute terms in GNP per capita. If, furthermore, worldwide defence expenditure fell to less than 2% of GNP as in Latin America, the region where defence expenditure is lowest on average, the benefits in terms of development and overall welfare would be substantial in the long term. Thus, in the industrialized countries, after some 50 years, the increase in GNP per capita would be 13.2%. For other regions such as Central and Eastern Europe, the benefits could prove even more substantial.

We are all familiar with the famous words of advice in the time-honoured adage: 'if you want peace, prepare for war'. We strongly dispute this illusory form of wisdom. We cannot give credit to the argument according to which defence expenditure is justified as it helps to increase the security of populations in a given territory. In the developing countries, 'the risks of death due to the inadequacies of welfare policies (malnutrition or the lack of health care), according to a United Nations report, are 33 times greater than the risks of dying during a war of aggression launched by a foreign State'.[28] According to the same report, the developing countries have on average 20 soldiers for every doctor and, all too often, the soldiers turn against the population. Whereas at the beginning of the century approximately 90% of all war victims were soldiers, today approximately 90% are civilians. Conflicts increasingly take on the guise of civil wars in which regular armies are involved, for partisan or ethnic reasons, and which result in massacre or even genocide. We must therefore state quite unequivocally: 'if you want peace, prepare for peace'.

According to the United Nations, one of the most pertinent indicators of political insecurity in a country is precisely and paradoxically the priority states give to military might. When a government is more concerned with strategic security than the security of its own citizens, an imbalance in budgetary options shows up clearly in the relationship between defence spending and social expenditure. For example, the two countries in which the relationship between defence spending and expenditure on education and health was most marked in 1980 were, by order of magnitude, Iraq (8 to 1) and Somalia (5 to 1). The UNDP observes that 'in these conditions, is it surprising that these two countries should have experienced serious problems during the 1980s and that those who provided them with arms some ten years ago are now attempting to disarm them?'[29] According to the World Bank, there also happens to be a strong correlation between conflicts and poverty: 16 of the 20 poorest nations in the world have experienced major conflicts since the beginning of the 1980s.[30]

There are times when we hear that research expenditure linked to the defence sector has positive spin-offs for development. According to an analysis of peace dividends published by OECD, several case studies (India, Brazil and the Republic of Korea) have shown that the civilian sector benefits only very slightly from the existence of a powerful arms sector. According to the authors of the OECD study, 'this form of industrialization has encouraged a section of human resources, which is already inadequate, to abandon the most productive activities'.[31] On the contrary, Japan and Germany have been able to devote most of their research efforts to civilian purposes since 1945 and have experienced growth rates far higher than those of the United Kingdom, for example, which has continued to invest a substantial part of its research resources in a much more powerful military sector.[32] What is more, the peculiarities of commercial transactions in the field of defence make it easy to exploit dominant positions on markets that are closed to competition, thereby introducing distortions into the economy. Equally frequently, the secrecy that surrounds these budgets gives rise to embezzlement for purposes of corruption, or facilitates the use of such funds for occult purposes as, for example, in the funding of paramilitary groups.[33] Sooner or later, it is democracy itself that may be threatened.

Above all, politicians and social players should, without exception, learn political lessons from this state of affairs: resources allocated to weapons are resources which are denied to the vital sectors of development, where needs are still sizeable. In 1994, the United Nations attempted to estimate the cost of defence expenditure for the developing countries. Out of a total of US$125 billion per year they spent in this field at the time, it would have been enough to levy 12% to 'provide basic medical treatment for all, vaccinate all the children, eliminate the most serious and reduce the most benign forms of malnutrition and supply everyone with drinking water'; 8% to 'provide a range of basic family-planning services to all couples who wanted them and to stabilize the world population by the year 2015'; and, more particularly, only 4% 'to reduce adult illiteracy by half, extend primary education to all and give women a level of education equivalent to that of men'.[34]

It must be emphasized that the amount of money allocated to arms imports by developing countries in 1997 was three times greater than that given to investments, which, had they been greater, would have ensured that all children in those countries had a basic education.[35] One more opportunity missed for development!

In this regard, each of us should dwell on the familiar example of Costa Rica which, having abolished the army as a permanent institution in 1949 and transferred its budget to the Ministry of Education, allocated only approximately 0.6% of its GDP to military and related expenditure during the 1980s.[36] The rate of infant mortality in Costa Rica has fallen to 16 per 1,000 viable births as compared with 8 per 1,000 on average in the member states of the OECD, while the income per capita in Costa Rica is ten times lower than the OECD average.

Since the end of the Second World War, between US$30 and US$35 trillion have been spent on the defence sector. The world would certainly have been a safer place if only a fraction of that sum had been allocated to other activities that contribute more to human security, such as education, health, housing, the fight against poverty and preservation of the environment.[37]

An Agenda for Action

If the international community intends to establish the culture of peace that UNESCO earnestly desires, it is vital that it should meet two challenges:

intensifying efforts to reduce defence expenditure and, more particularly, ensuring that such expenditure results in sustainable peace on a world scale, based on the intellectual and moral solidarity of humanity, rather than on any short-term reduction in, or stabilization of, weapons. We must become aware of the fact that arms reductions, the culture of peace, security and development are four concepts that are closely related in reality. Let us use the funds made available through the reduction of defence expenditure for building stable democracies in which the confrontation of ideas can take over from that of weapons and in which discussion, rather than war, can help to resolve conflicts at lower human cost.

What measures are to be taken today to ensure that this reduction in weapons is lasting? Up to now, the defence sector in the industrialized countries has benefited from sizeable production subsidies. Why couldn't these countries use such subsidies to reduce production instead of stimulating it? Some experts have already proposed the creation of a tax on arms sales. This tax would provide income that could be used specifically to fund part of the restructuring of that sector. For the reduction in weapons to be made acceptable in the producer countries, it would be necessary to encourage efficient retraining of workers in the military-industrial sector, as several million people are directly concerned. Some 8.3 million people lost their jobs in the weapons industry worldwide between 1987 and 1996, representing a reduction of 47% in the workforce, which stood at 17.5 million in 1987.[38]

According to Michael Renner of the Worldwatch Institute, retraining activities could be focused, in an imaginative and innovative manner, on the development of non-polluting production technologies, the promotion of renewable energy sources, the strengthening of public transport networks, access to preventive medicine and the improvement of public education services.[39] Renner also suggests that a forum be set up within the United Nations where the experience of every nation in the field of retraining could be made available to all.

Admittedly, redeployment is no easy task, as illustrated by the major problems raised by the reconversion of military bases for civilian purposes. Nevertheless, it does offer opportunities as shown by the policy pursued in the Philippines. When the American naval base in Subic Bay closed in 1992, the USA valued its infrastructure at $1.4 billion. On the negative side, in addition to massive job losses, there was another black spot, namely contamination of the environment, on account of the massive discharges of chemical residues and heavy metals into the bay and the infiltration over many years of crude oil and petrol into the ground. Seven years ago, the mayor of Olongapo helped to set up the Subic Bay Metropolitan Authority, the aim of which was to transform the naval base into a local 'Hong Kong'. By the end of 1993, the Authority had attracted $340 million and 33 investors to the base. Nevertheless, uncertainty regarding the real level of contamination of the environment in Subic Bay was the main obstacle to civilian development of the area.[40] A second example of reconversion is that of the city of Székesfehérvar in Hungary, which, thanks to a highly skilled labour force, employed in particular in the field of civilian and military electronics, succeeded in attracting US$1 billion of foreign investment between 1991 and 1995 and thereby contributed to lowering the unemployment rate from 30% to 10% in five years.[41] A third example is that of the missile launching site at Postavy in Belarus, which was recently converted into a home for children suffering from health problems in the wake of the Chernobyl nuclear disaster.[42] A fourth and particularly remarkable example is that of the American base at Fort Clayton in Panama, which was recently converted into a City of Knowledge with the help of UNESCO. The activities of the City of Knowledge are now being focused in four major fields: a technology park, a research centre, a higher education centre and a discussion forum, the purpose being to promote peace, democracy and culture through exchange and dialogue between various disciplines and professions.

Should economic and technical aid granted to a country take account of its leaders' efforts to reduce defence expenditure? That is what has been put forward in a United Nations report: granting of aid would depend on the relationship between military and social expenditure in the recipient country.[43] The greater the imbalance in that relationship, the lower would be the aid; in addition it would be appropriate to recommend a minimum level of social expenditure and a maximum level of defence expenditure.

Furthermore, the question of reducing military aid should be given priority attention by the donor countries and the main arms suppliers, especially the five permanent members of the Security Council, which, according to UNDP, in 1994 accounted alone for 86% of supplies of conventional weapons to the countries of the South.[44] Two-thirds of weapons were sold to ten developing countries, which included both emerging or newly industrialized countries enjoying rapid economic development and some of the poorest countries in the world. New ethics in this field would seem all the more called for in view of the fact that arms suppliers, by continuing to export arms to all centres of conflict throughout the world, are manifestly adding fuel to the fire.[45] The harmful consequences of military assistance are in fact numerous: they include exaggeratedly large numbers of soldiers and abundant defence equipment; a foreign debt burden when aid is provided in the form of loans; considerable ancillary expenditure – usually unproductive in nature – in terms of infrastructure, maintenance and spare parts; the development of 'grey areas' in the sphere of procurement contracts and the aggravation of political corruption. Fortunately, this form of aid has already been reduced, falling from US$21 billion to US$5 billion between 1987 and 1993. The number of foreign soldiers trained in the USA fell from 56,000 in 1975 to 4,500 in 1992.

Why not devote these substantial sums saved worldwide to the training of schoolchildren?

Cannot further steps be taken in this field? The Committee of Nobel Peace Prizewinners created on the initiative of Oscar Arias Sanchez, Nobel Peace Prizewinner and former President of Costa Rica, devised in 1997 an international code of conduct on the transfer of weapons which it will submit to the United Nations General Assembly in the hope that this may lead to an international treaty: 'Our children urgently need schools and health care centres, and not weapons or fighter planes,' declared the Committee.[46]

A third measure proposed in a slightly different form by François Mitterrand, then president of the French Republic, and by Oscar Arias Sanchez, would be to create a World Demilitarization Fund, which has also been advocated since then by a UNDP report and by the Global Governance Commission in the report *Our Global Neighbourhood*. The fund could be financed through the levying of taxes on the arms trade and cuts in the defence budgets of the industrialized countries. The developing countries would also contribute to the fund according to their means. The advantage of such a fund would be precisely to encourage countries in transition towards democracy, which have only very limited resources, by making available to them a share of the dividends of peace. Unfortunately, although this plan has been the subject of numerous discussions, no practical decision has been taken by the main actors.

In the developing countries, every initiative aimed at founding stable democracies should be encouraged. However, 'the greater the power of the army, the less likelihood there is that conditions for the exercise of democracy can be created'.[47] Furthermore, when the process of democratization has not been completed, it is the most vulnerable groups in society, namely women and children, who suffer most from excessive militarization. These groups do not have the political power required to make their voices heard when decisions are taken that are unfavourable to educational and social expenditure. Naturally, the very nature of the role of the army in society matters even more than the scale of defence budgets. In this regard, it should be emphasized that the armed services, in a democratic context, can also contribute significantly to development and nation-building by encouraging, for example, the development of infrastructure (roads, transport and communications), training, environmental protection, rural development and civil security. Through its projects for education focusing on a better understanding of the principles of democracy, human rights, tolerance and peace, UNESCO can play an important part in encouraging the emergence of civil society, in collaboration with all the actors in society, including the armed services.

All too often, in many developing countries the army is the only institution that offers real training opportunities to young people. Arms reductions should therefore be accompanied by policies aimed at gradually offering young people other means of access to education leading to stable employment. Such action is fundamental in countries recovering from a war. If the transition towards peace is to succeed, it is essential that the military be reincorporated into civilian life. In most instances, it is composed of young people who have been deprived of education and vocational training. It is necessary to transform demobilized soldiers rapidly into productive actors of development, not only because they deserve another future but also because they are likely to take up their weapons again if they are not offered a viable alternative.[48] In most cases, those countries that need to undertake redeployment measures are regrettably those that most lack the means of doing so. That is why we attach great importance to the project for the prevention of conflicts and the consolidation of peace, of which the three principal objectives are to promote a quest for efficient methods of preventing conflicts, to supply urgent assistance during the latter and to help to consolidate peace in their wake.

UNESCO has done much in recent years, in partnership with many military research and advanced training institutes,[49] to define a new approach to security, to see international security in a light different from that of the prospect of armed aggression and to free security from the culture of war in the framework of which it was devised and organized.[50] It is today absurd to spend astronomical sums on weapons intended to protect us against threats that no longer exist – while claiming to possess the necessary resources for relieving the misery of one-quarter of the world's population, which lacks the most basic goods and services. On the contrary, we should be investing in the safety of citizens and the institutions of democracy. In other words, we must choose: we cannot at one and the same time pay the price of war and that of peace.[51]

The real challenge is now to ensure the 'democratic security' of peoples, in terms of a 'global and indivisible' perspective that takes account of the challenges of dire poverty, degradation of the environment, epidemics and the various forms of discrimination and violation of human rights.[52] The aim is to break out of the 'repression–prevention' dichotomy and to ensure that security is gradually demilitarized, that it is returned to its primary task of protecting the citizen, that it works in the service of the general interest and is governed by democratic laws. Democracy should be neither vulnerable nor fragile. Security forces should be able to guarantee the strict observance of justice, complete freedom of opinion and respect for human rights.

Much has yet to be done. The transition towards sustainable peace is a process that would seem to have been triggered among the protagonists of the Cold War. Nevertheless, we must make sure that it is not merely an ephemeral illusion created – paradoxically – by budgetary austerity. In several countries, the destruction of nuclear arsenals will be very costly.[53] For many nations of the South, the transition towards peace still seems remote. The developing countries have been the theatre of 95% of major conflicts since the Second World War and these conflicts are increasingly internal, reflecting the fragility of societies that have spent too much on war and not enough on peace and which are the theatre of rivalry between the major powers and transnational economic interests.

The real danger today is that of 'bankrupt states' and conflicts that are played out without any regard for international legal standards, thereby making any attempt at mediation on the part of the international institutions extremely difficult. For example, out of the 82 armed conflicts that took place between 1989 and 1992, only three were inter-states conflicts. According to SIPRI, the number of major conflicts in 1997 (those in which more than 1,000 people died) stood at 25 and only one of them was between two different states.[54] If we take account of the conflicts of lesser intensity, the data reveal a constant increase in infra-state conflicts since the end of the Second World War.

We should not forget that, since 1945, wars and armed conflicts have caused the deaths of 20 million people. The children of this world will continue to pay the price of these conflicts for a long time yet, in terms of barbarous mutilations and unjust deaths. According to the estimates of experts, some 65 to 110 million mines are thought to be buried throughout the world, waiting to explode (see Box 18.1). 'The Cold War is not over: half of the task has yet to be completed.'[55]

It is not our intention to describe in detail the political and technical measures that should be taken in order to pursue the other half of the path: we believe that the United Nations and other forums, whether multilateral or regional, where agreements on the reduction of weapons and strategic strategy are discussed, are obviously the only context where such extremely complex agendas can be finalized. Suffice it to say that the outline of such agendas has already been drawn up, as in the case of the UNDP in 1994[56] or, in 1995, by the Commission on Global Governance, co-chaired by Ingvar Carlsson and Shridath Ramphal, in the report entitled *Our Global Neighbourhood*.[57]

As observed by that Commission, security can no longer be viewed from a strictly strategic or military angle. Today, security is an inextricable intertwining of political, economic, social, scientific, cultural, environmental, health, military and even spiritual components. With that view in mind, the notion of global security must henceforth encompass – beyond the narrow confines of the protection of states – the economic, social, cultural and human security of populations as well as planetary security. As already put forward by Olof Palme some 18 years ago in the introduction to a widely acclaimed report: 'Our alternative is common security ... international security must rest on a commitment to joint survival rather than on a threat of mutual destruction.'[58]

It is therefore vital to anticipate crises by strengthening the capacity of the system in that domain in order to respond to conflicts we have been unable to prevent. It is equally crucial to pay the price of peace and development, to avoid the threats of massive destruction and to count on the democratic pacification of human societies. Like many experts from both the North and the South, like the Ramphal–Carlsson Commission and the UNDP, we are convinced that governments should jointly adopt practical objectives, backed up by figures and dates, for the reduction of defence expenditure and that the arms trade should be more carefully controlled by the international community through the adoption of strict codes of conduct in that sphere. But political measures for a negotiated reduction in weapons are not enough. Measures of that kind were also taken during the inter-war period but were soon swept away by the unleashing of totalitarian violence – stirred up by economic, political and social causes, dire poverty, hatred of others and the mimetic logic of the arms race. What gives force and duration to treaties is not the paper on which they were drafted but the shared trust and faith in their beneficial effects for all.

The vital factor for ensuring sustainable peace is the task that lies at the heart of UNESCO's mandate, namely education, to which we might also add culture. But it is not education or culture of simply any kind. As pointed out by Léon Blum at the London conference that established UNESCO, it is education resolutely focused on peace that should lie at the heart of our endeavours. The genocide of Jews and gypsies took place in a nation that was probably the most highly educated in the world and boasted at the time the largest number of Nobel prizewinners. What matters therefore is the establishment of a culture of peace, a culture of non-violence. As noted by the Commission on Global Governance, 'militarization today not only involves governments, spending more than necessary to build up their military arsenals. It has increasingly become a global societal phenomenon, as witnessed by the rampant acquisition and use of increasingly lethal weapons by civilians – whether individuals seeking a means of self-defence, street gangs, criminals, political opposition groups, or terrorist organizations. An emphasis on the security of people requires the world to address the culture of violence in everyday life.'[59] The culture of violence turns everyday life into a microcosm of war, nightmare and aggression which, by turning the use of violence into a commonplace, prepares the ground for future large-scale conflicts.

The task of promoting a culture of peace is therefore an essential one. There can be no sustainable peace unless it is established lastingly in our hearts and minds. Do we really believe that global security can prevail thanks to the consultations of learned assemblies of diplomats when local insecurity is gaining ground everywhere? That is why we share the view of the Commission on Global Governance when it calls for the development of a culture of non-violence in terms which we believe should be quoted here:

We strongly endorse community initiatives to protect individual life, to encourage the disarming of civilians, and to foster an atmosphere of security in neighbourhoods. All have a role to play, including television, the cinema and other media. The task of promoting security in the global neighbourhood will be measurably harder if in societies around the world a culture of violence is on the rise and personal insecurity is pervasive.[60]

Governments throughout the world spent US$16 billion in 1994 on demilitarization or arms reduction measures, which amounted to approximately 2% of global military expenditure.[60] This expenditure has increased considerably in recent years. For instance, the USA alone spent $16.5 billion on conversion measures between 1993 and 1997.[62] Nevertheless, these sums are largely inadequate for coping with the whole range of needs. The cost of peace should be seen not as an additional budgetary heading but rather as an investment, the long-term benefits of which amply justify initial expenditure, if only in terms of lives spared. What is more, the prevention of conflicts costs considerably less than our occasional efforts at humanitarian assistance and peacekeeping and reconstruction, which, all too often, merely offer makeshift, short-lived solutions to the wounds that lie at the source of the conflicts.

Ultimately, the dividends of peace are development itself and the freedom ensuing from it. That is why the poorest countries must prepare a better future for themselves by ceasing to invest in war and by placing their hopes in the intelligence and well-being of their citizens, by educating them, caring for them and offering them an opportunity to accede to better living conditions. Admittedly, there is a price to be paid for peace, but the price is also that of development. It is the price of humanity's material and moral prosperity. There must be democratic security, efficient security, both internal and external. We must invest not in weapons but in helping to create a dialogue between individuals, to understand each other and thereby contribute to sustainable development.[63] We cannot be satisfied with extremely costly major international alliances when, at the same time, our citizens are exposed to insecurity in the streets and neighbourhoods.[64] What needs to be done is to consolidate a new approach to security that takes account of the roots of conflicts and the whole range of non-military threats to peace. The world is global and interactive. Security on a planetary scale cannot be based on glaring inequalities, intolerable impunity or recourse to violence. Awareness of interdependence and globalization is essential.[65] UNESCO has a part to play in disseminating the values of democracy, peace and tolerance, in promoting the culture of non-violence, in encouraging each country to enter the twenty-first century by relying on education and the training of young people. Let us give UNESCO the means to accomplish its tasks.

The Declaration on Science and the Use of Scientific Knowledge, adopted on the occasion of the World Conference on Science held from 26 June to 1 July 1999 in Budapest, Hungary, emphasized the essential role of the scientific community in this new approach to security by proclaiming in particular that 'worldwide cooperation among scientists makes a valuable and constructive contribution to global security and to the development of peaceful interactions between different nations, societies and cultures', and by stating in its preamble that 'there is now an opportunity to call for a reduction in the resources allocated to the development and manufacture of new weapons and to encourage the conversion, at least partially, of military production and research facilities to civilian use'. The time has come, through willpower and deeds, to fulfil the ancestral prophecy: 'they shall beat their swords into ploughshares, and their spears into pruning hooks: nation shall not lift up sword against nation, neither shall they learn war any more'.

Box 18.1 *Towards a Ban on Landmines*

In 1997, the Nobel Peace Prize was awarded to the 'International Campaign to Ban Landmines', an organization headed by Jody Williams that has now been joined by a thousand NGOs. Since then, international public opinion has become aware that these mines are an unbearable scourge: some 110 million active mines are scattered around some 70 countries; they kill or maim approximately 26,000 people a year, that is to say, a victim every 20 minutes. The injuries are atrocious, as the most common type of mine has a blast effect, thereby projecting into the legs and body of the victims metal fragments mixed with earth, pebbles and vegetation. When the victims are not actually killed through loss of blood, they suffer amputation and also experience secondary wounds to the face, eyes and other parts of the body. According to Handicap International, approximately one million people, including 600,000 civilians, have been killed by mines in the past 20 years. The countries most affected are Angola, Eritrea, Mozambique, Somalia, Sudan, Afghanistan, Cambodia, Iraq and Bosnia. In Cambodia, it is estimated that six to ten million mines are buried in the ground: one person in every 236 has had an amputation, which is the highest level worldwide. There are still over ten million mines in Angola, that is to say, one for every inhabitant. Some 70,000 Angolans, including 8,000 children, have had amputations. In its report on the impact of armed conflicts on children, UNICEF emphasized in 1996 their extreme vulnerability to mines: incapable of reading any warnings, children, by virtue of their size, are more likely to die from any injury than adults and among the survivors, there are few who can replace their artificial limb every six months as their body continues to grow: a child aged 10 years will require 25 artificial limbs if he or she lives to the age of 60, that is to say, an overall expense of more than US$3,000.

In the words of Boutros Boutros-Ghali, 'We are faced today, on account of landmines, with a crisis on a world scale, which goes beyond strictly military problems to reach the status of a humanitarian disaster.' Mines, or what might be called 'hidden killers', do not distinguish between a soldier, a child or a farmer: in some countries, women and children account for up to 30% of the victims. The proliferation of mines affects not only combat areas but also regions of civilian and commercial activity; mines are to be found near places as vital as farms, wells, fords, roads and paths, bridges, electricity power stations and water treatment stations. Apart from the human suffering they inflict on the populations, anti-personnel mines are therefore a distinct obstacle to development. The victims are mostly condemned to social and economic exclusion and weigh heavily on already inadequate health budgets. In countries where fertile agricultural land is scarce and infrastructure inadequate, the presence prevents exploitation of vast areas of land and the reconstruction of much infrastructure. In Libya, 20% of arable land is infested with mines dating back to the Second World War. This problem aggravates the dramatic circumstances of refugees (see Chapter 1) as it often prevents their return and condemns them to exile or poverty in suburban areas.

The health costs attributable to mines are extremely high and the financial, logistic and technical requirements for their removal are quite beyond the means of the countries most in need. Some mines, reputed to be the 'weapons of the poor', cost only a few dollars and can be mass produced. On the other hand, locating and destroying a single mine can cost between US$300 and US$1,000 and involves very significant human risks: at least 34 people have died during mine clearance operations conducted by the United Nations in Afghanistan. As the epitome of cynicism, it is sometimes the mine suppliers who offer their services, in return for payment, to undertake their destruction. It is possible to disseminate a thousand mines per minute but a full day's work is required for an experienced expert to clear 20 to 50 m^2 of contaminated ground. All too often, however, no plan is available of the danger areas. At the current rate of mine clearance in Cambodia – 10 km^2 per year since 1991 – two to three centuries would be required, in theory, to clear, defuse and destroy the mines that, in any case, would become inoperative after 75 years on average. Similarly, 4,300 years would be required for the mine clearance teams currently working in

Afghanistan in order to clear one-fifth of the country. In 1993, according to a study produced by the Défense Conseil International group (Paris), 100,000 mines had been neutralized throughout the world, whereas two million new mines had been dispersed over the five continents.

In December 1997, 122 countries meeting in Ottawa signed a treaty on a total ban on landmines. In September 1998, the number of countries increased to 132 and on 1 March 1999, the treaty came into force, 65 of the signatories having ratified it. Two months later, at the end of April 1999, the treaty had been signed by 135 countries, 77 of which had ratified it. Since the signing of the treaty, it is believed that 10 to 11 million mines have been destroyed, accounting for approximately 10% of stocks world-wide. Nevertheless, some 60 countries, including a number of mine-producers such as Russia, the USA, China, Syria, Israel, the two Koreas, India and Pakistan, have not yet signed the treaty and only twelve have actually completed the total destruction of their stocks. Each year, between five and ten million additional mines are produced. As we have stressed repeatedly, we must achieve a total ban on anti-personnel mines without further delay and without any exceptions. Any further delay – in the name of so-called national security interests or specious economic reasons – would constitute a dangerous exception but also a denial of justice and an intolerable breach of the right of all human beings to life, security and peace.

Sources: Boutros Boutros-Ghali, 'Les mines terrestres, un désastre humanit-aire', *Politique Etrangère*, Winter 1994–95. Reports from Handicap International (www.handicap-international.org) and the International Campaign to Ban Landmines (www.icbl.org). *Le Monde*, 2 March 1999, 11 October 1997, 17 January 1996.

Pointers and Recommendations

- Pursue the fight in favour of the eradication of poverty, a major cause of many intra-state conflicts.
- Encourage the creation at the international, regional and local levels of forecasting and early prevention capacity and impede the deterioration of conflictual situations.
- Promote the implementation of education and training programmes that encourage the reincorporation of demobilized soldiers into civilian life.
- Encourage the emergence of democratic societies through the implementation of educational projects focused on greater knowledge of the values of democracy, human rights, tolerance and peace.

- Proceed with micro-disarmament on the occasion of implementation of peace agreements.
- Encourage the adoption, within the United Nations, of an international code of conduct on the control and limitation of transfers of conventional weapons.
- Promote efforts undertaken within the United Nations Disarmament Committee with a view to the adoption of an international convention on disarmament, particularly for nuclear weapons.
- Increase human security through the redefinition, within all countries, of internal budgetary priorities in favour of investment allocated to education, health, housing and environmental conservation.
- Pursue efforts to sensitize and mobilize public opinion in favour of sustained reduction in defence budgets.
- Encourage the sharing between countries of information concerning successful efforts at reconversion.
- Promote a debate at international level on the creation of a World Demilitarization Fund, financed in particular through a tax levied on the arms trade and through savings made in defence budgets in the industrialized countries.
- Reduce military aid to the developing countries and link economic and technical aid to efforts at reducing defence expenditure and the concomitant definition of budgetary priorities in favour of social and human development (education, health, food security, etc.).

Notes

1. Vinceç Fisas, 'No farewell to arms', *UNESCO Courier*, April 1999. Sources: Stockholm International Peace Research Institute, *SIPRI Yearbook 1998. Armaments, Disarmaments and International Security*, SIPRI/Oxford University Press, New York, 1998; Arms Control and Disarmament Agency, *World Military Expenditures and Arms Transfers 1996*, ACDA, Washington, DC; Bonn International Centre for Conversion, *Conversion Survey 1998. Global Disarmament, Defense Industry and Conversion*, BICC, Oxford University Press, New York, 1998.

2. Ibid.

3. Jean-Claude Berthélemy, Robert S. McNamara and Somnath Sen, *The Disarmament Dividends: Challenges for Development Policy*, OECD Development Centre, Paris, 1994.

4. UNDP, *Human Devlopment Report 1994*, Oxford University Press, New York, 1994.

5. BICC, *Conversion Survey 1998*.

6. SIPRI, *SIPRI Yearbook 1998*.

7. Fisas, 'No farewell to arms'. Data for 1988–97.

8. SIPRI, *SIPRI Yearbook 1998*.

9. Gerard Baker, 'The product of peace', *Financial Times*, 18 August 1997.

10. UNDP, *Human Development Report*, Oxford University Press, New York, 1997.

11. UN, *Facts about the United Nations*, United Nations Information Service, DPI/ 1753/Rev.16, October 1998.

12. SIPRI, *SIPRI Yearbook 1998*.

13. Source: UNDP, *Human Development Report*, quoted by Fisas, 'No farewell to arms'.

14. Michael Renner, 'Budgeting for disarmament', *State of the World 1995*, World-watch Institute, Washington, DC, 1995.

15. Between 1960 and 1987, defence expenditure increased three times faster in the developing countries than in the industrialized countries, rising from US$24 to US$245 billion, and from 7% to 15% of worldwide defence expenditure; UNDP,*Human Development Report 1994*.

16. BICC, *Conversion Survey 1998*.

17. *UNESCO Courier*, April 1999.

18. BICC, *Conversion Survey 1997, Global Disarmament and Disposal of Surplus Weapons*, BICC, Oxford University Press, New York, 1997.

19. Bernard Adam, 'Armes légères, destructions massives', *Le Monde diplomatique*, April 1998.

20. *Message from His Holiness Pope John Paul II to mark the celebration of World Peace Day*, 1 January 1999, Libreria Editrice Vaticana, Vatican City.

21. SIPRI, *SIPRI Yearbook 1998*.

22. BICC, *Conversion Survey 1998*.

23. SIPRI, *SIPRI Yearbook 1998*.

24. Fisas, 'No farewell to arms'.

25. Patrice de Beer, 'Le président souhaite augmenter le budget de la défense', *Le Monde*, 5 January 1999; Stephen Fidler, 'Clinton seeks defence budget rise', *Financial Times*, 4 January 1999.

26. Baker, 'The product of peace'.

27. Malcolm Knight, Norman Loayza and Delano Villanueva, *The Peace Dividend: Military Spending Cuts and Economic Growth*, IMF Staff Papers, Vol. 43, No. 1, March 1997, International Monetary Fund, Washington, DC, 1996.

28. UNDP, *Human Development Report 1994*.

29. Ibid.

30. Steven Holtzman, *Post-conflict Reconstruction*, World Bank, Washington, DC, 1995; Françoise Lazare, 'Le mirage des marchés de la paix', *Le Monde*, 12 November 1996.

31. Berthélemy et al., *The Disarmament Dividends*.

32. *Economic and social situation in the world*, Economic and Social Council, United Nations, 1995.

33. Berthélemy et al., *The Disarmament Dividends*.

34. UNDP, *Human Development Report 1994*.

35. Fisas, 'No farewell to arms'.

36. Berthélemy et al., *The Disarmament Dividends*.

37. Renner, 'Budgeting for disarmament'.

38. BICC, *Conversion Survey 1998*.

39. Renner, 'Budgeting for disarmament'.

40. UNDP, *Human Development Report 1994*.

41. Yves-Michel Riols, 'Székesfehérvar, l'ancienne ville des rois symbolise le renouveau hongrois', *Le Monde*, 6 December 1995.

42. BICC, *Conversion Survey 1998*.

43. UNDP, *Human Development Report 1994*.

44. According to SIPRI data, the five permanent members of the Security Council jointly contributed to 80% of arms transfers between 1993 and 1997.

45. UNDP, *Human Development Report 1994*.

46. *UNESCO Courier*, April 1999.

47. Berthélemy et al., *The Disarmament Dividends*.

48. Renner, 'Budgeting for disarmament'.

49. In particular the Institut des Hautes Études de Défense Nationale (France).

50. Federico Mayor, preface to *What Kind of Security?*, UNESCO, Paris, 1998.

51. Federico Mayor, address given on the occasion of the awarding of the Joaquin Garrigues Walker Prize by the Salvador de Madariaga Foundation, Madrid, September 1997.

52. Moufida Goucha, introduction to *What Kind of Security?*, UNESCO, Paris, 1998.

53. Jacques Attali, *Economie de l'Apocalypse, Trafic et prolifération nucléaires*, Report to the Secretary-General of the United Nations, Fayard, Paris, 1995.

54. SIPRI, *SIPRI Yearbook 1998*.

55. UNDP, *Human Development Report 1994*.

56. Ibid.

57. Commission on Global Governance, *Our Global Neighbourhood*, Oxford University Press, New York, 1995.

58. Independent Commission on Disarmament and Security Issues, *Common Security: A Programme for Disarmament*, London, 1982.

59. Commission on Global Governance, *Our Global Neighbourhood*.

60. Ibid.

61. Renner, 'Budgeting for disarmament'.

62. BICC, *Conversion Survey 1998*.

63. Federico Mayor, address given at the fifth International Conference on Adult Education, Hamburg, July 1997.

64. Mayor, preface to *What Kind of Security?*.

65. Federico Mayor, address to the meeting of the Council of Ministers of the Western European Union (WEU), May 1997.

CHAPTER 19

What Future for the United Nations System?

§ THE United Nations organization has undergone substantial changes since its foundation, growing from 50 member states in 1945 to 188 today. Its mission too has expanded, to keep up with the changing needs of international security and development. When the United Nations Charter was drawn up, the problems of population, migration, food safety, poverty, the environment, and democracy, which lie at the very heart of the UN's concerns today, were not the major issues they have now become. Designed as it was to contend with the problems of the post-war period, the United Nations system seems ill-prepared today to take up the challenge of world development.[1] Furthermore, the system suffers from three major shortcomings:

- the lack of political will that characterizes its main protagonists;
- the lack of investment in the system, resulting in an almost permanent financial crisis; and
- the lack of forward vision, which condemns the system to react to crises as the need arises, and to adjust as best it can to changes as they happen, confining it to bureaucratic routine and no-win strategies.

Is it so surprising, then, that the system's workings are fraught with gross imbalances? The UN's main effort is focused too sharply on peacekeeping at the moment,[2] to the detriment of 'peace-building' – an expression that, as I see it, covers the restoration of peace and the prevention of conflicts, as well as development in its widest sense. In my opinion the UN has fallen victim to the tyranny of the short term and to urgency, condemning it to an essentially humanitarian role and, in the long run, to failure if remedial action is not taken soon. Can we seriously stand by and watch the organization whose Charter assigned it the task of delivering humankind from the scourge of war turn into a sort of Red Cross berated by the media for its ineffectiveness, and financially paralysed by the refusal of some of its largest contributors to pay their outstanding contributions?

In his report in July 1997, Secretary-General Kofi Annan stressed the importance of a reform of the United Nations system.[3] This effort must not be confined to the essential administrative revitalization measures that have already been set in motion: it is a question not just of bringing the system up to date, but of restoring strength and substance to the common ideals set forth in the Charter of the United Nations. It is vital now, based on an analysis of the changes the system has undergone in the last 50 years, to forge new prospects for the future and build the United Nations of the twenty-first century, giving the organization the financial means indispensable to the fulfilment of its mission. Let there be no doubt about it: in order to rise to the major challenges of the twenty-first century, some of which are referred to in this report, the world needs the United Nations more than ever.

Why the United Nations?

'Why the United Nations?' will ask the sceptics, the advocates of *Realpolitik*, stressing the increasing role of regional alliances. 'Why the United Nations?' will echo those indignant that the ideals of peace and development have too often been conveniently set aside by the international community, which has too often displayed inertia in the face of violence, genocide and human suffering. 'Why the United Nations?' will add with feigned candour those who believe in the *laisser-faire* approach and in a world providentially guided by the invisible hand of market forces. 'Why the United Nations?' will ask those who continue to believe that peace and security can be guaranteed by the sovereign state alone.

So, why the United Nations? First of all, *because the challenges of the future all have a global dimension*, and more than ever our world needs an international lookout agency and watchtower to make the ideals enshrined in the Charter of the United Nations prevail through dialogue and multilateral consultation. In a world characterized by interdependence and by a growing awareness of our common destiny, solving problems requires coordinated action on a worldwide scale. As former UN Secretary-General Boutros Boutros-Ghali once said, 'the United Nations Organization is destined to play an increasingly important role, because the international community will increasingly be faced with problems of global dimension that need to be solved on a global scale. And for the time being, the only institution which has the means of solving global problems is the United Nations.'[4] Provided that it receives the necessary support and resources from the member states, the United Nation system is destined to play a major role in conflict management and prevention, broadening the content of development aid and awareness of the increasing importance of the regional and transnational dimensions. In the face of these increasingly global challenges, we now know from experience that nations cannot, without serious consequences for the peace, well-being and security of all, hide behind a wall of sovereignty, unilateralism and nationalism. As the economist John Kenneth Galbraith has pointed out:

> Nothing is so accepted in our times as respect for sovereignty; nothing, on occasion, so protects disorder, poverty and hardship ... I do believe we need a much stronger role for international action, including, needless to say, the United Nations. We need to have a much larger sense of common responsibility for those suffering from the weakness, corruption, disorder and cruelty of bad government or none at all. Sovereignty, though it has something close to religious status in modern political thought, must not protect human despair. This may not be a popular point; popularity is not always a test of needed intelligence.[5]

In the face of an increasingly global market, we must henceforth advance resolutely towards an international democracy. Will we not be obliged one day, as Jacques Attali has suggested, to devise a democracy that 'like the market, is not limited by a territory, a democracy without frontiers in space and time'?[6] As I mentioned earlier, military action by NATO in Kosovo and Serbia set a very dangerous precedent, even in a context where human rights violations by the Serbian authorities were plain to see. Action must be taken in the only democratic framework that exists on an international scale, namely the United Nations. If the United Nations organization has been weakened in the course of time, it must be made strong again. But it is both inadmissible and incoherent to want to promote democracy at the national level while practising oligarchy at the international level, by trying to carry out justice oneself, so to speak. Only in the framework of the United Nations should international codes of conduct be adopted, or blue helmets be sent.

Why the United Nations? *Because our world has no memory.* That is why it needs institutions capable of ensuring the effective implementation of the international principles and commitments to which the United Nations member states have subscribed since the organization's foundation, and which were further developed by the summits organized by the system in the 1990s: human rights, the right to development, the right to education, the right to housing, children's rights, women's rights and many more besides, including one that I believe is fundamental, one without which all the others are dead letters, namely the human right to peace.[7]

Why the United Nations? *Because of the increasing inequality in our world.*[8] This is why it needs international organizations to make sure that everybody enjoys the right to dignity, freedom and security enshrined in the Universal Declaration of Human Rights. This is why it needs institutions that promote 'the economic and social advancement of all peoples' (Charter of the United Nations, preamble), institutions that strive to eradicate poverty, as the states party to the Copenhagen Declaration adopted in 1995 at the summit on social development have vowed to do, and that commit themselves to lifelong education for all, as recommended by UNESCO.

Why the United Nations? *Because our world is dominated by a culture of war, violence and oppression.* It is high time we laid the foundations for a culture of peace. The role of the UN and the system as a whole is 'to save succeeding generations from the scourge of war'; the only way to achieve this aim is to build peace on a day-to-day basis, brick by brick, by promoting development that is both human and sustainable, by promoting justice and strengthening democracy. The wealthy countries must realize what the options are: either they show solidarity – in which case they make friends and even win clients – or they do not, in which case they make enemies and generate radicalization, exclusion, aggressiveness and illegal immigration. We must learn to live together, as the Delors Commission urged in 1996.[9] United States President Abraham Lincoln once said: 'A house divided against itself cannot stand.'[10] The same applies to our world today, which is our common home. United we stand, divided we fall. *Learning to live together is therefore the greatest challenge of the twenty-first century. The United Nations system is the keystone of this common edifice.*

Why the United Nations? *Because our world is short-sighted.* It needs a completely reformed system to enable it to anticipate and prevent conflicts and crises, rather than a short-sighted approach consisting in taking emergency action too late and at too high a cost only to achieve what is invariably an unsatisfactory result. Our world needs foresight if it is to map out a lastingly fairer and more human course for future generations, based on solidarity. This cannot be achieved through unilateralism, egocentricity or short-sighted nationalism. Rehabilitation in the long term will be achieved only through dialogue, mutual respect, consultation and mediation.

Why the United Nations? *Because our world cannot build peace and security for all on the basis of economic precepts alone,* much less on dogmas whose impotence and harmfulness have recently been demonstrated by the international financial crisis. The mission of the United Nations is at the same time deeply ethical and political, as affirmed in its Charter and as proclaimed in visionary terms in the UNESCO Constitution, according to which peace 'must be founded upon the intellectual and moral solidarity of mankind'. In this perspective the decision of the United Nations General Assembly to make 2000 the International Year for a Culture of Peace was welcome. In the words of Kofi Annan:

for the United Nations there is no higher goal, no deeper commitment and no greater ambition than preventing armed conflict. The prevention of conflict begins and ends with the promotion of human security and human development. Ensuring human security is, in the broadest sense, the cardinal mission of the United Nations. Genuine and lasting prevention is the means to achieve that mission.[11]

Why the United Nations? *Because the problems of the world all have a universal and ethical dimension that transcends national borders, cultures and prejudices.* The principles of democracy and human rights, justice, sharing, solidarity and respect for the dignity of others belong to no single civilization or culture: they are part of our common ethical heritage. They are universal, indivisible aspirations that require us fully to assume our responsibilities, not only towards present generations but also, as highlighted by UNESCO, towards future generations.

A Stitch in Time

In the last ten years or so the nature of conflicts has changed: even when they are kindled by outside influences, they are generally confined within a state and involve opposing ethnic groups, political clans or even mafia or religious communities. In Chapter 18 it was pointed out that in 1995 most armed conflicts were intra-state conflicts.[12] The international system is still ill-prepared to respond to the extreme complexity of the present conflicts, as evidenced by the tragic failures and mistakes that marked the multilateral operations in Somalia, Rwanda and Bosnia. These shortcomings are compounded by a lack of motivation on the part of states reluctant to get involved in these operations, and by their lack of long-term outlook. As the foreign affairs minister of Côte d'Ivoire, Amara Essy, president of the 49th session of the United Nations General Assembly, rightly said, 'the short term always imposes its constraints on governments, which impose them on the UN'.[13]

With emergency action already gobbling up 80% of the United Nations system's resources (currently in the form of peacekeeping operations and emergency humanitarian aid) we must now strive to impose a long-term outlook, to anticipate and act in good time, in order to be proactive rather than ploddingly following the ups and downs of the current situation, and adapting and adjusting as best we can. We now know that if we do not act in time, future generations will have no time to act at all: they will be prisoners of processes beyond their control – population growth, the degradation of the environment, increasing inequalities, growing social and urban apartheid, the weakening of democracy, the spread of corruption and mafia activities, and the widening of the gap between the info-rich and the info-poor.

The stress placed on humanitarian-type missions today clearly shows that urgency prevails. But urgency hinders the solution of problems in the long term, and undermines the whole idea of a collective project. We spend colossal amounts on 'restoring' peace by deploying armies, then on restoring, repairing and rebuilding what war has destroyed. From now on we must tackle the very deepest roots of these conflicts: ignorance, intolerance and selfishness, economic hardship, social injustice, political oppression, discrimination and exclusion in every form.

True, forward vision is not a new idea. From Machiavelli to Max Weber, it is the virtue of princes *par excellence.* But it is now all the more necessary insofar as, at the dawn of the twenty-first century, new approaches are needed in the fields of peace and development in order to rise to the new challenges of globalization. The 1998 UNCTAD report strongly emphasizes the importance foresight can have in dealing with financial crises.[14] Preventive action is an indispensable investment for world security and, as Gareth Evans has pointed out, it would be wise to devote a large share of the security budgets traditionally earmarked for military spending to preventive measures instead.[15] Such preventive action is the very essence of UNESCO's vocation, since its essentially ethical mission is to 'construct the defences of peace in the minds of men', through education, science, culture and communication. It is therefore time we fully implemented the provisions of the Charter in the United Nations system and moved on from the idea of peacekeeping as the essential task of United Nations to a more responsible image of the organization, hinging on conflict prevention and peace building.[16]

To rise to the task that awaits it in the twenty-first century, the United Nations system must prove that it is capable of thinking and acting in a long-term perspective. The system's different agencies will have to enhance their powers of anticipation and act as a forward-looking think-tank to prevent conflicts from breaking out. These functions of anticipation, analysis and forward planning with a view to prevention and action, are an absolute priority. If it assumes them to the full, the United Nations system will be well equipped to light the way for politicians and to take timely action, before situations have time to degenerate, by setting up 'early warning systems'.[17] Only a long-term outlook and the corresponding action can guarantee peace and security in the world and foster development. Promoting a culture of peace, which is henceforth a priority of the system, is part of this approach and represents a new form of international cooperation geared to the notions of anticipation and prevention.

We are therefore glad to see that there is growing awareness of this need. Following his July 1997 reform plan, the secretary-general of the United Nations set up a Strategic Planning Unit. Similar long-term forecasting instruments have already been set up by the Commission of the European Communities and certain specialized agencies within the system, such as the FAO and, since 1994, UNESCO, where this function is fulfilled by the Analysis and Forecasting Office. This systematic strengthening of anticipation and

forecasting capability will fully bear fruit only if forecasting units or departments are provided with adequate means and are genuinely able to influence
the decision-making process.

For a Broader Approach to the Concept of Security

The concept of 'security' on a worldwide scale can no longer be confined
today to the traditional notion of the political/military security of states. In
its broadest sense, security means access to sustainable economic and social
development; it means banishing poverty from the face of the earth, as
recommended at the United Nations Summit on social development in Copenhagen in 1995. Establishing human security on these foundations is one of the
main aims of the United Nations system. The ministers of foreign affairs of
the Group of 77 stressed the need for the UN to play 'an active and central
role in examining the question of development based on an integrated
approach'.[18] In a similar spirit, at the Halifax Summit (June 1995), the G7
countries encouraged participatory development strategies, and at the Lyon
Summit (June 1996) they stressed the need to build a new global partnership
between developing countries, developed countries and multilateral institutions
and to rethink development policies and in particular development assistance,[19]
and recommended that the Security Council work in closer cooperation with
an Economic and Social Council (ECOSOC) with greater powers and a stronger
coordinating role.[20]

We believe that the global dimensions of security must henceforth be taken
into account at the highest level in the United Nations. True, significant
progress has been made in the 'multi-dimensional' approach to security[21] and
in gaining a broader vision of the threats to international peace and security.[22]
True, the Security Council does not deal only with political or strategic-cum-
military disputes. However, in view of the increasing interdependence of
political, economic, financial, social and environmental phenomena, other
threats to human security should be included more systematically in its
mandate: the degradation of the environment and living conditions, overpopulation, cultural and ethnic rivalries, all forms of human rights violations.
This reform is essential in order to make up some of the time the institutions
of world governance have lost in the face of rampant globalization, marked
by rapid change, often without any form of regulation.

It is vital to pursue this line of thinking – a process initiated by various fora
and encouraged by the international community. A proposal made by Jacques
Delors and subsequently taken up by the Commission on Global Governance
in its report entitled *Our Global Neighbourhood*, suggested setting up an Economic Security Council, which would be 'a global forum that can provide
leadership in economic, social, and environmental fields'. It would assemble,

under the auspices of the United Nations, the heads of state and government once a year, and in the interim the ministers primarily concerned, particularly those responsible for the economy and finance, to 'give political leadership and promote consensus on international economic issues where there are long-term threats to security in its widest sense' and to follow up the 'summits' and their resolutions.[23] The independent Working Group on the future of the United Nations, chaired by Moeen Qureshi and Richard von Weizsäcker, proposed a similar sort of mechanism: an Economic Council together with a Social Council, which would become main organs of the United Nations system as is the Security Council. These councils would help to forge a 'global alliance for sustainable development' to foster a comprehensive, global approach by member states, in the fields of monetary, financial and trade policy and also in environmental and social policy (reduction of poverty, social development, humanitarian questions, human rights, aid to states in distress).

In practical terms, we believe that the various threats that hang over us and jeopardize human security – degradation of the environment and living conditions, over-population, cultural and ethnic rivalries, human rights violations – should be included more systematically in the mandate of the UN Security Council, which has 'primary responsibility for the maintenance of international peace and security' (Article 24, paragraph 1 of the Charter). Extending the Security Council's powers in this way is justified by the spread of the notion of security in recent decades to encompass the social, ecological and even cultural fields. What is more, it would avoid the creation of new structures, and the concomitant extra cost, lost efficiency and duplication of effort they entail. It would make for clearer delimitation of the powers of the main organs of the United Nations, facilitating the coordination of their complementary activities. As we mentioned in Part II of this report, perhaps it would also be possible to form a corps of 'green helmets' to protect the environment, founded in particular on scientific know-how.

Improved coordination must also be achieved between the United Nations and the system's specialized agencies. As the representatives of the G7 countries stressed in Halifax, and again in Lyon, these agencies must once again become centres of authority in their fields. This means improving their interaction with national reflection groups, international scientific committees and research centres. Collaboration between the various specialized agencies will be effective only if it takes place in the field as well as at headquarters. The synergy between the system's institutions must be felt at the top – in discussions and decision-making – and also at the base, where decisions and programmes are put into action. More and more, the United Nations system and the institutions that compose it will have to function as networks, cutting down on bureaucracy and making use of the most modern means of information and communication. In the twenty-first century they will have to operate in an increasingly preventive spirit, both globally and in the field, developing their faculties of anticipation and forecasting, policy analysis and advice, and standard-setting.

The specialized agencies are not always able to rise to new challenges because of lack of interest on the part of the funding agencies. Closer co-ordination is needed between the Bretton Woods institutions and the rest of the system, hence the importance of the stance adopted by the G7 countries in favour of a new balance in relations between the United Nations and the Bretton Woods institutions, with the UN organizations acting as agents of intellectual cooperation, able to take part in the mobilization of funds in favour of specific projects.

In order for the organs of the United Nations system fully to recover their authority, they must have the support of governments and adequate financial means. Unfortunately, for a number of years now the policy of member states towards the United Nations has consisted mainly in cutbacks and reductions in the operating budget and in staff. 'Zero nominal growth' has become a byword; in practice it means doing more with less. The countries of the European Union acknowledged that 'it is the responsibility of the Member States to provide clear and coherent policy direction to the UN system as a whole'.[24] The support of the member states will be all the more effective and long-lasting if the institutions in the system are capable of making the most of their comparative advantages, and of carrying out the necessary reforms and getting rid of the dead wood of bureaucracy and routine.

Defending Human Dignity

Strengthening human security means protecting human dignity. Serious, repeated human rights violations – torture, summary executions and arbitrary imprisonment, sexual exploitation of children, child slave labour, discrimination and violence against women, persecution of ethnic and religious minorities, and so on – call for a commensurate response on the part of the international community. The United Nations has a fundamental arbitration role to play here: states must be encouraged to ratify the Rome Statute of 17 July 1998 on the establishment of an International Criminal Court to try individuals for heinous crimes affecting the international community, such as genocide, war crimes and crimes against humanity.[25] For there is perhaps something more important than economic globalization, namely the globalization of justice, law and democracy.[26] Furthermore, we believe it is the duty of the United Nations to take military action, under the supervision of the Security Council, when all other attempts at arbitration and negotiation have failed, particularly in the event of large-scale human rights violations, and where the state no longer exists and has been replaced by the law of the jungle. In such cases military intervention must be motivated solely by the need to protect people and property and to restore or establish the conditions necessary for lasting peace and development.

The United Nations must promote every dimension of human dignity: human rights include not only civil and political rights, but also economic, social and cultural rights, all of which are enshrined in the International Covenants on Human Rights adopted in 1966. Human rights must be considered universal and indivisible: we must combat oppression and violence on all fronts – combat extreme poverty and torture, hunger and political oppression, discrimination against women, and fight for access to education for all. The indivisible nature of human rights was reaffirmed by the United Nations Conference on human rights held in Vienna in 1993. The rights of the homeless people who live in the cities of the world's wealthiest countries must be as precious to us as the rights of those who are deprived of freedom of expression or association.

Stepping up Official Development Assistance

Official development assistance appears more essential now than ever, especially as we now know from experience that the countries that suffer most from internal strife are often those where economic conditions are hardest and the political system is unstable. Official development assistance cannot turn a blind eye to local conditions, which often limit its impact: it must even contribute actively to the creation of a favourable economic, social, institutional and human environment, and to enhanced resource use.

Official development assistance is all the more indispensable in that it helps to make up for the lack of private investment, which is too selective and contributes only marginally to the development of educational, sanitary and social infrastructure, and which is more sensitive to short-term economic trends (in 1998 private investment dropped by US$100 billion).[27] Furthermore, it seldom goes to the countries that need it most. In 1997, 72.3% of all direct private investment capital went to nine developing countries and one country in transition, namely, in decreasing order, China, Brazil, Mexico, Indonesia, Poland, Malaysia, Argentina, Chile, India and Venezuela;[28] between 1989 and 1992, only 2% of private capital went to the least developed countries.[29] The main flows of private funds thus largely bypass Africa: according to the World Bank, sub-Saharan Africa received only 1.8% of net private capital investment in low- and average-income countries in 1996.[30] 'Increasing private capital flows, it was rightly concluded, merely widens the gaps between Third World countries';[31] this tendency weighs all the more heavily on the future of the poorest countries insofar as this type of investment increasingly concerns the service sector, and in particular the strategic area of communication technologies.[32] The international organizations will therefore have a decisive role of arbitration to play in the future to strike the right balance between public and private investment, for spontaneous market trends alone cannot be relied on to fuel development in the least advanced countries.

There is no denying that current trends in this field are a source of concern. There has been a decline in international solidarity since the end of the Cold War, accompanied by a decrease in development assistance. At the present time only four countries – Denmark, Norway, the Netherlands and Sweden – have met the official target of 0.7% of GDP set by the United Nations conferences, i.e. by the member states themselves.[33] Public development assistance has declined for the member countries of the OECD's Development Assistance Committee, from an average of 0.38% of donor countries' GNP in 1980 to only 0.22% in 1997; according to the OECD, development cooperation budgets slumped much more sharply than other public spending, 'with the result that the share of Official Development Assistance (ODA) in total public spending fell from 0.8% to 0.6%' from 1992 to 1997: for the G7 countries assistance decreased by 27% in real terms from 1992 to 1997.[34] What is more, the effort is very unevenly distributed (the USA contributes only 0.09% of its GNP) and variable (Sweden plans to increase its ODA by 25% by 2002, while Japan intends to cut its assistance programme by 10% over three years). At the same time, countries are reducing their voluntary contributions to the United Nations system;[35] and this has resulted in a general decrease in the development assistance provided by the system from 1993 to 1997.[36]

As a matter of fact, with what they pay to service their debt, developing countries pay more to the industrialized countries than they receive from them. Can we, in all fairness, tolerate a situation where the rich thrive on the hardship of the poor? The ministers of foreign affairs of the Group of 77 urged the donor countries to improve the quality of official development assistance, in particular by reducing the cost of reimbursement.[37] While the Paris Club countries have agreed to go further than what was agreed in Naples and offer debt reductions of up to 80%, the USA grants only 6% of its total foreign aid to the African continent, i.e. 0.5% of its budget.[38] It has been stated that the initiative taken in 1996 by the world's richest countries to cancel up to 80% of the debt of the highly indebted poor countries (HIPC initiative) and the Cologne initiative adopted at the G7 Summit in June 1999 were two very encouraging steps in the right direction. But we must go further and cancel the debt of the poorest countries altogether – and include as many countries as possible in this measure.[39]

Also, is it not strange that two-thirds of the world's poor should receive less than one-third of all official development assistance? According to the UNDP, 'the wealthiest 40% of inhabitants of the developing world receive twice as much aid per person as the poorest 40%'.[40] The aid does not even always go to the most urgent priorities: in 1996 the OECD member states devoted only 16.8% of bilateral aid to education and health.[41] Official development assistance must not only be increased, it must above all be given a thorough overhaul, based on the recommendations of the United Nations social development summit (Copenhagen, 1995), which suggested strongly increasing the share of aid devoted to human development.

The industrialized countries will only succeed in solving their own problems in a global perspective based on solidarity, by contributing to the development of the countries of the South. In this way official development assistance will once again be a tool at the service of projects supported by informed and responsible partners and in keeping with genuine local needs.[42] In this context the United Nations Organization must 'promote awareness, build consensus and inform policy in every dimension affecting development and help rationalize and harmonize the multiplicity of public and private efforts worldwide'.[43] In other words, 'the UN must be the privileged instrument of a more human world economy'.[44]

The Role of Regional Cooperation Agreements

Regional cooperation and the resulting transfers of sovereignty have become one of the major geopolitical issues of recent years. Indeed, even if the notions of sovereignty and independence remain fundamental principles of relations between states, they alone are insufficient to contend with certain challenges that require concerted action and joint projects involving several states. Sovereignty is increasingly being transferred to regional organizations, be they primarily economic, political or strategic. We think we should welcome these processes with confidence and optimism, as long as they reflect the rejection of all hegemony and the free choice of responsible partners, aware of the potential benefits involved.

As well as stimulating development, regional cooperation can boost democracy and 'good governance', while contributing to the integration of minorities who have long been marginalized by the rigidity of traditional borders. But above all, it helps to overcome the temptation of self-centred nationalistic isolationism, as it contributes to the search for dialogue and consensus and makes it possible for states to work together. In the future, the regional level could be an intermediate step towards greater integration worldwide. The United Nations system should give more attention to this role, either by holding regular meetings with the regional organizations,[45] or by granting them observer status as it does to various states and NGOs.[46]

So we must encourage the integration process at the regional level, for this is a particularly effective means of alleviating tensions that can otherwise lead to conflicts. As Maurice Bertrand wrote, European construction 'has managed to make the outbreak of war between France, England, Germany, Spain,

Austria and Italy virtually unthinkable, when these countries were involved in countless conflicts prior to 1945, including two world wars'.[47] Cooperation agreements and security organizations are a major factor of political stability at regional level, as demonstrated today by such examples as MERCOSUR, the Organization for Security and Cooperation in Europe (OSCE) or the Association of South East Asian Nations (ASEAN). By contrast, it is in those regions or subregions of the world where integration has made slow progress or none at all that the most serious conflicts and tensions now prevail and the arms race is escalating.

Participation by Society

Establishing the conditions of peace and development at the international level requires genuine participation by every level of society. One trend that has marked the world in the last 20 years is the increasing contribution by the various social actors to debates hitherto confined to the political elite. This phenomenon is no doubt partially attributable to the extension of the work done by the United Nations and, to quote Leon Gordenker, 'to the penetration of the activities of the United Nations institutions into the very heart of national societies'.[48] Even today, however, governments are still the main protagonists of the United Nations system and society's influence on the elaboration of policies by the international community – and particularly the UN – remains very limited, because it is so piecemeal and disorderly. Most decisions continue to be taken at the national level, whereas nowadays, more often than not, problems need to be tackled and dealt with at the international level, whether they concern the environment, migration, currency, drugs or financial market regulation.

Certain organizations have long since brought society's representatives into the decision-making process: the ILO is a noteworthy example, as its governing bodies are tripartite bodies composed of representatives of governments, the private sector and the unions. At major international summit meetings too, the various social players are increasingly present, even if the governments do tend to debate and decide amongst themselves in Rio, Vienna, Cairo, Copenhagen and Beijing, while the non-governmental organizations meet away from the limelight of the official tribunes, in fora organized specially for civil society representatives. A particularly important innovation marked the United Nations Conference on Human Settlements (Habitat II, Istanbul, June 1996): for the first time the governments invited non-governmental partners to take part in the official discussions. A series of consultative fora was organized and the conclusions were reported to the plenary session or included in recommendations and were thus able to influence the talks directly. In this way representatives of cities, the private sector, women and young people, and also experts in long-term forecasting all contributed to the final decisions. The approach adopted in Istanbul should serve as an example: why does the United Nations system not take inspiration from it, for example during General Assembly sessions?[49]

The multilateral system would be all the more efficient and discussions would gain in transparency if key figures in the worlds of business and international associations as well as experts and scientists were allowed to have a say, even in an advisory capacity, at least where development strategies were concerned. This would mean first defining the framework of their participation and ensuring they did not trespass on the sovereignty of member states. Perhaps one might also envisage setting up international forecasting fora combining the economic and political approaches. In the United Nations system even more than elsewhere, it is important that all the member countries should be able to participate equitably in the discussion and decision-making processes.

It is important not to underestimate the role played by multinational firms in these times of globalization. Their turnover can easily exceed the GNP of certain small countries. Of the 200 main economic operators in the world today, only about forty are states. So it would no doubt be wise to involve multinational firms in deliberations on the challenges of development and in the implementation of solutions, rather than ignoring them: it is important to develop the sense of political and ethical responsibility of these major economic players, most of which, at present, are answerable for their actions only to the financial markets and their own shareholders. In the environmental field, for example, many multinationals have already taken a step in this direction and made an effort to adapt to the changes under way, either in response to public concern or in anticipation of the effects of new legislation to protect the biosphere.[50] These large business concerns are increasingly involved in the running and the research work of the main long-range forecasting institutes. So if multinational firms can be made more responsible by giving them an advisory role on national and international decision-making bodies, the effect could be beneficial for all concerned: the multilateral system, states and the firms themselves.

Financing the United Nations System

To quote Amara Essy again, 'the UN will not be able to rise to the challenges facing our planet until it is given the structural and financial wherewithal to accomplish its fundamental missions'.[51] The United Nations organization costs too much, some people say. But does it? The UN and its programmes and funds have an annual budget of US$4.8 billion for their social development activities, to help countries in the fields of education, health, agriculture, food distribution, etc. That is less than one dollar (about

81 cents) per human being; by comparison, the military spending of the world's governments in 1996 amounted to US$797 billion, the equivalent of US$135 per inhabitant of the world.[52] The total cost of the UN's peacekeeping operations represents less than 0.2% of military spending in the world; the total operating cost of the whole United Nations system – including the World Bank, the IMF and all the funds, programmes and specialized institutions – amounts to US$18.2 billion a year, which is less than the annual income of one large company like Dow Chemicals (over US$20 billion in 1997). The whole United Nations system worldwide, with the Secretariat in New York plus 28 other organizations, including UNESCO, employs 52,280 people. McDonald's has three times as many employees; Disney World and Disneyland employ 50,000 people.

For thousands of years we have invested in war; now we must pay the price of peace. The UN's financial problems must be resolved without delay, to enable the organization to get on with its job. The whole United Nations system must concentrate first and foremost on stepping up its preventive efforts and its forecasting work, as well as its advisory and initiative-taking role.

The sums required to remedy the funding problem no doubt exceed what the states alone can afford, so new sources of funding need to be found. Here one can imagine far more systematic partnerships with the non-profit sector and the private sector, together with voluntary contributions from citizens, foundations and firms. Several interesting proposals concerning alternative sources of funds have also been made in reports by the UNDP, the Commission for Global Governance and the Independent Working Group on the Future of the United Nations:[53] setting up a demilitarization fund, or levying taxes on the arms trade, international currency transactions and the exploitation of mankind's common resource heritage. Very careful thought should now be given to all these suggestions, for we cannot go on adding to the system's list of missions while continuing to strangle it financially.

Reforming the United Nations is no easy task. It took the European regional institutions 40 years to achieve any significant degree of intergovernmental cooperation, and even now it remains fragile. This reform is unavoidable, for it will modernize the project enshrined in the preamble of the United Nations Charter. The funding required to reform the system would be amply offset by the benefits to be gained from effective conflict prevention.[54] As emphasized in the report of the Independent Working Group on the Future of the United Nations, which had renowned historian and forecasting expert Paul Kennedy as its secretary, this is an essential investment for the future, the cost of which is nothing compared to the price we will have to pay if we just sit back and hope the world can weather the storms ahead.

The United Nations system is currently faced with deep unrest and a barrage of criticism. But we must pay no heed to the harbingers of doom who forecast its imminent collapse, or to its equally pessimistic opponents, who love to criticize its cumbersome inefficiency. In actual fact, the system is a formidable cooperation machine, an instrument of development and peace, which needs a thorough reform because it is working, in the words of Secretary-General Kofi Annan, 'in favour of a vast security project for all mankind'.[55] One need only remember the tragic consequences of the mistakes made in the period between the wars and the failure of the League of Nations to understand the danger that lies in a gradual loss of interest in the United Nations system on the part of the member states. It is high time, therefore, that all the actors on the international scene clearly and unequivocally reassert their commitment to giving moral and material support to the international organizations in order to build the future, not to wait for it.

The United Nations Millennium Assembly, scheduled for 2000 – the International Year for a Culture of Peace[56] – was a highly symbolic opportunity for us all to reaffirm the various commitments enshrined in the Charter of the United Nations and to highlight the ethical mission of the United Nations system on the threshold of the third millennium. The four contracts mentioned in this work – a new social contract, a natural contract, a cultural contract and an ethical contract[57] – form the core of UNESCO's contribution to the preparation of the new millennium Assembly.

Pointers and Recommendations

- Take into account the global dimensions of security by giving the Security Council economic, social and environmental powers – this will help to forge an international consensus on essential economic, financial, commercial, political, social, ecological and cultural issues, to examine the links between them, to provide effective 'summit' follow-up and to make sure that member states effectively honour their commitments.
- Protect human dignity in all its forms, by the effective implementation of civil and political rights, but also economic, social and cultural rights, as all these universal rights together make an indivisible whole.
- Encourage the states to ratify the Rome Statute on the establishment of an International Criminal Court to try individuals for heinous crimes affecting the international community, such as genocide, war crimes and crimes against humanity.
- Make the United Nations the instrument of a more human economic and social policy, for example by increasing official development aid, particularly in the fields of education and health.
- Pay the price of peace by providing proper financing for the United Nations system, by devising new forms of financing and also by devoting a larger share of security budgets to prevention.

- Adjust the balance of relations between the United Nations and the Bretton Woods institutions and improve coordination between the United Nations and the system's specialized agencies.
- Strengthen UNESCO's role as an instrument of intellectual, moral and scientific solidarity between nations.
- Erase the debt of the poorest countries, including as many countries as possible in this measure.
- Strengthen the anticipation and forecasting powers of the whole UN system.
- Encourage the integration process at regional level in order to allay the tensions that lead to conflicts.
- Increase the participation of civil society and private firms in the decision-making process and the work of the United Nations system.

Notes

1. Federico Mayor, 'Fifty years on', *UNESCO Courier*, October 1995.

2. 'Peace-keeping is the deployment of a United Nations presence in the field, hitherto with the consent of all the parties concerned, normally involving United Nations military and/or police personnel and frequently civilians as well.' Boutros Boutros-Ghali, *Agenda for Peace*, 1992, United Nations, New York, paragraph 20.

3. Kofi Annan, 'Renewing the United Nations: a programme for reform', Resolution of the General Assembly of the United Nations (A/RES/52/12).

4. Boutros Boutros-Ghali, *Le Nouvel Observateur*, 19–25 October 1995; presentation at the '21st Century Talks' on 6 April 1998, on the theme 'Ready for the 21st century?', organized by the UNESCO Analysis and Forecasting Office.

5. John Kenneth Galbraith, 'On the continuing influence of affluence', in UNDP, *Human Development Report 1998*, Oxford University Press, New York, p. 42.

6. Jerôme Bindé, 'Prêts pour the XXIe siècle?', *Le Monde*, 29 July 1998. Presentation by Jacques Attali at the '21st Century Talks' on 6 April 1998, on the theme 'Ready for the 21st century?', organized by the UNESCO Analysis and Forecasting Office.

7. 'The human right to peace', Statement of the Director-General of UNESCO, January 1997.

8. UNDP, *Human Development Report 1998*, Chapter 1.

9. *Learning: The Treasure Within*, report to UNESCO of the International Commission on Education for the 21st Century, chaired by Jacques Delors, UNESCO Publishing, Paris, 1996.

10. Speech marking the beginning of Abraham Lincoln's campaign for the US Senate, 16 June 1858.

11. Kofi Annan, 'The causes of conflict and the promotion of durable peace and sustainable development in Africa – Report of the Secretary-General to the Security Council of the United Nations Organization', 13 April 1998.

12. *Human Development Report 1994*, p. 47; *Human Development Report 1997*, Chapter 3.

13. Interview with Amara Essy, *Pôles*, April–June 1996.

14. The report stresses that a greater understanding of the causes and nature of financial crises is essential for their better management as well as for designing policies

to reduce their likelihood. UNCTAD, *Trade and Development Report, 1998*, UNCTAD, New York, 1998.

15. Gareth Evans, 'Cooperative security and intra-state conflict', *Foreign Policy*, No. 96, Autumn 1994.

16. Federico Mayor, 'Fifty years on', *UNESCO Courier*, October 1995, p. 7.

17. Recommendation made by the G8 countries at the Denver Summit (20–22 June 1997) in the peacekeeping field (paragraph 53 of the economic communiqué).

18. A/50/518, paragraph 43.

19. Economic communiqué, paragraph 33. Proposal also supported by the European Union countries in their October 1996 memorandum.

20. The Ministers of Foreign Affairs of the Group of 77 stated, *inter alia*, that 'the Economic and Social Council should play its role to the full, as defined in the Charter and in recent resolutions of the General Assembly', A/50/518, paragraph 45.

21. Evans, 'Cooperative security', note 8.

22. See also 'From partial insecurities to global security', proceedings of the symposium organized at UNESCO (12–14 June 1996) by UNESCO and the Institut des Hautes Etudes de Défense Nationale, France.

23. Commission on Global Governance, *Our Global Neighbourhood*, Oxford University Press, 1995, pp. 153–62. See also Jacques Delors, 'Economie: pour sortir de l'impuissance', *Le Nouvel Observateur*, 19–25 October 1995, and 'Appel à l'action: Summary of Our Global Neighbourhood: The Report of the Commission on Global Governance'*, Commission on Global Governance, Geneva, 1995.

24. Memorandum, October 1996.

25. First session of the Preparatory Commission for the International Criminal Court, 16–26 February 1999. Sixty ratifications are needed for the Rome Statute of the International Criminal Court to enter into force. On 12 June 2000, 97 countries had signed the Statute, but only twelve had ratified it.

26. See Mireille Delmas-Marty, *Pour un Droit commun*, Éditions du Seuil, Paris, 1994.

27. *The Economist*, 13 February 1999. The World Bank has predicted that private investment flows towards the developing countries will stagnate in the near future, in the wake of the Asian crisis; at the same time the private resources mobilized by NGOs in favour of the developing countries are in relative decline. World Bank, *Global Development Finance 1998*, 'Analysis and summary tables', and pp. 46 and 51.

28. World Bank, *Global Development Finance 1998*, p. 20.

29. UNDP, *Human Development Report 1994*, p. 66.

30. World Bank, *World Development Report 1998/99*, Oxford University Press, New York, 1999 ('Aid and financial flows'); the proportion is 2.7% for direct foreign investment.

31. Institut Français des Relations Internationales, *Ramses Report 98*, p. 224.

32. World Bank, *Global Development Finance 1998*, p. 21.

33. OECD, *Annual Report of the Development Assistance Committee, 1998*, OEDC, Paris.

34. OECD figures (James H. Michel, chair of the Development Assistance Committee, *Development Cooperation: Annual Report of the DAC 1998*, particularly Chapter V), and World Bank, *Global Development Finance Report*, p. 50.

35. According to the report of the secretary-general of the Assembly in May 1994, there was a general 10% to 20% drop in the voluntary contributions received by the

United Nations development agencies and programmes (figures cited by Essy, *Pôles*, p. 35). According to the 1998 DAC report, the DAC countries' contribution to the multilateral organizations decreased from 17.9 to 15.9 billion dollars from 1994 to 1997, a decrease of 10.5% (Michel, *Development Cooperation*). See also 'Le sommet de la terre tourne en rond', *Libération*, 28–29 June 1997.

36. From US$6.2 billion in 1993 to US$4.9 billion in 1997 (Michel, *Development Cooperation*).

37. A/50/518, paragraph 20.

38. 'Why Africa matters: the case for continued U.S. assistance to Africa', Summit on Africa Aid, 3 February 1995.

39. See Chapter 2 and World Bank, *Global Finance Development Report 1998*, pp. 54 and ff.

40. UNDP, *Human Development Report 1994*, p. 77.

41. Teaching received 10.8%, including 1.3% for basic education, 6% went to health and population and 6.6% to water distribution and sanitation. Source: OECD Development Assistance Committee report, 1998.

42. *Le Monde*, 9 May 1996.

43. *Confronting New Challenges*, Annual Report of the Secretary-General on the Work of the Organization, 1995, paragraph 183.

44. Interview with Amara Essy, *Pôles*, April–June 1996, p. 29. A 'more human approach' to globalization was also called for by the G7 countries at the Summit in Lyons.

45. Proposal made by the secretary-general in his *Agenda for Democratization*, paragraph 82.

46. Proposal by Amara Essy, *Pôles*, April–June 1996, p. 38.

47. Maurice Bertrand, 'The road to peace', *UNESCO Courier*, October 1995, p. 16.

48. Leon Gordenker, 'UN at 50: institutional development', *International Social Science Journal*, No. 144, June 1995.

49. The Commission for Global Governance (Ramphal–Carlsson commission) recommended starting by setting up a Forum of Civil Society to meet annually in the context of the preparation of the General Assembly session (*Our Global Neighbourhood*, pp. 258–60).

50. At the Rio Conference, for example, a number of multinational firms came together to form the Business Council on Sustainable Development and published a document entitled 'Changing course'.

51. Interview with Amara Essy, *Pôles*, April–June 1996, p. 37.

52. Source: UN, 'The UN: the truth in facts and figures', updated in October 1998.

53. *The United Nations in its Second Half-Century: The Report of the Independent Working Group on the Future of the United Nations*, 1995.

54. The United Nations basic annual operating budget totals US$1.3 billion, which represents about 4% of the annual budget of a city such as New York. The part of its budget the UN devotes to political and peacekeeping problems is the equivalent of 0.05% of the military spending in the world.

55. Kofi Annan, Davos speech, 31 January 1998.

56. Resolution 52/15 of the UN General Assembly.

57. See the Introduction in particular.

CHAPTER 20

Towards a Culture of Peace

§ AS made plain in the *Seville Statement on Violence*, drafted in 1986 by a group of experts representing a wide variety of disciplines, the idea according to which war and violence are inherent in human beings has no scientific foundation.[1] Far from being inherent in human nature, violence and war alter it profoundly as they deny the fundamental dignity of the human person and the capacity of that person to live in society. Far from being the mere 'continuation of politics through other means', as in the words of Clausewitz, war now symbolizes the interruption of politics in the modern and democratic sense of the term and above all its failure, in terms of participation, dialogue, negotiation, prevention, foresight, tolerance and, in the last resort, of education and democracy. As underlined in UNESCO's Constitution, 'wars begin in the minds of men'.

It is precisely because human beings can succumb to intolerance, racism, xenophobia and hatred that we must remind young people in particular that peace is never to be taken for granted. Our planet is replete with tears, as recalled in the inscription at the Women's House in Moscow.[2]

The major challenge facing humanity in the twenty-first century will be to create conditions favourable to a transition from a culture of violence to a culture of peace, in order to construct in the minds of men the 'defences of peace'.

We will define the culture of peace as UNESCO did in 1995:

- a culture of social interaction and sharing, based on the principles of freedom, justice and democracy, tolerance and solidarity,
- a culture that rejects violence, endeavours to prevent conflicts by tackling their roots and to solve problems through dialogue and negotiation,
- a culture which guarantees everyone the full exercise of all rights and the means to participate fully in the endogenous development of their society.[3]

George Bernard Shaw once said, 'Peace is not only better than war, it is infinitely more arduous.' For war, which is the worst option, is all too often the easiest one, at least in its opening salvoes. Victor Hugo put it well when he deplored 'the sinister easiness of dying': a sinister easiness indeed, for warmongering leaders and ideologues, of making young people die in their place. It is true that war breaks out very easily and peace is difficult. How, for instance, can peace be constructed when development is incomplete, inequitable and unevenly shared out; when democracy remains captive and modernity mutilated,[4] when the fundamental rights of every human being are flouted, and when the future is signed away for the sake of selfish, short-term gains? Peace is a long-term objective that presupposes that a close link has been established between peace, development, justice and democracy. How can we not see that such a dynamic process is impossible without the development of education for all, without the promotion of human rights, tolerance, cultural pluralism and dialogue between the constituent parts of society? Without a genuine commitment to peace on the part of every individual? Without bringing into play our energy, willpower and courage?

To the words *si vis pacem, para bellum*, we must gradually oppose the words *para pacem*: if you want peace, prepare for it and build on it. Do not accept the unacceptable. Be ever vigilant, but act according to your conscience: do not look around you for answers to fundamental questions, as those answers are in your own self. Preparing for peace means preparing for our future and that of our children. It means preparing for the twenty-first century. The role UNESCO has to play in this regard is all the more fundamental insofar as it is the only specialized institution in the United Nations system whose mandate refers explicitly to peace. Its task, under its Constitution, is 'to contribute to peace and security by promoting collaboration among the nations through education, science and culture in order to further universal respect for justice, for the rule of law and for the human rights and fundamental freedoms which are affirmed for the peoples of the world, without distinction of race, sex, language or religion, by the Charter of the United Nations'. UNESCO is also the only organization in the system whose Constitution refers to 'the democratic principles of the dignity, equality and mutual respect' of the human being, as war is made possible only by the denial of the key values of democracy.

We legitimately rejoice at the fact that the culture of peace has now been recognized by the international community as a fundamental priority: the United Nations General Assembly proclaimed 2000 the International Year for the Culture of Peace, and the decade 2001–10 as the International Decade for the Promotion of a Culture of Peace and Non-Violence for the Children of the World.[5] Furthermore, several intergovernmental institutions – such as the Organization of American States (OAS), the Organization for African Unity (OAU), the Economic Community of West African States (ECOWAS), the Council of Europe, the Association of South-East Asian Nations (ASEAN), the Commonwealth, and the International Organization of the Francophonie – together with many non-governmental organizations, have lent their support to this initiative.[6]

Facing up to New Forms of Violence and War

According to Pierre Hassner, the world as it stands after the destruction of the Berlin Wall in 1989 is faced with a new paradox, which replaces the one that Raymond Aron highlighted as a description of the Cold War: 'impossible peace, improbable war'. Today, while peace may seem less impossible, war would seem less improbable as many states continue to devote enormous sums to defence while not seeming to give much attention to the real dangers that jeopardize their future, which I have referred to in the previous chapters. We should take advantage of the unique opportunity provided to us by the end of the Cold War to invest the dividends of peace in human development through education, science and culture. Are we to let this opportunity go by? It has to be acknowledged that recent trends are hardly encouraging. During the last few years, international public aid for development has declined at a time when support for the United Nations system was decreasing.[7] Nevertheless, we shall be in a position to cope with the major challenges of our time only if we are prepared to allocate the means required for encouraging the growth of endogenous development at the national level and if we strengthen the United Nations system at the international level. We must also provide a democratic solution to the problem raised by the expansion of acute nationalism, fundamentalism and ethnic conflicts, in an increasingly fragmented world, where inequality is spreading at an alarming pace. In a word, we must learn to live in peace but also learn to persevere in expressing our disagreement, without ever imposing our point of view by force and, at the same time, without ever simply accepting the 'irremediable'.

New forms of violence and conflicts are tending to spread, 'within and outside States':[8] the phenomenon of intra-state confrontation is growing,[9] and has already become the typical form of conflict at the dawn of the twenty-first century. At the same time, there is evidence to suggest the expansion of terrorism and organized crime, which, though locally based, are rapidly acquiring global status. Civilians have become preferred targets for aggression and violence, large-scale massacres and rape devised as instruments of war in order to terrorize populations and destroy the image of the Other; war itself, planned by the military and politicians, is often conducted by civilians and particularly by children and young people. Clans and mafia groups, eager to cash in on enormous illicit profits, are playing an increasingly active role in these conflicts. The illicit war economy and the growing manipulation of local conflicts by major economic interests supported by corrupt 'warlords' are tending to cause such conflicts to become a lethal threat to the rule of law, institutions, democracy and development. Through this process of transformation, violence and war are taking on new forms, resorting to new weapons and players, and targeting new victims. The use of force is gradually becoming de-institutionalized, privatized, possibly professionalized; 'private armies' are prospering; 'war' is extending even into cyberspace. In some countries, armed violence, whether collective or individual, has already become commonplace even in schools, which are and should remain places of learning and peace. At the dawn of the twenty-first century, how can we not ponder the morbid influence exerted on young people by the culture of war, violence and domination?

At the beginning of the twenty-first century, we are also aware that other serious forms of violence and insecurity are becoming more threatening: the worst of these are undoubtedly injustice, poverty and social exclusion.[10] At the start of the third millennium, who could make do with a 'negative peace', defined as the mere absence of war? Who could be satisfied with peace guaranteed by the mere hegemony of empires? Peace embodies a far more complex reality: it is, by principle, a dynamic process. What we are striving for is 'positive peace' which, in the famous words of the philosopher Spinoza, 'is born out of fortitude, concord and justice'.[11] The culture of peace therefore presupposes a degree of sharing in order to attenuate imbalances in human development, eradicate poverty and bring to an end the exploitation of human beings, particularly that of women and children. We are convinced that the greatest danger that threatens us today is the triple gap that is widening between the countries of the North and those of the South, between the countries of the South themselves and between the very rich and the very poor within a given society. Will the twenty-first century be the century of new walls? Unless there is a significant reduction in major forms of inequality, which have grown worse over the last three decades, the peace and the development of all concerned are threatened and the rich will be increasingly tempted to defend their paradise by force, surrounded by high walls, whether material or electronic, and yet remain besieged.

Globalization or Fragmentation? Learning to Live Together in the Twenty-first Century

A legion of experts has observed another apparent paradox: the more the world becomes globalized the more it becomes individualized and fragmented. It is precisely because it is becoming globalized that fragmentation is occurring before our very eyes. In a market that is becoming global, fragmentation, far from involving penalties, is in fact profitable, and the mediating institutions on which social ties were founded – nation, work, family and school – are falling prey to a process of dissociation.[12] Admittedly, some observers believe that we are heading for times that Kant predicted would come about when he spoke of cosmopolitan law, based on tolerance and the capacity for peaceful coexistence, in which interdependency between states had progressed to such a degree 'that transgression of the law in any part of the world' would be 'experienced everywhere'.[13] Michael Doyle believes that the conditions for lasting peace have now been largely achieved or are on the point of being so.[14] Many experts have pointed out in support of this idea that, since the end of the nineteenth century, no genuine armed conflict has opposed two fully democratic regimes, although such an assertion is debatable and would not seem to be borne out by the facts. Nevertheless, the organization of major summits by the United Nations system, the endeavours, even thwarted, of the international organizations and the conclusion of world agreements such as those at the Earth Summit in Rio and the Kyoto Summit on the reduction of greenhouse gas emissions, and the decision to create an International Criminal Court would seem to suggest that a new phase has been reached. The international community would seem to be advancing towards the idea of 'concerted' management of the planet and greater respect for human rights. The number of democratic regimes is increasing steadily. Furthermore, genuine global awareness is emerging, strengthened by the development of the new information and communication technologies. There is a growing feeling that human beings share a common fate.

This process comes up against obvious limitations and failures: the absence of a political will has all too often compromised follow-up action after the major United Nations summits and the quantitative increase in the number of democratically elected regimes has not necessarily brought with it a qualitative improvement in democracy. What is more, the process itself is very fragile. While we may be convinced that it is possible to promote new forms of international cooperation which would prevent war once and for all, a number of factors can obstruct or frustrate that dynamic process. Today's world lacks bearings. Everywhere, roads are being built that do not lead anywhere. Will 'globalization' lead to the 'absence of a world' as prophesied by Hannah Arendt? Where can it lead us if it must mean the absence of universal values through a lack of vision and long-term objectives and through the decline of the idea of a common destiny? Does this world still convey a meaning when it has succumbed to the tyranny of short-term considerations and emergencies and on which, as emphasized by Paul Kennedy[15] in *Preparing for the Twenty-first Century*, weighs the hegemony of *laisser-faire* politics? Is it not devoid, as in the words of Emmanuel Lévinas, of promising perspectives?[16]

How then are we to recover the meaning of duration focused on the future? The development of forecasting and an anticipatory conception of democracy not only within nations but also on an international scale; the consolidation of a democracy that should reject social apartheid in order to reconstruct the public sphere on the basis of justice and the fight against inequality; and the social and individual construction of an ethics of the future therefore go hand in hand with the nurturing of a culture of peace. Only in this way can we measure up to the risks inherent in a process of globalization reduced to a new form of hegemony.

Another danger inherent in globalization is that of withdrawing into our own identity. The process whereby individuals are brought together ever more quickly can thus also lead to cultural and political fragmentation and leave excluded populations to their dreams of an imagined past. This tension concerning identity has been worsened, according to Benjamin Barber, by the real or supposed fear of cultural homogenization brought about by globalization.[17] As pointed out by Arjun Appadurai, the upsurge of violence is usually driven by a desire to assert a particular identity against other identities and 'in this opposition between various identities, the majority identity often becomes a "predator" for the minority identity'.[18] However, as René-Jean Dupuy puts it, 'when we cease to believe in the future and the future is dead, we tend to look back to the past. The future is then in the past. This attitude leads to fundamentalism through attachment to tradition regarded as sacred. It amounts to a "heritage history' in which we seek refuge.'[19] Naturally, there can never be any return to the past: a retrospective fixation on the past, instead of leading to a resurrection of the past, results in what the Iranian philosopher Daryush Shayegan rightly calls 'the ideologization of tradition',[20] and thus to a new form of ideology that, under cover of respect for the past, contributes to the unconscious Westernization of the world by borrowing Western patterns of ideology and action.

In this context of withdrawal into specific identities, where neighbours are often seen as enemies whereas they should be our friends, the principal challenge to humanity in the twenty-first century is undoubtedly the task of learning to live together, as highlighted by Jacques Delors in the report he coordinated on behalf of the International Committee on Education for the Twenty-First Century. It must be stated quite clearly that the culture of excluding the Other, imposed on societies in times of crisis in the name of fictitious and borrowed mythologies, could lead, if it were to prevail, to the fragmentation of the world into 'blood-based communities, based on exclusion and hatred, which would fetter democracy to the advantage of tyrannical paternalism or consensual tribalism'.[21]

Learning Peace: Education and Citizenship

Peace must not, however, be imposed solely from outside, through economic and political agreements; it must also find its sustenance in every one of us and within our cultures, on the basis of 'the moral and intellectual solidarity of humanity'. Peace cannot be imported from outside; it is an intimate part of ourselves and must thrive through our deeds and our attitudes. The culture of peace consists in developing our individual dispositions in favour of justice, which, in the words of Felipe E. MacGregor, is a vital tool for constructing the objective of peace.[22] With that aim in mind, UNESCO's fundamental role has been perfectly identified by René-Jean Dupuy:

> Nothing can tell us whether future generations will be more generous than we; they will perhaps, thanks to legal specialists, have better peace provisions and more sophisticated international organizations, but what is to be made of the structures of peace if they are not nurtured by a culture of peace? What this means is that the responsibility lies with us to ensure that future generations are better than ours. It is here that UNESCO's role emerges, its extraordinary mission to educate and train to which no limits in time can be seen and which should last for as long as humanity itself, as the future generations will always be current generations at a particular time. Consequently, this mission will continue to be relevant in the course of time, as unerringly as space probes launched into the heart of the galaxies.[23]

The culture of peace is an evolutionary concept but can be defined in terms of a number of fundamental principles:

- values, attitudes, forms of behaviour and lifestyles based on non-violence and respect for the rights and fundamental freedoms of every human being;
- a society attentive to its population that does not seek to dominate or to exploit but rather to protect the rights of its weakest members;
- understanding, tolerance and solidarity between cultures, rejection of all forms of xenophobia, racism and the attitude according to which others are seen to be enemies;
- the sharing and unrestricted flow of information; and
- the full and equal participation of women with the corresponding authority.[24]

It is, first and foremost, through education that the values of non-violence, tolerance, democracy, solidarity and justice, which are the very lifeblood of peace, can be passed on to individuals at a very early age. Education should promote open-mindedness, which is vital in a world where the interdependence of nations and peoples and their interactions are becoming increasingly important day by day. The task is not to combat what is different but to explain and understand it. As expressed by René-Jean Dupuy, what matters is 'to observe others and to watch them live with curiosity, seeking to be open-minded in order to understand them better, in order to grasp why it is they are alive, how they live and what are the relevant historical, sociological and religious reasons and how, therefore, they come to terms with the mystery of their existence'. It is open-minded observation and dialogue that are the foundations for promoting a culture of peace and an attitude of mutual acceptance of difference.

A particular concern for truth should also be the hallmark of history textbooks and teaching, since the same set of facts, according to the interpretation given of them, can either lend support to agreement and reconciliation or, conversely, nurture hate and the desire for revenge. We tend, all too often, to forget the influence that words can have on our consciousness and we should therefore grant them all the importance that they deserve. That is why it is important, at national as well as the international level, to promote education for peace, human rights, democracy, international understanding and tolerance. To achieve this, UNESCO has implemented programmes that deal as much with the content of formal and informal education as with the preparation and dissemination of teaching materials, and the creation of networks.

To that end, education should combine education for citizenship, and by that token for participation, and education for peace, and hence for tolerance. Every individual should be trained in respect for human rights and in inter-cultural understanding through the transfer and sharing of knowledge between the various cultures and societies, because it is through the contact of minds that positive peace may emerge. Our aim is education by all, for all and throughout people's lives, whereby they may acquire the values of dialogue, cooperation and non-violence and construct a new ethics that will necessarily be an ethics of the future. With this in mind, UNESCO has created university chairs for a culture of peace, the first of which was established in South Africa.

The media also play an essential role in promoting the fundamental principles of democracy and tolerance for the culture of peace. Whether as the source or the purveyors of information, the press, radio and television play a decisive part in acting on behalf of peace. That is why UNESCO is concerned with the educational and cultural dimensions of the media, especially the problem of violence on television and computer screens and its impact on young people in particular. Furthermore, the press is duty bound to refrain from taking part in any campaigns of open incitement to hatred or murder in regard to a particular nation or community. In this instance, I have in mind the tragic case of 'Radio-Télévision libre des mille collines' in Rwanda, which, in 1994, called for the massacre of the Tutsi ethnic group and Hutu opponents. UNESCO is lending its support to the efforts of the press in Rwanda and Burundi to foster reconciliation between the communities and is contributing to the creation and operating of free, independent media that endeavour to overcome the hatred and divisions in regions that are particularly torn by violence.

Cultivating Peace

Any culture of peace is first and foremost a *culture* and a dynamic current that aims at helping transformation by ourselves and in ourselves of our patterns of behaviour and our relations with others. Action in favour of intercultural pluralism and dialogue are therefore of crucial importance in building peace in the twenty-first century. Three attitudes can be adopted in regard to other people: the first is one of rejection – often the result of indifference and ignorance; the second involves bringing pressure to bear on others so that they 'convert' and renounce their own identity; the third involves becoming aware of difference, respecting it and welcoming it while remaining ourselves.[25] It is the third option that was chosen by UNESCO, whose endeavours focus in particular on intercultural dynamics within major urban concentrations, on pluri-lingualism and linguistic diversity at all levels of education, on the promotion of the cultural expression of minorities and native populations, and on the promotion of dialogue between cultures and between religions.[26]

Sceptics may well ask what culture has to do with a field that is pre-eminently political, namely the transition from war to peace. We cannot endorse such a point of view: for we humans cannot be reduced either to our biological nature or to that of the political animal described by Aristotle. We are fashioned by culture and if culture can be defined as the behaviour and attitudes of each of us, then peace cannot be built by neglecting culture, which fashions our relationship to the Other, whether it be positive or negative. Conflicts often arise before crises and smoulder over many years during which rejection of others is nurtured by the contagion of prejudice, the discourse of hatred and policies of marginalization and exclusion. That is why it is vital to act preventively and to strive to check the spiral of war and violence. Consequently, we cannot elude the immense responsibility that falls to us, namely that of passing on to the children of tomorrow, through education, culture and communication, the messages of tolerance and solidarity that they in turn, in the space of a generation, will have to convey to others.

Lasting peace cannot be constructed around a conference table unless it is deeply rooted in the minds of men. Nor can it be merely a matter of signing treaties, as history has made only too plain. It must be founded in the long term on the values handed down to young people by their families, teachers, social players, decision-makers and democratically elected representatives. According to Miguel de Unamuno, only educated people are free and the more cultured they are, the freer they become.

UNESCO's role in building a culture of peace is therefore essential: education and culture are the only durable guarantees for peace and human security, provided they are firmly rooted in an ethical approach based on the principles of democracy.

Building Peace: Development, Democracy and Anticipation

While war and violence are synonyms of destruction, peace means building up: it cannot be invented from scratch, but is built up, from day to day. It is a task that requires a long-term view and a daily struggle at individual, national and international levels.

Peace cannot be built on the basis of ideas alone. As stated by Boutros Boutros-Ghali in the *Agenda for Development*, 'Without development, however, there is no prospect for lasting peace.'[27] Peace is the fruit of economic and social, endogenous and equitable development that leaves behind all forms of frustration, jealousy or rivalry and ensures that a spirit of solidarity and cooperation prevails over the notion of the balance of power and competition. Peace therefore involves the elimination of poverty as 'social and human resource development makes social and economic relations more harmonious, facilitates inclusiveness and societal cohesion, and provides a solid and adaptable foundation for achieving long-term progress.'[28] Development therefore means an exchange (of wealth and resources, as well as ideas) and interaction not only between states but also between the various components of any given society.

The culture of peace must seek in particular to encourage development based on the notion of equity, by recognizing the rights of every citizen and particularly those of groups hitherto marginalized, by encouraging the participation of citizens in public debate so that they may express their demands more articulately, and by encouraging initiatives at community level which will enable development and democracy to advance hand in hand.

Nor can peace be established without a regulatory and institutional framework: as stated in Chapter 19, the establishment of this framework is lagging largely behind today's requirements. Without going so far as to hope to eradicate all threat of war, we are convinced that certain conditions are essential to prevent crises from degenerating into violent confrontation: the active participation of all citizens in appointing their government leaders; freedom of expression; the complete independence of the legislative, executive and judicial authorities, articulated within the context of democracy and the rule of law. Peace also presupposes the development of genuine 'multicultural democracy' (Néstor García Canclini), established on the basis of sustainable human development, mutual respect between cultures, the empowerment of citizens, and a change in patterns of behaviour, as violence must give way to the democratic regulation of conflicts.

In the words of Amartya Sen, 1998 Nobel prizewinner for economics, 'democracy is the best means of fighting against poverty'. Our task will be to give it stronger roots at national level but also to build it at international level. If, on account of its current membership and attributions, the Security Council cannot act with the required rapidity and authority, then its features must be changed and improved. Nevertheless, doing away with the United Nations would be tantamount to encouraging the discrepancy between the existence of democracies on a national scale for solving national problems and an oligarchy on a world scale for settling transnational issues. It should be acknowledged that the United Nations is the only stable international democratic structure capable of curbing violence and terror, which, all too often, are exacerbated by perverted interpretations of nationalist, religious and ideological feeling. The United Nations alone has the right to say that the international community will not recognize those who have seized power through bloodshed instead of obtaining it via the ballot box. The United Nations alone can legitimately intervene through the deployment of armed forces when there is patent evidence for the failure of a particular state or massive violation of human rights.

New opportunities should be opened up at national and international level for dialogue and exchange, arbitration and negotiation, prevention and anticipation. New non-governmental partners should be called upon to play an active role: sustainable peace and long-term stability are based on the participation of all those involved in the conduct of world affairs. No uniform, ideal model of democratization can be imposed. We should not overlook the fact that societies presented as exemplary in this regard, such as those of ancient Athens or the United States of America in the eighteenth century, were also societies that waged war, pursued conquest and practised slavery. The transition to democracy, which supposes the theorization and effective implementation of the universality of rights, is a complex process that requires lucidity: the democratic transition calls for adaptation that takes account of the specific traditions and peculiarities of each country in order to take root and to rest on sound foundations, without being limited to vague declarations of intent. It would be fanciful to see democracy as an institutional model that could be universally exported in a 'ready-made' form. It would undoubtedly be more useful to draw on the immense wealth of our experience, customs and traditions, those positive factors and the limited number of shared values on the basis of which a society can advance efficiently towards the ideal of justice. The consolidation of democracy presupposes not the elimination of conflict but merely its integration within a balance between power and rights. In the words of Paul Ricoeur, 'democracy is not a political regime without conflict but a regime in which conflicts are open and negotiable according to rules of arbitration'. Government must, for its part, concentrate on its role of guarantor of individual freedom and collective solidarity and thereby encourage national, regional and international cooperation based on common principles.

Peace cannot be achieved overnight. Unfortunately, it all too often begins to emerge when peoples have suffered too much and cannot go on killing each other. Genuine peace, sustainable peace, is the result of long-term action, based on solidarity and sharing. Can we really build that peace at a time when the industrialized countries, which commited themselves as early as 1974 to devote 0.7% of their GNP to public development aid and have since reiterated that commitment, continue to forget the promise they made? With the exception of some Nordic countries, the member states of OECD contributed only 0.22% of their GNP to aid in 1997, while the leading world power devoted only 0.09%. Shall we really build that peace if aid continues to be allocated to non-priority needs? In 1996, the OECD member states devoted only 16.8% of bilateral aid to education and health, including 10.8% to teaching as a whole and 1.3% to basic education. All too often, the West has forgotten the suffering and pain of violence and war; instead of consolidating peace, we have allowed the rationale of force to prevail once again over the force of reason and to prevail over prevention or the permanent effort of persuasion and dialogue. We have not yet learned to pay the price of peace and are once again in the process of paying the price of war.

The ethical imperatives of international solidarity require us to help countries ravaged by civil war or whose survival is seriously threatened. In this regard, UNESCO has developed national programmes whose purpose is to bring together the various parties involved in a conflict so that they can devise and implement development projects together. These programmes can prove extremely useful for gradually re-establishing trust and enabling progress to be made towards reconciliation. We have already implemented them in such countries as El Salvador, Mozambique and Burundi. In this way, the culture of peace makes it possible to renew methods of resolving conflicts, increase the diversity of approaches in regard to the peaceful settlement of conflicts and reduce the obstacles hindering the reconstruction of devastated countries by devising measures that gradually re-establish trust and create mechanisms for solidarity as well as mediation techniques at all levels of society.

Many statements have already ranked the culture of peace uppermost among the aspirations of the international community on the eve of the third millennium:

- the *United Nations General Assembly* has stressed that 'the task of the United Nations to save future generations from the scourge of war requires transformation towards a culture of peace, which consists of values, attitudes and behaviours that reflect and inspire social interaction and sharing based on the principles of freedom, justice and democracy, all human rights, tolerance and solidarity, that reject violence and endeavour to prevent conflicts by tackling their root causes to solve problems through dialogue and negotiation and that guarantee the full exercise of all rights and the means to participate fully in the development process of their society';[29]

- the *Organization of American States* has reaffirmed its intention 'to build a culture of peace, development and non-violence, recognizing the right to peace as inalienable and intrinsic to human dignity';[30]
- the *Organization for African Unity* has declared that the International Year for a Culture of Peace was 'a propitious occasion to substitute the culture of war and violence which characterized the last millennium of human history with a culture of peace by promoting values, attitudes and behaviours which constitute the foundations thereof';[31]
- the *Association of South-East Asian Nations* has also emphasized that 'the peaceful resolution of conflicts, the dialogue between cultures and religions, and the promotion of tolerance are, inter alia, key factors for giving a solid foundation to all endogenous development efforts, ensuring the participation of all', and added that 'in this framework, education has a key role to play in nurturing shared values and, in particular, education for co-operative peace, social justice, rule of law, tolerance and international understanding, which should be fostered at all levels of education';[32]
- the *Commonwealth* has also underlined that the UNESCO initiative for promoting a Culture of Peace, based on the principles set out in the United Nations Charter 'accords with the Commonwealth's own fundamental values of democracy, respect for human rights and the rule of law, respect for diversity and tolerance, equal rights for women and sustainable development', and called for international cooperation 'to contribute further to the global vision for a culture of peace and development';[33, 34]
- the *International Organization of the Francophonie* has declared that 'the preoccupation with peace and with the culture of peace which is a necessary prerequisite, has become essential to our organization as some of our Member States have been involved in dramatic internal or regional conflicts'.[35]

At a time when US$700 to US$800 billion are allocated annually to military expenditure, negotiated disarmament, which could be encouraged by the conclusion of regional and subregional alliances, is another fundamental stage in the building of a culture of peace. In this regard, it would be useful to reduce investment which retards social development (food security, education, health, etc.).[36] The elimination of nuclear weapons is particularly urgent so that the world may live without fear of the sword of Damocles that is a nuclear holocaust.[37]

If only we were to decide so democratically, the billions swallowed up in war and in preparing for war could henceforth be invested in practical action that would help to bring about sustainable peace: reducing massively and then eradicating poverty; ensuring education for all and gradually, on a lifelong basis, improving the quality of education; investing in scientific research that would be focused not on preparing for conflict but on technologies and expertise whereby every individual's quality of life could be improved; enriching the intercultural dialogue in order to combat prejudice and preconceived ideas that are so conducive to triggering war – such are some of the practical objectives that, if implemented, would serve as the best defence of peace and security. At the dawn of the twenty-first century, democracies have now reached the moment of truth: either they strive for peace and human development or they will ruin their reputation in the eyes of their citizens. If we know, through practical steps, how to promote the development of a culture of peace, then we shall restore a purer meaning to the words of the United Nations Charter, to those of UNESCO's Constitution and the humanist design contained therein. Let us recall the cruel words of the great Austrian writer Robert Musil who, shortly before the end of the First World War, stated: 'We have not yet devised a sufficiently exalting idea of the peace we yearn for.'[38] We believe precisely that a culture of peace can elicit, particularly among young people, a degree of enthusiasm that seems so often to be discouraged today. A culture of peace can alone give development a particular perspective, meaning and content and enable each of us to refuse the alternative between the cynicism of *Realpolitik* and the Utopia of perpetual concord. Peace was previously a fact or a concept: it has now become a right.[39]

Finally, it is the duty of memory. I recall today with emotion the time when I said, at Auschwitz and on the Island of Gorée – two sites that UNESCO has listed as part of the Human Heritage: 'Never again!' I also remember the time when, at the Cape, I could see Robben Island in the distance, the prison island where Nelson Mandela was detained for almost twenty-seven years, and I exclaimed: 'Never again!' And when we opened the Press Building in Kigali, the House of Peace in Bujumbura, and in Somalia, we repeated: 'Never again!' And then in Sarajevo, in Mostar, where they are starting to rebuild the bridges. Never again. I have often repeated the words: 'tomorrow is always too late'. But it is never too late for peace. That is why we must make a start in writing a historical record that is different, one that, for the time being, we can only describe. What better tribute could we pay to our children and to our children's children, whom in 1945 we promised to spare for evermore from the scourge of war?[40] Let us together offer them an opportunity for a new start.

Notes

1. UNESCO, *The Seville Statement on Violence*, UNESCO, 1991.

Box 20.1 The Manifesto 2000 for a Culture of Peace and Non-Violence

The Manifesto 2000 for a Culture of Peace and Non-Violence was written by the Laureates of the Nobel Peace Prize, in order to create a sense of responsibility starting on a personal level; it is not an appeal or petition addressed to a higher authority.

It is the responsibility of each and every individual to put into practice the values, attitudes and forms of behaviour which inspire the culture of peace. Everyone can contribute to this aim within their family, their area, their town, their region and their country by promoting non-violence, tolerance, dialogue, reconciliation, justice and solidarity on a daily basis.

The *Manifesto 2000* was made public in Paris on 4 March 1999, and is open for signature by the general public all over the world

The goal, at the turn of the millennium, was to present *100 million signatures* to the United Nations General Assembly meeting in September 2000.

Recognizing my share of responsibility for the future of humanity, especially for today's children and those of future generations, I pledge, in my daily life, in my family, my work, my community, my country and my region, to:

Respect the life and dignity of each human being without discrimination or prejudice;

Practise active non-violence, rejecting violence in all its forms: physical, sexual, psychological, economical and social, in particular towards the most deprived and vulnerable such as children and adolescents;

Share my time and material resources in a spirit of generosity to put an end to exclusion, injustice and political and economic oppression;

Defend freedom of expression and cultural diversity giving preference always to dialogue and listening without engaging in fanaticism, defamation and the rejection of others;

Promote consumer behaviour that is responsible, and development practices that respect all forms of life and preserve the balance of nature on the planet;

Contribute to the development of my community, with the full participation of women and respect for democratic principles, in order to create together new forms of solidarity.

(To sign the *Manifesto 2000*, go to the Internet site: http://manifesto2000. unesco.org)

2. 'Our planet has got enough tears' (Women's House, Moscow, April 1999).

3. Resolution 0.12 on the Medium-Term Strategy for 1996–2001, adopted at the 18th plenary session of the General Conference of UNESCO (1995).

4. See Daryush Shayegan, *Le Regard mutilé: schizophrénie culturelle: pays traditionnels face à la modernité*, Éditions de l'Aube, Paris, 1996.

5. Resolutions of the United Nations General Assembly 52-15 (20 November 1997) and 53-25 (19 November 1998).

6. See the UNESCO document entitled 'The culture of peace and UNESCO's action in Member States', 30 October 1998 (155 EX/INF.9).

7. See Chapters 18 and 19.

8. Pierre Hassner, 'Par-delà le totalitarisme et la guerre', *Esprit*, December 1998.

9. A major feature of the twentieth century was the gradual decline in inter-state war and the development of infra-state war, which has become the most common form of present-day conflicts (35 out of 38 in 1995). One author suggests that while 35 million victims of collective violence in the twentieth century were the victims of inter-state wars (including the two world wars), 150 million were the victims of their own governments. Rudolf Rummel, *Death by Government*, Transaction Publications, New Brunswick, 1995.

10. See Chapter 2.

11. Spinoza, quoted by Pierre Hassner, *La Violence et la paix: de la bombe atomique au nettoyage ethnique*, Editions Esprit, Paris, 1995.

12. Daniel Cohen, *The Wealth of the World and the Poverty of Nations*, trans. Jacqueline Lindenfeld, MIT Press, Cambridge, MA, 1998.

13. Kant, *Perpetual Peace*, US Library Association, Los Angeles, California, 1932.

14. Michael Doyle, 'Kant, liberal legacies and foreign affairs', *Philosophy and Public Affairs*, Princeton University Press, 1983.

15. Paul Kennedy, *Preparing for the Twenty-first Century*, HarperCollins, London, 1993.

16. Emmanuel Lévinas, interview with Roger-Pol Droit, *Le Monde*, 2 June 1992.

17. On this theme, see Benjamin R. Barber, *Jihad versus McWorld*, Ballantine Books, New York, 1996.

18. Arjun Appadurai, communication given at the *Twenty-First Century Dialogues*, organized at UNESCO (16–19 September 1998) by the Analysis and Forecasting Office.

19. René-Jean Dupuy, *Un monde dual*, note for the director-general of UNESCO, 1995.

20. Daryush Shayegan, see in particular *Qu'est-ce qu'une Révolution religieuse?*, Presses d'Aujourd'hui, Paris, 1982; *Le Regard mutilé*, Albin Michel, Paris, 1989; and a paper on the ideological interpretation of tradition at the Cordoba Symposium.

21. Barber, *Jihad versus McWorld*. See also Benjamin R. Barber, *Strong Democracy: Participatory Politics for a New Age*, University of California Press, Berkeley, CA, 1984.

22. Felipe E. MacGregor, 'Cultura de Paz: Apuntes sobre su naturaleza y dinamismo', contribution to the third meeting of the World Commission on Culture and Development, San José, Costa Rica, 22–26 February 1994.

23. René-Jean Dupuy, 'Security in the twenty-first century and the culture of peace', in *What Kind of Security*, UNESCO, Paris, 1998.

24. *UNESCO et la Culture de la paix: promouvoir un mouvement mondial*, UNESCO, Paris, 1996. CAB-95/WS/1. See also the collection of texts *From a Culture of Violence to*

a Culture of Peace, Peace and Conflict Issues Series, UNESCO, Paris, 1996, and Vicenç Fisas, *Cultura de paz y gestión de conflictos*, Prólogo de Federico Mayor Zaragoza, Icaria Antrazyt, Ediciones UNESCO, Paris, 1998.

25. Dupuy, *Un Monde dual*.

26. Among the examples of UNESCO's action in this field, reference can be made to the intercultural project the 'Slave Route'; the Barcelona Declaration 'On the Role of Religion in the Promotion of the Culture of Peace' (1994) and the project entitled 'Spiritual Convergence and Intercultural Dialogue' (a link between the 'Roads of Faith' and the 'Roads of Al-Andalus' projects). From 1988 to 1997, UNESCO also implemented the 'Silk Road' project, thereby promoting Euro-Asian dialogue between the European, Arab and Asian cultures.

27. A/48/935, § 11.

28. A/48/935, § 94.

29. Resolution adopted by the United Nations General Assembly on 19 November 1998 (A/RES/53/25), proclaiming the period 2001–10 as the International Decade for a Culture of Peace and Non-Violence for the Children of the World.

30. *Reaffirmation of Caracas*, 1 June 1998.

31. Decision AHG/DEC. 5 XXXIV, June 1998.

32. Statement on Peace in South-east Asia on the Eve of the Third Millennium, Jakarta, 12 September 1998.

33. Letter of 15 June 1998 from the Secretary-General, Emeka Anyaoku, to the director-general of UNESCO.

34. Note from the Secretariat on the UNESCO Draft Declaration and Programme of Action on a Culture of Peace, London, June 1998.

35. Letter of 11 May 1998 from UN Secretary-General Boutros Boutros-Ghali, to the director-general of UNESCO.

36. See Chapter 18.

37. 'The destructiveness of nuclear weapons is immense. Any use would be catastrophic ... The first requirement [for their elimination] is for the five nuclear weapon states to commit themselves unequivocally to the elimination of nuclear weapons and agree to start work immediately on the practical steps and negotiations required for its achievement ... Progressive extension of safeguards to nuclear activity in the nuclear weapon states, the undeclared weapon states and the threshold states will be needed with the end point being universal application of safeguards in all states' (Executive Summary of the Canberra Commission on the Elimination of Nuclear Weapons, transmitted to the secretary-general of the Conference on Disarmament on 26 August 1996).

38. R. Musil, *Prosa und Stücke*, Rowohlt, Hamburg, 1978.

39. Declaration by the director-general of UNESCO, 'The human right to peace', 21 February 1997 (UNESCO, SHS-97/WS/6). See also: Message from His Holiness Pope Jean Paul II for the celebration of World Peace Day, 1 January 1999.

40. See Federico Mayor, 'The duty of memory', published on 22 April 1999 in *El País* and subsequently in many leading newspapers in various parts of the world.

CONCLUSION
. . . .
Towards an Ethics of the Future

§ IN the light of the challenges referred to in this work, the reader will, we hope, be convinced that foresight and prevention, combined with forward thinking and action, are absolute imperatives if we really want there to be a twenty-first century and the human species to survive. Henceforth, the task that falls to the international community is to set up a vast network of intellectual and ethical fora focusing on the future, with the collaboration of scientists, creators, decision-makers, experts and society as a whole for, to quote Antonio Machado, 'neither tomorrow, nor yesterday, has yet been written'.[1] Such is the task that UNESCO set itself when, in 1995, the organization made forecasting and anticipation one of its major priorities. To recall the words of the Greek historian Thucydides quoted at the beginning of this book: a political leader should not only have clean hands but should also have clean eyes. Giving back to our vision its initial sharpness and clarity – or should one say its perceptiveness – is the role we assign to the ethics of the future.

'Our inheritance was not willed to us.' With these words, the French poet René Char reminded humanity, amid the ruins of the Second World War, of its basic responsibility towards history. Thus a generation of survivors took up the cause of future generations. This new approach, this quest for human solidarity in both space and time, has for over fifty years been the task of the United Nations in general and of UNESCO in particular. 'To save succeeding generations from the scourge of war' is the solemn commitment introducing the Charter of the United Nations. This, too, is the meaning of UNESCO's Constitution, which seeks to contribute to peace and security by promoting collaboration among nations through education, science and culture.

The world has changed, however, in the last 50 years, as have the issues, the challenges and, it must be acknowledged, the dangers of modernity. At the dawn of the twenty-first century, other wars are breaking out: we have experienced world wars, bloody conflicts between states; today we see fighting that tears peoples apart within nations. We shall not dwell today on other forms of violence – violence against hope and the future of human beings, against their dignity, and the latent conflicts between cultures and between generations. The scourge seems to be universal. All over the world, the citizens of today are claiming rights over the citizens of tomorrow, threatening their well-being and at times their lives, and we are beginning to realize that we are jeopardizing future generations' exercise of their human rights. More than ever, the ethics of the future requires us to devise and disseminate that culture of peace that was the aim of UNESCO's founders and to see that it is shared.

In the economic and social field, debt, division and instability make up the inglorious heritage, the poisoned legacy we leave to our successors. Let us look at the Earth and the natural environment: greenhouse gas emissions, desertification, pollution and the misuse of natural resources are signing away the future of the planet. And what better evidence can there be of the need for an ethics of the future than the calling into question of international agreements as witnessed from time to time in recent years? The essential, vital needs of our children – the earth, water and air and, too, knowledge, freedom and solidarity – are being sacrificed on the altar of short-term self-interest, ambition and gain, which encourage the easy options and the selfishness of times heedless of the future. Need I recall the famous saying attributed to the king of a world on the wane: '*Après moi, le déluge*'?

There are more serious matters still: it is not only society and the environment but the very essence and biological integrity of the human person that are imperilled. It is now possible for human beings to modify the genetic heritage of any species, including their own. They even possess the grim privilege of being able to plan their own extinction. With modern science we have almost reached the point of no return. Notwithstanding the arguments about the compensation in technological or financial terms, there will be no replacement since what is destroyed has no equivalent, and there will be no payout since what is destroyed is without price. Who can compensate for genocide? Who can compensate for ethnocide, for the extinction of cultures, languages and values? Who would dare to claim that we can pay for the earth, for the biosphere, for the extinction of species?

Faced with this sombre prospect and as a counterweight, mention should be made of a number of positive developments. We can observe a gradual trend towards *democracy*, towards conviviality based on the ideals of justice, liberty, equality and solidarity, as proclaimed in UNESCO's Constitution. The 'voice of the people' is making itself increasingly heard and we welcome greater awareness of the issues at stake in the future, which often leads to personal commitment.

If we want to protect our descendants, we must first of all recognize, accept and deal with this fundamental paradox: progress and civilization are one side of the coin, while the possibility of an apocalypse, of irreversible destruction, of chaos, is the other side. Such a lucid realization is the prime requirement of our responsibility to future generations. Agreeing to curb the now unbridled power of technology and economy by ethics and wisdom is henceforth the proper course. Montesquieu's dictum that 'absolute power corrupts absolutely' needs to be applied to technology and economy, while science needs to be reminded of Rabelais' saying that 'science without conscience is but ruination of the soul'.

But, one will object, where does science dwell and where wisdom? We are nowadays able to travel to the other end of the earth in a matter of hours, and we are able to see for ourselves that, while the great cities of the industrialized countries may possess the knowledge, it is in the remotest villages that the wisdom is to be found.

At the dawn of the twenty-first century, we at last have the ability to reconcile knowledge with wisdom and to combine their virtues. With this in mind, we at UNESCO have drawn up, with the assistance of the International Bioethics Committee, the Declaration on the Human Genome, which was adopted by the Organization's General Conference and, subsequently, by the United Nations' General Assembly. It is the first time that a universal declaration applies to science and lays down ethical principles in this field that remind every one of us that we are born free and equal.

We said earlier that we must agree – in the name of ethics and wisdom – to curb the power that technology gives to humans over humans. The issue looms large and the challenge is a real one. In an age of globalization and of the acceleration and multiplication of exchanges, the future appears if not dark, then at least unclear. Complexity and uncertainty are the key words of our time. We therefore invoke the virtues of an education to uncertainty, for uncertainty stimulates us whereas conformity and blind optimism benumb us. This, of course, assumes willingness on the part of the international community to observe and ask questions of the future.

Our temporal short-sightedness is often coupled with wilful blindness, when it does not serve as a justification for it. Trapped in the dizzy whirl of the quick fix, the tyrannical grip of short-termism, we do not take the time to shape our actions or think about their consequences. We are hurtling into the future, with no brakes and in conditions of zero visibility.

But the faster a car goes, the brighter its headlights must be: it is no longer, therefore, a question of adjusting or adapting – adjustment and adaptation always lag behind events, which move ahead more rapidly – but a matter of taking pre-emptive action. We must stop listening to conformist ideas preaching adjustment and adaptation. Let us adopt a clear-sighted, forward-looking approach and cast a future-oriented eye on the world. Let us plant today the seeds of the future, protecting them as they grow, so that tomorrow our children may harvest the fruits of our foresight. To foresee in order to prevent, and to foresee in order to build – these are our objectives.

Prevention is not merely a possibility; it is an obligation and a moral imperative. This concept has, moreover, already taken root in our global consciousness and in international law. It has even given rise to a new principle, enshrined in 1992 at the Earth Summit in Rio and incorporated in the Treaty of Maastricht and in some national standard-setting instruments: the principle of precaution. But the view of the principle of precaution that has prevailed has been that of a principle of inaction rather than one of vigilant action. Risk-taking without knowledge is dangerous, but knowledge without risk-taking is worthless. Today, alas, almost a decade after the Earth Summit in Rio de Janeiro, what has been the outcome, where are the results? The commitments then made have given way to evasiveness, and the action pro-gramme adopted at the time by the international community, *Agenda 21*, has largely remained a dead letter. 'Rio plus 7' is 'Rio minus 7'. We have to ponder this lesson and sow within democracy itself – and particularly within Western democracies, which have turned into a 'bloc' that is too closed, too uniform, too cautious, and too often inward-looking – the seed that can revitalize and recompose it. This seed is and can only be the ethics of the future, made central to decision-making, central to democratic deliberation, central to the kind of adversarial appraisal that, rather than obfuscating, appeasing or misleading opinion by serving vested interests, the authorities and the powerful, must enlighten the public and form its judgement.

Have we worked out the cost of inaction: inaction in regard to the natural environment, social inaction, cultural inaction and political inaction in regard to massacres and genocides? Why are we for ever paying the price of violence, of war, of immediate crises and emergencies, when what we should hence-forth be paying is the price of dialogue, the price of the future and the long term, the price of peace, the price – in a word – of prevention?

Preventing means first and foremost preserving. The ethics of the future is an ethics of the fragile and the perishable. We must hand down to future generations an inheritance that has not been damaged and polluted beyond all redress. We must bequeath to them the right to live in dignity in a world that is preserved. This concerns first of all our living environment, the new preoccupation of our era, and also such enduring universal values as health, education, culture, equality, freedom, peace, tolerance and solidarity.

The Catalan poet Salvador Espriù told his children: 'I have lived to preserve these few words which I bequeath to you: love, justice and freedom.' We are responsible not only for our tangible heritage; as regards our duties and responsibilities, what is essential is often invisible and intangible.

Hence the concept of heritage has taken on new meanings in recent decades; from the straightforward preservation of historic monuments to the Convention for the Protection of the World Cultural and Natural Heritage, adopted in 1972, and from the recognition of our non-material, symbolic and spiritual heritage to the work currently being done by the International Bioethics Committee on the protection of the human genome, the concept of being has gradually pervaded that of having: the real common heritage of humanity, our priceless universal birthright, is ourselves: in other words, the humanity of the human being. This is the prospect of the Declaration on Science and the Use of Scientific Knowledge (adopted unanimously by the World Conference on Science held in Budapest in July 1999 by UNESCO and the International Council for Science), which reaffirmed the ethical principles which should guide research and the application of scientific knowledge: 'scientific research and the use of scientific knowledge should respect human rights and the dignity of human beings, in accordance with the Universal Declaration of Human Rights and in the light of the Universal Declaration on the Human Genome and Human Rights'. The countries that were signatories to the Budapest Declaration emphasized that 'the ethics and the responsibility of science should be an integral part of the teaching and training provided to all scientists'.[2]

At the dawn of a new century and a new millennium, at a time when the global village no longer seems so remote, we must shoulder our responsibilities as citizens of the world. This means that we must become aware of our position, not only in spatial terms but also in relation to human time, and must reflect on our role on the planet and in history: love for one's neighbour is also measured by respect for those distant from us. Near or far, yesterday or today, other people are still fellow creatures; in space and in time, humanity spins its web and we are its threads. The philosopher Bergson, when commenting on the republican motto of 'liberty, equality and fraternity', remarked very judiciously that 'it proclaims liberty, it calls for equality and reconciles these two warring sisters by reminding them of the fact that they are sisters and by placing fraternity above all else'. There is one practice that sums up fraternity: sharing. There is one feeling that can convey it: love.

As René-Jean Dupuy so forcefully put it, 'We shall have to get more and more used to feeling ourselves to be within humanity, a part of *it*, as it is a part of us, and because humanity will be increasingly a part of us, we shall be more and more a part of it.' Our responsibility is what guarantees our identity, which is why the ethics of the future must be the memory of the future. Let us become humanity's boatmen, ferrying a universal humanity, one that transcends history, from one end of the world to the other and from shore to shore. Auguste Comte said that humanity was composed of more dead than living people, but it is also made up of those yet to be born, and those to come are also our brothers and sisters, members of the 'human family' mentioned in the first lines of the Universal Declaration of Human Rights. In that sense, humanity potentially comprises many more living than dead.

In our eagerness to preserve, let us not make the mistake of meddling.

The twenty-first century does not belong to us; it belongs to future generations. The men and women of the future are our brothers and sisters, not our doubles. They belong to another time whose challenges, dangers and desires we cannot know. The world does indeed change rapidly, and with it our preferences, our needs and our fears. It is highly probable that today's administrative, legal, scientific and intellectual structures will be ill-suited to the demands of tomorrow. To respect the men and women of the future means giving them the option, and the means, of being different.

In the words of the Guatemalan poet Otto René Castillo, 'it is a fine thing to love the world with the eyes of future generations'. To keep intact the universal heritage and guarantee the continuity and quality of human life is to bequeath to our children the capacity to understand a complex, varied, fast-moving world, one that is as yet beyond our grasp.

Scientific progress, knowledge and open-mindedness are part of the common heritage and hence they are a central concern of ours, which is why a draft Declaration on the Responsibilities of Present Generations towards Future Generations was submitted to the General Conference and was adopted by the member states of the organization in 1997.

It is also through its fields of competence that UNESCO helps to maintain the peace and security of future generations. Investing in education, science and culture means investing in the future. It is not enough to *protect* the future; we must also *build* it. And how can we make ourselves ready for it without the intelligence of science, without the knowledge of education, without creative forces and the capacity to link and to convey what is enshrined in culture? We cannot prepare for the future while turning our backs on 'sustainable development', a principle of solidarity among nations and between generations that, since the time of the Rio Summit, has been one of the main priorities for United Nations action – although that priority is now, regrettably, compromised by the absence, or lack, of an ethics of the future. How can we prepare for the future without concluding the four contracts we propose for the twenty-first century: a new *social contract* required by the third industrial revolution and its accompanying globalization; a *natural contract* that we should conclude with our environment; a *cultural contract* whereby the intangible treasures of cultures can be enhanced and their conviviality promoted; and finally an *ethical contract*, without which we shall never vanquish poverty and violence and without which we shall deprive future generations of their future. As emphasized elsewhere,[3] the United Nations has a vital role to play in this field. When every other form of arbitration and negotiation has failed, it is its duty to intervene for ethical or humanitarian reasons whenever massive violations of human rights occur or where the state no longer exists and has been replaced by the law of the jungle. But no country or group of countries, however powerful, can take justice 'into its own hands'. Since it constitutes the only democratic framework on a world scale, the United Nations must be respected and reinforced.

If we want to give the future a chance, then we must give the ethics of the future a chance. That role – training citizens to take responsibility for the future – belongs primarily to education, for it is education that chiefly nurtures the community and teaches us not only to know and to do, but also to be and to live together. The responsibility of UNESCO, like that of all educational institutions, is thus immense. The challenge is clear: to guarantee, with the help of the various active forces in society, 'education for all, and learning throughout life'. Such is one of the essential priorities that UNESCO has set itself, and we for our part should like education for all to become a reality by 2015, that is, within a generation.

Education – as we must remind those who rely too heavily on the role of computers – means first of all the acquisition of self-discipline and personal autonomy. Education means the capacity to reflect and to decide for oneself, without letting oneself be influenced. It means the acquired ability to think and hence to remember and compare, memory and comparison being two essential dimensions of any ethics. The importance of the Declaration of Human Rights cannot be over-emphasized as it in some way constitutes the 'moral framework' of humanity's future actions.

We have mentioned the responsibility of UNESCO and of educational institutions, but responsibility does not end there: responsibility at the political level is just as crucial. 'A politician's real concern', as Max Weber observed, is 'the future and responsibility in the face of the future'. It is the statesman's responsibility to know how to manage and structure time and expectations in regard to the future. From local action to international negotiations, every democratic debate on the future contributes in its own small way to the ethics of the future, since it is through profound changes in conceptions, in behaviour and in the link between knowledge, expertise, ethics and decision-making that lasting institutional change will come about, and not vice versa.

The ethics of the future[4] is an ethics that is not content with having fulfilled its obligations to the present. It is not simply a contractual undertaking, but imposes on political leaders and on citizens the duty to act in time, and thus to anticipate. The ethics of the future is a sibling of knowledge and wisdom.

Unfortunately, many of us have invested far too heavily in failure, in stop-gap measures, damage-limitation exercises and reconstruction rather than prevention. Everywhere, the prevailing rationale has been to react to emergencies and to fall back on short-term measures.

The ethics of the twenty-first century, however, will enable us to lay the foundations of genuine development. But we should not delude ourselves: development, in common with international stability and security, is contingent on a whole range of educational, scientific, technological, economic, financial and political measures that should, as stated in the UNESCO Medium-Term Strategy, 'be worked out of a common accord and applied at the right time'.[5]

What is needed is the courage to act in time. We should remember the words of Vaclav Havel: 'I thought I had all the time in the world; I was wrong.' We can no longer put off until tomorrow the decisions that have to be taken today. The world must stop waiting for Godot.

It was again Vaclav Havel who, at a lecture in Paris, said that waiting should not be confused with hoping: waiting is the sad daily lot of millions of people the world over, a wait all too often endless, interminable, repeatedly deferred, ended only by death. Hope is quite a different concept. We must act in time so that the world stops waiting for Godot and once again finds good reason to hope and to trust in the future.

In the final analysis, the issue goes beyond the political sphere and is one of culture, since culture is not just heritage and 'tradition', but also encompasses individual behaviour and attitudes and the power to create, innovate and give new meanings to the human adventure. The new millennium holds out an opportunity that we must grasp. Let us make sure, once and for all, that a special place is kept in the culture of the future for the education of our children; for are not today's children tomorrow's adults, who will uphold and sustain the ethics of the future? As Ilya Prigogine so admirably expressed it in his writings, we are all subject to 'time's arrow', which makes us discoverers of new worlds and, already, explorers of the century ahead. Quite simply, concern for the future must be so familiar a concern that it becomes second nature to us, bridging the gap between transmission and transformation.

We have only one heritage that is still intact: the future. It is there that our hope lies. Let us preserve the virgin lands of the future and start to sow the values of the future. Let us cultivate them and pass them on to our descendants. In so doing, we shall bequeath to our children a living, open legacy.

Notes

1. Antonio Machado, 'No está el mañana – ni el ayer – escrito'.

2. The UNESCO World Commission on the Ethics of Scientific Knowledge and Technology (COMEST) has the specific task of monitoring this issue in collaboration with the International Council for Science's Standing Committee on Responsibility and Ethics in Science.

3. See Chapter 19.

4. As regards the development of this concept, see Federico Mayor, *The Memory of the Future*, UNESCO, Paris, 1994, and J. Bindé, 'L'éthique du futur – Pourquoi faut-il retrouver le temps perdu?', *Futuribles*, December 1997, Paris. English translation, 'Toward an ethics of the future', *Public Culture*, Duke University Press, 2000.

5. Medium-Term Strategy 1996–2001 (28 C/4 Approved), Foreword, UNESCO.

Index